The Dynamics of Industrial Competition describes the internal dynamics of industries using new and unique longitudinal data that make it possible to track firms over time. It provides a comprehensive picture of a number of aspects of firm turnover that arise from the competitive process – the entry and the exit of firms, the growth and the decline of incumbent firms, and the merger process. Instantaneous and cumulative measures of market dynamics are provided.

Since the forces contributing to competition are varied and industries are affected by heterogeneous forces, different aspects of firm turnover are considered in order to provide a comprehensive overview of the competitive process. Entry is divided into that portion coming from the creation of new plants and that portion arising from the acquisition of existing firms. Differences are drawn between the effects of related and unrelated acquisitions and between the effects of take-overs made by domestic and foreign firms. Differences between large- and small-firm activity are also investigated.

The effects of turnover on productivity, efficiency, wage rates, and profitability are modelled. Using various measures of firm turnover to proxy the amount of competition, the study examines the relationship between industry performance and the intensity of the competitive process.

The dynamics of industrial competition

The dynamics of industrial competition

A North American perspective

JOHN R. BALDWIN

In association with

Paul Gorecki, Richard E. Caves, Tim Dunne,
John Haltiwanger, and Mohammed Rafiquzzaman

CAMBRIDGE
UNIVERSITY PRESS

Published by the Press Syndicate of the University of Cambridge
The Pitt Building, Trumpington Street, Cambridge CB2 1RP
40 West 20th Street, New York, NY 10011-4211, USA
10 Stamford Road, Oakleigh, Melbourne 3166, Australia

First published 1995

Printed in the United States of America

Library of Congress Cataloging-in-Publication Data
Baldwin, John R. (John Russel)
The dynamics of industrial competition: a North American
perspective / John R. Baldwin.
p.   cm.
Includes bibliographical references.
ISBN 0-521-46561-3
1. Corporations – Canada – Statistics – Longitudinal studies.
2. Canada – Industries – Statistics – Longitudinal studies.   3. Canada –
Manufactures – Statistics – Longitudinal studies.   4. Competition –
Canada – Statistics – Longitudinal studies.   I. Title.
HD2808.B27   1994
338.7′0971′021 – dc20   94-517
                                                                              CIP

A catalog record for this book is available from the British Library.

ISBN 0-521-46561-3 Hardback

CONTENTS

PREFACE

> Competition may be the spice of life, but in economics it has been more nearly the main dish.
>
> George Stigler (1968: 5)

The economics profession has offered a varied fare on its competition menu. Some have utilized an axiomatic approach to explaining perfect competition. Others have tendered the recipe as something workable though not perfect. Case studies have delved into the operations of particular markets. Hypotheses have been tested about the effect of market structure on performance. Market structure has received considerable attention – indeed, there has been so much food for thought that many of the audience have become satiated. Market performance has been studied but remains unconnected to underlying processes. The effect of innovation and technological change has provided the food for other courses.

There remains a serious gap in our empirical knowledge. There have been few attempts to measure the dynamics of competition – to study the internal dynamics of markets on a broad cross-sectional basis. We have only partial information on the importance of entry and exit, turnover due to mergers, and change in the incumbent-firm population and how it relates to performance. The topic has not been completely ignored by the profession. Partial insights have been offered by case studies that were limited in their generalizations and by simulations suffering from a lack of empirical evidence to sort out the important from the unimportant variants contained within them.

The gap in our understanding of the underlying dynamics of a broad range of industries is serious for a discipline that tries to combine analytical rigour with relevance. The purpose of this book is to accumulate a stream of empirical facts from a cross-section of industries that will improve our understanding of the process at work and that will provide the grist for theoretical innovations in the future.

The research is possible because of the creation of panel data that track firms and their establishments over time. Labour economists have long had such data at their disposal. Industrial economics is just now developing the longitudinal databases that make it possible to investigate phenomena that were previously difficult to study.

Knowledge gaps in industrial economics and the importance of panel data

The research agenda in industrial economics has been affected by the type of information available to researchers. Earlier generations of economists studying industrial organization had to rely on case studies. While they provided a wealth of detail, industry case studies generally preclude the type of generalizations that social science demands.

With the addition of econometrics to the tool bag of the industrial economics profession, cross-sectional studies of industry characteristics at a point in time became popular. This focus was primarily the result of a lack of panel data. Statistical agencies have concentrated on producing a set of industry statistics at a point in time. Linking these over time has been of secondary importance. Linking the micro-units at a lower level has received even less emphasis. Only recently has it become possible to use panel data to follow the micro-production units over time as computer technology and administrative practice have improved.

The lack of panel data on businesses has influenced the phenomena that can be studied. This has left large gaps in our understanding of the operation of the market system. Equally important, misconceptions have developed in some quarters because of studies that have relied on somewhat imperfect ad hoc databases or on a partial analysis of only one aspect of the adjustment process. The partial descriptions have in turn affected the depiction of the industrial system conveyed both in textbooks and in more popular articles.

The emphasis on market structure that has consumed so much empirical effort provides an example of many of these problems. Industrial economists have long been interested in summary measures of market structure. The most commonly used measure of structure depicts the firm-size distribution. Alternative measures that capture the dynamics of changes in firm size have been suggested, but require the researcher to follow plants and firms over time. An inability to do so has restricted attention to concentration measures. Since these measures show substantial stability, the industrial system has come to be characterized in many circles as being relatively rigid, and adaptation as difficult and slow. With structure being defined in a narrow sense to refer to firm-size distribution, change could be described as occurring "at the pace of a glacial drift" (Scherer, 1980: 70). In reality, there is a great deal of change in the relative position of firms in most industries – a view of the world that is different from that engendered by a reliance upon concentration statistics.

A second example of deficiencies occasioned by a lack of panel data can be found in merger studies. The lack of comprehensive panel data on businesses has forced many researchers to rely on small samples that were constructed from diverse sources containing unknown sample selection biases. In addition, the sheer effort of data collection has meant that coverage for more than a short period has rarely been possible. The result is that no clear picture of the effect of mergers has emerged in the literature (see Caves, 1987).

A third area that has suffered from the lack of good panel data consists of entry and exit studies. The entry of new firms has played a central role in many theories of industrial organization. Unfortunately, there are few quantitative studies of the phenomenon, since it is difficult to measure entry and exit accurately. Identifying the production units that are really new in administrative records has proven difficult. Because of the large number of changes in the corporate form of organization, production entities can appear to be new when only corporate control changes.

There is a second reason for the lack of quantitative studies of entry. Accurate measurement of the effect of entry requires panel data that can follow the new firm from birth onward. Generally entrants are small, and therefore the effect of entry in the short run is modest. Estimating the long-run effect of entry requires that entrants be tracked over time. The lack of panel data sets has generally precluded this from being done. As a result, studies that measure the importance of entry at time of birth have left the impression that entry is unimportant (see OECD, 1987) – even though the reverse is true (Baldwin and Gorecki, 1991).

Until the early 1980s, there were few quantitative studies of the process, thereby leaving the field to informed speculation about its importance. Since that time, there have been a number of studies of entry and exit using administrative databases. Unfortunately, many of these databases have severe limitations. The first problem lies in the quality of the data used.[1] In some cases, this is because the data are strung together from disparate sources and the extent of coverage bias is unknown. In other cases, births and deaths may be entirely false, because the identifiers attached to businesses in these files change for the wrong reason. In other cases, the updating of files may be so slow that births and deaths cannot be dated precisely.

Because of the difficulty in measuring specific aspects of the turnover process, few studies encompass several aspects of it. Not only does this mean that an overview of the dynamics of the competitive process has generally not been possible, but it has also been difficult to compare each aspect of turnover, like entry and exit, to other changes taking place. Any one turnover process may appear unimportant when taken by itself. It is, however, incorrect to conclude from this that intra-industry dynamics as a whole are unimportant.

Study objectives

This study addresses these deficiencies in two ways. First, it makes use of a comprehensive database that makes it possible to measure many aspects of intra-industry change with greater precision than before. Second, it examines a number of aspects of this change – entry, exit, incumbent market share, mergers – and thus presents a more complete picture of the internal dynamics of the competitive process than has previously been possible.

The Canadian manufacturing sector was chosen because it is possible to build a longitudinal panel from the Canadian Census of Manufactures that distinguishes different events and avoids many of the problems of previous studies.[2] Many databases are unable to define the nature of births precisely. Sometimes this is because identifier numbers attached to businesses change for random reasons. There are cases where a tax-related database changes identifiers if a firm changes chartered accountants. In other cases, identifiers can change if a merger or control change occurs. In these cases, merger entry and exit cannot be distinguished from greenfield entry and exit. Since the two have different characteristics, failure to distinguish between them can produce misleading results.

The Canadian data either do not suffer from the problems just outlined or these problems can be overcome. As a result, more precise data on entry can be obtained than in many previous studies. Entry by greenfield construction can be distinguished from entry by acquisition. The Canadian data can be used to follow entrants over time, so that measures of the cumulative effect of entry can be derived. The data allow the behaviour of incumbents to be examined over time. Since establishments under common ownership can be grouped, incumbent performance can be measured in both the short and the long run. This allows the dynamics of this group to be compared with the dynamics of entrants. In addition, since census characteristics can be attached to both entrants and incumbents, the performance as well as the dynamics of both groups can be examined. Finally, subgroups of each population can be chosen for study, since the micro-data can be aggregated to new classes with the aid of suitable identifiers. For example, the incumbent population can be divided into those experiencing control changes and those not doing so in order to examine the efficacy of merger activity. The business population can be divided into those under foreign control as opposed to domestic control in order to study the effects of foreign multinational enterprise both on the dynamics of industrial change and on performance.

ACKNOWLEDGEMENTS

This project was completed with the aid of several co-authors and two assistants. The most important co-author is Paul Gorecki, with whom I wrote the manuscript "Structural Change and Adaptation," which marked the beginning of my interest in the dynamics of change. He was instrumental in helping with the development of Chapters 2, 3, 4, and 7 and commented extensively on several others. Dick Caves at Harvard University contributed to Chapter 11 on foreign and domestic turnover. John Haltiwanger of the University of Maryland and Tim Dunne of the Center for Economic Studies collaborated on Chapter 6 comparing Canada and the United States. Mohammed Rafiquzzaman co-authored the entry model in Chapter 14. Equally important were two staff assistants at Statistics Canada. Bob Gibson provided programming assistance, and Jocelyne Bousfield provided the statistical support that was necessary to build the database.

I gratefully acknowledge comments on various parts of the manuscript by Dick Caves, Steve Davies, David Encoua, Paul Geroski, Zvi Griliches, Alan Hughes, David Mayes, Don McFetridge, Dennis Mueller, Frank Roseman, and Len Waverman.

The project would not have been finished without the support of Statistics Canada and the Economic Council. Statistics Canada recognized the untapped potential of the data under their control and supported the work by providing me both with a research fellowship that extended over several years and with research support. For this, I am indebted to the chief statistician, Ivan Fellegi, the assistant chief statistician, Stewart Wells, Michael Wolfson of the Analytical Studies Division, and Garnet Picot of the Business and Labour Market Analysis Group. In addition, the Economic Council of Canada provided a research fellowship, release time for my co-author Paul Gorecki, and computer support. David Slater, Peter Cornell, and Judith Maxwell from the Council supported the project throughout. Robert McGuckin of the Center of Economic Studies in the U.S. Bureau of the Census facilitated the joint project on turnover in Canada and the United States. Queen's University provided sabbatical support and an extended leave.

Applied economists must invest time and effort developing databases for research. This project was no different in that respect. What distinguishes this project from others is that the data development eventually required relocation from Queen's University to Statistics Canada. I owe the greatest debt to my family, who were uprooted from Kingston and moved to Ottawa so that I could pursue my research interests. I also am indebted to Adrianne, my wife, for editing the manuscript and shepherding it through the publication process.

1

The dynamics of competition

[The] process of incessant rise and decay of firms and industries . . . is the central – though much neglected – fact about the Capitalist System.

Joseph Schumpeter (1939: 70)

Introduction

This study sets out to measure the dynamics of the competitive process. It focuses on the performance of firm populations by analysing the components of firm turnover that affect the nature and the effectiveness of change within industries.

The dynamics of change within industries are complex. Firms are born and they die. Young firms mature, old ones decline. Growth and decline take place simultaneously in infants, adolescents, mature adults, and the elderly. Changes in size and efficacy occur both in individual units and in groups of firms. Family groups disband and are reconstituted as the result of mergers and control changes.

This study examines each of these components in detail. Both the magnitude and the effect of change on industry performance are measured. Each of the components is examined individually, and then the reinforcing effect of the various forces when taken together is calculated.

The research demonstrates that competition is a dynamic process, with various subcomponents, each of whose contribution is modest but meaningful. When taken together, they significantly change the industrial landscape. This change occurs gradually. It is rarely momentous. But it accumulates steadily to change the nature of an industry over relatively short periods.

Conceptual approaches to competition

Words in common usage tend to take on a variety of meanings. "Competition" is no exception. Although many nuances are attached to the term, most writers tend to view competition as either a process or a state of affairs.

1

When competition is described as a process, it is the competitive struggle that receives attention. In some treatises, entrepreneurs are described as the key to success. Hayek (1948) and Kirzner (1973), with their stress on the individual entrepreneur, epitomize this tradition. Schumpeter viewed the competitive struggle as one that revolved around innovation and economic progress. The most important form of competition comes from "the new commodity, the new technology, the new source of supply, the new form of organization" (Schumpeter, 1942: 84–85). Frank Knight (1921) emphasized the notion of risk. Risk-taking is the function of the entrepreneur, and the successful are rewarded for their efforts. The common thread in all of these analyses is that a competitive market system is one where entrepreneurs vie freely with one another for success. The struggle resembles a contest; markets in which the contest is intense are labelled competitive.

A second strand of this literature, found more frequently in business schools than economics departments, discusses the strategies that businesses can be expected to follow during their quest for success. Porter (1980, 1985) concentrates on the varied strategies related to the choice of market niche, advertising strategy, or technological path that lie behind the growth of successful companies. Carrol and Vogel (1984, 1987) also provide case studies, including some that describe how new firms find ways to break into established markets.

Economists have provided not only verbal descriptions of competition but also models of the processes. Simon and his colleagues stress that competition should be regarded as a stochastic process.[1] Steindl (1965) links the underlying stochastic events to the observed firm growth and decline process. Nelson and Winter (1982) develop a simulation model that captures the essence of the Schumpeterian process where investment in research and development affects firm success. Elliasson (1985) builds a simulation model for Sweden that allows the linkages between micro- and macro-economies to be explored more fully.

One pillar of the empirical tradition involves simulation of the underlying relationship between the nature of the innovative process, turnover, and market structure. The other pillar investigates the causal effects of innovation and technological change on turnover. Phillips (1956, 1966, 1971) documents how the nature of technological change, appropriability considerations, and the underlying science base affects product change and the turnover of firms in an industry. Different innovative capabilities lie behind the growth of some firms and the decline of others. Branch (1972–73) provides evidence that successful research and development as manifested in patenting activity is associated with increases in sales and thus with success. Mansfield (1983), in studying the effect of product innovations, noted that many were associated with reductions in concentration because the innovation was introduced by relatively small new firms. Gort and Klepper (1982), in their study of the diffusion of 48 new-product innovations, note that the structure of markets is shaped by a set of discrete events such as technical change that stimulate entry. Tilton's (1971) study of the semi-conductor industry in Silicon Valley stresses the connection between innovation and entry.

The alternative and more traditional way of describing competition is to view it as a state of affairs. The intensity of competition is assessed by taking a snapshot at a point in time. Those who ascribe to this position take the view that the dimensions of the competitive system can be classified by a set of structural attributes of the market. Adherents of this position place the emphasis on such characteristics as the number of firms, concentration, advertising ratios, and other structural variables.

These variables, which capture characteristics that describe the position of an industry at a point in time and not how it reached that position, are proxies for the intensity of the competitive process. Because they are proxies, substantial effort has been devoted to showing that these characteristics are related to cross-sectional differences in profitability. This is an indirect way of confirming that these measures are related to the intensity of the competitive process that has been postulated to affect cross-industry differentials in profitability.

At a conceptual level, the two approaches to analysing competition may not disagree as to what constitutes highly competitive markets. It is at the practical level of measurement that they differ. Those who have had to rely on measures of market structure and other static characteristics are, faute de mieux, focusing on a state of affairs. In using these measures, they presume such measures represent the intensity of competition within the industry.

Differences in practice often unwittingly lead to subtle divergences in attitudes that then influence the research agenda. Reid (1987) argues that during the evolution of the North American school of industrial organization, Marshall's concept of a representative firm was transformed into Viner's concept of the average firm. In the first case, the concept of a representative firm does not rule out intra-industry heterogeneity and an interest in the diversity of strategies that might be employed by the successful firm. In the latter case, the average-firm concept is associated with homogeneity, and issues of heterogeneity are placed low on the research agenda.

This distinction, far from being a matter of semantics, has influenced the issues that are considered worthy of investigation. When firm- and plant-cost data were first used to investigate the nature of cost curves, the exercise was greeted with criticism by Friedman (1955), who argued that inter-firm cost differences must be the result of measurement error. Later when Leibenstein (1966) argued that cost differences among firms within an industry warranted study, Stigler (1976) responded in much the same vein.

The dynamics of intra-industry change are generally ignored in empirical work. The lack of empirical work in turn has influenced theoretical developments. For example, the earlier limit-pricing models and the more recent contestability models focused on potential entry. With little empirical work being done on entry dynamics, entry appeared to be unimportant, and theorists turned to speculating on what would happen in a world where entry was possible but non-existent, because of optimal entry-deterring strategies being employed by incumbents.

Alternatively, entry was viewed as a phenomenon that was unimportant except when it moved an industry from one equilibrium situation to another. This view stemmed from a second common practice – that of focusing on equilibrium and comparative statics exercises. As useful as this view proved to be, it discouraged research into the dynamics of industry adjustment. If dynamics just influenced the pace of adjustment from one equilibrium to another, then it could only be of secondary interest unless disequilibrium persisted.

Measuring the dynamics of competition

At the heart of this study is the notion that speculation about the intensity and effects of the competitive process is no substitution for data that describe the outcome of the process. Various aspects of the turnover in firms are subject to measurement. Statistics that summarize these are referred to as mobility measures.[2]

The research strategy employed in this study is based on the presumption that much of what happens during the competitive process will be manifested by changes in relative firm position. Mobility measures provide a direct measure of the intensity of competition. As a result of the competitive struggle, firms will grow and decline, enter and exit from different markets. The successful will be separated from the unsuccessful. Measuring the extent to which this is the case sheds considerable light on the intensity of competition.

It is possible that some aspects of the competitive struggle will not be translated into a shift in relative market share. In some instances, an intensely bitter struggle may leave all parties in the same relative position as at the outset. However, it seems unlikely that there are a large number of intense struggles occurring in which no winner emerges. Providing new measures of turnover improves on the practice of just concentrating on the shape of the firm-size distribution.

Turnover is taken herein as an indication of the inability of suppliers to maintain impregnable market positions. It is one of the manifestations of the creative destruction that arises because innovation in technology and product markets permits some firms to grow at the expense of others. It is the way in which competition in ideas, in new methods, in new organizational techniques is transmitted to the structure of markets.

Turnover is not a direct measure of static allocative efficiency. There are static models of market outcomes where efficiency outcomes are produced with no turnover of market share. But these models bear little semblance to a world in which competition occurs in new products and processes and where uncertainty is the rule not the exception. Schumpeter questioned the importance of just studying static allocative efficiency when competition in new products and processes is so critical for economic progress and development.

Turnover measures also do not reflect only the intensity of the competitive process. Some change in market shares may result from the random sampling habits of consumers (Stigler, 1964). Dynamic limit-entry models (Gaskins, 1971) demonstrate how entry may be permitted by the rational leader with market power. Capital vintage effects also suffice to generate turnover.

Despite these caveats, turnover positively indicates the effectiveness of competition in a number of senses: the extent to which customer inertia due to switching costs is unimportant; how little entrenchment results from pre-committed production or other costs; the propensity for sellers to behave in aggressive ways that seize opportunities to the disadvantage of rivals.

Not all research in industrial organization has been aimed at measuring the static concept of the state of competition. Some studies have examined the extent of intra-industry dynamics. These studies suffer from two major deficiencies. First, they generally deal only with a small number of industries. Second, they examine only part of the turnover process. They investigate entry and exit, or turnover in incumbents, or the merger process.[3]

In order to overcome these deficiencies and to further our understanding of the dynamics of the competitive process, information was generated on all of these causes of firm turnover for a cross-section of Canadian manufacturing industries. The Canadian manufacturing sector was chosen since it is possible to build a longitudinal panel from the Canadian Census of Manufactures that is able to distinguish different events.[4] The aspects of turnover that were examined were greenfield entry and closedown exit,[5] turnover due to mergers,[6] and change in the relative position of incumbent producers. The period chosen for study was the decade of the 1970s. Rates of turnover were calculated for both the short and long run – that is, for periods of one year and for periods up to a decade. Turnover in this study is measured both in the short run and in the longer run so that we can investigate the permanence of the shifts that are taking place in different markets.

Many databases are unable to define the nature of births precisely. Sometimes this is because identifier numbers that are attached to businesses change for random reasons. There are cases where a tax-related database changes identifiers if a firm changes chartered accountants. In other cases, identifiers can change if a merger or control change occurs. In these cases, merger entry and exit cannot be distinguished from greenfield entry and exit. Since the two have different characteristics, failure to distinguish between them can produce misleading results.

Throughout the book, turnover is examined by looking at the relative size of firms, generally using four-digit Canadian industries.[7] The importance of entry is calculated as the share of shipments in a four-digit industry accounted for by new firms. Turnover in the incumbent population is measured as the share that is shifted from declining firms to growing firms.

While the four-digit industry level is the most detailed available in Canada, it is still rather aggregative and contains many different types of activities. In many, if not the majority of instances, entrants then are not producing exactly the same products as incumbents. Firms that gain market share may not be doing exactly the same things as firms that are losing share. There is considerable heterogeneity within industries because firms in every industry produce a range of products and use different technologies. Consequently, entry and exit, growth and decline, are not capturing just changes in relative shares of homogeneous products. They are also capturing variations in related product lines with similar technologies.

Entrants capture market share in this world because they produce existing products more efficiently (imitative entry) or because they produce new products or produce existing products with new technologies (innovative entry). Intra-industry mobility of incumbents results from the adoption of innovative products and technologies. The intensity of competition being measured is at least partially related to the Schumpeterian notion of competition in new products, new technologies, and new organizational forms.

The study has three objectives. The first is to provide basic statistics on the amount of turnover arising from three main sources and to provide an impression of the overall changes that are taking place. Chapter 2 focuses on greenfield entry and closedown exit, Chapter 3 on the amount of entry and exit activity that occurs as a result of acquisitions and the importance of related and unrelated mergers, and Chapter 4 on the amount of growth and decline in the incumbent population. Chapter 5 examines the pattern of change in the incumbent population.

The study then compares job turnover in Canada with that in the United States. Throughout the book, Canadian data are used to describe the turnover process. The comparison in Chapter 6 shows the similarity of the Canadian experience to a much larger and quite different U.S. economy and thereby suggests that much of what is demonstrated in this book is not unique to Canada. Further international comparisons, where warranted, are drawn in the Conclusion.

The second objective of this study is to ask what the different patterns of industry turnover tell us about the intensity of the competitive process and how it fills the gap in our present knowledge. The extent to which turnover is restricted to only a small number of industries is addressed in Chapters 2 to 4. Chapter 5 asks whether the patterns observed in turnover are likely to lead to ever-increasing concentration or whether larger firms on average are in decline and small ones are growing. Chapter 7 focuses on whether highly concentrated industries suffer much less turnover. Chapter 8 asks whether mobility tends to determine market structure. Chapter 14 models the entry process in order to estimate the extent to which structure affects turnover.

The third objective of this study is to evaluate the importance of turnover. Traditional approaches in industrial organization have relied upon profitability to measure performance and have estimated the extent to which market structure was related to profitability. These studies have been criticized for several reasons. First, market structure is an imperfect proxy for the intensity of competition. Second, by relying on industry-level data rather than micro-data, existing studies have not been able to rule out the possibility that the relationship between profitability and concentration is the result of the superior efficiency of the largest firms.

This study sets out to overcome these deficiencies in two ways. First, micro-data are used to evaluate the performance of the plants that fall into different turnover categories. Second, dimensions of market performance, other than profitability, are examined. An alternative measure that has long been emphasized as coming from the Schumpeterian tradition is technical progress. To this end, Chapter 9 examines the effect of various components of turnover on productivity. Chapter 12 investigates the extent to which turnover increases technical efficiency in an industry. The amount of technical efficiency depends on the dispersion of firm performance within an industry. It is a natural metric for the evaluation of turnover – a phenomenon deeply rooted in the notion of firm heterogeneity. Chapter 13 then examines the relationship between industry profitability and firm turnover.

Chapters 9, 12, and 13 focus primarily on the effect of entry and exit and on growth and decline in continuing plants. They do not look specifically at the effect of mergers. Chapter 10 examines mergers in general; Chapter 11 focuses on the difference in the effect of acquisitions by foreign and domestic firms.

2

Greenfield entry and closedown exit

> Most new firms are founded with an idea and for a definite purpose. The life goes out of them when that idea or purpose has been fulfilled or has become obsolete or even if, without having become obsolete, it has ceased to be new.
>
> Joseph Schumpeter (1939: 69)

Introduction

Economists have long focused on the process of entry and exit of firms. Many have emphasized its importance in facilitating the adaptation of industry to change. In the simplest of expositions, the acts of entry and exit serve to equate above- or below-normal profits with competitive rates. In other models, potential rather than actual entry serves to limit monopoly power. At one time included under the rubric of limit-pricing models, this argument has more recently been given theoretical elegance by contestability theory. The turnover that results from exit and entry is also seen as a conduit through which new ideas and innovations are introduced.

This view of entry is not shared by all. To some, the lack of entry indicates that entry is unimportant. Others have portrayed entry as an interesting but irrelevant curiosity. One such view depicts entrants as fringe firms that swarm into and out of an industry without having much impact. References to the entry and exit process as "hit-and-run" leave the impression, intentional or otherwise, of an unstable fringe that makes no contribution to such indicators of progress as productivity. Shepherd (1984), in a criticism of contestability theory, stresses that entry as an external force is usually secondary to internal conditions within an industry in determining the strength of competition.

While the importance of entry has been debated at length, little quantitative work has been done to measure the process directly. Most efforts have focused on quantifying barriers to entry, rather than on measuring entry itself. This focus reflects a preoccupation with static models in which interest centres on potential rather than actual entry (Bain, 1956; Bhagwati, 1970; Baumol, 1982).

8

Because of this emphasis on potential rather than actual entry, there have been few attempts to quantify the firm-turnover process.[1] On the one hand are studies that cover a small number of industries (Mansfield, 1962; Carroll and Vogel, 1987). Others, because of the difficulty of drawing general conclusions about the importance of the entry process from case studies, have attempted to measure the intensity of entry for a cross-section of industries. Many of these studies of entry have had to rely on data that were generated for other purposes and, as a result, yield estimates that were imprecise, less than comprehensive, or defective for other reasons.[2] Early studies had data for only the gross number of firms and, therefore, could not distinguish between entry and exit (Orr, 1974; Deutsch, 1975). The pioneering work of Birch (1979) and others, using Dun and Bradstreet data, also had problems.[3] More recently, studies have emerged that use national databases; but many of these, however, are either cobbled together from disparate sources[4] or use national census data without being able to evaluate fully the meaning attached to a birth and death by the census authorities or to modify it for the purpose of studying entry.[5]

Because of the dearth of empirical data on the entry process, the debate over its importance remains unresolved. Several studies have suggested that entry is relatively unimportant, because it rarely adds or subtracts more than a few percentage points to the population of firms or employment (e.g., Birch, 1981; Storey, 1985; Johnson, 1986; OECD, 1987). These studies suffer from a number of problems that have been documented by Baldwin and Gorecki (1990b). More recently, Dunne, Roberts, and Samuelson (1988), using data from the U.S. census, show that the cumulative effect of entry over five-year census periods is somewhat larger than was initially thought.

One of the difficulties of evaluating which view of entry and exit is correct and of placing the process in the context of overall change has been the lack of longitudinal panel data that follow firms through time. In order to understand the process of entry, more is required than snapshots taken at one- or five-year intervals. Some authors suggest that the relative importance of surviving entrants increases over time: Jovanovic (1982) introduces learning models where entrants start small and gradually approach the size of incumbents; Pakes and Ericson (1988) stress that the importance of learning and adaptation can be inferred from the relative size and importance of entrants at birth and from their subsequent history; Bevan (1974) shows how some entrants have carved out niches before expanding. If entry is to be labelled as quantitatively unimportant, both its instantaneous and its cumulative effects need to be measured. In addition, the entry and exit process needs to be set within a more general context of firm growth and decline and the long-run progress of entrants needs to be charted.

This chapter provides measures of entry and exit for the Canadian manufacturing sector that permit a comprehensive picture of the magnitude of the process. Attention is focused on firms that enter by plant opening (greenfield entry) and firms that exit by plant closing (closedown exit). Entry by acquisition and exit by divestiture are compared with greenfield entry and closedown exit in the next chapter. The quantity of entrants, both in the year of birth and subsequently, is presented here so as to contrast instantaneous or short-run measures with cumulative or long-run measures of the intensity of entry and exit. The chapter focuses on the growth paths and exit rates of entrants, thereby permitting a better picture of the trajectory followed by surviving entrants as they mature to become established firms.

Measurement issues

Comprehensive Census of Manufactures data for Canada overcome many of the problems that beset previous work. In order to generate entry and exit statistics from this potentially rich data source, several decisions relating to measurement had to be taken. The nature of the entry and exit statistics produced will depend on the level of industry aggregation used, the time period selected, the definition of a production unit adopted, and the method of entry and exit chosen for measurement. In previous studies the methods that could be chosen for measuring entry were limited by the nature of the data. The database that was constructed for this study overcomes these limitations. Understanding what options were available and how they were chosen not only serves as an introduction to the results, but also is a necessity if the differences between the results reported here and those in other studies are to be fully understood.

Industry level of aggregation

Entry and exit can be measured either at the level of the manufacturing sector as a whole or for individual industries. In the first case, entry is defined as a new firm in the manufacturing sector; in the second case, as a new firm in a particular four-digit industry.

Measures that are derived using different levels of industry aggregation capture different aspects of entry and exit. Even when the individual industry measures are averaged for the manufacturing sector as a whole, the two measures are unlikely to be the same. When defined at the level of the manufacturing sector, measures of entry catch only entry by outsiders. Entry into a particular industry may come partly from firms already in other manufacturing industries. Such entry is not counted when the manufacturing sector as a whole is used to define entry, but is included when entry is measured at the level of the individual four-digit industry.

Normally, more rather than less detail is valued. But in economics, succinctness is as much a virtue as it is in statistical reporting. In this chapter, entry is examined first at the manufacturing-sector level in order to provide a broad overview. As the resulting measure does not encapsulate all entry, this approach is supplemented with entry rates calculated at a more detailed industry level.

Time period

Entry and exit can be measured by comparing two adjacent points in time using annual data, or by using end-points that are further apart. The first procedure yields instantaneous rates of entry – short-run rates; the second provides measures of the cumulative effect of entrants – long-run rates. The two rates can be compared by using the annual equivalent value of the cumulative rate – the value that, when compounded, gives the cumulative rate.

A comparison of short- and long-run rates reveals the extent to which entry is ephemeral or long-lasting in its effect. If the turnover process is essentially marginal, if entrants operate at the fringe of each industry, and if they are relatively short-lived, then the entry rate derived from annual data will be small and the same as the cumulative rate when measured with end years further apart (and higher than the equivalent annual rate derived from the cumulative rate). The instantaneous and the cumulative rates will be similar in this instance if most entrants die shortly after birth and the survivors do not experience much growth. On the other hand, if some entrants have enough of an advantage over incumbents that they are able to survive and grow to be of substantial importance, and there are enough such firms, then long-term cumulative entry rates (and possibly their equivalent annual values) for a particular group of entrants will exceed or equal short-term entry rates.

In order to investigate which characterization of the entry process is correct, both shorter- and longer-run periods are used for the calculations. Short-run rates are equated here with year-to-year changes; longer-run rates are derived from comparing years 6, 9, and 11 years apart.

Choice of production unit

Interest in the firm- and plant-turnover process centres on its relationship with the evolution of industry profit, innovation, and productivity over time.[6] Such considerations suggest that the firm rather than the individual production unit – the establishment, the plant, or the factory – be used to define entry and exit. It is the firm, not the plant, that makes the decision to enter or exit an industry. Therefore, this chapter concentrates primarily on firm entry and exit.

Firms are composed of plants, however, and it is the fate of plants that determines the fate of firms. Therefore, much of the data will be presented in terms of the plants that experience change. For example, new plants will be divided into those associated with new firms and those belonging to continuing firms. Plant entry rates are useful for two other reasons.[7] First, since they give a broad overview of the magnitude of *all* new plants, it may be this variable, rather than just new-firm plant births, that has the greater influence on the equilibrating process that drives down supra-normal industry profits or increases profits when they fall below average. Second, by focusing on the fate of all plants, the importance of several categories can be compared with one another.

Gross and net entry measures

Entry can be defined either gross or net of exits. Many previous studies (e.g., Orr, 1974; Deutsch, 1975) have used the net measure. Such a definition measures expansion rather than entry. It understates entry by the amount of exit. For this study, gross entry rates and exit rates are calculated separately so as to evaluate their relative magnitude, both over time and across industries.

Unit of measurement

The magnitude of entry and exit can be assessed using the number of firms, or the share of an industry's sales captured by entrants. Since measures of market structure so often stress the significance of the number of firms in an industry, the magnitude of entry and exit is measured here both as a percentage of existing firms and as a percentage of shipments or employment in entrants or in exits.[8]

Types of entry and exit

Discussions of entry and exit often proceed as if distinguishing among different methods of entry and exit were unimportant.[9] Entry can occur through the acquisition of existing capacity or the building of new capacity – acquisition as opposed to greenfield entry; equally, exit can occur through the divestiture of existing capacity or the closure of capacity – divestiture and closedown exit. Changes in industry capacity through plant opening (entry) and closure (exit) have the potential to affect the industry supply curve and industry performance immediately and directly. How acquisitions and divestitures affect the supply curve is more difficult to predict because they do not affect capacity in the first instance. Such entry may disturb existing patterns of oligopolistic co-ordination, and at the same time introduce innovative methods and products. On the other hand, it may reinforce oligopolistic co-ordination if the leading firms in an industry already compete with each other in several other industries as the result of diversification (Scott, 1982). In view of the potential differences between the two methods of entry and exit, they are measured separately here. This chapter focuses on greenfield entry and closedown exit; Chapter 3 examines entry by acquisition and exit by divestiture.

Data sources and definitions
Measuring entry and exit

This chapter uses establishment-based data, extending from 1970 to the early 1980s, that are derived from the Canadian Census of Manufactures. This census is discussed in detail in Statistics Canada (1979), while the measurement of entry and exit is detailed in Appendix A.

The advantage of using this database is that it is an annual census of virtually all manufacturing establishments in Canada and, therefore, provides comprehensive coverage. Each establishment and enterprise[10] – defined as a group of establishments under common control – is linked. Plants and firms have been assigned identifiers that they retain over their lifetime. Because they can be followed through time, entry, exit, and continuing-firm activity can be tabulated. In addition, plants under common ownership can be linked together into firms at different levels of aggregation. For industry analyses, the four-digit level (all plants in a four-digit industry under common control) is chosen here. For analyses at the aggregate level, a firm is defined as all plants anywhere in the manufacturing sector that are under common control.

Defining categories of entry, exit, and continuing firms

A summary of the various entry, exit, and continuing-firm classifications used at the four-digit industry level is presented in Table 2-1, along with the numerical designations that will be used to identify each group. Establishments are classified as births, deaths, continuing, transferred, acquired, or divested. They are then aggregated into firms, which are defined as consisting of all establishments that are under common control. This classification, in turn, allows firms to be grouped into new firms, exiting firms, and continuing firms on the basis of the status of their plants.

New firms are divided into three groups: those that entered by building new plant (cell 23), by acquiring existing plant (22), and by transferring plant from another industry (26). Similarly, exiting firms are divided into those that exited by divesting themselves of plant (31), by closing plant (34), and by transferring plant to another industry (37). Finally, the plants of continuing firms are divided into those that were newly built (13), those that were transferred into an industry (16), those that were closed (14), those that were transferred to another industry (17), those that were divested (11), those that were acquired (12), and those that stayed continuously in the industry without a change in ownership status (15). Because of the classification scheme used, the plant creation and destruction process for continuing firms can be compared with that for the entering and exiting segment (e.g., 13 and 23, 14 and

Table 2-1. *Plant and firm classification matrix used to study entry and exit*

Plant status	Firm status		
	Continuing	Entrants	Exits
Divested	11	—	31
Acquired	12	22	—
Births	13	23	—
Deaths	14	—	34
Continuing	15	—	—
Transfer in	16	26	—
Transfer out	17	—	37

Definition	Cell	Description
Entrants	22	Firms that entered the industry by acquiring one or more plants between t and $t + n$
	23	Firms that entered the industry by opening one or more plants between t and $t + n$
	26	Firms that entered the industry by transferring one or more plants from another industry to the given industry between t and $t + n$
Exits	31	Firms that left the industry by divesting one or more plants between t and $t + n$
	34	Firms that left the industry by closing one or more plants between t and $t + n$
	37	Firms that exited the industry by transferring one or more plants out of the given industry to another between t and $t + n$
Continuing	11	Continuing firms that divested themselves of one or more plants between t and $t + n$
	12	Continuing firms that acquired one or more plants between t and $t + n$
	13	Continuing firms that built one or more plants between t and $t + n$
	14	Continuing firms that closed one or more plants between t and $t + n$
	15	Continuing firms that owned at least one plant that existed in both t and $t + n$
	16	Continuing firms that transferred plants into the given industry
	17	Continuing firms that transferred plants out of the given industry

34). Similarly, the merger process for continuing firms (horizontal) can be compared with the process that brings new firms into an industry through acquisition (e.g., 12 and 22). In each case, the importance of a category is measured by the number or the size (shipments) of plants belonging to firms in that category.

All of the categories in Table 2-1 are used when measuring entry into and exit from a four-digit industry. When entry and exit are measured at the level of the manufacturing sector as a whole, two main categories are chosen – entry by plant creation (23) or exit by plant closure (34), and entry by acquisition (22) or exit by divestiture (31). The categories arising from transfers – 16, 17, 26, and 37 – are not considered when entry and exit are measured at the aggregate level.

The magnitude of greenfield entry and closedown exit

The nature of the entry and exit process has implications for the efficacy of the market system and the strength of the competitive process. However, basic patterns of entry and exit have not been extensively documented. This section begins to correct this deficiency. It analyses the extent of greenfield entry and closedown exit and addresses the following questions. Are entry and exit limited to a competitive fringe? Are they confined to the smaller-sized groups? What is the length of life of an entrant? Are short- and long-run results similar? Throughout, the emphasis is on understanding entry and exit as parts of a dynamic process that needs to be described by examining the evolution of firms.

In Chapter 3, greenfield entry and closedown exit are compared with entry and exit by acquisition. Then both are contrasted in Chapter 4 with the amount of change that takes place in the continuing-firm population.

Entry and exit measured in the short run

In order to measure the effect of short-run entry, annual rates of entry and exit are calculated for 1970–82 (Table 2-2).[11] Rates are measured first as the percentage of the number of firms in the particular entry or exit category, and second as the percentage of total employment accounted for by these firms. Entry and exit are defined as firm entry into and exit from the manufacturing sector as a whole. Thus, for 1970–71, entrants are those firms that possessed plants in manufacturing in 1971 but not in 1970, and exits are those firms that possessed plants in manufacturing in 1970 but not in 1971. All rates are estimated relative to the first of the two years (e.g., 1970 for 1970–71). On average, during the 1970s, greenfield entrants accounted for 4.3 per cent of the stock of firms each year in the manufacturing sector. During the same period, 5.3 per cent of all firms became closedown exits each year.

Table 2-2. *Greenfield-entry and closedown-exit rates measured using number of firms and employment, 1970–82 (per cent of base year)*

Period	Entry rate (greenfield)		Exit rate (closedown)	
	Number of firms	Employment	Number of firms	Employment
1970–71	3.4	1.2	5.6	1.1
1971–72	4.6	1.0	4.8	0.9
1972–73	4.8	1.1	5.5	0.6
1973–74	5.7	1.2	4.3	0.9
1974–75	5.9	0.8	6.3	0.9
1975–76	3.4	0.4	5.1	1.2
1976–77	1.7	0.3	5.3	1.5
1977–78	4.4	1.2	5.0	1.6
1978–79	3.4	0.7	3.8	1.0
1979–80	4.7	1.2	4.6	1.2
1980–81	2.9	0.6	5.5	1.4
1981–82	6.3	1.1	8.3	1.7
Mean	4.3	0.9	5.3	1.2

Note: An entrant is defined as a firm present in manufacturing in the end year, but not the initial year of the period; an exit is the reverse. Rates are calculated relative to initial-year firm and employment numbers. Greenfield entry occurs when the appearance of a firm corresponds with the appearance of its first plant assigned to an industry. Closedown exit occurs when the exit of a firm corresponds with the disappearance of its plants from manufacturing.

When measured in terms of employment, the importance of both greenfield entry and closedown exit falls. On average, greenfield entry contributed 0.9 per cent annually to total employment. Closedowns employed 1.2 per cent of the labour force.

An examination of average annual entry and exit rates over the period 1970–82 reveals more clearly the difference between the firm number and the employment measures (Figure 2-1). The two measures differ in relative size because greenfield entrants and closedown exits are much smaller, on average, than a typical firm. Over the period 1970–82, the average sizes of the firms exiting by plant closure and entering by greenfield construction were 18 and 21 per cent of the manufacturing average, respectively.

It is clear from this evidence that annual rates of entry are quite small. When measured by employment affected, the instantaneous rate of greenfield entry is not large enough to suggest that even moderate change is occasioned by entrants at birth.

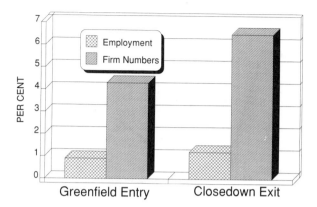

Figure 2-1. Rate of greenfield entry and closedown exit (annual average, 1970–82).

The maturation process for entrants

The short-run or instantaneous greenfield entry and closedown exit rates are not surprising. They confirm the casual impression that entrants rarely dominate an industry in their first year of operation. Whether this is an accurate depiction of the magnitude of entry depends on the long-run share of a particular cohort of entrants. This, in turn, depends on the exit rate of its members, the average length of life, and the growth rate after birth of all entrants in that cohort. If entrants either experience a relatively short life due to high infant mortality rates or a relatively slow growth rate during adolescence, then the long-run or cumulative impact of entry may be unimportant. On the other hand, surviving entrants may grow enough to outweigh the effect of exits and allow a cohort's share to increase over a substantial period of time. In this case, the cumulative effect of entry will be greater.

Length of life of new firms. Evidence on the length of life of new firms indicates that greenfield entrants have a high infant mortality rate and that they tend to fail at higher rates than do older firms, but also that a significant percentage are alive a decade after birth (Figures 2-2, 2-3, and 2-4).

The exit rates of firms that existed in 1970 and the exit rates of the 1971 cohort of greenfield entrants over the period 1971–80 are presented in Figure 2-2. Exit is defined at the level of the manufacturing sector as a whole. Exit rates are calculated as a percentage of the number of firms in the opening period – 1970 for incumbents, and 1971 for entrants. The hazard rate for each group is also included. The hazard rate is the percentage of remaining firms in each group that fail. It is the probability of death, conditional on surviving

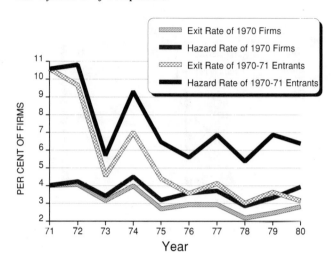

Figure 2-2. Enterprise exit and hazard rates: a comparison of the experience of 1970 firms with 1971 greenfield entrants (1971–80).

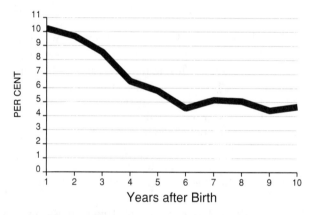

Figure 2-3. Average rates of exit of greenfield entrants by age class (percentage of firms).

to the particular period being examined. It provides a measure of the risk of death in any period for the group that has survived to that period.

The initial exit rate for 1971 greenfield entrants starts at 10 per cent. This is well above the initial exit rate calculated for 1970 incumbents, which is 4 per cent. By the end of 10 years, the exit rate for 1971 entrants is not much above the exit rate for incumbents, but there is still a substantial difference in the hazard rate and, therefore, in the risk of exit faced by those in each

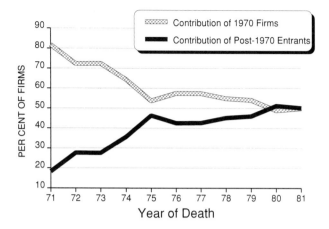

Figure 2-4. The origin of exits by plant closedown: entrants since 1970 vs. 1970 firms (1971–81).

group who have survived to the end of the period. The hazard rate of a 1971 entrant falls to between only 5 and 7 per cent, while the hazard rate of 1970 incumbents stays generally in the range of 3.5 to 4.5 per cent. While some progress is made in reducing risk in the remaining entrant population, this group cannot be said to have reached the same risk level as older firms at the end of their first decade of life.

The complete set of survival rates for all greenfield entry cohorts between 1971 and 1981 is presented in Table 2-3. As with Table 2-2, the turnover process is evaluated at the manufacturing-sector level. Table 2-3 lists each year's entrants between 1971 and 1981 and includes the number and percentage that exit in each subsequent year and that remain in existence in 1982. The average exit rate for all cohorts declines over time.[12]

These data, then, show that new firms die in large numbers. Equally, they show that some entrants in a given year have an impact that lasts well beyond that particular year. Of the 1,427 entrants by plant creation in 1971, 10.6 per cent exited within the first year; nevertheless, 40.2 per cent were still alive in 1982. The data presented in Table 2-3 were used to estimate the implied average length of life of greenfield entrants. A Weibull function was used to estimate the hazard function that depicts the exit rate as a function of age. The average length of life of a greenfield entrant implied by this distribution and the estimated parameters was about 13 years.

Length of life of exiting firms. There is a second way of showing that entry and exit are not confined to a fringe of firms that affect only the margin of

Table 2-3. Exit profile of firms that enter the manufacturing sector[a] by building new plant, 1971–81 (firm numbers and percentages)[b]

Year of exit[d]	Year of entry[c]										
	1971	1972	1973	1974	1975	1976	1977	1978	1979	1980	1981
1971	151 (10.58)	—	—	—	—	—	—	—	—	—	—
1972	138 (9.67)	118 (14.32)	—	—	—	—	—	—	—	—	—
1973	65 (4.56)	71 (8.62)	64 (7.38)	—	—	—	—	—	—	—	—
1974	100 (7.01)	66 (8.01)	100 (11.53)	110 (10.69)	—	—	—	—	—	—	—
1975	63 (4.41)	41 (4.98)	59 (6.81)	101 (9.82)	101 (13.20)	—	—	—	—	—	—
1976	51 (3.57)	40 (4.85)	52 (6.00)	94 (9.14)	95 (12.42)	32 (7.60)	—	—	—	—	—
1977	59 (4.13)	42 (5.10)	54 (6.23)	88 (8.55)	72 (9.41)	35 (8.31)	31 (13.84)	—	—	—	—
1978	43 (3.01)	31 (3.76)	31 (3.58)	34 (3.30)	29 (3.79)	28 (6.65)	17 (7.59)	126 (7.22)	—	—	—
1979	52 (3.64)	40 (4.85)	54 (6.23)	53 (5.15)	44 (5.75)	18 (4.28)	10 (4.46)	116 (6.65)	50 (6.35)	—	—
1980	45 (3.15)	33 (4.00)	49 (5.65)	54 (5.25)	32 (4.18)	28 (6.65)	20 (8.93)	106 (6.07)	73 (9.26)	86 (10.87)	—
1981	87 (6.10)	51 (6.19)	48 (5.54)	69 (6.71)	48 (6.27)	24 (5.70)	21 (9.38)	145 (8.31)	93 (11.80)	103 (13.02)	51 (10.49)
Alive in 1982	573 (40.15)	291 (35.32)	356 (41.06)	426 (41.40)	344 (44.97)	256 (60.81)	125 (55.80)	1252 (71.75)	572 (72.59)	602 (76.11)	435 (89.51)
Total	1,427 (100.00)	824 (100.00)	867 (100.00)	1,029 (100.00)	765 (100.00)	421 (100.00)	224 (100.00)	1,745 (100.00)	788 (100.00)	791 (100.00)	486 (100.00)

[a] The manufacturing sector is defined using the 1970 Standard Industry Classification for the years 1971–81.
[b] Numbers in parentheses are percentages.
[c] The first year that the enterprise's code appeared.
[d] The last year that the enterprise's code appeared.

each industry. Instead of examining the fate of an entry cohort, the age of firms in every exit cohort can be tabulated. Evidence on the source of close-down exits suggests that they are not confined to recent entrants, an inference that could all too easily be drawn from the high infant-mortality rates.

The distribution of deaths by year of birth is tabulated for each year be-tween 1971 and 1981 in Table 2-4 for firms that exited by plant closure. In 1971, 18.3 per cent of deaths by plant closure were entrants of the same year, and 81.7 per cent were from the population that existed at the beginning of the year. Even by the end of the decade, about 50 per cent of deaths came from the original 1970 population. It is true that there is a tendency for a slightly larger percentage of deaths in any one year to come from the imme-diately preceding years, but these years do not overwhelm the total. Exits, then, are not restricted just to recent entrants.

These data were used to construct Figure 2-4, which plots the percentage of deaths that are attributed to entrants since 1970 as opposed to firms in existence in 1970, as a longer and longer time period is used to measure retrospectively the effect of entrants. The cumulative effect of entrants is the sum of contributions of all entry cohorts since 1970 to deaths in a particular year, and the effect of incumbents is the contribution made by the 1970 group of firms to deaths in that year. The cumulative effect of entrants to exit rates increases rapidly at first as the period of measurement is increased from 1 to 5 years. But, after 5 years, the contribution of entrants increases only slightly year by year. Conversely, the contribution of incumbents declines rapidly at first, but after 5 years levels out. After a decade, incumbents (firms in exist-ence 10 years previously) are contributing over half of all deaths.

While many entrants, then, disappear after entry, this has all too frequently been interpreted to imply that entrants do not matter. The data presented to this point suggest that the issue is more complex. While entrants have a high mortality rate at birth, there are still many left a decade later. The ultimate effect of these entrants depends on the growth rate of the survivors.

Growth of entry cohorts. In order to characterize the experience of surviving entrants in the 1970s, the data on entry into and exit from the manufacturing sector as a whole were used to calculate the share of each entry cohort as it matured. Data for each entry cohort from 1971 to 1980 were used to calculate the average share of the number of firms and value-added for each age class of each entry cohort. The results are plotted in Figure 2-5 for greenfield entrants. All shares are expressed in index form as a percentage of the share in the year of birth.

Because there is immediate exit from each greenfield entry cohort, the average percentage of all firms accounted for by each entry cohort declines continuously as the cohort ages. In contrast, the average value-added share[13]

Table 2-4. *Distribution of firms that exit the manufacturing sector[a] by closing plant according to year of entry, 1971–81 (firm numbers and percentages)[b]*

Year of entry[c]	Year of exit[d]										
	1971	1972	1973	1974	1975	1976	1977	1978	1979	1980	1981
1971	143 (18.31)	131 (14.70)	60 (8.70)	89 (9.03)	61 (7.65)	40 (4.93)	49 (6.03)	31 (4.93)	46 (5.97)	33 (3.61)	78 (5.81)
1972	—	115 (12.91)	66 (9.57)	64 (6.49)	45 (5.65)	38 (4.69)	36 (4.43)	25 (3.97)	39 (5.06)	31 (3.39)	44 (3.28)
1973			64 (9.28)	93 (9.43)	56 (7.03)	50 (6.17)	52 (6.40)	26 (4.13)	47 (6.10)	42 (4.60)	45 (3.35)
1974			—	106 (10.75)	104 (13.05)	94 (11.59)	78 (9.61)	31 (4.93)	46 (5.97)	49 (5.36)	60 (4.47)
1975				—	103 (12.92)	96 (11.84)	70 (8.62)	22 (3.50)	37 (4.80)	25 (2.74)	43 (3.20)
1976					—	27 (3.33)	32 (3.94)	24 (3.82)	14 (1.82)	29 (3.17)	21 (1.56)
1977						—	29 (3.57)	14 (2.23)	13 (1.69)	16 (1.75)	17 (1.27)
1978							—	111 (17.65)	96 (12.45)	96 (10.50)	123 (9.16)
1979								—	44 (5.71)	71 (7.77)	94 (7.00)
1980									—	76 (8.32)	102 (7.00)
1981										—	46 (7.59)
Alive in 1970	638 (81.69)	645 (72.39)	500 (72.46)	634 (64.30)	428 (53.70)	466 (57.46)	466 (57.39)	345 (54.85)	389 (50.45)	446 (48.80)	670 (49.89)
Total	781 (100.00)	891 (100.00)	690 (100.00)	986 (100.00)	797 (100.00)	811 (100.00)	812 (100.00)	629 (100.00)	771 (100.00)	914 (100.00)	1,343 (100.00)

[a] The manufacturing sector is defined using the 1970 Standard Industrial Classification for the years 1971–81.
[b] Numbers in parentheses are percentages.
[c] The first year that the enterprise's code appeared.
[d] The last year that the enterprise's code appeared.

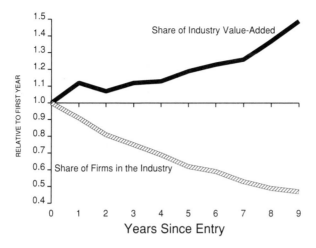

Figure 2-5. The post-entry performance of greenfield entrants (average of 1971–80 cohorts, indexed on initial share).

increases throughout the 10-year period studied here. The growth rate of surviving entrants, then, more than offsets the high death rate experienced by each cohort in the early years of its existence.

Long-run measures of entry are derived by counting the market share that has been accumulated by entrants since an initial year. The total share of all entrants will increase over time because more cohorts are being added, but this tendency may be offset if the market share of existing cohorts declines. If, on average, each cohort adds n per cent to employment starting in period zero and then declines by a constant m percentage points per year, the maximum cumulative value that entry can have is in the n/mth period.

The cumulative effects of greenfield entry are plotted in Figure 2-6. The average market share – using value-added – of each entry cohort from 1971 to 1981 was used for the starting point. The average share trajectory corresponding to Figure 2-5 was then applied to each cohort. The resulting total market share captured by entrants is a representation of how the effect of entry accumulates, on average. Over the decade studied, there is no downturn in an average cohort's share and the cumulative effect of entry continuously increases. Despite their high mortality rate, entrants remain to make themselves felt as a group.

Cumulative effects of greenfield entry and closedown exit

The previous analysis describes how the magnitude of entry accumulates, but it is based on averages and on a definition of entry into the manufacturing sector as a whole that may understate the amount of entry that

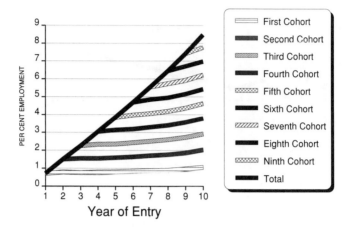

Figure 2-6. The cumulative market share of greenfield entrants: a representation.

occurs because it misses movements by firms originally in one manufacturing industry into another. More comprehensive measures of the cumulative effect of entry over a period of years can be generated. This is done first by measuring the cumulative amount of entry into and exit from the manufacturing sector as a whole over 6- and 11-year periods. Second, more detailed analyses at the four-digit level that compare end-points 9 years apart are conducted to avoid the aggregation bias inherent in defining entry into and exit from the manufacturing sector as a whole.

Using measures of entry to the manufacturing sector as a whole. Two 6-year periods, 1970–76 and 1975–81, and one 11-year period, 1970–81, are selected to examine longer-run entry and exit rates in the Canadian manufacturing sector. The long-run rates of change for each period are calculated by comparing the status of firms in the initial and terminal years. Thus, for the period 1970–81, the entry rate is calculated as the 1981 employment in manufacturing firms that were not in the manufacturing sector in 1970 divided by 1970 employment in the manufacturing sector. This measure captures the cumulative effect of all entrants between 1970 and 1981 that were extant in 1981.

The longer-run greenfield-entry and closedown-exit rates and the average rates derived from measuring the instantaneous entry and exit rates within each of the 6- and 11-year periods are presented in Table 2-5. Long-run entry and exit rates are presented in the first two panels of Table 2-5. Panel A contains the cumulative rates of change. Panel B contains the equivalent annual rates derived from these cumulative rates of change. For comparative

Table 2-5. *Cumulative greenfield-entry and closedown-exit rates, selected periods, 1970–81 (per cent)*[a]

Period	Greenfield-entry rate		Closedown-exit rate	
	Number of firms	Employment	Number of firms	Employment
A. Cumulative change from comparing end-points				
1970–76	23.7	5.1	22.5	5.3
1975–81	21.6	6.1	23.7	7.8
1970–81	35.5	10.9	35.0	10.5
B. Implicit annual rates of change from panel A				
1970–76	3.6	0.8	4.2	1.0
1975–81	3.3	0.9	4.4	1.3
1970–81	2.8	0.9	3.8	1.0
C. Average of annual rates within each period				
1970–76	5.2	0.7	4.9	0.9
1975–81	4.5	1.0	4.8	1.3
1970–81	5.1	0.9	4.9	1.1

[a] Entrants are defined as those firms that were not in any manufacturing industry in the base year (i.e., 1970 for 1970–76) but were there in the final year (i.e., 1976 for 1970–76); exits are the reverse. All rates are expressed as a percentage of base-year firm numbers or employment in the manufacturing sector.

purposes, panel C provides the corresponding average annual rates derived from the year-to-year comparisons.[14]

The longer-run entry and exit rates presented in panel A indicate that when cumulated over periods of 6 to 11 years, greenfield entry and closedown exit are processes of considerable magnitude. For example, 35 per cent of the 1970 population of firms had exited the manufacturing sector by 1980 because of plant closings. These exits accounted for 11 per cent of sector employment in 1970. Greenfield entrants into the manufacturing sector during the same period also had a substantial effect. The number of entrants equalled 36 per cent of the 1970 firm population. Their employment in 1981 was equal to 11 per cent of total employment in 1970.

Using measures of entry at the four-digit SIC level. While the data for entry into the manufacturing sector indicate that decadal turnover is not insignificant, they may understate the magnitude of entry because they focus only on entry by firms outside the manufacturing sector. Therefore, more detailed

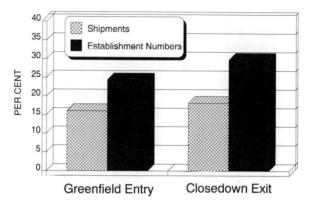

Figure 2-7. Cumulative rates of greenfield entry and closedown exit (1970–79, four-digit industry mean value).

estimates of longer-run entry and exit rates were made for the period 1970–79 using the categories presented in Table 2-1 by measuring this process at the finer four-digit industry level. The initial year was 1970 and the terminal year was 1979.

The cumulative magnitude of entry captures the importance in 1979 of successive cohorts of entrants from 1971 to 1979. The cumulative magnitude of exit captures the effect on the 1970 firm population of exits in 1970 through 1978. In this exercise, greenfield entrants are defined as firms that entered either by opening new plant or by transferring it from another industry. Closedown exits are defined as those firms that exited either by closing plant or by transferring it to another industry.[15]

The rates of entry and exit so defined are presented in Figure 2-7, first by the proportion of the number of establishments involved, and second by the relative proportion of the new and closed plants' shares of industry shipments. In each case, the proportion is the mean taken across 167 four-digit industries.

These data confirm the magnitude of the entry and exit process that was found using turnover data for the manufacturing sector as a whole (see Table 2-5). The cumulative effect of greenfield entry and closedown exit over the decade of the 1970s was large. By 1979, greenfield entrants since 1970 accounted for, on average, 24.4 per cent of all establishments and 16.1 per cent of shipments in that year. Closedown exits over the decade accounted for, on average, 29.8 per cent of the number of establishments in 1970 and 18.2 per cent of shipments.

These four-digit measures of entry and exit are considerably higher than those measured at the aggregate level of the manufacturing sector as a whole.

Entrants over the period 1970–79 that are still alive in 1979 are only five years old, on average. The earlier exercise placed the cumulative share of entry after five years at around 5 per cent (Figure 2-6 and Table 2-5). This is only about a third of the rate calculated at the more detailed four-digit level.

In summary, the long-run data reveal that the cumulative effect of successive waves of greenfield entry over a decade is considerable. On an annual basis, entry is not large. Moreover, a considerable proportion of recent entrants exit the industry. These two stylized facts should not be used to infer that the greenfield-entry process is generally unimportant. When entrants are tracked longitudinally, the story changes. Those entrants who do not die in early childhood grow sufficiently to offset the departures.

Entry and exit by size-class

The previous sections have focused on aggregate measures of change at the industry level. They ignore how entry and exit are distributed across size-classes. An examination of the importance of entry and exit by size-class provides information on the extent to which these processes are restricted to the fringe or whether they have a more general effect across the size distribution of all firms.

To answer this question, it is necessary once again to distinguish between the short and the long run. In the short run, the smallest size-classes may dominate exits; but if the cumulative impact of exit over several years is calculated by size-class, the relative importance of small firms will be less once large firms decline to the point where they begin to exit. In the short run, entry rates in smaller size-classes may be larger than those for larger size-classes, but only because entrants have not yet had the opportunity to grow to maturity. To reduce the possible biases associated with calculating the size distribution of entry and exit using short-run data, long-run entry and exit rates are calculated.

In order to investigate the distribution of longer-run entry and exit rates by size-class, both rates are calculated at the detailed four-digit industry level for the period 1970–79. Using the finer level of industry detail also reduces the aggregation bias inherent in the more aggregate statistics – when calculated across all industries, entry and exit rates may be higher in smaller size-classes if entry and exit rates are higher in industries with smaller average firm sizes. Quintile groups are chosen to define the size-classes for each industry, with firms ranked on the basis of shipment shares. Exits are assigned to the size-class in which they fell in 1970; entrants are assigned to their size-class as of 1979. The entry and exit rates plotted in Figure 2-8 are averages calculated across 167 four-digit industries. Both are expressed in terms of percentage of firms per quintile group.

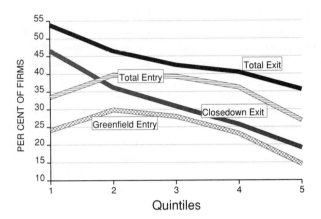

Figure 2-8. Entry and exit rates by size-class (1970–79, four-digit industry mean value).

The data reveal that while exit is generally a small-firm phenomenon, it is not restricted to small firms. Closedown exit rates are not zero for the larger size-classes.[16]

The cumulative long-run entry rate also generally declines across size-classes and closely follows the pattern of the exit rate, except for the smallest classes. Here entry rates increase while exit rates decline. This reflects the fact that by 1979 entrants in the smallest size-classes have an opportunity to move upward over time since their birth rates are being calculated using 1979 status. Nevertheless, while entry rates in the smaller size-classes are twice those in the largest, the latter, at some 15 per cent, are not inconsequential.

In summary, the entry process, like the exit process, is ubiquitous, but it is not equally concentrated across the spectrum of firm size-classes. The largest size-classes are subject to less greenfield entry and closedown exit; they are not, however, completely protected from them.

Conclusion

Controversy about the efficacy of the entry process is not resolved just by measuring greenfield entry and closedown exit. Providing basic data on its importance does, however, further the debate.

The importance of entrants depends upon the probability of entry, the size of entrants, and their growth rate after birth. It has been shown here that all three have to be examined to appreciate fully the role that entry and exit play. If year-to-year data on entry and exit are examined and a narrow definition of entry is used, the process appears to be insignificant. At birth, greenfield entrants rarely account for more than 1 per cent of employment. Moreover, these entrants are initially small, on average, and therefore of little immediate threat to large firms.

Entry turns latent or potential competition into actual competition. The arrival of real plant and machinery serves to make the reality of potential competitors that much more substantial. But entrants are not immediately successful. The maturation process is often slow and painful. The infant mortality rate is high. Upwards of 50 per cent of greenfield births die by the end of the decade. Nevertheless, the survivors grow sufficiently to offset the deaths of their siblings. As a result, the share of each greenfield entry cohort increases slowly over time, and as more and more cohorts of entrants are added with the passage of time, the importance of new firms accumulates.

It is true that post-entry growth matters. But to refer to this as internal competition rather than competition from entrants is to place too narrow an interpretation on entry. If an industry is regarded as being divided into classes and having barriers that reduce movement between different size-classes, then post-birth growth is synonymous with entry into the larger size-classes. Models that rely on internal rivalry rather than latent rivalry from potential entrants may still be more appropriate for some purposes. But industries do not remain static over time. The conventional industrial-economics literature – with its focus on large-firm shares and concentration ratios – all too easily gives the impression of minimal change and, therefore, of static markets. The gradual accumulation of entry and exit depicted here should begin to dispel this mistaken impression.

While the data presented here reveal much about the entry and exit process, they tell only part of the story. Not all firm entry involves new-plant creation. Entry is also accomplished by acquiring assets or through merger. Exit occurs through the divestiture of assets. The next chapter focuses on the magnitude and characteristics of this second method of entry and exit.

3

Entry, exit, and the merger process

Introduction

Different processes contribute to the dynamics of intra-industry growth and decline. Firm turnover transfers resources from one group to another. The emergence of new firms causes some firms to exit and others to decline.

Greenfield entry and closedown exit is the process that changes the firm population in the most obvious way. When a firm enters by building new plant or when it leaves by closing plant, the effect on jobs and productive capacity is immediate.

Resources are also transferred as a result of ownership-control changes. Control is shifted from one group of owners to another in a variety of ways. One firm may purchase all of the shares or assets of another and subsume the acquired operations into its own; or it may maintain them as entirely separate entities. Control can also be shifted when only a controlling interest is acquired. In this case, control of the firm has changed hands, although the firm has not been entirely acquired.

Changes in control are often, though not invariably, associated with a merging of the interests of two companies. Control can be shifted without such a merging of two firms' interests – for example, when different factions of shareholders, who do not represent other firms' interests, rearrange the majority coalition that controls the company. But this situation is not common in this database. Thus, for all intents and purposes, changes in control that are examined here are those accomplished by mergers and acquisitions of some type.

It is ironic that greenfield entry and closedown exit, whose short-run impact is readily apparent, have received little attention. Mergers, on the other hand, have been the focus of many studies. Much of this attention has been directed at horizontal mergers because of their potential for anti-competitive consequences, even though they did not account for the majority of merger activity in the Canadian manufacturing sector in the 1970s. Between 1971 and 1973, only 43 per cent of all mergers in the Canadian manufacturing sector were horizontal, and between 1977 and 1979 only 30 per cent were in this category.[1] In the majority of cases studied here, the transfer of a plant from one firm to another resulted in a firm exiting or entering an industry. These are broadly classified as diversifying mergers – where a firm acquires facilities in an industry in which it has no interest.[2]

This chapter examines the merger process in the manufacturing sector. Other studies have tried to provide comprehensive evaluations of the merger process, focusing on the profitability, productivity, and growth paths of merged firms (Cowling et al., 1980; Mueller, 1980; Ravenscraft and Scherer, 1987). Few of these studies have attempted to place the merger process in context. This chapter does so by comparing the merger process with other changes that affect industry dynamics – in particular, greenfield entry and closedown exit.

Comparing the merger process with these alternatives serves to provide a framework within which the importance of that process can be better understood. Importance here will be judged in terms of both the size of the phenomenon and the pattern of its occurrence. The efficacy of the merger process, measured in terms of its effect on both productivity and profitability, is examined in Chapter 8.

The work reported here is unique, not only in terms of its approach, but also in terms of the databases used.[3] There have been other studies of the Canadian merger process (Eckbo 1986, 1988; Jog and Riding, 1986).[4] But most have had to rely on relatively limited samples of mergers and use stock-market or balance-sheet data. This chapter relies on the same establishment-based Census of Manufactures data files that were used to measure the importance of greenfield entry and closedown exit. Because of the comprehensive nature of the Canadian census, these data have the potential to overcome the deficiency of earlier Canadian merger studies. It also allows the industry in which the merger occurs to be specified more precisely.

The importance of mergers

Methodology issues

Comparisons of mergers with firm turnover can use long- or short-run data, aggregated or disaggregated industry data. Measurement can focus either on firms or on establishments. The amount of recorded merger activity depends on which set of factors are chosen for the measurement.

Two separate analyses are employed here. The first focuses on the short run and compares the yearly entry rate of firms that build new plants with that of those that acquire plants. Entry is defined as occurring at the aggregate level of the manufacturing sector; that is, entrants are defined as firms that did not previously have a presence in the manufacturing sector. The second comparison adopts a longer-run focus by comparing firms and their plants in 1970 and 1979. It uses a less aggregated industry level of definition. Entrants are defined as firms that are new to a four-digit manufacturing industry. The longer-run database allows a comparison of the characteristics of different types of plants (entrants, exits, acquisitions) in these two years.

Throughout the analysis, entry and exit of plants and establishments are defined by the appearance and disappearance of identifiers attached to producers. These identifiers allow plants and firms in the Census of Manufactures to be tracked over time. A greenfield entrant is defined in this study as the appearance of a new-firm identifier in an industry associated with a new plant. An acquisition or merger entrant is defined in this study as the appearance of a new-firm identifier in an industry associated with an existing plant. In the latter case, the firm has entered by acquiring assets – and is referred to as an acquisition or merger entry.

"Merger or acquisition entry" is a broad generic term and describes a myriad of corporate changes – as does the term "merger". New-firm identifiers are assigned when the firm is acquired by new controlling owners or when there is another major form of corporate reorganization. The change may involve just the purchase of a plant; it may involve the subsuming of one company under another; it may involve the integration of two corporate entities into a completely new one. For the purposes of this study, the various forms of control changes are not distinguished. Appendix A discusses the concepts and measurement problems in detail.

Short-run estimates of merger entry

Short-run rates of enterprise entry into and exit from the manufacturing sector as a whole,[5] defined in terms of both number of firms and employment affected, are presented in Table 3-1 for the period 1970–82. Entry by plant creation (greenfield entry) and by plant acquisition are tabulated separately. So too are exit by plant closure (closedown exit) and by plant divestiture.

Over the period 1970–82 the annual greenfield entry rate averaged 4.3 per cent of the firm population examined; the annual entry rate through acquisition averaged only 0.6 per cent. The average size of a new firm that was created through acquisition, however, was larger than that of a greenfield entrant. As a result, the employment entry rates for the two categories were quite similar.[6] Greenfield firm entry averaged 0.9 per cent and firm entry through acquisition averaged 1.1 per cent of total employment per year. Figure 3-1 is a bar chart of average annual entry rates over the period that reveals the different results when entry rates are calculated using firm numbers as opposed to employment measures.

A similar picture emerges on the exit side. Closedown firm-exit rates are several times those of exit rates by plant divestiture – 5.3 and 1.2 per cent of

Table 3-1. *Comparison of annual firm-entry and -exit rates, by category of entry and exit, 1970–82 (per cent)*[a]

| | Entry | | | | Exit | | | |
| | Via plant creation | | Via acquisition | | Via plant closedown | | Via divestiture | |
Period	Number of firms	Employment	Number of firms	Employment	Number of firms	Employment	Number of firms	Employment
1970–71	3.4	1.2	0.8	0.4	5.6	1.1	0.2	0.2
1971–72	4.6	1.0	0.4	0.7	4.8	0.9	1.4	1.5
1972–73	4.8	1.1	0.2	0.4	5.5	0.6	0.6	0.9
1973–74	5.7	1.2	0.3	2.4	4.3	0.9	0.9	3.0
1974–75	5.9	0.8	0.3	0.2	6.3	0.9	1.1	1.6
1975–76	3.4	0.4	0.2	0.4	5.1	1.2	0.6	0.6
1976–77	1.7	0.3	0.4	0.4	5.3	1.5	0.9	0.6
1977–78	4.4	1.2	0.9	2.4	5.0	1.6	1.7	3.3
1978–79	3.4	0.7	1.1	1.8	3.8	1.0	1.6	2.4
1979–80	4.7	1.2	1.1	1.9	4.6	1.2	1.8	2.8
1980–81	2.9	0.6	0.9	1.2	5.5	1.4	1.5	5.4
1981–82	6.3	1.1	1.0	1.1	8.3	1.7	1.8	2.0
Mean	4.3	0.9	0.6	1.1	5.3	1.2	1.2	2.0

[a] An entrant is defined as a firm present in manufacturing in the end year, but not the initial year of the period. Exit is the reverse. Rates are calculated relative to the number of establishments and employment in the initial year. Entry and exit are defined as entry to manufacturing and exit from manufacturing as a whole. Greenfield entry occurs when the appearance of a firm in the manufacturing sector corresponds to the appearance of a plant. Closedown exit occurs when a firm's disappearance corresponds to the disappearance of its plant(s).

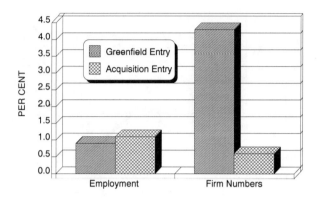

Figure 3-1. Relative rates of entry: greenfield vs. acquisition (annual average, 1970–1982).

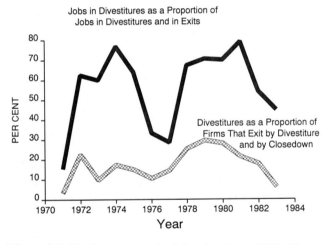

Figure 3-2. The importance of exit by divestiture (1971–83).

the firm population, respectively, over the period. However, when employment is used to measure the intensity of the processes, firm-exit rates by divestiture average 2.0 per cent compared with 1.2 per cent by plant closing.

While the average level of acquisition entry and divestiture exit, defined at the aggregate manufacturing level, is more important than entry through plant creation or exit through plant closure in terms of jobs affected, its importance varies substantially over time. In Figure 3-2 the percentage of jobs affected by divestiture exit is plotted along with the percentage of all firms that exited. Although divestiture exit affected an average of 53 per cent of all jobs in exiting firms, this figure varies from less than 20 per cent to almost 80 per

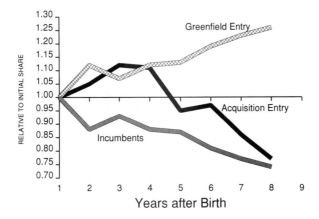

Figure 3-3. The growth in post-entry share: greenfield vs. acquisition entrants (average of 1971–80 cohorts, indexed on initial value-added share).

cent. Acquisitions come in erratically timed waves. This means that the importance of entry through plant creation and entry through acquisition may well differ across time because of variations in the type and intensity of merger waves in each period.

It is evident that considering acquisition entry in addition to greenfield entry doubles the annual rates at which the firm population turns over. But since the base that is being doubled is relatively small, total entry from both sources, calculated on an annual basis, is still relatively small – affecting about 2 per cent of employment per year.

Transition from the short run to the long run

In the preceding chapter, it was demonstrated that the instantaneous or short-run rates of greenfield entry concealed the true magnitude of the process. To appreciate its long-run magnitude, the history of each cohort since birth had to be tracked in order to measure the ultimate dimensions of the cohort.

The same procedure was followed for acquisition entrants. In order to characterize the experience of surviving entrants in the 1970s, the yearly data on the number and size of acquisitions that resulted in entry to the manufacturing sector as a whole were used to calculate the share of each entry cohort as it matured. Data for each entry cohort from 1971 to 1980 were used and the average share, in terms of value-added, was calculated for each age class of each entry cohort. These results are plotted in Figure 3-3 for greenfield and acquisition entrants, by age class. All shares are expressed in index form as a percentage of the share in the year of birth.

The two entry processes followed very different paths. The average share initially increased for each, but while that of greenfield entrants continued to grow, that of acquisition entrants began to decline. After five years it had fallen below its initial level.

The growth rate of surviving greenfield entrants, then, more than offset the high death rate experienced by each cohort in the early years of its existence. This is not the case for acquisition entrants. That the two groups of entrants did not experience the same post-entry success is not surprising in light of the differences between them. Only greenfield entrants can be classified as true infants that have the potential for rapid growth and maturation. Merger entrants are better characterized as mature firms looking for rejuvenation. Because of their larger initial size, there is less possibility for continued post-entry growth.

Despite this, there is evidence of some initial success among merger entrants after entry. To demonstrate more clearly the degree to which this is so, the normal path of market share for existing plants at any point in time is also plotted in Figure 3-3. It is just one minus the share of entrants. It is evident that normally an incumbent would expect its share to decline more or less continuously. By way of contrast, plants that have been merged experience a short-run increase in their market share before they follow the downward path that is normally followed by incumbents. Whether the merger effect is temporary or permanent depends on whether the eventual downward path causes the merged plant to lose market share at a faster rate than do incumbents. At present, there is insufficient data to determine whether this is the case. It does appear that the merged plants had almost returned to the normal growth path by the end of the period, because once they started to lose market share, they did so at a faster rate than did incumbents. Whether the average trajectory of merged plants passed below that of incumbents and, thus, whether the merged plants lost the short-run gains experienced shortly after merger is a matter that must await data for a longer period.

The course followed by an entry cohort over time reveals how successful one group of entrants is; but it is the cumulative effect of succeeding years of entrants that indicates the extent to which the process ultimately has an impact on the industrial structure. The cumulative effects of acquisition entry are plotted in Figure 3-4. The average market share, using value-added, of each entry cohort from 1970 to 1981 was used for the starting point. The average-share trajectory corresponding to Figure 3-3 was then applied to each cohort. The resulting total market share captured by acquisition entrants is a representation of how the effect of entry accumulates, on average. It is only a representation because the initial share varies over time – especially in the case of acquisition entry. Despite the reversal in the effects of acquisition entry after a short period, the cumulative effects of adding successive cohorts of acquisition entrants offset this tendency for at least a decade.

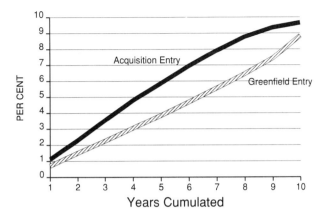

Figure 3-4. The cumulative growth of acquisition entrants vs. greenfield entrants (average of 1971–80 cohorts, indexed on initial share of industry value-added).

The cumulative effect of successive cohorts of greenfield entrants is also presented in Figure 3-4. It also cumulates inexorably over the first decade of measurement. Despite the high mortality rate of young greenfield entrants, the survivors grew at a sufficient rate to increase the overall share of a cohort, on average. Even though the paths of the average cohort of acquisition entrants and greenfield entrants depicted in Figure 3-3 differ dramatically, their cumulative effects are remarkably similar after the first ten years of life. The difference in their growth paths is reflected in different curvatures of the two cumulative-growth trajectories in Figure 3-4. The trajectories are about to cross at the end of the decade, suggesting that greenfield entrants will emerge in the lead in the second decade of their existence.

Cumulative effects of entry and exit

Merged firms, then, experience a modicum of success that is characterized by a short-run increase in market share. While the long-run cumulative effect of several cohorts of acquisition entrants has already been presented, more precise measurement of these long-run effects is presented here. Long-run entry rates are obtained by comparing the status of firms and the plants they own, not in adjacent years, as for the short run, but for two years that are further apart.

Using measures of entry into the manufacturing sector as a whole. In order to calculate the magnitude of acquisition entry in the long run, the annual enterprise database that defines entry as firms that are new to manufacturing

Table 3-2. *Cumulative firm-entry rates, by category of entry, selected periods, 1970–81 (per cent)*[a]

Period	Total entry rate		Greenfield rate		Acquisition rate	
	Number of firms	Employment	Number of firms	Employment	Number of firms	Employment
A. Cumulative change from comparing end-points						
1970–76	25.4	9.8	23.7	5.1	1.8	4.7
1975–81	25.2	15.1	21.6	6.1	3.6	9.0
1970–81	39.9	25.5	35.5	10.9	4.5	14.6
B. Implicit annual rates of change from panel A						
1970–76	3.9	1.6	3.6	0.8	0.3	0.8
1975–81	3.8	2.4	3.3	0.9	0.6	1.4
1970–81	3.1	2.1	2.8	0.9	0.4	1.3
C. Average of annual rates within each period						
1970–76	5.6	1.5	5.2	0.7	0.4	0.7
1975–81	5.3	2.4	4.5	1.0	0.8	1.4
1970–81	5.7	2.0	5.1	0.9	0.6	1.1

[a] Entrants are defined as those firms that were not in any manufacturing industry in the base year (i.e., 1970 for 1970–76) but were in an industry in the final year (i.e., 1976 for 1970–76). All rates are expressed as a percentage of firms or employment in the base year.

was used.[7] The status of manufacturing firms was compared in the periods 1970–76, 1975–81, and 1970–81. The cumulative rates of employment change are reported in Table 3-2 for entry and Table 3-3 for exit. Thus, for the period 1970–81, the entry rate is calculated as the 1981 employment in manufacturing firms that were not in the manufacturing sector in 1970 divided by the 1970 employment in the manufacturing sector. This captures the cumulative effect of all entrants to manufacturing from 1970 to 1981 that were extant in 1981. In order to set acquisition entry and divestiture exit in context, the greenfield-entry rate and the closedown-exit rate presented in Chapter 2 are repeated in Tables 3-2 and 3-3.

   The longer-run entry and exit rates confirm the picture that is presented in Figure 3-4. When accumulated over periods of 6 to 11 years, acquisition entry and divestiture exit are processes of considerable magnitude and are approximately equal in effect to greenfield entry and closedown exit. The 1981 employment in all firms entering during the period 1970–81 was equal

Table 3-3. *Cumulative firm-exit rates, by category of exit, selected periods, 1970–81 (per cent)*[a]

	Total exit rate		Closedown rate		Divestiture rate	
Period	Number of firms	Employment	Number of firms	Employment	Number of firms	Employment
A. Cumulative change from comparing end-points						
1970–76	26.6	12.6	22.5	5.3	4.2	7.3
1975–81	30.3	20.5	23.7	7.8	6.6	12.7
1970–81	43.6	28.1	35.0	10.5	8.6	17.7
B. Implicit annual rates of change from panel A						
1970–76	5.0	2.2	4.2	1.0	0.7	1.3
1975–81	5.8	3.7	4.4	1.3	1.1	2.2
1970–81	5.1	3.0	3.8	1.0	0.8	1.8
C. Average of annual rates within each period						
1970–76	5.7	2.3	4.9	0.9	0.8	1.3
1975–81	6.1	3.8	4.8	1.3	1.3	2.5
1970–81	6.0	3.1	4.9	1.1	1.1	2.0

[a] Exits are defined as those firms that were not in any manufacturing industry in the final year (i.e., 1976 for 1970–76) but were in an industry in the first year (i.e., 1970 for 1970–76). All rates are expressed as a percentage of base-year firm numbers or employment in the manufacturing sector.

to 25.5 per cent of 1970 employment; for greenfield entry, it was 10.9 per cent; for entry by acquisition, it was 14.6 per cent. The same relationship held for exit. Closedown exits over the period 1970–81 accounted for 10.5 per cent of employment in 1970; exit through divestiture accounted for 17.7 per cent of 1970 employment.

Using measures of entry at the four-digit SIC level. The previous analysis describes how the magnitude of entry accumulates inexorably; but it is based on averages and on a definition of entry to the manufacturing sector as a whole that may understate the amount of entry that occurs because it misses movement by firms originally in one manufacturing industry to another. More comprehensive measures of the cumulative effect of entry were estimated at the industry level in order to avoid the aggregation bias inherent in defining entry into and exit from the manufacturing sector as a whole.

Detailed estimates of longer-run entry and exit rates were made using data

Table 3-4. *Average share of number of establishments and of shipments[a] across four-digit manufacturing industries by category of entry and exit, 1970 and 1979 (per cent)[b]*

Firm category	Share of industries	Share of number of establishments		Share of shipments	
		1970	1979	1970	1979
All firms	100.0	100.0	100.0	100.0	100.0
All entrants[c]	—	—	33.2	—	26.8
By plant birth	95.0	—	24.4	—	16.1
By acquisition	90.0	—	8.7	—	10.7
All exits[d]	—	39.8	—	30.8	—
By plant closing	97.0	29.8	—	18.2	—
By divestiture	93.0	10.0	—	12.7	—
All continuing firms[e]	100.0	60.2	66.8	69.1	73.2
Continuing establishments[f]	100.0	55.3	59.2	63.4	65.0
Divested	32.0	0.6	—	1.1	—
Acquired	53.0	—	2.2	—	3.0
Plant closures	76.0	4.3	—	4.6	—
Plant births	77.0	—	5.3	—	5.3

[a] The sample consists of long-form establishments (see Appendix A). The average is calculated across all 167 four-digit industries.
[b] A discussion of the database used for this table can be found in Appendix A.
[c] Firms that entered a four-digit SIC industry between 1970 and 1979 by plant birth, plant acquisition, or transferring a plant from another industry. Each sub-category contains entry due to transfers.
[d] Firms that exited a four-digit SIC industry between 1970 and 1979 by closing a plant, divesting themselves of plant, or transferring plant to another industry. As with entry, transfers are included.
[e] Firms that existed in both 1970 and 1979. Firms are defined as unconsolidated enterprises at the four-digit SIC industry level.
[f] Continuing establishments are those that existed in the industry in both 1970 and 1979 and did not undergo a change in ownership that led to firm entry or exit.

that compare the status of plants in 1970 and 1979 and link plants to firms. This database permits the investigation of the importance of the categories presented in Table 2-1. The magnitude of the various cells of Table 2-1 is presented in Table 3-4, first by the proportion of the number of establishments involved, and second by the relative proportion of the new, acquired, divested, and closed plants' shares of industry shipments. In each case, the proportion is the mean taken across 167 industries.

The individual industry-level data presented in Table 3-4 confirm the magnitude of the entry and exit process that was found using turnover data for the manufacturing sector as a whole. The cumulative effect of entry and exit[8] over the decade of the 1970s was large.

In 1979, some 24.4 per cent of all establishments in a four-digit industry, on average, were opened by firms that were created after 1970. Only 8.7 per cent of establishments in 1979, on average, had been acquired by firms that entered by acquisition since 1970. On this basis, greenfield entry is of greater magnitude than acquisition entry in the long run. When shipments are used, however, acquisition entry is only of slightly lesser magnitude than greenfield entry. Establishments that were created since 1970 by new firms accounted for 16.1 per cent of shipments on average in 1979; but establishments that were acquired over the decade accounted for 10.7 per cent of shipments, on average, in 1979. Acquisition entry is quantitatively significant.

Continuing firms: horizontal mergers and plant creation

Differences among the alternative forms of expansion and contraction of continuing firms are just as interesting as differences among methods of entry. Firms continuing over the decade are those with a presence in both the opening and closing year. Turnover among continuing firms is divided here into two main categories. Continuing firms can expand their operations to new plants by either building plant (Table 2-1, category 13) or by buying establishments (Table 2-1, category 12). They can reduce the number of plants operated either by closing plant (Table 2-1, category 14) or by divesting plant (Table 2-1, category 11). The data in Table 3-4 show that horizontal acquisitions are an important form of expansion for continuing firms. The share of 1979 industry shipments in plants acquired in horizontal mergers was about 60 per cent of shipments in newly created plants in the continuing-firm sector. Plants in these two categories accounted for 3 and 5.2 per cent, on average, of shipments in 1979.

While the horizontal merger process is important relative to the continuing-firm new-plant-creation process, it is not as important as the acquisition process that brings new firms into an industry. Significantly fewer plants are acquired by continuing firms than by entering firms. The 1979 share of shipments in plants acquired by continuing firms is about one-quarter that of plants acquired by entrants.

Nevertheless, the horizontal merger process plays a critical role in preventing existing firms from losing market share. Continuing firms expanded their market share, on average, by 4 percentage points from 69.1 to 73.2 per cent of shipments between 1970 and 1979 (see Table 3-4). Some of this – 0.8 of a percentage point – was generated because of the difference between the share of new plants in 1979 and closed plants in 1970. Some – 1.6 percentage points – came from the internal expansion of continuing plants. The remaining

1.8 percentage points came from the merger process.[9] This is considerably above the contribution to expansion of continuing firms made by the closure and opening of plants, or by the expansion of existing establishments.[10]

Summary

New participants in an industry are introduced in one of two different ways. On the one hand, new plants are created, either by new firms or by existing firms. On the other hand, existing plants are acquired by new firms and by existing firms. Whether it be new or continuing firms, over the decade of the 1970s the transfer of ownership was almost as important as the creation of new plants in terms of renewal. Any study of the effect of renewal on productivity growth and other aspects of industry performance needs to devote as much attention to mergers as to plant birth and death.

Mergers compared with plant creation and destruction

While take-overs are about as important a method of entry for new firms and expansion for existing firms as is the building of new plant, the merger process does not affect all industries or all groups of firms within industries equally. At the aggregate level of the manufacturing sector, the similarity in the relative importance of the two methods of expansion suggests they may be good substitutes. But on more detailed examination, substantial differences that show they are not perfect substitutes become apparent. Merger entry is concentrated in the largest size-classes and in industries where entry barriers are high. Entry by new-plant creation decreases in magnitude as size-class increases and is negatively related to concentration. The differences between the two forms of entry for new firms and the two methods of expansion for existing firms are examined next.

Size-class differences

Methods of entry and exit. The previous sections focus on aggregate measures of change at the industry level. They ignore how entrants and exits are distributed across size-classes. While greenfield and acquisition entry are of similar magnitude, they do not affect all size-classes equally. When measured annually over the period 1970–84 at the level of the manufacturing sector as a whole,[11] the greenfield entrant had 20 employees, on average, upon entry; the acquisition entrant had 255 employees, on average, in its first year after take-over. Only 1.4 per cent of greenfield entrants owned more than one plant; 17 per cent of acquisition entrants were multi-plant firms. Exits present a similar picture. Firms that exited through plant closure had 26 employees, on average, at closedown; firms that exited by divestiture had 168 employees, on average.

Entry through plant creation and acquisition, therefore, affect different parts of the firm-size distribution. Firm entry through plant creation and firm exit through plant closedown are concentrated at the smaller end of the size distribution. By way of contrast, failure at the upper end of the size distribution is less likely to result in death by plant closure; rather, the market for corporate control overcomes the problem of failing management in larger firms, and these firms are more likely to transfer plant to others than to close plant.

An examination of the magnitude of entry and exit by size-class provides information on whether these processes are restricted to the fringe or whether they have a more general effect across the size distribution of all firms. To answer this question, it is necessary once again to distinguish between the short and the long run. Firms that exit may have been in decline for some time. Measuring such firms' size in the year of death will give the incorrect impression that large firms do not decline and then die. Similarly, entrants, which may have started out quite small, may achieve substantial size after several years' growth. Measurement of size at birth, then, will underestimate the eventual impact of entrants.

Short-run firm exit by size-class. To investigate differences in firm exit across size-classes, the yearly exit data on firms at the level of the manufacturing sector as a whole were used. Since firms that exit through plant closure were much smaller than those doing so through divestiture, it is important, when examining the intensity of firm exit by size-class, to treat the types of exit separately.

The two methods of exit by firm size-class are presented in Table 3-5. The average distribution of shares for each exit category, by size-class, for all years from 1970 to 1982, is presented in columns 1 and 2, and the average distribution of firm employment for the period is in column 3. The relative importance of divestiture is given by the proportion of all jobs affected by exit (both closing and divestiture) that are in plant divestitures (column 4).

The percentage of employment affected in firms exiting by closure in the three smallest classes is greater than the percentage of employment in these classes. In this sense, exit by closure is concentrated among small firms. The magnitude of divestitures increases by size-class. It accounts for only 1.8 per cent of all employment in the smallest class; but it accounts for 47.7 per cent of employment in the largest class. However, even though firms in the largest size-class have the highest percentage of employment affected by divestiture, the percentage is still less than the percentage of total employment in this class. For firms in the two middle size-classes, divestiture is more heavily concentrated than is employment.

Considered by itself, exit by plant closure decreases the magnitude of the smallest size-class – though to the extent that entrants cause these exits and

Table 3-5. *Distribution of annual employment loss associated with firm exits by size-class, 1970–82 (per cent)*

	Mean value of distributions calculated annually[a]			
Employment size-class	Exit by divestiture (1)	Exit by closing (2)	All employment in continuing firms[b] (3)	Employment in exiting firms accounted for by divestiture[c] (4)
1–19	1.8	21.8	4.2	11.0
	(0.3)	(1.6)	(0.1)	(1.2)
20–99	17.8	41.7	14.8	38.0
	(2.8)	(1.7)	(0.1)	(2.6)
100–499	32.7	22.4	18.9	68.0
	(3.9)	(1.3)	(0.1)	(3.0)
500+	47.7	14.1	62.1	79.0
	(6.2)	(3.0)	(0.3)	(7.2)
All size-classes	100.0	100.0	100.0	—

[a] Standard error of the mean is in parentheses.
[b] Employment in firms continuing between adjacent years.
[c] Column 4 is the ratio of column 1 to the sum of columns 1 and 2.

generally appear first in the smaller size-classes, the actual effect of plant openings and closings on the firms in a particular size-class cannot be determined by examining closedowns alone.[12]

It is certainly the case that the effect of exit by divestiture on the firm-size distribution cannot be inferred without knowledge of the distribution by size of the acquirer. When the size of the acquirer is considered, the divestiture and acquisition processes are found to favour the larger firms. Baldwin and Gorecki (1986b) classify both the origin and destination of all acquisitions within manufacturing during the 1970s using three firm size-classes based on number of employees (0–99, 100–499, and 500+). The smallest and the middle-size firms lost employment as a result of redistribution due to divestiture and acquisition; the largest gained employment. If there is an inevitable rise and decline of firms due to natural tendencies, the merger process will tend to ease this process and to cushion the decline of large firms.

Average annual exit rates by size for firm closedowns and divestitures based on the same database used to generate Table 3-5 are presented in Figure 3-5. Annual exit rates are calculated from employment in exiting firms in a particular size-class divided by employment in that size-class. The average exit rate is then calculated for the period 1970–82. Exit rates by plant closure are largest for the smallest firms and decline as firm size increases.

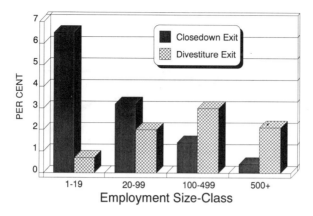

Figure 3-5. Proportion of jobs affected by exit, by size-class: closedowns vs. divestitures (average of annual rates, 1970–82).

Firm exit rates by plant divestiture do not display this monotonic relationship. They are lowest for the smallest firms and highest for firms in the third size-class; but there is little difference between firms in the second and fourth size-classes.

Longer-run firm exit and entry rates by size-class. The patterns of exit across firm size-classes in the long run and the short run need not be the same. In the short run, the smallest firms may dominate exits, but in the longer run, this will be less noticeable to the extent that large firms decline to the point where they begin to exit.

Differences in the intensity of exit and entry across different firm size-classes were investigated using data that compared the status of plants and firms in 1970 and 1979 at the industry level of aggregation. In order to generate the entry measures, each industry was divided into 10 size-classes by ranking all plants by shares of shipments. The plants were then grouped into decile classes in ascending order of market share. Then exit and entry were calculated for each size-class as the total number of plants in each entry category in a size-class divided by the total number of plants in the same size-class. Exits were assigned to the size-class into which they fell in 1970; entrants were assigned to the size-class into which they fell in 1979. Average entry and exit rates for each size-class were then calculated across the sample.[13]

The degree of exit for each form of exit and the total of the two are graphed in Figure 3-6. In the smallest size-class, 37.7 per cent of all plants in 1970 were closed because of firm exits by 1979; only 6.4 per cent of plants in this group were divested by 1979 by exiting firms. But in the four largest

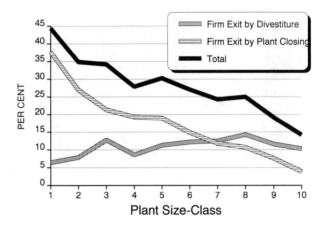

Figure 3-6. Exit by size-class: divestiture vs. closedown exit (per cent of establishments affected).

plant size-classes, which accounted for over 80 per cent of 1970 employment, more plants were affected by divestiture than by plant closure.

In Chapter 1, it was noted that closedown exits are much less prevalent in larger firms. This fact, if taken alone, can be misinterpreted to imply that large firms are relatively immune to failure. While larger firms are less likely to exit by closedown, they are more likely to exit by divestiture. When the total of both forms of exit are examined, it is apparent that the rate of exit still declines as firm size increases, but it does not decline as much as does the closedown-exit rate alone.

The two forms of entry are graphed by plant size in Figure 3-7. In the smallest plant size-class, entry by new-plant creation accounts for over 20 per cent of plants; acquisition entry affects only 4 per cent. But the magnitude of firm entry by plant birth declines rapidly, while acquisition entry increases – though not in a monotonic fashion – across size-classes. Acquisition entry is just as important, or more so, than entry by plant creation in the three largest size-classes – the classes that contain over 78 per cent of 1979 total employment. As was the case with the exit process, the addition of acquisition-entry rates to greenfield-entry rates leaves less of an impression that the largest size-classes are immune to entry.

In conclusion, although entry by acquisition is about as important as entry by plant creation at the industry level, it is greater among firms in the larger size-classes. While firms that enter on a small scale by building plant may expand later to rival the largest firms already in the industry, entry by acquisition immediately places the new firm in the upper cohorts of an industry.

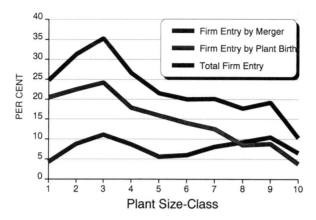

Figure 3-7. Entry by size-class: acquisition vs. greenfield entry (per cent of establishments affected).

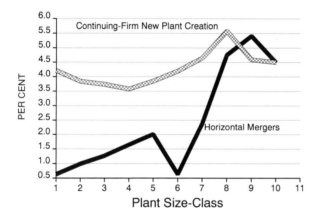

Figure 3-8. Continuing-firm plant addition: merger vs. plant creation by size-class (per cent of establishments affected).

By method of continuing-firm expansion. Continuing firms can expand by building new plant, by acquiring plant, or by expanding existing plants. The different types of expansion by continuing firms into new plants, using the share of establishments affected, is plotted in Figure 3-8 across plant size-classes. The calculations were made in the same fashion as for Figures 3-6 and 3-7. Horizontal mergers, like diversifying mergers, become more important as plant size increases. By way of contrast, while greenfield entry was inversely related to size, new-plant creation by continuing firms was not.

While there may be entry barriers to plant creation by the smallest newcomers relative to the largest, there appear to be few barriers to expansion by building new plant. The intensity of continuing-firm new-plant creation is relatively constant across size-classes when measured in terms of the share of establishments in this category. In the largest plant size-class, the two methods of continuing-firm expansion (plant creation and merger) are of about equal magnitude – whether number of establishments or share of shipments is used.

Differences across industries

That mergers are concentrated in the larger firms suggests that they are imperfect substitutes for entry or expansion through plant creation. They serve to facilitate entry where normally it is difficult because of the existence of scale economies. Since the distribution across size-classes was calculated in such a way as to avoid industry aggregation bias, the differences observed were not due to a particular concentration of take-overs in those industries that have larger firms. Nevertheless, it may be that acquisition entry is concentrated in some industries. If this is the case, the pattern of cross-industry differences may explain the reason for these intra-industry differences.

Entry by merger and by plant birth. Many studies in the field of industrial organization have stressed the connection between performance and entry barriers. Several applied studies have found that entry in Canada is inversely related to such barriers (e.g., Orr, 1974). Early studies did not test whether this phenomenon affected only entry by plant creation or also entry by acquisition, because the databases used did not allow for such distinctions to be made. But using data from the Canadian manufacturing sector that does permit such a distinction, Baldwin and Gorecki (1987b) point out that acquisition entry is less affected by entry barriers than is entry by new-plant creation.

Entry by acquisition and by plant creation across manufacturing industries are inversely related. Across the 167 industries, the rate of acquisition entry over the period 1970–79 is inversely correlated with the rate of entry by new-plant creation – whether the rate is defined as the percentage of plants, employment, or shipments affected. For example, the correlation coefficient between the two, using the share of 1979 employment affected, is −.18 with a significance level of .026.

Acquisition entry is plotted along with entry by plant creation in Figure 3-9 by industry grouping. Entry rates are measured by employment in the number of plants affected divided by total industry employment. Each manufacturing industry was ranked on the basis of the intensity of acquisitions and then all industries were divided into five equal-sized groups. The means of acquisition entry and greenfield entry for each group are plotted in Figure 3-9 – the five classes ranging from left to right in order of the rate of acquisition

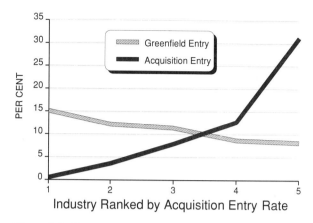

Figure 3-9. Entry intensity by industry: acquisition vs. greenfield entry (per cent of employment affected).

entry. Entry by acquisition increases in magnitude as entry by plant creation decreases.

This comparison is two-dimensional. It does not suggest the reason for the differences in the behaviour of the two series. In order to do so, multivariate regression analysis is used. Work by Baldwin and Gorecki (1987b), who focus on the number of firms that entered and exited an industry between 1970 and 1979, is extended here to measure the share of industry shipments accounted for by establishments in the two entry categories.

The data used for the regression analysis come from the 1970 and 1979 database that was developed to examine long-run entry and exit. The dependent variables used are defined as follows: SH23 is the employment in new establishments (measured as of 1979) created between 1970 and 1979 by firms entering during the period, divided by total 1979 industry employment. SH22 is the employment in establishments (measured as of 1979) acquired between 1970 and 1979 by firms that were not in the industry in 1970 but were in 1979, divided by total 1979 industry employment.

Baldwin and Gorecki (1987b) examine the effect of a large number of regressors. The variables they use fall into four groups: (1) growth, (2) profitability, (3) barriers to entry, and (4) miscellaneous factors (other than the standard entry-barrier variables) that describe the openness of markets (such as trade penetration). A subset of the variables that they found had the strongest explanatory power was chosen for the present analysis.[14] The definitions of the regressors used here can be found in Appendix B.

The first variable (G) is the rate of growth in industry shipments between 1970 and 1979. The second variable (PRSMALL) measures profitability in

Table 3-6. *Inter-industry differences in entry intensity by acquisition vs. plant creation: coefficients from multivariate analysis*

Regressors[a]	Entry[b]	
	By plant opening	By acquisition
G	0.105 (.0001)	−0.035 (.373)
VAR	0.011 (.0001)	−0.001 (.664)
CR4	−0.025 (.0001)	0.016 (.0003)
PRSMALL	0.579 (.2970)	−0.145 (.792)
PRFTGR	−0.036 (.7420)	0.241 (.037)
R^2	.32	.13
F	12.38	3.82
prob > F	.0001	.0031
N^c	141	141

[a] For definitions of the regressors, see Appendix B.
[b] The regressand in each case was the intensity of entry by plant creation or by acquisition measured in terms of share of employment in the category. The probability value of the t statistic ($|t| > 0$) for the null hypothesis that the coefficient is zero is in parentheses.
[c] N is the number of observations used in the regression.

1970. It is an interaction term that captures both continuing-firm profitability and the difference between large- and small-firm profitability. The third variable (PRFTGR) is a measure of profitability growth over the decade. These profit variables are included to capture both the state of economic well-being in the early part of the period and how it changed during the period. If entry responds to well-being, the sign on each of the variables is expected to be positive. The fourth variable (VAR) measures the variability in sales around the trend growth rate. An industry with a high value of VAR provides greater short-run temporary opportunities for new firms, and therefore might also be associated with higher entry. The fifth variable (CR4) is the four-firm concentration ratio and is used to proxy entry-barrier effects. In earlier work, several variables were included to catch various entry barriers; but for the purposes of this exercise, these various effects are grouped together with this proxy.

The regression results are reported in Table 3-6. The sample chosen excludes 26 industries that were classified as miscellaneous. Since the dependent variable is bounded by zero and one, a logistic transformation was performed[15] and an ordinary-least-squares (OLS) technique was used.[16]

Greenfield and acquisition entry react quite differently to the explanatory variables. The former responds significantly in a positive fashion to industry growth but not to the profitability variables. Acquisition entry is not

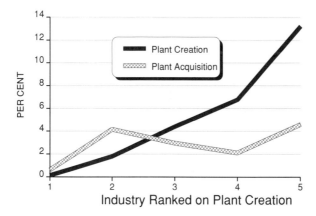

Figure 3-10. Continuing-firm expansion intensity: new-plant creation vs. plant acquisition by industry (per cent of employment affected).

significantly related to growth but is related to changes in industry profitability. Greenfield entry is negatively related to concentration, while acquisition entry is positively related to it. The coefficients in both cases are highly significant. Finally, greenfield entry is higher in industries with greater volatility but acquisition entry is not.

In conclusion, acquisition entry is greater where entry barriers and profitability are high in general. These are industries where greenfield entry is either less or no greater than elsewhere. It is the merger process that brings new owners into those industries where greenfield entry is least likely, and therefore least able, to exert a competitive check on monopolistic power if it exists. Whether acquisition serves the same equilibrating function often attributed to greenfield entry is examined in Chapter 13. The impact of mergers on productivity is examined in Chapter 8.

Expansion by horizontal merger and by plant construction. Just as entrants can choose to build new plant or acquire plant, continuing firms have the option of expanding through plant construction or by acquiring plant in the same industry. The differences between the latter two processes are less marked than are the former. The intensity of horizontal merger activity and of continuing-firm plant creation are positively, not negatively correlated, though the relationship is not significant. Continuing-firm plant creation and horizontal acquisitions are plotted in Figure 3-10.[17] Manufacturing industries are ordered on the basis of continuing-firm new-plant creation, arranged by quintile groups, and ranked from left to right in order of increasing importance of plant creation. Horizontal mergers in each quintile group are then plotted using the same ordering system. It is apparent that there is little relationship between these two forms of continuing-firm plant expansion.

Regression analysis was used to examine the relationship between each form of expansion by existing firms and certain industry characteristics. As in the case of the entry regressions, the magnitude of each form of expansion was measured by share of industry employment accounted for by new and by acquired plants. Most industries – around 95 per cent – experience greenfield entry.[18] However, only 53 per cent of the industries have horizontal acquisitions; only 77 per cent have plant creation by continuing firms. Therefore, in the case of continuing-firm activity, two separate regressions were employed. The first uses a binary variable that takes on a value of one where there is plant creation or acquisitions and zero where there is none. It is used to investigate the industry characteristics that are associated with some as opposed to no entry (the existence equation). The second regression uses the share of employment in plants created by continuing firms and acquired by continuing firms, but only for industries where the share is positive (the intensity equation). It is used to investigate the industry characteristics that are associated with increasing amounts of plant creation or acquisition by continuing firms where it exists. The data come from the database that compares plant and firm status in 1970 and 1979. The same variables that were used in the entry regressions were employed here. The results are presented in Table 3-7. Columns 1 and 2 are the estimated coefficients for the existence equations; the third and fourth columns are the coefficients of the intensity equations.

In the case of plant creation by continuing firms, the coefficients in both equations (columns 1 and 3) are not very significant. The binary dependent variable equation shows that continuing-firm plant creation occurs less frequently where variability in growth is higher. This is the same variable that was related to a greater intensity of entry by new-plant creation. When the intensity of plant creation is used as the dependent variable (column 3), only the concentration variable is at all significant, and the associated coefficient is positive. It is negative, though insignificant, for entry by plant creation. Thus, high variability of the growth process and low concentration are associated with more new-firm plant creation but less continuing-firm plant creation.

In the case of horizontal-merger activity, the binary existence variable is negatively related to concentration and profit growth. On the other hand, when the dependent variable measures merger activity, only growth rates are significant, with a negative coefficient.

The fact that, in the existence and the intensity equations, horizontal mergers are negatively related – either to growth in output or in profitability – suggests that a rationalization process may be at work here. Baldwin and

Table 3-7. *Inter-industry differences in mergers and plant creation by continuing firms: coefficients from multivariate analysis*

Regressors[a]	Dependent variable[b]			
	Binary variable		Employment intensity for the category	
	By plant creation (1)	By merger (2)	By plant creation (3)	By merger (4)
G	0.009 (.881)	0.063 (.274)	−0.011 (.725)	−0.095 (.066)
VAR	−0.011 (.018)	−0.005 (.262)	−0.000 (.991)	0.005 (.139)
CR4	−0.006 (.533)	−0.025 (.002)	0.009 (.051)	0.004 (.479)
PRSMALL	1.601 (.354)	−0.105 (.305)	0.619 (.251)	0.047 (.948)
PRFTGR	0.385 (.099)	−0.368 (.067)	0.019 (.868)	−0.072 (.683)
P[c]	.096	.007	.344	.214
N[d]	141	141	105	105

[a] For definitions of the regressors, see Appendix B.

[b] The regressand in the first case was 0 if there was no activity and 1 if there was activity; in the second case, the intensity of plant creation or merger is measured in terms of share of employment in the category. The probability value of the t statistic ($|t| > 0$) for the null hypothesis that the coefficient is zero is in parentheses.

[c] P is the probability value of the model likelihood ratio chi-square for the binary variable.

[d] N is the number of observations used in the regression.

Gorecki (1986b) report that the number of horizontal mergers was significantly related to a variable that captures the extent to which the optimal number of plants was falling because of an increase in minimum-efficient-plant scale. The share equations used here also suggest that rationalization was the motive behind some horizontal mergers.

That the existence of horizontal mergers but not their intensity is negatively related to concentration may be ascribed to Canadian competition law. While merger law was weak during this period, it may nevertheless have had a restraining effect in the most concentrated industries. On the other hand, that concentration did not affect merger intensity where mergers existed suggests that, below a certain threshold, rationalization was the motive behind mergers.

One of the variables that consistently appears in the various equations with a significant coefficient is concentration. The relationship between an industry's merger or plant-creation intensity and the industry level of concentration

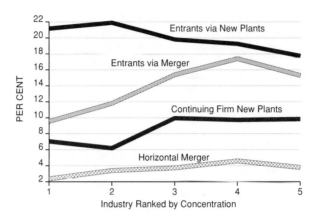

Figure 3-11. Individual turnover activity ranked by industry concentration (per cent of establishments affected).

serves to clarify the differences among the various entry and expansion categories. The two forms of entry and the two methods of continuing-firm expansion on the one hand, and industry concentration on the other, are presented in Figure 3-11. The industries were ranked from lowest to highest concentration using the Herfindahl index, and divided into quintile groups. Average entry and acquisition were calculated and then plotted for all the quintile groups, which are ranked from left to right in Figure 3-11 on the basis of increasing average concentration.

It is striking that concentrated industries cannot be classified as static from the point of view of plant turnover (where turnover is defined as the percentage of plants in 1979 that were either newly created or acquired between 1970 and 1979). Concentrated industries may be protected from outside entry by new-plant creation; but this is more than offset by increased activity by merger entrants, by horizontal-merger activity, and by incumbent-firm new-plant creation. In Figure 3-12, the total intensity of these four activities is plotted against concentration for the same five concentration classes used in Figure 3-11. As concentration increases, total turnover goes up except for the most concentrated class; nevertheless, it is still larger here than for the two classes with the lowest levels of concentration.

Success as measured by exit rates

Much has been made of the fact that not all mergers succeed. Market share has been used as one criterion to measure success in some studies. The loss of market share is an indicator – at best, of failure, and at worst, of the restriction of output associated with the monopolistic exploitation of markets.

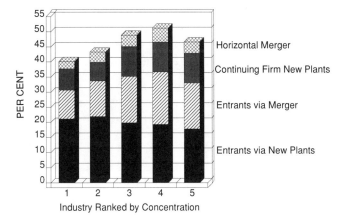

Figure 3-12. Cumulative turnover activity ranked by industry concentration (per cent of establishments affected).

Another criterion is the extent to which acquisitions fail and are subsequently sold again.

Post-merger divestiture figures prominently in the literature that evaluates the success of diversifying mergers (Royal Commission on Corporate Concentration, 1978; Ravenscraft and Scherer, 1987).[19]

The post-merger divestiture rate should not be used to evaluate the success of mergers without reference to some control group. The failure of some mergers is to be expected. Entry by acquisition involves entry into new markets. The progress of new firms that enter by building new plant has already been extensively examined in Chapter 2. Greenfield entrants fail at a very high rate during the early years of their existence. Less than half normally survive over the first decade. Take-over entry offers an alternative method of entry into an industry. It should not be surprising, therefore, if entry by merger also is less than completely successful. The interesting question is not whether some merger entry is unsuccessful or even whether it is, on average, unsuccessful; the important question is whether entry by merger is more or less successful than greenfield entry.

The most drastic decrease in market share for an entrant occurs when it subsequently exits. It is therefore important to compare the exit rates of the two entry processes. The annual database that defines entry at the level of the manufacturing sector as a whole was used for this purpose. Each acquisition entrant into the manufacturing sector between 1971 and 1981 was tracked subsequent to entry. The date of exit, by either divestiture or closure, was noted. Then the experience of acquisition entrants was summarized by year of entry. The percentage of each entry cohort that exited in each subsequent

Table 3-8. *Exit profile of firms that enter the manufacturing sector by acquisition, 1971–81 (per cent)*[a]

Year of exit	Year of entry									
	1971	1972	1973	1974	1975	1976	1977	1978	1979	1980
1971	15.33	—	—	—	—	—	—	—	—	—
1972	0.73	1.43	—	—	—	—	—	—	—	—
1973	5.84	1.43	17.24	—	—	—	—	—	—	—
1974	8.76	1.43	3.45	5.26	—	—	—	—	—	—
1975	3.65	7.14	0.00	8.77	14.29	—	—	—	—	—
1976	6.57	7.14	0.00	3.51	8.16	0.00	—	—	—	—
1977	36.50	8.57	3.45	7.02	4.08	7.89	4.48	—	—	—
1978	12.41	4.29	3.45	12.28	4.08	10.53	7.46	2.96	—	—
1979	0.00	8.57	3.45	1.75	8.16	7.89	11.94	2.96	28.96	—
1980	0.00	2.86	10.34	7.02	4.08	7.89	4.48	11.85	3.28	8.84
1981	2.19	4.29	0.00	5.26	2.04	0.00	5.97	4.44	7.10	10.50
Alive in 1981	8.03	52.86	58.62	49.12	55.10	65.79	65.67	77.78	60.66	80.66

[a] This table gives the percentage of entrants from a particular year that exited in a subsequent year. Exit takes place both through divestiture and closedown exits. The year of entry is defined as the first year that the enterprise's code appeared. The year of exit is the last year that the enterprise's code appeared.

year and the percentage that remained in the final year are presented in Table 3-8.

The results confirm the findings of other analysts. Many of the firms that enter an industry by merger exit shortly thereafter. On average, 10 per cent of acquisition entrants exit within a year, 15 per cent within two years, and 58 per cent by the end of nine years.[20] Entry by acquisition, then, is no guarantee that a firm will remain in an industry. Acquisition entry is part of a process of experimentation. Not all such entry experiments are successful and some firms will exit shortly after they have entered.[21] The same result for greenfield entrants was described in Chapter 2.

The important question is whether acquisition entrants leave at a higher rate than do greenfield entrants. In order to investigate this issue, it is necessary to compare the two processes more carefully. The cumulative exit rates for greenfield and acquisition entry are plotted by years of life in Figure 3-13. It is evident that, in the short run, acquisition entry is more successful than entry by new-plant creation. A smaller proportion of the former exited over the first eight years of life; by the end of the period, the differences are small. Nevertheless, only in the three middle years are acquisitions significantly

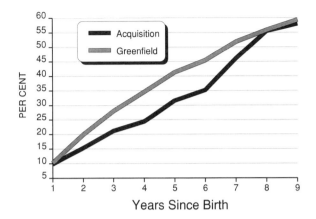

Figure 3-13. Cumulative rates of exit: entrants by acquisition vs. plant birth (per cent of establishments affected).

more successful. This does not make a strong case for merger entry having an advantage over entry by new-plant creation.

The data presented in Figure 3-13 have not been corrected for the effects of macro-economic conditions. Mergers come in waves. If greenfield and acquisition entry react somewhat differently to economic conditions, as the results of the regressions in Tables 3-6 and 3-7 suggest, it is possible that the calculated relative exit rates will reflect these factors rather than the underlying exit process itself. Therefore, separate correction factors were estimated to capture the "cyclical" part of each exit process.[22] These were then applied to the original series to remove the cyclical factor. These correction factors were estimated to account for general cycles in the underlying processes that might be related to macro-economic factors. The "corrected" cumulative exit rates for entrants are plotted in Figure 3-14. A slightly different picture is presented in this chart than in Figure 3-13 – though the same inferences are drawn. Over the first five years of their existence, there is very little difference between the two series; after five years, a higher percentage of acquisition entrants leave, on average.

The reason for the differences that develop between the two series after five years can be found in Figure 3-15, which plots the "corrected" hazard rates for greenfield and acquisition entry. The hazard rate for a given year is the probability of exit, conditional on a firm surviving to that point in time. The hazard rates are remarkably similar for most of the period. The two types of entry alternate in having the higher hazard rate. But the explosion of exits in the seventh and eighth years of life, which corresponds to a period of intense merger activity, pushes the hazard rate for acquisition entrants to

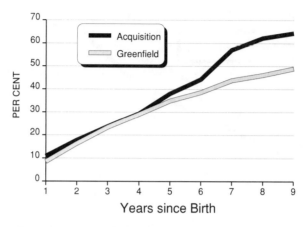

Figure 3-14. Corrected cumulative exit rates: entrants by acquisition vs. plant birth (per cent of establishments affected).

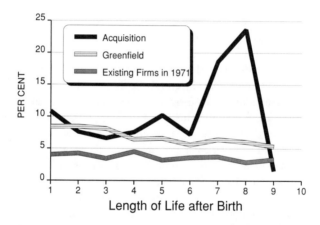

Figure 3-15. The hazard rate of entrants: acquisition vs. greenfield entry.

unprecedented levels in those years and causes the average of the cumulative exit rate of mergers to move well above that of firms that entered the manufacturing sector by building new plants.

In summary, the exit rates of firms that have entered an industry through acquisition are high when cumulated over a longer period. High death rates in this category have also been found in the United States. The high exit rate for mergers has been implicitly used to argue that such entry is peculiarly unsuccessful. The comparisons presented here indicate that this is not the case – at least in Canada. The patterns of exit associated with greenfield and acquisition entry are remarkably similar. With more data, meaningful differences may emerge. But for now, the conclusion must be that on the whole there is no significant difference between the two processes.

At first glance, this result is surprising. A priori, we might expect the failure rate of acquisition entrants to be lower than that of greenfield entrants. The former is purchasing a going concern with an established position in the industry; the latter is both starting a new firm and entering a new industry. However, similarity between their exit rates does not mean that they are equally unsuccessful. Some of the divestitures of acquired entities will be the result of successful turn-around situations. Thus, similarity between the two exit profiles certainly indicates that merger entry is at least as successful as, probably more successful than, greenfield entry. (More evidence of the success of mergers is adduced in Chapter 10, where the productivity and profitability effects of mergers are examined.)

Conclusion

Mergers can be studied by themselves or as part of a larger phenomenon. The latter approach has been taken here, since mergers are only one way that firms can enter an industry or expand within it. In this study, mergers are divided into two groups – diversifying mergers, which bring new firms into an industry, and horizontal mergers, which allow existing firms to expand within an industry. Each is compared with an alternative. Diversifying mergers that result in entry are compared with entry by plant birth. Horizontal mergers are compared with plant creation by continuing firms.

Entry by acquisition over the decade of the 1970s generally affected more workers each year than did entry by plant creation. But mergers come in waves, and their importance varies significantly over time. Entry by plant creation proceeds more steadily and cumulates slowly over time. When the effects of both are cumulated over the decade, they account for a significant proportion of an industry's shipments.

Greenfield and acquisition entry are also very similar when the exit histories of the groups are compared. Entrants do not all remain in an industry. The rates at which the two classes of entrants leave an industry are about the same in periods when merger activity is not extremely high. The cumulative exit rates of the two types of entry over the first five or six years of life are also about the same.

While there are considerable similarities between the diversifying-merger entry process and entry by plant creation, there are also differences that suggest that they are substitutes rather than complements. First, acquisition entry is higher among larger firms. This can be explained in one of two ways. On the one hand, there may be mobility barriers that make it difficult to enter with a large plant. On the other hand, it could simply be that larger plants that are failing tend to be purchased for turn-around rather than closedown. Second, there is more entry by acquisition and less entry by plant birth in concentrated industries. Once again, this may be the result of acquisition entry overcoming entry barriers or the fact that there tend to be larger-than-average firms in concentrated industries, and when these firms begin to fail, they tend to be divested rather than closed.

The horizontal-merger process, as a method of expansion for a continuing firm, is important relative to the alternative of building a new plant. Horizontal mergers are more frequent among larger firms, as is merger entry. Once again, this supports the failing-firm hypothesis. Not all large firms that begin to falter will be purchased by new participants in an industry; some will be acquired by existing firms as part of a horizontal merger.

The intensity of horizontal mergers and that of continuing-firm new-plant creation are not inversely related as are the intensities of acquisition and greenfield entry. Nor is continuing-firm new-plant creation inversely related to size-class as new-firm plant creation is. There may be barriers to greenfield entry among larger firms; but once established, firms of different sizes do not create new plants at significantly different rates. Since there are no barriers to building new plants as size increases, there is less incentive to choose the alternative method of expanding – through the acquisition of new plant through horizontal merger. The two processes, then, bear no simple relationship one to another. The researcher must look to alternative explanations of the inter-industry pattern of horizontal mergers. Indeed, the regressions that were used to investigate inter-industry differences between entry through plant creation and merger have less explanatory power for horizontal mergers and for continuing-firm plant creation. While it is true that both horizontal mergers and entry through merger increase in concentrated industries, this too is consistent with the existence of a component of the horizontal-merger process that is related to the failing-firm motive.

This chapter has demonstrated the significance of a second aspect of entry – the merger process that brings firms into and takes them out of different industries. As such, the chapter reinforces a theme that is developed throughout this study. Competition is a complex process with several parts, each with different characteristics and with different effects. It is only by examining how the various parts contribute to the whole that a complete picture of the dynamics of the process can be developed. The next chapter evaluates the changes that take place in incumbent firms.

4

The rise and fall of incumbents

One tree will last longer in full vigour and attain a greater size than another, but sooner or later age tells on them all. Though the taller ones have a better access to light and air than their rivals, they gradually lose vitality, and one after another they give place to others.

Alfred Marshall (1920: 316)

Introduction

The entry and exit of entire firms account for only part of the turn-over that transfers market share from one firm to another. Entry occurs at the beginning of a firm's life, exit at the end. In the interim, infra-marginal change within the body of an industry occurs as incumbents grow and decline. In Chapters 2 and 3, the magnitude of entry and exit is described in detail. This chapter outlines the amount and pattern of turnover in incumbent firms – those that continue from one period to another – and compares it with the amount of turnover occasioned by entry and exit.

The amount of turnover can be expressed either in terms of absolute expansion and contraction in firm size or in terms of relative change such as shifts in market shares. In the first section, the pattern of change is examined using rates of growth and decline in firms defined at the level of the manufacturing sector as a whole;[1] in the second section, the market share being shifted from those gaining to those losing relative position within a four-digit manufacturing industry is examined.

Appreciating the magnitude of the entry and exit process requires a comparison of instantaneous and cumulative rates of change. Entrants, who are barely noticeable in the short run, reach a respectable size when the process is allowed to cumulate over time. Because important insights into the entry process are gained by comparing the long and the short run, this procedure is followed here. As in the investigation of the magnitude of entry and exit, continuing-firm turnover is first investigated at an aggregate level, where a firm is defined as encompassing all manufacturing operations that are under

61

Table 4-1. *Rate of change[a] in employment in expanding and contracting continuing firms,[b] 1970–82 (per cent)*

Period	Expanding	Contracting	Net change
1970–71	5.19	6.10	−0.91
1971–72	8.46	4.69	3.77
1972–73	9.36	3.93	5.43
1973–74	8.18	4.89	3.29
1974–75	5.72	7.69	−1.97
1975–76	6.67	5.80	0.97
1976–77	6.68	6.75	0.07
1977–78	8.95	5.56	3.39
1978–79	10.50	5.61	4.89
1979–80	6.95	7.87	−0.92
1980–81	13.38	5.87	7.51
1981–82	3.59	10.60	−7.01
Mean	7.80	6.28	1.53

[a] Change in employment is calculated as a proportion of total manufacturing employment in the initial year.
[b] A continuing firm is one that owned at least one establishment in the manufacturing sector in both the initial and terminal year. All statistics were calculated using employment of consolidated manufacturing firms.

common control. Then it is summarized at a less aggregated level, where a firm is defined as including just those operations in a particular four-digit manufacturing industry.

The rise and fall of firms in the short run
Annual rates of firm growth and decline
    In order to estimate the contribution of continuing firms to turnover, employment in manufacturing firms in the period 1970–82 was compared. Employment was measured for consolidated firms.[2] Firms were divided on the basis of whether their employment expanded, contracted, or remained constant between adjacent years. Then the change in employment in each of the expanding and contracting sectors relative to total manufacturing employment in the base or initial year was used to measure the rates of growth and decline.

    Growth and decline among continuing-firms can stem from three separate sources: the expansion and contraction of existing establishments, the opening and closing of plants, and the acquisition and divestiture of plants. The joint effect of all three over the period 1970–82 is reported in Table 4-1.[3]

    The amount of underlying change within the continuing-firm sector is

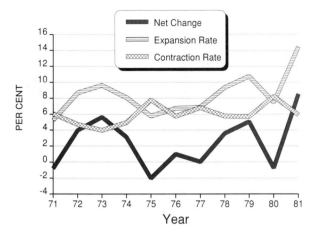

Figure 4-1. Contraction and expansion rates of continuing firms 1970–81).

considerably larger than year-to-year change in net employment would indicate. On average, net growth in continuing firms between 1970 and 1982 was about 1.5 per cent per year. But this was accompanied by an average annual gain in employment in expanding firms of 7.8 per cent and an average annual loss in contracting firms of 6.3 per cent.

The annual rates of firm growth and decline in the period 1970–81, along with the net rate of change derived from the two processes, are graphed in Figure 4-1. Both the expansion and contraction rates have a cyclical component, though the expansion rates have slightly more cyclical variability than the contraction rates.[4]

Despite this volatility, there is a component of both expansion and contraction that is not affected by the phase of the business cycle. This component reflects specific idiosyncratic effects that cause random yearly fluctuations in firm output. Even when expansion rates are at their peak, a large proportion of firms contract with non-negligible rates of decline. For example, there was strong economic growth in the period 1972–73. Over 65 per cent of firms expanded during that time at an average rate of 9.6 per cent; nevertheless, in the same period, 34 per cent of the firm population declined, and the average rate of contraction of these firms was 4 per cent. Short-run contraction and expansion are not just functions of overall cyclical conditions. There is a process at work that constantly leads to the expansion of some firms and the contraction of others.

The growth and decline of incumbents lead to considerably more short-run churning than do entry and exit. Figure 4-2 is a bar-chart that depicts the size

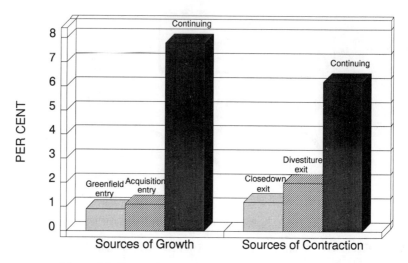

Figure 4-2. Rates of expansion, acquisition, contraction, and divestiture, by source (annual average for 1970–82).

of the two sources of growth and decline in the short run. It consists of the average annual expansion rate of continuing firms, the average annual greenfield- and acquisition-entry rates for the period 1970–82, as well as the average annual contraction rate in continuing firms, and the average annual closedown- and divestiture-exit rates. Growth due to expansion is about eight times that of either entry category. Rates of continuing-firm contraction also dominate exit rates, in the short run.

Variability of the components of change

The annual expansion and contraction rates may mask considerable variability in the underlying process. The rate of change in employment depends on the proportion of firms in a category, the change in employment of firms in this group, and the average size of firms in this category. For example, the expansion rate in growing firms, which is defined as

$$(\text{employment expansion}) / (\text{total employment}), \tag{4-1}$$

can be identically written as

$$(\text{number of firms growing}) \times (\text{average expansion}) /$$
$$(\text{total number of firms}) \times (\text{average size of all firms}), \tag{4-2}$$

or

$$(\text{number of firms growing}) / (\text{total number of firms}) \times (\text{average}$$
$$\text{expansion}) / (\text{average size of those growing}) \times (\text{average size}$$
$$\text{of those growing}) / (\text{average firm size of all firms}). \tag{4-3}$$

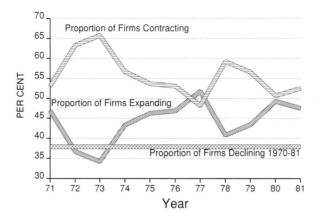

Figure 4-3. The proportion of firms with employment change that expand and contract (1970–81).

In order to investigate the process further, firms with a change in employment were examined. The proportions of those firms that expanded and those that contracted from 1970 to 1981 are presented in Figure 4-3. Also included is the proportion that had lower employment in 1981 than in 1970. The latter represents the proportion of firms in long-run decline. It provides a lower bound on the annual contraction rates, since the latter will contain some firms that are only temporarily experiencing difficulties.

Cyclical, transitory factors dominate the short-run results. Firms that increase employment one year tend to reverse direction the following year. Therefore, it is not surprising that, in the short run, growing and declining firms are split quite evenly. On average, 55.2 per cent of all firms expanded on a year-to-year basis and 44.8 per cent contracted. The proportions of firms in long-run decline can be derived from comparing the employment status of firms over longer periods – 1970–76 and 1970–81. Over these periods, the proportions of firms declining are still substantial – 37.1 and 37.9 per cent, respectively. These are close to the proportions that characterize short-run decline during 1973 and 1978, years of rapid expansion.

Regression to the mean

While the magnitude of growth and decline indicates that turnover is large, its importance to the competitive process is revealed by the patterns that emerge. One such pattern is the extent to which short-run change can also be found in the long run. Another is the tendency of large firms to decline and small firms to grow – the regression-to-the-mean phenomenon.

Both aspects can be found in characteristics of the growth and decline

Table 4-2. *Employment characteristics of expanding and contracting continuing firms in the manufacturing sector, 1970–81 (per cent)*[a]

	Expanding firms			Contracting firms		
Period	Average rate of change[b]	Average change	Average size[c]	Average rate of change	Average change	Average size
1970–71	12.6	13.0	103.3	11.2	16.8	149.5
1971–72	15.6	16.9	107.9	11.6	15.6	135.2
1972–73	13.9	18.4	132.4	14.2	14.3	100.7
1973–74	14.3	20.0	140.4	13.7	15.5	112.8
1974–75	15.0	13.8	91.6	13.4	21.0	156.5
1975–76	14.2	16.3	114.4	12.0	15.7	131.5
1976–77	15.1	18.6	122.9	13.3	17.3	130.2
1977–78	16.4	21.0	127.7	14.8	18.7	127.0
1978–79	18.0	24.5	136.4	15.9	16.8	105.6
1979–80	16.3	19.3	117.9	15.5	22.0	141.8
1980–81	28.6	35.7	125.1	13.6	16.7	122.8
Mean	16.4	19.8	120.0	13.6	17.3	128.5
Longer-run comparisons						
1970–76	44.3	41.9	94.4	24.2	38.9	161.3
1970–81	73.5	77.3	105.2	31.9	51.3	160.6

[a] All statistics were calculated using employment of consolidated manufacturing firms.
[b] The rate of change is calculated as the growth (contraction) divided by base-year employment in just those continuing firms growing (contracting).
[c] Average size is measured in the initial year.

process listed in Table 4-2. The table contains several components of equation 4-3 – the average annual employment change, average firm size for each of the expanding and contracting sectors for the years 1970–81, and the rates of change in employment in each of the growing and declining groups. Rates are calculated relative to the employment base in the growing and declining groups. In addition, data for the same variables are reported for the longer periods – 1970–76 and 1970–81.

The short-run data show a remarkable symmetry in annual growth and decline. Expanding firms increased employment by 16.4 per cent, on average; declining firms contracted by 13.6 per cent. Expanding firms grew by 19.8 employees, on average; contracting firms declined by 17.3 employees. These minor differences between annual growth and decline are due to the asymmetry of merger and plant creation. When the same statistics are calculated for growing and declining establishments, as opposed to firms, average annual growth is the same as the average decline – 13.6 and 13.4 employees, respectively.[5]

The nature of the change in the relative positions of firms is evident when the average size of a declining firm is compared with the average size of an expanding firm. Using annual data from 1970 to 1981 for measurement, the average size of a firm in decline is 129 employees and the average size of a firm that expanded is 120 employees. Thus, even in the short run, there is a regression-to-the-mean phenomenon.

In the longer periods 1970–76 and 1970–81, expansion and contraction were less symmetrical. Firms that had lower employment in 1981 than 1970 lost 51 employees, on average; firms that grew over the same period expanded by some 77 employees. The asymmetry is not as important as the fact that the expansion and contraction rates were considerably greater in the long run than in the short run. Not only did a third of the firms contract over the longer periods, but the amount of contraction was substantial. Turnover, when measured over a decade, leads to substantial change in firms' relative positions.

The difference between the average sizes of the gainers and losers increased over the longer periods (1970–76 and 1970–81). Although the difference in average size is only 9 employees when annual data are used, it is over 50 employees in each of the longer periods. The regression-to-the-mean process is more than just a short-run phenomenon. What is present in the year-to-year data is even more visible over the longer periods. The turnover process caused the largest firms to decline and the smallest to grow.

The change in average firm size in the declining and growing sectors was large. The cumulative rates of growth and decline between 1970 and 1981 were 74 and 32 per cent, respectively. More importantly, the magnitude of the change caused the relative mean size of the two groups to change. Contracting firms declined from an average of 161 to 109 employees; expanding firms grew from an average of 105 to 183 employees. As Figure 4-4 indicates, this is a dramatic change in the relative average sizes of the two groups.

In the short run, then, the proportion of firms that grew and declined is relatively similar, and the amount of employment change was small – some 17 to 20 employees, on average. The stochastic process at work here would not have had a great impact on relative firm rankings. The long-run changes, however, indicate that the process at work contains more than a transitory component.

Research showing that rates of firm growth in adjacent years are negatively correlated can all too easily be interpreted to mean that all short-run change is reversed in the long run. This is incorrect. More than a third of firms declined over the period 1970–81. In 1970, these firms were, on average, some 50 per cent larger than those that subsequently expanded over the same

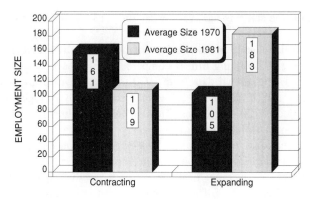

Figure 4-4. The change in average size of firms that contracted and expanded between 1970 and 1981.

period. The amount of growth and decline was large enough to change the average relative sizes of the two groups by 1981.

Long-run rates of change in firm size

Expansion and contraction of incumbents dominate entry and exit in the short run. Whether they do so in the long run depends upon whether the short-run rates are sustained in the longer run. While the annualized values of the decadal entry and exit rates in the 1970s are virtually the same as the short-run rates,[6] there is no reason to expect short- and long-run rates in the continuing-firm sector to be the same. Indeed, the short-run situation, when about half of firms contract or expand by 6 to 8 per cent, is unlikely to be sustainable in the longer run without the type of rapid and dramatic reversals in the relative positions of firms that are rarely observed.

Several other studies of the annual growth rates of firms suggest that the short-run fortunes of continuing firms are reversed fairly quickly (Leonard, 1987). The predominance of annual reversals need not imply that little long-run change is taking place. This section presents additional evidence that cumulative expansion and contraction over a decade is substantial.

In order to contrast the relative magnitude of change in the continuing-firm sector in the short and the long run, the status of manufacturing firms was examined in the periods 1970–76, 1975–81, and 1970–81. The rates of change in employment in growing and declining firms are reported in Table 4-3. Three sets of results are tabulated. Panel A contains the cumulative rates of change obtained from comparing the employment in firms at the beginning and end of each period. Panel B contains the equivalent annual rates derived from these cumulative rates of change. Panel C contains the average annual rates derived from the year-to-year changes, calculated within each period.

Table 4-3. *Cumulative rates of growth and decline[a] of expanding and contracting continuing firms, 1970–81 (per cent)*

Period	Expansion	Contraction
A. *Cumulative change from comparing end-points*		
1970–76	19.06	10.47
1975–81	23.14	10.41
1970–81	27.21	11.00
B. *Implicit annual rates of change from panel A*		
1970–76	2.95	1.83
1975–81	3.53	1.82
1970–81	2.21	1.05
C. *Average of annual rates within each period[b]*		
1970–76	7.26	5.52
1975–81	8.86	6.24
1970–81	8.18	5.89

[a] The rates of growth and decline are calculated as the difference in total employment of consolidated manufacturing firms between the initial and terminal years divided by total employment in the base year.
[b] The firms that are used to calculate panel C differ from those in panels A and B. Panel C is calculated by taking all firms that expanded or contracted in any year of the subperiod. Panels A and B use those firms that expanded or contracted over the entire subperiod listed.

The year-to-year rates of growth and decline for continuing firms are considerably greater than the rates for firms that grew or declined over the longer periods, as can be seen by comparing panel C with panel B. For example, the yearly rates of contraction were between 5 and 6 per cent in each of the six-year periods; the equivalent annual rate of contraction in the long run was only about 1.8 per cent in each of these periods. The yearly expansion rates were between 7 and 9 per cent in each of the six-year periods; the equivalent annual expansion rate in the long run was between 3 and 4 per cent in each period. Substantial reversals in the short-run fortunes of continuing firms took place.

While continuing-firm expansion and contraction dominate the churning that takes place in the short run (see Figure 4-2), this is not the case in the decadal comparison. Because the long-run expansion and contraction rates declined from their high short-run values, and the longer-run entry and exit rates stayed at their short-run values, the two processes are about equally

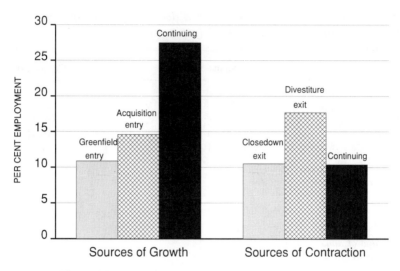

Figure 4-5. Rates of expansion, acquisition, contraction, and divestiture, by source (cumulative change, 1970–81).

important in the long run. Over the period 1970–81, the equivalent annual expansion rate for continuing firms was 2.2 per cent; the equivalent annual entry rate of acquisition and greenfield entry combined was 2.1 per cent. The equivalent annual rate of contraction was 1 per cent; the equivalent rate of annual closedown exit was 1 per cent.

Just as important as the relative magnitude of the two processes is their cumulative effect. Figure 4-5 is a bar chart depicting the total cumulative contribution made to employment by continuing-firm expansion, greenfield and acquisition entry, continuing-firm contraction, and closedown and divestiture exit between 1970 and 1981. Greenfield entry added 10.9 per cent and expansion in the continuing sector 27.2 per cent to 1970 employment. Acquisition entry affected 14.6 per cent of 1970 employment. Closedown exits led to the disappearance of 10.5 per cent of 1970 employment, and employment contracted in declining firms by an amount equal to 11 per cent of initial total employment in all firms. Divestitures affected 17.7 per cent of 1970 employment. While it is true that short-run changes in firm size are mainly transitory, there is nevertheless a large subset of firms that contracted, and the cumulative change in these firms was substantial. Combined with the fact that some firms also experienced substantial growth, this means the relative size of firms in each group reversed itself during the 1970s.

The differences between the short- and long-run results provide a fundamental insight into the nature of the growth and decline process.[7] Just as there are opposing views of the importance of entry and exit, there are two different views of the importance of growth and decline in the continuing-firm sector. The first is that most change in the continuing-firm sector is transitory: large firms remain large and small firms remain small, except for minor disturbances in their relative shares. The second is the Marshallian view that the growth and decline of firms is important. In this view, the lives and deaths of firms are likened to those of trees in a forest. While birth, maturation, and death are common, the outward appearance of the forest remains unchanged to the casual observer.

In the first view, the cumulative long-run results would be the same as the short-run results. That this is not the case supports the Marshallian view. More support for this view is provided by the regression-to-the-mean phenomenon. The difference in the average sizes of declining and growing firms might be expected under either view. If change in continuing firms is regarded primarily as transitory – except for small marginal firms that are apt to exit when they decline – then the average size of a contracting firm will go up over time as the marginal firms are removed. But this view is not compatible with the considerable increase in the average amount of contraction in the long run, nor with the change in the relative positions of expanding and contracting firms. The evidence on this aspect of change supports the position that there is considerable expansion and contraction across the firm-size distribution.

Turnover as measured by change in market share

The rates of growth and decline, as already outlined, show the extent to which absolute firm-size changes are taking place in the population of firms. However, they have several shortcomings for several reasons.

First, they do not capture change in relative size. In an economy that is growing rapidly, only a few firms may decline in absolute size, but there may be substantial changes in relative firm position. An investigation of the strength of the competitive process requires a measure such as the change in market share to evaluate the extent to which some firms supplant others in the struggle for dominance. Therefore, this section focuses on the extent to which market share is shifted from one group of firms to another.

Second, they measure employment at the consolidated-firm level. Some of the expansion and contraction observed at this level may come from change in the relative size of the industries within which these firms operate. Analysis at an industry level is required to show more precisely what is happening to relative firm size within more narrowly defined markets.[8]

To measure change in market share, data at the level of the individual four-digit Canadian manufacturing industry were used to compare the status of plants and firms in 1970 and 1979. The longer period was chosen so as to minimize the amount of transitory change that the short-run estimates have been shown to contain. Measures that are derived from the longer period capture the cumulative effect of change over the period. They measure the 1979 share of entrants that were born between 1970 and 1979 and were still alive in 1979. They capture the 1970 share of exits that left sometime between 1970 and 1979. They measure the changes in share of continuing establishments in 1970 and in 1979 that had either higher or lower shares (defined in terms of industry shipments) in one period than another.

Establishments in the two years are classified as births, deaths, acquired, divested, transferred, or continuing without a change in ownership. Establishments are then aggregated into firms. A firm is defined as consisting of all the establishments at the four-digit SIC industry level that are under common control (see Appendix A). Enterprises are grouped into new firms, exiting firms, and continuing firms on the basis of the status of their plants (see Table 2-1 for more details on these categories).

These categories permit the calculation of the importance of the different sources of turnover and a comparison of the magnitude of entering and exiting firms with that of continuing firms. Table 4-4 details the various categories, measured as the shares of plants in a particular category. In each case, the share is the mean taken across all industries.

As already pointed out in Chapters 2 and 3, the amount of cumulative entry and exit over the long term is substantial. Firm exits due to closings, transfers, and divestitures over the decade accounted for 30.8 per cent of 1970 shipments on average. In addition, some 4.6 per cent of shipments were in plants that were closed or transferred by continuing firms and another 1.1 per cent were in plants divested by continuing firms. Finally, those continuing plants that did not have a change in ownership experienced substantial share changes. Those in decline lost 12.6 percentage points of market share. Some 49 per cent of 1970 shipments turned over due to plant closings, divestiture, or continuing plants losing share.

Turnover is equally large if share gain is examined. Firms that entered since 1970 accounted for, on average, 26.8 per cent of 1979 shipments. Continuing-firms' plant births and transfers accounted for 5.3 per cent and acquired plant accounted for 3.0 per cent of 1979 shipments. Finally, those continuing plants that were not acquired or divested but that were gaining share acquired 14.1 percentage points, on average.

Incumbents contributed a relatively minor proportion of the gain and loss of share from plant births and closures. The various firm entry and exit categories were more important than comparable categories for the continuing-firm sector. Plant births were much more heavily concentrated in the entrant sector than in the continuing sector. For example, new plants (both births and transfers) of continuing firms accounted for only 5.3 per cent of

Table 4-4. *Average share of shipments across four-digit manufacturing industries, by entry and exit category, 1970 and 1979 (per cent)[a]*

Firm category	1970	1979
All firms	100.0	100.0
All entrants[b]	—	26.8
By plant birth	—	11.5
By acquisition	—	10.7
By plant transfer[c]	—	4.6
All exits[d]	30.8	—
By plant closing	13.3	—
By divestiture	12.7	—
By plant transfer[c]	4.9	—
All continuing firms[e]	69.1	73.2
Continuing plant[e]	63.4	65.0
Gaining share	26.4	40.5
Losing share	37.1	24.5
Divested plant	1.1	—
Acquired plant	—	3.0
Plant closures	3.8	—
Plant births	—	4.4
Plant transfers[c]	0.8	0.9

[a] The sample consists of long-form establishments. (See Appendix A for definition.)

[b] Entrants are firms that were in a four-digit industry in 1979 but not in 1970.

[c] Plant transfers are those whose four-digit industry classification changed because the principal product changed.

[d] Exits are those firms in 1970 that were no longer in the same four-digit industry in 1979.

[e] Continuing firms and plants were in the same four-digit industry in both 1970 and 1979. Firms are defined as unconsolidated enterprises at the four-digit SIC industry level.

shipments in 1979, while the new plants of entering firms (both births and transfers) accounted for 16.1 per cent of shipments in 1979. Diversified mergers were also more important than horizontal mergers. The market share of plants acquired by firms in the same industry was, on average, 3 per cent in 1979, but it was, on average, 10.7 per cent for plants acquired by firms outside the industry.

The continuing sector may not have played a major role in plant creation and closing or acquisition and divestiture. Nevertheless, the continuing sector's contribution to share turnover was substantial because of the share gain and decline in continuing plants. This is demonstrated in Figure 4-6, which plots the sources of share gain and decline from plant entry and exit and from

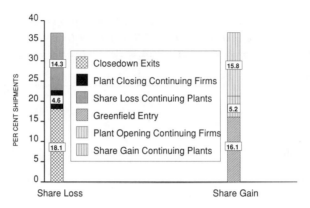

Figure 4-6. The components of establishment turnover: market-share loss and gain (cumulative change, 1970–79).

all continuing-establishment share changes – including the continuing establishments that were acquired or divested and were included under the entry and exit categories in Table 4-4. Some 18.1 per cent of share is lost due to plant closure by firms exiting an industry, but the continuing-firm sector lost 18.9 per cent of market share – 4.6 percentage points from continuing-firm plant closures (both deaths and transfers) and 14.3 percentage points from share loss by continuing establishments. In contrast, firm entry by plant opening (both births and transfers) led to a gain in market share of 16.1 percentage points and the continuing sector in one form or other gained 21 percentage points in market share – 5.2 percentage points from the opening of new plants (both births and transfers) and 15.8 percentage points from continuing plants.

Share turnover as presented in Table 4-4 and Figure 4-6 is considerable, but the measures presented have two drawbacks. First, they are calculated at an establishment level and it is the firm that is most relevant for discussions of competition policy. Second, the variety of change that takes place at the establishment level is so diverse that it is difficult to digest. To overcome these problems, a summary statistic of turnover at the firm level was calculated.

The index that is used to measure market-share change is a dissimilarity index of firm shares between two periods for each firm in the industry.[9] It is defined as half the sum of the absolute value of the 1979 share minus the 1970 share for all firms being considered. This measure captures the market share that is transferred from those firms that are declining to those that are growing in relative importance. When all firms in an industry are used in the calculation, it varies from 0 to 100 and, therefore, provides a metric by which the amount or severity of change can be readily measured.

Since the relative size of market-share turnover due to entry and exit as

Table 4-5. *Average change in market share due to turnover of entrants, exits, and continuing firms[a] in four-digit manufacturing industries, 1970–79 (per cent of total shipments)[b]*

Cause of turnover	Entry and exit due to acquisition omitted[c]	Entry and exit due to acquisition included
Entry and exit[d]	20.1 (1.1)	30.3 (1.2)
Growth and decline in continuers[e]	16.0 (0.4)	13.9 (0.4)
Total	36.1 (1.2)	44.2 (1.2)

[a] Firms are defined as unconsolidated enterprises at the four-digit SIC industry level.
[b] Standard error of the mean is in parentheses.
[c] For the first column, all firms that were acquired or divested were treated as continuing during the decade and changes in their shares are included in the second row.
[d] Share change is calculated as half the sum of entry plus exit for each industry and then averaged across four-digit manufacturing industries.
[e] Share change is half the sum of the absolute value of the difference between the shares of all continuing firms measured in 1970 and 1979.

opposed to continuing-firm expansion and contraction is of interest, three values of the dissimilarity index were calculated. The first captures the amount of market-share[10] transfer that is due to the entry and exit of firms (TURNE). The dissimilarity index in this case is simply half the sum of the entry shares for 1979 and the exit shares for 1970. The second measures the amount of share transfer within the continuing-firm sector alone (TURNC), and the third takes account of all changes in share – for continuing firms as well as for entrants and exits. The mean values of each of these indices are presented in Table 4-5.

Two variants of the index are provided. The first includes only greenfield entry and closedown exit in calculations of the share transfer due to entry and exit.[11] The second includes, in addition to these, entry by acquisition and exit by divestiture in the market-share transfer due to entry and exit.[12] Entry by acquisition and exit by divestiture are treated differently in these two calculations since there are legitimate differences of opinion as to the importance of acquisition and divestment. On the one hand, they change the ownership of the firm, and since new owners may institute new policies, they may thus be regarded as a new force. On the other hand, ownership change may not involve any modification in the operating entity and its policies, only a change in the legal entity. Since, a priori, it is not certain how this form of entry and exit should be treated, the share-turnover measure was calculated twice – once including acquisition and divestiture as entry and exit, and once excluding them.[13]

In the long run, the amount of share change from all sources is substantial. Consider first the values of the index when entry by acquisition and exit by divestiture are excluded. Greenfield entry and closedown exit led to an average shift in market share from declining to growing firms over the decade of 20 percentage points. About the same market share – some 16 percentage points – was transferred as continuing firms changed relative position. Thus, 36 percentage points of market share were transferred.

When acquisition entry and divestiture exit are included, the amount of share transfer due to entry and exit increases from 20 to 30 per cent. In total, 44 per cent of market share is shifted from one group of firms to another when acquisition entry and divestiture exit are included in the total.

Changes in size-class and market share

Turnover is often regarded as unimportant, either because it is viewed as not being very large, or because it is seen to affect mainly small firms at the margin of an industry. It has been demonstrated in this chapter that the first view is incorrect; total turnover from both entry and continuing-firm expansion and contraction is quantitatively important. The second view has only partially been addressed. The presence of entrants across a range of size-classes, detailed in Chapter 2, demonstrates that entry is not restricted to small and marginally insignificant industries. This section complements the analysis in Chapter 2. It asks whether growth and decline are also relatively widespread within the continuing-firm population.

In order to examine the extent to which continuing-firm share change differs across size-classes, firms in each industry (unconsolidated firms) in 1970 were divided into quintile groups based on a ranking of their shipments in 1970. Then the firms in each of the five groups were divided into those whose share increased and those whose share decreased between 1970 and 1979. The share change between 1970 and 1979 of firms in each industry was calculated as the ratio of the mean increase or decrease in the shares of each group divided by the mean share in 1970 of the group whose shares increased or decreased – giving the mean rate of share change.

The means of these ratios are presented in Table 4-6. The mean rate of share change, whether for gainers or losers, decreases across size-classes. For the smallest size-class, the ratio of share gain to opening-period share was 1.66. It was 0.39 for the largest quintile group. For the smallest size-class, the ratio of share loss to opening-period share was 0.49. It was 0.35 in the largest quintile group. While the rate of share change in the largest size-class was

Table 4-6. *Average[a] change in market share, by size-class, 1970–79[b]*

Size-class (small to large)	Ratio of mean change in share[c] to mean 1970 share[d]		Ratio of mean share gained to mean share lost[c]	Ratio of mean share of gainers to mean share of losers in 1970[c]
	Gainers	Losers		
1	1.66 (0.13)	−0.49 (0.01)	3.97	1.26
2	1.10 (0.09)	−0.43 (0.01)	2.42	0.96
3	0.85 (0.07)	−0.40 (0.01)	1.26	0.73
4	0.62 (0.05)	−0.37 (0.01)	1.04	0.87
5	0.39 (0.03)	−0.35 (0.01)	0.49	0.54

[a] The means are taken across four-digit manufacturing industries.
[b] Firms acquired by entrants and divested by exiting firms are treated as continuing firms.
[c] Share change is measured between 1970 and 1979.
[d] Standard error of the mean is in parentheses.

less than that in the smallest, large firms experienced significant changes in market share.

Table 4-6 also includes a variable that measures the ratio of growth to decline in each size-class (third column). It is the total share gains divided by the total share losses for each quintile group. For all size-classes but the largest, more market share was gained than lost. In the largest size-class, about twice as much was lost as was gained. The tendency for small firms to grow and large firms to decline was observed in the data on the rate of employment change for consolidated firms. Firms that declined in absolute terms were larger, on average, than those that grew. Here, a similar regression-to-the-mean phenomenon was observed for market-share gains in unconsolidated firms.

The same regression process can be seen in the difference between shares of each quintile group in 1970 for those that eventually gained market share and those that lost market share. The mean ratio of the shares in the opening year of those gaining share to the shares of those losing share over the subsequent 10 years is given in the fourth column of Table 4-6. The percentage of 1970 gainers' market share declines as the size-class increases. For the largest size-class, firms that experienced subsequent market-share increases had only about half the market share of those about to experience a loss in market share. A relatively large percentage of the market share of the smallest size-classes is in firms that grew. This indicates that there is relatively more dynamism in smaller firms.

In conclusion, when turnover data by size-class are examined, it is apparent that there is relatively more growth in smaller firms and more decline in larger firms. Despite this differential, the data show that there is substantial change in firms of all sizes.

A comparison of the sources of turnover in market share

When measured at yearly intervals, most turnover comes from continuing firms. But the longer the time period examined, the greater the importance of entering and exiting firms. Continuing firms in long-term decline exit, thereby increasing the importance of entering and exiting firms. Entrants, which start relatively small, begin to grow.

The previous section has shown that, in general, there is turnover in market share due to entry and exit as well as to the growth and decline of incumbents. In this section, the relationship between the two measures in a cross-section of industries is examined. This, once again, places the entry and exit process in the context of the change that is taking place in the continuing-firm population.

While the turnover that occurs from both sources is sufficiently large that neither can be dismissed, it is nevertheless important to ask whether they capture the same phenomenon – whether the same industry characteristics determine the significance of marginal and infra-marginal change. If they do, either can be used to rank industries on the basis of the amount of mobility they exhibit. If they do not, then analyses of market dynamics need to consider more than one aspect of intra-industry change.

It would not be surprising to find that the two processes were manifestations of the same forces. Where decline occurs in the short run, exit is probable in the longer run. As firms contract, they begin to exit. Where there is a large amount of growth in incumbents, there is likely to be room for entrants to grow.

In order to assess the relationship between the two sources of turnover, the data on long-run change derived from a comparison of 1970 and 1979 firm market shares were used. Short-run changes in market share derived from annual comparisons were not used because the transitory change in the share of the continuing-firm sector tends to dominate long-run changes in share when annual data are used. The measure of change used is the dissimilarity index – half the sum of the entry and exit shares or half the sum of the

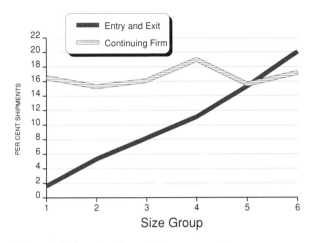

Figure 4-7. A comparison of the sources of turnover by size-class: market share change due to entry and exit vs. continuing-firm growth and decline (long run, 1970–79).

absolute value of the changes in the shares of continuing firms. The entry and exit shares include only greenfield entry and closedown exit.

The two measures calculated for four-digit industries were correlated. The correlation coefficient between the two sources of turnover was .06. Figure 4-7 provides a graphic depiction of the relationship between the two measures. All industries were ranked on the basis of the entry and exit turnover measure, and were grouped into six equal size-classes on the basis of this measure. Then the average turnover measure for entry and exit (as opposed to that for continuing firms) was calculated for each group. In Figure 4-7, the averages for each group are plotted from left to right in ascending order of importance of entry and exit turnover. It is evident that turnover from continuing firms is not closely related to that from entering and exiting firms. While turnover from entering and exiting firms varied from a low of about 2 per cent in the first group to over 20 per cent in the last group, turnover among continuing firms was relatively constant, staying in the range of 15 to 19 per cent. Whatever industry characteristics determined the amount of entry and exit, they do not have the same effect on the amount of change in incumbent firms.[14]

Concentration measures have long been the mainstay for those trying to characterize the structure of an industry. Their failings have been widely discussed. It is well known that they provide only a partial picture in that they capture the distribution of firms and not movements of firms within an industry. Two measures of mobility that overcome some of these difficulties have been presented here. Both yield important and different information. That they are not closely related confirms the criticism that has long been levelled at the concentration measure: there are a variety of changes taking place within industries and no single measure adequately summarizes these changes. Just as the concentration measure by itself is inadequate, so too is a simple measure of entry and exit or of incumbent-firm mobility.

Conclusion

This chapter has provided a basic description of turnover in continuing firms and compared it with that resulting from entry and exit. These two types of turnover have quite different long- and short-run characteristics. Greenfield entrants, as a class, start small but then inevitably grow. Estimates of the importance of greenfield entry in the short run, then, can all too easily lead to the false impression that entry and exit are insignificant. Exactly the opposite occurs in the continuing-firm sector. Here, growth and decline in the short run is large. But much of this is transitory. When measured over a decade, the annualized rate of change for the continuing sector is about one-fifth the rate yielded by yearly comparisons.

Some of the difference between the annualized long-run and the short-run rates of change in the continuing-firm sector is due to transitory phenomena – changes that are quickly reversed. However, some is due to the change in the composition of the continuing-firm population associated with long-term structural change in the rankings of firms. For example, when the measurement is taken over a longer period, there will be fewer incumbent firms to decline, because more will have exited. The remaining firms will be the more successful and will have lower rates of decline. We might, therefore, expect the cumulative rate of contraction to reach an asymptote and the annualized rate of decline that is calculated from it to approach zero.

The same conclusion also applies to the expanding segment, but for different reasons. Initially, cumulative expansion should be high, reflecting growth opportunities for younger, more efficient firms that are expanding. But eventually, as the period of measurement is lengthened, young firms become old and begin the process of decline. Cumulative growth will peak and then fall. The equivalent annual rates will approach zero.

Since in the long run the equivalent annualized rates of entry, exit, growth, and decline all approach zero, interest must focus on the rapidity of the process. In this chapter, only 6- and 11-year periods have been used to measure the long-run effect. It is not sensible to project the ultimate time paths of growing and declining firms on the basis of two observations.

Nevertheless, useful information is provided by these statistics. They reveal that the cumulative value of growth and contraction is significant. Over a decade, entries and exits contributed about the same amount of change as did continuing firms. Together, they shifted over a third of market share from gainers to losers over the period. These figures do not include the resources that were transferred from one firm to another as a result of take-overs and mergers. When they are included, some 44 per cent of market share is real-located, on average. This indicates a large degree of mobility.

This chapter has also demonstrated that the degree of turnover due to entry and exit does not correlate highly with the amount of incumbent-firm turno-ver. Whichever industry characteristics determine the extent of external com-petition from entry and exit, they do not also appear to influence the amount of internal competition. Analysts in the field of industrial organization have often devoted special attention to modelling the effect of entry. Implicit in these exercises is the notion that the disciplining influence exerted by entry is different from internal pressures that come from incumbent firms. If entry and exit are just marginal manifestations of a general turnover process at work, then there is little need to treat them separately. The differences found here reinforce the need to investigate separately the determinants of the two processes. They also emphasize the fact that there are several dimensions to the concept of mobility that need to be more fully delineated. These are considered at length in the next chapter.

5

Patterns of large- and small-firm mobility

Even in the world of giant firms, new ones arise and others fall into the background. Innovations still emerge primarily with the "young" ones, and the "old" ones display as a rule symptoms of what is euphemistically called conservatism.

Joseph Schumpeter (1939: 71)

Introduction

The preceding chapters outline the amount of turnover in the industrial population. They focus on a relatively aggregate level – presenting, for the most part, statistics that summarize the average levels of various components of firm turnover. These include greenfield entry and closedown exit, share change in continuing firms, and the frequency of mergers.

The amount of turnover depends on the amount of shifting that takes place in market shares and also on the pattern of these changes. It is possible that the turnover that occurs as one firm supplants another is completely random. This could occur if large and small firms had equal probabilities of growing or if the rates of growth did not depend on the size of the firm. On the other hand, there may be a pattern to the turnover in market share. Large firms may supplant small firms or small firms may grow at the expense of large firms.

The pattern of market-share change has important implications for competition policy. The reasons for this vary, depending on which conceptual framework is used.

One such framework is the stochastic-growth model associated with the work of Simon and Bonini (1958), Steindl (1965), and Prais (1976). This literature stresses the importance of determining the relationship between the amount of growth or decline and firm size. If growth and decline are unrelated to firm size, then the stochastic process that is associated with the operation of markets will lead to ever-increasing variance in firm size. The distribution of firm sizes will become more and more unequal and large firms will become increasingly dominant. On the other hand, if large firms tend to

82

decline and small firms tend to grow, then the process that leads to ever increasing inequality in firm size will be attenuated or reversed. These two possibilities have different implications for the competitive environment.

There are also numerous alternatives to stochastic theories, where the relative performance of large and small firms is also important. Some of the earlier static dominant-firm and oligopoly-leadership models implicitly assume the continued presence of large firms. In other models, existing dominant firms are portrayed as being able to adopt pre-emptive strategies that protect their market position. Still other game-theory models are built around the notion that the outcome of competition will be the development of coordinated strategies that allow existing firms to maintain their position relative to outsiders. Descriptions of the extent to which dominant firms maintain their position are helpful in evaluating the relevance of these various models. Finding that large firms decline suggests that these models suffer from a serious deficiency.

The goal of this chapter is to provide descriptive material to guide the focus of theoretical models. Evidence of the continued existence of larger firms is taken by many to imply something quite different than evidence of their decline. Gort (1963: 51), for example, emphasizes that in evaluating the degree of competition, the ability of leading firms to maintain their market share "is probably more significant than the extent of concentration at a single point in time". It is, thus, not just the magnitude of change as much as its pattern – in particular, the extent to which the largest firms decline and the smallest grow – that provides evidence of the intensity of competition in an industry.

Limited evidence on the pattern of change was presented earlier (see Chapters 2 and 3). Different types of entry were shown to affect different segments of the firm-size distribution. Greenfield entry and closedown exit have a greater impact on smaller firms. Entry by acquisition and exit by divestiture are concentrated in larger firms.

A more detailed investigation of the pattern of change that takes place within industries is, however, required. This chapter focuses on several aspects of intra-industry change by examining the extent to which firms of different sizes replace one another and the rapidity of the process. The first question posed is whether the largest firms are spared the turnover process. There is an impression given by earlier work in the United States (Gort, 1963) and the United Kingdom (Prais, 1976) that large firms are quite stable in terms of their relative position and market share over time. The second question that the chapter asks is whether market share exhibits a Galtonian regression to the mean. Finally, the chapter describes the amount of growth and decline in different-sized firms so that the pervasiveness of change can be fully appreciated.

For the purposes of analysis, industries are divided into large- and small-firm groups. Grouping firms by size-class has several justifications. Caves and Porter (1977) stress that mobility barriers may exist that divide industries into subgroups within which competition takes place. Small firms are prevented from growing by industry characteristics that impede the transition from small to large size-classes. Barriers do not provide the only explanation for the existence of variety of firm sizes within an industry. Others treat the coexistence of small and large firms as resulting from heterogeneity of specialization that allows small and large firms to exist side by side. Differences may exist in innovative potential with small firms enjoying a comparative advantage in innovative activity while large firms have advantages in utilizing production techniques that exploit economies of scale and scope. This is a theme emphasized in Jewkes, Sawers, and Stillerman (1958), and Neumann, Bobel, and Haid (1982). On the other hand, the small-business economics literature emphasizes that small firms coexist with larger firms because of the advantages that small firms possess in service, quality and flexibility (Ibrahim and Goodwin, 1986). In the same spirit, Mansfield et al. (1977: 16) conclude that small firms focus on areas requiring "sophistication and flexibility and catering to specialized needs" while larger firms have their advantage in products where scale economies exist in production, advertising, or technological advances.

The primary focus of the chapter is on the pattern of change within industries.[1] For this purpose, aggregate measures are employed that summarize the amount of change that exists on average across all industries. Since aggregate measures can hide important detail, the last part of the chapter details the extent to which the processes described are present in all industries, not concentrated in just a few. While the patterns of intra-industry change clearly vary across industries, with some industries experiencing considerably less change than others, the majority of Canadian manufacturing industries experience substantial turnover.

Mobility patterns within industries
Market-share change for large firms

Until now, the amount of market share that is transferred from declining to growing firms has been used to characterize the amount of mobility. During the 1970s, turnover in market share was about equally divided between entrants and incumbents. Since entry is concentrated among small firms, this type of turnover does not directly affect large firms. This observation raises the possibility that the phenomenon being measured here is only important at the margin – that turnover has virtually no effect on the largest firms in an industry.

If turnover in market share has no impact on the market share of the largest firms, it is more difficult to argue that it will have an effect on the competitive behaviour of the dominant firm in the industry. If some small firms are constantly replacing other small firms and there is no effect on larger firms, there is little reason to suppose that large firms must consider the possibility that they will lose market share and act in a way that will forestall this possibility.

While there are models that suggest that potential entry may be sufficient to affect the behaviour of dominant firms, it is difficult to conceive of a world in which potential entry exists without the presence of actual entry. The concept of potential entry becomes excessive baggage when actual entry is large. Likewise, the notion of stable dominant firms is superfluous when there is evidence of their demise. Central to the current study is the notion that speculation about the intensity and effects of competition is no substitute for data that describe its outcome. Change in relative firm position is one source of such data. This section, therefore, focuses on the question of whether large firms experience much market-share turnover.

The first measure used to capture turnover is the sum of the absolute value of the change in share experienced by a category – the leading firm or a group of leading firms, large firms, or small firms. The advantage of this measure is that it captures the totality of market-share change and is related to the dissimilarity index that was used in Chapter 4. When all categories are considered together, half the value of the sum of these measures yields the dissimilarity index used in Chapter 4. Thus, half the value of this measure for a particular category can be used to calculate the contribution the category makes to the dissimilarity index calculated from total market-share change in an industry.

The second group of measures attempts to capture the direction of change by taking either the sum of all market-share changes and thus allowing positive and negative values to offset one another, or by examining only the amount of negative or positive share changes. Since each category that is examined here starts with a different market share (the leading firm's market share varies across industries), the amount of decline is sometimes translated into a rate of share change by dividing by the original market share of the category. This initialization procedure permits more meaningful inter-group or inter-industry comparisons.

The weighted dissimilarity index. In Chapter 4, turnover among continuing firms has been measured with a dissimilarity index that captures the extent to which market share is transferred among firms in an industry. One way to investigate the importance of change in larger firms is to recalculate the dissimilarity index, with weights attached to each firm's market-share change

$[Sh_{79}(i) - Sh_{70}(i)]$, where the weights are the initial market shares of firms in each industry $[Sh_{70}(i)]$. In this case, the index is written

$$\text{Index} = \sum \left| \left[Sh_{70}(i) \times \left\{ Sh_{79}(i) - Sh_{70}(i) \right\} \right] \right|. \tag{5-1}$$

Share changes in larger firms are given more emphasis in this summary statistic.

The unweighted dissimilarity index has well-defined bounds between 0 and 1, so the intensity of change in a particular industry can be readily assessed. A value of .44 for the unweighted dissimilarity index indicates that market-share turnover between 1970 and 1979 accounted for 44 per cent of the maximum that could potentially be shifted. The maximum amount of change for the weighted dissimilarity index can also be calculated, though it is more complicated, and the upper bound is no longer 1.[2]

The weighted index was calculated twice for each manufacturing industry – once including entry and exit through acquisition and divestiture as a share change and once excluding them. In the first case, the mean value of the weighted index relative to its upper bound was .39. In the second case, the mean value of the index relative to its potential maximum was .33. The mean values of the same two unweighted statistics were .44 and .36, respectively.

The actual market-share change, when calculated as a percentage of the maximum change that could have taken place, is significant. Moreover, the change indicated by the index that weights the amount of turnover by initial market share is just as important as that given by the index that does not. Taking into account the size of the firm that loses or gains market share does not affect the conclusion that market-share turnover is significant. On the basis of this evidence, share change is not completely restricted to smaller firms.

Share change in the largest firms. Summary statistics, like the dissimilarity index, that encompass the activity of all firms in an industry encapsulate information in an efficient fashion; but in order to do so they often drastically reduce the dimensions of the data. The resulting statistics are not susceptible to easy interpretation.

Another way to describe the extent to which change is not restricted to smaller firms is to concentrate directly on the success of the leading firms in an industry. This was done by calculating the sum of the absolute share changes for only the largest firms in 1970 using shipments.[3] Estimates for three different groups of the largest firms are presented in Table 5-1. The first uses the 10 largest firms; the second uses the 5 largest firms; and the third uses those firms that make up the top 75 per cent of shipments.

The 10 largest firms accounted for 75 per cent of the market on average;

Table 5-1. *Average share change of the largest manufacturing firms between 1970 and 1979, four-digit industry level*

Measure of share change[a]	Ten largest firms, 1970	Five largest firms, 1970	Firms accounting for top 75 per cent of shipments[b]
Share change (unweighted percentage points)	28	21	27
Share of sample (per cent)	75	61	71
Ratio of share change to initial share (per cent)	38	36	37

[a] Share change is the sum of the absolute values of individual firm change.
[b] The mean of the sample is less than 75 per cent because of the truncation routine used.

their average share change was 28 percentage points and the mean ratio of their share change to their initial share was 38 per cent. The 5 largest firms, accounting for 61 per cent of the market, on average, had a 21-percentage-point share change, which averaged 36 per cent of their original share.

Because the Canadian manufacturing sector is small, a few firms generally account for a large proportion of each industry. There is, therefore, the danger that reliance on the 5 or 10 largest firms could provide misleading results. When a constant number of firms is used to define the index, the turnover that is captured comes from varying proportions of different industries. If turnover differs across the size distribution, the average measure for any industry calculated from a constant number of the largest firms will partially reflect the extent to which these firms dominate the industry.

To overcome this potential problem, the share-change indices were also calculated for those firms that made up 75 per cent of industry shipments for each industry. Market-share change in this segment (the sum of the absolute value of all changes) averaged 27 percentage points. This was 37 per cent of the original market share, on average. The two methods, then, yield a similar picture of the amount of change that is taking place in the largest firms. They indicate that change over a decade in the largest firms, as a percentage of their initial market share, is substantial.

These share-change indices will not have the same bounds as those in Chapter 4 because only the largest firms in 1970 (and not in both 1970 and 1979) are included; however, the bound for the maximum change in the four largest firms can be calculated.[4] On average, the total share change was 13 per cent of the maximum. Within the incumbent population, 16.6 per cent of market share was transferred (see Chapter 4). The four largest firms experienced

Table 5-2. *Mean share change*[a] *between 1970 and 1979 of the four largest manufacturing firms as of 1970, four-digit industry level*

Measure of share change	Rank of firm in 1970			
	First	Second	Third	Fourth
1970–79 share change	−5.5	−3.1	−2.6	−1.2
(percentage points)	(0.7)	(0.4)	(0.3)	(0.3)
Average 1970 share (per cent)	24.4	14.6	9.8	7.1
	(1.1)	(0.6)	(0.4)	(0.3)
Share change divided	−24.2	−25.2	−30.5	−16.5
by original share	(3.1)	(2.7)	(3.1)	(4.7)
Absolute value of share change	36.3	34.7	40.6	41.9
divided by original share	(2.2)	(1.9)	(2.2)	(3.6)

[a] Standard error of the mean is in parentheses.

slightly less change, relative to the maximum, than the entire continuing-firm population.

In conclusion, the dissimilarity index for the leading firms in an industry shows that these firms experienced considerable change. It is only slightly less than that experienced by all incumbent continuing firms.

Share change in the four largest firms. Since the largest firms are so important in many industries and the dissimilarity indices obscure what is happening to individual large firms, the experience of each of the four largest firms was examined in more depth.[5] To do so, the average change in market share and the sum of the absolute value of the changes for each group of firms were calculated for the period 1970–79.

The average change – the net change due to growth and decline – was chosen because the direction of the net change is of particular interest in assessing the long-run success of the leading firms. The results are reported in Table 5-2. Each of the four largest firms experienced a decline in market share, on average. For each of these firms, the mean value of the change calculated at the four-digit level is significantly less than zero. The average reduction in market share declines monotonically from 5.5 percentage points for the largest firm to 1.2 percentage points for the fourth largest firm; but when the average decline is calculated as a percentage of the initial share (third row), there is no significant difference between the mean rate of decline in the shares of the three largest firms. On average, the three largest firms lost between 25 and 30 per cent of their initial market share over the decade.

There is, thus, little tendency for the average rates of decline of the four largest firms to differ. But the average rate is calculated by taking the net effect of growth in some firms and decline in others. Using it may mask differences in underlying volatility. To investigate this possibility, the absolute value of share change divided by original market share is presented in Table 5-2, fourth row. Total share change ranges from some 35 per cent of the original market share for the first two firms to over 40 per cent for the third and fourth. The third and fourth firms now both show more volatility than the first two, and these differences are weakly significant.

A comparison of market-share change in large and small firms

Differences in the market shares of the four largest firms show that volatility increases with the rank of the firm. This suggests that smaller firms are in general more volatile than larger firms. This proposition was investigated by comparing the total amount of change in large and small firms between 1970 and 1979. Firms in each industry were sorted on the basis of output size and then were divided at the firm that accounted for 50 per cent of output.[6] Then the amount of change in the continuing group and from entry and exit was calculated.

The dissimilarity index – half the sum of the absolute value of all share changes – was used to measure share change for the larger continuing firms (TOPCHG) and the smaller continuing firms (BOTCHG).[7] The dissimilarity indices for the two firm-size groupings are presented in Table 5-3, along with the value of the index that is derived from all firms, both large and small, in each category. Panel 1 divides the sample on the basis of 1979 firm size for each industry; panel 2 divides the sample on the basis of 1970 firm size. There was a significant difference in the amount and direction of change in large compared with small continuing firms. The dissimilarity index for continuing firms measured 7.4 per cent for the large firms and 8.8 per cent for small firms, when firm size in 1979 is used to divide the sample. This corresponds to a change in total share of 14.8 and 17.6 per cent, respectively. The differences are statistically significant, though not large. The stochastic process, therefore, affects larger firms less than smaller firms – a result that was also found in the comparison of just the largest four firms.

While the dissimilarity index reveals differences in volatility, it does not indicate the direction of change. In order to do so, the total share change was also calculated. Since it allows positive share change to offset negative change, its sign reveals the direction of net change – positive or negative. The measure for large firms (TOPGR) and for small firms (BOTGR) is calculated on the basis of 1970 firm size.[8] When the sum of all share changes was taken, large firms lost 11.6 percentage points of market share, on average; small firms gained 13.9 percentage points. This is equivalent to a 25.3 per cent rate of decline in market share for large firms and a 31 per cent rate of gain for the smaller firms. Generally, large firms are declining and small firms are growing.

Table 5-3. *Average contribution of large and small firms[a] to dissimilarity index, 1970–79, four-digit industry level (per cent of shipments)[b]*

Firm category	Large firms	Small firms	Total
1. Sorting on 1979 size			
a. Acquisitions considered as ongoing entities			
Continuing	7.4 (0.31)	8.8 (0.30)	16.2
Greenfield entrants	2.8	7.7	10.4
Total	10.2 (0.47)	16.5 (0.31)	26.6
b. Acquisitions considered as entrants			
Continuing	6.8 (0.31)	7.7 (0.27)	14.5
Greenfield	2.8	7.7	10.5
Acquisition entrants	2.6	2.0	4.6
Total	12.2 (0.50)	17.4 (0.43)	29.6
2. Sorting on 1970 size			
a. Divestitures considered as ongoing entities			
Continuing	6.8 (0.35)	9.5 (0.26)	16.3
Closedown exits	3.7	7.4	11.1
Total	10.5 (0.51)	16.9 (0.43)	27.4
b. Divestitures considered as exits			
Continuing	5.8 (0.32)	8.3 (0.25)	14.1
Closedown exits	3.7	7.4	11.1
Divestitive exits	2.6	2.5	5.1
Total	12.1 (0.55)	18.2 (0.49)	30.3

[a] To divide large from small firms, all enterprises were ranked by shipments and the dividing point chosen was the firm that accounted for 50 per cent of output.
[b] Standard error of the mean is in parentheses.

The sources of market-share change in large and small firms. While the growth and decline process affects small firms more than large firms, it is only one of the dynamic processes that works to change the firm-size distribution. Greenfield entry and closedown exit, and acquisition entry and divestiture exit have different impacts on large compared with small firms. An appreciation of the effect of each requires that the joint impact of all three processes on large and small firms be compared.

In order to do so, large and small firms are defined by ranking firms by size and by using the mid-point of cumulative output. The effects of each of the different aspects of turnover on large and small firms are compared in Table 5-3 by calculating the contribution that a particular category made to the overall dissimilarity index. This is half the sum of the absolute value of the share changes of firms in that category. Panels 1 and 2 present the results for large and small firms based on rankings for 1979 and 1970, respectively. The results for 1979 reveal how much change large and small firms experienced from growth, decline, and entry over the previous decade. For 1970, the results reveal how much change occurred over the following decade because of growth and decline in continuing firms and because of exit. Results are calculated separately for 1979 and 1970 in order to separate the effects of entry from exit.[9]

Within each panel, there are two sets of results. In panel 1, the entry category in set A includes the effects of greenfield entrants only; it does not include entry by acquisition. Such firms are treated as ongoing in this set of results. Then, the effects of greenfield and acquisition entry are calculated separately in set B. Since acquisitions are included in the population of entrants in set B but not in the population of continuing firms in set A, estimates of growth and decline in the continuing sector for sets A and B will be different because a different population is being used for the measurement. Similarly, in panel 2, the first exit category in set A includes the effects of closedown exits only; then, in set B, separate estimates of closedown exit and divestiture exit are calculated.

Greenfield entry and closedown exit have the greatest differential effect on large and small firms. The dissimilarity index indicates that some 10.4 per cent of market share was transferred as a result of greenfield entry. Of this, 2.8 per cent occurred as a result of the entry of large firms, and 7.7 per cent as a result of the entry of small firms. The results are equally skewed for closedown exit – 3.7 per cent came from large firms and 7.4 per cent came from small firms.

The differential between the dissimilarity index for large and small continuing firms is less than that for greenfield entry and closedown exit – though the size of the differential depends on the year. In 1970, the differential was larger – 6.8 per cent for large firms and 9.5 per cent for small firms; in 1979, it was 7.4 per cent for large firms and 8.8 per cent for small firms. This difference reflects the transition of what were small firms in 1970 to large-firm status in 1979. In 1970 small firms experienced more change, growing on average, and in 1979 some of the change in the large-firm category came from small firms that were small in 1970 and had become large by 1979.

The categories with the smallest differential effects are acquisition and divestiture associated with entry and exit. The total market share that shifted only as a result of acquisition that led to entry is about 4.6 percentage points, on average. Of that, 2.6 per cent came from large firms and 2 per cent came from small firms. The total contribution to the dissimilarity index from divestitures associated with exit is 5.1 per cent; of that, 2.6 per cent came from large firms and 2.5 per cent came from small firms.

Smaller firms exhibit more market-share turnover than do larger firms. Most of the market-share turnover among small firms comes from entry and exit. This should not be interpreted to mean that dominant firms do not change. On average, the largest firm loses almost a quarter of its market share over a decade.

This section has shown that there is more change among small firms than among large firms. On average, large firms decline and small firms grow. Competition serves to sort the worthy from the undeserving. During the sorting process, a significant amount of churning takes place among small firms, primarily as a result of entry and exit. The large firm must sort through complex signals before it can discern which of the newly arrived is likely to offer it the greatest threat. This is not a picture of a world in which market leaders can afford to be complacent; nor is it one in which they can easily develop policies against specific intruders.

Change in firm ranks

Share-change indices have provided the focus for the previous section. There is another measure, which is based on the rank change of firms, that has been used by Joskow (1960) to measure intra-industry mobility. Rank changes have not been used in this study for a number of reasons. First, as a measure of instability, market share is more relevant to most firm decision-making. Share changes directly translate into lost sales and, therefore, into lost profits. Rank change, on the other hand, is a discontinuous variable that is not monotonically related to lost sales and profits. Since it is the loss in sales and profits that is relevant to decision-making, rank change is an imperfect measure of the amount of uncertainty that large firms face. Second, as a measure of the importance of the leading firm that varies across industries, the market share of that firm, and not its rank, is the appropriate measure.

The share-change indices show that there was substantial overall movement, especially among the largest firms. These firms can lose substantial market share without changing their relative ranking. Because the firm-size distribution is skewed, the largest firm has to lose considerable market share before it drops to second. On average, in 1970 the largest firm in an industry possessed some 10 percentage points more market share than the second firm. Differences in the average market share of a firm decline as the rank increases; between the second- and third-ranked firm, there is a 5-percentage-point difference; between the third- and fourth-ranked firm, there is a 3-percentage-point difference.

Because the rate of market-share change is about the same for the largest firms and because of the degree of skewness in the size distribution, the

Table 5-4. *Distribution of rank changes between 1970 and 1979 among the four largest firms as of 1970, four-digit industry level (per cent)*

Rank change	Rank of firm in 1970			
	First	Second	Third	Fourth
+3	—	—	—	6.6
+2	—	—	4.8	16.8
+1	—	15.0	12.0	25.7
0	64.7	39.5	28.1	16.8
−1	19.8	15.0	15.0	9.0
−2	4.2	8.4	6.6	3.6
−3	1.2	3.6	3.6	3.6
−4	0.6	5.4	4.2	1.8
−5	1.2	2.4	6.0	1.2
−6 or more	8.3	10.7	19.7	14.9

amount of rank change should be inversely related to the market share of the firm. Large market-share change should have less effect on rank among larger firms than among smaller firms.

In order to investigate the effect of market-share change on the relative positions of the largest firms, the ranks of the four largest firms in each manufacturing industry were calculated for 1970 and 1979. The distribution of the change in the ranks of each of the four largest firms is tabulated in Table 5-4. As predicted, the largest firms experienced the greatest stability. Over 64 per cent of the largest firms in 1970 were still the leaders in 1979, despite the fact that they lost an average of about one-quarter of their market share over the decade. The next three ranks do not exhibit the same stability. There is an inverse relationship between the rank and the percentage of firms that maintain their rank over the decade. Only 16 per cent of those firms that were fourth in 1970 occupied the same position in 1979.

These results confirm that rank changes have to be used carefully. Hymer and Pashigian (1962) note that the amount of rank change in two industries can be different, even though they experience a similar amount of market-share shifting at the individual-firm level. This can occur if there are more firms in one industry than another and the differences among the shares of firms is smaller. It is clear from Table 5-4 that, although the rate of market-share loss is similar for the three largest firms, the degree to which this causes a shift in firm rank differs dramatically because of the skewed nature of the firm-size distribution.

This demonstrates the shortcomings of using rank changes alone to characterize the amount of intra-industry change. It does not mean that measures of rank change should be completely discarded. When used appropriately, they can provide important additional information on a dimension of change for which market-share statistics are less suited.

There are several interesting dimensions to the change. The first is the amount and direction of that change. The share-change data reveal that the cumulative amount of change is large and that large firms tend to decline in relative terms. Another important dimension is the speed of change. Here, the rank-change statistics are a useful complement to rates of market-share decline.

The average rate of share loss among the leading firms is between 30 and 40 per cent over a decade. This is one indicator of the speed of change. The data on change in rank (Table 5-4) can also be used to characterize the rapidity of change. They give an indication of the average length of time that a firm might expect to remain at a particular rank. Prais (1955) shows that, with the appropriate assumptions, the proportion of firms remaining in a given category can be used to estimate the average time a firm stayed in that category.[10] Using this approach, the average length of stay of each of the four largest firms is 28, 17, 14, and 12 years. This confirms the casual impression that change is not apocalyptic. The leading firm in an industry today is likely to be the leading firm for quite a long time. Nor is the situation that it faces static. In 35 per cent of the cases, the leading firm is supplanted by another firm within a decade. On average, it loses about a third of its market share over the decade – both to newcomers and to existing firms.

Transitional probabilities across firm size-classes

The preceding section has demonstrated that change is not restricted to the smallest firms and that there is a general regression-to-the-mean phenomenon. Unfortunately, focusing only on the rank of the four largest firms obscures what is happening to the rest of the firm population. In order to track the extent to which smaller firms change position, more detailed data that show the extent to which firms grow and decline and the variability in the experience of different-sized firms over a longer time period are required.

This type of information can be derived from a transitions matrix that reveals the percentage of firms moving from one size-class to another between two periods.[11]

In order to calculate the transitions matrices for the Canadian manufacturing sector, each industry was divided into quintiles based on the ranks of the firms in 1970 and in 1979. The proportions of firms in that class that were in the same class, another class, or that had exited by 1979 were then calculated. The proportions reported in the transitions matrices were calculated including and excluding entry and exit through acquisition and divestiture,

Table 5-5. *Mean duration that firms stay in a size-class, four-digit industry level (years)[a]*

	Size-class				
Alternate measures	1	2	3	4	5
Entry and exit through merger included	12.1 (0.4)	12.4 (0.4)	13.3 (0.4)	15.5 (0.5)	23.3 (0.7)
Entry and exit through merger excluded	12.2 (0.4)	12.9 (0.4)	13.9 (0.5)	16.8 (0.6)	30.0 (0.8)

[a] Based on a transition matrix calculated for 1970 and 1979. See text for details of how the size-classes were derived. Standard error of the mean is in parentheses and was derived from the individual variances of the mean duration of stay in each industry.

and were used to calculate the average time firms stayed in a particular quintile group.

The average length of stay is reported in Table 5-5. Several important points emerge. First, the average length of stay increases as the size of firm increases – from about 12 years to over 20 years in the largest class. The average length of stay in the four smallest firm size-classes varies from 12 to 17 years. Second, the average length of stay is not greatly affected by the inclusion or exclusion of entry and exit by acquisition and divestiture, except among the largest firms. If entry and exit by divestiture is excluded, the mean duration of stay for firms in this class is some 30 years; if they are included, it is 23 years.

The transitions matrices are presented in Table 5-6. These matrices are calculated for continuing firms only. Panel A divides firms into their size-class as of 1970 and calculates the proportions of each that had moved to another class by 1979. Panel B divides firms into their size-class in 1979 and calculates the proportion coming from a different size-class as of 1970. The distribution of the 1979 destination of the firms according to their 1970 quintile groups is graphed in Figure 5-1. Some 55 per cent of continuing firms that started in quintile group 1 were still there in 1979, but over 20 per cent moved up one class. Two other points are noteworthy. First, there is more inter-class movement in the small size-classes than in the large size-classes, which is not surprising since there would have to be a dramatic decline in the largest firms for them to end up in the smaller classes. Second, a substantial percentage of stayers moved up or down at least one size-class.

Table 5-6. *Distribution of continuing firms by size-class in 1970 and 1979, by quintile group at the four-digit industry level (per cent)*

	Size-class, 1979					
Size-class, 1970	1	2	3	4	5	Total
A. Destination of 1970 size-class						
1	54.3	30.7	12.3	2.1	0.6	100.0
2	17.6	39.3	30.8	10.8	1.6	100.0
3	5.1	15.4	39.8	33.4	6.2	100.0
4	1.1	3.3	16.9	51.7	26.9	100.0
5	0.3	0.5	1.9	13.8	83.5	100.0
B. Origin of 1979 size-class						
1	54.5	19.5	5.9	0.7	0.3	
2	30.5	48.9	25.6	6.6	0.8	
3	11.0	25.0	44.5	25.6	0.4	
4	2.9	5.8	21.3	51.2	20.1	
5	0.6	0.8	2.7	15.9	74.8	
Total	100.0	100.0	100.0	100.0	100.0	

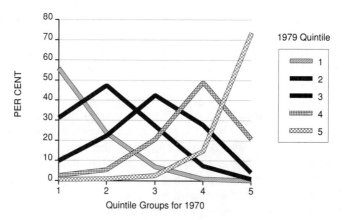

Figure 5-1. The distribution of 1970 continuing firms by 1979 quintile class.

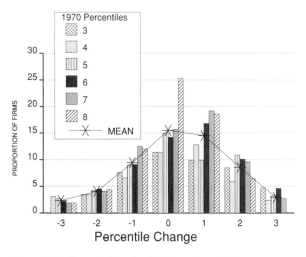

Figure 5-2. Cumulative distribution of transitions across size-classes between 1970 and 1979.

For example, while some 40 per cent of continuing firms that were in quintile group 3 in 1970 stayed in that group, almost 50 per cent moved up or down one class.

In order to test the sensitivity of these results to the level of aggregation used, the sample was divided into 10 percentiles and the analysis was performed once again. The results are reported in Figure 5-2. This time the transition probabilities are calculated against all firms, not just continuers. The largest firm size-classes and the two smallest firm size-classes were excluded and the percentage of each group that moved was plotted against the number of decile changes. A change of zero denotes no movement. On average, 15 per cent experienced no change, 10 per cent dropped by one group, 4 per cent dropped by two groups; 14 per cent moved up one group, 9 per cent moved up two groups. These values are lower than the quintile proportions reported in Figure 5-1, both because they are calculated for finer percentiles and because they are calculated for all firms, including exits; but they show that the percentage moving relative to the proportion staying is large. It must be noted, however, that moves upward are primarily to the next two decile groups. Only relatively small proportions of these middle-percentile groups manage to grow more than three classes over the decade.

Regression to the mean in market shares

Focusing on the fate of the largest firms provides a picture of only part of the change that is taking place. This section focuses more generally on comparing the pattern of change in large and small firms. In particular, it investigates the tendency for large firms to decline and small firms to grow relative to one another – the Galtonian regression-to-the-mean phenomenon.

Chapter 4 demonstrates that, for manufacturing as a whole, there was a substantial regression to the mean. This finding, however, was based on an analysis done on consolidated firms. It could, therefore, have been the result of changes in the size of different industries rather than shifts within industries.

The regression-to-the-mean phenomenon plays an important role in stochastic growth models (see Prais, 1976: ch. 2). Some of the most important are those models that embody the law of proportionate effect. They essentially assume that the growth rate is independent of size. If firm growth and decline is presumed to follow such a process, then the size of a firm in one period can be related to that in the previous period by

$$\log(Q_1) = \log(Q_0) + G, \tag{5-2}$$

where Q_1 and Q_0 are the firm size in period 1 and 0, respectively, and G is the logarithmic growth rate of the firm. Then the variance of the size of firms in two adjacent periods can be written as

$$S_1^2 = S_0^2 + \text{var}(G), \tag{5-3}$$

where S_{i1}^2 is the variance of the firm size when expressed as logarithms in period $i1$.

After t periods, the variance of the logarithm of firm sizes is

$$S_t^2 = S_0^2 + t \times \text{var}(G). \tag{5-4}$$

Therefore, the variance of the firm-size distribution will grow over time unless there is some process at work other than that described by equation 5-2. Moreover, the rate at which it grows is a function of the variance in the growth rates of firms in an industry. It is this finding that provides the anomaly that the competitive process can sow the seeds of its own destruction. If a competitive market structure promotes competition and the competitive process leads to a diversity of growth rates across firms, then the original market structure will inevitably become more concentrated if firm growth follows the law of proportionate effect.

Ever-increasing concentration need not develop from a stochastic growth model. A sufficient though not a necessary condition for stability in the firm-size distribution is the tendency for extreme values of the firm-size distribution to regress towards the mean – for large firms to shrink and small firms to grow.

If instead of equation 5-2 the growth process is characterized by

$$\log(Q_1) = b \times \log(Q_0) + G, \tag{5-5}$$

then the variance in firm sizes in two adjacent periods is given by

$$S_1^2 = b^2 \times S_0^2 + \text{var}(G). \tag{5-6}$$

If b is less than one, firms regress towards the mean. If b is sufficiently small,[12] then the variance or inequality in firm size will not increase over time. It is, therefore, important to estimate the extent to which the Galtonian regression coefficient differs from one, on average, and how widespread this phenomenon is in different manufacturing industries.

Regression and correlation analysis can be used to measure the importance of the Galtonian regression phenomenon. Regression analysis provides an estimate of the magnitude of the Galtonian regression tendency. Correlation analysis can be used to complement this procedure in order to indicate the *goodness of fit* of the simple bivariate relationship.

Stability of market share is measured in this way by Gort (1963), who examines the relationship between the market shares of the 15 leading firms in 205 U.S. manufacturing industries between 1947 and 1954. Correlation coefficients are found generally to be above .8, and 78 of 197 regression coefficients are between 0.9 and 1.1. On the basis of this evidence, Scherer (1980: 74) concludes that there is little movement in relative firm size.

Unfortunately, the correlation and regression statistics are not well suited to describing how much change occurs. The regression coefficient only describes the pattern of change that is taking place. A value of one for the Galtonian coefficient b in equation 5-5 could result from many firms changing their market share or from all firms retaining the same market share over the period. In order to distinguish the first from the second situation, knowledge of the variance of the estimated parameter or the goodness of fit of a linear relationship (given by the correlation coefficient) is required. It is, therefore, important to know both the pattern of share change and how much variation in the pattern exists.

The correlation and regression coefficients have to be interpreted jointly with the dissimilarity indices that measure the amount of share change. Mean regression coefficients such as those found by Gort, which ranged from 0.9 to 1.1, are not sufficient to prove that there is little change taking place. The cumulative value of market-share turnover, as indicated by the weighted and unweighted share-shift statistics, can still be large.

One way to demonstrate this point is to note that the square of the correlation coefficient is just the coefficient of determination for the regression of final-year share on initial-year share. If the correlation coefficient is .80, only 64 per cent of the variability of final-year share is "explained" by initial-year share. A large component of final-year share is not explained by a linear relationship between initial- and final-year share. Thus, even a finding that the regression coefficient was not significantly different from one would not by itself indicate that there was little change taking place among firms in the industry.

In order to investigate whether the same impression would be produced by regression and correlation analysis using Canadian data, despite the relatively large shift in market shares exhibited by the unweighted and weighted dissimilarity indices, and to investigate the pattern of market-share change, correlation and regression analyses were performed for 167 Canadian manufacturing industries using 1970 and 1979 market shares.

Much of the literature on the existence of the law of proportionate effect uses only the performance of incumbent firms, primarily because of the lack of more comprehensive data. This has necessitated complicated corrections for sample selection bias (Hall, 1987). If exits and entrants are omitted and they are characterized by different growth and decline patterns than incumbents, then the estimated regression-to-the-mean coefficients will not represent the behaviour of the population as a whole.

Because of the nature of the data being used here, there is no reason to omit the information available for entrants and exits. Using this information, however, requires that a slightly different format be adopted for the estimation procedure. Normally, the existence of a size effect is obtained from a regression of

$$\log(Q_2/Q_1) = b + c \times Q_1. \tag{5-7}$$

If this formulation is used, then all entrants and exits must be omitted since the logarithm of zero is undefined. Therefore, market shares are used at first to outline the course of the regression phenomenon – both for the entire population and then for just the continuing population. The estimating equation is

$$Sh_t = a + b \times Sh_{t-1}. \tag{5-8}$$

The results for the traditional equation 5–7 are also presented to show the similarities between the two approaches.

The extent to which there is regression to the mean can be examined by using plant or firm data. The use of plant data reveals the extent to which the production units maintain their position over time. Focusing on the firm allows the success of the operating entity to be assessed. The two need not have the same tendency to regress towards the mean. Large firms may possess plants that lose market share, but nevertheless the firms may maintain their position by acquiring new plants.

Table 5-7. *Relationships between 1979 and 1970 firm market share
estimated for four-digit industries in the manufacturing sector*

	All firms			Continuing firms		
Mean regression coefficient[a]	Mean coefficient (1)	Standard error mean (2)	Per cent ≠ 1[b] (3)	Mean coefficient (4)	Standard error mean (5)	Per cent ≠ 1[b] (6)
COR	.756	(.017)	—	.876	(.009)	—
OLS	0.758	(0.021)	73.0	0.905	(0.023)	56.0
INST	0.656	(0.022)	64.0	0.949	(0.018)	24.0
MSE	0.768	(0.022)	69.0	0.961	(0.021)	38.0

[a] The columns present the mean values of regression coefficients. The terms used are defined as follows: COR is the correlation coefficient of Sh_{79} with Sh_{70}; OLS is the coefficient derived from OLS regression of Sh_{79} on Sh_{70}; INST is the coefficient derived from instrumental regression of Sh_{79} on Sh_{70} using the 1970 ranks as the instrument; MSE is Feldstein's (1974) minimum-mean-squared-error coefficient.
[b] A two-tailed test with 5 per cent significance level was used.

Regression to the mean: firm data. The mean values of several correlation and regression statistics that use firm shares in 1970 and 1979 for all firms and for continuing firms are presented in Table 5-7. Differences between the two may be used to infer the bias in studies that concentrate only on incumbent firms. The mean value of the correlation coefficient between initial- and final-period firm shares is .76 for all firms; it is .88 for continuing firms. This suggests a fairly stable relationship between firm market shares at the beginning and end of the 1970s.

Estimation of the Galtonian regression coefficient must allow for the possibility that the assumptions required for the ordinary-least-squares (OLS) technique to be linear-unbiased estimates may be violated. Chapter 3 demonstrates that the amount of change in the continuing sector in the short and long runs are different – even when that change is reported in terms of equivalent annual rates of change. There is a short-run, transitory component in firm sales that is reversed in the longer run. Thus, observed share (Sh_t) is made up of a long-run component (L_t) and a short-run cyclical or transitory component (C_t):

$$Sh_t = L_t + C_t. \tag{5-9}$$

It is the pattern of the long-run component (L_t) that needs to be tracked; that is, the required Galtonian coefficient is b in the following equation:

$$L_t = a + b \times L_{t-1}. \tag{5-10}$$

Unfortunately, only the observed share (Sh_t) values are available in any one year. This means that any attempt to obtain the Galtonian regression coefficient using Sh_t rather than L_t will suffer from a classic errors-in-variable problem. Observed firm share will equal true long-term share plus an error term that consists of the transitory component. Coefficients that are estimated using OLS techniques will tend to be biased downward.

Several methods are adopted here to correct for the inconsistency that accompanies an errors-in-variable problem. Table 5-7 contains the means, calculated across all industries, of three different estimates of the regression coefficients (second, third, and fourth rows) of a linear relation between 1979 and 1970 share. The mean OLS regression coefficient is 0.76 for all firms. Only 15 per cent of the estimates are greater than one, and only one-third of these are significantly different from one. Of the 85 per cent that are less than one, about 80 per cent are significantly less than one. The tendency to regress towards the mean is generally strong enough to overcome the imprecision of the estimation process caused by the relatively small number of firms in some industries.

When only continuing firms are used, the mean value of the OLS estimate increases to 0.91, the proportion of values greater than one increases to some 30 per cent, and the overall percentage of values that are significantly different from one falls to about 56 per cent. Continuing firms, then, also show a regression to the mean, but it is much less pronounced. Omitting the effect of entry and exit when calculating the Galtonian regression tendency leaves a false impression of stability.

The other regression coefficients reported in Table 5-7 were obtained by different methods that correct for the errors-in-variable problem. The INST coefficient reported in the third row of Table 5-7 is an instrumental estimator.[13] The MSE estimate uses Feldstein's (1974) mean-squared-error estimator. While the mean values of the estimators differ, the differences are not such as to affect the overall impression that initial- and final-year firm shares, a decade apart, are related, or that there is a regression-to-the-mean phenomenon taking place. That they are related, of course, does not imply that there is little aggregate turnover in market shares.

These three techniques all yield mean estimates that are less than one. The modifications to the OLS technique result in estimates that are only slightly different from those produced by the OLS technique itself, suggesting that the errors-in-variable problem is not particularly important when shares are compared for years a decade apart.[14] The conclusion that most of the co-efficients are significantly less than one is also not markedly affected by the technique used.

Correlation and regression coefficients are useful for an examination of the extent to which Galtonian regression towards the mean exists – whether large firms tend to lose share and small firms tend to gain it (see Prais, 1976). The regression coefficients in this case suggest that a regression to the mean is evident in the Canadian manufacturing sector in the 1970s. The mean values of the coefficients that relate 1979 and 1970 share, derived by the various techniques, are significantly less than one. The values of the individual industry coefficients are also generally less than one. It is, therefore, evident that a firm that was large in 1970 regressed toward the mean by 1979; a small firm tended to increase its share.

The coefficients derived from the regression analysis can be used to ask what proportion of market-share change is the result of the Galtonian regression toward the mean and what proportion is the result of random movement in market shares. For instance, if

$$Sh_{79} = A + (B \times Sh_{70}), \tag{5-11}$$

then, since the dissimilarity index is written as

$$\sum \left| \left(Sh_{79} - Sh_{70} \right) \right|, \tag{5-12}$$

substituting equation 5-11 into equation 5-12 means that the market-share change due to the regression-to-the-mean phenomenon can be written as

$$\sum \left| \left[A + (B - 1) \times Sh_{70} \right] \right|. \tag{5-13}$$

The value of market share due to the regression-to-the-mean phenomenon can be obtained by substituting the OLS value from Table 5-7, column 2 and its associated intercept into equation 5-13. This yields a measure of about .15 and not the level of .36 that is provided by the dissimilarity index. This implies that less than half of the total share change is accounted for by the regression-to-the-mean phenomenon. The remainder is the random component due to the residual in the estimating equation.

Rates of growth and firm size. Singh and Whittington (1975) address the existence of the Galtonian regression phenomenon by regressing the rate of growth of individual firms against initial size (equation 5-7). Studying a sample of 2,000 British firms between 1948 and 1960, they find that there is no tendency for regression towards the mean. Indeed, their finding of a positive coefficient on firm size suggests that large firms tend to have a higher growth rate.

The results of the previous section have already shown that firms in Canadian manufacturing industries exhibited a distinct tendency to regress towards the mean – though the strength of the result is weakened when only continuing firms are used in the analysis. The analysis was therefore repeated by regressing the growth rate on initial firm size so that a comparison could be made with the results of others. Only those firms that continued over the decade were examined. This is the strategy that is generally adopted because there is a paucity of data on entrants and exits. The logarithm of the ratio of final-year to initial-year market share [log (Sh_{79}/Sh_{70})] was regressed on initial share (Sh_{70}), a binary variable taking a value of one when a plant's share was greater than the mean for the industry in which it was located (Mnplant), and a set of industry binary variables. The binary variable (Mnplant) allows for a non-linearity in the regression effect. The use of the logarithm of the ratio of market shares allows for fixed industry effects, since

$$\log(Sh_{79}/Sh_{70}) = \log(Q_{79}/Q_{70}) - \log(T_{79}/T_{70}) \tag{5-14}$$

where

$$Sh_{79} = Q_{79}/T_{79}. \tag{5-15}$$

Thus, the results yielded by the regression used here will be equivalent to those yielded by one that uses a more standard formulation with the growth rate of output [$\log(Q_{79}/Q_{70})$] as the regressor, but that allows for inter-industry differentials in growth rates [$\log(T_{79}/T_{70})$] as the mean around which growth rates for individual firms fluctuate within each industry. Whether this captures all the fixed industry effects was examined by including industry binary variables as well. Only about 10 per cent of these coefficients were significant. When fixed industry effects were also included for the binary variable that defined the shift in the intercept that occurred above the mean (Mnplant), these too proved to be generally insignificant. Therefore, fixed effects for the intercepts were excluded from the regressions reported here that use the logarithm of market shares as the dependent variable.[15]

The results are reported in Table 5-8. Two different samples were used. One sample is continuing firms that did not experience a change in ownership. The other sample consists of all firms. When observations from all industries are combined, the growth rate of large firms is negatively related to initial size in both samples. As well, allowing for a discontinuity at the mean caused the share variable to become insignificant. Larger firms have lower growth rates than do smaller firms, but when this effect is included, initial-year market share is no longer significant.

Regression to the mean: plant data. When all firms are single-plant enterprises and mergers are unimportant, then if the law of proportionate effect holds at the plant level, it should also apply at the firm level. Firm growth rates may, however, follow a different pattern from plant growth rates if firms are made up of both large and small plants or if mergers and acquisitions are used to buy market share.

Table 5-8. *Regression coefficients for firm-growth equation*

Regressors[a]	Dependent variable [$\log(Sh_{79}/Sh_{70})$]			
	All firms	Continuing firms	All firms	Continuing firms
Intercept[b]	n.s.	n.s.	n.s.	n.s.
Sh_{70}	−0.94*	−0.89*	−0.37	−0.41
	(0.23)	(0.25)	(0.14)	(0.27)
Mnplant	—	—	−0.13*	0.11*
			(0.02)	(0.02)
F	17.10	12.91	24.52	16.43
prob > F	.0001	.0001	.0001	.0001

Note: Standard error of the estimated parameter is in parentheses.
[a] See text for definition of regressors.
[b] n.s. – not significant.
* Significantly different from zero at the 1 per cent level.

In order to investigate whether there is regression to the mean at the plant level, a regression was performed using data on plants. The logarithm of the ratio of final-year to initial-year market share [$\log (Sh_{79}/Sh_{70})$] was regressed on initial share (Sh_{70}), a binary variable taking a value of one when a plant's share was greater than the mean for the industry in which it was located (Mnplant), the plant's market share when this occurred (TOPSH = Mnplant × Sh_{70}), and a set of industry binary variables. The results are reported in columns 1 and 2 of Table 5-9. Large and small plants are not differentiated in column 1. The coefficient attached to the original market share (Sh_{70}) is negative and significant. When the sample is divided in each industry at the mean, the regression coefficient attached to market share for both small and large firms is insignificant; but the larger plants' intercept (Mnplant) is significantly negative. Within each of the segments, growth is independent of market share; but large plants have significantly lower growth rates. The regression coefficients for plants indicate that the regression-to-the-mean effect for them is slightly greater than for firms.

The regressions were also run with plant market share in 1979 as the dependent variable; the results are reported in columns 3 and 4 of Table 5-9. Industry binary variables were included, since about a quarter were found to be significant and it is no longer as evident that there should be few industry effects. The results reveal the same picture. When no allowance is made for differing effects among large and small firms (column 3), there is regression to the mean. When allowance is made for different effects (column 4), the

Table 5-9. *Regression coefficients for plant-growth equations*

Regressors[a]	Dependent variable			
	$\log(Sh_{79}/Sh_{70})$		Sh_{79}	
	(1)	(2)	(3)	(4)
Intercept	0.0001	0.034*	—[b]	—[b]
	(0.0086)	(0.010)		
Sh_{70}	−1.97*	−1.33	0.85	0.99[c]
	(0.293)	(1.52)	(0.02)	(0.03)
Mnplant	—	−0.13*	—	0.014*
		(0.02)		(0.0002)
TOPSH	—	0.30	—	−0.146*
		(1.54)		(0.029)
Industry dummies	No	No	Yes	Yes
R^2	.0036	.0077	.79	.78
F	45.2	33.	273.3	271.4
prob > F	.0001	.0001	.0001	.0001

Note: Standard error of the estimated parameter is in parentheses.
[a] See text for definition of regressors.
[b] Not relevant since industry dummies were used.
[c] Not significantly different from one at 1 per cent level.
* Significantly different from zero at 1 per cent level.

share of the largest firms (TOPSH) has a significantly lower coefficient than for smaller firms (Sh_{70}).

Inter-industry differences
Turnover occurs among firms of all sizes. Whether it is pervasive across industries is the subject of this section.

Total market-share change in the four largest firms. The experience of the largest group of firms is examined by considering total changes in the four largest firms taken together. Whether market-share change for a fixed number of firms or for those firms that accounted for a particular fraction of sales is used does not particularly affect the picture of change that emerges. Since the four largest firms form the basis for one of the most commonly used concentration statistics, this group is chosen here. Market-share change for each of the four largest firms was calculated; two indices were generated to measure the magnitude of change. One is the ratio of the sum of the absolute value of all share changes divided by the sum of the original share of the four largest firms. Across the manufacturing industries examined, this averaged

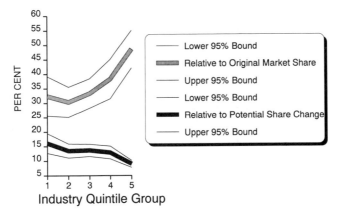

Figure 5-3. Cross-industry differences in the value of the total market-share change between 1970 and 1979 of the top four firms by industry quintile group. Market-share change is the sum of the absolute value of the change in market share of each of the top four firms. Quintile groups are created by inversely ranking four-digit industries on the basis of the share of the leading firm.

36.7 per cent. The other index is the sum of the absolute share change divided by the maximum potential change in share. It averaged 13 per cent across the same set of industries.

To examine cross-industry differences in these measures, industries were ranked on the basis of the market share of the leading firm and divided into quintile groups. Figure 5-3 plots the two instability indices along with confidence intervals for the means in each quintile group. These groups are ranked from left to right in Figure 5-3, in descending order of the importance of the leading firm. The average share of the largest firm varies substantially from 46 per cent in the top quintile group to 8 per cent in the bottom quintile group.

In the top three quintiles, the first index (sum of absolute value of share change as a fraction of original share) takes a value between 30 and 33 per cent. It increases markedly in the fourth quintile group and reaches a level of some 49 per cent in the fifth quintile group where the largest firm is least important.

The second index – the absolute value of share change as a percentage of total share-change potential – takes on about the same value in the first three quintile groups. But then the index declines. The market share of the four largest firms may change more in industries where the leading firm is not as dominant; but the increase in these industries is not as great as the increased potential for change.

In conclusion, the industry-wide averages hide some industries where market-share change is quite different from the mean – but these differences occur primarily in unconcentrated industries. For the three or four industry quintiles where the leading firm is most dominant, the amount of market-share change is quite similar to the average. In the quintile with the least important dominant firm, the amount of market-share change, calculated as a percentage of original market share, is about 50 per cent greater than the change in the quintile where the dominant firm has the highest market share. Examining industry-level data, then, strengthens the conclusion that market-share turnover in the largest firms is important.

Market-share change for the leading firm. It is important to consider not only inter-industry differences in the performance of the four largest firms as a group and differences in the performance of individual members of this group.

This section examines whether the fate of the leading firm depends critically upon its level of dominance and whether the leading firm experiences less change in industries where its share is very large.

In order to investigate differences across industries in the success of the largest firm, manufacturing industries were divided, as before, into quintile groups on the basis of the market shares of the largest firm. The average *rate* of share change for the leading firm was calculated for each quintile group. This is the sum of the market-share change (absolute values are not taken here) divided by the initial market share. On average, share change is negative for large firms. Figure 5-4 plots the average market share of the leading firm in each industry quintile group against the mean value of the rate of share decline of the largest firm. Although the average share of the largest firm varies substantially – from 46 to 8 per cent – the calculated rate of share decline for the leading firm for the first four quintile groups falls within a narrow band from 17.1 to 24.6 per cent. It is not until the fifth quintile group that the rate of share decline for the largest firm is substantially higher at 32 per cent. These data indicate that the performance of the largest firm derived from the cross-industry average rate of share loss can be found in a wide range of industries.

The relative constancy of share change for the largest firm in all industries was confirmed by regressing the rate of market-share change for the largest firm on the market share of the leading firm. The estimated coefficient was not significantly different from zero. Having a large market share does not protect a leading firm from declining at the same rate as do leading firms with smaller market shares.

The magnitude of change in market share can be measured either in terms of an average or in terms of a dispersion. Measuring the average rate at which

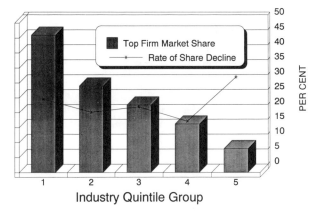

Figure 5-4. Leading-firm market share (1970) and share change (1970–79) across industries by industry quintile group. Quintile groups are created by ranking industries inversely by the market share of the largest firm. The rate of the share decline is the sum of share loss and gain divided by initial market share.

market share is lost cannot capture the extent to which there is considerable variability of experience within a particular group. To do so, market-share change for the leading firm was divided into components that separately capture market-share losses as opposed to market-share gains. Figure 5-5 plots the mean rates of share loss and share gain for the leading firm using the same industry quintiles employed in Figure 5-4. Once again, the quintile groups are ranked from left to right in descending order of the leading firm's market share.

Gains are not expected to be the same everywhere if there are constraints that prevent leading firms from becoming even larger. Where the market share of the largest firm is already high, the ability to increase its share further is constrained. The evidence confirms this. The rate of share gain has a tendency to increase as the share of the leading firm declines. The rate of share loss also increases, but not as dramatically over the first four quintile groups. In the quintile group where the leading firm is the least important, share loss of the leading firm is dramatically higher. Thus, the average expected change in the market share of the largest firm is similar across most industries, but the variance around the mean is smaller where the leading firm is very dominant, primarily because rates of share gain are less. It is in this more limited sense that increasing dominance leads to greater stability.

In industrial economics, the stability of the leading firm has sometimes been taken to imply that large firms partially exploit their power by reducing the volatility of their sales patterns. The results suggest that the greater stability

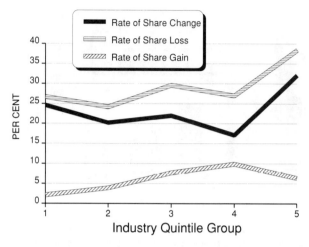

Figure 5-5. Rates of share gain and loss between 1970 and 1979 for the top firm across industry quintiles ranked by share of the top firm. Quintile groups are created by ranking industries inversely by the importance of the leading firm. Average share change is the sum of share gain and share loss.

observed may partly be a statistical phenomenon having to do with truncated growth possibilities, rather than lower rates of share loss. The largest firms enjoy greater stability either partially or entirely as a result of the type of stochastic process they face, rather than as a result of conscious decision-making.

Differences in the behaviour of the four largest firms. The cross-industry variation in the volatility of the largest firm raises two questions. Do similar patterns exist in the other three largest firms? Does the performance of the other large firms depend upon the level of dominance of the leading firm?

To answer these questions, the rate of share loss – the sum of all share losses divided by initial market share – was calculated for each industry for each of the four largest firms. The average rate of share loss was then calculated for all industries divided into quintile groups based on the market share of the first, second, third, and fourth firm. These averages are plotted in Figure 5-6. The tendency for rates of share loss to increase for industries as the share of the firm declines is evident. When the rates of decline at the industry level for all four firms are regressed on average firm share, the regression coefficient is significantly negative. This is not the case for either the rates of net share change or the rates of share gain.

When industries are ranked successively according to the share of the first,

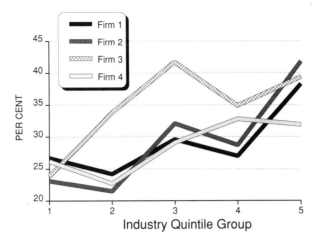

Figure 5-6. Average rate of share loss between 1970 and 1979 for each of the top four firms, by industry quintile. The rate of share loss is the amount of share loss divided by initial market share. Quintiles are obtained by ranking industries inversely by market share of the firm that is being used to calculate share loss.

second, third, and fourth firm, respectively, as was done in Figure 5-5, the quintile groups cannot be directly compared. Industries where the fourth largest firm's share is greater than in other industries may not be the same industries where the leading firm's share is also larger than in other industries. In order to compare the performance of the largest firms for the same industries, industries were placed in quintile groups on the basis of the share of the leading firm. The average rates of loss and gain for each of the four largest firms were calculated separately and are graphed in Figures 5-7 and 5-8, respectively. Each line in these graphs connects the four largest firms within an industry quintile group. The slope of the line allows us to distinguish between the performance of different ranks within an industry quintile group. If the slope is positive, then smaller firms have a higher rate of loss or gain. The differences between the lines allow us to distinguish between the performance of these groups where the industry quintiles are distinguished by the importance of the leading firm. The higher the line, the greater is the rate of share loss or gain for the largest firms in the particular industry group being considered.

Figure 5-7, which details rates of share loss, indicates that it is not generally the case that the leading firm is less likely to lose market share than are the other leading firms. In the three industry groups where the leading firm is most dominant, there is little difference between the positions of the

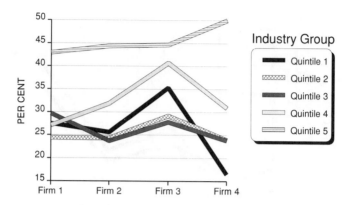

Figure 5-7. Average share loss between 1970 and 1979 for each of the top four firms, by industry quintile. The rate of share loss is the amount of share loss divided by initial market share. Quintiles are obtained by ranking industries inversely by the market share of the firm that is being used to calculate share loss.

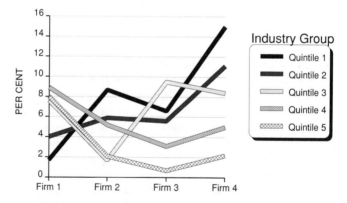

Figure 5-8. Average share gain between 1970 and 1979 for each of the top four firms, by industry quintile. The rate of share loss is the amount of share loss divided by initial market share. Quintiles are obtained by ranking industries inversely by the market share of the firm that is being used to calculate share loss.

leading and the second firm. While the third firm loses a greater percentage of initial share, the fourth firm does not. There is one notable exception. Share loss for all firms is considerably greater in the group with the smallest leading firms. Here, also, there is evidence of a significant difference between the behaviour of industries in the group that is least concentrated and that of all other industries.

There are substantial differences among the patterns of share-gain changes in industry quintile groups (Figure 5-8). In the groups with the largest leading firms, the rate of share gain increases monotonically as the rank of the firm decreases. In the two groups with the smallest leading firms, the rate of share gain is less for the lower-ranked firms. The pattern that emerges is one where the third- and fourth-ranked firms are likely to grow more in industries where the largest firm is dominant. In the middle groups, there is no discernible pattern of growth and decline. In the two industry groups where the largest firm is least dominant in the first period, the two largest firms have greater growth. Because of the lack of pattern in share loss, this suggests that in industries where the two largest firms dominate, their position is declining, and in industries where the two leading firms are relatively small, their relative market share is increasing. Thus, industries, like firms, go through life cycles in which the dominance of the leading firms changes over time.

Differences between large and small firms. When industries are grouped on the basis of concentration, several aggregate measures of change – the instability index for the four largest firms taken together, the average rate of share loss of the largest firm – are often quite similar across most industries, with the exception of a small number of industries where concentration is low. Other measures have shown more variation across industries. Thus, the dissimilarity index shows much more change in industries where concentration is low for the second-, third-, and fourth-ranked firms, because they experience more growth than the largest firms. This investigation can be extended by asking whether the amount of change in large and small firms and the difference between them varies across concentration classes.

All industries were assigned to quintile groups on the basis of the four-firm concentration ratio, and the total amount of market-share change was calculated for large and small firms. The absolute value of all share change was calculated for incumbents, for greenfield entrants, and for closedown exits. The results are reported in Table 5-10, in Figure 5-9 for incumbents, and in Figure 5-10 for entrants and exits.

Incumbent market-share change for large firms is inversely related to concentration – though much of the variation occurs as a result of less change in the industry group with the highest levels of concentration and more change in the group with the lowest levels of concentration. In contrast, incumbent market-share change in smaller firms is not related to concentration. As a result of these two patterns, the difference between incumbent change in large and small firms decreases markedly as concentration decreases (Figure 5-9). This should not be interpreted to mean that concentration affects large firms in general differently than smaller firms, unless the effect of entry and exit acts in a comparable fashion.

Table 5-10. *Market-share turnover in large and small firms across concentration classes, by component (sum of absolute value share change) (per cent of shipments)*

	Concentration class[a]				
Category	1	2	3	4	5
Continuing firms[b]					
Large	9.5	12.7	14.4	13.7	16.3
Small	18.4	20.8	17.4	20.3	17.6
Exiting firms[b]					
Large	5.6	2.2	7.0	8.4	11.5
Small	9.4	11.6	16.5	15.0	19.8
Entering firms[b]					
Large	5.1	3.5	4.2	4.7	9.8
Small	13.6	10.0	15.4	15.1	20.1
All change					
Large	20.2	18.4	25.6	26.8	37.6
Small	41.6	42.4	49.3	50.4	57.5
Difference	21.4	24.0	23.7	23.6	19.9
Dissimilarity index[c]	30.9	30.4	37.5	38.6	47.6

Note: The data reported here were corrected for the fact that the calculated changes covered slightly less than 50 per cent of market share for both large and small firms because of the method used to divide the sample into large and small firms. All plants acquired by entering firms or divested by exiting firms were considered as part of ongoing firms for the purpose of calculating change in continuing firms.
[a] 1 is the highest concentration class, 5 the lowest.
[b] The definition of large and small firms can be found in Table 5-3. Continuing and exiting firm sizes are based on ranking firms on basis of 1970 size; entering firm sizes are based on 1979 size.
[c] Dissimilarity index is half the sum of the absolute value of all market-share changes.

A similar pattern is exhibited for large- and small-firm entries and exits across concentration classes (Figure 5-10). Exit increases as concentration declines. Entry increases generally across industry groups as concentration declines. As a result, when total change from incumbents, entrants, and exits is calculated, there is an inverse relationship between change and concentration for both large and small firms. Nevertheless, the amount of change in the most concentrated class is not insignificant. The dissimilarity index implicit in these numbers is about 30 per cent in the two most concentrated classes.

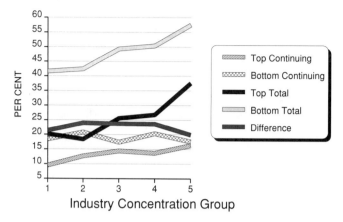

Figure 5-9. The relationship between large- and small-firm market-share change and concentration. Groups are ranked from left to right in order of decreasing concentration.

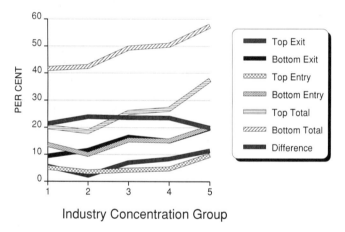

Figure 5-10. The relationship between large- and small-firm entry and exit and concentration, 1970–79. Industry groups are ranked from left to right from highest to lowest concentration.

The difference between the total market-share change in the largest and the smallest firms does not vary significantly across concentration classes, with the exception of the least concentrated class, where it is smallest. This is contrary to the results produced by incumbent firms alone and shows the necessity of examining incumbents, entrants, and exits simultaneously. In the case of both large and small firms, the amount of change from the incumbent population is inversely related to that from exit and entry. As firms exit, there are fewer incumbents to lose or gain market share. When the proper comparison is made, concentration is found not to protect the large firms in concentrated industries any more than it does small firms. The effect of concentration is felt more or less equally in large and small firms, as defined here, in all industries.

The apparent relationship between concentration and both large- and small-firm turnover does not mean that large- and small-firm change are closely related. Indeed, just the opposite is true. The correlation of incumbent market-share change between large and small firms in an industry is not significant. Market-share changes that arise from entry and exit in large and small firms are only weakly related. The correlation between entry intensities in large and small firms is only .39; for exit intensities, it is .37. Perhaps more importantly, the entry and exit intensities of smaller firms are not strongly correlated with incumbent change in larger continuing firms. Exit intensity in smaller firms has a correlation of only .26 with change in larger continuing firms; entry intensity in smaller firms has a correlation of only .15 with change in smaller continuing firms. A relationship would be expected if exit among the smaller firms resulted in some share gain among the larger firms. That the relationship is not very strong indicates that there is a considerable dichotomy between the forces that affect large and small firms and the forces that offset each of the entering, exiting, and continuing-firm sectors. While a relationship was found between overall change and concentration in large- and small-firm size groupings, the most important message to be drawn from this data is that the forces that affect different industries and firms of different sizes within the manufacturing sector are heterogeneous.

Differences across firm size-classes. That there are differences across different industries in the degree of market-share change between large and small firms has been established. Differences across industries can also be investigated by considering whether the rapidity by which firms change size-class varies by size-class. In order to do this, the mean duration of firm stay in each of five quintile groups was calculated for each industry. The quintiles were based on the market share of firms in each industry.[16] Then the industries were grouped into one of four concentration categories:[17] (1) atomistic, (2) low-grade oligopolistic, (3) moderately concentrated, and (4) highly concentrated. In order to examine how performance differs across quintiles, the mean duration of stay in a firm-size quintile group was calculated for each industry concentration group. Figure 5-11 plots the mean stay for each quintile group by industry group. The difference within a quintile group shows the impact of concentration on the average time a firm would expect to remain in the quintile group.

The difference between each industry concentration group within a quintile

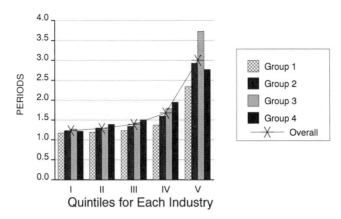

Figure 5-11. Average length of stay by quintile for industry
concentration groups, by periods. A period is about nine years.

group is relatively minor for the first three size groups. Concentration does
not greatly affect the extent to which small firms stay small. The differences
begin to widen in the fourth quintile group and become quite large in the fifth
– though the most concentrated class is not the one with the longest mean
duration. Once again, this confirms that concentration has a greater effect on
inter-industry differentials in larger firms than on those in smaller firms.

Conclusion

Understanding the dynamics of the market system requires that the
importance of change from entry and exit, continuing-firm turnover, and
mergers be outlined. Previous chapters present general information on the
magnitude of each of these categories. Greenfield entry and closedown exit
are shown in Chapter 2 to be relatively unimportant when measured on a
yearly basis, but to accumulate to significant levels after a decade. Entrants
do not swarm into and out of an industry. They settle and acquire a significant
portion of market share. Acquisition entry is shown in Chapter 3 to be as
important a force in changing the composition of an industry as greenfield
entry. Growth and decline in continuing firms are shown in Chapter 4 to shift
as much market share as do entry and exit.

As impressive as the magnitude of this change might be, establishing
magnitude is not sufficient. It does not show that all firms, or that large firms
in particular, experience much change. By focusing on intra-industry detail,
this chapter deals with this issue.

It shows that turnover is not restricted to the smaller firms in an industry.
The picture presented is rather one of growth that varies over the firm's life
cycle. There is turnover among large firms and among small firms. While

large firms are more stable than small ones, the difference is not enormous. More importantly, the major difference is that large firms decline and small firms grow, on average. Regression to the mean is taking place. The industrial system is being renewed, not only by the constant arrival of entrants in the small end of the size distribution, but also by the growth of small firms to supplant the older large firms.

The chapter also shows that in the midst of the ocean of change, there are islands of stability. Transitions matrices indicate that movement across the size distribution is not instantaneous. Most moves are to adjacent positions, and the average duration spent in a given size rank can be quite long. Small firms cannot expect to move out of their quintile for about a decade. The largest firms have a mean stay in their position of three decades. Growth and decline may be inevitable; it does not occur with blinding speed. It is this fact that makes appreciating the dynamics of the competitive system so difficult. When the pattern is measured over short periods, it is difficult to appreciate its magnitude. And when longer periods are examined, the amount of change is difficult to measure because the identity of so many of the participants has changed. The result is that many studies have been forced to rely on a very unrepresentative sample that consists of the entities that can be easily followed over a long period.

Industries are complicated entities. They are characterized by fluidity and stability. A large amount of churning occurs on the margin. There is an extremely large number of firms that enter the fray only to retreat as exits. Once established, small firms move up and down within their segment, trading share among one another. Many in turn exit; some manage to grow. At the top of the distribution are large firms that maintain their ranks for substantial periods and that give the false impression that industries are stable. But these firms inevitably give way to smaller firms that emerge from the pack. When a long enough period is examined, Marshall's analogy of the forest becomes relevant. It is apparent that old growth is thinned out by the emergence of new stock. As part of that process, the mature firms are continuously being pruned through acquisition and divestiture.

The chapter also focuses on cross-industry differences in the intra-industry patterns of change and their relationship to measures of industry concentration. Generally, it was only the most atomistic industries, accounting for only one-fifth of the population, that experienced distinct differences. In these industries, large firms lost significant market share and there was less difference between turnover in large and small firms. Market structure is related to patterns of turnover in the continuing sector but not very strongly. Since analysts in the field of industrial economics have placed much emphasis on the relationship between market structure and the intensity of competition, this subject is investigated in depth in Chapters 7 and 8.

6

Plant turnover in Canada and the United States

This book focuses on the nature of the competitive process. Canada was chosen to illustrate how this process functions because a unique database permits analyses that are not possible for most other countries. The Canadian experience should not, however, be regarded as atypical. To illustrate this point, this chapter focuses on the extent to which competition in the United States is similar to that in Canada. It compares the dynamics of growth and decline in the two countries' manufacturing sectors by measuring the rate of job growth among entrants and growing plants, and the rate of job destruction among exits and declining plants.

In the past, industrial economists have used international comparisons to examine the connection between market size and firm or plant size.[1] Other studies have examined the extent to which international differences in concentration are rooted in production technology or are related to differences in market size.

The difference in the sizes of Canadian and U.S. markets, along with other factors such as tariff protection, have long been cited as reasons for differences in the intensity of competition. Considerable Canadian research, therefore, has focused on the connection between smaller markets, openness to trade, and the effects of oligopolistic coordination operating behind tariff barriers (Hazledine, 1990). These studies have focused on the determinants of price differences (Hazledine, 1980), differences in scale and diversity (Baldwin and Gorecki, 1987a), and differences in productivity (Caves et al., 1980; Baldwin and Gorecki, 1986a). The current comparison of the differences in job creation and destruction that are captured by turnover measures provides a dimension that has not previously been examined. It provides a more direct measure of the degree to which the internal dynamics within industries differs between Canada and the United States.

Research on job growth and job loss associated with firm and plant turnover that uses recently developed data has provided new stylized facts for both industrial and labour economics. International comparisons provide the opportunity to replicate these findings in quite different environments (Schmalensee, 1988) and to ask how different economic structures, legal systems, cultures, languages, histories, and customs affect plant-level job turnover.

Many economic factors are likely to affect heterogeneity in plant-level employment dynamics. Technological differences in plants and industries contribute to plant heterogeneity. The technology-related factor should produce similarities in plant dynamics in the United States and Canada, since both countries draw from the same technological sources. By way of contrast, Canada and the United States differ in many other respects. For example, the market size and structure of the two countries are not the same. Employment and output are more concentrated in Canada.[2] Canadian plants are smaller than U.S. plants. Exposure to international markets differs, since import penetration of markets and export shares of industry output are higher in Canada than in the United States. Finally, unionization rates, government taxation, and labour-market policies also differ between the two countries.

The higher concentration of output, smaller market size, and higher unionization rates in Canada all suggest that there should be less volatility and lower plant-level job turnover in Canada than in the United States. The greater trade exposure and smaller plants in Canada suggest there should be greater volatility. Alternatively, if technological factors are the primary source of volatility in both countries, then the commonality of the technological choices and shocks facing plants should lead to similar patterns of plant-level job turnover.

A comparison between Canada and the United States provides an opportunity for evaluating the role of these factors. The focus is on plant-level job turnover that is generated through the creation of jobs in newly opened and expanding plants and the destruction of jobs in closing and contracting plants. The primary goal of this chapter is to determine the similarities and differences in gross job turnover (gross job creation, gross job destruction, and their sum) in Canada and the United States. The analysis has four parts.

First, patterns of gross turnover are compared by investigating annual rates of job creation and destruction in the Canadian and U.S. manufacturing sectors. Analysing annual rates permits characterization of short-run plant dynamics, including cyclical behaviour. Annual job-destruction rates are closely linked to permanent worker separations (Baldwin and Gorecki, 1990b) and largely represent permanent job losses (Davis and Haltiwanger, 1992).[3]

Second, short-run (annual) and long-run (five-year) job flows are compared, so as to evaluate the extent to which similarities in the short run are carried through to the long run. Short-run dynamics are influenced both by underlying structural shifts and the macro-environment. Long-run rates of job turnover are less influenced by the macro-economy and, therefore, better reveal long-term trends.

Third, industry job-turnover measures are related to industry characteristics describing size distribution, trade exposure, productivity growth, and unionization. This allows us to examine the factors related to Canada–U.S. differences in plant-level job turnover.

Fourth, the amount of plant job turnover is divided into two groups – job shifts between industries and those within industries. This provides evidence on the extent to which inter- or intra-industry change occurs most frequently in both countries and the extent to which structural change occurs mainly because of shifts in the relative importance of industries or because of shifts in the relative importance of firms within industries.

Data considerations

Many international comparisons of job turnover have suffered from a lack of comparability.[4] This is mainly because of differences in the way statistical agencies collect and organize data on firms and their plants. The collection methods used by national statistical agencies have been primarily designed to produce an accurate reflection of a population of firms at a given point in time. They were not devised to develop the type of longitudinal panels of firms and their plants that are required to measure job turnover.

Measuring job turnover involves tracking individual plants from year to year. This is done in two basic steps. First, longitudinal identifiers are assigned to business entities. Second, the business population is divided, on the basis of these identifiers, into those plants that continue, those that die, and those that are born.

Since the process of transforming sequential sets of cross-sections into longitudinal panels differs from country to country, international comparisons must be made cautiously.[5] Countries often differ in the circumstances used to change a business identifier and, thus, in the definition of a birth and death. The most important difference that is relevant here involves the extent to which business-entity identifiers change when mergers or control changes occur and whether these changes result in these events being classified as births. If so, births can include both greenfield births and births due to mergers.

This chapter uses data collected by the official statistical agencies of Canada and the United States. Both countries conduct an establishment-based census of the manufacturing sector and, therefore, produce a comprehensive picture of the firm population. The principal statistical agencies in Canada and the United States collect data on similar variables and use similar definitions of births and deaths to develop longitudinal data; that is, they link establishments and firms and distinguish between ownership transfers and the birth and death of establishments. The latter distinction is critical because of the tendency that some administrative databases have to change the identifiers used to track firms over time when mergers occur and to register a death and a birth. Without this distinction, it is impossible to differentiate greenfield entry – entry due to new-plant construction – from entry due to merger.

In order to assure comparability between the Canadian and U.S. turnover rates, the samples and definitions used for the estimates were carefully harmonized. For the Canadian data, this meant using a larger sample than was used in previous chapters;[6] for the U.S. data, it meant using a more restrictive definition of births and deaths than Dunne, Roberts, and Samuelson (1988, 1989) used.[7] As a result, the turnover estimates contained in this chapter for Canada do not precisely match the calculations in previous chapters, nor do those for the United States correspond exactly to the estimates reported by Davis and Haltiwanger (1992).[8]

The Canadian data cover the period 1970–87 and come from an annual census of the manufacturing sector. The U.S. data come from contiguous five-year panels with annual data on many manufacturing establishments, plus census-year data for all manufacturing establishments. Census years for the United States were 1972, 1977, and 1982.

Measurement of job creation, destruction, and reallocation

Either input or output share can be used to measure intra-industry dynamics. Previous studies show that market share and input share yield similar pictures of the amount of change.[9] Change is measured here using employment.[10]

Growth and decline are measured in terms of jobs gained and jobs lost, defined as the difference in establishment employment between two years. Establishments are divided into those where employment is growing and those where employment is declining. The resulting summary measures capture the extent of job turnover. Some job creation and destruction will reflect growth and decline in market share, and some will reflect differences in the extent to which plants improve productivity.

Total job-creation measures for Canada and the United States are calculated by summing employment gains at expanding and new establishments within a sector between years $t - 1$ and t; total job destruction is calculated by summing employment losses at shrinking and dying establishments within a sector between years $t - 1$ and t. Rates of growth between years $t - 1$ and t (POS_t) and rates of decline (NEG_t) are calculated by dividing total job creation and destruction by sector size (X_t). Sector size is calculated as the average of employment between years $t - 1$ and t in the case of the year-to-year calculations and for the year $t - 1$ in the case of the five-year calculations. The difference between POS_t and NEG_t is net employment growth (NET_t).

The sum of POS_t and NEG_t is used to measure the total job-turnover rate

(SUM$_t$) of a sector between years $t - 1$ and t. It has been interpreted to represent an upper bound on the number of workers who change jobs in response to establishment-level employment changes (OECD, 1987; Davis and Haltiwanger, 1990). Part of the change measured by SUM$_t$ is occasioned by the net growth or decline in jobs. The measure EXCESS$_t$, defined as SUM$_t$ minus the absolute value of NET$_t$, is the amount of job reallocation in excess of that required to facilitate net employment changes. It measures that component of growth and decline related to "pure" turnover within an industry. This component, of course, need not be constant across the business cycle. If higher net growth, whether it be positive or negative, leads to less inter-firm competition, EXCESS$_t$ and the absolute value of NET$_t$ will be negatively related. On the other hand, if higher net growth is associated with greater internal restructuring, the correlation will be positive.

Annual rates of job turnover

Overall measures for the manufacturing sector

Table 6-1 presents annual rates of job creation (POS), job destruction (NEG), net employment growth (NET), and the total turnover rate (SUM) for Canada and the United States. The Canadian data are based on differences in annual employment levels between 1972 and 1986. The data for the United States are based on changes in establishment-level employment from March to March, in the same years.

Baldwin and Gorecki (1990b) and Davis and Haltiwanger (1990) stress that in both countries job creation and destruction occur simultaneously. This is clearly demonstrated in the data presented in Table 6-1. In Canada, when net change is negative in 1975, 1977, 1982, and 1983, there is also substantial positive job creation – more than 7 per cent in each of these years. The same pattern is evident in the United States, where there is substantial job creation even when net rates of change are negative.

The two countries differ in terms of average annual net job creation. The Canadian manufacturing sector experiences small but positive growth over the period being studied; manufacturing in the United States declines at a rate of 1 per cent annually. The higher average net growth rate in Canada occurs partially because of higher job growth (POS averages 10.6 per cent in Canada and 9.2 per cent in the United States) and partially because of lower job loss (NEG averages 10.0 per cent in Canada and 10.4 per cent in the United States). The average annual gross change is higher in Canada than the United States. The total turnover rate (SUM) averages 20.6 per cent for Canada and 19.6 per cent for the United States. The range of this variable is similar, varying from a low of 17 per cent to a high of 23 per cent. The larger net job-change rate in the United States means that the average excess-job-

Table 6-1. *Annual net and gross job-change rates in the manufacturing sector, Canada and the United States, 1972–86 (per cent)*[a]

	Canada				United States			
Period	Job gain (POS)	Job loss (NEG)	Net change (NET)	Total turnover (SUM)	Job gain (POS)	Job loss (NEG)	Net change (NET)	Total turnover (SUM)
1972–73	11.1	6.6	4.5	17.6	11.9	6.1	5.7	18.0
1973–74	9.7	7.7	2.0	17.4	9.0	9.3	–0.3	18.3
1974–75	9.4	11.9	–2.5	21.2	6.2	16.5	–10.3	22.6
1975–76	9.4	9.3	0.1	18.7	11.2	9.4	1.8	20.6
1976–77	7.8	10.1	–2.2	17.9	11.0	8.6	2.3	19.6
1977–78	13.3	8.3	5.0	21.6	10.9	7.3	3.6	18.2
1978–79	12.1	8.5	3.6	20.6	10.3	7.0	3.3	17.4
1979–80	9.8	10.1	–0.3	19.9	8.0	9.1	–1.1	17.1
1980–81	9.7	9.6	0.2	19.4	6.3	11.4	–5.0	17.7
1981–82	7.6	15.4	–7.8	23.0	6.8	14.5	–7.7	21.3
1982–83	10.7	12.9	–2.2	23.7	8.4	15.6	–7.2	23.9
1983–84	12.8	9.3	3.0	21.7	13.3	7.6	5.7	20.9
1984–85	12.0	9.4	2.6	21.3	7.9	11.1	–3.2	19.0
1985–86	12.9	10.5	2.4	23.3	10.4	12.1	–4.2	20.1
Mean[b]	10.6	10.0	0.6	20.6	9.2	10.4	–1.2	19.6
	(1.8)	(2.2)	(3.5)	(2.1)	(2.2)	(3.3)	(5.2)	(2.1)
r (POS, NEG)[c]		= –.47 [.09]				= –.78 [.001]		
r (NET, SUM)		= –.23 [.42]				= –.54 [.046]		
r (EXCESS, ABNET)		= –.54 [.04]				= –.66 [.010]		

[a] The unit of measurement is the individual establishment.
[b] Standard deviation of the mean is in parentheses.
[c] Probability value of the correlation is in brackets.

reallocation rate (EXCESS) is also higher in Canada than in the United States – 20 per cent versus 18.4 percent. As a whole, the Canadian manufacturing sector is slightly more volatile than the U.S. sector.

There are some notable differences in the pattern of movements of the net and gross job-flow rates in Canada and the United States. The rate of job creation is negatively correlated with the rate of job destruction in both countries, but the relationship is more pronounced in the United States. The correlation is –.78 for the United States and –.47 for Canada. During a downturn, fewer jobs are created and more jobs are destroyed. The overall rate of turnover (EXCESS) is negatively related to the absolute value of net job creation (ABNET) in both countries, though once again the correlation is lower (–.54) for Canada than the United States (–.66). When net job change

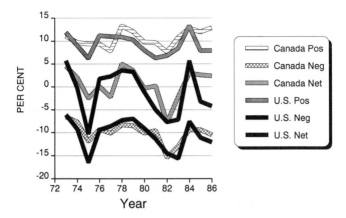

Figure 6-1. Job-turnover rates for Canada and the United States: job gain, job loss, and net change (annual, 1972–86).

is particularly large, whether it be positive or negative, excess job reallocation is less.

Annual net job-change rates (NET), job-gain rates (POS), and job-loss rates (NEG) are plotted in Figure 6-1. Net change in the two countries follows a very similar pattern (the correlation is .68). Job loss in the two countries is also highly correlated (.83). However, job gain is only correlated at .35. This confirms the finding of previous studies that job-loss rates are more closely correlated across regions in both Canada and the United States than are job-gain rates.[11]

Excess-turnover rates for the two countries are graphed in Figure 6-2. Because of the differences in the job-growth rates, the correlation between excess turnover in Canada and the United States is only .23. It is noteworthy that the Canadian excess job-turnover (EXCESS) series has a pronounced upward trend, while that of the United States exhibits no trend. In Canada, the rate of total job turnover (SUM) averages 18 per cent between 1970 and 1974 and 22 per cent between 1981 and 1985; excess job reallocation (EXCESS) increases from 15 to 20 per cent. Fitting a simple linear time trend to the total turnover series (EXCESS) for both countries yields a trend coefficient (prob value) of 0.36 (.01) for Canada and 0.02 (.86) for the United States.

Entry and exit

Job creation and job destruction can be broken down into the portion caused by growth and decline in continuing plants and the portion caused by entrants and exits. That portion caused by entry and exit is particularly

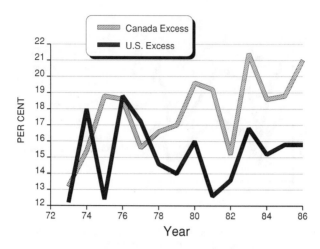

Figure 6-2. A comparison of total turnover rates for Canada and the United States (annual, 1972–86).

interesting for several reasons. First, exit results in the permanent loss of jobs and affects all workers in a plant, whereas job destruction in the continuing sector affects only part of a plant's work-force and the employment loss may be only temporary if the plant reverses its decline. Second, entry and exit are more closely related to traditional structural statistics – such as concentration – that proxy structural impediments to competition than to other measures of intra-industry mobility that are constructed from the amount of job creation and destruction occurring in continuing firms (see Chapter 7). Thus, if differences between concentration in Canada and the United States affect the dynamics of competition, this should be manifested more in different entry and exit rates than in different total turnover measures (SUM or EXCESS).

Figure 6-3 presents the average annual job-turnover rates due to entry and exit for the manufacturing sector as a whole.[12] On average, Canadian entry rates are just as high as those of the United States, and exit rates are also about the same.

The relative dynamics can also be gauged by the proportions of total job change accounted for by entry and exit. If the Canadian economy suffers from reduced competition associated with greater concentration, a greater proportion of Canadian growth might be expected to come from incumbents than from entrants. This is not the case. The mean ratio of job creation in births to that in growing continuing plants over the period 1970–85 is 27 per cent in Canada and 21 per cent in the United States. On this basis, too, births are just as important in Canada as in the United States.

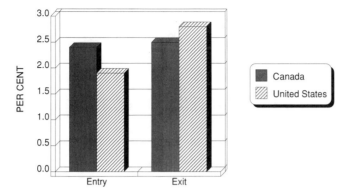

Figure 6-3. Average annual plant entry and exit rates for Canada and the United States (select years, 1972–86).

Variation in average annual rates at the two-digit industry level

Aggregate job-turnover rates may hide substantial differences between Canada and the United States at the industry level. In order to investigate differences in industry performance, annual job-turnover rates were calculated for two-digit industries. Table 6-2 presents the average annual rates for total job loss (NEG), net job change (NET), and excess job reallocation (EXCESS) for two-digit manufacturing industries in Canada and the United States. In both countries, there is pervasive growth and decline in all sectors. Moreover, the cross-industry patterns are closely related. The cross-country correlations of POS, NEG, NET, and EXCESS are .89, .69, .81, and .86, respectively.

The close relationship in the cross-industry pattern of excess job-reallocation rates of the two countries at the two-digit industry level is demonstrated in Figure 6-4. Industries are ranked from left to right in descending order by concentration in the Canadian industry. Turnover in both countries increases in industries with lower levels of concentration, but there is no apparent relationship between the difference in job-turnover rates and Canadian concentration levels.[13]

Correlations of the time series of POS and NEG at the two-digit industry level confirm the story told by the aggregate figures. The mean value for the United States is −.69 but only −.31 for Canada. Seventeen of the correlations are significantly different from zero (5% level) for the United States; only seven are for Canada.

The reason for this difference between Canada and the United States lies in the relative volatility of the job-loss rates. The means of the variances of job gain for two-digit industries are about the same in the two countries – 8.7

Table 6-2. *Annual net and gross job-change rates by two-digit manufacturing industry, Canada and the United States, 1972–86 (per cent)*

Industry	Canada				United States			
	Job gain (GAIN)	Job loss (NEG)	Net change (NET)	Total turnover (EXCESS)	Job gain (GAIN)	Job loss (NEG)	Net change (NET)	Total turnover (EXCESS)
Food	9.2	9.0	0.2	18.0	8.5	9.8	-1.3	17.0
Tobacco	4.7	6.8	-2.1	9.4	5.8	7.9	-2.1	11.6
Textiles	8.8	10.0	-1.3	17.6	6.5	9.6	-3.1	13.0
Knitting mills	10.1	11.2	-1.1	20.2	9.2	12.0	-2.8	18.4
Apparel	13.3	13.8	-0.5	26.6	10.8	14.8	-4.0	21.6
Lumber	13.3	12.5	0.8	25.0	12.6	14.7	-2.1	25.2
Furniture	13.9	12.6	1.3	25.2	10.3	11.2	-0.9	20.6
Paper	5.4	5.3	0.1	10.6	6.3	7.0	-0.7	12.6
Printing	11.6	9.0	2.6	18.0	8.9	8.2	0.7	16.4
Chemicals	9.3	7.8	1.5	15.6	6.6	7.5	-0.9	13.2
Petroleum	7.0	7.1	-0.1	14.0	6.3	8.4	-2.1	12.6
Rubber	11.5	8.5	3.0	17.0	10.8	10.5	0.3	21.0
Leather	10.4	11.7	-1.3	20.8	8.7	14.3	-5.5	17.4
Stone, clay, glass	10.5	10.4	0.1	20.8	9.2	11.3	-2.1	18.4
Primary metals	6.4	7.0	-0.6	12.8	6.5	10.3	-3.8	13.0
Fabricated metals	13.1	11.5	1.6	23.0	9.6	11.1	-1.5	19.2
Non-electrical machinery	13.7	12.5	1.2	25.0	10.0	10.9	-0.9	20.0
Electrical machinery	11.2	11.4	-0.2	22.4	10.0	9.8	0.2	19.6
Transportation	10.8	9.4	0.6	18.8	9.5	9.5	0.0	19.0
Miscellaneous	13.4	12.4	1.0	24.8	9.9	10.7	-0.8	19.8

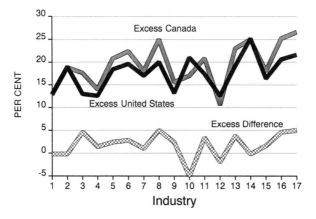

Figure 6-4. Average annual rates of gross turnover by two-digit industry for Canada and the United States (1972–86).

for Canada and 7.3 for the United States. The variance of the job-loss rates is 50 per cent higher in the United States (15.9) than in Canada (10.6). Therefore, job-loss rates are more volatile in the United States than are job-gain rates. The two have about the same volatility in Canada.

In order to estimate the extent to which there are synchronous movements in job gain or job loss across industries within each country, the time series of POS and NEG are correlated across all two-digit industries within Canada and then within the United States. The resulting mean correlation shows the extent to which job growth and job decline across different industries move in step with one another over the business cycle. In Canada, the mean correlation for POS is .34 and for NEG .49; in the United States, it is .56 and .64, respectively.

In both countries, NEG has a higher mean correlation than does POS. Job-loss rates are more closely synchronized than are job-gain rates. The number of important factors that affects change, outside cyclical ones, is greater for job gain than for job loss. For both POS and NEG, the average Canadian correlations are lower than those for the United States. The business cycle then has a greater effect in the United States in causing more synchronous change across sectors both in terms of job gain and job loss.

Gross turnover is also found to be negatively related to the absolute size of net job change (ABNET) using two-digit industry-level data in both countries. The mean correlation of EXCESS and ABNET is −.63 for the United States, −.50 for Canada. Sixteen of the 20 U.S. industry correlations are negative and significantly different from zero (5% level) compared with 12 of the Canadian two-digit correlations.

In order to further investigate differences in the relationship between Canada and the United States, regression analysis is used to test whether the relationship between EXCESS and ABNET differs for Canada and the United States and for positive and negative values of NET. EXCESS is regressed on the absolute value of NET (ABNET), the value of ABNET when NET is positive (PABNET), dummies for 20 two-digit industries, a U.S. dummy, an interaction term between the U.S. variable and ABNET (USABNET), and an interaction term between the U.S. variable and PABNET (USPABNET). The results are reported in equation 6-1.

$$\text{EXCESS} = 18.33 - 0.593 \text{ ABNET} - 0.039 \text{ PABNET}$$

$$s = \quad 0.62 \quad 0.066 \quad\quad\quad 0.081$$

$$\text{prob} = \quad .0001 \quad .0001 \quad\quad\quad .595$$

$$+ .078 \text{ USABNET} - .154 \text{ USPABNET} - 1.632 \text{ US} \qquad (6\text{-}1)$$

$$.081 \quad\quad\quad\quad .103 \quad\quad\quad\quad .432$$

$$.339 \quad\quad\quad\quad .134 \quad\quad\quad\quad .0002$$

There is no significant difference between the effect of positive and negative values of NET on EXCESS since the coefficient of PABNET is not significantly different from zero. The degree to which churning declines with an increase in the amount of employment change is the same irrespective of the sign in the employment change. The relationship is also the same in the two countries. When a U.S. dummy is included to account for the fact that EXCESS is generally lower in the United States, the interaction terms, USABNET and USPABNET, are not significantly different from zero.

Thus, the component of gross turnover in excess of that which is required to facilitate net change is significantly lower when net change is large. This confirms that there is less restructuring in periods of rapid growth and decline. Job turnover is the result of some firms growing at the expense of others. With rapid increases in employment, firms have all they can do to keep up with general growth. There is less inter-firm shifting. When an industry is in rapid decline, firms focus on keeping their own customers and pay less attention to acquiring the customers of others.

Excess job turnover is generally higher in Canada than in the United States for all sectors combined. This result could stem from quite different underlying causes. Differences at the aggregate level may be the result of different time patterns due to different levels of macro-economic cyclicality. They may be the result of similar patterns over time but greater volatility in all industries. Or it may be that differences occur for most industries in only one or two years – perhaps at the cyclical trough – or in only one or two industries in most years.

To examine the origin of the apparent cross-country differences in the volatility of job turnover, job-gain, job-loss, and the excess-turnover rates at the two-digit level for the years 1972 to 1986 are regressed on an industry, a year, and a general Canada–U.S. effect variable. Interaction terms for Canada–U.S. differences on both industry and year are also included. The results are presented in Table 6-3 for each of job gain, job loss, net change, and excess turnover, respectively.

For job loss, the U.S. coefficient is positive (0.48) and significant (prob $|t|$ > 0 = .037) when only separate year and industry effects are estimated. For job gain, the U.S. effect is negative (–1.56) and significant (prob $|t|$ > 0 = .0001). Thus, on average, the United States has more job loss and less job gain than does Canada.

In the case of job loss, industry-interaction terms are all insignificant at the 5 per cent level; on the other hand, three of the year-interaction terms are significant at the 5 per cent level. Figure 6-5 plots the year effects for Canada and for the United States with asterisks being used to denote the three periods that are significant at the 5 per cent level – 1974–75, 1982–83, 1984–85. These are the years when U.S. job loss is particularly high.

In the case of job gain, only 4 of the industry-interaction terms are significant at the 5 per cent level, but 10 of the year-interaction terms are significant at the 5 per cent level. Figure 6-6 plots the year effects for Canada and for the United States with asterisks being used to denote the years that are significant at the 5 per cent level. Significant differences here occur both for high and low levels of job gain.

In the case of both job gain and job loss then, Canada differs from the United States not so much because industries consistently differ; rather there are several years in which job turnover is significantly different in Canada than in the United States. Higher job loss occurs in the United States in three separate years. Lower job growth is also more closely associated with year than with industry effects. It is not that industries were less dynamic in the United States during the period being studied; the economy was affected more by the business cycle in the United States.

That there are fewer significant industry effects for job loss than for job gain confirms once more that regions resemble one another more in terms of job-decline rates than they do in terms of job-growth rates. The non-cyclical component of job decline is a random process that does not vary across industries as much as does job growth, which depends more on the technological regime, the entry conditions, and the growth path of the industry.

Cumulative five-year employment-turnover measures
Manufacturing-sector turnover measures

Short-run growth and decline are dominated by change in continuing firms. In the longer run, a larger proportion of turnover is made up of entry and exit. In order to compare growth over longer periods, intra-industry change

Table 6-3. Regression of POS, NEG, NET, and EXCESS on industry, year, and country effects

	POS		NEG		NET		EXCESS	
Variable	Parameter estimate	Probability value	Parameter estimate	Probability value	Parameter estimate	Probability value	Parameter estimate	Probability value
INTERCEP	9.53	.000	5.44	.000	4.09	.002	13.14	.000
IND21	-4.46	.000	-2.14	.024	-2.32	.115	-8.12	.000
IND22	-0.41	.060	1.05	.267	-1.46	.323	-1.59	.142
IND23	4.13	.000	4.83	.000	-0.70	.636	7.90	.000
IND24	4.11	.000	3.54	.000	0.57	.699	3.33	.002
IND25	4.78	.000	3.60	.000	1.18	.422	3.38	.002
IND26	-3.76	.000	-3.72	.000	-0.04	.978	-8.76	.000
IND27	2.47	.002	0.06	.947	2.41	.103	0.92	.396
IND28	0.13	.871	-1.17	.215	1.30	.378	-1.68	.122
IND29	-2.21	.006	-1.86	.049	-0.35	.814	-9.42	.000
IND30	2.36	.003	-0.46	.626	2.82	.057	-1.21	.263
IND31	1.25	.116	2.70	.005	-1.44	.329	1.43	.188
IND32	1.36	.097	1.42	.133	-0.06	.969	0.49	.648
IND33	-2.77	.000	-1.96	.039	-0.81	.582	-6.81	.000
IND34	4.04	.000	2.53	.008	1.51	.307	3.32	.002
IND35	4.49	.000	3.49	.000	1.00	.497	3.75	.001
IND36	2.01	.012	2.42	.011	-0.41	.780	1.42	.189
IND37	1.63	.041	0.40	.676	1.24	.402	-1.66	.126
IND38	0.97	.225	2.18	.021	-1.21	.411	0.05	.967
IND39	4.21	.000	3.38	.000	0.83	.572	6.03	.000
INT21	1.74	.123	0.23	.866	1.51	.469	1.93	.210
INT22	-1.68	.137	-1.25	.349	-0.43	.838	-4.50	.004
INT23	-1.80	.110	0.16	.904	-1.97	.346	-4.58	.003

INT24	-0.07	.951	1.37	.305	-1.44	.490	0.22	.885
INT25	-3.00	.008	-2.20	.101	-0.80	.701	-4.26	.006
INT26	1.51	.181	0.94	.482	0.57	.784	2.42	.114
INT27	-2.09	.064	-1.68	.210	-0.42	.842	-2.31	.133
INT28	-2.07	.066	-1.15	.389	-0.92	.658	-3.19	.038
INT29	-0.07	.948	0.47	.724	-0.55	.794	4.01	.009
INT30	-0.08	.943	1.18	.378	-1.26	.546	-0.07	.963
INT31	-1.08	.336	1.77	.186	-2.85	.172	-1.32	.391
INT32	-0.73	.519	0.05	.969	-0.78	.709	-1.19	.437
INT33	0.70	.535	2.44	.069	-1.74	.405	-0.32	.834
INT34	-2.92	.010	-1.18	.378	-1.74	.403	-4.33	.005
INT35	-3.02	.008	-2.37	.077	-0.65	.755	-5.68	.000
INT36	-0.48	.667	-2.43	.070	1.94	.353	-3.45	.025
INT37	-0.68	.546	-0.71	.596	0.03	.989	-1.34	.383
INT38	-0.31	.781	0.07	.956	-0.39	.853	0.20	.894
INT39	-2.86	.012	-2.49	.062	-0.37	.861	-5.83	.000
T74	-0.97	.145	1.10	.162	-2.08	.093	0.91	.317
T75	-1.46	.029	4.88	.000	-6.34	.000	5.10	.000
T76	-1.67	.013	3.20	.000	-4.87	.000	3.07	.001
T77	-3.18	.000	4.07	.000	-7.24	.000	0.63	.487
T78	2.45	.000	2.00	.012	0.45	.718	3.76	.000
T79	0.96	.152	1.93	.015	-0.97	.431	3.42	.000
T80	-1.23	.066	3.17	.000	-4.40	.000	4.14	.000
T81	-0.69	.299	2.68	.001	-3.37	.007	3.93	.000
T82	-3.46	.000	8.80	.000	-12.26	.000	1.80	.047
T83	0.06	.933	6.27	.000	-6.21	.000	6.12	.000
T84	0.95	.153	3.27	.000	-2.31	.062	4.97	.000
T85	0.61	.361	3.47	.000	-2.86	.021	4.51	.000
T86	2.46	.000	4.67	.000	-2.21	.074	7.80	.000
I74	-1.57	.096	1.78	.112	-3.35	.055	2.49	.053
I75	-3.89	.000	5.35	.000	-9.24	.000	-5.78	.000

Table 6-3. (cont.)

Variable	POS		NEG		NET		EXCESS	
	Parameter estimate	Probability value	Parameter estimate	Probability value	Parameter estimate	Probability value	Parameter estimate	Probability value
I76	1.82	.055	-0.79	.478	2.61	.136	1.09	.396
I77	2.34	.013	-1.63	.145	3.97	.023	3.36	.009
I78	-3.42	.000	-0.82	.463	-2.60	.138	-1.53	.234
I79	-2.64	.005	-0.95	.395	-1.69	.333	-1.80	.161
I80	-2.54	.007	-0.27	.811	-2.27	.195	-2.82	.028
I81	-3.83	.000	1.88	.092	-5.71	.001	-4.07	.002
I82	-1.08	.254	-0.71	.526	-0.37	.832	-0.85	.508
I83	-2.84	.003	2.03	.070	-4.88	.005	-2.10	.103
I84	0.47	.621	-1.77	.114	2.24	.200	-2.19	.088
I85	-4.71	.000	2.11	.060	-6.81	.000	-3.12	.015
I86	-6.01	.000	1.27	.257	-7.28	.000	-4.93	.000
US	1.38	.180	0.82	.816	1.09	.564	1.22	.379
R^2	.67	—	.64	—	.54	—	.70	—
$F(494, 65)$	18.63	—	16.42	—	11.06	—	20.91	—
prob > F	.0001	—	.0001	—	.0001	—	.0001	—

Note: Variables are IND – industry effect; INT – additional industry effect for the United States; T – year effect; I – additional year effect for the United States; US – country effect for the United States.

134

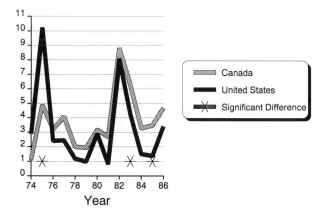

Figure 6-5. Differences in annual job-loss rates for Canada and the United States (year effects from regression analysis, 1972–86).

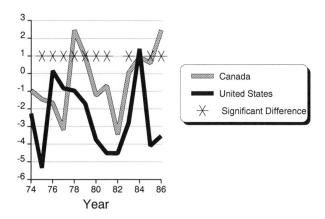

Figure 6-6. Differences in job-gain rates for Canada and the United States (year effects from regression analysis, 1972–86).

in relative plant size is measured over two five-year periods: 1972–77 and 1977–82. Change over these five-year periods provides an estimate of long-run change that is associated with the net accumulation of job flows. Employment creation is divided into job gain in growing, continuing establishments and into firm births. Employment destruction is divided into job loss in contracting, continuing establishments and into firm deaths. Rates of change are calculated using the initial year as the base period. The total turnover rates for the two periods are presented in Table 6-4; for births and deaths in Table 6-5.

Table 6-4. *Average five-year cumulative net and gross job-change rates, by two-digit manufacturing industry, Canada and the United States, average of 1972–77 and 1977–82 (per cent)[a]*

Industry	Canada				United States			
	Job gain (POS)	Job loss (NEG)	Net change (NET)	Total turnover (SUM)	Job gain (POS)	Job loss (NEG)	Net change (NET)	Total turnover (SUM)
Food	22.3	20.7	1.6	43.0	24.3	26.7	–2.4	51.0
Textiles	15.2	27.1	–11.9	42.3	13.5	25.9	–12.4	39.4
Knitting mills	17.3	31.1	–13.8	48.3	22.6	34.3	–11.7	56.9
Apparel	29.3	34.9	–5.6	64.2	30.8	37.7	–6.9	68.5
Lumber	26.7	29.3	–2.7	56.0	31.3	39.9	–8.6	71.2
Furniture	29.7	30.7	–1.1	60.4	27.0	29.9	–2.9	56.9
Paper	12.6	12.1	0.5	24.7	16.7	19.0	–2.3	35.7
Printing	30.3	19.4	10.9	49.7	32.5	22.4	10.1	54.9
Chemicals	28.1	18.2	10.0	46.3	21.8	19.9	2.0	41.7
Petroleum	25.7	8.0	17.7	33.8	19.8	17.0	2.8	36.8
Rubber	28.0	20.6	7.4	48.7	30.9	27.7	3.2	58.6
Leather	22.9	29.4	–6.5	52.3	19.0	32.8	–13.8	51.8
Stone, clay, glass	21.9	26.0	–4.1	47.8	21.8	29.4	–7.6	51.2
Primary metals	14.7	15.0	–0.3	29.7	12.0	24.2	–12.2	36.2
Fabricated metals	29.4	23.9	5.5	53.3	25.6	26.9	–1.3	52.5
Non-electrical machinery	34.1	26.7	7.5	60.8	33.1	24.2	8.8	57.3
Electrical machinery	27.6	28.8	–1.2	56.4	31.0	23.4	7.6	54.4
Transportation	22.4	22.9	–0.5	45.2	20.3	23.4	–3.1	43.7
Miscellaneous	31.3	28.1	3.2	59.4	33.5	26.6	6.9	60.1
Total	24.2	23.3	0.9	47.6	25.8	26.5	–0.7	52.3

[a] Rates are calculated as a proportion of beginning-period employment.

Net growth in manufacturing employment averages –0.3 per cent in Canada over the two periods compared with –0.7 per cent in the United States.

In contrast with the short run, in the long run Canada experiences less total job change than does the United States for all of the manufacturing sector. Total job creation and destruction (SUM) is only 47.6 per cent in Canada; it is 52.3 per cent in the United States. This difference also occurs for the long-run excess-turnover rate (EXCESS).

There are differences between the two countries in all categories. Job growth is 1.6 percentage points lower and job destruction 3.2 percentage points lower in Canada. There are also differences in birth, death, growth, and decline in continuing plants. At this aggregate level, U.S. labour markets undergo about

Table 6-5. *Comparison of birth and death rates,[a] Canada and the United States, two-digit industries, average of 1972–77 and 1977–82 (per cent)*

| Industry | Canada | | United States | |
	Birth	Death	Birth	Death
Food	7.4	10.1	9.3	13.9
Textiles	8.2	11.8	5.7	9.9
Knitting mills	6.9	16.1	10.4	16.3
Apparel	15.7	19.2	18.3	22.2
Lumber	12.7	13.2	18.9	20.2
Furniture	16.3	17.3	13.4	14.1
Paper	4.6	4.0	6.7	7.2
Printing	14.1	9.4	14.7	10.9
Chemicals	13.4	6.5	7.4	6.9
Petroleum	6.0	2.8	7.3	5.6
Rubber	12.2	6.9	14.6	12.4
Leather	9.6	13.7	8.0	17.1
Stone, clay, glass	10.6	9.2	11.6	11.7
Primary metals	5.8	2.5	4.7	6.6
Fabricated metals	14.3	10.3	12.0	10.0
Non-electrical machinery	16.2	12.1	14.1	8.7
Electrical machinery	13.6	9.6	11.9	7.8
Transportation	8.2	8.0	5.7	6.5
Miscellaneous	16.6	13.0	14.4	12.4
Total	10.9	9.8	11.3	11.0

[a] All rates are calculated as a proportion of beginning-period employment.

10 per cent more change in the long run than their Canadian counterparts in all of these dimensions.

Variation in cumulative five-year turnover measures calculated at the two-digit level

Employment turnover during the five-year period at the two-digit level is also examined to see whether the aggregate cross-industry differences are a general phenomenon or are to be found in only a small number of industries. The average rates of job gain (POS), job loss (NEG), net change (NET), and excess turnover (EXCESS) by two-digit industry are presented in Table 6-4. Once more, job turnover is closely related at the industry level in the two countries. The cross-country correlations of POS, NEG, NET, and EXCESS are .86, .78, .74, and .78, respectively.

While long-run job-turnover rates calculated for all of manufacturing suggest

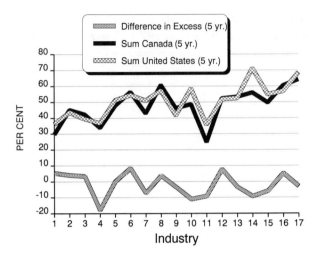

Figure 6-7. Cumulative five-year turnover rates for two-digit industries in Canada and the United States (average of 1972–77 and 1977–82).

that there is less change in Canada, the two-digit data do not bear out this picture. Two-digit Canadian industries do not in general have lower overall turnover rates. They are split about equally between those with lower EX-CESS rates and those with higher rates. There is no significant difference between the means of the excess-turnover rates for Canada and the United States. There are, however, two industries where Canada has undergone much less long-run job turnover than their U.S. counterparts. The industry with the largest difference is the petroleum sector. The second largest difference occurs in rubber and plastics. Both of these were influenced by Canadian policy, which protected firms in these industries from increases in the price of materials inputs as the result of a national energy policy that kept Canadian crude oil prices significantly below world market prices for most of the 1970s after the OPEC crisis in 1973.

The average rate of long-run job reallocation (SUM) at the two-digit level is plotted in Figure 6-7, along with the difference in the excess rate. Industries are ranked from left to right in descending order of level of concentration. The cross-industry similarities found in the annual rates are also present in the longer run.

As with short-run job reallocation, long-run job reallocation is inversely related to concentration. However, while most Canadian industries experience higher turnover than their U.S. counterparts in the short run, this is not the case in the longer run. Morever, there is no apparent tendency for the more concentrated Canadian industries to lag behind their counterparts in the

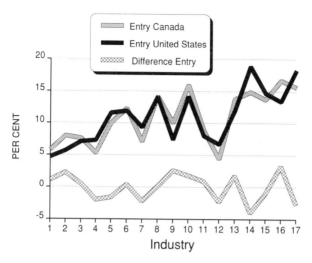

Figure 6-8. Cumulative five-year entry rates for two-digit industries in Canada and the United States (average of 1972–77 and 1977–82).

United States. Indeed, Canadian industries that are the most concentrated are more likely to have higher turnover than comparable U.S. industries.

Variation in cumulative five-year birth and death rates calculated at the two-digit level

Birth and death rates are at the heart of the renewal process. The data suggest that in the long run the relative importance of births and deaths is about the same in Canada and the United States. Job growth from births accounts for 44 per cent on average of total growth in the United States and 45 per cent in Canada. On average, job destruction from plant death over the periods 1972–77 and 1977–82 accounts for 42 per cent of total job destruction in the United States compared with 42 per cent in Canada.

In order to investigate differences further, the cumulative five-year birth and death rates at the two-digit industry level are calculated (Table 6-5). The birth and death rates in similar industries in the two countries are closely related (see also Figure 6-8). Births and deaths in the two countries have correlations of .76 and .79, respectively.

Job turnover and industry characteristics

The forces generating job change produce very similar patterns in the two countries. These similarities are noteworthy, especially given the differences between the two economies in trade, plant size, and other dimensions.

To test to see whether industry characteristics have similar effects, job turnover is regressed on structural and trade characteristics.

Previous work has shown that the most important characteristic affecting turnover in an industry is average plant and firm size. Three separate measures of the size distribution are employed. The first size measure is concentration (HF) – measured as the Herfindahl index, not corrected for trade flows. The second is the average plant size (AVPLSZ), which is total employment divided by total number of plants. The third is the employment-weighted average plant size or the co-worker mean (AVGSZE).[14] This represents the average plant size for a typical worker. Since these three measures are highly correlated, only one is kept for the analysis – the co-worker mean – which consistently had the highest correlation with all aspects of job turnover.

Two trade variables that capture the openness of the economy are used to test whether volatility from exposure to foreign trade influences the level of job change. The first trade variable is export share (EXP) – defined as exports divided by domestic production. The second trade variable is import share (IMP) – defined as imports over domestic disappearance – domestic shipments minus exports plus imports.

The annual rate of labour productivity growth (LABOUR) is used to capture the factors displacing labour that are associated with labour productivity growth. The degree of unionization is used to test whether differences in industrial climate associated with unionization are related to differences in turnover.

The two-digit shares of employment in the two countries are presented in Figure 6-9. These shares have a correlation coefficient of .75. While the overall similarities are striking, there are two differences. Canada has a considerably larger share of employment in food and wood products than does the United States. The United States has a larger share of employment in electrical and non-electrical machinery than does Canada.

While the industrial structure, as measured by employment share, is quite similar, industry characteristics are not. The average Canadian plant size – the co-worker mean – is 755, while the average U.S. co-worker mean is 1,383. Canadian average export intensity is 26 per cent; U.S. average export intensity is only 7 per cent. Canadian average import intensity is 26 per cent; U.S. average import intensity is only 9 per cent. Despite the differences in level, industry characteristics are correlated across industries. The co-worker plant means have a correlation coefficient of .72; the correlation for export intensity is .62; for import intensity, .40.[15]

In order to investigate the way in which these industry characteristics are related to job turnover, pooled cross-sectional data from 18 two-digit industries in each country are used.[16] The two-digit data on turnover are regressed

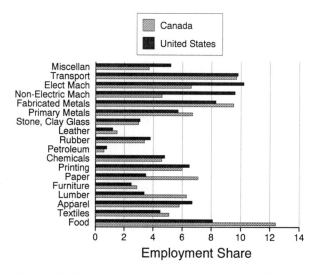

Figure 6-9. Employment shares for Canada and the United States at the two-digit level (average 1972–84). Knitting mills is included in Textiles, and Scientific instruments in Miscellaneous.

on productivity, exports, imports, and the log of the co-worker mean – average size – for the period 1972–84. The regression is performed first with these four variables alone, then with a set of fixed industry effects, then a set of time effects, and finally with both industry and time effects. The results for Canada and the United States are reported in Tables 6-6 and 6-7, respectively, for each of POS, NEG, EXCESS, and NET.

Larger plant size is associated with lower job gain and job loss, is highly significant in both countries, and has a coefficient that is not significantly different in the two countries. When industry effects are included, the coefficient changes sign for both Canada and the United States, thereby indicating that the temporal variation in average plant size is positively related to turnover. A secular increase in industry average plant size is associated with more job turnover.

Higher levels of labour productivity are associated with more job gain and less job loss in both countries when industry and year effects are not included; however, the relationship is generally only significant for Canada. The coefficient is still significant in the Canadian case after year fixed effects are included.

Both exports and imports are positively associated with job gain when industry and year effects are omitted. For Canada, the inclusion of industry effects reduces the effect of exports and imports for the job-gain equation.

Table 6-6. *Determinants of annual rates of job turnover in Canada,*
1972–84: coefficients from multivariate analysis

	Labour	Exports	Imports	Avg. size	R^2
POS					
1	0.0008 (.0001)	0.017 (.10)	0.049 (.0001)	−0.011 (.0001)	.24
2	0.0008 (.0001)	−0.025 (.57)	0.028 (.56)	0.044 (.0009)	.44
3	0.0004 (.0410)	0.022 (.02)	0.049 (.0001)	−0.012 (.0001)	.45
4	0.0004 (.0371)	−0.021 (.65)	0.020 (.64)	0.041 (.0039)	.56
NEG					
1	−0.0010 (.0004)	0.023 (.11)	0.065 (.0001)	−0.024 (.0001)	.30
2	−0.0012 (.0001)	0.053 (.37)	0.138 (.03)	−0.128 (.0001)	.53
3	−0.0007 (.0130)	0.013 (.28)	0.065 (.0001)	−0.022 (.0001)	.57
4	−0.0008 (.0006)	0.006 (.92)	0.119 (.02)	−0.080 (.0001)	.67
EXCESS					
1	0.0009 (.0018)	0.022 (.16)	0.096 (.0001)	−0.028 (.0001)	.44
2	0.0009 (.0003)	−0.007 (.91)	0.113 (.09)	0.018 (.34)	.54
3	0.0004 (.1670)	0.025 (.09)	0.096 (.0001)	−0.028 (.0001)	.48
4	0.0004 (.1380)	0.029 (.66)	0.059 (.33)	0.022 (.27)	.65
NET					
1	0.0017 (.0001)	−0.006 (.77)	−0.016 (.35)	0.013 (.004)	.12
2	0.0020 (.0001)	−0.079 (.40)	−0.111 (.27)	0.172 (.0001)	.28
3	0.0011 (.0036)	0.009 (.58)	−0.016 (.25)	0.009 (.006)	.50
4	0.0012 (.0013)	−0.026 (.77)	−0.099 (.23)	0.122 (.0001)	.50

Note: Probability value $|t| > 0$ is in parentheses. In each group of four rows, the first uses characteristics only as regressors; the second, characteristics plus industry effects; the third, characteristics plus year effects; and the fourth, characteristics plus industry and year effects.

Industries with higher export and import intensity have greater job gain, but upward trends in exports do not appear to be increasing the rates of job gain. Indeed, the sign on exports in Canada, after allowing for industry effects is negative, although the coefficient is insignificant. Thus, job gain is declining in those industries experiencing increases in exports.

For the Canadian job-loss equation, both exports and imports have positive coefficients. When industry effects are included, the significance of exports is reduced. This is also the case for import intensity though it remains significant at the 5 per cent level. On a cross-sectional basis, industries with more imports have greater turnover, and any increase in imports over time is associated with greater job loss.

The effect of the trade variables for the United States is similar qualitatively to that for Canada. However, the negative effect of export intensity on

Table 6-7. *Determinants of annual rates of job turnover in the United States, 1972–84: coefficients from multivariate analysis*

	Labour	Exports	Imports	Avg. size	R^2
POS					
1	0.0008 (.005)	0.38 (.44)	0.06 (.048)	−0.010 (.0002)	.10
2	0.0005 (.021)	−0.75 (.0001)	0.20 (.0002)	0.060 (.0001)	.44
3	−0.00009 (.72)	0.16 (.0001)	0.04 (.0869)	−0.014 (.0001)	.46
4	−0.00023 (.28)	−0.29 (.0019)	0.07 (.137)	0.028 (.0022)	.70
NEG					
1	−0.00019 (.63)	0.15 (.025)	0.13 (.0008)	−0.020 (.0001)	.15
2	−0.00015 (.69)	0.80 (.0001)	0.05 (.54)	−0.104 (.0001)	.29
3	0.000067 (.83)	0.08 (.089)	0.13 (.0001)	−0.017 (.0001)	.61
4	−0.000065 (.82)	0.42 (.0009)	0.09 (.17)	−0.065 (.0001)	.71
EXCESS					
1	0.0006 (.08)	0.10 (.099)	0.13 (.0002)	−0.025 (.0001)	.28
2	0.0004 (.21)	−0.20 (.112)	0.22 (.0006)	−0.002 (.865)	.53
3	−0.00004 (.89)	0.16 (.003)	0.12 (.0002)	−0.027 (.0001)	.42
4	−0.0003 (.35)	0.05 (.672)	0.18 (.004)	−0.020 (.098)	.69
NET					
1	0.0010 (.81)	−0.11 (.260)	−0.07 (.199)	0.010 (.0794)	.02
2	0.0007 (.21)	−0.15 (.0001)	0.15 (.233)	0.164 (.0001)	.15
3	−0.0002 (.71)	0.08 (.229)	−0.09 (.0139)	0.003 (.386)	.63
4	−0.0002 (.72)	−0.72 (.0003)	−0.02 (.857)	0.094 (.0001)	.64

Note: Probability value $|t| > 0$ is in parentheses. In each group of four rows, the first uses characteristics only as regressors; the second, characteristics plus industry effects; the third, characteristics plus year effects; and the fourth, characteristics plus industry and year effects.

job growth after allowing for industry effects is significantly larger than for Canada and, by way of contrast, is significantly different from zero. It is also the case that, for the United States, exports have a positive and significant coefficient in the job-loss equation, which increases in size and significance after the fixed industry effects are added. In contrast to the Canadian case, import intensity loses its significant positive association with job loss when industry effects are added. Thus, in Canada, a temporal increase in imports is associated with increasing job loss; in the United States, exports have that effect.

In both Canada and the United States, total turnover in excess of that required to facilitate net employment change (EXCESS) is positively related to labour productivity and to both export and import intensity, as well as negatively related to average plant size. Export intensity has a larger coefficient and is more significant for the United States. The inclusion of industry and year fixed effects makes all but imports insignificant for the United States and all but labour productivity insignificant for Canada.

The similarities in the determinants of job turnover outweigh the differences. The coefficients on average size, productivity, and imports do not differ significantly in the two countries. The countries differ only in the extent that exports are associated with less job gain and more job loss in the United States after fixed industry and year effects are included. As a result, exports have a greater influence on the excess-turnover rate in the United States than in Canada.

It is noteworthy that the United States generally has more turnover than Canada both before and after industry characteristics are taken into account. When the two data sets are pooled and just a country effect included, POS is 1.9 percentage points higher in the United States, NEG is 0.8 percentage points higher, and EXCESS is 1.8 percentage points higher. When industry characteristics are also included, POS, NEG, and EXCESS for the United States are 3.8 percentage points, 3.6 percentage points, and 5.6 percentage points higher, respectively.

In order to pursue the similarities further, the same industry characteristics are used for a regression of long-run turnover (POS, NEG, and EXCESS) in each two-digit industry and for long-run estimates of birth and death rates. The long-run measures are averages of the results for the 1972–77 and 1977–82 period. The industry characteristics are averages for the period 1973–84.

The average job-growth, job-loss, and excess-turnover rates calculated at the two-digit level for Canada and the United States are pooled and regressed first on a country-effect variable for the United States and then on this same variable, import intensity, the logarithm of average plant size, and the square of the logarithm of plant size. Each of these industry characteristics is included as an interaction term with the U.S. country effect. Only those interactions that are significant are reported.

In order to provide a point of comparison to the pooled results, regressions are also estimated using the average of the short-run turnover measures calculated for the period 1972–86. The coefficients from the longer five-year turnover estimates are adjusted, by dividing by five, to provide estimates that are comparable to the yearly estimates. The results are reported in Table 6-8.

Three variables are found to have little or no significance in the regression analysis that uses two-digit averages and are omitted from the reported results. These are unionization, labour productivity, and export intensity. Unionization is negatively correlated primarily with job growth but not job decline and is highly collinear with plant size. As is the case with the pooled time series before industry fixed effects were removed, labour productivity

Table 6-8. *Cross-sectional regressions for two-digit industry averages of turnover variables*

Period	U.S.	Avg. size	Avg. size^2	IMP	IMP $\times$ U.S.	R^2
Short run						
POS	−1.51					
	(.07)					
	0.96	−13.64	0.89	0.062		.53
	(.21)	(.001)	(.003)	(.005)		
NEG	0.58					
	(.46)					
	2.82	−14.09	0.90	0.07	0.08	.69
	(.003)	(.0001)	(.0005)	(.0002)	(.13)	
EXCESS	−1.62					
	(.29)					
	3.10	−28.70	1.89	0.11		.54
	(.029)	(.0002)	(.0005)	(.005)		
Long run						
POS	−0.11					
	(.80)					
	0.70	−1.57	0.07	0.02		.10
	(.22)	(.57)	(.74)	(.18)		
NEG	0.67					
	(.15)					
	2.47	−8.51	0.55	0.04	−0.005	.63
	(.0001)	(.0002)	(.0007)	(.0005)	(.882)	
EXCESS	0.40					
	(.62)					
	2.82	−11.60	0.74	0.06		.36
	(.003)	(.01)	(.02)	(.02)		
Five-year births and deaths						
BIRTHS	−0.05					
	(.85)					
	1.05	−3.00	0.17	0.02	−0.05	.41
	(.005)	(.056)	(.12)	(.01)	(.07)	
DEATHS	0.29					
	(.37)					
	1.45	−5.53	0.33	0.02	0.002	.72
	(.0002)	(.0001)	(.0008)	(.0008)	(.86)	
EXCESS	0.31					
	(.57)					
	2.15	−8.91	0.55	0.03		.63
	(.0001)	(.0005)	(.0023)	(.08)		

Note: Probability value $|t| > 0$ is in parentheses.

has a positive sign for job gain and job loss in both countries, but with fewer observations and the lack of time series variation, it is not significant. Exports are not significant for the cross-sectional averages, but then they are only weakly significant in the pooled cross-section.

For both the short- and long-run results, plant size is negatively associated with all aspects of turnover and is generally significant. The effect of plant size is found to differ slightly for job growth in Canada and the United States when entered in linear form. Job growth does not decline as quickly for small plant sizes in the United States. Entering plant size in a non-linear form serves to indicate that Canadian turnover reaches a floor at a smaller plant size than does job growth in the United States. There is no significant difference in the effect of plant size on job loss.

Import intensity has a positive coefficient for job growth and job decline for Canada and for the United States in both the short and the long run. The import interaction term for the United States is significant for job loss but not for job gain in the short run. In the case of short-run job loss, import intensity has a significant positive effect for both countries but the effect is significantly larger for the United States.

What then can be said about the difference in turnover in the two countries in light of differences in industry characteristics? The inherent difference in the two countries can be inferred from the sign of the industry effect. When industry characteristics are not considered, short-run job growth (POS) in the United States is significantly lower than for Canada, and job loss (NEG) is not significantly different. When industry characteristics are taken into account, the country effect becomes positive but insignificant for job growth (POS) and significant for job loss (NEG) and total turnover (EXCESS).

On average, Canadian and U.S. turnover rates are about the same; but Canadian industry is characterized by a smaller plant size and greater trade intensity. Both are factors that, on a cross-sectional basis, increase turnover. Therefore, correcting for differences in these characteristics, the United States experiences more turnover than does Canada in the short run.

The long-run results are much the same. There is slightly less job growth and more job loss, but neither difference is significant when industry characteristics are not included. When they are taken into account, both job growth and job loss are higher in the United States; but the difference is only significant for job loss. Consequently, total turnover (EXCESS) is only significantly different in the two countries when industry characteristics are considered. Most of the difference in total turnover (EXCESS) then comes from higher rates of job loss in the United States, not higher rates of job growth.

Of some significance is the finding that the long-run differences attributed to country of origin for job growth (0.7 of a percentage point), for job loss (2.4 percentage points), and for excess turnover (2.8 percentage points) are smaller than for the short run (1.0, 2.8, and 3.1 percentage points, respectively). Short-run turnover is influenced by many factors that are transitory in nature such as the business cycle and exchange rate adjustments. Long-run turnover is more closely related to structural change associated with firms changing their relative position within an industry. That the differences are slightly greater in the short run accords with previous findings that the macrocycle affects job turnover more in the United States than in Canada.

Most of the previous conclusions that arise in comparisons of long-run job growth and job loss also apply to the birth and death equations that are reported in Table 6-8. There is a differential size effect for births but not deaths. There is no significant country effect when industry characteristics are excluded; there is when they are included. Imports lead to more deaths in Canada and the United States. The one significant difference is that, in the United States, import intensity is associated with fewer births than in Canada.

The importance of inter-industry labour reallocation

Job reallocation is commonly considered to be caused by industrial restructuring. Employment problems are perceived to arise because of the need to transfer workers from declining to growing industries. Research into job turnover in Canada and the United States has addressed this question in quite different ways.

In Canada, Baldwin and Gorecki (1993) used a dissimilarity index to measure the extent to which job turnover is associated primarily with intra-industry or inter-industry shifts in the relative importance of plants. The dissimilarity index is the sum of the absolute value of the employment-share change of all plants in the population divided by two. When calculated using shares of industry employment relative to total manufacturing employment, the index captures inter-industry shifts in relative importance. When measured for all plants in a particular industry using shares of that industry's employment, it captures the extent of change within an industry. When measured for all plants in manufacturing using a plant's share of total manufacturing employment, it captures the extent of change from both intra-industry shifts and inter-industry reallocation.

If S_{ij} stands for the share of the jth establishment located in the ith industry as a percentage of total manufacturing-sector employment and the subscripts 1 and 0 stand for the two time periods being compared, then these dissimilarity measures can be written as

Total change: $\dfrac{1}{2}\left(\sum_i\sum_j\left|S_{ij1} - S_{ij0}\right|\right),$

Inter-industry change: $\dfrac{1}{2}\left(\sum_i\left|\sum_j S_{ij1} - \sum_j S_{ij0}\right|\right),$

Table 6-9. *Decomposition of share-change index for manufacturing, 1970 vs. 1979 (per cent)*

Calculated	Dissimilarity index[a]
1. Across all plants	31
2. Across industries	7
3. Average within-industry component across 167 industries	33

Note: The indices are calculated using total-sector employment for the years 1970 and 1979. Small plants and headquarters are not used.
[a] The dissimilarity index is defined in the text.

Intra-industry change for industry:
$$\frac{1}{2}\left(\sum_j \left| \frac{S_{ij1}}{\sum_j S_{ij1}} - \frac{S_{ij0}}{\sum_j S_{ij0}} \right|\right). \qquad (6\text{-}2)$$

The values of the dissimilarity index for these three categories are presented in Table 6-9. The minimum value of each index is 0; the maximum value is 1. The index compares manufacturing-sector establishment shares in 1970 and 1979 and uses the Canadian four-digit industry level of aggregation.

Some 31 per cent of total employment is transferred from losers to gainers in total (index 1). Only 7 per cent is transferred if industry shares are used (index 2). This is less than one-quarter of the value of the total change produced using index 1. If the dissimilarity index is calculated within each of the 167 industries (index 3), 33 per cent of an industry's employment (as opposed to total manufacturing-sector employment), on average, is transferred from losers to gainers. Whether the proportion of total change accounted for by inter-industry shifts or the relative size of the average intra-industry and inter-industry reallocation is used for evaluation, intra-industry reallocation dominates the adjustment process.

Studies of U.S. turnover (Dunne, Roberts, and Samuelson, 1989; Davis and Haltiwanger, 1992) also report that most turnover occurs as a result of displacement of labour within industries rather than across industries. The U.S. studies focus on total turnover that is in excess of net expansion and contraction arising from shifts in employment across different manufacturing plants. This excess is divided into components that capture shifts among plants within a particular category and across a category (i.e., an industry) using the following identity:

$$\text{SUM} = T_p(t) - |\Delta L(t)| + \left[\sum_j |\Delta L_j(t)| - |\Delta L(t)| \right]$$
$$+ \sum_j \left[T_j(t) - |\Delta L_j(t)| \right], \qquad (6\text{-}3)$$

where $L_j(t)$ is the net change in employment within cell j at time t and $T_j(t)$ is the total turnover (the sum of total job creation and destruction) in cell j at time t.

The first term in equation 6-3 is the turnover arising from the net expansion or contraction of the manufacturing sector. The second term is the turnover resulting from shifts of employment across cells with different characteristics minus the turnover resulting from the net change in manufacturing employment. The final component is the intra-industry employment turnover summed across all cells. When cells are defined as industries, change is divided into that caused by jobs shifting from industry to industry and that caused by jobs shifting among plants within industries.

Dunne, Roberts, and Samuelson (1989) use this framework to decompose change for five-year periods. A cell is defined as a two-digit industry. Averaged over the periods 1972–77 and 1977–82, the proportion of total turnover accounted for by net change in employment in manufacturing as a whole is 5.5 per cent, that accounted for the inter-industry component is 6.9 per cent, and that accounted for by intra-industry reallocation is 87.9 per cent. Davis and Haltiwanger (1992) use a similar method to decompose annual change in turnover. When industries are defined at the two-digit level, inter-industry movement accounts for only 1.5 per cent of excess job reallocation. When employment shifts among some 450 four-digit industries are used, the importance of inter-industry reallocation increases to only 12 per cent of the total.

This type of decomposition has been applied to take into account additional characteristics. When Dunne, Roberts, and Samuelson (1989) define cells at the level of the industry and the region, the importance of inter-cell reallocation increases to about 19 per cent. Most turnover is still accounted for by intra-industry regional combinations. Turnover is primarily associated with heterogeneity among plants at the industry level. Some plants are able to adapt to changes in their environment, and others are not. One difference among plants that can be measured is age. When age is added to industry and region in defining a cell, the importance of inter-cell reallocation increases to 54 per cent.

Davis and Haltiwanger (1992) also investigate the extent to which a finer degree of disaggregation changes the conclusion that inter-cell reallocation is relatively unimportant. When cells are defined using plant age, size, region, ownership type, and industry, the importance of shifts between cells increases to 39 per cent of excess job reallocation in the annual data. The addition of age accounts for a considerable proportion of this increase.

Conclusion

This comparison between Canada and the United States yields four major conclusions. First, the factors affecting change in the reallocation of labour in the two countries that relate to industrial structure are basically the same. Second, differences between the two countries are more often the result of differences in cyclical than of industry effects. Third, there is evidence that the Canadian economy has become more volatile over time. Fourth, change within industries dominates the inter-industry reallocation of labour.

Similarities in industrial dynamics

Job creation, job destruction, total job reallocation, job creation due to entry, and job destruction due to exit in the two countries exhibit a number of similarities. First, the aggregate levels of turnover for all of manufacturing and for two-digit industries in both the short and the long run are equal in magnitude. Second, industry correlations reveal that cross-industry patterns are similar in the two countries. Third, when the yearly or cyclical components are removed in the short run, they become even more comparable.

These similarities are remarkable in light of the many differences between Canada and the United States. Although they occupy the same continent, there are significant differences in their political, legal, social, and economic systems. Canada has about one-tenth the population of the United States. The Canadian economy is subject to more foreign competition, its exports account for more domestic production, and its imports account for more of the domestic market. A larger percentage of the Canadian manufacturing sector is foreign-controlled, there are higher levels of unionization in Canada, and Canadian markets are more concentrated than U.S. markets.

It is not that these variables do not affect turnover. The cross-section regressions found that they do so. But the relationship between each of these characteristics and the various turnover measures is very similar in the two countries. Moreover, after these variables are considered, the industry effect that captures the mean residual difference is not large. It is not significant for job gain either for the short-run or long-run estimates. At most, one can say that, after the effect of industry characteristics are considered, Canada appears to have less job loss. In reality, of course, because of the Canadian environment, Canadian job turnover is generally just as high as that of the United States.

Since Canadian plant turnover is very similar to that of the United States, the explanation of turnover rates is to be found in common, not different factors. This is strongly suggestive that the principal determinants of turnover are to be found in the technology base of an industry, since the two countries' manufacturing sectors are different in so many other dimensions. The major commonality is the production and marketing technologies that determine a firm's competitiveness.

Differences in cyclical effects

The cross-industry variation in turnover rates is not the only place where similarities can be found between the two countries. Time-series correlations indicate that the cyclical behaviour of net and gross job-flow rates are also closely related. The cyclical variation in total turnover (EX-CESS) relative to the absolute value of net change (NET) is similar. In both countries, there is less overall job turnover when there are large absolute values of net employment change in both countries.

There are also some striking differences in the time-series patterns. First, U.S. turnover is different from Canadian turnover because of specific year effects often associated with cyclical downturns. There is evidence to suggest that gross turnover rises more in the United States at the downturn because job decline is greater and job growth is less. The variance of job loss is also considerably higher relative to the variance of job gain in the United States than in Canada. Change at the industry level is not as synchronous in Canada as in the United States.

Second, total and excess job-turnover rates exhibit a positive trend in Canada from the 1970s through the 1980s, while there is essentially no trend in the United States. This finding is significant. Canada's unemployment rates during the 1980s are 2 per cent higher, on average, than those of the United States. In the 1970s, there is much less difference between the rates in the two countries. Explanations for the higher Canadian unemployment rate have generally focused on the supply side.[17] Differences in the volatility of demand have not garnered the same attention. The process of plant growth and decline is associated with factor reallocation in labour markets. Higher job turnover is associated with greater turbulence in labour markets as workers are forced to separate more frequently from those enterprises that are shedding labour and to find jobs in those hiring new workers.

Cyclical versus structural differences

Another notable finding pertains to the differences found between Canada and the United States in excess job-turnover rates.

The Canadian economy has alternately been described as either more rigid or more volatile than the U.S. economy. Problems with the Canadian economy have sometimes been ascribed to rigidity arising from differences in market structure, culture, and customs that make competitiveness less of a priority in Canada than in the United States. Rigidity is manifested in less dynamic change and less job creation and destruction. By way of contrast, the Canadian economy has been described as more volatile, because of its openness to trade flows and its greater reliance on basic commodity markets and semi-processed raw materials.

Both views may be correct. Job turnover in the short run is at least as high and growing in Canada relative to that in the United States. There are no significant differences in the longer-run measures for a sample of two-digit industries. But when industry characteristics are taken into account, Canada experiences lower job turnover. Based on the regressions, if Canada had the same average plant size, labour productivity change, and trade intensity, it would have lower turnover both in the short run and the long run. The differences, however, when corrected for the different periods used, are smaller in the longer-run estimates. Canada is, therefore, inherently somewhat less dynamic, but this natural tendency is offset by industry characteristics that increase the level of job creation and destruction to U.S. levels.

The data also suggest that the long-run differences are not related to industry structure as traditionally thought. Canadian concentration ratios are higher than U.S. concentration ratios, on average; but the Canadian job-turnover rate in the long run is relatively high in the most highly concentrated industries and relatively low in industries with lower concentration. Market structure as it is traditionally measured is not closely related to differences in turnover between the two countries.

7

Measures of market structure and the intensity of competition

> Let us remember that measures of concentration, whether they try to measure the concentration of ownership, profits, or market policies within an industry, are only one among many possible indexes of oligopoly power.
>
> Tibor Scitovsky (1955: 101–2)

Introduction

Mobility statistics directly measure the extent to which firms replace one another during the course of the competitive struggle. Measures of market structure have tended to focus on inequalities in firm size during the course of the struggle. The two measures therefore address quite different questions about the competitive process. This chapter asks how they are related. In doing so, it provides evidence that the two measures need to be used in conjunction with each other rather than separately because the information they produce is complementary. This chapter asks whether the dimensions of intra-industry mobility are captured by concentration statistics.[1] Chapter 8 reverses the question and asks whether mobility statistics explain concentration levels.

Concentration statistics: the conventional wisdom

In the field of industrial organization, market structure is seen as having considerable stability. This is based on two inter-related but mutually reinforcing factors, one empirical, the other theoretical.

The measure of market structure that is most widely used in the United States, the United Kingdom, and Canada is a measure of concentration. The most commonly used concentration measure is the percentage of output (or any other indicator of industry size, such as employment or assets) accounted for by a small number of the largest firms – typically four in North America. Measures of concentration capture characteristics of the firm-size distribution at a point in time. The size distribution changes slowly over time and so do the associated measures of concentration. These results are found in a series of U.S. studies, such as those by M. A. Adelman (1951) and Mueller and Hamm (1974), which are summarized as follows by Scherer in his widely used textbook:

> Average industry concentration levels in U.S. manufacturing apparently increased quite modestly during the quarter century following World War II. Less solid evidence suggests that the increase was slight even when compared to the levels prevailing at the turn of the century. As Professor Adelman concluded in an earlier study of concentration trends, "Any tendency either way, if it does exist, must be at the pace of a glacial drift". (1980: 70)

In his recent survey of industrial organization, Schmalensee (1988: 644) reiterates this position when he refers to market structure as "relatively stable".

With its almost exclusive emphasis on concentration to measure market structure, Canadian work is squarely in the mainstream of the profession. Rosenbluth's classic studies (1955, 1957) for the National Bureau of Economic Research (NBER) were the foundation of a generation of research. Subsequent work continued to emphasize static market-structure concepts and not dynamic market-turnover characteristics that offer an alternative view of the strength of the competitive process.[2]

Canadian studies, like U.S. studies of changes in concentration, give the impression of market stability since they show slow changes in concentration in the manufacturing sector. In a study that examines the period 1948–72, Khemani (1980: 54, Chart 4-2, panel 1) finds, for a sample of 57 comparably defined industries, that the mean level of the four-firm concentration ratio only increased from 44.4 to 48.3 per cent. Marfels (1976), using a larger sample of 103 manufacturing industries for the period 1965–72, reports little change in mean concentration levels. Krause and Lothian (1988: 1), in reviewing these and other Canadian studies, conclude: "Over time this analysis produced a body of statistics which concluded that up to the mid-1970s concentration though fairly high had remained constant".

The empirical generality that emerged from these concentration studies, both in Canada and abroad, was consistent with the "most influential" (Reid, 1987: 11) paradigm used in industrial-organization studies over most of the post-war period. Developed in the 1930s at Harvard by Mason (1939) and subsequently extended by Bain (1956, 1968), the structure-conduct-performance (SCP) paradigm of industrial organization treats industry structure as being determined primarily by exogenous factors such as technology and public policies.[3] Industry structure, in turn, influences industry conduct and ultimately performance.[4]

This framework guided a number of case studies and, with the introduction of econometrics, many inter-industry cross-sectional empirical studies of the SCP relationship. Canadian work in this area has tended to be an extension of U.S. work, both in spirit and methodology. While those who utilized the SCP framework recognized that market structure possessed several important dimensions – for example the number and size distribution of sellers and buyers, product differentiation, and entry barriers – "the concentration characteristic, particularly with respect to sellers rather than buyers, has received by far the greatest attention" (Reid, 1987: 12). This measure has varied little over time and its use, therefore, has contributed to the impression conveyed to outside observers that markets are stable.

The relationship between structure and mobility

Despite the preoccupation of industrial economists with stability, the existence of change has not been ignored. It has long been recognized that market structure, as measured by concentration ratios, may be stable at the same time as there is considerable underlying change in the number of firms, their size distribution, and the identity of the leading firms. A number of recent developments have placed much greater emphasis on market dynamics, on intra- rather than inter-industry analysis, and on firm rather than industry analysis. The traditional unidirectional SCP model has been modified to consider relationships between performance and structure. Nevertheless, industry performance is generally regarded as having only a second-order effect on industry structure. "Structure" rather than "dynamics" has provided the framework for many analyses.

As part of the ongoing debate, the shortcomings of the concentration ratio, both as a measure of market structure and as an indicator of the degree of competition, have been argued at length.[5] Concern has been expressed that the concentration ratio may not reveal the extent of underlying change, and other measures of the size distribution of firms have been proposed. Some emphasize one aspect of the size distribution, such as the variance in the logarithms of firms' sizes (Hart and Prais, 1956; Hart, 1971, 1975, 1979); others try to provide measures that summarize several dimensions of the size distribution (Hannah and Kay, 1977). Boyle and Bailey (1971), Grossack (1965, 1972), and Kilpatrick (1967) all have sought to define an optimal concentration index. A wide range of these measures is defined in Appendix B.

Another response to the deficiencies inherent in concentration statistics has been to suggest that mobility indices better capture the impact of this dynamic process. They are direct measures of the manifestation of competition – the extent to which the successful supplant the unsuccessful. Analysts have suggested that indices that more directly measure fluctuations in market share and the rank of producers be used (Joskow, 1960; Hymer and Pashigian,

1962; Gort, 1963). Early work by Gort (1963) on changes in market-share stability seems to suggest that between 1947 and 1954 there was very little mobility. Despite the fact that the post-war period is somewhat unusual, Scherer (1980) used Gort's results to argue that mobility measures add little to concentration statistics.

The calls for greater use of mobility measures have largely been ignored because of these early results, because of the easy availability from census publications of concentration ratios for a wide variety of industries, and because of the untested assumption that concentration is closely related to mobility. Concentrated industries are depicted as having formidable barriers to both entry and internal mobility. As a result, even today, most expositions of structure focus almost exclusively on concentration measures rather than on mobility measures that capture the extent of intra-industry movement.

An evaluation of concentration statistics

Concentration statistics were devised to produce summary measures of a complex phenomenon. They were designed to relay information on dominance and the potential for competition. Like most summary statistics, they deliberately reduce complex phenomena to their bare essentials and are not intended to represent the complexity of individual situations. They also suffer from being misapplied on occasion. As is often the case, they have come to be used for purposes to which they are less well suited – for instance, to infer changes over time in competitive conditions. Even for their main purpose of ranking industries by the potential for anti-competitive behaviour, they are not perfect statistics.[6]

Information on mobility statistics offers additional insights on the intensity of competition. For those who believe that concentration statistics already do a moderately good job, mobility statistics can provide a useful incremental addition to our knowledge. For those who consider concentration statistics as static concepts with little relationship to the real conditions of competition, mobility statistics provide absolutely critical and new information.

An evaluation of the additional information provided by mobility statistics can adopt one of two approaches. It can ask whether the impression given by concentration statistics, when they are used as a summary representation of reality, is adequate in light of the picture provided by mobility statistics. This is the approach followed by this chapter. It is directed to those who want to know how the dimensions of market structure differ from the internal dynamics of markets. Or it can abandon the treatment of concentration as a simple summary statistic to be used by itself and ask how the information it provides can be used in conjunction with turnover measures to provide a picture of the intensity of competition. This approach is followed in Chapter 8.

Change in concentration levels

Examining the firm-size distribution to make inferences about the degree of competition in an industry is commonly practised by those who use trends in concentration to assess changes in the intensity of competition.[7] Implicit in this approach must be the view that the more vigorous the competitive process, the greater the expected change in concentration.[8] Mergers, entry, exit, and the rise and fall of incumbents should all lead to changes in the size distribution of firms and, hence, changes in concentration. Entry of smaller firms may lead to a decrease in concentration. Shake-outs may lead to an increase in concentration.[9] These changes may occur not only as a result of increases in international competition due to falling transportation costs and tariff barriers, technological change, and shifts in demand, but also because of oligopolistic interaction and the dynamics of market competition.

Studies for some industrial countries, such as that by Hart and Clarke (1980) for the United Kingdom, find that there are periods when marked trends in concentration are evident. Such marked trends have not occurred in North America since the turn of the century.

In order to update these concentration studies of Canada's manufacturing sector, data are presented here for 167 industries at the four-digit level for the years 1970 and 1979.[10] First, trends are inferred by a comparison of mean levels of concentration at different points in time; and second, changes in individual industry-concentration indices through time are estimated and summary statistics presented. As concentration is but one measure of structure, the stability of other indices of structure and other methods of characterizing the size distribution of firms is briefly investigated. Before measuring concentration change, however, some discussion of the appropriate index is needed.

Measuring concentration

One of the longest-standing debates in industrial economics concerns the appropriate method of summarizing the size distribution of firms in an industry.[11] The literature is replete with indices named after their originators – Herfindahl, Hall–Tideman (1967), Horvath (1970), and Hannah and Kay (1977). Such a vigorous search for the optimal measure reflects a number of factors: the absence of a generally accepted theoretical model that links structure, behaviour, and performance from which un index can be derived, and the fact that in the absence of such a model, different people attach different weights to the various dimensions of market structure.

Despite a lack of consensus as to which market-structure index is superior, there is widespread agreement that the index should take into account at least two dimensions of the size distribution of firms: the number of firms and the variance in the size of firms. Therefore, many indices have the property that they increase if either the number of firms falls or the degree of inequality in firm size increases.

Indices of market structure are divided into two broad categories: discrete and summary indices.[12] The two are differentiated in the set of points from the size distribution of firms that are used to derive the index. The discrete measures use data on the market share of a small number of the largest firms. The widely used concentration ratio (CR) uses the leading four (CR4) or eight (CR8) firms. In contrast, the summary measures, as the name implies, use all the data points in the size distribution. The summary indices differ one from another primarily in how they weight individual firms' market shares. The Herfindahl index weights each market share by itself, while the entropy index uses the log of share as the weight.

Several criteria can be used to select indices of market structure. When economic theory is used, the approach has been to postulate a behaviourial relationship that governs the type of interaction among the largest firms and to derive an identity that links a measure of structure and performance. Some have derived the Herfindahl index (Cowling and Waterson, 1976; Stigler, 1964); others have derived the discrete indices, particularly the concentration ratio (Saving, 1970). This approach does not directly link structure to performance. Instead, it links behaviour to performance, and an index of structure that is related to performance results from the analysis. Since it is not known, in general, what the appropriate behavioural assumption for a particular industry should be, nor how it relates to structure, it is difficult to use this approach to select the appropriate index.

Alternatively, a set of axiomatic criteria can be used to derive the concentration index. Unfortunately, it is difficult to obtain general agreement on the criteria to be used. One index based on axiomatic criteria is that proposed by Hannah and Kay (1977). It satisfies seven axioms. These include the following: concentration should increase because of mergers or if the law of proportionate effect (LPE) holds; it should decrease if there is entry of firms that are below some size threshold. The Hannah and Kay index is related to the entropy index and under certain circumstances reduces to the numbers equivalent of the Herfindahl index.

In this section, two statistics – the four-firm concentration ratio (CR4)[13] and the summary Herfindahl (HF) measure – are selected to evaluate trends in the size distribution of firms. The CR4 and HF measures were chosen not only because they have some theoretical underpinning, but also because such ratios (particularly the CR4) are often produced by statistical agencies, which facilitates comparisons with earlier studies.[14]

The stability of Canadian concentration levels

While measures of concentration were devised primarily to evaluate differences across industries in the competitive environment, changes in

Table 7-1. *Industry concentration in the manufacturing sector, 1970 and 1979*[a]

Concentration measure	Unweighted mean		Ratio of 1979 to 1970	
	1970	1979	Mean	Median
CR4	50.91	49.86	1.0007	0.979
	(23.71)	(23.51)	(0.2356)	—
CR8	65.46	64.42	0.9929	1.037
	(24.84)	(25.05)	(0.1567)	—
HF	.1149	.1144	1.0428	1.122
	(.0956)	(.1119)	(0.4440)	—

[a] CR4 and CR8 are the proportion (per cent) of industry size accounted for by the leading four and the leading eight firms, respectively. HF is the Herfindahl index of concentration. Market share is measured using shipments. Standard error of the mean is in parentheses.

concentration over time have been used to analyse long-term trends in the competitive environment. When this is done for the Canadian manufacturing sector, very little change appears to be taking place. The mean level of concentration in Canadian manufacturing industries changed imperceptibly in the 1970s. Over the decade, the mean proportion of industry shipments in the four leading firms declined by 1.05 percentage points from 50.91 to 49.86 per cent. The distribution around the mean, measured by the standard deviation, also showed little change (Table 7-1). The same picture of stability was painted by the CR8 and HF measures.[15]

Since the CR4 and CR8 measures involve an arbitrary selection of the number of firms used to create a summary statistic of concentration, the analysis of trends in mean levels of concentration was taken one step further. CR1 to CR10 were estimated for each of the manufacturing industries. The mean level of CR1 to CR10 in 1970 and 1979 for these industries is presented in Figure 7-1. It is evident that the stability shown by the CR4 and CR8 measures is not some quirk of the particular number of firms selected to define concentration. It holds for all of the CR measures.

The use of trends in the mean value of concentration may hide considerable underlying change in the concentration levels of individual industries. In order to see whether this is the case, the ratio of 1979 to 1970 concentration was calculated. Its mean across the sample is 1.0007. The corresponding ratios for CR8 and HF measures also have mean values very close to unity (see Table 7-1). This is further evidence of the stability of market structure.

Despite this evidence of stability, the structure of Canada's manufacturing industries in the 1970s has not been completely rigid. There is some

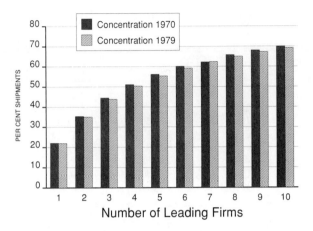

Figure 7-1. A comparison of leading-firm concentration measures (1970 vs. 1979).

inter-industry variability in the ratio of 1979 to 1970 concentration. To characterize the extent of change, a transition matrix was estimated that shows the number of industries moving from one concentration class to another. Industries were assigned to a concentration class in 1970 and 1979 using a fourfold classification system that divides industries into the following CR4 classes: highly concentrated oligopoly (75.0–100.0); moderately concentrated oligopoly (50.0–74.9); slightly concentrated (or low-grade) oligopoly (25.0–49.9); and atomism (0–24.9).[16] Similar classification systems exist for the HF index.[17] However, in view of the similarity in findings, only tabular results for CR4 are presented here (Table 7-2).

The table confirms the existence of considerable market-structure stability. Of the 167 industries, 79 per cent or 132 remained in the same CR4 class. In the case of the threefold HF classification, 81 per cent, or 135, remained in the same class. Furthermore, of those industries that did change concentration classes, movement was almost always to an adjacent class. Only one industry moved more than one class, and this occurred using only the HF concentration grouping.

The stability of other structural indicators

Characterizing market structure using the concentration ratio suggests that it changes very little in dimension. However, there are other ways of representing the structural traits of an industry. Some, such as the cost structure, are quite separate from concentration. Others, while based on the size distribution of firms, refer to different aspects of that distribution and are thought to measure the intensity of competition more accurately. Reliance has

Table 7-2. *Relationship between four-firm concentration ratios, 1970 and 1979 (per cent)*

CR4 class, 1970	CR4 class, 1979				
	0–24.9	25.0–49.9	50.0–74.9	75.0–100.0	Total
0–24.9	24.20	3.00	0.00	0.00	27.00
	14.37	1.80	0.00	0.00	16.17
	88.89	11.11	0.00	0.00	—
	92.31	4.76	0.00	0.00	—
25.0–49.9	2.00	51.00	7.00	0.00	60.00
	1.20	30.54	4.19	0.00	35.93
	3.33	85.00	11.67	0.00	—
	7.69	80.95	14.58	0.00	—
50.0–74.9	0.00	9.00	31.00	4.00	44.00
	0.00	5.39	18.56	2.40	26.35
	0.00	20.45	70.45	9.09	—
	0.00	14.29	64.58	13.33	—
75.0–100.0	0.00	0.00	10.00	26.00	36.00
	0.00	0.00	5.99	15.57	21.56
	0.00	0.00	27.78	72.22	—
	0.00	0.00	20.83	86.67	—
Total					
Observations	26.00	63.00	48.00	30.00	167.00
Per cent	15.57	37.72	28.74	17.96	100.00

Note: In each group of four rows, the first is the number of observations in the cell; the second, the per cent of the total in the cell; the third, the per cent of the row's total in the cell; and the fourth, the per cent of the column's total in the cell.

usually been placed on concentration as the indicator of structure, because it was thought to be a useful proxy for these other dimensions. This section examines whether these other indices also confirm the pattern of stability portrayed by the CR4 and HF measures.

Concentration measures, such as the CR4 or HF indices, are designed to incorporate at least two dimensions – the number of firms and their inequality – of the size distribution of firms. There are, however, a number of other measures of the size distribution that rely only on one aspect of it.[18] Proponents of these measures feel they capture more precisely the intensity of competition, either when used separately or in conjunction with the traditional measures. Some of these measures focus only on inequality – such as the variance of the size of all firms (VARS),[19] the Pareto coefficient (PAR) used to characterize inequality in the upper tail of the firm-size distribution,[20] or the coefficient of variation of the eight leading firms (CVAR8).[21] Others are concerned with the number of competitors. Numbers of competitors can be used in absolute form (NF, NP) or, when used as a quotient to divide the numbers-equivalent derived from some concentration measure, to provide a relative measure. These relative-number measures vary inversely as the numerical importance of small firms increases relative to the numbers equivalent and, therefore, assess the skewness in the distribution.[22] Still others have advocated the use of the marginal-concentration ratio – the share of the firms ranked five to eight (MCR8)[23] – or the size of this group relative to the top four (REL84) to capture the importance of competition from a secondary group of firms.

Market structure is also sometimes described with measures that are not derived directly from the size distribution of firms. Such measures include cost structure, Canadian ownership, and minimum-efficient-sized plant as a percentage of industry size. Some of these can be classified as entry-barrier variables. As such, they are likely to influence the size distribution of firms and can be regarded as proxies for concentration.

The impression of stability in market structure that the CR4 and HF measures convey is also found with respect to many of these other dimensions of structure (Table 7-3). Even though these secondary measures of concentration exhibit slightly more change than either CR4 or HF measures (see Table 7-1), they have generally changed by only a few percentage points over the decade. The median values of the ratio of these structural measures in 1979 to 1970 vary between 0.90 and 1.12.

Intra-industry mobility

When viewed from the outside using dimensions of market structure, markets do not appear to have changed much in the 1970s. While structure was not completely static, there were few visible changes. This is in marked contrast to the change that was going on within industries as firms grew and declined. The degree of instability on the inside can be depicted by using measures developed in Chapter 5. These measures describe the size of the market share transferred from losers to winners over the 1970s as well as the relationship between a firm's market share in 1970 and 1979.[24]

On average, 36 percentage points of market share were transferred from firms that lost market share to those that gained it within an industry (see Table 4-5). The minimum value was .06, the maximum value .72. Total turnover of market share is divided into the change occurring in continuing firms (TURNC), and the change due to greenfield entrants and closedown exits (TURNE).[25] Total share change over the decade of the 1970s was about equally divided between TURNE and TURNC – 20.1 and 16 per cent,

Table 7-3. *Selected indicators of the stability of market structure, 1970–79*[a]

	Mean		Ratio of 1979 to 1970	
Measure of market structure	1970	1979	Mean	Median
Size distribution of firms				
Coefficient of variation of the market shares of the leading eight firms (CVAR8)	0.7126 (0.3134)	0.7233 (0.3490)	1.1092 (0.6189)	0.9786
Marginal concentration ratio (MCR8)	14.55 (6.30)	14.56 (6.14)	1.1740 (1.4083)	1.0368
Number of plants (NP)	191.1 (313.1)	207.1 (314.3)	1.1414 (0.3064)	1.1207
Number of firms (NF)	173.0 (297.2)	186.9 (298.7)	1.1422 (0.3280)	1.1125
Other structural variables				
Minimum efficient plant size as a proportion of industry size[b] (AVSZT)	8.54 (8.00)	7.76 (9.24)	0.9373 (0.3144)	0.9115
Proportion of industry sales accounted for by Canadian firms (CDN)[c]	55.17 (30.03)	58.89 (29.29)	1.3125 (1.6023)	1.0502
Cost structure: proportion of value-added accounted for by wages and salaries (CST)	51.96 (12.66)	47.88 (12.13)	0.9366 (0.1939)	0.9057

[a] For nominal tariff protection, 1978 was used instead of 1979. Standard deviation is in parentheses.
[b] Minimum-efficient-size plant is defined as the average size of the largest plants accounting for 50 per cent of industry employment. Plant size is measured in shipments.
[c] Estimated for 166 industries, since 1 industry had no Canadian ownership in 1970.

respectively. These numbers show that a considerable amount of underlying change occurs within an industry. It is certainly substantially more than the 1 percentage point by which the market share of the leading four – the CR4 index – declined over the decade of the 1970s.

Some analysts have emphasized that it is not just the amount of market share that is being shifted but also the pattern that is important.[26] Gort (1963: 51), for example, emphasizes that in evaluating the degree of competition, the ability of leading firms to maintain their market share "is probably more significant than the extent of concentration at a single point in time". The extent to which the largest firms decline and the smallest grow has been described in Chapter 5. Regression and correlation techniques applied to shares at two different points in time provide summary statistics of this pattern.

Two indices are used here to determine whether the picture of market-share stability of the four leading firms applies across all firms in an industry. The first, CORSH, is the correlation coefficient of the firm's market share in 1970 and 1979; the second, REGSH, is the regression coefficient relating 1979 and 1970 market share.[27] REGSH reflects the extent to which firms, on average, regress toward the mean (REGSH < 1) or experience no change (REGSH = 1), or the extent to which centrifugal forces cause large firms to get larger relative to small firms (REGSH > 1). The correlation coefficient (CORSH) measures the degree to which market shares at one point are linearly dependent on those at another point, and is directly related to the co-efficient of determination in a bivariate regression. As such, it can be taken to represent the extent to which the residual error of prediction from the share regression is large or small. The stronger the dependence, the closer the index is to unity and the smaller are the residual errors.

A high value of CORSH – defined here as .9 to 1.0 – is consistent with REGSH showing that firms generally lose, gain, or maintain their relative position. Equally, a value of REGSH that is close to one – defined here as 0.9 to 1.1 – which indicates no regression to the mean, is consistent with either low or high values of CORSH. Hence, industries that have high values of CORSH *and* in which REGSH is centred on unity are defined here as those whose market share is stable. In order to examine the extent to which this is the case, a two-way classification of CORSH and REGSH was performed using the bounds .9 to 1.0 and 0.9 to 1.1, respectively (Table 7-4).[28] Only in 25, or 15 per cent, of Canadian manufacturing industries are both of these two conditions for stability met (the bottom-right quadrant of Table 7-4). Stability of market share, based on both REGSH and CORSH, is the exception rather than the rule. This confirms the picture drawn in Chapter 5 of the extent to which there was a regression to the mean. When all firms in 1970 and 1979 are used, the OLS estimate of REGSH is significantly different from one in about 75 per cent of the cases.

Concentration and mobility

The picture painted by mobility statistics is one of substantial intra-industry change, as firms enter, exit, grow, and decline. Concentration statistics paint a very different picture. They tend to remain relatively constant and, therefore, give the impression of a static universe. While it is possible to find some movement in concentration indices, the amount of change is small relative to what is taking place within each industry.

It may still be, of course, that changes in concentration are strongly related

Table 7-4. *Regression and correlation analysis of the stability of firm market share, 1970–79*

CORSH[a]	REGSH[a]		
	Increasing/decreasing[b]	Stable[c]	Totals
Low[d]	96	8	104
	57.83	4.82	62.65
	92.31	7.69	
	72.18	24.24	
High[e]	37	25	62
	22.29	15.06	37.35
	59.68	40.32	
	27.82	75.76	
Total			
Observations	133	33	166
Per cent	80.12	19.88	100.00

Note: In each group of four rows, the first is the number of observations in the cell; the second, the per cent of the total in the cell; the third, the per cent of the row's total in each cell; and the fourth, the per cent of the column's total in the cell.
[a] See text for definition.
[b] Increasing/decreasing is defined as values of REGSH from 0.00–0.89 and 1.10 and higher.
[c] Stable is defined as values of REGSH from 0.90–1.09.
[d] Low is defined as values of CORSH from .00–.89.
[e] High is defined as values of CORSH from .90–1.00.

to the turnover that occurs within an industry. To test this, all industries were ranked on the basis of the amount of concentration change – using the difference between 1979 and 1970 four-firm concentration ratios. The industries were then grouped into eight equal classes on the basis of the amount of concentration change, and the average turnover ratios for entry and exit (TURNE) and for continuing firms (TURNC) were calculated for each group. In Figure 7-2 the groups are arranged from left to right in ascending order of concentration change – with the leftmost observations representing decline in concentration and the rightmost representing increases in concentration.

There is no simple linear relationship between the turnover measures and changes in concentration. If anything, there is a U-shaped relationship between total turnover and concentration change. Where concentration decreased most, turnover from entry and exit was largest; where concentration increased most, turnover from the continuing sector was largest. Concentration changes

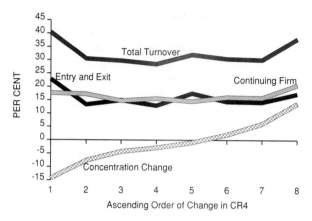

Figure 7-2. The intensity of turnover vs. change in concentration (1970–79).

then are broadly indicative of two different underlying phenomena. On the one hand, declines in concentration are associated with greater turnover arising from entry and exit. Entry and exit occur generally at the margin of the industry in smaller firms. This parallels the findings of Mukhopadhyay (1985), who reports that for U.S. markets concentration ratios decreased in technologically progressive industries because the net rate of entry was much higher in these industries. On the other hand, where concentration is increasing, it is turnover in the incumbent population that is larger than normal. These are situations where a shake-out among the largest firms is taking place.

Change in concentration reflects particularly large turnover of different types. But it would be wrong to conclude that in industries where concentration did not change, the internal dynamics of firm turnover indicated little change was taking place. Where there was virtually no concentration change, there was considerable turnover. Concentration change may be indicative of underlying turnover; lack of concentration change is not.[29] It is, therefore, better to focus on both the amount of internal mobility as well as on concentration measures to depict the amount and type of change taking place within an industry.

Concentration and mobility as indicators of the state of competition

Assessing trends in concentration is only one of the uses made of concentration statistics. More frequently, concentration indices are used to rank industries according to their degree of competition. Since mobility indices provide another metric, it is important to ask whether they rank industries quite differently than do concentration measures.

This question, initially, is examined in two ways: first, by correlating mobility and concentration measures; and second, by examining the pattern of mobility across different market structures. Attention then turns to whether concentration and mobility indices identify the same subset of "problem" industries, since interest in concentration indices often centres on their ability to isolate industries where the competitive process is most likely to malfunction.

Does concentration predict mobility?

In order to compare the way concentration and mobility statistics rank industries, correlation coefficients are used.[30] For the correlation analysis, total turnover of market share is separated into the change occurring in continuing firms (TURNC) and the change due to greenfield entrants and closedown exits (TURNE). This distinction is made because the two sources of turnover have been treated as having different effects on the intensity of competition. There is a long-standing tradition in industrial economics to treat oligopoly and entry models quite separately.

Four other statistics are used to measure the extent to which firm market shares in 1970 and 1979 are related. CORSH and REGSH have already been described. In addition, since stability is to be found in those values of REGSH centred on unity, STAB1 is defined as the absolute value of (1 – REGSH). The lower the value of this index, the greater the degree of stability in market share. Second, a binary variable (STAB2) is formulated that takes a value of one when REGSH is significantly different from one. STAB1 captures the degree to which market share deviates from its original value over time; STAB2 captures the extent to which this deviation is statistically significant.

The correlations between concentration in 1970 and these mobility estimates for the period 1970–79 are presented in Table 7-5. Both the four-firm concentration ratio (CR4) and the Herfindahl (HF) index are used to test the sensitivity of the results to the particular concentration measure employed.

The signs of the correlation coefficients in Table 7-5 indicate that if an industry ranks high in terms of concentration, then it is also more stable; moreover, the correlation coefficients are significantly different from zero – using a 5 per cent significance level – for all of the mobility variables used. There is less turnover and more stability in highly concentrated industries. Therefore, concentration indices capture, albeit imperfectly, some aspects of the turnover that is internal to industries.

The two sources of turnover – entry/exit and incumbent-firm change – are of about equal quantitative importance over the decade being measured, but they are not equally correlated with concentration. The correlation between concentration and the turnover associated with entry and exit (TURNE) is –.5, but the correlation between concentration and turnover in the continuing sector (TURNC) is only –.2.

Table 7-5. *Correlation coefficients between concentration in 1970 and mobility indices for the period 1970–79*

Mobility indices	Concentration indices[a] (1970)		
	CR4[b]	CR4[c]	HF[b]
TURNE	−.541	—	−.469
	(.0017)		(.001)
TURNC	−.242	—	−.275
	(.001)		(.001)
CORSH	+.421	+.393	+.386
	(.001)	(.001)	(.001)
REGSH	+.243	+.017	+.232
	(.001)	(.82)	(.003)
STAB1	−.264	−.106	−.216
	(.001)	(.17)	(.005)
STAB2	−.442	−.360	−.381
	(.001)	(.001)	(.001)

Note: Probability value for the correlation coefficients is in parentheses.
[a] See text for definitions.
[b] Correlations are between concentration and turnover measures calculated for all firms.
[c] Correlations are between concentration and turnover measures calculated for continuing firms only.

In order to test the extent to which the correlation between concentration and the other variables – CORSH, REGSH, STAB1, and STAB2 – was being driven by entry and exit, the measures were reestimated using only the continuing-firm sample. The correlations with the four-firm concentration ratio (column 2 of Table 7-5) are much lower and generally not significant.

While significant correlations are found between concentration and turnover measures, the correlations are not high and they differ considerably. Cross-industry differences in the entry and exit process are more closely related to industry concentration than is turnover in the continuing sector. Even in those cases where a statistically significant correlation coefficient is found, concentration explains or accounts for only a small percentage of the variance of the mobility measure – about a third in the case of the 1970 CR4 and TURNE indices.

This exercise is carried further by examining the relationships between concentration and total share change in large and small continuing firms. Two measures are employed. The first is a measure of volatility – the sum of the absolute values of share change among large firms (TOPCHG) and among small firms (BOTCHG) between 1970 and 1979. These two variables had correlations with the four-firm concentration ratio of −.30 (significant) and −.07 (not significant), respectively. Thus, volatility in large firms is lower in more concentrated industries; volatility in small firms is not related to concentration. The second measure captures the direction of change – the sum of the value of market-share changes among large firms (TOPGR) and small firms (BOTGR) calculated as a rate of initial market share. The rate of decline for large firms was lower in concentrated industries. The rate of small-firm share growth was not significantly correlated with concentration.

The continuing sector does not have the same relationship with concentration as do entry and exit. The reason for this becomes apparent when the continuing sector is broken down into large and small firms. Large-firm turnover responds more than small-firm turnover to concentration, and small-firm turnover substantially weakens the overall response of incumbents to concentration.

Concentration classes and their mobility experience
Correlation analysis performed on a broad cross-section of industries may miss non-linear patterns in the data. For example, the relationship between concentration and continuing-firm turnover across the entire sample may be low, but there may be a significant difference between turnover in highly concentrated industries and that in less concentrated industries, due to clustering at different mean levels.

In order to examine this possibility, the average values of the mobility measures were calculated for groups of industries ranked by concentration class. The market-structure classification system that was used earlier to divide industries into groups based on their CR4 values is adopted. The mean and standard error of the mean for each of these groups are presented in Table 7-6. It is evident that most of the variation in market-share turnover across concentration classes comes from entry and exit (TURNE) rather than from share gain and share loss in the continuing sector (TURNC). The difference between the two is evident in Figure 7-3, which graphs the means and a 95 per cent confidence interval for each.

An analysis-of-covariance test was employed to determine whether there are significant inter-group differences for both of these mobility measures. In the case of entry and exit turnover, the mean of TURNE in each concentration class is significantly different from those in adjoining classes. In the case of continuing-firm turnover, TURNC, the bottom three concentration classes are different from the most concentrated class; but similar to one another. Thus, while entry and exit turnover declines significantly across all

Table 7-6. *Correlation between concentration and various measures of mobility, by concentration class, 1970–79*

CR4 class	Measure of mobility (class mean)				
	TURNE	TURNC	CORSH	REGSH	STAB1
0–24.9	.327	.169	.574	.610	.411
	[.023]	[.007]	[.041]	[.051]	[.044]
N = 27	(.120)	(.035)	(.212)	(.267)	(.231)
25.0–49.9	.228	.172	.743	.767	.303
	[.016]	[.006]	[.023]	[.037]	[.027]
N = 60	(.124)	(.050)	(.180)	(.288)	(.212)
50.0–74.9	.161	.162	.793	.775	.250
	[.017]	[.007]	[.034]	[.073]	[.032]
N = 44	(.114)	(.053)	(.228)	(.245)	(.219)
75.0–100.0	.109	.133	.869	.836	.231
	[.021]	[.009]	[.037]	[.048]	[.040]
N = 36	(.126)	(.054)	(.224)	(.291)	(.240)

Note: N is the number of industries in each class. Numbers in parentheses are standard deviations, and those in brackets are standard errors of the mean.

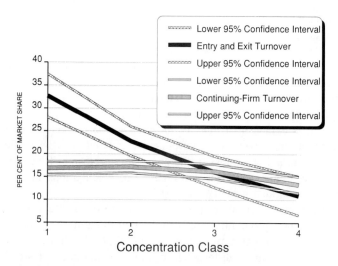

Figure 7-3. Market-share turnover by concentration class.

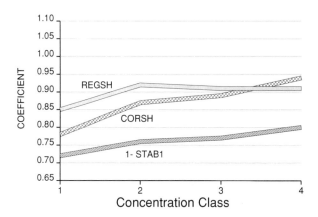

Figure 7-4. The relationship between concentration and share-stability measures. These measures were calculated with continuing firms only.

concentration classes, continuing-firm turnover only does so for the highest concentration class.

A major criticism of the concentration index has been that any level of concentration may be consistent with a wide range of mobility patterns. It is argued that industry growth rates, their variability, and other mobility characteristics are likely to vary considerably among industries that have the same value of concentration. The data confirm that this is the case.[31] For example, while the mean values of entry and exit turnover (TURNE) in the two most concentrated industry groupings are 10.9 and 16.1 per cent, the standard deviation is between 8 and 12 per cent (see Table 7-6). This is large, relative to the values ranged along the locus of points that join the means of the two top groupings. While it is true that there is enough between-group variation relative to the total variation in the sample that the difference in group means is significant, this should not obscure the basic point that there is considerable variation in the turnover measure within each concentration group.

The other measures – CORSH, REGSH, STAB1 – show more or less continuous variation across classes.[32] But much of the cross-industry variation in these measures is a result of entry and exit.[33] To eliminate the effect of entry and exit, these measures were calculated only for continuing firms (Figure 7-4). Concentration is still inversely related to stability but much more weakly. Moreover, for all the measures, the greatest difference is between the least concentrated class and the other three. The discontinuity occurs not between a small number of concentrated industries and all others, but between a small number of highly atomistic industries and the vast majority of the manufacturing sector. This is additional evidence that concentration does a poor job in providing a continuous metric to gauge the amount of change taking place within industries. Mobility measures provide important information that cannot be derived from concentration measures alone.

Problem industries: do concentration and mobility indices provide the same answers?

When the extent to which concentration and mobility are related in a broad cross-section of industries is examined, concentration is shown to be only imperfectly related to mobility. However, concentration statistics are not always used to rank all industries along a continuous scale from the least to the most competitive. A number of analysts have examined the extent to which there is a critical concentration ratio that groups industries into two classes – those with a potential monopoly or oligopoly problem and those without it.[34]

This section examines the extent to which concentration and mobility measures identify the same set of potential problem industries. The CR4 classification was used to define potential problem industries – those with a CR4 measure between 75 and 100 per cent in 1970. In this way, 35 industries were identified.[35] In order to compare the results produced by the CR4 and mobility indices, all industries were ranked using each of these measures. A high rank for the 1970 CR4 index indicates the industry is more rather than less concentrated; a high rank for the mobility indices denotes stability. If the 35 top-ranked industries are the same for the 1970 CR4 and mobility indices, this means that mobility statistics add little information to that already captured by concentration data.

Since there are a number of different interpretations that can be attached to stability, several mobility measures are employed. Three indices – TURNE, TURNC, and STAB1 – are used.

Table 7-7 provides data on the degree to which the same potential problem industries are found using the 1970 CR4 and these mobility indices. The 35 problem industries identified using the 1970 CR4 are ranked first and the remaining columns give the overall rank of each of these 35 industries using TURNE, TURNC, and STAB1. The first row indicates, for example, that the industry with the highest level of concentration in 1970 was ranked 5th in terms of TURNC, but 38th in terms of TURNE. In contrast, the 31st-ranked industry using the 1970 CR4 is ranked 55th using TURNE and 108th using TURNC.

It is evident that concentration and mobility statistics do not identify the same set of problem industries. The final row of the table shows that a substantial percentage of the 35 problem industries were not ranked among the 35 industries with the greatest stability. Entry turnover (TURNE) ranks 57 per cent and continuing-firm turnover ranks 49 per cent in the top 35. The

Table 7-7. *Top 35 manufacturing industries ranked by CR4 index for 1970 and their comparable rankings by three mobility indices*[a]

Concentration index, CR4	Ranking using mobility indices			
			STAB1	
	TURNE	TURNC	All firms	Continuing firms
1.0	38	5	53	51
2.0	3	69	64	113
3.0	12	58	98	127
4.0	5	1	17	19
5.0	8	54	15	16
6.5	32	8	80	106
6.5	1	141	11	13
8.0	18	2	69	26
9.0	19	3	13	15
10.0	45	32	77	90
11.0	131	159	154	136
12.0	9	7	20	22
13.0	105	142	147	161
14.0	20	45	49	89
15.0	17	20	68	81
16.0	6	4	12	14
17.5	71	10	55	55
17.5	7	22	37	60
19.5	76	30	41	120
19.5	79	153	113	132
21.0	16	21	33	58
22.0	31	12	14	30
23.0	4	149	70	116
24.5	2	119	8	11
24.5	81	96	75	84
26.0	11	65	103	125
27.0	89	121	145	156
28.0	165	27	167	121
29.5	30	34	31	35
29.5	160	74	162	143
31.0	55	108	124	146
32.0	13	67	44	52
33.0	98	11	62	44
34.0	68	150	100	115
35.0	54	102	71	25
Proportion ranked in top 35 using given index (per cent)				
100.0	57.1	48.6	28.6	31.4

[a] A high rank in a mobility index represents greater stability; a high rank in the concentration index represents higher levels of concentration.

deviation of the share coefficient from one (STAB1) ranks about 30 per cent in the top 35. If combinations of mobility rankings are taken, even fewer industries would be included. Only 11 of the 35 most concentrated industries are among the 35 most stable industries on the basis of *both* TURNE and TURNC, only 7 on the basis of TURNE, TURNC, *and* STAB1.

It must be concluded that concentration statistics need to be used in conjunction with measures of the intensity of firm turnover if industries with potential competition problems are to be identified.

Conclusion

The four-firm concentration ratio and other market-structure statistics are static measures of the size distribution of firms. They provide a picture of the outside of a box. Inside the box, the competitive process is at work, as firms constantly vie for competitive advantage.

If measures of the size distribution – the outside of the box – were sufficient to describe the intensity of what goes on inside the box, turnover measures could be disregarded. Mobility statistics, which characterize the internal workings of the box, would not add useful information to that provided by concentration statistics.

This chapter has reviewed the picture of competition portrayed by concentration statistics on Canada's manufacturing sector in the 1970s and compared it with that presented by mobility statistics. Since both the levels and changes in the levels of concentration statistics are commonly used to infer the intensity of competition, they are examined separately.

The picture that emerges from the examination of changes in concentration statistics is one of considerable stability. This finding accords with earlier studies of trends in concentration for the United States and Canada. This picture of stability does not reflect the degree of change that is taking place within industries – what is going on inside the industry box. Contrary to the impression given by concentration measures, mobility statistics suggest considerable change and instability.

This chapter also investigates whether concentration measures can be used to infer the degree of intra-industry mobility, by examining the extent to which the two sets of measures are highly correlated and whether they capture the same "problem" industries – industries where competition may be constrained. Concentration statistics were found to rank industries imperfectly on the basis of the amount of change going on inside those industries.

Concentration measures are inadequate by themselves because there is more than one dimension to the competitive process. Inter alia, these dimensions include the extent to which firms change rank, larger firms regress toward the mean, entry and exit are important, and how much market share is redistributed among continuing firms. Concentration is related more closely to some mobility measures than others. In particular, it appears to be more closely related to the amount of turnover associated with entry and exit than with dimensions of change associated with the incumbent-firm population.

The impression of change in the size distribution of firms is quite different depending on whether the inside or outside of the box is examined. A scholar looking at the outside of the box might decide to design models of industry behaviour that emphasize reasons for stability, such as market-sharing arrangements, as well as incumbent behaviour that seems able to deter entry. Attention would be devoted to equilibrium games with static solutions. In contrast, a scholar who peers inside the box would focus on those factors leading to entry and exit, as well as the rise and fall of incumbents. Such a scholar would acknowledge the necessity of modelling incumbent behaviour toward entrants, as well as how incumbents interact with each other. Furthermore, given the magnitude of share change and the lack, in many cases, of any pattern to this change, any model of firm behaviour would have to incorporate some notion of the considerable uncertainty of market outcomes.

The results of this analysis can serve as a guide both for theorists and for policy-makers in the field of competition policy. Concentration and mobility measures have been treated as substitutes, rather than complements. This, reflects, in part, the preoccupation of economists with finding a relatively simple concentration measure to use as a straightforward index that can gauge the state of competition and the lack of effort devoted to measuring the internal dynamics of markets. The intensity of competition in the real world is not amenable to simplification because there is such a wide variety of events occurring within individual industries. The concentration and mobility indices are related, but only imperfectly. They reveal different aspects of the competitive process. In order to detect those industries where competition problems may arise, mobility and concentration indices need to be used together.

8

The relationship between mobility and concentration

Introduction

Two different but complementary approaches have been taken to the study of market processes. On the one hand, competition is described as a process by which entrepreneurs vie freely for success. Firms experiment with strategies to produce new and better goods. They take risks as they commit resources to the process. Gambles are taken when advertising campaigns are mounted to persuade the consumer to sample new product lines. Successful firms wrestle market share away from unsuccessful firms. This approach, occasionally but not exclusively associated with the Austrian school, emphasizes that it is the intensity of this contest that must be the basis of evaluating the process.

An alternative view is that competition can be approached as a state of affairs. According to this view, the dimensions of the competitive system, as complex as they might be, can be meaningfully reduced by means of a suitable classification system. This tradition emphasizes the use of statistics that summarize a state of affairs rather than a process. It uses measures of market structure derived from the firm-size distribution as proxies for the intensity of competition. The firm-size distribution is a measure that depicts the state in which an industry finds itself, rather than the process that has brought it to that position.

At the conceptual level, the two sides may not disagree as to what constitutes highly competitive markets. It is at the practical level of measurement that they differ. Those who use measures of market structure are, faute de mieux, focusing on a state of affairs. In using these measures, they are making certain strong assumptions about the ability of such measures to represent the intensity of competition within the industry.

The potential weakness of the structuralist school lies in the measures that are commonly used by members of this school. In the best traditions of social science, the school's exponents moved beyond verbal descriptions of the intensity of competition to measurement. But the picture of competition that

176

emerged was determined by the limited data that were used: data related to firm-size distributions at a point in time were available, while longitudinal data that follow a firm over time were not. As a result, the structuralist school has had to rely on measures of concentration to represent the intensity of the competitive process.

This study starts with the assumption that much of what happens during the competitive process is manifested in change in relative firm position and that it is important to estimate mobility measures since they shed additional light on the intensity of competition. As a result of the competitive struggle, firms grow and decline, and enter and exit from different markets. The competitive process separates the unsuccessful from the successful.

It is demonstrated in Chapter 5 that the four-firm concentration statistics commonly used by the structuralist school provide only a partial image of the intensity of competition for several reasons. First, this concentration measure suggests stability. In reality, there is considerable underlying change. Second, it is not strongly correlated with several of the key dimensions of intra-industry turnover. Therefore, when used alone, it fails to adequately describe the competitive process. It fails because the competitive process has too much variety to be easily summarized by a single measure.

The contention that it is important to examine turnover within industries does not preclude an interest in the relationship between the intensity of turnover and the market structure of an industry. While the four-firm concentration measure by itself does an imperfect job of describing the variety of competitive situations, it would be wrong to conclude that the state and the process of competition are unconnected. The evidence in Chapter 5 demonstrates a relationship between the four-firm concentration ratio and various measures of mobility, but it is complicated, and the four-firm ratio should not be relied on solely to describe the intensity of the competitive process.

This chapter investigates the relationship further. Despite their failings, concentration statistics should not be discarded. In conjunction with mobility statistics, they can enhance our understanding of the competitive process. Before the two types of statistics can be combined, however, a better picture of their relationship with mobility is required. This chapter will explore these relationships by using statistics that summarize both market structure and mobility. The relationship between concentration and mobility is examined using principal-component analysis, canonical-correlation analysis, and regression analysis.

Principal-component analysis is employed to measure the number of independent dimensions of concentration and mobility. It is also used to determine whether the dimensions of each of the data sets are sufficiently different to argue that mobility statistics add to the information provided by concentration statistics.

While the principal-component analysis finds generally that concentration and mobility statistics contain different dimensions, there are links between the two sets of measures. These are explored further with canonical-correlation analysis, which examines the correlation between the different dimensions of concentration and mobility.

Principal-component and canonical-correlation analyses explore the broad relationships between the concentration and mobility measures with no reference to causality. It is important to consider the effect of other variables, in order to determine whether the variation in concentration is equally well accounted for by variation, not in mobility, but in plant and firm scale. Therefore, regression analysis is used to investigate the relationships between concentration and mobility measures and to "explain" the level of concentration and changes in concentration over the decade of the 1970s. Regression analysis is used to investigate whether the contents of the box – the extent and the pattern of intra-industry firm mobility – reveal the shape of the outside of the box – the market structure.

Attempting to explain the causes of concentration with mobility measures originates in the work of economists like Simon and Bonini (1958) who model markets as stochastic processes and demonstrate that certain measures of mobility may determine the degree of concentration. For explanatory variables, the regression analysis uses not only technical factors, such as scale economies, but also various mobility indicators. Mobility is found to be related to concentration even when the scale factors are taken into account.

The relationship between concentration and mobility
Investigating the dimensions of mobility and concentration statistics

Several facets of intra-industry competition have been used to produce mobility statistics – the extent of entry and exit (Baldwin and Gorecki, 1991), the amount of market-share exchange in the continuing-firm population (Hymer and Pashigian, 1962), the extent of change in ranks (Joskow, 1960), the degree to which market shares regress to the mean (Gort, 1963; Prais, 1976), and the extent of inter-group mobility (Prais, 1955).

Just as there are numerous mobility measures, there are many concentration statistics (Curry and George, 1983). Some capture several aspects of the firm-size distribution – both the number of firms and the difference in firm size. Others focus on select aspects of the distribution, that is, its variance.

The multiplicity of mobility and concentration measures complicates an investigation of the relationship between the two. Since both concentration and mobility have been represented by a large number of summary statistics, the choice of a measure for the analysis is arbitrary. The results of the investigation may, however, be sensitive to the particular measure chosen. This problem can be avoided if the measures are considered as a whole and the relationships between the two groups are then investigated.

Consideration of a set of concentration and mobility statistics may founder on another criterion, that of comprehensibility. The complexity involved in the joint consideration of a set of variables may obscure the relationships between key variables. This problem can be overcome by establishing how many key dimensions exist in each data set and then by delineating the relationships between the different principal dimensions.

The first requirement is to ascertain whether the different measures of concentration and mobility capture related or unrelated dimensions of the same phenomena. This can be done by, first, measuring the primary dimensions of each set of measures or reducing those dimensions with the appropriate statistical technique. To do so, principal-component analysis is used to ask how many significant but unrelated dimensions exist in each data set and to interpret each of the major dimensions in terms of the original variables.[1] The second step is to perform a principal-component analysis on the concentration and mobility variables together, to determine whether the characteristics of the mobility set are captured, submerged, or otherwise overwhelmed by the principal components of the concentration statistics when the two are combined. If the mobility and concentration variables are weighted heavily in different components of the combined set of concentration and mobility statistics, then they possess different dimensions – the outside of the box is generally different from the inside. If, however, the mobility variables are subsumed under the concentration variables, then the inside of the box does not add much information beyond that captured by the outside.

Principal-component analysis. Principal-component analysis provides a set of weights that, when applied to the original variables, creates a set of new variables that are orthogonal to one another, that exhaust the variance in the original set of variables, and that are hierarchically ordered in terms of their variance. Thus, the principal components [$PMOB(i)$] of a set of n mobility variables (m_i) are written as

$$PMOB(i) = w_1 \times m_1 + \cdots + w_n \times m_n \qquad (8\text{-}1)$$

and the set of principal components [$PCON(i)$] of a set of k concentration statistics (c_i) as

$$PCON(i) = r_1 \times c_1 + \cdots + r_k \times c_k, \qquad (8\text{-}2)$$

where w_i, $i = 1, \ldots, n$ and r_i, $i = 1, \ldots, k$ are the weights (the eigenvectors) that sum to 1 and are applied to the original variables to create the new variables – the components.

The first principal component of each set is the linear combination of the original variables that maximally discriminates – has the largest variance – among the industries in the sample. Each succeeding component accounts for the largest sample variance possible, subject to the constraint that it be uncorrelated with previous ones.

The principal-component procedure is suited to analysing a situation in which a number of different but related measures of a phenomenon exist and for which a reduction in the dimensionality of the data set is required. Principal-component analysis will determine how much independence there is in a data set. It also measures the ability of each of the independent components to discriminate, since the variance of a component is a measure of the extent to which industries differ in their score on that component. Maximal power to discriminate should not be confused, however, with maximal explanatory power. The linear combination of a set of concentration or mobility variables that maximizes differentiation may not be the same as the linear combination that correlates most highly with a criterion such as market performance.

Principal-component analysis of concentration and mobility. There are a large number of indices that can be chosen for any study involving concentration. Some of these indices, like the four-firm concentration ratio, use only a select number of firms; others, like the Herfindahl index, use information on all firms. The relevance of some of these indices can be related to specific assumptions about behavioral relationships among oligopolists (Cowling and Waterson, 1976; Dansby and Willig, 1979); or it can be derived from an axiomatic approach like that adopted by Hannah and Kay (1977).

Because there is no consensus on the most desirable index, a large number of concentration statistics were calculated for the years 1970 and 1979 for 167 four-digit Canadian manufacturing industries. Some were chosen from the group known as comprehensive statistics – those that combine the dimensions of firm numbers and firm-size inequality in different ways. They include such indices as the Herfindahl, the entropy, the Hall–Tideman, the Horvath, the Hannah and Kay, and the top-four-firm-market-share index. Others were chosen from secondary measures that focus on single characteristics of the firm-size distribution. The Gini coefficient or the variance of the log of firm size captures inequality. So too do measures that use numbers-equivalent estimates of the number of firms – the inverse of the Herfindahl index or the Hannah and Kay numbers-equivalent divided by the actual number of firms in the industry. The marginal-concentration ratio or the size of the firms from positions five to eight relative to the largest four firms captures the extent to which competition from a secondary grouping may be important.

Preliminary investigation revealed that many of the major comprehensive concentration measures were capturing the same dimension.[2] This is surprising, since so much effort has been devoted to generating additional measures

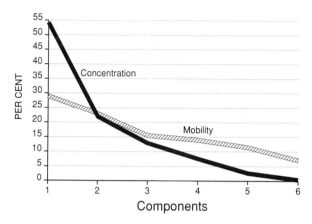

Figure 8-1. The relative importance of the principal components of concentration and mobility statistics.

of concentration, but it accords with the findings of Aaronovitch and Sawyer (1975) and Vanlommel, de Brabander, and Liebaers (1977). The various comprehensive measures basically possess the same information. Therefore, only a subset of the available concentration measures was analysed here.[3] It includes the four-firm concentration ratio (CR4), the Herfindahl index (HF), the marginal-concentration ratio of the second group of four firms (MCR8), the size of the second group of four relative to the first four (REL84), the relative-redundancy ratio based on the entropy index (RELRED), the relative-firm-numbers ratio using the Hannah and Kay numbers-equivalent (RELNUM),[4] and the variance of the logarithm of firm size (VARS).[5]

Six mobility measures were used: market-share turnover arising from entry and exit (TURNE); that arising from continuing-firm growth and decline (TURNC); that arising from entry through acquisition and exit through divestiture (TURNM); the variability in rank change for firms in an industry (RANK);[6] the variance in growth rates of continuing firms (GROW); and the coefficient that captures the regression of market share toward the mean (REGSH). All mobility statistics were calculated by comparing the position of manufacturing firms in 1970 and 1979.[7] The concentration and mobility variables are defined in Appendix B.

Since a principal-component analysis generates new variables – the components – in decreasing order of importance, the extent to which a small number of components dominate the others can be used to evaluate how many important independent dimensions exist. The importance of each of the principal components for both the concentration and mobility variables is presented in Table 8-1 and graphed in Figure 8-1, where importance is defined in terms of the proportion of total sample variability accounted for by each.[8] When the concentration or mobility variables are highly correlated one with another, the first principal component of each set of variables will account for most of the sample variability and will dominate the other components.

The first component is much more important for the concentration statistics than for the mobility statistics. The former accounts for 54 per cent of total sample variance; the latter accounts for 29 per cent. The rate of decline in importance of the succeeding components is greater as well for the concentration principal components. Relatively few important orthogonal components are therefore captured in the various concentration statistics. The mobility variables, by way of contrast, offer a more diverse set of characteristics.

The eigenvectors derived from the principal-component analysis are also presented in Table 8-1 – PCON(i), the concentration components, and PMOB(i), the mobility components. The eigenvectors are the weights (w_i and r_i in equations 8-1 and 8-2) that, when applied to the original variables, yield the principal components. A high eigenvector value for a particular mobility or concentration component indicates that a variable receives a heavy weight in this component. The various components can be interpreted in terms of the original variables by identifying the variables with the highest weights per component.

The first concentration component is equally weighted on both the discrete and summary measures (CR4, HF), the relative measures (RELRED, REL84), and to a lesser extent, the variance in firm size (VARS). This is the general component where high concentration and inequality matter. That the discrete measure CR4 is as important as the Herfindahl index, which uses all firms' market shares, confirms the findings of Aaronovitch and Sawyer (1975) and Vanlommel, de Brabander, and Liebaers (1977) that the CR4 measure does as well – that is, is weighted as heavily – as more elaborate but less accessible measures. This accords with the finding of many structure-performance studies that, because of the high inter-industry zero-order correlations among the standard concentration measures, the choice of concentration measure does not matter. The second concentration component represents situations where the market shares of the top four and of the next four firms (MCR8) are large, and where the relative-numbers variable (RELNUM) is large – that is, where there is no tail of small firms. The third component represents situations where the second foursome (MCR8) is important and where there is a tail of small firms. The fourth component primarily weights inequality as measured by VARS.

These results indicate that there is more than one dimension to market structure. Though the most commonly used concentration statistics, such as the four-firm concentration ratio and the Herfindahl index, are designed to

Table 8-1. *Principal-component analysis performed on concentration and mobility variables separately, 1970–79[a]*

				Eigenvector			
Concentration variable[b]	PCON1	PCON2	PCON3	PCON4	PCON5	PCON6	PCON7
CR4	-0.4304	0.4171	0.0307	-0.1200	-0.1697	0.6607	0.4001
HF	-0.4451	0.3158	-0.1259	-0.0562	0.6124	-0.4920	0.2570
MCR8	0.1521	0.4644	0.7794	-0.2081	-0.1779	-0.2723	-0.0683
REL84	0.4565	-0.0292	0.3042	0.2705	0.6542	0.3873	0.2172
RELNUM	0.1917	0.6723	-0.3570	0.2902	0.0560	0.1073	-0.5337
VARS	-0.3710	-0.0809	0.2770	0.8597	-0.1744	-0.0976	0.0091
RELRED	0.4591	0.2264	-0.2811	0.2066	-0.3210	-0.2760	0.6611
Proportion of total sample variability accounted for	54.3	22.0	12.9	7.6	2.7	0.4	0.2

				Eigenvector		
Mobility variable[c]	PMOB1	PMOB2	PMOB3	PMOB4	PMOB5	PMOB6
TURNE	0.6499	-0.0873	-0.0701	0.1024	0.1508	0.7292
TURNC	0.0797	0.6583	0.0194	0.2338	-0.7003	0.1217
TURNM	-0.2088	0.4586	-0.6819	0.2333	0.4741	0.0447
GROW	0.2788	0.4315	0.0069	-0.8398	0.1387	-0.1069
REGSH	-0.3746	0.3503	0.6744	0.0818	0.3931	0.3478
RANK	0.5564	0.1994	0.2738	0.4104	0.2972	-0.5648
Proportion of total sample variability accounted for	29.0	23.0	15.5	13.9	11.5	7.1

[a] The sample consisted of 166 four-digit industries.
[b] Measured for 1979. These terms are defined in the text.
[c] Measured for 1970–79. These terms are defined in the text.

capture both the number-of-firms dimension and the inequality dimension, they dominate but do not exhaust all the dimensions of the concentration data. The ancillary components embody the importance of a second group of firms. In the past these measures have been discounted, partly because there is always the danger that they capture the same phenomenon as the dominant measures. That these alternative measures are included as separate components, orthogonal to the first, demonstrates that they represent a different dimension of market structure.

In contrast with the concentration components, the mobility components are not dominated by the first principal component. The first principal component of the concentration statistics accounted for 54 per cent of total sample variability; that of the mobility statistics accounted for only 29 per cent of total sample variability. The mobility components are also easier to interpret, since there are a small number of dominant variables in each component. The first mobility component reflects turnover that arises from entry and exit (TURNE) and change in the rank of continuing firms (RANK). The second component reflects turnover in the continuing sector (TURNC) and merger turnover (TURNM). The third component reflects merger turnover (TURNM) and regression to the mean (REGSH). The fourth captures variability in growth rates (GROW). The fifth represents turnover in the continuing sector (TURNC).

This is a rich set of characteristics describing the change that is taking place within industries. It confirms the complexity of the competitive process. The conventional tendency to summarize these aspects with single statistics such as the concentration ratio leaves the impression that the intensity of competition is unidimensional or that the various characteristics that describe the outcome of the competitive process must be closely correlated across industries – that is, industries where there is greenfield entry are also those where the market shares and the relative ranks of incumbents are changing. The orthogonality of these different dimensions demonstrates this is not the case.

Principal-component analysis of a combined data set of concentration and mobility statistics. Whether the mobility and concentration measures capture different dimensions of the same phenomenon can be determined by performing a principal-component analysis jointly on both and by investigating the pattern of interdependence among the original components, noting which of the original concentration and mobility components appear together in the combined set. The eigenvectors associated with this exercise are presented in Table 8-2 – PRIN1 to PRIN13. The mobility measures are not completely subsumed into the concentration components. The only exception is the first component (PRIN1) of the combined set that includes both PCON1 (the main

Table 8-2. *Principal-component analysis, performed on concentration and mobility variables together, 1970–79*[a]

Variable	Eigenvector						
	PRIN1	PRIN2	PRIN3	PRIN4	PRIN5	PRIN6	PRIN7
CR4[b]	-0.4209	0.2139	-0.0848	0.0724	0.1583	0.1855	0.0650
HF	-0.4122	0.0846	-0.1503	-0.0026	0.1962	0.2601	0.1251
MCR8	0.0790	0.5083	0.2120	0.4402	-0.1669	-0.1204	-0.0396
REL84	0.4075	0.1283	0.1024	0.1264	-0.2328	-0.1058	0.1234
RELNUM	0.1303	0.5490	-0.2865	-0.1336	0.2296	0.3886	0.1684
VARS	-0.3306	-0.1417	0.1057	0.0990	-0.1940	0.1553	0.2518
RELRED	0.3978	0.2861	-0.1240	-0.1444	0.0818	0.1202	0.0188
TURNE	0.3095	-0.1988	-0.2710	0.2310	0.2173	0.1029	0.2218
TURNC	0.1094	-0.0208	0.4855	-0.2577	0.4522	0.2254	-0.5370
TURNM	-0.0809	0.1386	0.4331	0.2033	0.5478	-0.3976	0.4274
GROW	0.1312	-0.1797	0.3977	0.4075	-0.1382	0.6745	0.1074
REGSH	-0.0459	0.2081	0.3887	-0.5978	-0.3643	0.0622	0.3669
RANK	0.2499	-0.3662	-0.0122	-0.2280	0.2320	0.0658	0.4525
Proportion of total sample variability accounted for	34.5	14.4	11.6	8.1	7.8	5.9	5.4

Table 8-2. (*cont.*)

			Eigenvector			
Variable	PRIN8	PRIN9	PRIN10	PRIN11	PRIN12	PRIN13
CR4	0.1100	-0.1999	-0.0463	-0.2217	0.6560	0.4090
HF	0.1106	-0.2054	0.0261	0.5680	-0.4880	0.2504
MCR8	0.4667	-0.3054	-0.0885	-0.2359	-0.2700	-0.0727
REL84	0.2254	0.1679	-0.0043	0.6563	0.3872	-0.2253
RELNUM	-0.0235	0.2132	-0.0610	0.0613	0.1169	-0.5315
VARS	0.4145	0.7049	0.1423	-0.1647	-0.0913	0.0092
RELRED	-0.1663	0.2749	-0.0800	-0.2783	-0.2908	-0.6561
TURNE	0.1570	-0.1968	0.7438	-0.1172	0.0157	0.0166
TURNC	0.3273	0.0698	0.1594	0.0527	0.0389	0.0082
TURNM	-0.2824	0.1476	0.0379	0.0364	-0.0116	-0.0109
GROW	-0.3424	-0.0913	-0.1222	-0.0071	0.0058	-0.0098
REGSH	-0.0514	-0.2496	0.3265	-0.0560	-0.0131	0.0043
RANK	0.4190	-0.2061	-0.5073	-0.1116	-0.0105	-0.0195
Proportion of total sample variability accounted for	4.1	3.7	2.8	1.3	0.2	0.1

[a] The sample consisted of 166 four-digit industries.
[b] For variable definitions, see text.

concentration component) and PMOB1 (the entry and exit component) as presented in Table 8-1. Concentration and turnover from entry and exit are closely related.

The remaining components of the combined data are basically one of the original components of either the concentration or mobility data, with a few variables from the other set added. The combined principal components (PRIN2–7) are, in order, PCON2, PMOB2, PCON3, PMOB3, PMOB4, and PMOB5 from Table 8-1. Where new variables are added to one of the original components, the additional information corroborates or extends, in a sensible manner, the original interpretation placed on the component. For example, the continuing-firm turnover and merger-turnover component of the mobility data PMOB2, is combined with MCR8 in the third component when the concentration and mobility measures are merged together for the analysis. Having a second tier of large firms (firms 5–8), then, is an important structural attribute of those situations where continuing-firm turnover is large. The second-tier concentration component, PCON3, weighting primarily MCR8, is combined in the fourth joint component with the mobility variables GROW and REGSH. Larger variance in growth rates associated with regression to the mean is accompanied by a larger market share for the second foursome.

This confirms that the primary relationship between structure and mobility can be found in the inverse relationship between concentration and the extent of entry and exit. The other important dimensions of mobility are not closely related with the main or primary dimension of concentration. Rather, they are related to structural measures that have received a secondary emphasis in the literature – measures that capture the importance of a second tier of firms.

The fact that concentration and mobility generally have separate dimensions confirms the existence of enough cross-sectional differences in the concentration and mobility measures to warrant the use of both for exercises that attempt to classify industries on the basis of potential and actual competitiveness.

The link between concentration and mobility measures
Canonical-correlation analysis. Concentration and mobility statistics are, on the whole, sufficiently different from each other that both are needed to describe structure. It would, however, be incorrect to claim that there is no relationship between the two. This section more directly investigates the nature of these relationships.

Principal-component analysis is designed to establish the dimensionality of the data set, but it creates variables for each data set that may or may not be related across the sets. It is therefore not as well suited for describing the relationships between sets; these have to be inferred from the weights attached to the variables that make up the components in each set.

An alternative way to reduce the dimensionality in both the concentration and mobility statistics and to investigate the relationship between the two is to perform a canonical-correlation analysis. When performed on the concentration and mobility statistics, canonical-correlation analysis finds weights for each of the concentration statistics and then for each of the mobility statistics that create pairs of new variables (the canonical correlates) – one associated with each data set, CANCON and CANMOB. These variables are correlated with themselves, but not with other pairs of correlates. The canonical correlates [CANMOB(i)] of a set of n mobility variables (m_i) are written as

$$CANMOB(i) = y_1 \times m_1 + \cdots + y_n \times m_n. \tag{8-3}$$

The canonical correlates [CANCON(i)] of a set of k concentration statistics (c_i) are written as

$$CANCON(i) = z_1 \times c_1 + \cdots + z_k \times c_k, \tag{8-4}$$

where y_i, $i = 1, \ldots, n$, and z_i, $i = 1, \ldots, k$ are the weights applied to the original variables to create the new variables – the correlates. The correlations between corresponding pairs of the canonical variables form a decreasing sequence – that is, the first canonical variable has the highest correlation, the second has the second highest.

Canonical-correlation analysis is better able to depict the relationships across data sets than is principal-component analysis, but is less able to define the dimensionality within each data set. An additional advantage of canonical-correlation analysis is that significance tests are available to judge whether the nth and succeeding pairs are significantly related. When they are not, the relationships can be disregarded.

Applying canonical-correlation analysis. The canonical-correlation analysis was performed twice – first on the principal components that were generated from each of the concentration and mobility data sets, and then on the original variables.

When canonical-correlation analysis was performed on the principal components of each data set (see Table 8-3), three pairs of canonical variables were produced where the correlation between each pair [CANMOB(i), CANCON(i)] is significantly different from zero. The first set (CANMOB1, CANCON1) primarily links PCON1 to PMOB1 and inversely relates the principal dimension of concentration to the entry component. Once more, this emphasizes the importance of the connection between industry structure and entry. The second set primarily relates PCON2 and PMOB6. The third set links PCON3 and PMOB4, or MCR8 (the importance of the second foursome) to GROW (the variance in growth rates of continuing firms).

It should be noted that while some linkages between the principal components of the concentration and mobility statistics do exist, only in the case of

Table 8-3. *Correlations between canonical variables and the concentration and mobility components, 1970–79*[a]

	Canonical variable					
Concentration component[b]	CANCON1	CANCON2	CANCON3	CANCON4	CANCON5	CANCON6
PCON1	.7979	.3791	.2984	.2264	.1540	.2236
PCON2	-.4468	.6739	-.1108	.4042	.1907	.1607
PCON3	-.2952	-.1180	.8549	.3237	-.0488	-.2184
PCON4	.0758	-.2576	-.0302	.3721	-.6743	.4282
PCON5	.2521	-.1688	-.2478	.4697	.0962	-.7152
PCON6	-.0969	-.2720	-.2935	.5712	-.2282	.2559
PCON7	.0045	-.4703	.1420	-.0348	.6398	.3434

	Canonical variable					
Mobility component[c]	CANMOB1	CANMOB2	CANMOB3	CANMOB4	CANMOB5	CANMOB6
PMOB1	.9051	-.0842	.0395	-.1135	.1099	-.3835
PMOB2	.1574	-.0949	.7254	-.1965	.2290	.5907
PMOB3	.3332	-.1375	-.2347	-.2299	-.6980	.5243
PMOB4	.1572	.2062	-.6179	-.2062	.5314	.4754
PMOB5	.0342	-.4224	-.0131	.8074	.4073	.0498
PMOB6	.1380	.8626	.1876	.4486	-.0030	.0219

[a] The sample consisted of 166 four-digit industries.
[b] Based on concentration measures for 1979. These terms are defined in the text.
[c] Based on turnover measures for 1970–79. These terms are defined in the text.

Table 8-4. *Correlations between canonical variables and the concentration and mobility variables, 1970–79[a]*

	Canonical variable					
Concentration variable[b]	V1	V2	V3	V4	V5	V6
CR4	−.9452	−.0064	−.2891	.0214	.0713	−.0538
HF	−.7591	.0793	−.4409	−.0186	−.0028	−.3255
MCR8	−.2631	−.4773	.6976	.4194	.1978	−.0284
REL84	.7205	−.1521	.4245	.5233	.0406	.0366
RELNUM	.0516	−.7056	−.2982	.4132	.0596	.3512
VARS	−.5824	.5175	.0252	.0691	−.5763	.0825
RELRED	.6517	−.5228	.0618	.1897	.1235	.4794

	Canonical variable					
Mobility variable[c]	W1	W2	W3	W4	W5	W6
TURNE	.8215	−.3236	.0050	.2025	.2172	−.3636
TURNC	.2478	−.2731	.4516	−.6374	.0523	.5010
TURNM	−.3325	.0346	.4030	.0609	.8257	.2008
GROW	.2884	.3471	.8407	.0801	−.2089	−.1986
REGSH	−.1113	.0136	.1186	.4744	−.2420	.8305
RANK	.8054	.4649	−.1671	−.1121	.2509	.1782

[a] The sample consisted of 166 four-digit industries.
[b] Measured for 1979. These terms are defined in the text.
[c] Measured for 1970–79. These terms are defined in the text.

the first canonical correlate are the most important components linked. This confirms that the two sets generally contain different dimensions.

While using the principal components as input into the canonical-correlation analysis serves to illustrate how the separate orthogonal dimensions within each of the two data sets are related across sets, the relationship between the original variables has to be inferred indirectly when working at the level of the principal components. These inferences may miss links that can only be ascertained after following a complex path that sometimes crosses two or more principal components.

To overcome this problem, the canonical technique was also applied directly to the underlying variables. Once more, three significant sets of canonical variables were generated; the correlation coefficients between each of the canonical variables [V(i), W(i)] and the original variables in the two data sets are presented in Table 8-4. The first set of canonical variables (V1, W1) inversely relates the most popular concentration indices (CR4 and HF) as well as several others (VARS, MCR8) to turnover from greenfield entry and closedown exit (TURNE) and rank change (RANK). The second set (V2, W2) relates the secondary concentration measures (MCR8, RELNUM) to entry (TURNE), continuing-firm turnover (TURNC), variability of growth rates (GROW), and rank change (RANK). The third set (V3, W3) relates marginal concentration (MCR8) to continuing-firm turnover, turnover from merger entry and exit, and variance in growth rates – TURNC, TURNM, and GROW.

These results confirm the dichotomy that emerged in the principal-component analysis between the traditional measures of concentration and the tertiary measures that focus on the importance of a second tier of firms. The most commonly used measures of concentration are related closely to only two of several equally important mobility measures – greenfield entry and closedown exit and the amount of rank change in the continuing-firm population. The other dimensions of mobility are related to the secondary measures of concentration that capture the number and importance of firms outside the top four. The canonical-correlation analysis shows that various measures of the importance of a secondary group of firms (MCR8, RELNUM) are related to internal conditions of competition – the extent to which there is continuing-firm turnover (TURNC) and variability in growth rates (GROW).

The results of the principal-component and canonical-correlation analyses suggest that concentration and mobility are related in the way that some stochastic-growth models would suggest. The most important dimension of concentration is negatively related to the entry and exit dimension of mobility. This is the relationship that emerges from the model proposed by Simon and Bonini. Not only does this suggest that at least some aspects of the outside of the box can be related to the dynamics of the competitive process, but it strongly points to entry as the most important correlate of structure.

On the inside looking out: the influence of mobility on concentration

The questions that have been posed to this point are in keeping with the traditional approach, with its emphasis on the causal relationship flowing from structure to intensity of competition. There is another approach that is followed here. Rather than asking whether concentration serves to describe the intensity of competition, this chapter asks how the nature of turnover affects concentration.

The determinants of concentration: a framework

A number of theories have been proposed to explain the level of concentration in an industry. They can be divided into two groups. One sees concentration as a reflection of production characteristics such as entry barriers and scale and scope economies. A variant of this theory has been dubbed the technological explanation, in which concentration is a function of the minimum-efficient-sized plant (Davies and Lyons, 1982). This explanation does not always provide a point estimate of the level of concentration, but sometimes gives a lower bound for it instead. In the case of the technological explanation using plant-scale economies, the lower bound for CR4 is four times the ratio of the minimum-efficient-sized plant divided by market size.

The second type of explanation models the workings of the competitive process by the use of stochastic processes. It predicts that the degree of concentration should be a function of the amount of mobility in an industry. One variant starts with a version of Gibrat's law, or the law of proportionate effect (LPE), which states that all firms, irrespective of their size, have the same probability of growing or declining. The application of this law to a given population of firms results in the prediction that inequality in firm size should constantly increase.

Since concentration does not appear to be trending upward without limit, various mechanisms have been added to the stochastic-growth model so that it does not result in ever-increasing levels of concentration. For example, Prais (1976: 34–39) relies on the concept of a regression to the mean in firm size to offset the LPE. Simon and Bonini (1958) take another approach. In their model, the LPE applies only to firms above minimum efficient size (MES), where it is assumed that costs are constant. The particular mechanism that prevents ever-increasing concentration is entry just above MES. The greater the degree of entry, the lower is the equilibrium level of concentration.

These stochastic explanations of the causes of concentration are mechanistic. But they can be made more purposive using underlying behavioral and technical characteristics of markets. For example, low turnover due to entry and exit can in turn be related to entry barriers. Or the variance of firm-growth rates can be associated with the underlying technological regime. The technological environment sometimes permits new firms to take advantage of innovations and move ahead of incumbents in a short period of time (Nelson and Winter, 1978). This is just one example of situations where entry barriers associated with firm-appropriable successes increase the variability of firm "draws", increase the variability of firm-growth rates and, thus, ultimately the degree of concentration in an industry. These characteristics have often been referred to as being research and development related, but they encompass a broader range of barriers that permit unusual successes dependent upon the mastery of expertise either in the innovation and technology areas, in marketing, or in organizational forms.

Empirical studies of the determinants of turnover stress underlying causes related to the technological characteristics of industries. Gort and Klepper (1982) in their study of the diffusion of 48 new product innovations note that the structure of markets at any point in time is shaped by a set of discrete events such as technical change that stimulates entry. Mansfield's (1983) study of the extent to which technological changes were associated with scale-augmenting or concentration-decreasing effects finds that product innovation often decreased concentration because innovators were entrants and relatively small firms.

The issue of the underlying causes of turnover is important and will be investigated in later chapters. Here we investigate the extent to which concentration depends just on technical conditions such as scale economies or also is a function of mobility characteristics as the stochastic literature hypothesizes.

The determinants of concentration: the evidence

In the preceding sections, clear evidence of the empirical relationship between mobility and structure emerged. This section examines whether this relationship adds anything to the explanation of concentration that technical considerations do not.

Two approaches can be taken in choosing the form of equation with which to estimate the determinants of concentration. On the one hand, a tight model can be formulated and tested. On the other hand, a loose structure can be used. The advantage of the tight model is that it is elegant; the disadvantage is that reality has to be so simplified that the model cannot be expected to fit exactly.

The simplest model is Simon and Bonini's. If the growth and decline of all firms above a certain minimum size follow the law of proportionate effect and new firms are born into the smallest size-class at a constant rate, then the firm-size distribution will be skewed and its upper tail can be approximated by a Pareto distribution with parameter r, where

$$r = 1/(1 - a), \tag{8-5}$$
$$a = G_n/G, \tag{8-6}$$

and G_n is the part of net growth G due to new firms.

This expression provides a direct and testable hypothesis of the relationship between a parameter that measures the size distribution and the rate of entry.

Simon and Bonini (1958) test this relationship for the United States by calculating r from the firm-size distribution and a from entry data, and find that the two-point estimates were quite similar. Davies and Lyons (1982) indirectly test this relationship for the United Kingdom by transforming it into one between the four-firm concentration ratio and several other variables – the Pareto parameter r, the ratio of the amount of suboptimal capacity, and others. They also report evidence suggesting that Simon and Bonini's model has some validity.

The relationship was tested directly for the Canadian manufacturing sector. An estimate of a was obtained by measuring the size of all firms that entered between 1970 and 1979 that were still extant in 1979 and dividing this plant size by industry growth between 1970 and 1979. The parameter r was estimated from the firm-size distribution. The mean size of all plants above the plant size that just accounts for 50 per cent of employment was calculated. Then r was estimated by dividing the estimate of the top 50 per cent by the plant size that just accounts for 50 per cent of employment. This is equal to $a/(a - 1)$ (Davies, 1980a, 1980b). The median value of the Pareto parameter was 1.69. The median value of the right side of equation 8-5, based on entrants' market share, was 1.20.[9] These are significantly different from one another. Moreover, the correlation between the two, across 167 industries, was only .004 and insignificant.

The failure of Simon and Bonini's model, as it is specified here, is to be expected. The model was not meant to apply everywhere. In the first place, not all Canadian industries satisfy Gibrat's law. In some, there is a very significant regression to the mean. Second, the particular variant of the model that results in equation 8-5 was derived for the situation where there is positive growth in the economy. Only 80 per cent of Canadian manufacturing industries at the four-digit SIC level had positive growth in real output in the 1970s.

Given the variety of competitive conditions that exist in an industry, it is unlikely that any single model can be found that applies across all industries and is empirically tractable. Therefore, a technique was adopted that is more in keeping with the existing literature on the causes of concentration. Correlates of concentration were examined using a set of predetermined instruments that, a priori, should affect concentration. To this end, concentration was regressed on a number of the mobility statistics and a set of variables that represent the degree to which scale economies at the firm and plant level might influence the level of concentration, that is,

$$\text{Concentration} = f(\text{Mobility, Scale}). \tag{8-7}$$

In this analysis, the four-firm concentration ratio was used as the dependent variable since it is heavily weighted in both of the first two principal components of market structure. It is measured for 1979. At issue is the extent to which it is explained by technical factors in 1979 or by mobility characteristics measured over the preceding 10 years. The mobility variables used in the principal-component and canonical-correlation analyses were employed as regressors. Turnover due to mergers was also included in the list of mobility variables.[10]

Many analyses of the determinants of concentration have suffered from important conceptual and measurement problems. As Caves et al. (1980: 41–43) point out, the four-firm concentration ratio is just the product of three terms: the ratio of four divided by the number of firms; the ratio of the average plant size of the four largest firms to the industry average; and the multi-plant activity of the four largest firms relative to industry average multi-plant ownership. If CR4 is regressed on variables that are proxies for these three terms, the resulting relationship will be close to an identity. This problem is not solved by using only one of the proxies, since the regression coefficient on this variable will then represent only a weighted average value of the omitted variables. Nevertheless, this is what a large number of studies of the determinants of concentration have done.[11]

The scale variable that is commonly used involves an estimate of the minimum-efficient-plant size. Typically this is not measured by some best-practice engineering estimate, but comes from the size distribution of plants. One such widely used proxy is the average size of the larger plants (those accounting for 50 per cent of industry employment) divided by market size. Yet this is likely to be identical or very closely related to one of the three terms that make up the concentration identity. In the Canadian situation, this proxy is closely related to the average size of the plants of the four largest firms. For 1979 the correlation at the four-digit level between these two was .9862. Thus, using this term is equivalent to using a variable that is part of the concentration identity. CR4 will equal four times this scale proxy times the number of plants of each of the four largest firms, and the coefficient attached to this variable, when it is regressed on concentration, is just a weighted average of the number of plants owned by the four largest firms. Davies (1980b: 287) observes that such MES proxies are "better interpreted as measures of concentration". Finding a close relationship between CR4 and this proxy for scale economies does not provide evidence of the importance of scale economies.

Davies and Lyons (1982) point out another problem with using the average size of plants accounting for the top 50 per cent of sales divided by market size to proxy scale effects. When the plant-size distribution is Pareto, this proxy variable reduces to a function of the coefficient characterizing the Pareto distribution. Thus, the proxy for scale is just a measure of inequality. Finding a regression relationship between CR4 and this variable only confirms that inequality and concentration measures are related – as the principal-component and the canonical-correlation analyses reveal. It does not demonstrate the extent of the connection between concentration and scale effects.

Independent evidence of the extent of scale economies is required. It was obtained here from four different statistics. The first, SCALE, is an estimate of the extent of scale economies at the plant level that was derived from the estimate of a production function using plant-level data for each of the 167 manufacturing industries.[12] The second, BMES, is an estimate of the branching minimum-efficient-plant size divided by market size. The problems with an MES estimate that is based on the average size of larger plants are overcome by directly estimating the minimum-efficient-plant size. In order to do so, Lyons' (1980) method, which uses information on the size at which firms begin to build a second plant to infer the size at which plant economies are exhausted, is employed.[13] The third is CDR, a variable that measures the cost disadvantage of small plants.[14] It is the ratio of value-added per worker in small plants relative to large plants. Finally, the capital–labour ratio, KL,[15] is employed as a proxy for the extent to which scale economies are likely to be important.

Several variables that proxy the determinants of multi-plant operations, and therefore of firm economies, were also included. These were advertising (ADV) and research and development (RD).[16]

The different variables used for scale effects were sufficiently correlated that they all appear to be capturing a similar phenomenon. Therefore, the regression was performed in two steps. In the first stage, all variables were included. In the second, a principal-component analysis was performed separately on the scale variables and on the mobility variables, and the resulting principal components from each set were then used as regressors for CR4.

When all variables are included in their original form, both mobility and scale variables are significant, as the estimates in column I in Table 8-5 indicate. High mobility from entry and exit (TURNE), continuing-firm turnover (TURNC), and rank change (RANK) are all associated with lower concentration. While all of the plant-scale effects have positive and significant correlations with CR4, only BMES and the capital–labour ratio (KL) are significant when all scale variables are included together in the regression. This is the result of multicollinearity between the scale variables.

In order to overcome this problem, principal components for each of the mobility and scale variables were generated [PMOB(i) and PSCL(i), respectively] and then used in the regression. The components are presented in Table 8-6 and the regression coefficients in Table 8-7. The regression results using the principal components (column I) demonstrate that more than two dimensions of scale matter. The second, third, fourth, and fifth components of the plant-scale coefficients are all significant; SCALE and CDR weigh heavily in these components, as do BMES and KL. Moreover, RD is also important.

The regression with all the variables included accounts for about 64 per cent of the variation in the values of the four-firm concentration ratio across the 162-industry sample used. This is a substantially better fit than other

Table 8-5. *Determinants of concentration, measured as CR4 for 1979, coefficients from regression analysis*[a]

Independent variable[b]	I OLS[c]	II TSLS[d]
Intercept	0.3382	0.5571
	(3.75)*	(3.59)*
TURNE	−0.8005	−1.6189
	(−6.36)*	(−3.94)*
TURNC	−0.1881	−0.2750
	(−1.12)	(−1.27)
GROW	−0.0262	−0.0252
	(−1.38)	(−1.27)
RANK	−0.0038	0.0001
	(−1.28)	(0.15)
REGSH	0.1214	0.0917
	(2.08)**	(0.99)
SCALE	0.0092	0.0272
	(0.20)	(0.47)
BMES	2.543	2.603
	(9.61)*	(5.05)*
CDR	52.96	55.76
	(1.14)	(0.92)*
KL	0.0011	0.0009
	(3.94)*	(2.64)*
ADV	0.2006	−0.8447
	(0.26)	(0.41)
RD	−6.943	−94.68
	(−0.09)	(−0.80)
R^2	.64	.44
F-ratio	27.13*	12.05*

Note: Numbers in parentheses are *t* statistics.
[a] The sample consisted of 162 four-digit industries.
[b] See text for variable definitions.
[c] OLS denotes ordinary least squares.
[d] TSLS denotes two-stage least squares.
* Significantly different from zero at 1 per cent level.
** Significantly different from zero at 5 per cent level.

attempts to explain the cross-sectional variation in Canadian concentration that rely on scale-related measures alone.[17] The mobility and the scale variables as a group were about equally important in this regression. Omitting all of the mobility or all of the scale variables reduced the coefficient of determination to 44 and 31 per cent, respectively.

While this suggests that both mobility and scale effects are important, it is

Table 8-6. *Principal-component analysis performed on scale and mobility variables separately*[a]

Scale variable[b]	Eigenvector					
	PSCL1	PSCL2	PSCL3	PSCL4	PSCL5	PSCL6
SCALE	0.5527	−0.0503	−0.4595	0.2816	−0.3593	0.5219
BMES	0.1608	0.5092	−0.4542	−0.4816	0.5173	0.0949
CDR	0.6680	−0.2477	−0.0334	0.0862	0.2088	−0.6635
KL	0.3928	0.0277	0.7011	−0.0114	0.3702	0.4649
ADV	−0.1075	0.5029	−0.0274	0.8034	0.2809	−0.1018
RD	0.2376	0.6505	0.2986	−0.1891	−0.5862	−0.2276
Proportion of total sample variability accounted for	24.5	20.6	19.2	15.8	11.2	8.7

Mobility variable[c]	Eigenvector				
	PMOB1	PMOB2	PMOB3	PMOB4	PMOB5
TURNE	0.6404	−0.2169	0.1022	0.0975	0.7231
TURNC	0.1655	0.6658	0.0999	−0.7080	0.1344
GROW	0.3296	0.4242	−0.7609	0.3488	−0.1041
RANK	0.5769	0.1428	0.5147	−0.2332	−0.5722
REGSH	−0.3480	0.5562	0.3684	0.5596	0.3474
Proportion of total sample variability accounted for	34.2	25.3	16.9	15.0	8.5

[a] The sample consisted of 166 four-digit industries.
[b] Measured for 1979. These terms are defined in the text.
[c] Measured for 1970–79. These terms are defined in the text.

not conclusive; for the stochastic theories of market structure may have as their foundation explanations of differences in turnover that are related to technical characteristics of an industry. For instance, the existence of scale economies may lead to considerable turnover as some firms find the strategy that allows them to exploit these economies, move down the cost curve, and gain market share while the less successful fall further and further behind. Or entry barriers related to economies of scale may raise concentration by precluding turnover due to entry or exit. If this explanation of the relationship between turnover and scale is correct, some of the explanatory power of the mobility statistics really lies in the scale effects. In order to test this, the principal components were calculated for the mobility and scale variables

Table 8-7. *Determinants of concentration, measured as CR4 for 1979, coefficients from regression analysis*[a]

Independent variable[b]	I	Independent variable[b]	II
Intercept	0.5005	Intercept	0.5021
	(45.48)*		45.47*
PMOB1	−0.1134	PRIN1	0.1672
	(−9.39)*		(15.09)*
PMOB2	0.0182	PRIN2	0.0186
	(1.60)		(1.68)
PMOB3	0.0015	PRIN3	−0.0380
	(0.14)		(−3.43)*
PMOB4	0.0046	PRIN4	0.0174
	(0.40)		(1.58)
PMOB5	−0.0321	PRIN5	−0.0446
	(−2.72)*		(−4.02)*
PSCL1	0.0594	PRIN6	0.0170
	(5.02)*		(1.533)
PSCL2	0.0667	PRIN7	−0.0091
	(5.73)*		(−0.826)
PSCL3	−0.0246	PRIN8	−0.0088
	(2.15)**		(−0.792)
PSCL4	−0.0527	PRIN9	0.0038
	(−4.65)*		(3.47)*
PSCL5	0.0687	PRIN10	0.0035
	(5.90)*		(0.32)
PSCL6	0.0185	PRIN11	−0.0513
	(1.64)***		(−4.63)*
R^2	.6410	—	.6410
F-ratio	27.13	—	27.13

Note: Numbers in parentheses are t statistics.
[a] The sample consisted of 162 four-digit industries.
[b] See text for variable definitions.
* Significantly different from zero at 1 per cent level.
** Significantly different from zero at 5 per cent level.
***Significantly different from zero at 10 per cent level.

together (Table 8-8) and the components were used as regressors (Table 8-7, column II).

There was very little overlap between the components of the original two sets. On the whole, the components that were visible by themselves are still separate components of the combined set.[18] The two explanations of concentration are complementary rather than competing hypotheses. That is not to say there are no links between them. The first joint component in Table

Table 8-8. *Principal-component analysis performed on scale and mobility variables together*[a]

| | Eigenvector | | | | | |
Variable	PRIN1	PRIN2	PRIN3	PRIN4	PRIN5	PRIN6
TURNE[b]	−0.5035	−0.2678	−0.1844	−0.0130	0.0040	0.2709
TURNC	−0.1240	0.2768	0.5400	0.3226	−0.0190	0.0504
GROW	−0.2702	0.2136	0.1235	0.4230	0.3463	0.2673
RANK	−0.4894	0.0050	0.1546	−0.0137	−0.0075	0.1102
REGSH	0.1934	0.5180	0.0758	0.2177	−0.4395	−0.1900
SCALE	0.2119	−0.3990	0.1405	0.5720	0.0956	−0.1534
BMES	0.2277	−0.0620	−0.5183	0.3286	−0.2930	0.3601
CDR	0.2764	−0.5154	0.3125	0.1277	0.0770	0.0438
KL	0.3138	−0.0066	0.3873	−0.4642	0.1047	0.2643
ADV	0.1159	0.2145	−0.3012	0.0395	0.7068	−0.3780
RD	0.3100	−0.2511	−0.0524	0.0280	0.2739	0.6607
Proportion of total sample variability accounted for	19.5	13.4	12.5	10.1	9.3	8.6

| | Eigenvector | | | | |
Variable	PRIN7	PRIN8	PRIN9	PRIN10	PRIN11
TURNE	0.1330	−0.1046	0.3345	−0.0620	0.6502
TURNC	0.1155	0.6666	0.0437	0.2220	0.0244
GROW	−0.5826	0.2957	0.1423	−0.1876	−0.1157
RANK	0.5587	0.3612	0.1324	0.1603	−0.4882
REGSH	0.1336	0.4116	0.3200	0.0322	0.3481
SCALE	0.3599	0.0548	−0.0711	−0.5267	0.0359
BMES	−0.0002	−0.2497	0.3830	0.0964	−0.3658
CDR	−0.1426	0.2539	0.1908	0.6353	0.1067
KL	0.0335	−0.0471	0.5392	−0.3890	−0.0989
ADV	0.2146	−0.0859	0.3463	0.1780	0.0278
RD	0.3201	0.1339	−0.3836	0.1075	0.2160
Proportion of total sample variability accounted for	7.3	6.1	5.8	4.5	3.0

[a] The sample consisted of 166 four-digit industries.
[b] For variable definitions, see text.

8-8 contains the first mobility component (low entry – PMOB1 from Table 8-6) but also is characterized by scale economies; the third joint component is basically the second scale component (a high weight for BMES – PSCL2) but inversely weights continuing-firm turnover. The fifth joint component is the fourth scale component (advertising – PSCL4) and also is positively related to the amount of regression to the mean in firm market shares.

The regressions using the joint components produce the same qualitative results as previously in that both the mobility and scale components matter. The joint components that are significant are the first, third, fifth, ninth, and eleventh. They represent PMOB1, PSCL1, PSCL4, PSCL5, and PMOB5. Low entry leads to lower concentration. Scale effects, which are accompanied by high MES relative to market size, lead to higher concentration.

Until now, the problem of simultaneity has been ignored. Mobility and scale characteristics are presumed to determine concentration. This is contrary to the position long taken by traditional structuralists. The structure-conduct-performance tradition emphasizes that entry and mobility are likely to be affected by structure. The possible effect of simultaneity on the coefficients estimated here needs to be considered.

In order to do so, a two-stage least-squares regression was employed. The various exogenous variables in the larger set of regressions that determined both concentration, entry and exit, and internal mobility were used as instruments on both TURNE and TURNC, the two variables that were posited to be endogenous. Variables chosen as exogenous were the industry growth rate, the variability of the growth rate, a regional dummy variable, a producer-goods dummy variable, foreign ownership, imports, and the comparative advantage of an industry. The exogenous variables were transformed into principal components. The SCALE variables used before were again assumed to be exogenous. The results of the equation that uses this technique are reported in Table 8-5, column II. It is evident that the entry and exit variable is still significant.

It may, therefore, be concluded that both technological and stochastic-growth theories of market structure are relevant. Scale economies have an undeniable effect on market structure, but the amount of firm turnover, whether it be from entry and exit or from continuing-firm growth and decline, also has an impact.[19] This is consistent with the argument that technical considerations provide a lower bound on concentration and that the characteristics of the stochastic processes inherent to an industry influence the degree to which concentration exceeds these bounds.

Changes in concentration. The analysis of the determinants of concentration was taken one step further by examining changes in concentration. Concentration, like firm size, exhibited a tendency to regress to the mean during the

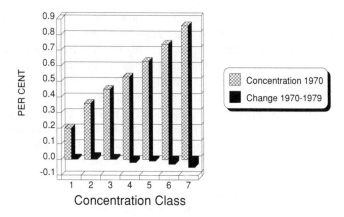

Figure 8-2. Changes in concentration between 1970 and 1979 ranked by industry using 1970 concentration levels.

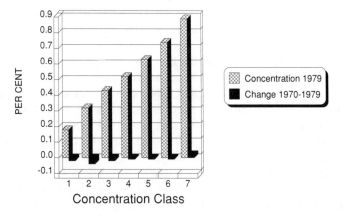

Figure 8-3. Changes in concentration between 1970 and 1979 ranked by industry using 1979 concentration levels.

1970s. In Figure 8-2, industries are ranked on the basis of their 1970 concentration ratio and divided into seven equal-sized groups. The average change in concentration is also included. It is evident that concentration increased in industries with low levels of concentration in 1970. It decreased in industries with high initial levels of concentration.

It is also true that for some industries below the highest concentration level, concentration was increasing and for some above the lowest concentration level, concentration was decreasing. Figure 8-3 ranks industries on the basis of 1979 concentration values and graphs the average 1979 values and the average change $[C(t) - C(t - 1)]$. Industries that were in the low end of the concentration spectrum in 1979 experienced declines in their concentration since 1970, on average. Those in the high end experienced increases over the decade.

Martin (1979) and Geroski, Masson, and Shaanan (1987) model changes in concentration as

$$C(t) - C(t - 1) = L \times [(C_e) - C(t - 1)]; \qquad (8\text{-}8)$$

that is, the change in concentration is assumed to follow a partial adjustment process with parameter L, where $C_e - C(t - 1)$ is the difference between the permanent or equilibrium level of concentration (C_e) and last period's value of concentration. Using this formulation, other studies have produced an estimate of the adjustment parameter that is quite small. Martin (1979) and Geroski, Masson, and Shaanan (1987) produce estimates of around 10 per cent over a five-year period. These imply a long period of adjustment.

When equation 8-8 was estimated using the 1979 and 1970 concentration ratios for the Canadian manufacturing sector and the predicted long-run concentration values (C_e) derived from equation 8-7, the estimated value of the adjustment parameter was 0.38 with a standard error of 0.11, thereby suggesting that the adjustment process in Canada was also relatively slow.

These results need to be treated cautiously. An error-in-variable problem arises in the course of estimating equation 8-8 that will bias the estimated adjustment coefficient. The main reason to expect a measurement error in the regressor is that the estimate of the long-run equilibrium level towards which the system is adjusting, C_e, must contain an error as it is estimated from a regression. The standard formula for bias in the face of measurement error for a two-variable regression indicates that the estimated adjustment coefficient L derived from equation 8-8 will be biased downward. Less than instantaneous adjustment will be suggested even when adjustment is almost immediate.

Two methods were chosen to overcome the problem of measurement. Since actual change is not subject to measurement error and long-run change is, the reverse regression should provide an unbiased estimator of the inverse of the adjustment coefficient. This procedure yielded an estimate of 0.84 with standard error of 0.12. This estimate of the adjustment coefficient is not significantly different from one.

The second method is to choose an instrument that is correlated with the true long-term change and not with the error in measurement. An instrumental variable using the rank of the independent variable is commonly used to correct for the error-in-variable problem. It is useful only if the error is not correlated with the rank of the observation. It is doubtful that this is the case here.

The nature of the adjustment process can be seen in Figure 8-4, which graphs the mean value of the predicted required long-run change, $C_e - C(t - 1)$, and

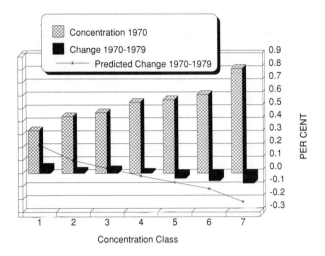

Figure 8-4. Actual and predicted required changes in concentration between 1970 and 1979 ranked by industry based on predicted required changes in concentration.

the actual change, $C(t) - C(t - 1)$, between 1970 and 1979 for industries ranked on the basis of the required change and grouped into seven categories. The average value of concentration in 1970 for each group is also presented. Both required and actual changes show that there is a regression to the mean. The greatest increase in concentration occurs in industries with low values of concentration in 1970. The greatest decrease in concentration occurs in industries with the highest levels of concentration in 1970. In both cases, the actual change in the tails of the distribution, $C(t) - C(t - 1)$, is much less than that required to reach long-run equilibrium, $C_e - C(t - 1)$.

The reverse regression suggests that there is really no significant difference in the actual change and the change required to reach long-run equilibrium. On the basis of Figure 8-4, then, it would appear that the error in $C_e - C(t - 1)$ is larger for larger values of this variable and that the error is also correlated with $C(t - 1)$. The rank of both variables, therefore, is likely to be unsuitable for use as an instrument. On the other hand, the rank of the actual change, $C(t) - C(t - 1)$, is likely to be related to the true variable and less correlated with the error, and may therefore provide a suitable instrument. In order to evaluate this possibility, the data were ranked on the basis of the actual change in concentration and grouped into seven classes (Figure 8-5). The average actual change and the average predicted required change are graphed along with the average 1970 concentration class.[20] There is much less difference between the two series when the grouping is done on the basis

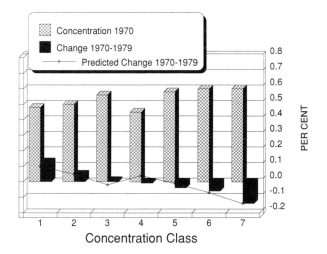

Figure 8-5. Actual and predicted required changes in concentration between 1970 and 1979 ranked by industry based on actual changes in concentration.

of the actual change. A regression that uses the rank of the actual change in concentration yielded a coefficient of adjustment of 1.16 with standard error 0.17. The coefficient of adjustment was not significantly different from one. Alternatively, using the rank of $C(t) - C(t - 1)$ to divide the sample into three groups, removing the middle group, and then using the means of the samples in the remaining two tails to calculate the adjustment parameter produced an estimate of 1.11.[21]

In summary, the evidence suggests that change in the outer shell of the box called market structure follows the same stochastic pattern as firm growth does. There are both centripetal and centrifugal forces at work. It is also probable that the changes in structure that are required by changes in basic conditions are fully encapsulated in market structure within the decade. Market structure is relatively stable compared with mobility measures – but the changes that are warranted are brought about fairly quickly.

Conclusion

The first objective of this chapter is to demonstrate that mobility statistics have an important relationship to industry structure and thereby confirm the importance of the contention that the underlying structure is endogenous not exogenous.

Mobility statistics have tended to be ignored because of the school of thought that maintains that entry, exit, and other aspects of intra-industry change are important only in the case of disequilibrium phenomena. According to this view, when fundamental characteristics related to scale economies change, then entry and exit occur as an industry moves from an old to a new market structure. Inter-industry differences in measures like market-share turnover do not reflect quasi-permanent differences in the intensity of the competitive process but a reaction to exogenous phenomena that requires adapting from one equilibrium to another.

This view is incorrect. It is true that changes in structure are associated with net entry or exit and with large firms gaining or losing market share. But it is also true, as the stochastic-growth theorists hypothesize, that there is a causal relationship between mobility and concentration. Taken together, technical characteristics relating to the importance of scale and the various dimensions of mobility predict concentration quite well.

Mobility measures, then, are significant for two reasons. The evidence indicates that mobility statistics are important determinants of the box that is used to describe industry structure. They are also independent estimates of the degree of market rivalry that is taking place within industries and offer an important complement to structural characteristics.

This chapter is also meant to contribute to the rich, applied industrial-economics literature that has examined the performance and structure of industries. Mobility statistics can be used to complement the point-in-time measures and static analyses that predominate in the literature and to either confirm or reject propositions contained in that literature.

Sections of the last two chapters have argued that mobility statistics extend our understanding of the operations of markets in important ways by enumerating the amount of change taking place in markets. On the assumption that these statistics provide important information about the intensity of competition, we also argue that this should correct false impressions that some users of concentration ratios have left.

These chapters demonstrate how the outside and the inside of the industry box are related so as to improve our understanding of how markets operate and adapt. Decreases in concentration are shown to be associated with higher rates of entry and exit. Increases in concentration are associated not so much with lower rates of entry but with shake-outs in the continuing-firm population.

The evidence indicates that the traditional concentration measures are negatively associated more with entry than with continuing-firm turnover, thereby justifying an interest in the determinants of entry, which will be pursued in later chapters. The lack of a close relationship between normal measures of concentration and incumbent-firm turnover suggests other measures must be sought that better capture the latter phenomenon. The canonical-correlation analysis suggests that one such measure is the importance of a second tier of firms. Miller (1971) suggests the importance of marginal-concentration measures and Kwoka (1979) shows that one such measure negatively affects price–cost margins. The results of this chapter suggest a reason for this – that in situations where the second tier of firms is particularly large, there is less internal turnover.

These findings have relevance both for future research and for empirical practice in antitrust economics. While mobility statistics are a powerful tool for analysis, they are not always available. Analysts will continue to use measures of market structure in these circumstances. This chapter provides a guide for this practice. It demonstrates that when structural measures are sought to proxy the internal competitive conditions, they should come from at least two different sets. The first should come from the comprehensive measures that concentrate on the importance of the largest firms – such as the four-firm concentration ratio, or the Herfindahl index. These measures are related to cross-industry differences in the extent of entry and exit. A second concentration statistic should be chosen from those measures that capture the importance of a second tier of firms – such as the market share of firms in positions five to eight or a relative-redundancy variable. These measures are closely related to inter-industry differences in turnover among continuing firms.

9

Turnover and productivity growth

> Like human beings firms are constantly being born that cannot live. Others may meet what is akin, in the case of man, to death from accident or illness. Still others die a "natural" death, as men die of old age. And the "natural" cause, in the case of firms, is precisely their inability to keep up the pace in innovation which they themselves had been instrumental in setting in the time of their vigour.
>
> Joseph Schumpeter (1939: 69)

Introduction

Productivity growth and technical change have often been described as disembodied – a type of manna from heaven. Studies of productivity in the Solow growth-model tradition tend to ignore the contribution that the worldly process of competition makes to growth. This is not the picture of Schumpeter's world where innovation and turnover are linked. While some progress has been made by writers like Nelson and Winter (1982) and Scherer (1983) in dispelling the belief that technical change is bestowed in some ephemeral form, much remains to be done. When technical progress is described in a more earthly form, the narration proceeds in terms of such concrete phenomena as the aggregate labour and machines employed in an industry. While the endogeneity of innovation and technical change was stressed by Schumpeter (1942) and more recently by Rohmer (1986), improvements in productivity are rarely related, at least in empirical studies, to the dynamics of firm turnover.

Industrial economics has taken several tentative steps to measure certain aspects of this relationship; but none fits the various pieces of the puzzle together. One branch investigates the relationship between changes in concentration and efficiency; for example, Peltzman (1977) examines the relationship between changes in industry unit costs and concentration, and Martin (1988) examines the relationship between the share of the four leading firms and their relative productivity. Others have studied how productivity change

208

relates to innovation and technological change. In this literature, productivity change involves not just the application of existing knowledge but the creation of new knowledge and depends on the innovative capabilities of firms. Scherer (1983) uses the U.S. Federal Trade Commission's line of business data to demonstrate the association of research and development decisions and long-run productivity growth. Geroski (1989) investigates the relationship at the industry level between patenting activity and productivity growth.

While these fledgling attempts are aimed in the right direction, substantial gaps in our knowledge remain. The literature does not examine firm turnover directly. Instead of using data on firm turnover, concentration statistics are used for inferences about the effect of market structure. As is shown in Chapter 7, concentration measures are poor proxies for many aspects of the intensity of the competitive process.

In an attempt to remedy these deficiencies, this chapter focuses directly on the link between industry-productivity growth and turnover. It builds on the previous chapters by focusing on turnover and calculates the proportion of the total increase in productivity that is due to the turnover process.

Productivity and plant turnover

Earlier chapters outlined the amount of turnover that takes place in the producer population. Producers expand and contract as the successful replace the unsuccessful. This process leads to considerable change in relative positions within industries and a concomitant transfer of resources over a decade. Between 1970 and 1979, some 37 per cent of market share was transferred from plants that either closed or contracted to new plants or plants that expanded.

The importance of entry and exit as well as expansion and contraction in the continuing sector can be judged not only by the share of shipments transferred by the turnover process, but also by its effect on a measure of industry performance. This chapter demonstrates that the turnover process contributed significantly to total productivity growth during the 1970s.

The amount of entry and exit varies in the short and the long run. At birth, the share of entrants is small; greenfield entrants that were new to the manufacturing sector as a whole accounted only for an average of 0.9 per cent of employment annually between 1970 and 1982. Infant mortality rates in this group were high. Over the same period, the average death rate in the first year after birth was about 10 per cent. Over 50 per cent died within the first decade. Nevertheless, the remaining greenfield entrants in a cohort grew sufficiently rapidly that the total share of the cohort expanded over the decade.

While the market share of a cohort of entrants increased, its progress was slow. This was also the case for productivity improvements. Figure 9-1 depicts the relative progress of greenfield entrants in terms of size and productivity.

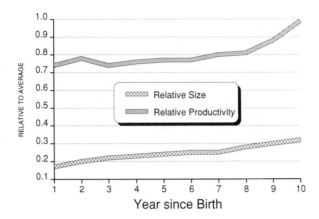

Figure 9-1. Average relative productivity and size of greenfield entrants, by age.

The graph plots the ratio of the mean value of the size (employment) and productivity (value-added per worker) of firm entrants that opened new plants divided by the mean for all firms in the manufacturing sector.[1] An entrant is defined as a firm that is new to the manufacturing sector.

Greenfield entrants commence operations at a relatively small size. At birth, their average plant size was only about 17 per cent of that of existing firms. They increased in relative size slowly to about 33 per cent of that of existing firms by the end of their first decade of life. At birth, the labour productivity of greenfield entrants averaged about 73 per cent of incumbents; after a decade, the productivity of these two groups was about equal. The effect of entry and exit on overall industry productivity, then, is likely to emerge more strongly in the longer run and should be measured over a relatively long period.

There is a second reason that a longer period should be used to capture the effects of turnover on productivity. The performance of continuing establishments varies considerably in the short run and the long run. In the short run, change in this sector is not consistent. An increase in one year could be followed by a decrease in the next. As demonstrated in Chapter 4, it is only when examined in the longer run that permanent change in the relative market share of the continuing sector can be clearly observed.

In order to evaluate the effect of entry and exit on the productivity of an industry, the years 1970 and 1979 were chosen and the productivity of plants in these two years was compared. Productivity was measured as value-added per worker and changes were measured in real terms.[2] More comprehensive (multi-factor) measures of productivity were not employed for several reasons.

The first is that this study focuses on the impact of turnover on output per worker, because this measure is closely associated with well-being. Moreover, since the pioneering work of Salter (1966), this measure has been shown to be closely correlated with other measures of productivity. Second, more comprehensive measures of productivity have, as one of their goals, accounting or correcting for other factors that cause output per worker to increase. More complex measures were not used because the purpose of this chapter is to establish the connection between firm turnover and increases in output per worker.

The effect of plant and firm turnover on productivity is of interest because of what it reveals about the competitive process and how it functions. In the next section a broad overview of the relationship between plant turnover and productivity differentials is developed. First, all plants are divided equally on the basis of value-added per worker, and information is sought by asking such questions as the following: Was there a higher proportion of exits from the least productive plants than from the most productive plants? Was there a higher proportion of births in the most productive segment than in the least productive segment? Did continuing plants that gained market share also gain relative productivity?

There are potential shortcomings to this approach. First, success and failure depend on many factors other than productivity. Second, productivity involves dimensions other than output per worker. Thus, differences in output per worker may not be very closely associated with the tendency of plants to exit or to enter. Third, the test uses the rankings of firms during only one year to capture relative position. If there are considerable fluctuations in relative plant productivity due to transitory shifts in output that are not matched by labour reductions, the rankings in any one year may not correspond to long-run productivity differentials. Despite these shortcomings, the dynamics of the competitive process clearly emerge.

By focusing on probabilities of success and failure, this section establishes the relationship between the pattern of replacement and relative productivity differences. The following section provides a measure of the extent to which the turnover process enhances productivity.

Relative productivity and firm growth and decline

If turnover is related to productivity gains, then entry, exit, expansion, and contraction should be related to relative-productivity differentials. A pattern should emerge that shows exits and contracting establishments to be the least productive, entrants and expanding establishments to be more productive. The relationship between plant turnover and relative-productivity differentials is investigated by attempting to answer a series of questions.

Table 9-1. *Proportion of plant entrants and exits above and below the median plant classified on the basis of labour productivity (per cent)*[a]

Category	In bottom 50 per cent	In top 50 per cent	Significance of differences[b]
New firm, new plant			
Plant birth (23)	18.02	20.42	< .001
Plant transfer (36)	5.20	4.32	.004
Continuing firm, new plant			
Plant birth (13)	2.87	5.19	< .001
Plant transfer (16)	0.52	0.76	.04
Exiting firm, exiting plant			
Plant closure (34)	29.36	21.39	< .001
Plant transfer (37)	4.56	4.36	.47
Continuing firm, exiting plant			
Plant closure (14)	3.23	3.80	.028
Plant transfer (17)	0.36	0.54	.040

[a] The plants in each of the 167 industries were divided equally on the basis of labour productivity, and the number of entrants in each group was counted. The proportions reported are the sum of all such entrants or exits divided by the sum of all plants above or below the median. Calculating the proportion by industry and taking the mean across all industries yields basically the same results.
[b] The minimum significance level required to reject the null hypothesis that the proportions are the same.

Is exit a purely random process or does it remove the less efficient? This issue was approached by examining whether plants that were less productive also tended to exit more frequently. The population of plants in each industry in 1970 was divided equally into two parts on the basis of output per worker. Then the number of closures was calculated among the most productive and least productive plants for each industry to standardize for industry-specific factors. Exiting plants were divided first into two categories: those associated with exiting firms and those made by continuing firms.[3] Each of these categories was in turn divided into two categories: plants that closed (deaths) and those that left an industry and moved to another (transfers).[4]

The probability of exit calculated across the whole sample is reported in Table 9-1. The probability of exit through plant closure by exiting firms is significantly higher for the less productive plants. This is not the case for plant closures by continuing firms.

Are entrants concentrated in the most productive segment? This issue was addressed by asking whether the more productive plants in 1979 had a higher proportion of entrants than the less productive segment. The universe of plants in each four-digit industry in 1979 was divided equally on the basis of labour productivity and the number of entrants above and below the median was tabulated. Entrants were sorted first into new plants associated with new firms and then into those associated with continuing firms. Each of these categories was then subdivided into newly opened plants (births) and plants that were transferred from another industry (transfers).

Table 9-1 contains the proportion of all plants in each of these entrant categories according to productivity.[5] Plant births for both new and continuing firms made up a larger proportion of the more productive than the less productive segment. The difference is greatest among new plants of continuing firms. As was the case with the exiting categories, transfers did not follow the same pattern. Plant transfers by continuing firms were more likely to be in the more productive segment in 1970 and to end up in the more productive segment in 1979. Plant transfers that caused a firm to exit one industry and to enter another were equally likely to be in either segment in 1970 but were more likely to end up in the less productive segment in 1979.

Do growth and decline depend on initial productivity? This question was addressed by examining whether the plants that were more productive in 1970 tended to grow faster over the subsequent decade than plants that were less productive. The output growth rate was calculated for each continuing plant. Plants in each industry in 1970 were divided equally into two parts on the basis of productivity and the proportion in each of the two groups that experienced high growth rates was calculated.[6]

Table 9-2 contains the proportions of the more and less productive plants that experienced an above-average rate of output growth. Two samples were used to rank continuing plants as being above or below median productivity. The first excluded exits and thus considered only continuing plants. The second included exits. The conclusions are not affected by the sample chosen.

In 1970, the more productive segment had a significantly smaller proportion of plants that subsequently had high growth than did the less productive segment. Thus, if a plant was relatively more productive in 1970, it had not only a reduced likelihood of exit but also a diminished probability of market-share gain compared with that of other continuing plants over the subsequent decade. Gains in market share within this group depended on superior performance in more than one year. This accords with studies showing that the performance of continuing producers, in other than adjacent years, is not correlated.[7]

Table 9-2. *Proportion of continuing plants above and below the median plant classified on the basis of labour productivity that gained market share between 1970 and 1979 (per cent)*

	Sample used to define median plant	
Year of comparison	Continuing plants	All plants
1979		
Percentage above median gaining share	59	44
Percentage below median gaining share	38	31
1970		
Percentage above median gaining share	47	31
Percentage below median gaining share	51	35

Note: The plants in each of the 167 industries were divided equally on the basis of labour productivity, and the number of plants gaining share in each group was counted. The proportions reported are the sum of all such plants divided by the sum of all plants above or below the median. Calculating the proportion by industry and taking the mean across all industries yields basically the same results. The differences between the proportions reported here are significant at the 1 per cent level.

Are the most productive plants at the end of the period more likely to have gained market share over the decade? This issue was addressed first by examining whether plants that were more productive in 1979 grew faster over the decade than did plants that were less productive in the same year. Plants were divided equally on the basis of labour productivity, and the proportions of continuing high-growth plants above and below the median level of productivity were calculated. A much higher proportion of plants in the most productive half of the 1979 distribution grew more rapidly during the decade. In contrast, growth over the decade was not related, or only weakly related, to 1970 productivity performance. Success, then, as measured by gains in market share, was associated with superior productivity performance, where the latter was measured at the end rather than at the beginning of the decade.

The relative productivity of exits, entrants, and continuing plants

The pattern of entry, exit, and turnover in continuing plants between 1970 and 1979 should have improved productivity. The less productive plants in 1970 were more likely to exit. Plants born since 1970 made up a greater proportion of the more productive than the less productive segment in 1979.

Continuing plants that gained market share increased their productivity relative to those losing market share.

The contribution that turnover makes to total growth in productivity depends on several factors. First, it is a function of the market share of entrants and exits, and the shift of shares within the continuing segment between those establishments whose relative productivity is growing and those whose relative productivity is declining. Second, it depends on the relative productivity of the various components.

Exits. A comparison of the productivity of exits relative to that of continuing firms at the beginning of the period gives an indication of the potential gains from exits. Continuing plants that did not have a change in ownership are examined.[8] Plant exits are divided into four different categories: the closed and transferred plant of exiting firms, and the closed and transferred plant of continuing firms. Table 9-3 contains the mean and the standard error of the ratio of the median productivity[9] of each of these exit categories to the median productivity of continuing plants[10] for manufacturing industries. A test of significance for the difference in the two medians is also presented.

Closed plant associated with exiting firms had the lowest relative productivity. On average, they were only 79 per cent as productive as continuing plants in 1970. The difference between the two is significant. Ceteris paribus, establishment closedowns associated with exiting firms improved industry productivity as the less efficient were weeded out.

A simple comparison of average productivity differences at the four-digit industry level may conceal the true significance of exits, especially if they are concentrated in only a portion of all four-digit industries. Moreover, it does not standardize for other factors.

The primary difference between exiting and continuing plants is size. Generally, smaller plants are less productive than larger ones. Therefore, exiting plants may be less productive only because they are small.[11] To investigate this issue, a regression of 1970 productivity (PROD) on size (SIZE), as measured by employment and using dummy variables for the various exit categories, was estimated across the entire plant sample. Industry dummies and interaction effects with size were also included to allow for different industry effects such as differing capital–output ratios.[12] The results are reported in Table 9-3, where the estimated coefficients are the ratio of the productivity of plants in an exit category to the productivity of plant in the continuing category that did not change ownership, and the probability value is the significance level required to reject the null hypothesis that the exit category is no less productive than the continuing-establishments category. Plant closures and plant switches associated with exiting firms were significantly less productive than was the continuing segment.

Table 9-3. *Relative labour productivity of plant entrants and exits compared with that of continuing plants[a] for 167 four-digit manufacturing industries*

	Mean[b]	Significance of sign-rank test for first differences[c]	Regression coefficient[d]
Exits			
Exiting firms			
Closed plant (34)	0.79	< .001	0.89
	(0.02)		[.009]
Plant transfer (37)	0.96	.001	0.97
	(0.04)		[.018]
Continuing firms			
Closed plant (14)	0.96	.003	1.01
	(0.04)		[.020]
Plant transfer (17)	0.99	.280	1.07
	(0.07)		[.054]
Entrants			
Entering firms			
Plant births (23)	1.04	.173	1.16
	(0.03)		[.010]
Plant transfer (36)	0.95	.003	0.98
	(0.04)		[.018]
Continuing firms			
Plant births (13)	1.15	.006	1.31
	(0.05)		[.020]
Plant transfer (16)	0.93	.146	1.09
	(0.06)		[.048]

[a] Productivity is measured for plant exits as of 1970 and for entrants as of 1979 relative to continuing plants that did not change ownership.
[b] The mean is the average of the ratio of the median estimate of the productivity of each class divided by the median estimate of the productivity of the continuing class. Standard error of the mean is in parentheses.
[c] The probability of a greater absolute value of the signed-rank statistic for the mean difference between the medians of productivity in each entry or exit class and in the continuing class under the null hypothesis of no difference.
[d] The probability value, in brackets, is the minimum level of significance required to reject the null hypothesis that the productivity of the category relative to the continuing sector is 1.

It is noteworthy that the productivity disadvantage of plant closures by exiting firms remains even after the size effect has been removed. Exiting plants may, on the whole, be smaller than the population average, but they suffer even more of a productivity disadvantage than might be expected given their size. Plants do not exit just because their smallness causes a productivity disadvantage.

Entrants. Table 9-3 also contains the mean of the ratio calculated by dividing the median productivity in 1979 of plant births by the median productivity of plants that survived the decade without a change in ownership. Plant in both birth categories were more productive than continuing plants, but the only significant advantage occurred for plant births of continuing firms.

These averages take no account of productivity differences that might be expected because of size differences. Despite the increase in relative size since birth, greenfield entrants in 1979 were considerably smaller than existing plants. A regression of productivity comparable to that done for exits was estimated across the entire plant sample for entrants. Productivity in 1979 was regressed against employment (a measure of size) and dummy variables for both industries and entry categories (see Table 9-3). Once again, the coefficients represent the productivity of the entry category relative to establishments that were in the same industry in both 1970 and 1979 and that did not change ownership. When corrected for size, the productivity of greenfield entrants is now significantly higher than that of continuing plants. Continuing-firm new plants are still significantly more productive. Plant transfers associated with entry by firms are not significantly different from continuing plants. Plant transfers among continuing firms are more productive.

An additional regression was estimated for the two plant-birth categories alone. Jovanovic (1982) as well as Pakes and Ericson (1988) have formulated models of entry that incorporate a learning process. In a world where adaptation and learning occur, entrants that succeed gradually approach the size and productivity of continuing firms.

Figure 9-1 depicts the annual progress in relative productivity made by each entry cohort as it matured. These estimates are calculated at a relatively aggregated level for greenfield entrants that were new to the manufacturing sector as a whole.

Data at the four-digit industry level in 1979 for all entrants since 1970 can also be used to track the progress of entrants. Plant entrants as of 1979 can be dated by their year of entry. Therefore, the 1979 size (measured in employment) of all plants that entered between 1970 and 1979 and that were still alive in 1979 was regressed on binary variables for year of birth and industry dummies to test for the learning effect. The estimated coefficients for each of the year-of-birth variables and a 95 per cent confidence interval are plotted

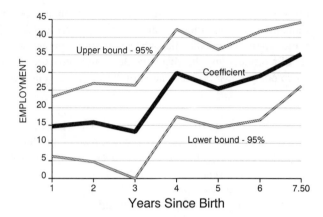

Figure 9-2. The regression coefficient of employment size on age for 1979 entrants. Entrants are greenfield births between 1970 and 1979 that are still alive in 1979.

in Figure 9-2. These micro-data confirm the results of the analysis using aggregate data. Table 9-4 contains the regression results of a slightly different formulation. Size of entrant was regressed on a trend variable ($T = 1, 2, \ldots,$ 9) to capture the age of the entrant and industry dummies. In both analyses, age is highly significant. As entrants age, they get larger. The results suggest that successful entrants grew at about 8 per cent per year. The relative size of entering plants increased slowly but steadily over the decade.

Since some of the increase in productivity depicted in Figure 9-1 may just be a result of increases in size, the productivity of 1979 entrants was also regressed on size, industry dummies, and a time trend. Two different productivity variables were used – shipments per worker and value-added per worker. The estimated coefficients for the time variable are reported in Table 9-4. Even with plant size controlled, time still had a significantly positive coefficient. The results depicted in Figure 9-2 and Table 9-4 are consistent with the adaptive model. Entrants can appear with lower than average size and productivity, but they successfully increase their relative size and productivity over time. There are distinct productivity gains that are separate from those one might expect just from the tendency of surviving entrants to grow larger over time.

Continuing plants. Over the decade of the 1970s, almost as much share changed hands as a result of expansion and contraction in continuing establishments as by entry and exit. There were also substantial changes in relative productivity in the continuing sector. In order to measure the extent to which

Table 9-4. *Relationship between size or productivity and age for 1979 entrants*

| Dependent variable | Regressor | | | |
	Intercept	Log of employment	Time since birth	R^2
Employment	15.05	—	3.65	.17
	(1.45)		(8.16)	
	[.148]		[.0001]	
Log of employment	2.63	—	0.083	.24
	(20.87)		(15.46)	
	[.0001]		[.0001]	
Log of shipments/ employee	—	0.065	0.021	.48
		(0.752)	(5.71)	
		[.452]	[.0001]	
Log of value-added/ employee	—	0.074	0.013	.27
		(0.878)	(3.61)	
		[.380]	[.0003]	

Note: The regression coefficients were estimated from the entire sample of long-form establishments that entered between 1970 and 1979 and were extant in 1979. The *t* statistic is in parentheses and the associated probability value ($|t| > 0$) is in brackets.

changes in relative productivity were taking place, the continuing-plant population was divided into those that increased and those that decreased market share between 1970 and 1979. The mean of the ratio of the productivity of the gainers to the losers in 1970 is 0.98[13] (the standard error of the mean is 0.02), which is not significantly different from unity. The mean of the relative productivity of the two groups in 1979 is 1.34 (the standard error is 0.09), which is significantly different from unity. Plants that grew more quickly over the period did not start with an advantage in productivity, but by the end of the decade, they were 34 per cent more productive on average than those losing market share. The growth and decline in the continuing-plant segment also enhanced the average level of productivity over the decade.

Taken together, the results on the relative productivity of exiting plant and entering plant demonstrate a pattern. Continuing firms are not closing plant that is relatively unproductive, but they are opening plant that is very much more productive than the average. It is this group that is at the frontier of new knowledge and techniques. A plant does not have to be substandard for it to be closed when the opportunities to make a substantial gain in productivity

Mean Share Loss			Mean Share Gain
18.1	Closed Plant of Exiting Firms (Category 34) ⟶	Plant Birth of Entering Firms (Category 23)	16.1
4.6	Closed Plant of Continuing Firms (Category 14) ⟶	Plant Birth of Continuing Firms (Category 13)	5.3
12.6	Continuing Plant Losing Market Share (Category D) ⟶	Continuing Plant Gaining Market Share (Category U)	14.1

Figure 9-3. A schematic representation of a simple replacement process.

are known. Exiting firms that close plant and entering firms that open plant show a different pattern, but one that has the same effect on productivity. The closed plant of exiting firms is much less productive than the average, even when allowances are made for plant-size differences. These firms are the failures. Firms that enter with newly opened plant are initially not more successful than the average continuing plant. A learning process takes place that gradually increases the size and productivity of the successful entrant. To the extent that these entrants replace the exiting firms of below-average productivity, industry-average productivity will be enhanced by the turnover associated with the entry and exit process.

Measuring the effect of plant turnover on productivity growth

The results presented here so far reject the view that the turnover of plants is quantitatively unimportant and that the process makes no contribution to overall productivity growth. The size of the contribution is the subject of this section.

In order to measure the effect of each of the entry categories, it is a useful first approximation to adopt a trade-off process akin to that depicted in Figure 9-3, with each entry category replacing one exit category – the new plant of entrants replacing closed plant of exiting firms; new plant of continuing firms replacing closed plant of continuing firms; and share increases in continuing plants replacing share decreases in the continuing sector.

There are several reasons for postulating this replacement pattern. First, the individual components of each pair are symmetrical, by definition. Moreover, pairs are sufficiently different in concept that inter-group rivalry might not be expected to be very strong. Finally, the respective losses and gains of each category are similar, though not identical.

This characterization of the replacement process generates a straight-forward measure of the productivity gains contributed by each turnover category. The performance of each category that gained market share can be set against one category that lost market share. For instance, in 1979 the new plants of entrants were more productive than continuing plants, while in 1970 the closed plants of exiting firms were less productive than continuing plants. The ratios were 1.04 and 0.79, respectively (Table 9-3). Plant births of continuing firms were also more productive in 1979 relative to the continuing-plant population than were the closed plants of continuing firms relative to the continuing-plant population in 1970 – a ratio of 1.15 in 1979 against 0.96 in 1970. Finally, continuing plants that gained market share became 1.34 times as productive, on average, as those that lost market share over the decade. In 1970, there was no significant difference between the two.[14]

The productivity gains that were being generated can also be measured by means of a comparison between the increase in productivity between 1970 and 1979 within each category and the productivity increase among the losers in the continuing sector – the plants that lost market share to other continuing plants. The latter provide a convenient standard of comparison in that they continued to exist over the decade, even though they were not able to maintain their market share. Plant turnover associated with entering and exiting firms produced a mean productivity gain (the 1979 productivity of the former minus the 1970 productivity of the latter) equal to 1.43 (standard error of mean = 0.09) times that in the contracting sector. Productivity growth in continuing-sector plants that gained market share was on average 1.49 (standard error of mean = 0.08) times that in the declining sector. Productivity growth associated with plant turnover by continuing firms (the productivity of new plants in 1979 minus that of closed plants in 1970) was, on average, 1.56 (standard error of mean = 0.10) times that in the declining sector.

The effect of individual entry categories

Measuring the effect of entry and exit is approached here in two ways. First, total growth in labour productivity is mechanically decomposed into that caused by entry and exit. There are several ways to do this and, thus, several ways to measure the effect of entry and exit. Second, an explicit simplifying assumption is made about the way entry affects exits compared with its effect on continuing plants. This is referred to as the replacement assumption. Then, the formula from the first exercise that corresponds with the various replacement assumptions is identified. The appropriateness of each replacement assumption is empirically tested, and the correct one is then used to measure the contribution of each category to total productivity growth.

At first only the effects of entry and exit are considered. All plants in the continuing sector are grouped together. No distinction is made between continuing plants that gained market share and those that lost it. Then this restriction is relaxed and the replacement assumption is examined in more detail.

In order to evaluate the contribution that exits and entrants make to changes in average productivity per worker, the change in this variable can be decomposed into components that measure the effect of entry and exit. Total growth in average productivity per worker (TOT) is

$$TOT = (SHE_9 \times APE_9 + SHC_9 \times APC_9) - (SHE_0 \times APE_0 + SHC_0 \times APC_0), \tag{9-1}$$

where APE represents output per worker in the entering/exiting sector and APC is the output per worker in the continuing sector. SHE and SHC are the labour shares of each category and the subscripts 9 and 0 refer to the years 1979 and 1970, respectively. Thus, APE_9 refers to the productivity of entrants in 1979 and APE_0 refers to the productivity of exits in 1970. Total productivity growth is equal to the difference in productivity in 1979 and 1970, where the productivity in each of these periods is the weighted average of the productivity in each sector – entrants and continuing plants in 1979, and exits and continuing plants in 1970.

Equation 9-1 can be rewritten so as to capture the effect of entry in a number of different ways. Perhaps two of the most intuitive – derived from an orthogonal transformation of change – are

$$TOT = SHE_9 \times (APE_9 - APE_0) + SHC_9 \times (APC_9 - APC_0) + (SHC_9 - SHC_0) \times (APC_0 - APE_0), \tag{9-2}$$

and

$$TOT = SHE_0 \times (APE_9 - APE_0) + SHC_0 \times (APC_9 - APC_0) + (SHC_9 - SHC_0) \times (APC_9 - APE_9). \tag{9-3}$$

These two expressions divide the total change into three terms, and differ only in the extent to which base- or end-year shares are used as weights. The first term captures the change that is due to the productivity difference between entrants and exits. It is the entry (exit) share multiplied by the difference between the productivity of entrants and exits. The second term represents the growth in productivity due to progress in continuing plants. It is simply the share of continuing plants multiplied by the growth in their average productivity. Both the first and second terms capture the component of total change that is due to entry or continuing-plant progress, assuming shares are held constant. The last term captures the effect of share changes.

There are a number of other ways to rewrite the total productivity change in equation 9-1. For example, it can also be written as[15]

$$\text{TOT} = (\text{APC}_9 - \text{APC}_0) + \text{SHE}_9 \times (\text{APE}_9 - \text{APC}_9)$$
$$+ \text{SHE}_0 \times (\text{APC}_0 - \text{APE}_0). \tag{9-4}$$

In this formulation, the first term measures productivity growth in the continuing sector, the second and third terms measure the difference between productivity in entrants or exits and the continuing sector. The second and the third terms can be interpreted as capturing the effect of entry and exit, respectively. The differences between equations 9-4 and either equations 9-2 or 9-3 occur because each originates from a different assumption as to whether entrants supplant exits or continuing plants.

Instead of arbitrarily breaking down productivity growth into components as is done in equations 9-2, 9-3, and 9-4, a different approach that starts with explicit assumptions about the effect of entry and exit on the share of the continuing population can be utilized. Suppose that entrants replace exits. This is equivalent to assuming that, in the absence of entry, exiting plants would not have disappeared. Then, productivity growth can be written in the same form as equation 9-1, except that the values of the entrants' share and/or average productivity are replaced with comparable values drawn from the exits. In this case, the increase in productivity that would have occurred in the absence of entry can be written as

$$(\text{SHC}_9 \times \text{APC}_9 + \text{SHE}_9 \times \text{APE}_0) - (\text{SHC}_0 \times \text{APC}_0 + \text{SHE}_0 \times \text{APE}_0), \tag{9-5}$$

or

$$(\text{SHC}_0 \times \text{APC}_9 + \text{SHE}_0 \times \text{APE}_0) - (\text{SHC}_0 \times \text{APC}_0 + \text{SHE}_0 \times \text{APE}_0). \tag{9-6}$$

Equation 9-5 is just equation 9-1 with the productivity of entrants in 1979 being replaced by exits in 1970. Equation 9-6 is equation 9-5 with the share of entrants in 1979 replaced by that of exits for 1970. Equation 9-5 assumes that, without entrants, continuing firms would have made the same share gains or losses that did occur. Equation 9-6 assumes that without entrants, relative shares of continuing and exiting firms would have stayed at 1970 levels.[16] Both are approximations, since a combination of an increase in productivity among continuing firms and no increase in productivity among exiting firms would no doubt have resulted in a loss of market share by the latter in 1979. Both assumptions are used to test the sensitivity of the results.

The difference between total growth (equation 9-1) and growth without entry (equation 9-5 or 9-6) is the effect of entry. It is given by the first term in equation 9-2 for the assumption embedded in equation 9-5 and the sum of the first and third terms in equation 9-3 for the assumptions of equation 9-6.

Alternatively, it could be assumed that if there had been no entry, the exits would still have occurred. This is equivalent to assuming that entrants replace continuing plants; that is, they cause continuing plants to lose market share they would otherwise have captured, since exits are presumed to fail in any case. In this instance, the increase in productivity that would have occurred without entry is just the average productivity of continuing firms in 1979 minus the average productivity of all firms in 1970. This is

$$APC_9 - (SHC_0 \times APC_0 + SHE_0 \times APE_0). \tag{9-7}$$

Similarly, if it is assumed that there would have been entrants without exits, the amount of total growth not due to exit is

$$(SHC_9 \times APC_9 + SHE_9 \times APE_9) - APC_0. \tag{9-8}$$

Subtracting equations 9-7 (the amount of growth not due to entry) and 9-8 (the amount of growth not due to exit) from equation 9-1 (actual growth) yields the second and third terms of equation 9-4 (the amount due to entry and exit, respectively).

If the effects of entry and exit are to be evaluated, then the conditions for the counterfactual exercise must be clearly stated. The assumptions embodied in equations 9-5, 9-6, 9-7, and 9-8 are quite different. Which of these formulations is chosen depends on our view of the economic process and is ultimately a matter for empirical investigation.

If entrants displace exits, then the formulations in equations 9-2 and 9-3 are closer to the truth. The work reported in Chapter 2 suggests that exits are related to entry in the sense that the more entry there has been in the recent past, the higher exit rates will be today. In this sense, entrants and exits are closely associated. However, it is also true that the share of entry does not correspond exactly with the share of exits. Some displacement must occur between continuing firms and entrants or exits.

If entrants generally replace continuing plants, equation 9-4 is the appropriate one;[17] but only if the continuing plants whose market share declined as a result of entry had average levels of productivity. This last qualification reveals the importance of another implicit assumption contained in this growth-accounting exercise – share changes do not affect relative average productivity levels. If entrants are assumed to replace continuing plants, it may be inappropriate to measure the effect of no entry with equation 9-7, which presumes that the level of productivity in the continuing segment with entry is the same as without. If entry eliminates the least productive continuing plants, as seems likely, the average level of productivity of the continuing segment would be lower without entry and the second term of equation 9-4 would understate the effect of entry.

While different assumptions about the direction of the replacement pattern yield quite different estimating formulae, the answers that are produced may

Table 9-5. *Average contribution of entry, exit, growth, and decline in the continuing sector to productivity growth between 1970 and 1979 (per cent)[a]*

Source of productivity growth (assumptions[b] of equation 9-5)	Contribution to total productivity growth[c]
New plant of new firm replaces closed plant of exiting firm	24.0
	(3.2)
New plant of continuing firm replaces closed plant of continuing firm	5.1
	(1.8)
Growth in continuing plants	68.8
	(3.1)

[a] The reported ratios are calculated for a sample of 167 four-digit industries where real productivity growth was positive during the period 1970–79.

[b] The assumptions contained in the formulation are discussed at greater length in the text.

[c] Column does not sum to 100 because medians were used. Standard error of the mean is in parentheses.

not differ greatly. To see whether this was the case, all three assumptions (equations 9-5, 9-6, and 9-7) are used to provide a first approximation of the effect of entry and exit.[18] Only new-plant creation by new firms and continuing firms is considered. The results for equation 9-5, which presumes that the new plants in a firm category (new firms or continuing firms) replace closed plants in the same firm category, are reported in Table 9-5. The contribution is expressed as a percentage of the total change in productivity.[19]

When plant creation by entrants is presumed to displace plants closed by exiting firms, replacement accounts for some 24 per cent of total productivity growth, on average. When plants opened by continuing firms are presumed to replace plants closed by continuing firms, replacement accounts for 5 per cent. Together, plant openings and closings contributed 29 per cent of productivity growth. If the assumptions of equation 9-6 are applied instead, then the joint effect of all plant openings and closings is 30 per cent. The results, then, are not very sensitive to differences between the assumptions embedded in equations 9-5 and 9-6.

If the contributions of entry and exit are assumed to occur using the assumptions embedded in equation 9-8 – with less productive entrants replacing more productive continuing plants (equation 9-4) – then the contribution of entry falls dramatically. The contributions of entry and exit are −5 per cent and 14 per cent, respectively, for a joint contribution of 9 per cent. The result produced by equation 9-8 – that entry contributes negatively to productivity growth – is similar to that reported by Hazledine (1985), who used a similar formula but studied shorter periods in the mid-1970s.[20] The assumptions implicit in this formulation are the least realistic, as will be demonstrated later in this chapter.

Where entrants are treated as replacing exits, the contribution that they make jointly is not unimportant. How important it is depends on the standard chosen to measure it. It is certainly important enough to eliminate any notion that entry and exit make no contribution, that they are only marginal. But can we say they contribute more than might be expected if they were treated as ongoing firms that would also have experienced productivity growth? To examine this issue, the distribution of the share of productivity growth derived from entry using equation 9-5 was compared with the distribution of the entry category's share of shipments. Their ratio will be one if the share of the entry category is the same as its contribution to productivity growth. The median of this ratio was 1.24 for new plants of new firms in industries with positive real productivity growth. It was 1.39 for new plants of continuing firms. A Wilcox non-parametric signed-rank test was carried out to determine whether the contribution of each entrant was greater than its share. The null hypothesis that they were the same was rejected in each case in favour of the alternative hypothesis that each entry category made a significantly greater contribution to productivity growth than might have been expected in light of its market share.

The effect of displacement in the continuing sector

The exit of some and the entry of others is not the only way in which market share is transferred from the less to the more successful. Among continuing firms, some plants lose market share, and others gain it. The difference between the labour productivity of gainers and losers by the end of the 1970s is substantial. The effect of this part of the plant-turnover process can be calculated by considering the replacement process here to be independent of that taking place elsewhere – in this case, of the amount of entry and exit. Productivity growth in the continuing sector (TOTC) is

$$TOTC = APC_9 \times APC_0 = (SHCU_9 \times APCU_9 + SHCD_9 \times APCD_9)$$
$$- (SHCU_0 \times APCU_0 + SHCD_0 \times APCD_0), \qquad (9-9)$$

where SH refers to the employment share, AP refers to average labour productivity, the suffixes CU and CD refer to the segment of the continuing sector that increases market share and that decreases market share between 1970 and 1979. The subscripts 9 and 0 refer to the years 1979 and 1970, respectively.

Table 9-6. *Average contribution of growth and decline in the continuing-firm sector to productivity growth between 1970 and 1979 (per cent)*[a]

Source of productivity growth[b]	Contribution to productivity growth in the continuing-firm sector[c] (1)	Contribution to total productivity growth (2)
Displacement effect	37.9	26.9
Growth in plants gaining share	43.2	38.9
Growth in plants losing share	18.8	3.0

[a] The breakdown in column 1 was estimated using equation 9-10 in the text. Column 2 was estimated from the second term of equation 9-2.
[b] The sample contains only those industries where growth in real output per worker was positive over the period 1970–79.
[c] Column does not sum to 100 because medians were used.

The growth in labour productivity (TOTC) that originates in the continuing sector can be rewritten in a form comparable to equations 9-2 and 9-3 as

$$\text{TOTC} = \text{SHCU}_0 \times (\text{APCU}_9 - \text{APCU}_0) + \text{SHCD}_0 \\ \times (\text{APCD}_9 - \text{APCD}_0) + (\text{SHCU}_9 - \text{SHCU}_0) \\ \times \text{APCU}_9 + (\text{SHCD}_9 - \text{SHCD}_0) \times \text{APCD}_9, \quad (9\text{-}10)$$

or

$$\text{TOTC} = \text{SHCU}_9 \times (\text{APCU}_9 - \text{APCU}_0) + \text{SHCD}_9 \\ \times (\text{APCD}_9 - \text{APCD}_0) + (\text{SHCU}_9 - \text{SHCU}_0) \\ \times \text{APCU}_0 + (\text{SHCD}_9 - \text{SHCD}_0) \times \text{APCD}_0. \quad (9\text{-}11)$$

In both equations, the first and second terms capture the productivity growth that comes from growth in the expanding and contracting sectors, respectively. The third and fourth terms capture the effect of share displacement – the effect of the expanding segment displacing the losing segment. The difference between equations 9-10 and 9-11 lies in whether base- or final-year shares are chosen as weights. The mean values of the first, second, and the sum of the third and fourth terms expressed as a proportion of total productivity growth in the continuing sector (TOTC) are reported in Table 9-6, (first column) for equation 9-10.[21] Some 38 per cent of productivity growth in the continuing sector comes from displacement of declining plants by growing plants; 43 per cent comes from productivity growth in plants gaining share; only 19 per cent comes from those losing market share.

Instead of starting with an arbitrary breakdown as in equations 9-10 and 9-11, the effect of turnover can be estimated using the counterfactual approach by specifying what productivity growth would have been in the absence of a particular event. For instance, if it is assumed that in the absence of productivity growth in the expanding sector, market shares in 1979 would have been the same as in 1970 and only the declining sector would have had productivity growth, then the growth in labour productivity in the continuing sector would have been

$$(SHCU_0 \times APCU_0 + SHCD_0 \times APCD_9) - (SHCU_0$$
$$\times APCU_0 + SHCD_0 \times APCD_0), \tag{9-12}$$

and the difference between actual productivity growth in the continuing sector (TOTC) and the amount yielded by equation 9-12 is the amount of productivity growth due to those plants in the continuing sector that gained market share:

$$TOTC = SHCU_0 \times (APCU_9 - APCU_0) + (SHCU_9 - SHCU_0)$$
$$\times APCU_9 + (SHCD_9 - SHCD_0) \times APCD_9. \tag{9-13}$$

This is the first, third, and fourth terms of equation 9-10. It accounts for 81 per cent of productivity growth in the continuing sector (TOTC).

The displacement effect due to share change can be measured by postulating the counterfactual where both sectors manage to achieve their actual productivity growth, but where there is no share change – that is, shares remain in 1979 what they were in 1970. In this case, the displacement effect is the sum of the third and fourth terms of equation 9-10. It amounts to 38 per cent of productivity growth in the continuing sector (TOTC).

The difference between the amount of productivity growth due to those plants in the continuing sector that gained market share and the amount due to displacement is the effect of no growth in the expanding sector extrapolating from the displacement effect – just the first term in equation 9-10. It is 43 per cent of productivity growth in the continuing sector.

Finally, the effect of no growth in the declining sector can be estimated by assuming a comparable counterfactual to equation 9-12. The effect, then, of growth in the losing segment would be the sum of the second, third, and fourth terms in equation 9-10. It makes up 57 per cent of the total. Once again, it includes the effects of both productivity growth and share change. Subtracting the displacement effect gives only the effect of productivity growth in the losing sector – 19 per cent.

Examining total productivity growth in the continuing sector (TOTC) is useful, but it does not, by itself, tell us how much of total growth in productivity comes from the continuing sector components. An estimate of this can be derived by substituting the components of equation 9-10 into the second term of equation 9-2, multiplying by SHC_9, and calculating each component as a percentage of total productivity growth (TOT). The mean values of these ratios for industries with positive real productivity growth are reported in Table 9-6 (second column). The sum of the three components just equals the contribution reported in Table 9-5 for the continuing sector – some 69 per cent of the total. The contribution arising from the displacement of some continuing plants by others is 27 per cent. Productivity growth in those plants gaining market share contributes 39 per cent of the total. Productivity growth in plants losing market share is relatively unimportant – only 3 per cent of the total. It is noteworthy that the latter category loses its relative importance when its contribution to total productivity growth, as opposed to growth in only the continuing sector, is calculated. Where losers are relatively important in the continuing-firm sector, the share of the continuing-firm sector is lower; if losers in the continuing-firm sector are important, the continuing-firm sector as a whole is not.

In conclusion, when the continuing-firm sector is treated independently of other sectors, plant turnover (this time through share displacement rather than through openings and closings) accounts for 27 per cent of total productivity growth. This suggests, when considered together with the results in Table 9-5, that total turnover contributes almost half of productivity growth.

The contribution of total firm turnover

Assessing the role of entry and exit or of expansion and contraction in the continuing sector separately is difficult and unsatisfactory, for several reasons. The counterfactuals involve making choices between entrants replacing exits or entrants supplanting continuing plants. Reality lies somewhere in between. But when continuing plants are taken as a group, the difficulty in treating entrants as replacing continuing plants – which are, on average, about as productive as entrants – is all too evident.

When the continuing sector is broken into plants that gained market share and plants that lost it, the direction of the replacement process is easier to conjecture. Table 9-7 contains the ratio of the productivity of new plants in 1979 to the productivity of continuing plants that gained and lost market share, respectively.[22] New plants are divided into those associated with new firms entering an industry and those associated with continuing firms. Each of these categories is, in turn, divided into plant births and plant transfers. New plants in all four categories were more productive than were the continuing plants that lost market share; but only new plants of continuing firms were more productive than continuing plants that gained market share. The new plants of new firms, both births and transfers, were significantly less productive than the gainers.

On the basis of relative productivity differentials, it is reasonable to consider entrants as replacing not only exits but also continuing plants that lost market share. Continuing plants that gained market share should have done

Table 9-7. *Relative productivity of plant entrants compared with that of continuing plants that gained and lost market share for 167 four-digit manufacturing industries*

Category	Mean[a]	Probability value of rank test for first differences[b]
Relative to continuing plants gaining share		
Entering firms		
Plant birth (23)	0.97 (0.03)	<.001
Plant transfer (36)	0.90 (0.04)	<.001
Continuing firms		
Plant birth (13)	1.08 (0.04)	.532
Plant transfer (16)	0.86 (0.05)	.004
Relative to continuing plants losing share		
Entering firms		
Plant birth (23)	1.24 (0.07)	.015
Plant transfer (36)	1.09 (0.05)	.771
Continuing firms		
Plant birth (13)	1.32 (0.06)	<.001
Plant transfer (16)	1.10 (0.08)	.256

[a] The mean was calculated across the ratio of the median estimates of the productivity for each class relative to the median estimate of productivity for the declining class. Standard error of the mean is in parentheses.
[b] The minimum significance level required to reject the null hypothesis that the productivity of the plant-birth categories is the same as that for continuing firms.

so both at the expense of declining continuing plants and also of exits. The nature of the trade-off was estimated using regression analysis.

The share of entrants (SHE_9) was calculated for two categories – entering-firm new plants (SH23) and continuing-firm new plants (SH13).[23] The share of exits (SHE_0) was also estimated for two categories – the closed plants of exiting firms (SH34) and the closed plants of continuing firms (SH14).[24] The increase in market share of continuing plants that gained (U) is the difference between the share of this group in 1970 and 1979 (i.e., $U = SHCU_9 - SHCU_0$). The decrease in the market shares of losers (D) is the difference between the share of this group in 1970 and 1979 (i.e., $D = SHCD_9 - SHCD_0$). By definition, the sum of the market shares of entrants and continuing plants gaining market share must just offset the share lost by the others; that is,

$$SH23 + U + SH13 = SH34 + D + SH14. \tag{9-14}$$

In the preceding section, the following restrictive assumptions were made about the direction of the replacement process: that SH23 replaced SH34, that

Table 9-8. *Relationship between share loss and share gain at the establishment level: coefficients from regression analysis*

Regressor	Independent variable			R^2
	SH23	U	SH13	
SH34	0.673	0.832	−0.067	.88
	(0.037)	(0.053)	(0.116)	
	[.0001]	[.0001]	[.5640]	
D	0.296	−0.026	0.718	.58
	(0.035)	(0.049)	(0.108)	
	[.0001]	[.601]	[.0001]	
SH14	0.034	0.193	0.340	.44
	(0.024)	(0.035)	(0.077)	
	[.2181]	[.0001]	[.0001]	

Note: The variables are defined in terms of shipments. SH34 is the share of exiting plant of exiting firms, SH14 is the share of exiting plant of continuing firms, D is the share loss of continuing plants losing relative share, SH23 is the share of plant births of entering firms, SH13 is the share of plant births of continuing firms, and U is the share gain of continuing plants gaining relative share. Entrants and exits contain transfers. Standard error of the parameter estimates is in parentheses and the probability value ($|t| > 0$) is in brackets.

U replaced D; and that SH13 replaced SH14. As intuitively attractive and as empirically tractable as the assumptions underlying this approach are, they need to be investigated more fully.

Table 9-8 reports the coefficients estimated by regressing the market shares of each of the displaced categories (SH34, D, SH14) on the market shares of the entrants and the continuing-plant gainers (SH23, U, SH13);[25] that is,

$$SH34 = a_0 \times SH23 + a_1 \times U + a_2 \times SH13,$$
$$D = b_0 \times SH23 + b_1 \times U + b_2 \times SH13,$$

and

$$SH14 = c_0 \times SH23 + c_1 \times U + c_2 \times SH13. \qquad (9\text{-}15)$$

Each of these coefficients indicates the extent to which a 1 per cent change in a growing category results in the replacement of a declining category. The coefficients sum to one in each column. They indicate that the gainers in each category do not just replace the losers in that category – the diagonal elements[26] are not the only coefficients significantly different from zero. Nevertheless, some replacement patterns are stronger than others. The new plant of new firms (SH23) has a greater effect on the exiting plant of exiting firms

(SH34) than on the declining plant of the continuing-plant population (D). A 1-percentage-point change in SH23 leads to a 0.67-percentage-point change in SH34 but only a 0.30-percentage-point change in D. The effect of an increase of 1 percentage point in the market share of gaining continuing plants (U) is also distributed more heavily on SH34 than on D – 0.83 on SH34, 0 on D, and 0.19 on SH14.

These coefficients allow the displacement effects that were only hinted at previously to be more precisely modeled.[27]

Total productivity growth is broken into its separate components. Let

> SH_j represent the 1979 share of plants in category j (SH23, SHCU$_9$, SHCD$_9$, SH13),
> SH_i represent the 1970 share of plants in category i (SH34, SHCU$_0$, SHCD$_0$, SH14),
> AP_i, AP_j represent the average productivity of categories i and j, respectively; and let
> $i = 34$ represent the closed plants of exiting firms,
> $i = 14$ the closed plants of continuing firms,
> $i = CD_0$ the continuing plants as of 1970 that lose share,
> $i = CU_0$ the continuing plants in 1970 that subsequently gain market share,
> $j = 23$ the new plants of entering firms,
> $j = 13$ the new plants of continuing firms,
> $j = CD_9$ the continuing plants as of 1979 that lose share, and
> $j = CU_9$ the continuing plants as of 1979 that gain market share.

Then the total change in average productivity is written as

$$\text{TOTAL} = \sum_j (SH_j \times AP_j) - \sum_i (SH_i \times AP_i). \qquad (9\text{-}16)$$

The relationship between the categories gaining and losing shares, which is presented in Table 9-8, is represented as

$$SH_i = \sum_j (a_{ij} \times SH_j), \qquad (9\text{-}17)$$

where SH_j is {SH23, U, SH13} and SH_i is {SH34, D, SH14}.

The effect on average productivity of one of the categories j gaining share as a result of displacing plants in a category i losing share is written as

$$\text{PROD}_{ij} = a_{ij} \times SH_j \times (AP_j - AP_i). \qquad (9\text{-}18)$$

In this formulation, each gainer is allowed to affect each loser to some extent. The change due to any one entrant, then, consists of the sum of its effects across all exit components, i. The sum of the components (PROD_{ij}) across all exit classes, i, is

$$PROD_j = SH_j \times \sum_i \left[a_{ij} \times \left(AP_j - AP_i \right) \right];^{28} \qquad (9\text{-}19)$$

that is, the effect of new firms building new plants (category 23) is

$$PROD_{23} = SH23[a_0 \times (AP_{23} - AP_{34}) + b_0 \times (AP_{23} - AP_{CD0})$$
$$+ c_0 \times (AP_{23} - AP_{14})]. \qquad (9\text{-}20)$$

Finally, the total effect of all turnover in all "entry" classes, j, is

$$TURN = \sum_j \left(PROD_j \right). \qquad (9\text{-}21)$$

The sum of the various components derived from equation 9-21 (TURN) along with the growth in the productivity of the growing and declining segments is equal to the estimated change in average productivity (TOTEST):

$$TOTEST = TURN + SHCU_9 \times (AP_{CU9} - AP_{CU0})$$
$$+ SHCD_0 \times (AP_{CD9} - AP_{CD0}). \qquad (9\text{-}22)$$

TOTEST equals the change given by equation 9-16 plus an error term, due to the fact that equation 9-17 is estimated with an error, that is,

$$TOTEST = TOTAL + U, \qquad (9\text{-}23)$$

where U is a stochastic error term.

The first term in equation 9-22 (TURN) represents the productivity growth due to the replacement process associated with competition – the displacement of exiting and declining plant with new and growing plant. The second term represents the productivity growth that occurred in the continuing sector that gained share (CU). The third term represents the growth that occurred in the continuing sector that lost share (CD).[29]

Each component was expressed as a percentage of total growth (TOTEST).[30] The means of these ratios across the reduced sample are reported in Table 9-9.[31] New plants of entering firms contribute 20 per cent of the total, on average, continuing-firm plant births 7 per cent, and the replacement process due to market-share transfer in continuing plants 21 per cent. In addition, 48 per cent comes from productivity growth among market-share gainers and 4 per cent from productivity growth in market-share losers. The contribution made by each component is presented in Figure 9-4. Also presented in Table 9-9 are the results derived using the assumption that entrants replace exits and growing continuing plants displace declining continuing plants. The difference between the two sets of results are relatively small. Treating entrants as primarily replacing exits yields basically the correct answer. Treating entrants as replacing continuing firms does not.

The contribution that turnover made to growth in output per worker can be examined in reverse. Instead of calculating the effect of a particular entry or expansion category, the effect of an exit or contraction category can be

Table 9-9. *Plant turnover and the average proportion of productivity growth accounted for by each entry source (per cent)*

Source of productivity growth	Assumption regarding replacement[a]	
	Complex	Simple
Share growth due to new-plant entry[b]		
By new firms	19.5	24.0
	(2.8)	(3.2)
By continuing firms	7.0	5.1
	(1.7)	(1.8)
Share growth by growing continuing plants	20.9	26.9
	(2.0)	(9.7)
Productivity gains in growing continuing sector	48.2	38.9
	(6.3)	(4.8)
Productivity gains in declining continuing sector	4.4	3.0
	(4.6)	(5.1)

Note: The sample includes only those industries where growth in real output per worker was positive. Standard error of the mean is in parentheses.
[a] The complex replacement assumption uses the trade-offs from equation 9-17 and the estimates from Table 9-8. The simple replacement assumptions come from equations 9-2 and 9-10 and are presented previously in Tables 9-5 and 9-6.
[b] New plants include both plant openings and plant transfers.

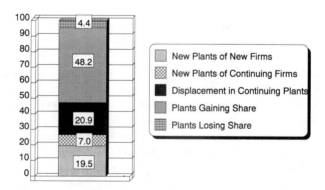

Figure 9-4. Productivity growth: the importance of the components of plant turnover.

Table 9-10. *Plant turnover and the average proportion of productivity growth accounted for by each exit source (per cent)*

Source of productivity growth	Components breakdown[a]
Share growth due to plant exit[b]	
By exiting firms	31.8
	(2.9)
By continuing firms	8.1
	(2.1)
Share loss due to decline in continuing plants	7.4
	(1.4)
Productivity gains in growing continuing sector	48.2
	(6.3)
Productivity gains in declining continuing sector	4.4
	(4.6)

Note: The sample includes only those industries where growth in real output per worker was positive. Standard error of the mean is in parentheses.
[a] The results use the complex replacement assumptions derived from equation 9-17 and the estimates from Table 9-8.
[b] Plant exits include both plant closings and plant transfers.

estimated in an analogous fashion – except with the effects $PROD_{ij}$ in equation 9-18 summed across all entry classes j (Table 9-10). Displacement of plants closed by exiting firms (category 34) accounted for 32 per cent of total productivity growth, on average, closure of continuing-firm plants for 8 per cent, and market-share loss by continuing-firm plants for 7 per cent.

Productivity growth as manna from heaven

While occasionally accused of being too worldly because of their interest in material matters, economists often manifest a tendency to rely on the extra-terrestrial. Earlier monetary economists, with their helicopter bond drops, have long been infamous in this regard. Most of those who do research into productivity in the Solow growth tradition are no exception. Their emphasis on disembodied progress is symptomatic of this abstraction from reality.

This chapter depicts a world in which a Darwinian replacement process is at work. Progress is made as the successful displace the unsuccessful. Whether the economic sectors are considered separately or together, some 40 to 50 per cent of productivity growth is due to plant turnover. That is not the image of disembodied technological progress that many studies depict.

Can we say anything about the degree to which progress is "exogenous", or naturally bestowed on the manufacturing sector? One measure of the amount of exogenous technical progress is the proportion of total growth that occurs in those plants whose market share declines over time. These plants make some progress, but not enough to maintain their market share. The losers' rate of technical progress, then, can be seen as the rate that is bestowed naturally on the industry – a type of Rawlesian patrimony. Winners succeed because they improve on what even losers can manage. If this definition of exogenous technical progress is used, then only 4 per cent of total growth is disembodied.

This definition presumes that the technical progress of losers is independent of winners. It may be that losers learn from winners and that there is a spillover effect. There is little quantitative evidence that such a demonstration effect is very significant. A regression of the change in productivity of the losers on the gainers produces an insignificant regression coefficient of about 0.05. Thus, as a first approximation, the progress made by losers can be considered to be exogenously determined.

While the estimate of exogenous technical change is not unduly biased if the demonstration effect is ignored, there is an alternative way to measure exogenous technical change that generates a more generous estimate of this component. One estimate presented here presumes that if exits had not been replaced, the affected plants would have made no gains in productivity. It also presupposes that all growth in the continuing-plant sector that gained market share was due to the special efforts of plants in this group. It may also be assumed that each of these groups would have had the same rate of productivity growth as the continuing segment that lost market share. In this case, the amount of productivity gain due to exogenous forces can be written as

$$\text{PEXOG} = \sum_i \left(\text{SH}_i \times \left[\text{AP}_i / \text{AP}_{\text{CD0}}\right] \times \text{AP}_{\text{CD9}}\right) - \sum_i \left(\text{SH}_i \times \text{AP}_i\right). \qquad (9\text{-}24)$$

In this formulation, all segments also are assumed to maintain their 1979 market shares at their 1970 level. The mean estimate of the contribution of PEXOG to total productivity gain (TOTAL) for those industries with positive productivity growth is 19 per cent.

The residual can then be divided into that which is due to each entry category. This time the formula for the growth of the entry component, j, is

$$\text{PRODEXOG}_{ij} = a_{ij} \times \text{SH}_j \times \{\text{AP}_j - [(\text{AP}_i / \text{AP}_{\text{CD0}}) \times \text{AP}_{\text{CD9}}]\}. \qquad (9\text{-}25)$$

When this is done for those industries with positive real growth in productivity, new plants of entering firms accounted for 12 per cent of total productivity growth, new plants of continuing firms for 8 per cent, and the gainers in the continuing segment for 21 per cent. In addition, productivity growth in the continuing segment that gained market share accounted for 40 per cent of total productivity growth. The impression of the importance of the turnover to productivity growth is not affected by this assumption about what would have happened in its absence.

To assume that productivity in all plants would have grown at the same rate as that in the continuing sector that lost market share provides a generous estimate of exogenous change. Even so, it indicates that without the turnover process that replaces less productive with more productive plants, productivity growth would have been reduced by 80 per cent, on average. The cumulative effect of this type of difference over a long period is substantial.

The second counterfactual is quite misleading. In fact, turnover was associated with much of the productivity growth. What would have happened in the absence of this competitive process is somewhat moot. What did happen is that growth came as new and expanding plants supplanted exiting as well as declining plants. Some 45 per cent of the total growth in productivity, on average, came from this displacement process. About 50 per cent came from productivity growth in that sector of the continuing-plant population that gained market share. Very little, less than 5 per cent, came as the result of productivity growth in plants that were being supplanted, and of course, none came from those that exited because another more productive plant took its place. In fact, the turnover process mattered very much.

Conclusion

Entry and exit may be viewed either as the engine of progress or as an interesting but irrelevant curiosity. In the first view, entry is seen as bringing new and dynamic firms into the market, and exit as eliminating incompetent ones. In the second view, entry is portrayed as bringing into an industry a group of fringe firms that leave quickly without having made much impact. References to the entry and exit process as "hit and run" give the impression of an unstable fringe that makes no contribution to overall progress.

In a related vein, the competitive process that leads to growth and decline in the continuing sector can be viewed as constructive or destructive, stable or unstable. Gort's (1963) work on the stability of the largest U.S. firms between 1947 and 1954 suggests that there was little turnover among the largest firms. It is not surprising, therefore, that little work has been done on the amount of productivity growth that is due to changes in relative firm position.

Preceding chapters have demonstrated that careful measurement is necessary if the extent of entry and exit is to be fully appreciated. In the short run, the market share transferred by entry and exit is less than that transferred by expansion and contraction in the continuing sector. Short-run estimates of entry and exit, therefore, suggest that the process is not very important. Because most studies have had to rely on such estimates, the impression has been that entry and exit are insignificant. Conclusions about the significance of entry have been based on theoretical constructs rather than empirical evidence. The development of panel data for the Canadian manufacturing sector has meant that such indirect methods are not the only method of evaluating the effect of entry. These panel data show that over time the importance of entry and exit accumulates inexorably and can no longer be dismissed as either absolutely or relatively unimportant.

This chapter looks directly at the contribution of entry and exit and other sources of turnover to productivity growth. It does not rely on correlation or regression analysis to examine the relationship between entry intensity and productivity. Rather, it looks directly at the relative productivity of entrants and exits and calculates the contribution that they make to productivity growth. It extends the previous analysis from simply delineating the magnitude of entry and exit to measuring one dimension of its importance. Previous work with Canadian data (Hazledine, 1985) gives the impression that the effect of entry on productivity is unimportant, indeed that it is negative. This chapter shows that this conclusion is wrong. Entry and exit make a healthy contribution to total productivity growth.

The chapter also shows that industries are not homogeneous – a point that Marshall stresses but that has often been ignored. Entrants arriving in industries are much smaller than the average. While they do grow, they still are well below the average plant size by the end of 10 years, even though they have increased their labour productivity to the average by this time. More importantly, the pattern of substitution is one of new plants of new firms supplanting closed plants of exiting firms, and new plants of continuing firms supplanting closed plants in the same sector. While there is some interaction between the two groups, there is clearly a distinction between them. It is useful, therefore, to differentiate between inter-group and intra-group rivalry (Caves and Porter, 1977). This is important for analysts attempting to model entry. Most work that is based on the early research by Orr (1974) has some more or less complicated version of a limit-entry model behind it, in which entrants and leading firms interact. The results of the analysis in this chapter suggest that entrants have little effect on incumbents; instead, they replace other small firms that exit. Shepherd (1984) is correct when he observes that large existing firms do not initially have to worry about entry. At first, entrants replace small firms. Large market leaders generally only have to worry about which of the large number of entrants will move out of the fringe and challenge them.

10

Merger success

Introduction

Whether the turnover that results from mergers produces real gains is a controversial topic. Mergers are seen to fulfil a number of roles. The most favourable view of their role comes from the theory of corporate control, which holds that mergers and related transactions shift control of business assets into the hands of more efficient managers. According to this theory, gains in performance can be traced to various sources. Changes in control can reduce inputs or salary and wage costs. They can shift resources to better managers and thus produce more value to the firm.

Although the theory is clear on the potential value of the market for corporate control, sceptics in the United States and Britain suggest that there are reasons, both theoretical and empirical, to doubt its efficacy. Markets for corporate control only work when there are sufficient arbitrageurs to take advantage of management lapses and when control can be wrestled from the managers. Some doubters suggest that there are not enough arbitrageurs. Others argue that managers in widely held firms are relatively immune to take-over. Still others claim to have detected serious defects in the performance of the take-over market, thereby suggesting that the market for corporate control works rather ineffectively.

Evidence on the negative effect of large diversifying mergers in the United States was first produced by studies of the popular conglomerate merger movement of the 1960s. Studies using data from the 1960s and 1970s indicate that acquisitions by large firms failed to raise the profitability of the acquired business units. Indeed, Ravenscraft and Scherer (1987) find that profitability was reduced as a result of mergers. Mueller (1985) finds that the market shares of business units transferred through larger mergers over the period 1950–72 fell substantially. Until recently, most of the evidence on ex post merger performance in the United States has been negative.[1] The losses associated with mergers are attributed to the motives of managers of large firms and imperfections in the market for corporate control.

The tenor of Canadian studies is similar, as exemplified by the work of the Royal Commission on Corporate Concentration (1978). The commission finds evidence that unrelated diversification, usually pursued through mergers of some type, had at best neutral effects on firm profitability. The report acknowledges the play of managerial motives that might not maximize stockholder wealth as well as the traditional reasons for increased efficiency in resource use.

Other Canadian studies have produced much the same results. Laiken (1973) finds no association between acquisition activity and financial performance among Canadian firms. Lecraw (1977) finds that large firms that were classified as unrelated diversifiers and were heavily engaged in merger activity tended to report lower profits over the period 1960–75 than did less diversified firms. Jog and Riding (1988) and Tarasofsky (1991), using a sample of mergers obtained from the merger register of the Department of Consumer and Corporate Affairs involving acquirers that were listed on the Toronto Stock Exchange, find about equal numbers of post-merger failures and successes, where success is equated to profitability.

In contrast to these negative findings on the ex post success of mergers, there is much positive ex ante evidence on the efficiency of the market for corporate control. Ratios of market to book value are found to be low for firms acquired in merger transactions, and stock-market returns prior to their acquisition are subnormal. The substantial premiums paid for control of targets over their market values as free-standing firms attests to anticipated increases in value. However, the near zero or negative values placed, on average, on the transactions by the acquirers' shareholders leaves in doubt the existence of expected gains to acquiring and acquired firms taken together.

Here too, the Canadian evidence confirms the patterns found elsewhere. Eckbo (1986, 1988) reports that studies of stock-market valuations done for Canada show that shareholders of both target and acquiring firms benefit. The result for target firms corresponds with findings from the United States, while the result for acquiring firms does not. Together the two results support the efficiency theory of the market for corporate control. Eckbo attributes the difference to the fact that Canadian acquiring and target firms differ in size less than do those of U.S. merger partners, thus making it easier in Canada to separate the gains due to a merger from other influences.

The advantage of census data

This chapter attempts to solve this conundrum by looking once more at the ex post results of changes in control by using data from the Canadian Census of Manufactures[2] on the performance of the merged entities. These data have often been ignored. They reveal that there is much greater concordance between the ex ante financial studies and what happens ex post.

The chapter examines selected measures of success associated with these changes in control. Various aspects of post-merger performance are examined: market share, labour productivity, worker remuneration, and profitability. An establishment-based data file using the Canadian Census of Manufactures principal statistics is employed for the analysis.

Other studies have examined the effect of mergers by focusing on the firm using data from company balance sheets. Unfortunately, balance-sheet information on a firm is difficult to assign to a particular industry because balance sheets often cover operations in a number of different industries.[3] It is also difficult to deal with a wide range of mergers in these circumstances, especially when part of an operation is spun off. Because balance-sheet information is usually provided only at an overall company level, the performance of the parts that are divested cannot be examined prior to the divestiture.

Another source of data for merger studies is stock prices of the merged parties before and after the acquisition (Eckbo, 1986). While providing useful information, these so-called event studies suffer from several disadvantages. First, as is the case with studies that use balance-sheet data, the stock-market event studies measure financial performance. At this level, stock prices may change because of anticipated productivity gains associated with the production process, because of anticipated tax savings, and because of financial innovations.[4] One of the questions left unanswered by stock-market event studies is whether the gains that accrue from mergers are the result of "real" or "financial" effects (Caves, 1987; Scherer, 1988). Second, stock-market data do not permit a very fine level of industry detail to be used in cross-industry analyses because quoted companies often have operations spanning more than one industry.

This chapter uses plant data from the Census of Manufactures to measure the effects of mergers. Size and industry characteristics can, therefore, be assigned relatively precisely. By using these data, this chapter focuses on the real as opposed to the financial characteristics of merged firms. Because census data track the identity of firms and their plants over time, this study promises to be more comprehensive than others that rely on identifying mergers from the financial press. It has the disadvantage that it does not permit financial characteristics to be measured. In light of the recent debate on the meaning of balance-sheet information,[5] this may not be a serious handicap.

A study of the effect of mergers could focus on a short period before and after the merger (see Mueller, 1980). Chapters 2 through 4 indicate why problems will develop with a research strategy that focuses *only* on the short run. In the short run, there is a large amount of transitory change. Shipments increase and decrease quite dramatically and it is difficult to distinguish trend movement from transitory change. Studies that only focus on a short time before and after a merger suffer from not knowing whether the characteristics of a merged firm just before or just after the merger arise from strictly cyclical phenomena. Longer-run studies like those included in Mueller (1987) or performed by Ravenscraft and Scherer (1987) are needed to complement the short-run studies.

In this study, both short- and long-run data are used. Most of the results are based on the latter, which are derived from a comparison of the status of plants and firms in 1970 and 1979. It is often claimed that the fruits of mergers are not harvested immediately but take a period of years to come to fruition. Examining two years about a decade apart allows this to occur. The method is not perfect.[6] But it is an efficacious research strategy when used in conjunction with information on short-run trends. Data on performance in the short run are used to both guide the longer-run analysis and corroborate its findings.

In evaluating the merger process, this chapter first explores the success of mergers by comparing the change in market shares of merged plants to the market-share changes experienced by other plants in the population. It then investigates the effect of mergers on productivity, wage rates, and profitability by comparing them with a control group. Since turnover from changes in control are about as important as turnover from the opening and closing of plant, the performance of merged plant is also compared with the changes that occur as a result of plant births and deaths.

Market-share change for mergers

The success of mergers has been judged in terms of market-share changes after purchase. On the one hand, market-share changes have been invoked as evidence of anti-competitive behaviour. In a horizontal merger, decreases in supply are sometimes used as evidence of the exploitation of monopolistic power. On the other hand, market-share loss may also be of interest where monopoly power is not predicted to emerge from the merger. Diversified mergers, where a new firm enters a market by acquisition, are not generally perceived to have the same anti-competitive consequences as horizontal mergers. Market share is examined to gauge the success of a diversified merger in a different sense. Loss of market share is seen as partial evidence of management's loss of control. Caves (1987: 158) calls Mueller's (1985) finding that mergers in the United States lost market share "blatantly inconsistent with any persistent efficiency gain from mergers".

In order to see whether the same results occurred in Canada, the data on plant and firm status in 1970 and 1979 were used to track what happens to the market share of merged plants. Previous investigations of the effectiveness of mergers in Canada have found that the success of the transaction was higher in related than in unrelated mergers.[7] Related mergers occur when firms acquire others in lines of business that are complementary – either because their final products are related or because of a vertical relationship. This distinction can be best made by considering whether the acquiring firm was already in the same industry. Canadian four-digit industries are defined broadly enough that only a small portion of intra-industry mergers are likely to be strictly horizontal. Therefore, we refer to intra-industry mergers as related rather than horizontal. If the acquiring and acquired firm are not in the same industry, the merger is classified as unrelated. In addition, whether the divesting firm stayed in the industry may also be relevant. These divestitures involve spin-offs of parts of firms that do not completely disappear. Spin-offs can also be divided into those that involve related or unrelated acquiring parties. In the former, the acquiring firm is already in the same industry and the merger involves a type of rationalization. In the latter, the acquiring firm is not in the same industry.

Plants that were divested after 1970 by exiting firms (Table 2-1, category 31) were divided into those that were acquired by entering firms (category 31D) and those that were acquired by continuing firms (category 31H). Plant divestitures by continuing firms (category 11) were divided into those that were acquired by entering firms (11D) and those that were acquired by continuing firms (11H). Similarly, plants as of 1979 that were acquired by entering firms (category 22) were divided into those that were divested by exiting firms (22D) and those that were divested by continuing firms (22H). Plant acquisitions by continuing firms (category 12) were divided into those that were divested by exiting firms (12D) and those that were divested by continuing firms (12H). Then the market shares of the plants in each category in 1970 and 1979 were compared.

The groupings that match plants in 1970 to 1979 are 22D and 31D (unrelated mergers); 22H and 11D (pure spin-offs); 12H and 11H (related spin-offs); and 12D and 31H (related mergers). They are presented in Figure 10-1. Market shares are calculated at the industry level and then averaged to correct for industry effects. Unrelated mergers accounted for an average of 10.1 per cent of shipments in an industry in 1979 and were, therefore, the most important. Related mergers accounted for an average of 2.6 per cent, unrelated spin-offs for an average of 0.6 per cent, and related spin-offs for an average of 0.3 per cent.[8]

Figure 10-2 allows the 1970 and 1979 shares of shipments of each group to be compared. The mean shares in 1970 and 1979 are presented for each category. The means for each category are calculated only across industries with non-zero observations in that category. Pure spin-offs lost market share. In this category (11D, 22H) the average share fell from 3.05 per cent to 2.65 per cent. The same fate befell related spin-offs. Market share decreased from 2.09 to 1.63 per cent for plants transferred from one set of continuing firms to another – categories 11H and 12H. Unrelated mergers show neither success

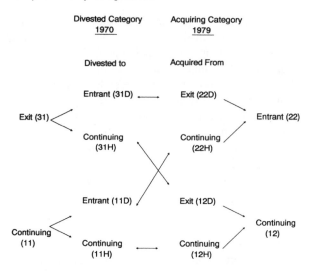

Figure 10-1. Acquisition and divestiture categories.

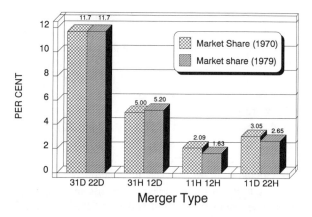

Figure 10-2. The effect of mergers on market shares. (For definitions, see Figure 10-1.)

nor failure based on market share. When plants were transferred from exiting to entering firms (31D, 22D), average market share remained constant at 11.7 per cent. It increased from 5.0 to 5.2 per cent on average only for plants acquired by continuing firms from exiting firms (categories 31H and 12D). Thus, related mergers are the only category to show success based on market share.

These are not large changes when measured in terms of absolute values, but the rates of decline are large, especially for related spin-offs – categories 12H and 11H. The results accord with previous findings that merged plants

Table 10-1. *Regression of market share in 1979 on 1970[a]*

Independent variable	Parameter	Standard error	t for H_o parameter = 0	Significance[b]
Share 1970	0.8859	0.0044	198.8	.0001
Category 22H	−0.001587	0.0017	−0.929	.3530
Category 22D	0.000488	0.00044	1.109	.2675
Category 12H	−0.003040	0.00177	−1.711	.0871
Category 12D	0.000347	0.00068	0.513	.6078
Old 12H	−0.001872	0.00105	−1.781	.0749
Old 12D	0.001288	0.00059	2.199	.0279
Old 11H	−0.001081	0.00121	−0.890	.3734
Old 11D	0.000219	0.00132	0.166	.8683

[a] The regression used all plants in the manufacturing sector in 1970 and 1979. The categories are defined in the text.
[b] The probability value ($|t| > 0$) for the null hypothesis that the coefficient is zero.

often tend to lose market share. However, these averages do not standardize for the fact the mergers involve the larger plants in the population, and on average, larger plants lose market share.

In Chapter 5, plant share in 1979 is regressed on plant share in 1970. The coefficient is found to be significantly less than one. Larger plants lost market share and smaller plants gained it over the 1970s. In order to set the market-share change of merged plants in context, the share regression was repeated with a binary variable for each of the four merger categories. The 1979 category is the variable name – category 12H for related spin-offs, category 12D for related mergers, category 22H for unrelated spin-offs, and category 22D for unrelated mergers (Table 10-1). Only the coefficient on plants acquired by continuing firms from continuing firms (12H) is close to being significant and it is negative. Since the reversion-to-the-mean process is non-linear (see Chapter 5), a number of non-linear functional forms were used here. When various forms were tried that allowed for greater reversion to the mean on the part of the largest firms, the fit improved and the coefficient attached to plants involved in related spin-offs – categories 12H and 11H – became significant at the 5 per cent level.

After size of plants is taken into account, the only share effects of note occur in related spin-offs. Here market share falls – the direction that would be predicted if anti-competitive accommodations were being made. Of course, examining the share of acquired plants is not sufficient to make this point. The acquiring firm may have used the opportunity to expand its existing plant while contracting its newly acquired plant. In order to investigate this, binary variables were entered in the share regression for the existing plant of the acquiring and the divesting firms in the four relevant categories. These are the plants that were neither acquired nor divested by the two parties to the merger but that continued throughout the decade in the same industry. These variables are as follows:

> Old 12H – the existing plant of continuing firms that acquired plant from other continuing firms (related spin-offs)
>
> Old 12D – the existing plant of continuing firms that acquired plant from exiting firms (related mergers)
>
> Old 11H – the existing plant of continuing firms that divested plant acquired by other continuing firms (related spin-offs)
>
> Old 11D – the existing plant of continuing firms that divested plant acquired by entering firms (unrelated spin-offs)

The coefficients for these variables are also reported in Table 10-1. When both parties to the merger continue in the industry, negative coefficients on Old 12H and Old 11H indicate that both lost more market share than might be expected. In the case of the existing plant of the purchaser (Old 12H), this is significant. Thus, related spin-offs are accompanied by lower share both for the acquired plant (Category 12H) and the other existing plants of the acquiring firm (Old 12H). This reinforces the potential for anti-competitive results from related spin-offs. In the case of the related merger where the divesting firm exits (Category 12D), the acquired plant increases market share,[9] but the other existing plant (Old 12D) also increases market share and the latter effect is significant. Related mergers, then, are accompanied by market-share expansion rather than contraction. These contrasting results are not surprising. When both parties remain in the industry after the merger, there is more opportunity or necessity for mutual accommodation. When the divesting firm leaves an industry, there is no need for accommodation and the acquirer can act more aggressively to gain market share.

Mergers and productivity

If mergers have relatively little effect on market share, they may have a more discernible impact on other measures of performance. Market share, after all, is an indirect measure of performance. It is not easy to interpret changes in market share in isolation. To some observers, a decline in market share indicates failure; to others, it suggests anti-competitive accommodation.

A more direct measure of performance is productivity. Reallocations that lead to increased productivity are potentially welfare enhancing. Several analyses have, therefore, examined the effect of mergers on productivity as a proxy for the cost-decreasing effects of mergers (Newbould, 1970; Cowling et al., 1980). This issue can be examined for Canada by following the performance of mergers in both the short and long run. For the short-run analysis,

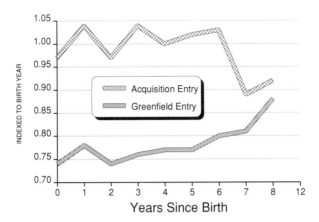

Figure 10-3. Average relative productivity of greenfield and acquisition entrants, by age.

the yearly data on acquisition entrants into the manufacturing sector as a whole were employed. Value-added per worker in acquired firms was tracked over the first seven years after the merger and compared with the value-added per worker in all other plants.[10] The mean relative value-added per worker of all merger entrants between 1970 and 1981 is plotted in Figure 10-3, along with the experience of greenfield entrants. The productivity of acquisition entrants is slightly below the mean at the time of the merger; it experiences a short-run increase that keeps it generally above the control group in the first six years after the merger and then it falls below the norm. In contrast, the productivity of greenfield entrants starts well below the mean and continuously increases over the decade.

The aggregate nature of these data may conceal greater change at the four-digit industry level. Therefore, a longer time horizon and more detailed industry data were used to investigate the issue further. The labour productivity in 1970 of plants that were merged some time during the decade was compared with their productivity in 1979.

Several tests were used to examine the productivity change associated with mergers, because it is important to know how robust the results are to different methodologies, and also because the tests reveal different information on the success of the merger process. The first two tests summarize information at the industry level and then take industry averages to summarize the impact of mergers. Industry averages give an indication of the central tendency of the process. But knowledge of the central tendency can be inadequate and misleading in some circumstances – especially when distributions are skewed. Therefore, the last two tests summarize information from all plants directly.

Table 10-2. *Proportion of merged plants in the manufacturing sector above and below the median plant, classified on the basis of labour productivity, 1970 and 1979 (per cent)*[a]

| | | Proportion | | |
| | | Top | Bottom | Significance of |
Category	Year	50 per cent	50 per cent	differences[b]
Divested by exiting firm				
Related mergers				
12D	1979	2.64	1.67	.0143
31H	1970	2.25	1.77	.0001
Unrelated mergers				
22D	1979	5.52	5.25	.0001
31D	1970	5.79	4.32	.0001
Divested by continuing firm				
Related spin-offs				
12H	1979	0.44	0.18	.0012
11H	1970	0.36	0.21	.0543
Unrelated spin-offs				
22H	1979	0.42	0.24	.0340
11D	1970	0.34	0.26	.2695

[a] The plants in each industry were divided equally on the basis of labour productivity and the number of merged plants in each group was calculated. The proportions are the sum of all merged plants in a category divided by the sum of all plants above or below the median. Calculating the proportion by industry and taking the mean across all industries yields basically the same results.
[b] The minimum significance level required to reject the null hypothesis that the proportions above and below the median plant size are the same.

Differences in the proportion of plants merged. The first test splits the plant distribution on the basis of productivity in 1970 and 1979 and calculates the percentage of the most and least productive plants that were merged. The mean proportion of the most and the least productive plants accounted for by a particular merger category is presented in Table 10-2 along with the significance level of a non-parametric test that the two proportions differ.

In all cases, a higher proportion of the most productive than the least productive plants in 1970 were involved in mergers, and with the exception of unrelated spin-offs – the categories that contain plants divested by continuing firms (22H and 11D) that were acquired by new firms – the differences are significant. By 1979, the proportions in the more productive half that were involved in mergers had gone up for all categories except for unrelated mergers – plants divested by exiting firms and acquired by entering firms (31D and 22D). Moreover, for the three categories where the proportion in the more productive half increased, the differences between most productive and least productive halves became more significant. This evidence suggests that merged plant tended to be more productive and that changes in control were associated with an increase in productivity – except for unrelated mergers.

Differences in average productivity of merged plants. For the second test, the average productivities of merged plants in an industry in 1970 and 1979 were compared. In order to standardize for industry-specific effects on productivity, the relative productivity of merged plants was compared with that of plants that continued throughout the decade without a change in ownership.[11] The mean relative productivity ratio for all four-digit industries is presented in Table 10-3. Also reported is a test that the merged plants differ in productivity from the continuing plants.

The data confirm that merged plants in 1970 were already more productive than continuing plants that did not merge – though only the related spin-off category (11H) is significantly different from the continuing-plant control group. By 1979, all merger categories had increased their relative productivity – though unrelated mergers (31D, 22D) once more experienced the least change. The three other categories experienced substantial increases in their relative productivity, and by 1979 there is a statistically significant difference between their productivity and that of the plants in the control group.

The economic significance of these changes can be appreciated when they are compared with those resulting from the opening and closing of plant – whether by greenfield entry, closedown exit, or by continuing firms' new plant. The increases in the average industry ratios for all but unrelated mergers are less than those for plant openings and closings – but they are not so small that they can be dismissed. For example, related mergers (31H, 12D) contribute about the same productivity increase as the plant openings and closings of continuing firms and about 70 per cent that of the greenfield entry and closedown exits.

Regression analysis across the entire plant sample. Industry averages such as those presented in Table 10-3 may conceal important information if merger intensity differs substantially across industries. If mergers are concentrated in industries where they are most successful, industry averages will hide the extent to which mergers are successful. Cross-industry averages may also miss changes that are entirely due to other factors. Productivity and changes in productivity may be higher for larger plants because of their greater capital intensity. One way to incorporate all the information in the sample – to allow for these effects within industries and at the same time to allow for industry

Table 10-3. *Average labour productivity of merged plants in the manufacturing sector relative to that of continuing plants, 1970 and 1979*

Category	Year	Mean relative productivity[a]	Standard error of mean	Significance[b]
Divested by exiting firms				
Related mergers				
12D	1979	1.20	0.05	.0001
31H	1970	1.03	0.04	n.s.[c]
Unrelated mergers				
22D	1979	1.13	0.04	n.s.
31D	1970	1.09	0.03	n.s.
Divested by continuing firms				
Related spin-offs				
12H	1979	1.32	0.12	.015
11H	1970	1.15	0.06	.040
Unrelated spin-offs				
22H	1979	1.32	0.13	.016
11D	1970	1.13	0.06	n.s.
Plant birth/death category[d]				
Greenfield entrant (23)	1979	1.04	0.03	.173
Closedown exit (34)	1970	0.79	0.02	.0001
Continuing-firm plant birth (13)	1979	1.15	0.05	.006
Continuing-firm plant death (14)	1970	0.96	0.04	.003

[a] Productivity is measured relative to continuing plants that did not change ownership. It is the average of the ratio-of-the-median estimate of the productivity of plants in each class divided by the median estimate of the productivity of plants in the continuing-plant class that did not change ownership over the decade.
[b] The probability of a greater absolute value of the signed-rank statistic for the mean difference between the median of productivity in each merger class and that of the continuing class.
[c] Not significant at a 5 per cent level.
[d] For plant birth and death categories, see Table 7-3 or Table 2-1.

differences – is to regress the productivity of each plant on size and binary variables representing entry, exit, and merger categories.

The formulation used was

$$\log(\text{Prod}) = b_0 + b_1 \times \log(\text{Emp}) + b_2 \times D(i) + b_3 \times I(j) \dots,$$

$$(10\text{-}1)$$

where Prod is productivity,[12] Emp is employment, the $D(i)$ are the binary variables for each category i, and the $I(j)$ are the binary variables for each industry j.

Equation 10-1 can be interpreted as a production function that relates output to labour. The regression was estimated three times; first, for all observations in 1970, then for all observations in 1979, and finally for both years pooled together. In the last case, a binary variable was used to allow the intercept and the slope coefficient on employment size to vary between years. In all three regressions, industry effects were also included with the use of binary variables. When suitably transformed, the estimated coefficients attached to the binary variables that represent each merger category provide an estimate of the productivity of the category relative to the omitted category.[13] The omitted category is the continuing-plant population that did not experience a change in ownership. Thus, the transformed coefficients are directly comparable with those reported in Table 10-3, which were derived from industry averages.

The results of the three regressions are presented in Table 10-4. The first row of each category contains the results for 1979; the second row, for 1970; the third row, the coefficient representing the added effect of that category in 1979 over that in 1970 – it measures the change over the decade in the relative position of merged plants. Also included are the probability values indicating the level that would have to be adopted to reject the null hypothesis that the estimated parameter was equal to one – that there was no productivity difference between the particular merger category and plants that did not change ownership.

The regression coefficients tell a similar story to that told by the industry averages presented in Table 10-3. The least change is in unrelated mergers, which are already significantly more productive than the control group in 1970. All the coefficients in the other categories are higher in 1979 than in 1970.

The estimated value of the increase is important when set against the productivity changes due to entry and exit that are given by the coefficients in Table 10-4 attached to the entry and exit categories (34, 14, 23, and 13). In Chapter 9, it was demonstrated that the contribution made to productivity growth by new plants could be approximated by assuming that greenfield entrants replace closedown exits, and that continuing firms' new plants replace continuing firms' closed plants. Using this assumption, it is evident that turnover contributed substantially to productivity. Exiting firms closed plants that were only 89 per cent as productive as continuing plants and were replaced by entrants that opened plants that were 116 per cent as productive – a gain of 27 percentage points, on average. In the continuing-firm sector, the difference between closed and opened plant produces an average gain of 30 percentage points.

Plants in related mergers (12D, 31H) produce a gain of some 14 percentage points; plants involved in related spin-offs (12H, 11H) increase their relative productivity by 12 percentage points on average; unrelated spin-offs (22H,

Table 10-4. *Regression coefficients for labour productivity of entry, exit, and merger categories relative to those for continuing plants, 1970 and 1979[a]*

Category	Year	Coefficient[b]	Significance[c]
Divested by exiting firms			
Related mergers			
12D	1979	1.09	.004
31H	1970	1.01	.666
Ratio (1979/70)		1.14	.001
Unrelated mergers			
22D	1979	1.03	.077
31D	1970	1.05	.001
Ratio (1979/70)		1.01	.753
Divested by continuing firms			
Related spin-offs			
12H	1979	1.20	.012
11H	1970	1.12	.065
Ratio (1979/70)		1.12	.252
Unrelated spin-offs			
22H	1979	1.11	.154
11D	1970	1.02	.760
Ratio (1979/70)		1.09	.334
Plant birth/death category			
Greenfield entrant (23)	1979	1.16	.010
Closedown exit (34)	1970	0.89	.009
Continuing-firm plant birth (13)	1979	1.31	.020
Continuing-firm plant death (14)	1970	1.01	.020

[a] See Table 2-1 and text for definitions of categories.
[b] The estimated coefficient in the first two rows of each category is the productivity of the category relative to that of continuing plants that do not change ownership during the decade. The coefficient in the third row of each category is the additional effect of that category in 1979 relative to 1970.
[c] The probability value for a two-tailed test of the null hypothesis that the coefficient is one.

11D) gain some 9 percentage points relative to that of continuing firms that did not change hands. These gains are smaller than those derived from opening new plants and closing plants, but they are still important.

Weighted averages of average productivity. Regression analysis makes use of all the information in the census on the effect of mergers, but like industry averages, it provides only a summary statistic that indicates the central tendency of the process. In order to determine the total effect, the weighted averages of the relative productivity of all merged plants were calculated across the entire population.[14] The weighted averages were calculated using different weights for 1970 and 1979,[15] because it is appropriate to measure success not only by the amount of change but also by whether the plants that are making progress increase their value-added and their market share.[16]

The results are reported in Table 10-5, both for the merger categories and for the turnover categories (plant birth and death). The results show a considerable productivity increase in both these turnover categories – though the absolute levels of productivity are somewhat lower in the two years because of the weighting process. Overall, the weighted relative productivity of all merged plant increased by about half of that of greenfield entrants and closedown exits and by about one-quarter of that of continuing-firm plant openings and closings.

The differences between the weighted and unweighted averages for productivity generally accord with what is expected from the changes in market shares. Related and unrelated spin-offs show poorer performance when weighted averages are taken; they also experienced share loss during the period. Related mergers still show a positive gain, but unrelated mergers now do equally well. That unrelated mergers do somewhat better when weighted averages are examined means that the most productive in this group were gaining market share at a greater rate than the most productive in the control group. The weighted averages show the importance of taking into account the total effect of mergers in a given category. When this is done, both types of mergers show positive gains.

Mergers and labour costs

Enhanced efficiency that results from changes in corporate control may arise from the reduction in costs. The area of labour costs has garnered particular attention.[17] Labour costs may be reduced either by economizing on labour inputs or by reducing wage rates. Lichtenberg and Siegel (1989a) show that U.S. mergers over the period 1977–82 tended to reduce head office personnel. Brown and Medoff (1988) focus on the extent to which mergers affect labour costs.

The effect of mergers on labour costs in Canada was evaluated by comparing three separate determinants of these costs before and after the merger. These variables were the wage rate paid to production workers,[18] the salary rate paid to non-production workers,[19] and the percentage of the work-force that were non-production workers. These variables were calculated in 1970 and 1979 relative to the control group – continuing plants that were not affected by a change in control. For each characteristic, two summary statistics

Table 10-5. *Weighted averages[a] of labour productivity of new, closed, and merged plants relative to those of continuing plants, 1970 and 1979*

Category	Year	Productivity[b]
Greenfield entrant	1979	0.85
Closedown exit	1970	<u>0.68</u>
Difference		0.17
Continuing firm		
New plant	1979	1.11
Plant closure	1970	<u>0.79</u>
Difference		0.32
Merged plant		
All acquired	1979	0.95
All divested	1970	<u>0.87</u>
Difference		0.08
Related mergers		
12D	1979	0.98
31H	1970	<u>0.87</u>
Difference		0.11
Unrelated mergers		
22D	1979	0.95
31D	1970	<u>0.87</u>
Difference		0.08
Related spin-offs		
12D	1979	0.89
11H	1970	<u>0.86</u>
Difference		0.03
Unrelated spin-offs		
22H	1979	0.82
11D	1970	<u>0.85</u>
Difference		−0.03

[a] The weighted average is the ratio of the weighted value-added per person in a category relative to that of plants that continued over the decade without a change in ownership. It is calculated as the ratio of the sum of value-added to the sum of production workers in the entrant/merger category divided by the same ratio for continuing plants.
[b] Value-added per person.

were estimated. The first – a weighted average – was estimated for each category. The second was derived from a regression of the labour-cost characteristic on a variable that allows for plant size, on industry binary variables, and on merger-category binary variables. The formulation used was

$$\log(W) = b_0 + b_1 \times \log(\text{Emp}) + b_2 \times D(i) + b_3 \times I(j) \ldots, \quad (10\text{-}2)$$

where *W* is wage rate, salary level, or percentage of non-production workers; Emp is employment; the $D(i)$ are the binary variables for each category; and the $I(j)$ are the binary variables for each industry.

The same procedure used for equation 10-1 was employed here. The estimated coefficients attached to the binary variables that represent each merger category provide an estimate of the wage rate of the category relative to that of the omitted category. The omitted category was the continuing-plant population that did not experience a change in ownership.

The effects of mergers on labour costs using both the weighted average and the regression approach are reported in Table 10-6, along with data on the effect of the plant births and deaths on the same variables. Greenfield entry and closedown exit generally contribute to an increase in both wages and salaries – irrespective of the technique used. Ceteris paribus, continuing-firm plant births and deaths contribute to an increase in salaries but not in wages. When the weighted averages that consider share changes are calculated, incumbent plant creation and destruction also contribute to higher wages. Plant openings and closures also contribute to a reduction in the proportion of workers in non-production jobs.

The effect of mergers on wages is different from their effect on salaries. Overall, the weighted averages show there is little effect on wages[20] and a decrease in salaries. They do have an effect similar to plant turnover in reducing the proportion of non-production workers. An examination of the underlying components reveals that few of the individual categories show an effect – with the exception, once more, of related mergers. Here mergers increase wage rates from significantly below the norm to the average level; they decrease salaries that are at the norm to significantly below the norm; and they also decrease the percentage of non-production workers from the norm to significantly below the norm. Unrelated mergers also have a downward effect on salary rates when the regression technique is used, but this disappears when the weighted average that considers share changes is calculated. These results and those of the regression analysis demonstrate that it is the unrelated mergers with the highest value-added per worker and the higher salary rates that do best in terms of share gains over the period.

Mergers and profitability

Profitability serves as another widely used standard of performance for merger studies. It has long been stressed that an evaluation of the welfare effects of mergers must consider the trade-off between efficiency gains due to cost reductions and the welfare losses due to the exploitation of monopoly power. The productivity gains examined in the preceding section are a proxy for the cost-reducing effects of mergers – measured at the plant level.

Table 10-6. Wage rates, salary levels, and proportion of work-force in non-production employment of new, closed, and merged plants relative to those of continuing plants, 1970 and 1979

Category	Year	Wage rate[a] Weighted average[d]	Wage rate[a] Regression coefficient[e]	Salary level[b] Weighted average	Salary level[b] Regression coefficient	Non-production workers[c] Weighted average	Non-production workers[c] Regression coefficient
Greenfield entrants	1979	0.86	1.00	0.93	0.96*	0.44	0.94*
Closedown exit	1970	0.81	0.97*	0.88	0.91*	0.41	1.01
Continuing firms							
New plant	1979	0.98	1.04*	0.98	0.99	0.88	0.90*
Closed plant	1970	0.93	1.05*	0.93	0.95*	1.00	0.98
Merged plants							
Related mergers							
12D	1979	1.01	1.01	0.95	0.95*	1.30	0.92*
31H	1970	0.98	0.98*	0.99	0.99	1.30	0.97
Unrelated mergers							
22D	1979	1.00	0.99	0.93	0.96*	1.04	1.01
31D	1970	1.00	0.99	0.93	1.01	1.77	0.98
Related spin-offs							
12H	1979	1.02	1.06*	0.99	1.00	2.09	0.92
11H	1970	1.02	1.04	1.04	0.98	2.76	1.07
Unrelated spin-offs							
22H	1979	0.97	0.99	0.94	0.99	1.30	1.02
11D	1970	0.98	1.02	0.97	0.97	1.35	1.08
All mergers	1979	0.99	—	0.95	—	1.32	—
	1970	0.98	—	0.98	—	1.42	—

[a] Defined as production worker remuneration divided by total number of production workers.
[b] Defined as salaries paid to non-production workers divided by number of non-production workers.
[c] Defined as number of non-production workers divided by total employment (production and non-production workers).
[d] The weighted average is calculated as the sum of wages divided by the sum of all production workers in a category divided by the same ratio for all plants that continued through the decade without a change in ownership.
[e] The regression is equation 10-2.
* Significantly different from one at the 1 per cent level.

Profitability changes may be, but are not necessarily, a proxy for changes in monopoly power.

Profitability can change after a merger for several reasons other than just the accumulation of market power. On the one hand, acquired firms may have less than average levels of profitability, and acquisition may return profit levels to industry norms. Thus, increases in profitability may be a sign that inefficiency has been overcome. On the other hand, a decline in profitability may indicate that the merger has resulted in loss of control. Several studies have suggested that post-merger profitability declines and that mergers are, therefore, unsuccessful. Investigating whether this is so, on average, is one way to address how widespread such a failure might be.

This section explores whether the trends that others have found of decreasing post-merger profitability[21] are present in the Canadian manufacturing sector. As in the investigation of productivity, the effect of mergers on profitability is examined by first using industry-wide ratios of pre- and post-merger profitability, and then by employing regression analysis that considers the changes in profitability of all plants. In each case, merged plant is compared with continuing non-merged plant within the same industry to standardize for general changes that are occurring within an industry. Profitability is defined as profits divided by shipments[22] – what is commonly referred to as the price–cost margin in empirical studies.

The price–cost margin is widely used to measure performance, because in a monopoly model it is equal to the inverse of demand elasticity and, therefore, provides a measure of monopoly power. It is used here for a different reason. It is an efficient way of separating the effects of a merger on productivity from profitability. If a merger allows total value-added to increase, it may also increase profits. Suppose the production function is

$$Q = f[L, K] \times \exp[b_2 \times D(i)], \tag{10-3}$$

and for purposes of simplicity $f(L, K)$ is a Cobb–Douglas function. The term $\exp[b_2 \times D(i)]$ catches the productivity effects of the mergers category $D(i)$ on the production function. Then the partial profit function is

$$\text{Profit} = m \times f[L, K] \times \exp[b_2 \times D(i)].^{[23]} \tag{10-4}$$

Thus, if productivity is increased by merger category $D(i)$, profits will be similarly affected. In order to test whether profitability was higher than might be expected on the basis of the earlier productivity result, an additional term must be added to allow for such an effect.

In this case, the profit formulation is written

$$\text{Profit} = m \times f[L, K] \times \exp[b_2 \times D(i)] \times \exp[d_2 \times D(i)], \tag{10-5}$$

where $\exp[d_2 \times D(i)]$ is the additional effect of a merger on profitability that does not stem just from an increase in productivity.

The effect of mergers on profitability can be separated from their effect on productivity by dividing equation 10-5 by equation 10-3. Under the previous assumptions about functional form and profit-maximizing behaviour, profits divided by shipments (PCM) is a function only of the binary variables that determine the effect of a merger category on profits; that is,

$$\log(\text{PCM}) = C + d_2 \times D(i) + \cdots, \tag{10-6}$$

where d_2 represents the coefficient that measures the pure profitability effect from equation 10-5.

Table 10-7 contains ratios of the relative profitability (profits divided by shipments) of merged plants calculated at the industry level. These relative-profitability estimates are derived by calculating, for each industry, the median estimate of profitability of merged plants divided by that of all continuing plants that did not change ownership over the period, and then calculating the mean of these ratios across all industries where there were plants in the particular merger category. Also reported in Table 10-7 are the standard error of the mean and the probability of the non-parametric signed-rank test that the mean difference between the median profitability in each merger class and the continuing sector is non-zero. Finally, in each case the mean difference between the profitability relative to the merger category before a merger (in 1970) and after a merger (in 1979) is presented, along with its standard error and the probability that the mean difference in the ratios is non-zero using a non-parametric signed-rank test.

The results show that the profitability of the merged plants does not differ significantly from that of the control group prior to merger. They are all more profitable after the merger. However, the increase in relative profitability is only highly significant for related and unrelated mergers – plants that are divested by exiting firms (31H and 31D). When this information is combined with the relative productivity ratios from Table 10-3, it is evident that related mergers experience a significant improvement in unweighted average industry productivity and profitability. For unrelated mergers, unweighted average productivity does not increase, but profitability does.

Plants divested by continuing firms (spin-offs) react in the same way whether productivity or profitability statistics are used. On average, the increase in relative productivity and profitability is of at least the same magnitude as that of the divested plants of exiting firms, but it is not as significant because of the larger standard error of the mean.

In order to investigate whether the industry averages in Table 10-7 underestimate the significance of the changes that were taking place because they involved aggregation to the industry level, regression analysis using the plant

Table 10-7. *Mean profitability of merged plants relative to that of continuing plants*

Category	Year	Mean relative profitability[a]	Standard error of mean	Significance[b]
Divested by exiting firms				
Related mergers				
12D	1979	1.23	0.08	.006
31H	1970	1.02	0.06	n.s.[d]
Difference[c]		0.21	0.10	.007
Unrelated mergers				
22D	1979	1.26	0.07	.0003
31D	1970	1.10	0.05	n.s.
Difference		0.16	0.07	.03
Divested by continuing firms				
Related spin-offs				
12H	1979	1.24	0.14	.09
11H	1970	0.91	0.09	n.s.
Difference		0.33	0.17	.10
Unrelated spin-offs				
22H	1979	1.22	0.11	.29
11D	1970	0.91	0.10	n.s.
Difference		0.31	0.15	.14

[a] Profitability (profits/shipments) is measured relative to continuing plants that did not change ownership. The mean is calculated across 167 four-digit industries. It is the average of the ratio of the median estimate of the profitability of plants in each class divided by the median estimate of the profitability of plants in the continuing class that did not change ownership over the decade.

[b] The probability of a greater absolute value of the signed-rank statistic for the mean difference between the median of profitability in each entry class and that of the continuing class under the null hypothesis of no difference.

[c] The third line in each panel represents the difference in relative profitability of the category. The associated level of significance is the probability of a greater absolute value of the signed-rank statistic for the mean difference between the median of productivity in each merger class and that of the continuing class.

[d] Not significant at a 5 per cent level.

as the unit of observation and equation 10-6 were employed to test for significant profitability differences. The coefficients d_2 associated with each of the merger categories that are estimated from equation 10-6 are reported in Table 10-8. Once again, three regressions were estimated for each formulation. The first used 1970 data, the second used 1979 data, and the third pooled the two data sets. The coefficient estimates reported for the pooled data set are estimates of the *additional* effect of the merger category in 1979. In each

Table 10-8. *Regression coefficients for relative profitability of merger categories, 1970 and 1979*[a]

Category	Year	Coefficient[b]	Significance[c]
Divested by exiting firms			
Related mergers			
12D	1979	1.17	.001
31H	1970	1.04	.312
Ratio (1979/70)		1.16	.009
Unrelated mergers			
22D	1979	1.13	.000
31D	1970	1.03	.233
Ratio (1979/70)		1.14	.001
Divested by continuing firms			
Related spin-offs			
12H	1979	1.24	.044
11H	1970	1.03	.762
Ratio (1979/70)		1.23	.153
Unrelated spin-offs			
22H	1979	1.14	.185
11D	1970	1.02	.839
Ratio (1979/70)		1.15	.361
Plant birth/death category			
Greenfield entrants (23)	1979	1.19	.001
Closedown exits (34)	1970	0.94	.001
Continuing-firm			
plant birth (13)	1979	1.31	.001
Continuing-firm			
plant death (14)	1970	0.92	.001

[a] See Table 2-1 and text for definition of categories.
[b] The estimated coefficient in the first two rows of each category is the productivity of the category relative to that of continuing plants that do not change ownership during the decade. The coefficient in the third row is the additional effect of that category in 1979 relative to 1970.
[c] The probability value for a two-tailed test of the null hypothesis that the coefficient is one.

case, the original coefficient was transformed into a value that measures the effect of the category relative to the control group. The control group consists of continuing plants that were not merged over the period. As such, the coefficients are comparable with those reported in Table 10-7, which were derived from industry averages.

The data in Table 10-8 confirm the finding that divested plants in all categories were not significantly more or less profitable than the control group in 1970 (Table 10-7). Moreover, the plants that are divested by exiting firms had become more profitable than the control group by 1979. The profitability of exiting firms' plants, then, is turned around by the merger process. The transfer of plant from one continuing firm to another (11H, 12H) has the same effect.

Conclusion

Mergers can be studied by themselves or as part of a larger phenomenon. The latter approach has been taken here, since mergers are only one way that firms can enter an industry or expand within it. This chapter shows how mergers contribute to growth and decline.

In Chapter 3 the merger process was compared with greenfield entry and closedown exit. Similarities and differences between mergers and other aspects of the turnover process were examined in order to avoid the tendency to treat mergers in isolation of other events. When the death or dissolution rate of mergers is compared with the death rate of alternative forms of entry, merger entry no longer appears as unsuccessful when treated by itself. It is only one of several ways that entrepreneurs enter an industry and all of these bear considerable risk of failure.

This chapter shows that mergers are successful in another sense; that they have a "real" effect. The short-run effect of mergers – defined at a relatively aggregated level – on plants acquired by entrants was to increase their market share and productivity. But this effect is less than that experienced by greenfield entrants. The longer-run effects of mergers are then investigated by examining the relative performance of merged plants both before and after the merger. The results confirm that mergers have a real effect.

Caves (1987) and Scherer (1988) stress the dichotomy between financial-event studies that show stockholders gain from mergers, on the one hand, and industrial-organization studies that often do not find changes that are strongly suggestive of real gains associated with mergers. Using a comprehensive micro-economic database, this chapter provides evidence of such gains. Of the four merger categories studied here, the productivity or profitability levels of three increased from being not significantly different from the norm prior to the merger to being significantly greater than the norm after the merger.

In the largest category – plants that are transferred from firms exiting an industry to firms entering an industry (unrelated mergers) – the divested plants were generally more productive both before and after the merger, with no change in unweighted productivity over the period but some increase in weighted average productivity. Profitability that was not significantly different from the norm before the merger had become so afterward; moreover, the increase was significant.

The category of related mergers – plants that are divested by exiting firms but are acquired by continuing firms – provides the strongest evidence that mergers are associated with real change. Here market-share gains were positive both for the acquired plant and for the other plant of the acquiring firms. While neither profitability nor productivity were significantly different from the norm prior to merger, both were significantly so after the merger and both increases were significantly greater than zero.

Spin-offs provide weaker evidence that real changes are taking place. In the case of related spin-offs, plants prior to divestiture were more productive than the norm but not more profitable. After the merger their profitability increased to become significantly higher than that of the control group. On the other hand, unrelated spin-offs show less evidence of success based on standard statistical criteria. The changes affecting them are basically the same in sign and sometimes in magnitude to those experienced by related spin-offs, but they are not as statistically significant – primarily because of the smaller number of observations in this merger category.

These results suggest that there is no conflict between the ex ante and ex post evidence on the efficiency of large mergers. When comprehensive data on mergers such as these are employed, mergers no longer appear to be generally unsuccessful. This accords with other evidence: Kaplan (1989) presents evidence that sell-offs and spin-offs have value-creating potential; Lichtenberg and Siegel (1987) use a comprehensive database for the United States similar to the one used here and also report beneficial results of mergers.

This chapter also confirms the evidence based on balance-sheet data presented by the Royal Commission on Corporate Concentration (1978), Caves et al. (1980), and Lecraw (1977) that related mergers are the most successful. In addition, it demonstrates that they are not the only type of merger to affect productivity and profitability.

Finally, it has been shown here that mergers in the 1970s had very little effect on labour costs. While productivity and profitability were increasing, there is little evidence that this was at the expense of production workers. Indeed, related mergers – which had the greatest impact on productivity, profitability, and market share – also had a positive impact on wages. Mergers did, however, have a negative impact on the proportion of the labour force classified as non-production workers and on their remuneration. This result also accords with results reported by Lichtenberg (1992) for the United States.

11

Turnover in domestic and foreign enterprises

Introduction

There is considerable diversity in the type and intensity of turnover both across and within industries. On the one hand, the rates of entry, exit, and continuing-firm displacement differ across industries. On the other hand, there is considerable heterogeneity within industries; firms are not subject to the same uncertainties. Age and size are two characteristics that have been shown in previous chapters to affect the performance of different firms within industries. This chapter examines whether the nationality of a firm also differentiates firms and affects intra-industry firm performance.

Foreign-controlled firms are seen to embody a different form of organization than are domestic-controlled firms, to be able to coordinate larger operations, to possess superior technologies, to access strategic sources of raw materials more efficiently (Rugman, 1980). As a result, there are substantial differences between the plants of domestic-controlled and foreign-controlled firms in the Canadian manufacturing sector. The parents of foreign-owned plants were more diversified across industries (Table 11-1). Within each industry, the foreign-owned plants were more specialized. Combined with their larger average size, the greater degree of specialization in foreign plants meant that their production runs were longer and economies of scale in product lines easier to exploit. Concomitantly, foreign-owned plants had higher labour productivity and higher remuneration rates. While the salary paid to non-production workers was much the same in the two populations, foreign-owned plants employed a larger proportion of their work-force in higher-paid white-collar jobs, since a larger proportion of their total work-force was classified as non-production workers.

These differences indicate that foreign and domestic firms are drawn from different populations. Variations in size and productivity suggest that foreign firms may not be subject to the same competitive forces that lead to entry and exit, growth and decline.[1]

This chapter focuses on differences in turnover between foreign-controlled

263

Table 11-1. *Ratio of selected characteristics of foreign- to Canadian-owned plants[a] for the manufacturing sector, 1979*

Characteristics	Mean ratio of foreign- to Canadian-owned plants[b]
Firm specialization[c]	0.80
	(0.02)
Plant specialization[d]	1.18
	(0.03)
Average plant size[e]	2.66
	(0.04)
Value-added per employee[f]	1.41
	(0.04)
Shipments per employee[f]	1.43
	(0.07)
Income per production worker[g]	1.07
	(0.01)
Income per salaried worker[h]	1.01
	(0.02)
White-collar jobs as a proportion of industry employment[i]	1.08
	(0.01)

[a] Only plants filling out the long census forms were used, since indices of specialization were being calculated. Use of all plants does not affect the direction of the differences in other cases.
[b] The ratios were calculated by taking the mean value of a characteristic for foreign and domestic plants in each four-digit industry and dividing the former by the latter, then taking the average across all four-digit industries in the particular industry grouping. The standard error of the mean is in parentheses.
[c] The Herfindahl index of the parent's specialization across all four-digit industries in manufacturing, mining, and logging.
[d] The Herfindahl index of the plant's shipments at the four-digit ICC commodity level.
[e] Calculated using employment.
[f] Employees used in this calculation include production and salaried workers.
[g] Income is wages paid to production workers.
[h] Income is salaries of non-production workers.
[i] The number of non-production workers divided by total employment.

and domestic-controlled firms. Differences in both the intensity and the impact of turnover on market share, productivity, and wage rates are considered. Two different types of turnover are investigated – plant birth/death and control changes. The latter receive special emphasis. The extent to which the effects of control changes are determined by factors that give foreign firms a general advantage or just an advantage in certain industrial sectors is examined by asking whether differences in the experience of foreign firms are the result of the industries in which they are located, rather than of ownership.

Analytical background: multinational enterprises

The theory of multinational enterprises provides the analytical framework that is used to predict which industries are likely to attract multinational firms, and how entry is likely to occur (Caves, 1982; Dunning, 1993). The fact that a substantial portion of Canada's manufacturing sector is foreign-controlled has been attributed to various factors. Foreign investment in Canada is ascribed to a desire to overcome high Canadian tariffs, to control scarce resources, to exercise monopoly power, and to take advantage of synergies in assets.

Synergy in asset use, which assumes the existence of lumpy or intangible productive assets that can be used simultaneously in more than one market,[2] has been used by Caves (1982) to develop a theory of the expansion of multinationals. To the extent that the lumpy or intangible qualities of an asset prevent the owning firm from utilizing it fully in a single market, they confer on that firm a lower opportunity cost of entering another market than an entrant who must pay full cost for the lumpy asset. In this case, entry by established firms prevails over de novo entry.

This view underlies the internalization theory of foreign direct investment as a transaction that links markets across a national boundary. It appears as a theory of diversification when mergers or other transactions forge links between business units in different product markets within the same nation. In both cases, the lumpy asset must be of multiple use: its services must be portable between product markets in the case of diversification and between geographic markets in the case of foreign investment.

Diversification and foreign direct investment can be accomplished by means of either greenfield entry or the acquisition of a firm or plant that is a going concern. A corollary stemming from this theory suggests that foreign entry should occur more often as a result of acquisition than of greenfield entry. If a specialized asset cannot be fully exploited in the original home market of the foreign company, then the Canadian market for it is also likely to be small relative to firm size. Such markets are relatively concentrated, and entry into them occurs more frequently through acquisition than by greenfield entry.[3]

Closely related is the theory that argues that the connection between the possession of a special asset and the high transaction costs of exploiting that asset partly explains the evolution of multinational enterprise.[4] When the cost of transferring an asset owned by a firm from one country to another is high, the favoured way to maximize the value of the asset is to invest directly abroad rather than indirectly by means of an arm's-length transaction such as a licence agreement or sale. Transfer costs are assumed to be high where an asset resides in an individual or a research team and is not easily communicated or separated. When the asset is on the leading edge of technology, there may not be agreement on the value of the asset. This increases the transaction costs associated with reaching any agreement on price and other terms and conditions for sale or licence. Marketing expertise may also not be easily transferable because tastes vary from country to country.

Empirical research on foreign investment in Canada (Caves, 1974) has confirmed the predictions of this analysis. The causal factors verified in Canada include not only the importance of lumpy and intangible assets but also an industry's affinity for multi-plant operations within the United States. DeMelto, McMullen, and Wills (1980) confirm the role of the multinational in Canada as an arbitrageur of its parent's innovations. Baldwin and Gorecki (1986a) observe the positive net effect of the prevalence of foreign investment on total-factor productivity in Canada.[5]

The internalization theory of multinational enterprise coincides with one aspect of the theory of the market for corporate control: mergers are an efficient way to redeploy business assets – the expected gains coming from better utilization of lumpy assets. Mergers should therefore increase productivity through improved competence or incentives for managers – especially where they lead to the exploitation of lumpy assets. Set against this prediction is an important caveat. The effectiveness of managers probably depends on their familiarity with the country's ambient language, culture, polity, and traditions. If a Canadian firm is ripe for take-over because of its managers' underperformance, a multinational not presently operating in Canada may be less able to improve that firm's performance. Multinationals that are already operating in Canada may have less of a disadvantage.

Finally, it should be noted that the negative impact of large corporate mergers in the United States in the era of conglomerates may have spilled over into Canada. Multinational enterprises tend to be large, and large firms' managers tend to be less closely monitored than those of small public companies. Some international mergers may have had poor value-creating potential. Canadian businesses that were acquired incidentally as part of these transactions may have become less productive.

These considerations and differences in the characteristics of foreign and domestic firms yield the following predictions about foreign turnover in Canada.

Foreign entry by means of firm acquisition should be more important than foreign entry by means of building new plant. Differences in the rates between low- and high-foreign-ownership industries should be greater in high-foreign-ownership industries than in low-foreign-ownership industries, since the latter have more of the characteristics that would lead entry by acquisition to be preferred to greenfield entry.

Acquisition by foreign continuing firms should increase as foreign ownership increases but at a lower rate than foreign entry by acquisition. The former should be less related to the percentage of foreign-ownership in an industry since they will involve more situations where product-line complementarity is being exploited. These opportunities are less likely to be related to the percentage of foreign ownership in a sector.

Domestic firms should enter more by greenfield entry than by acquisition. Their general advantage is not so much that they possess specific marketing and research assets that are efficiently transferred through mergers, but that they know the local markets.

Foreign greenfield entrants should be larger and more productive than domestic greenfield entrants. It is not clear whether the difference between the productivity of entrants and exits will be larger among foreign firms than among domestic firms. Turnover should increase productivity in both.

To the extent that mergers improve the use of lumpy and intangible assets, they should occur more often in industries with heavy foreign investment. Foreign firms should be active as buyers and sellers, although not necessarily in disproportion to their average share of an industry's activity. Mergers involving foreign enterprises should support productivity gains for the transferred assets at least as large as those due to purely domestic mergers.

To the extent that mergers are driven by improvements in managerial performance, multinational firms should be underrepresented as buyers, except when changes in control in Canada occur incidentally as a result of mergers between enterprises outside of Canada. The amount of change in control involving foreign multinationals should be relatively independent of the proportion of activity in a sector accounted for by foreign-controlled business units. Wholly domestic mergers should generate productivity gains at least as large as those involving foreign enterprises.[6]

If international mergers in Canada occur because of nonmaximizing or "managerial" behaviour in large multinational firms, they should be concentrated in industries that are extensively foreign-owned, but should not be more productive than mergers involving domestic enterprises. The same prediction pertains to changes in control in Canada that occur as the result of mergers or other strategic changes occurring outside Canada.

Entry activity of multinationals in Canada

The categories used to distinguish different forms of entry and control change were greenfield entry and closedown exit, continuing-firm plant opening and closing, and acquisitions and divestitures of plants. Changes in control are distinguished by whether an establishment passed from one continuing firm in the industry to another (a related spin-off), whether it passed from a continuing firm to an entrant (an unrelated spin-off), whether it passed from an exiting firm to an entrant (an unrelated merger), and whether it passed from an exiting firm to an incumbent (a related or horizontal merger). Changes in control include not only mergers and acquisitions but also sell-offs of businesses from one firm to another, spin-offs to shareholders, and buyouts.

Because they represented limited and special situations, changes in control involving plants divested by firms that continued in the industry – related and unrelated spin-offs – were eliminated. That left the question of whether to divide plants divested by exiting firms into those acquired by continuing firms (related mergers) and those acquired by entrants (unrelated diversification). Some related mergers increase the effective concentration of producers and also prices, so that any apparent gains in productivity could stem partly or wholly from increased monopoly rents. The related merger category was nevertheless retained. Because of the relatively aggregated nature of even the four-digit SIC industry level, many of the mergers in this category are, no doubt, closely related diversifications or transfers of control to managements with experience in the acquired plants' operations, and not mergers intended to create monopoly gains. Since these control changes may result in real productivity gains, they were not discarded; but neither were they included in the unrelated-take-over category. The emphasis is on the results of the divestitures that are associated with unrelated take-overs. The calculations are repeated for related mergers and reported separately where they differ from unrelated control changes.

Transfers of control can also involve a change in nationality. Therefore, each of these categories was divided into four groups: transfers of control between domestic firms, between foreign firms, from foreign to domestic firms, and from domestic to foreign firms.

Average plant turnover of domestic and foreign firms for all four-digit manufacturing industries is summarized in Table 11-2.[7] Turnover is divided into greenfield entry and acquisition entry, the creation of new plants, and the acquisition of plants by continuing firms. Two rates are calculated. Aggregate industry rates are calculated by dividing the shipments of the domestic or foreign enterprises in a particular category (e.g., greenfield entry) by all shipments. Individual population rates for domestic and for foreign populations are calculated using, as denominator, domestic shipments and foreign shipments, respectively. This allows a comparison between the extent to which domestic firms and foreign firms are renewed by a particular turnover category.

As was hypothesized, foreign firms tended to enter by means of the acquisition rather than the construction of plant (5.3 compared with 4.5 per cent of shipments). Domestic firms tended to enter more by means of greenfield entry than acquisition (14.3 compared with 5.1 per cent). Differences between

Table 11-2. *Average plant-birth and acquisition rates of domestic and foreign-controlled firms, 1970–79 (per cent)[a]*

Category	Industry shipments	
	Aggregate[b]	Disaggregated[c]
Greenfield entrants[d]		
Domestic	14.3 (1.1)	26.4 (1.6)
Foreign	4.5 (0.5)	15.9 (1.9)
Acquisition entrants[e]		
Domestic	5.1 (0.7)	10.6 (1.3)
Foreign	5.3 (0.7)	14.7 (1.7)
Continuing-firm new plants[f]		
Domestic	2.7 (0.4)	4.7 (0.6)
Foreign	2.4 (0.3)	5.7 (0.8)
Continuing-firm acquired plants		
Domestic	1.5 (0.3)	2.3 (0.4)
Foreign	1.3 (0.2)	2.9 (0.5)

[a] Firms are defined as unconsolidated enterprises at the four-digit level. The average industry turnover rate is calculated across 167 four-digit industries. Standard error of the mean is in parentheses.

[b] Aggregate rates use total industry shipments as the denominator.

[c] For disaggregated domestic rates, shipments in domestic firms are used as the denominator; for disaggregated foreign rates, shipments in foreign firms are used as the denominator.

[d] Firms that entered a four-digit industry between 1970 and 1979 by constructing plant.

[e] Firms that entered a four-digit industry between 1970 and 1979 by acquisition of a plant.

[f] Continuing firms are firms that owned plants in an industry in 1970 and 1979.

the importance of the two types of entry are greater for the domestic population, where greenfield entry rates are about three times greater than those of entry by acquisition. The difference between the rate of domestic and foreign continuing-firm new-plant creation is small.

In order to demonstrate differences in the effect of domestic and foreign turnover, the labour productivity, wage rate, salary level, and percentage of employment accounted for by non-production workers, as well as domestic and foreign new, closed, and merged plants were compared.[8]

Comprehensively weighted averages (within and between industries) were calculated summing the indicated variable across the particular entry, exit, or merger category of foreign and domestic plants – summing it across all continuing plants that did not undergo a change in control, and dividing the former by the latter.[9] Characteristics of the plants that continued with no change in control (foreign and domestic taken together) were used to normalize data for plants that experienced changes in control, entry, or shutdown. Plant-size-weighted averages were used because the important question for economic welfare is whether changes in control raise or lower average productivity or average remuneration; large establishments, ceteris paribus, matter more for aggregate welfare, and weighted averages are more appropriate than unweighted averages.

The results are reported in Table 11-3. New plant of domestic greenfield entrants was 79 per cent as productive as continuing plant in 1979 and their closed plant was 62 per cent as productive as continuing plant in 1970, an increase over the period of 17 percentage points.

The productivity of births and deaths is greater for foreign than for domestic firms for greenfield entrants, closedown exits, continuing-firm new plants, and continuing-firm closed plants, as would be expected considering the difference in the productivity of continuing foreign and domestic plants.[10] The process of replacing closed plant by new plant increases productivity for both foreign and domestic firms. The contributions of greenfield entry and closedown exit among domestic and foreign plants are about equal at 18 percentage points. The contributions of new and closed plant made by continuing firms are greater than for greenfield entrants and closedown exits and are larger in the foreign (36 percentage points) than in the domestic segment (28 percentage points).

All four changes in control improved productivity, and there was little difference between the two main categories – foreign-to-foreign and domestic-to-domestic transfers. These summary statistics demonstrate that the effect of control changes among domestic and foreign firms on productivity was quite similar.

There is less similarity between sectors in the effect of changes in control on wage rates, salary levels, and the proportion of employment accounted for by non-production workers. Plant turnover associated with greenfield entry and closedown exit resulted in a greater increase in wage and salary rates and the percentages of non-production workers in the domestic than the foreign sector. Plant turnover associated with continuing firms resulted in higher wage and salary increases, and less of a decline in the proportion of non-production workers in foreign firms than in domestic firms. There was a similar but weaker tendency for foreign firms to increase remuneration in plants affected by control changes. Plants acquired in foreign-to-foreign

Table 11-3. *Characteristics of establishments subject to control changes, start-ups, or shut-downs between 1970 and 1979 normalized by characteristics of all continuing Canadian plants, 1970 and 1979 (weighted mean ratio)*

		Characteristic[b]							
		Productivity[c]		Wage rate[d]		Salary[e]		Non-production workers[f]	
Category[a]	Year	Domestic	Foreign	Domestic	Foreign	Domestic	Foreign	Domestic	Foreign
Greenfield entrant	1979	0.79	1.01	0.85	0.89	0.94	0.92	0.36	0.95
Closedown exit	1970	0.62	0.82	0.79	0.88	0.85	0.93	0.31	1.05
Difference		0.17	0.19	0.06	0.01	0.09	-0.01	0.05	-0.10
Continuing firms									
New plant	1979	0.96	1.24	0.92	1.05	0.94	1.01	0.77	1.00
Closed plant	1970	0.68	0.88	0.91	0.96	0.90	0.95	0.91	1.09
Difference		0.28	0.36	0.01	0.09	0.04	0.06	-0.14	-0.09
Acquisitions and divestitures									
Foreign acquired from foreign	1979	0.96		0.96		0.93		1.43	
Foreign divested to foreign	1970	0.90		0.93		0.94		1.52	
Difference		0.06		0.03		-0.01		-0.09	
Foreign acquired from domestic	1979	0.87		0.92		0.90		0.95	
Domestic divested to foreign	1970	0.80		0.87		0.93		1.02	
Difference		0.07		0.05		-0.03		-0.07	

Table 11-3. (cont.)

		Characteristic[b]							
		Productivity[c]		Wage rate[d]		Salary[e]		Non-production workers[f]	
Category[a]	Year	Domestic	Foreign	Domestic	Foreign	Domestic	Foreign	Domestic	Foreign
Domestic acquired from foreign	1979	0.99		1.02		0.99		1.70	
Foreign divested to domestic	1970	0.82		0.82		1.04		2.18	
Difference		0.17		0.20		−0.05		−0.48	
Domestic acquired from domestic	1979	0.95		1.01		0.96		1.29	
Domestic divested to domestic	1970	0.89		1.03		0.97		1.28	
Difference		0.06		−0.02		−0.01		0.01	

[a] Each statistic in this table consists of the ratio of two weighted averages. Thus, for the relative salary of entrants, the numerator is the sum of all salary remuneration to non-production workers in entrant firms divided by all non-production workers in entrant firms. The denominator is the same statistic for all continuing plants that did not experience an ownership change.

[b] For a definition of the categories, see text.

[c] Productivity is defined as value-added per employee.

[d] Wage rate is defined as gross earnings of production workers divided by the number of production workers.

[e] Salary level is defined as salaries paid to non-production workers divided by their number.

[f] The proportion of total industry employment (production and non-production workers) accounted for by salaried workers.

transfers generally showed larger wage gains than plants involved in domestic-to-domestic transfers.

In conclusion, turnover enhances productivity in domestic and foreign firms. There are, however, differences in the effect of turnover on wages, salaries and the proportion of white-collar workers. Foreign firms tend to pay higher wages and salaries and use a greater percentage of non-production workers than do domestic firms. This difference is reinforced by turnover associated with continuing firms – plant births and deaths as well as control changes.

Empirical evidence on industry differences

In order to determine the frequency and effect of turnover arising from plant births and deaths as well as mergers involving foreign enterprises, while controlling for the characteristics of industries that are likely to make foreign acquisition more productive, four-digit industries were ranked by the proportion of shipments accounted for in 1970 by foreign-controlled establishments. They were then divided into those with low, medium, and high levels of foreign shares. The turnover of establishments in 1970 and 1979 was then observed for industries in each foreign-ownership group. This simple procedure allows the incidence and consequences of plant birth and death as well as changes in control involving foreign and domestic firms to be estimated while taking account of which industry characteristics are attractive to multinational enterprises. If turnover involving foreign firms differs from that involving domestic firms, this may reflect differences in domestic and foreign market structures or the firms themselves. Evidence of the first will be differences between foreign and domestic firms that vary across the foreign-ownership industry groups. Evidence of the second will be differences that are basically the same across these industry groups.

Select characteristics of foreign-ownership industry groups

Previous research has shown that the prevalence of multinational enterprises or their subsidiaries in an industry is closely associated with underlying elements of its market structure. The averages of a range of industry characteristics are reported by foreign-ownership industry group in Table 11-4.

The internalization theory has successfully predicted the association of foreign ownership with several traits of market structure – with the intensity of advertising, the amount of research and development, and with the extent of multiple-plant ownership activity in the counterpart U.S. industry. Advertising and research and development intensity increase across foreign-ownership industry groups as the share of foreign ownership increases. The average number of plants per firm of each of Canadian industry's four leading firms, on the other hand, decreases.[11] Because these predictors of foreign ownership

Table 11-4. *Average characteristics[a] of industries and changes in selected characteristics, by foreign-ownership group, selected years*

| Characteristic | Year | Foreign-ownership group | | | All industries |
		Low	Medium	High	
Foreign-ownership share[b]	1970	11.9	41.0	81.1	44.4
	1979	12.5	36.8	73.9	40.9
Advertising/sales	1975	0.8	1.1	1.7	1.2
R&D/employees (per cent)	1975	0.12	0.73	1.43	0.76
Plants per firm,[c] leading firms	1970	3.16	3.67	3.02	3.29
	1979	2.97	4.06	3.23	3.43
Plants per enterprise	1970	1.16	1.32	1.33	1.27
	1979	1.16	1.33	1.34	1.27
Four-firm concentration	1970	38.2	51.7	63.1	50.9
	1979	37.1	50.7	62.0	49.9
Number of products classified	1970	9.2	13.7	20.0	14.4
Nominal tariff rate	1970	15.3	10.3	9.2	11.6
	1978	13.3	9.0	7.9	10.1
Effective tariff rate	1966	17.6	13.9	14.1	15.2
	1978	15.5	10.3	10.1	12.0
Domestic disappearance[d]/ shipments	1970	1.06	1.10	1.27	1.14
	1979	1.11	1.15	1.31	1.19
Exports/shipments	1970	10.4	15.1	20.4	15.3
	1979	13.4	18.2	26.2	19.3

[a] Average characteristics are calculated across all four-digit industries within a foreign-ownership group.
[b] Foreign ownership is based on shipments under foreign control. A firm is defined as foreign-controlled if there is effective foreign control, although less than 50 per cent of the stock may be owned by the foreign parent.
[c] A firm is defined as all plants under common control within a four-digit industry.
[d] Domestic disappearance is shipments minus exports plus imports.

are also predictors of concentration among producers, concentration (shipments accounted for by the four largest firms) increases with foreign ownership.

There is also substantial variation among the foreign-ownership industry groups in the complexity and diversity of the industry product lines, shown by the average number of census-defined products classified to each industry. It is more than twice as large in the highest-foreign-ownership group as it is in the lowest-foreign-ownership group. The ability and perhaps the necessity to combine products at the plant level so as to exploit economies of scope in product-line distribution increases with foreign ownership. This is consistent with the role of the foreign subsidiary as a distribution conduit for product lines assembled from both its own output and those of its foreign affiliates.

Tariff protection historically has served to promote foreign investment in Canada, but this was not apparent in the 1970s. Nominal tariffs decreased with foreign ownership, although effective tariffs for the medium- and high-foreign-ownership categories did not differ.

Import intensity is shown by means of the ratio of domestic disappearance (domestic shipments minus exports plus imports) to domestic shipments. On balance, each foreign-ownership industry group is import-competing, especially the high-foreign-ownership group. Export intensity increases with foreign ownership, so industries with high foreign ownership also exhibit high levels of intra-industry trade.

Because turnover partially consists of mergers and acquisitions that occur across industry boundaries and result in a diversified enterprise, information on the specialization of companies classified to each industry was also analysed (Table 11-5). The average Herfindahl (inverse) index of specialization in panel A captures the extent to which firms operate in several industries.[12] Higher values of the index indicate less diversification or more specialization, and lower values indicate more diversification or less specialization.[13] Foreign-controlled enterprises are more diversified than domestic ones in all groups. Diversification increases with foreign investment overall, partly because domestic companies are less diversified in industries with little foreign ownership, but mainly because the proportion of more diversified foreign-controlled companies increases with foreign ownership.

Like enterprise specialization, plant specialization is highest (for all establishments taken together) in industries with low foreign ownership, and lowest for those with high foreign ownership. Plant specialization decreases across foreign-ownership groups, as one would expect, on the basis of the number of products classified to an industry. There is a slightly greater tendency for foreign plants to specialize less in the higher-foreign-ownership categories.[14]

Differences in characteristics of foreign and domestic firms across foreign-ownership industry groups

Some of these variations in industry characteristics may be associated with varying proportions of foreign and domestic firms across foreign-ownership industry groups; some may be the result of the widening gap in the differences between domestic and foreign firms across groups. In order to distinguish the effect of industry from ownership, a regression was estimated across all plants in the manufacturing sector using a select group of plant characteristics as regressors (Table 11-6). The characteristics were the degree

Table 11-5. *Average diversity characteristics of consolidated enterprises and plants, industries classified by foreign-ownership group, 1979[a]*

	Foreign-ownership group			All industries
Characteristic	Low	Medium	High	
Herfindahl measure of inter-industry diversification, enterprise level[b]				
All enterprises	.89	.77	.72	.80
Domestic	.90	.82	.82	.84
Foreign-controlled	.74	.64	.64	.67
Ratio of enterprise diversification for domestic and foreign enterprises	1.28	1.34	1.35	1.33
Average number of four-digit census products classified to industry[c]				
Number	9.21	13.66	20.02	14.41
Inverse	0.27	0.23	0.22	0.24
Average Herfindahl measure of plant-level diversification within industry[d]				
All establishments	.80	.79	.76	.79
Domestic	.80	.80	.77	.77
Foreign-controlled	.81	.78	.75	.63

[a] Average characteristics are calculated across all four-digit industries within a foreign-ownership group.
[b] Enterprise-level specialization is the parent's specialization calculated across all four-digit manufacturing, mining, and logging industries.
[c] Number of products is the number of four-digit ICC commodities (2,326 in total) per industry.
[d] Plant specialization is the Herfindahl index of plant shipments at the four-digit ICC commodity level.

of firm and plant specialization, labour productivity, wage and salary levels, and the importance of white-collar jobs. These characteristics were separately regressed on binary variables representing the domestic ownership of the plant (Domestic) and whether it was in the medium- or the high-foreign-ownership group (T2 and T3). Interactive variables, Dom × T2 and Dom × T3, were also included. They capture whether other disadvantages (advantages) were experienced by domestic plants in the industries with higher foreign ownership.

The first row in each set reports the results only with the nationality of ownership variable, and so gives the average difference between domestic-

Table 11-6. *Regression of plant characteristics on ownership and industry group, 1979*

	Regressor				
Regressand	Domestic	T2	T3	Dom × T2	Dom × T3
Firm specialization	1.50*				
	1.44*	0.89*	0.89*		
	1.57*	0.96**	0.99	0.93*	0.87*
Plant specialization	1.03*				
	1.01	1.05*	0.94*		
	0.97	1.02	0.89*	1.02	1.07*
Labour productivity	0.69*				
	0.76*	1.12*	1.34*		
	0.78*	1.10*	1.42*	1.03	0.91*
Production-worker income	0.92*				
	0.95*	1.06*	1.10*		
	0.94*	1.05*	1.08*	1.01	1.01
Salary level	0.94*				
	0.97*	1.06*	1.10*		
	0.97*	1.07*	1.08*	0.98	1.03
White-collar jobs as	0.86*				
a proportion of	0.91*	0.99	1.21*		
total employment	0.94*	1.06*	1.10*	1.01	1.02

Note: All coefficients indicate the effect of the category relative to the omitted category. Dom is domestically controlled establishments; T2 and T3 are the middle and highest foreign-ownership groups, respectively; and Dom × T2 and Dom × T3 represent domestic plants in groups 2 and 3, respectively. The exponents represent the significance level of the estimated coefficients for the null hypothesis of no difference.
* Significant at 1 per cent level.
** Significant at 10 per cent level.

and foreign-controlled plants when industry group is not considered. The second row includes the effects of the foreign-ownership industry group.

The regression coefficient for domestic identity alone (the first row in each category) indicates that domestically owned plants, compared with foreign-owned plants, were part of a parent that was considerably more specialized in terms of industries within which they owned plants, were slightly more specialized themselves in terms of products produced, had much lower labour productivity, paid lower wages and salaries, and had a lower proportion of non-production workers.

Adding the variables for foreign-ownership industry group (T2 and T3) leaves most of these differences intact. The exception is plant specialization. Most of the difference between domestic and foreign firms, then, is not simply the result of their operating in different sectors.

The interaction terms for each characteristic (third row) show that there is also some variation in the performance of domestic and foreign-owned plants across foreign-ownership industry groups. Domestic plants in the highest-foreign-ownership group were more specialized, belonged to parents that were more diversified, and suffered more of a productivity disadvantage than did their domestic counterparts in other industries. On the other hand, the differential between the annual incomes of production workers in domestic plants and foreign plants was not greater in industries where there was a high level of foreign-ownership, nor was the differential in salaries or the percentage of non-production workers greater.

The difference between foreign-owned and domestically owned plants' characteristics may be related to size differences. Size is a proxy for a number of variables that determine success. Capital stock may be less costly in foreign-controlled firms. They may have more efficient management. Being more diversified, foreign-controlled firms may be able to specialize more at the plant level and take advantage of product-line scale economies.

In order to test for the extent to which differences between domestic and foreign plants are related to size, the regression was repeated with the addition of a size variable – the rank of a plant within a four-digit industry, based on shipments. Adding this variable, however, did not affect the results.

In conclusion, the differences between foreign and domestic plants cannot simply be ascribed to the fact that they operate in different industries. There are differences between foreign and domestic plants across all the foreign-ownership industry groups. Moreover, the foreign-industry-group variables that represent the environment are almost always significant. The interaction terms that capture the extent to which the differences between domestic and foreign firms vary across industries are significant less frequently. The environment matters as much as, if not more than, nationality.

Turnover differences across foreign-ownership industry groups

Differences among industry characteristics were used to hypothesize that there should be differences across foreign-ownership industry groups in the amount and type of turnover. Table 11-7 presents measures of the overall intensity of turnover for foreign and domestic plants by foreign-ownership level. The rate of activity is based on shipments by plants.

The hypothesis that foreign firms enter more frequently by acquisition than greenfield entry and that domestic firms do the reverse is confirmed. The relative frequency of turnover due to greenfield entry and closedown exit declines sharply with foreign ownership, and turnover associated with the acquisition of firms is less important in industries with low foreign ownership.

Table 11-7. *Average market shares[a] of establishments opened, closed, and changing control, by status of firm and extent of foreign ownership, 1970 and 1979 (per cent)*

Characteristic	Foreign-ownership group		
	Low	Medium	High
Establishments closed by exiting firms (1970)[b]	27.0	18.3	11.3
	(2.1)	(1.9)	(1.5)
Establishments opened by entering firms (1979)[c]	24.9	18.5	13.1
	(2.3)	(2.0)	(1.7)
Plants closed by continuing firms (1970)[d]	3.6	5.1	5.0
	(0.6)	(0.9)	(0.8)
New plants opened by continuing firms (1979)[e]	3.2	6.1	5.9
	(0.5)	(0.8)	(0.9)
Plants divested by exiting firms (1970)	9.1	14.8	13.7
	(1.6)	(1.6)	(1.6)
Plants acquired by entering firms (1979)	7.6	11.9	11.7
	(1.5)	(1.6)	(1.6)
Plants divested by continuing firms (1970)	1.2	0.8	1.2
	(0.4)	(0.2)	(0.5)
Plants acquired by continuing firms (1979)	2.2	4.0	2.4
	(0.5)	(0.7)	(0.6)

[a] These data are based on plant shipments and include all plants except head offices. The calculations in this table are unweighted averages at the four-digit industry level. Standard error of the mean is in parentheses.
[b] Establishments closed are those plants in existence in 1970 in a particular four-digit industry that were no longer in that industry in 1979. Some were physically closed; others were switched to another industry.
[c] Establishments opened are plants that existed in a four-digit industry in 1979 and not in 1970. Some were plant births; others were transferred from another four-digit industry.
[d] All divested plants were in the same four-digit industry in 1970 and 1979.
[e] Entering firms are those that owned a plant in a four-digit industry in 1979 but not in 1970. Exiting firms are those that owned a plant in a four-digit industry in 1970 but not in 1979. Continuing firms owned plants in an industry in 1970 and 1979.

It was also hypothesized that changes in control whose purpose was to improve management efficiency would have little relationship with the amount of foreign control. Related acquisitions are independent of foreign owner-ship. Either this category includes a substantial number of mergers aimed at improving managerial efficiency, or the tendency to acquire complementary product lines is not closely related to the industry characteristics that attract foreign firms.

Overall, changes in control in continuing establishments are more important, and greenfield entry and closedown exit are relatively infrequent in industries with high foreign ownership. Entry by new enterprises has less of a role in stimulating efficiency in industries with greater foreign ownership than it does in those with less, leaving a larger role for the market for corporate control and for competition from abroad.

Variation in the overall rate of turnover across foreign-ownership groups is the result of differences between the turnover of foreign- and domestic-owned plants. The turnover rates of domestic and foreign firms are presented in Table 11-8. These rates are calculated as the shipments in foreign or domestic entrants divided by total industry shipments. Turnover rates may vary among industries because domestic or foreign firm rates are changing or because the proportions of domestic or foreign firms in foreign-ownership industry groups differ.

The decline in the greenfield entry rate across foreign-ownership groups is primarily the result of a decline in the domestic-entry rate from 22.4 to 14.0 to 6.6 per cent as foreign ownership increases. Domestic entrants, then, reacted negatively to characteristics like concentration and more advertising and research and development, characteristics of the high-foreign-ownership industries. Greenfield-entry rates of foreign firms increase across the foreign-ownership levels, from 2.5 to 4.5 to 6.5 per cent.

The rate of entry by acquisition increases with foreign ownership primarily because of the increase in the number of foreign firms. The increase in the rate of foreign greenfield entry across foreign-ownership groups is somewhat less than that of the rate of acquisition entry by foreign firms, confirming the hypothesis that foreign firms would generally choose to acquire rather than build – especially in those sectors where industry characteristics attract foreign firms.

The plant birth rate of domestic continuing firms shows no monotonic relationship across foreign-ownership industry groups. The plant birth rate of foreign firms increases with foreign ownership.

Plant acquisition by continuing domestic and foreign firms differs across foreign-ownership industry groups much as the underlying populations do. The hypothesis that the related-merger rate for foreign firms would not increase across foreign-ownership groups as much as the unrelated-merger rate is confirmed.

Table 11-9 focuses on change in the shares of shipments by *firms*, as opposed to establishments operating in 1970, 1979, or both. For each industry, the dissimilarity index – one-half the sum of the absolute value of share changes – was calculated:

$$INDEX = \Sigma\left(\left|SH79_i - SH70_i\right|\right)/2, \tag{11-1}$$

Table 11-8. *Average plant-birth and acquisition rates in domestic and foreign-controlled firms, by foreign-ownership group, 1970–79 (per cent)*[a]

Category[b]	Aggregate rates by foreign-ownership group[c]			Disaggregated rates by foreign-ownership group[c]		
	Low (1)	Medium (2)	High (3)	Low (4)	Medium (5)	High (6)
Greenfield entrants						
Domestic	22.4 (2.2)	14.0 (1.5)	6.6 (1.1)	24.9 (2.3)	22.6 (2.2)	31.9 (3.6)
Foreign	2.5 (0.6)	4.5 (0.7)	6.5 (1.2)	19.1 (4.0)	15.4 (2.9)	13.1 (2.8)
Acquisition entrants						
Domestic	4.3 (1.2)	7.6 (1.3)	3.5 (0.8)	5.0 (1.5)	11.9 (1.9)	14.9 (2.8)
Foreign	3.3 (0.8)	4.4 (1.1)	8.1 (1.4)	18.1 (3.6)	13.2 (2.4)	12.6 (2.4)
Continuing-firm new plants						
Domestic	2.7 (0.4)	3.2 (0.6)	2.0 (0.8)	3.4 (0.5)	5.3 (1.0)	5.3 (1.5)
Foreign	0.5 (0.2)	2.9 (0.6)	3.9 (0.6)	4.6 (1.4)	7.5 (1.8)	4.9 (0.8)
Continuing-firm acquired plants						
Domestic	1.7 (0.4)	2.4 (0.6)	0.5 (0.2)	2.1 (0.5)	3.5 (0.8)	1.4 (0.5)
Foreign	0.5 (0.2)	1.6 (0.4)	1.9 (0.5)	2.4 (0.7)	2.6 (0.8)	3.8 (1.1)

[a] Firms are defined as unconsolidated enterprises at the four-digit level. The average turnover rate is calculated across all four-digit industries in a foreign-ownership category. Standard error of the mean is in parentheses.

[b] For definitions of categories, see text.

[c] Aggregate rates use total industry shipments as the denominator. For disaggregated domestic rates, shipments in domestic firms are used as denominator; for disaggregated foreign rates, shipments in foreign firms are used as the denominator.

Table 11-9. *Average turnover^a of market share^b among firms by source of turnover and extent of foreign ownership, 1970–79 (per cent)*

Category of firm turnover	Foreign-ownership group		
	Low	Medium	High
Greenfield entry and closedown exit	25.8	18.4	12.1
Growth and decline of continuing firms^c	16.6	16.6	14.7
Total^d	42.4	35.0	26.8

^{a} Average turnover is calculated across all four-digit industries within a foreign-ownership group.
^{b} Market share is based on shipments.
^{c} Firms are defined as all establishments including head offices under common control in a four-digit industry. Head offices are omitted from the first line.
^{d} Total turnover does not include the effect of acquisition entry and divestiture exit.

where $SH79_i$ is the ith firm's share of industry shipments in 1979 and $SH70_i$ is its share in 1970.

In the first row, this index is calculated for greenfield entrants and exits only. The second row presents these calculations for continuing firms. The change in the market share of continuing firms is the result of plant births and deaths, acquisitions and divestitures, and the growth and decline of their plants. Industries with high foreign ownership exhibit much less turnover in their market share due to entry and exit, and there is also slightly less turnover in the market share of incumbents that persisted in the industry throughout the decade.

Control changes and performance

In this examination of the structural conditions surrounding turnover, the main contention is that industries with extensive foreign ownership provide the greatest scope for "lumpiness", intangibility of assets, and product-line complexity. They also exhibit the most turnover as a result of control changes. Most of the hypotheses about the relative intensity of different forms of entry and change in control and its relationship to the intensity of foreign ownership have been confirmed.

The effect of change in control has been hotly debated both in Canada and abroad. It is not clear whether Canada was spared the productivity losses experienced in the United States as a result of diversifying acquisitions by large firms, although there is certainly evidence that, in Canada, firms that merged extensively or engaged in unrelated diversification were not particularly profitable.[15] Evidence on the motives of firms undertaking acquisitions in Canada indicate that there is generally an expectation of positive productivity from mergers, but with qualifications for large-scale acquisitions by large enterprises.[16]

The effect of these control changes, both overall and by firm nationality, is examined here. The establishments that were in operation from 1970 to 1979 and that underwent changes in control during the period are grouped according to whether the changes were between domestic companies, between foreign companies, or between foreign and domestic companies. The effect on market shares, productivity, and factors that affect labour costs was considered.

Market shares

Market shares provide one metric to gauge the relative success of plants affected by merger. The market shares of establishments affected by control changes were summed for 1970 and for 1979 in each industry, and unweighted averages of the resulting industry sums were calculated (Table 11-10). The average relative plant size of acquired plant as of 1979 was also calculated. The size of plants that experienced a change in control is measured relative to plants that had no change in control.

Turnover among larger firms tends to take the form of mergers and other changes in control while smaller ones experience greenfield entry and closedown exit (see Chapters 2 and 3). This tendency for mergers to affect larger firms is confirmed by the fact that acquired plants in 1979 were, on average, larger than plants that continued over the decade without a change in ownership. There is a marked difference among the relative sizes of acquired plants across the foreign-ownership groups. It is greater than one in the low-foreign-ownership category and falls to less than one in the high-foreign-ownership category. Plants that are divested and acquired by foreign firms are generally larger than plants that are divested and acquired by domestic firms, partially reflecting the differences in the underlying populations.

Because large plants or firms tend to lose market share (through the regression process outlined in Chapter 5), the market shares of the larger establishments undergoing changes in control should have declined. The reverse was expected for smaller establishments that are acquired. What matters, therefore, is deviations from this expected pattern.

Changes in market share as a result of domestic-to-domestic transfers accord with our expectations. Market-share loss occurred in the low-foreign-ownership group, where acquired plants are larger than continuing plants, and

Table 11-10. *Average combined market shares and average relative plant size of establishments subject to changes in control,[a] by nationality and extent of foreign ownership, 1970 and 1979 (per cent)[b]*

Type of control change	Year	Foreign-ownership group			Total
		Low	Medium	High	
Average market share					
Domestic to domestic	1979	3.24	5.60	1.46	3.45
	1970	3.55	5.74	1.33	3.55
Domestic to foreign-controlled	1979	1.96	1.70	1.56	1.74
	1970	2.16	1.86	1.41	1.81
Foreign-controlled to domestic	1979	0.80	1.80	1.89	1.50
	1970	0.73	1.89	2.38	1.66
Foreign-controlled to foreign-controlled	1979	1.12	2.69	6.50	3.42
	1970	1.01	2.16	6.22	3.11
All divested plants	1979	7.14	11.79	11.41	10.10
All acquired plants	1970	7.44	11.66	11.33	10.14
Average relative plant size[c]					
Domestic to domestic	1979	1.22	1.36	0.76	1.15
Domestic to foreign-controlled	1979	1.53	1.26	0.71	1.14
Foreign-controlled to domestic	1979	2.13	1.29	0.82	1.28
Foreign-controlled to foreign-controlled	1979	2.58	3.59	1.15	2.22
All acquired plants	1979	1.67	1.78	0.94	1.44

[a] For plants divested by exiting firms and acquired by entering firms (unrelated mergers).
[b] The calculations in this table are unweighted averages at the four-digit industry level.
[c] Size of plants subject to control change relative to plants that continued in the same industry between 1970 and 1979 without a change in control.

market-share gains occurred in the high-foreign-ownership group, where the affected plant is smaller than other continuing plant. In contrast, plants involved in foreign-to-foreign transfers experienced a small market-share gain across all groups, even though the relative size of the acquired plant differs across foreign-ownership groups in much the same way as do plants involved in domestic-to-domestic transfers. These results suggest that mergers between foreign enterprises generally have favourable effects because such control changes often involve the type of asset transfer described in the theory of the multinational firm. That the effect of transfers among domestic enterprises is generally unfavourable in industries where domestic control is high, and where acquired plants are relatively large, suggests that there is a strong component here of transfers that involve difficult turnaround situations.

To see whether any patterns emerge when related acquisitions are considered, Table 11-10 was recalculated to take into account change in control that transfers plant from exiting firms to firms that persist in the industry throughout the decade. Among related mergers, foreign-to-foreign transfers are less successful in the high-foreign-ownership group and more successful in the low-foreign-ownership group. The other changes were basically the same. This confirms the hypothesis that closely related mergers by foreign firms are less successful, especially among firms in the high-foreign-ownership group since more of these mergers probably were incidental to control changes abroad.

The market-share changes that occurred among divested and acquired plants may be partially explained by the nature of the stochastic process at work rather than by the effect of mergers per se. To investigate this possibility, a growth equation that allows for the regression-to-the-mean phenomenon was estimated for all plants in the manufacturing sector. The dependent variable chosen for the analysis was the log of the ratio of 1979 share to 1970 market share of all continuing plants. This was regressed against the 1970 market share and a binary variable that takes on a value of one when the plant is larger than the median plant in an industry. Both of these had significant and negative coefficients, indicating that growth was inversely related to plant size. Also included were binary variables for the foreign-ownership group, the nationality of the control change (foreign-to-foreign, domestic-to-domestic, domestic-to-foreign, and foreign-to-domestic), and whether the control change was a related merger. Four merger categories were defined. They were based on whether the acquiring and divesting firms continued in the industry over the period. Divesting and acquiring firms were classified as entrants–exits (unrelated control changes), continuing-firm–exits (related mergers), entrants–continuing firm (unrelated spin-offs), and continuing firm–continuing firm (related spin-offs).

The core regression included only the initial market share and the binary variable that divided each industry at the median. Binary variables were added first for each foreign-ownership industry group, then for each type of merger category, then for the nationality of the transaction. When the foreign-ownership industry group is considered alone, the two with the highest foreign ownership have a negative coefficient, indicating that there was more market-share loss among these plants than would have been expected on the basis of the regression-to-the-mean process. This is primarily the result of the interaction with merger type. When related mergers and interaction terms for the foreign-ownership industry group are included, the result is a significant positive coefficient in the lowest-foreign-ownership group and a significant

negative coefficient on the highest-foreign-ownership group for related mergers (the continuing-firm–exits category), which accords with the finding that
these mergers are more successful in the domestic group and less successful
in the high-foreign-ownership group. On the other hand, the coefficients attached to the unrelated-merger category (entrants–exits) show that the low-
est- and highest-foreign-ownership groups are not markedly different from all
continuing establishments. Differences in the market share change among all
plants in the unrelated-merger category are explained by the regression-to-
the-mean process. Finally, the related-merger type, nationality, and foreign-
ownership-group variables were all entered to test whether there were
significant differences in the performance of each related-merger type by
nationality of the transfer among foreign-ownership industry groups. None of
the components of the merger class on which this chapter primarily focuses
(unrelated mergers) showed a pattern in market-share changes that could be
distinguished from that of continuing plants.[17]

In conclusion, the analysis using unweighted microeconomic data demonstrates that once the regression-to-the-mean phenomenon is considered, the
pattern of market-share change does not vary systematically with the level of
foreign ownership. The ability of transferred units to maintain their market
shares is related to their initial position. Nevertheless, transfers in the domestic sector are different from those in the foreign sector because the relative
sizes of their plants are different. The hypothesis cannot therefore be rejected
that the transfer of plants between foreign enterprises has a favourable effect
on industries with high foreign ownership while the transfer of plants between domestic enterprises has an unfavourable effect on industries with high
domestic ownership.

Productivity effects

Market shares can change for many reasons. From the point of view
of Darwinian reasoning, an increasing market share suggests an improvement
in productivity. This was confirmed in Chapter 9 for the population as a
whole. In order to examine whether market share change had differential
effects for domestic as opposed to foreign plants, selected characteristics of
new, closed, and merged plants in each sector were compared.[18] The characteristics were labour productivity, wage rate, salary level, and percentage of
non-production workers. To investigate the effect of control changes on productivity (and other variables), each industry was divided into establishments
that did not experience a change of control between 1970 and 1979 and those
that did. Characteristics of the plants that did not experience a change in
control (foreign and domestic) were used to normalize data for entrants, exits,
and plants that underwent changes in control.

A comprehensively weighted average similar to that used in Table 11-3 was calculated for each foreign-ownership industry group by summing the indicated variable across the particular entry, exit, or merger category in one of the foreign-ownership industry groups, summing it across all continuing plants without changes in control in the same industry group, and dividing the former by the latter. The results are reported in Table 11-11.

There were larger productivity gains in the highest-foreign-ownership group. In the high-foreign-ownership industries, the productivity of plants that experienced a control change increased from 69 to 80 per cent of the productivity of the control group, a gain of 11 percentage points. In contrast, in the lowest-foreign-ownership group, the productivity of plants experiencing a control change increased only 5 per cent. The pattern of productivity change, as expected, corresponds with that of market-share change (see Table 11-10). Industries that are most disposed toward extensive foreign ownership are those in which changes in control have the most positive effects. This is consistent with the internalization theory of foreign investment and diversification, which argues that it is in these industries where changes in control can contribute the most to the utilization of lumpy and intangible assets.

When these calculations were performed only on the related-merger component, the results were exactly the opposite. Productivity gains of 14 percentage points were due to control changes in the lowest-foreign-ownership group, 11 percentage points in the middle group, and 6 percentage points in the highest group. This also accords with the market-share changes recorded for this category of mergers across foreign-ownership industry groups. This pattern conforms with the interpretation offered for Table 11-10: where foreign ownership is low, the productivity of mergers depends on the close similarity of activities between the acquiring and acquired units.[19]

These increases need to be set in the context of the gains made by plant exit and entry, which led to considerably larger productivity gains than did control changes. The gains stemming from the replacement by continuing firms of closed plants with new plants were 36, 31, and 20 percentage points across the three foreign-ownership industry groups, low to high. When exiting firms that closed plants were replaced with entrants that opened plants, productivity increased by 15, 16, and 13 percentage points across the three industry groups, low to high. In both cases the largest increase was in the lowest-foreign-ownership group. In contrast, changes in control had the greatest impact in the highest-foreign-ownership group.

Labour costs

A change in control might be profitable to the acquirer because it can curb the payment of above-market wages or salaries. However, only in industries with low foreign ownership are both wages and salaries initially higher in establishments that change control than in all continuing

Table 11-11. *Characteristics of establishments subject to control changes, start-ups, or shut-downs normalized by characteristics of continuing plants, by extent of foreign ownership (weighted mean ratio), 1970 and 1979*[a]

		Foreign-ownership group		
Characteristic by category	Year	Low	Medium	High
Productivity (value-added per employee)				
Acquired continuing plants[b]	1979	1.02	1.03	0.80
Continuing plants divested[b]	1970	0.97	1.04	0.69
New plants of greenfield entrants	1979	0.89	0.91	0.80
Closed plants of exiting firms	1970	0.74	0.75	0.67
New plants of continuing firms	1979	1.22	1.05	1.00
Closed plants of continuing firms	1970	0.86	0.74	0.80
Average remuneration per production worker[c]				
Continuing plants acquired[b]	1979	1.07	0.97	0.88
Continuing plants divested[b]	1970	1.08	1.00	0.87
New plants of greenfield entrants	1979	0.89	0.85	0.86
Closed plants of exiting firms	1970	0.87	0.80	0.81
New plants of continuing firms	1979	0.88	0.99	0.99
Closed plants of continuing firms	1970	1.00	0.89	0.92
Annual salary per non-production worker				
Continuing plants acquired[b]	1979	1.06	0.94	0.89
Continuing plants divested[b]	1970	1.01	0.97	0.94
New plants of greenfield entrants	1979	0.98	0.90	0.94
Closed plants of exiting firms	1970	0.93	0.87	0.89
New plants of continuing firms	1979	0.91	0.95	0.99
Closed plants of continuing firms	1970	0.90	0.87	0.92
Percentage of non-production workers[d]				
Continuing plants acquired[b]	1979	1.53	1.48	0.77
Continuing plants divested[b]	1970	1.76	1.48	0.78
New plants of greenfield entrants	1979	0.43	0.56	0.33
Closed plants of exiting firms	1970	0.53	0.48	0.33
New plants of continuing firms	1979	0.82	0.92	0.59
Closed plants of continuing firms	1970	1.31	1.05	0.65

[a] These data are the ratio of two weighted averages. Thus, for the relative salary of greenfield entrants, the numerator is the sum of all salary remuneration to non-production workers divided by the number of entering firms in a group; the denominator is the same statistic for continuing plants that did not experience an ownership change.
[b] Only unrelated control changes – plants divested by exiting firms and acquired by entering firms – were used. See Chapter 10.
[c] Gross earnings of workers. Workers are defined in person-year equivalents.
[d] The proportion of total industry employment accounted for by salaried workers.

establishments. In those industries, changes in control pull wages down toward the norm but increase salary remuneration. Sectors with medium and high foreign investment tend to constrain salaries. The normalized percentage of non-production workers decreased between 1970 and 1979 in plants subject to control change in industries with low foreign ownership: thus, it was primarily in the low-foreign-ownership group that new owners reaped pecuniary gains by squeezing out excess costs (i.e., non-production staff and compensation).[20]

The results were the same when calculations were redone for the related mergers. Related mergers among firms in industries with high domestic ownership were accompanied by wage and salary declines (5 and 6 percentage points, respectively) and decreases in the percentage of non-production workers (49 percentage points). Among firms in industries with high foreign ownership, related mergers were accompanied by much smaller decreases in the percentage of non-production workers (6 percentage points).

There is no evidence that the plant creation and destruction process effects labour-cost savings. Indeed the opposite is the case. The difference between greenfield entry and closedown exit produces a wage and salary gain across all foreign-ownership industry groups. The opening and closing of plants by continuing firms also has a beneficial effect on all but the low-foreign-ownership group. Plant turnover weeds out the inefficient; in doing so it generally improves the remuneration rates of workers.

Industry differences in productivity

Plant-size-weighted averages[21] depend both on the distribution of change across firms and industries and on the size of the firms and the industries in which the mergers are occurring. Thus, the question of whether the results depended on the weights used arises. To examine this question, the industry-level weighted averages of the gain in productivity from changes in control were correlated with several industry attributes for all industries and for industries in each foreign-investment industry group.[22] There was relatively little association between the productivity gains and various measures of unit size. What stands out is that the productivity gains decreased with the productivity of to-be-divested plants relative to that of continuing plants in 1970. The shortcoming of large mergers in the domestic sector may have been not so much the limited ability of management to raise productivity in the purchased units as the fact that units purchased had little scope for improvement. This result is similar to that found for differences between the success of foreign and domestic firms in maintaining market shares. Domestic mergers were primarily concentrated in plants with a large market share whose decline was caused by the natural regression process.

All four-digit industries were divided by the degree of foreign ownership in order to stratify industries on the basis of the multitude of factors that are associated with foreign ownership. This strategy is useful if the factors that affect foreign ownership also affect the efficacy of mergers. According to the results, this is partly true. This should not be misconstrued; it does not mean that no factors other than those determining foreign investment influence the effect of mergers, or that there are some reasons for foreign investment that might not be conducive to the success of mergers.

In order to investigate the extent to which other factors affect the success of mergers and of foreign ownership, all four-digit manufacturing industries were divided into five categories. These are natural-resource-based, labour-intensive, scale-related, product-differentiated, and science-based industries. This uses a taxonomy outlined by the OECD (1987: chap. 7, annex A). Canadian industries were assigned to the OECD classification using the Statistics Canada concordance between the Canadian SIC and the ISIC used by the OECD. A discriminant analysis was performed using variables such as wage rate, proportion of value-added accounted for by labour remuneration, concentration, economies-of-scale estimates, research and development intensity, and advertising–sales ratios to verify the classification; corrections were made when the original assignment was shown to be wanting. Finally, the same weighted-average-relative-productivity variable used in Table 11-11 was calculated for each of the five OECD industry groupings, cross-classified by foreign-ownership group. Changes in the relative productivity of each category are reported in Table 11-12, panel A. Panel B reports the number of industries classified to the cell and the proportion of foreign ownership in each.

The effect of mergers on productivity differed substantially across the sample, both for industry totals and across foreign-ownership groups. In natural-resource-based industries and labour-intensive industries, the overall effect of mergers on productivity was negative. Scale-related industries experienced a small gain from control changes. Product-differentiated and science-based industries exhibit the greatest productivity gains. Assets primarily associated with marketing and innovation generated the greatest gains from mergers.

Differences across the five sectors in the highest-foreign-ownership group mirror the overall total. Few gains were made in natural-resource-based and labour-intensive industries or even in scale-related industries; all of the gains were in the product-differentiated and science-based industries. The industries with the highest domestic ownership made more gains in the natural-resource-based and scale-related sectors but did poorly in the product-differentiated sector compared with the high-foreign-ownership industries. Domestic ownership yielded lower gains in science-based industries from control changes.

Table 11-12. *Change in relative productivity[a] of plants that experienced unrelated control changes and foreign ownership, by industry type and foreign-ownership group, 1970–79*

Industry type[b]	Foreign-ownership group			Total
	Low	Medium	High	
A. *Percentage points of change in relative*				
productivity (value-added per employee)				
Natural-resource-based	0.08	−0.19	0.02	−0.02
Labour-intensive	−0.24	0.03	−0.06	−0.09
Scale-related	0.31	−0.01	−0.08	0.09
Product-differentiated	−0.09	0.65	0.14	0.33
Science-based	−0.14	0.28	0.22	—
B. *Level of 1979 foreign ownership (per cent)*				
and number of industries (in parentheses)				
Natural-resource-based	13.0 (21)	37.0 (15)	82.0 (16)	41.0 (52)
Labour-intensive	10.0 (28)	42.0 (18)	76.0 (8)	30.0 (54)
Scale-related	13.0 (6)	42.0 (13)	82.0 (14)	54.0 (33)
Product-differentiated	16.0 (1)	44.0 (8)	80.0 (8)	58.0 (17)
Science-based	—	41.0 (2)	83.0 (9)	75.0 (11)
Total	11.0 (56)	41.0 (56)	81.0 (56)	44.0 (167)

[a] Relative productivity is defined as the productivity of plants experiencing control changes divided by the productivity of continuing plants that did not experience a control change. A weighted mean was calculated for productivity in each category and then the ratio of the two was computed. The value of the change in relative productivity is the difference in this ratio between 1979 and 1970.
[b] Industry groupings are defined in OECD (1987).

The effect of nationality on the impact of mergers by foreign-ownership tranche

The basic relationship between the prevalence of foreign ownership in an industry and increases in productivity that result from changes in the control of establishments has been established. During the 1970s, mergers increased productivity. Where foreign ownership was low, gains seemed to come from containing excess costs. Where foreign ownership was high, they seemed to stem from improved usage of lumpy and intangible assets.

There remains the important question of whether those gains came specifically from control changes involving foreign enterprises or whether they were independent of the firms' nationalities, especially for the industries with high foreign ownership. To answer this question, establishments that underwent control changes between 1970 and 1979 were divided into those subject to the four classes of control changes – foreign-to-foreign, domestic-to-domestic, foreign-to-domestic, and domestic-to-foreign. Changes in labour productivity, production- and non-production-worker remuneration, and the proportion of the work-force employed as non-production workers were calculated (Table 11-13).

Several conclusions emerge. First, although the largest productivity gains were in the industries with high foreign ownership, domestic-to-domestic and foreign-to-domestic transfers both performed well in this group. Gains involving domestic enterprises as buyers were just as large as those involving foreign firms as buyers. Where foreign ownership is high, the environment affects both domestic and foreign take-overs beneficially. Second, in the lowest-foreign-ownership group, foreign firm take-overs do well. Foreign-to-foreign and domestic-to-foreign take-overs led to productivity gains, even though domestic-to-domestic take-overs led to losses. This suggests that foreign take-overs in all sectors involved lumpy-asset transfer, whereas more domestic take-overs involved lumpy-asset transfer in high-foreign-ownership industries.

These calculations were also carried out using the categories introduced in Table 11-12 – natural-resource-based, labour-intensive, scale-related, product-differentiated, and science-based industries. All cells where there were particularly large losses or gains were chosen and differences between productivity gains for domestic-to-domestic and foreign-to-foreign take-overs were examined. The differences were found to be small. The environment, rather than nationality, was the primary determining factor of productivity change associated with control changes.

Control changes were associated with a decrease in above-average wages in industries with low foreign ownership, while in industries with high foreign ownership control changes were associated with an increase in below-average wages (see Table 11-11). The "excess" wages[23] in low-foreign-ownership industries appeared mainly in domestic establishments and decreased most in domestic-to-domestic mergers (Table 11-13). Where foreign ownership is high, changes in control tend to increase wages, except for transfers of control to domestic firms. Thus, with regard to wages, both environment and nationality matters in control changes.

Take-overs were associated with an increase in salaries in industries with low foreign ownership and a decrease in those with high foreign ownership (see Table 11-11). The tendency to increase salaries came from domestic acquisitions in the low-foreign-ownership sector (see Table 11-13). The salary rate was compressed in high-foreign-ownership industries following changes in control in every category other than foreign-to-foreign changes. As was the case with wage rates, the effect of control changes on salary rate

Table 11-13. *Effects of changes in control on continuing establishments (relative to continuing establishments without control changes), by nationality of firm and foreign-ownership group (weighted mean ratio), 1970 and 1979[a]*

		Foreign-ownership group			
Characteristic by category	Year	Low	Medium	High	Total
Productivity (value-added per employee)					
All acquired continuing plants	1979	1.02	1.03	0.80	0.95
All continuing plants divested	1970	0.97	1.04	0.69	0.87
Domestic acquired from domestic	1979	1.05	1.12	0.68	0.96
Domestic divested to domestic	1970	1.06	1.16	0.61	0.94
Domestic acquired from foreign	1979	1.12	1.01	0.86	1.01
Foreign divested to domestic	1970	0.86	0.95	0.55	0.76
Foreign acquired from domestic	1979	0.95	0.87	0.80	0.86
Domestic divested to foreign	1970	0.87	0.77	0.73	0.77
Foreign acquired from foreign	1979	0.93	0.92	0.83	0.89
Foreign divested to foreign	1970	0.85	0.91	0.79	0.83
Average remuneration per production worker					
All continuing plants acquired	1979	1.07	0.97	0.88	0.97
All continuing plants divested	1970	1.08	1.00	0.87	0.98
Domestic acquired from domestic	1979	1.12	1.02	0.79	0.99
Domestic divested to domestic	1970	1.20	1.05	0.79	1.02
Domestic acquired from foreign	1979	1.09	0.98	0.91	0.99
Foreign divested to domestic	1970	0.96	1.02	0.98	1.01
Foreign acquired from domestic	1979	0.99	0.80	0.88	0.89
Domestic divested to foreign	1970	0.89	0.82	0.87	0.86
Foreign acquired from foreign	1979	0.97	0.95	0.92	0.96
Foreign divested to foreign	1970	0.98	0.94	0.87	0.93
Annual salary per non-production worker					
All continuing plants acquired	1979	1.06	0.94	0.89	0.94
All continuing plants divested	1970	1.01	0.97	0.94	0.97
Domestic acquired from domestic	1979	1.14	0.94	0.85	0.96
Domestic divested to domestic	1970	1.08	0.96	0.91	0.96
Domestic acquired from foreign	1979	1.13	1.02	0.92	0.99
Foreign divested to domestic	1970	1.06	1.04	0.99	1.03
Foreign acquired from domestic	1979	0.91	0.89	0.86	0.88
Domestic divested to foreign	1970	0.91	0.91	0.98	0.93
Foreign acquired from foreign	1979	0.91	0.91	0.90	0.91
Foreign divested to foreign	1970	0.93	0.98	0.90	0.93

Table 11-13. *(cont.)*

Characteristic by category	Year	Foreign-ownership group			Total
		Low	Medium	High	
Percentage of non-production workers					
All continuing plants acquired	1979	1.53	1.48	0.77	1.30
All continuing plants divested	1970	1.76	1.48	0.78	1.35
Domestic acquired from domestic	1979	1.62	1.55	0.64	1.24
Domestic divested to domestic	1970	1.72	1.56	0.57	1.23
Domestic acquired from foreign	1979	1.71	1.19	1.05	1.30
Foreign divested to domestic	1970	1.46	1.39	1.39	1.40
Foreign acquired from domestic	1979	1.21	0.92	0.60	0.93
Domestic divested to foreign	1970	1.71	1.01	0.50	0.98
Foreign acquired from foreign	1979	1.78	1.95	0.80	1.57
Foreign divested to foreign	1970	2.23	1.67	0.78	1.52

[a] Only unrelated mergers were considered. All summary statistics presented here are weighted averages, defined in Table 11-11.

differed across foreign-ownership industry groups, and the differential effect was greatest in the domestic-to-domestic sector.

Changes in control were associated with reductions in the salaried component of the work-force (non-production workers) where foreign ownership was low, but there was virtually no change where it was high (see Table 11-11). These reductions where foreign ownership was low are evident in all sectors except the domestic-to-foreign changes (Table 11-13). Where foreign ownership was high, the proportion of non-production workers was unaffected by foreign-to-foreign control changes but increased where a domestic acquirer was involved.

In conclusion, when nationality is examined, neither type of acquirer (foreign versus domestic) appears systematically to outperform the other. In the high-foreign-ownership group, domestic-to-domestic transfers are characterized by higher productivity gains and increases in the proportion of non-production workers, but lower wage and salary gains compared with those of foreign-to-foreign transfers. In the lowest-foreign-ownership group, foreign-to-foreign transfers result in higher productivity gains and lower wage-rate losses than do domestic-to-domestic transfers, but greater decreases in salary gains and in the proportion of non-production workers.

There is also evidence of a division of labour between domestic-to-domestic and foreign-to-foreign transfers. Domestic enterprises achieve more containment of costs. When control changes across all groups are considered, domestic-to-domestic take-overs result in either a decline or no change in their relative wage, salary, and non-production-worker proportions; the reverse is generally the case in foreign-to-foreign transfers. Foreign enterprises effect more relocations of resources that might lead to synergistic gains. Their productivity gains extend across all industries, whereas these gains happen only in the high-foreign-ownership group for domestic-to-domestic take-overs. There is a difference between the types of opportunities for productive control changes that arise in industry structures that are congenial to foreign ownership and those that are not.

Conclusions

This chapter has investigated the difference between turnover among domestic- and foreign-controlled firms. The theory and previous research on turnover and on mergers suggest that the effect of changes in control should vary with the extent to which multinational enterprises exist in an industry. The same opportunities for the synergistic deployment of lumpy and intangible assets that foster foreign investment also create opportunities for beneficial changes in control. If mergers serve to increase efficiency in the use of inputs, no such association should appear. The data support the following conclusions.

The proportion of an industry's output that is subject to changes in control increases with the importance of foreign ownership. Greenfield entry by new firms and closedown exit by incumbents decreases sharply with foreign ownership, so that industries with high foreign ownership experience less pressure from this source to improve efficiency. They also experience a bit less turnover of market share among incumbents. Roughly speaking, producers in industries with high foreign ownership feel more pressure to achieve efficiency from control changes and less from domestic product-market competition than those in industries with low foreign ownership.

Differences in the type of entry used by foreign and domestic firms primarily reflect differences in the industries in which they function. Foreign firms tend to enter more commonly by means of plant acquisition than by construction of plant in high-foreign-ownership industries but not in low-foreign-ownership industries. On the other hand, the tendency of domestic firms to rely more on greenfield entry is greater in the lowest-foreign-ownership group than in the highest.

Foreign and domestic firms are different, but turnover in both contributes to productivity growth. Plant turnover associated with entry and exit results in about the same productivity growth for domestic and foreign firms, but entry and exit of domestic plants lead to greater wage-rate gains. For plant births and deaths associated with continuing firms, foreign firms produce greater productivity, wage, and salary gains than do domestic firms.

Changes in productivity and remuneration levels due to plant birth and death are large relative to those associated with control changes. Nevertheless, control changes have a positive impact on both.

Industries with low and high foreign ownership differ sharply in the opportunities they afford for gains through changes in control. Where foreign ownership is high, so are opportunities for the synergistic deployment of lumpy and intangible assets. Where it is low, the opportunities for productive changes in control lie more in cost containment and improved use of the establishment's existing input flow.

The favourable effects of changes in control increase with the amount of foreign ownership in an industry. Changes in control lead to increases in relative market share and relative productivity that are greater in the highest-foreign-ownership group than in the lowest.

While industries with high foreign ownership show gains in productivity associated with control changes, there is wide variation in the effects of control changes across industries within this foreign-ownership industry group. In particular, productivity gains are larger in product-differentiated and science-based industries, and smaller in the natural-resource-based industries.

Productivity gains in high-foreign-ownership industries do not come only from foreign acquisitions. They also come from acquisitions by domestic firms who make important contributions in this sector. This accords with the hypothesis that the predominant reason for control change in industries with a high level of foreign ownership relates to the synergistic merging of assets.

Productivity gains in foreign firms are not restricted to the high-foreign-ownership group. They also occur in the sector with the highest level of domestic ownership. This supports the contention that most control changes affecting multinational firms involve the transfer of specialized assets.

Transfers between foreign firms in the industry group with the highest foreign ownership are beneficial on several counts. Foreign-to-foreign transfers here lead to productivity gains and are not accompanied generally by wage and salary losses for production workers, or a decline in the proportion of non-production workers.

There are sectoral differences in the function of transfers that change the nationality of control. These suggest a specialization of function by nationality across foreign-ownership groups. In terms of productivity, wage and salary gains, and increases in the proportion of non-production workers, foreign-to-domestic transfers do better in industries with high domestic ownership than those with high foreign ownership, and domestic-to-foreign transfers do better in the high-foreign-ownership group.

Domestic-to-domestic transfers in industries with low foreign ownership have many negative features – share losses, productivity losses, wage losses, non-production-worker losses.

The conclusions that follow from these quantitative findings are clear. Control changes typically have a favourable effect on productivity and efficiency. Foreign and domestic enterprises bring different skills to the task of resource reallocation. Some foreign-to-foreign changes in control in Canada were probably adjuncts of suspect mergers that occurred elsewhere, but they had few deleterious effects on foreign-controlled units within the country. Finally, it is probably more costly to discourage control changes in industries with high foreign ownership because they are highly concentrated and subject to attenuated pressures for efficiency from actual and potential competition.

12

Industry efficiency and firm turnover in the Canadian manufacturing sector

The instruments of labour are largely modified all the time by the progress of industry. Hence they are not replaced in their original, but in their modified form. On the one hand the mass of the fixed capital invested in a certain bodily form and endowed in that form with a certain average life constitutes one reason for the only gradual pace of the introduction of new machinery etc., and therefore an obstacle to the rapid general introduction of improved instruments of labour. On the other hand, competition compels the replacement of the old instruments of labour by new ones before the expiration of their natural life, especially when decisive changes occur.

Karl Marx (1966: vol. 1, 381)

Introduction

While both Marx and Marshall recognized the diversity of production techniques that were likely to be employed at any given time, recent studies of industry performance generally fail to recognize the diversity of firms within an industry. For example, productivity growth is generally measured at the industry level with almost complete disregard for the underlying production entities, probably because of the widely accepted concept of a representative or average firm. As Reid (1987) points out, in industrial organization the Vinerian concept of the representative firm has been dominant at the expense of the more complex notion of the diversity of firm performance stressed by Marshall. As a result, the mainstream of industrial organization has had trouble in coming to grips with the reality of heterogeneity of firm performance within industries.

One of the few areas of applied industrial economics that acknowledges firm heterogeneity is the literature on X-inefficiency. On the one hand, analysts such as Leibenstein (1966) argue, from observation, that inefficiency deserves attention. On the other hand, economists such as Stigler (1976) argue that profit maximization makes it unlikely that inefficiency can exist for

298

long and that the analyses of those who claim to observe it must be based on incorrect measurement.

Despite this existential debate, econometricians who were working on the estimation of frontier production functions began to investigate how the error structure of these production functions could be used to characterize the degree of efficiency in an industry. As a result, there is now an impressive body of empirical evidence on the nature and correlates of efficiency.[1] Most of these empirical studies were limited to a small number of industries, until the work of Caves and Barton (1990), who looked at a broad cross-section of U.S. manufacturing industries in the 1970s. But there are few studies that allow an assessment of how fleeting the phenomenon is (one of Stigler's criticisms), or what causes efficiency to change. This chapter investigates both issues.

First, the methodology used to measure industry efficiency is examined and a summary statistic is chosen for the analysis. Then, the extent to which the chosen measure is related to the industry characteristics that were found to be important determinants of efficiency in Caves and Barton's study is investigated. The dynamics of industry change are then explored, with a focus on the role played by turnover in changes in efficiency. Finally, regression analysis is used to examine the determinants of the forces that reduce turnover and to look at the commonalities between the determinants of inter-industry variability in efficiency levels and the forces that change these levels.

Measuring efficiency

Measures of efficiency have typically been divided into two categories: technical and allocative efficiency.[2] Technical efficiency occurs when a firm makes the best use of its inputs. A firm is technically inefficient when it obtains less than the maximum output possible from the bundle of inputs it chooses to utilize. Allocative efficiency occurs when a firm employs its inputs in the correct proportions. A firm is allocatively inefficient when, given the prices of its inputs and the marginal products of the inputs, it does not employ these factors in the optimal proportions. Like the majority of studies, this chapter focuses on technical efficiency. A series of snapshots of technical efficiency when related to the amount of turnover provides a picture of dynamic efficiency.

Recent work in measuring efficiency uses production functions estimated from plant and firm data.[3] The production-function approach attempts to correct for differences in output caused by differences in inputs and in size. The residuals are then utilized to produce an "average" measure of efficiency.

The current study uses the same concept of efficiency, but a simpler measurement technique. Efficiency is measured as the ratio of actual output to potential output. Potential output is calculated as the efficient level of output per person multiplied by the level of employment in each establishment, summed over all establishments. As such, the measure of efficiency used here is size-weighted. The efficient level of output per person is defined as the sum of output divided by the sum of all employment in the most productive establishments accounting for a specified proportion of total output: 10, 20, 30, or 40 per cent.

This method is more direct, though less elegant, than an estimate of efficiency derived from the residuals of a production function. It may also be the more appropriate research strategy. Estimating the average level of efficiency from a production function presumes that it is appropriate to correct for differences in productivity that are the result of different establishment sizes or factor proportions. This is not always the case. If the cause of inefficiency is the existence of suboptimal-sized plants, then part of the estimated inefficiency is being eliminated by the use of a production function.

The measure employed here will avoid some of these problems. By focusing directly on output per worker, it presumes that society's goal should be to maximize product per worker and that firms setting the lead in this area can and should be emulated. Whether this view is justified depends on the extent to which intra-industry differences in factor proportions and plant sizes are efficient. It might be argued that different factor proportions within an industry are justifiable in terms of different factor prices. If differences in capital–labour ratios are optimal because of different factor costs, or because of different vintage effects, inefficiency as measured here will be overstated. It also might be argued that small, inefficient firms provide externalities that compensate for their inefficiencies and make their existence desirable – that they provide external discipline for large firms and in some cases become the next generation of large, efficient firms.

These views are very much akin to the notion that the concept of efficiency is misplaced. The issue will not be resolved here. Nevertheless, the dispersion of relative productivity among plants within an industry – irrespective of the term applied to the phenomenon – has intrinsic interest. To the extent that productivity levels in less productive plants can be brought up to those in the most productive plants, productivity gains will ensue. How this occurs warrants further investigation.[4]

Since the use of production functions to estimate efficiency measures has become widespread, a word or two is required in defence of the efficiency measure used here. As a practical matter, the potential problems with the measure adopted here – failure to correct for differing factor proportions or firm size – may be unimportant if the measure used closely correlates with others. Unfortunately, there are no comparative analyses of how closely this measure relates to others. But there is an increasing amount of evidence to suggest that alternative measures of efficiency in general are highly correlated (Caves and Barton, 1990: 53) and that using different measures has a relatively minor effect on isolating the determinants of efficiency (Caves and Barton, 1990: 107–10). In this respect, it has been observed that skewness measures of efficiency – from which the measure used here is derived – are closely correlated to other efficiency measures derived from the residuals of production functions.

There are several additional reasons to adopt the measure used here. First, its inter-industry variance is relatively unaffected by the industry sample chosen to define optimal output-per-person ratios. The measure is not greatly affected by outliers and is less likely to be affected by the number of observations used to estimate it than are most measures that are derived from the production-function approach. Second, it is correlated with many of the variables that other studies find to be correlated with alternative inefficiency measures. Its inter-industry variability, therefore, appears to be closely related to the more complex and more costly measures of efficiency that are derived from production functions.

Efficiency in Canadian manufacturing
Choice of sample

When industry efficiency is defined using output per person in the most productive plants, as it is here, some subset must be chosen to define maximum potential productivity. If the inter-industry variability is sensitive to the sample chosen, then the choice of subset becomes critical. In order to examine this issue, different cut-off points based on the proportion of industry shipments covered were used to define the plants considered to be efficient, frontier output per person was calculated for plants above each cut-off point, and the correlations between the various efficiency estimates associated with each cut-off were calculated. The sample consisted of 167 industries classified at the four-digit SIC level. The years chosen were 1970 and 1979. Output per person was defined alternately as shipments per worker and value-added per worker.

For the first measure (EFF1), the efficient output per person was defined as the sum of output over the sum of labour input of the most productive plants that accounted for 10 per cent of output. Levels of 20, 30, and 40 per cent of industry output were also used, yielding the efficiency measures EFF2, EFF3, and EFF4, respectively.

The levels of efficiency for the various cut-off points are, on average, substantially different. Figure 12-1 plots the mean value of efficiency for each cut-off point, as well as its upper and lower bounds in 1970, using value-added as the output measure. When the most productive plants that account for 10 per cent of value-added are used to define maximum potential

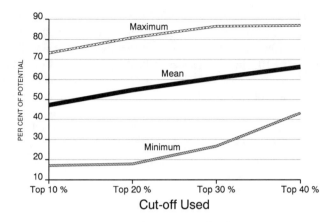

Figure 12-1. Industry-efficiency measures for 1970 by cut-off point.

output per person, production is only 47 per cent of potential. This increases to 55, 61, and 66 per cent when the most productive plants, accounting for 20, 30, and 40 per cent of value-added, respectively, are used for the cut-off. Comparable measures based on shipments per worker are 44, 52, 57, and 63 per cent. Since there is little difference between the value-added-based and the shipments-based measures, only the former are reported here.[5]

In light of the lack of consensus as to the most appropriate methodology for measuring efficiency, international comparisons of the *levels* of inefficiency are hazardous. Nevertheless, analysts make such comparisons. Caves and Barton (1990) summarize several studies that use the stochastic-production-function technique and that find efficiency estimates ranging from 50 to 90 per cent for such disparate countries as Colombia, Indonesia, and France. They report mean values for efficiency in the U.S. manufacturing sector as different as 63 and 99 per cent using two variations in the stochastic-production-frontier approach (1990: 50). The differences among these values indicate the degree to which estimates of *levels* of efficiency are sensitive to the technique used.

Although Caves and Barton find large differences in the level of efficiency in the United States, the cross-industry variability of their two most important estimates is quite similar. The partial correlation coefficient of these measures is .96, and the regressions that examine the relationship between an industry's efficiency and its characteristics using each of these measures tell the same story.

The measures of efficiency that are derived here for the Canadian manufacturing sector produce similar results. While the mean values of the efficiency measures for the four cut-off points are different, they are highly

Table 12-1. *Correlations between efficiency estimates, 1970 and 1979[a]*

	1970				
	EFF1	EFF2	EFF3	EFF4	1979[b]
EFF1	1.0	.91	.82	.77	.61
EFF2		1.0	.89	.84	.51
EFF3			1.0	.92	.55
EFF4				1.0	.52

Note: For definitions of the variables, see text.
[a] All correlations are significantly different from zero at the 1 per cent significance level.
[b] The correlations for 1979 are between the 1970 and 1979 estimates of efficiency that use the same cut-off point.

correlated. The correlation matrix for the four 1970 measures derived using the 10, 20, 30, and 40 per cent cut-off points is presented in Table 12-1. The correlations are all high and, for adjacent cut-off points, are about .90. This pattern suggests that the cut-off chosen is not critical. This supposition was tested and confirmed by using several values of the efficiency measure at different stages of the analysis. Since the conclusions were generally the same, the measure that corresponds with the 40 per cent cut-off point was arbitrarily chosen here.

Characteristics of the efficiency measure

The efficiency estimates vary considerably among industries. Figure 12-2 contains the mean estimates across industry deciles where industries are ranked by the efficiency measure. The mean efficiency value is 53 per cent for the industry in the first decile and increases to 77 per cent at the tenth decile. The preferred efficiency measure in Caves and Barton's study ranges from 46 per cent to 81 per cent over the same range (1990: 51).

The inter-industry differences in efficiency change over time. The last column of Table 12-1 contains the estimates of the correlation of the efficiency estimates in 1970 and 1979. Correlations between .5 and .6 indicate that, while patterns of cross-industry efficiency differentials persist, they are not immutable. The mean values of the 1970 and the 1979 efficiency estimates based on the decile ranking of the 1970 estimates are plotted in Figure 12-2. There is a tendency for industries to regress to the mean.

What is most striking is the increase in the dispersion of industries that are grouped in the same decile in 1970. The bottom line shows the range in 1970 (of course, small by construction). The range in 1979 for each of the industries

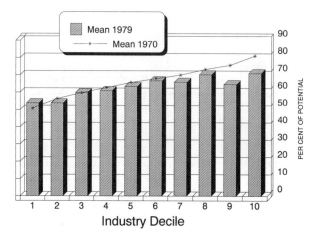

Figure 12-2. A comparison of the mean efficiency measures for 1970 and 1979, ranked by an industry's efficiency measure for 1970.

in a particular 1970 decile is much greater than the range in 1970. The increase in variability is largest in the industries that were most and least efficient in 1970. The world does not stand still. Industries where most firms have moved close to the maximum potential output are those where something, perhaps new technology, is likely to result in some firms gaining an advantage over others in the future. Industries where efficiency is lowest make the greatest improvements.

Industry characteristics associated with efficiency

The industry characteristics associated with efficiency are important because they shed light on the reasons for inter-industry differences in efficiency and because they verify the usefulness of the efficiency measure adopted here. Since this measure is not identical to others, it is important to ask whether it is similarly related to industry characteristics found to be important determinants of efficiency in other countries.

In order to make this comparison, the taxonomy of industry characteristics developed by Caves and Barton in their extensive U.S. study is used. Industry characteristics are divided into six broad groups. In the first group are competitive conditions such as concentration and exposure to international trade that, it is posited, produce centripetal pressures that reduce firm heterogeneity. The second group consists of product-differentiation characteristics that are used to control for the likelihood that efficiency is measured with error. Efficiency measures are generally based on the value of shipments or value-added – variables that combine both output and price. It is normally assumed that prices are reasonably similar across firms. If there are differences in the prices buyers pay, some of the measured differences in efficiency will actually be due to differences in rents accruing to firms. Product-differentiation variables control for this possibility. The third group of variables captures the occurrence of change and, therefore, the centrifugal forces that might allow plants' productivity levels to diverge. The fourth group represents characteristics that permit heterogeneity due to differences among markets. The fifth group includes organizational influences that exert pressures on management – the extent of diversification, multi-plant operation, large plant size, and certain labour characteristics such as the degree of unionization and the use of full-time as opposed to part-time workers. Finally, the sixth group of variables serves to control for influences that have been omitted. Some of these variables – such as the vintage of capital or the variation in capital–labour ratios – proxy factors that have been missed in estimating a simplified production function. Other variables, such as the number of observations on which the production function is based, are used to account for the bias that arises because of a purely statistical factor. Technical efficiency, as it is defined in most studies, depends inversely on the highest observed value of a distribution. The theory of order statistics suggests that the larger the number of observations (i.e., plants in an industry) the greater the range and thus the lower measured efficiency will be (Caves and Barton, 1990). Since the efficiency measure used in this study is size-weighted, this problem is likely to be less important here. The variables that were employed are listed in Table 12-2. They were defined to resemble those used in Caves and Barton's study.[6]

The correlations between industry characteristics for 1970 and the measure of efficiency for the same year are reported in Table 12-3.[7] These correlations reveal a situation similar to that reported by Caves and Barton. Several of what they classified as core variables have high correlations with the Canadian efficiency measure. As is the case in the United States, the higher the proportion of an industry's sales that are controlled by firms with their main interests elsewhere (COVE), the lower the efficiency. Similarly, the greater the diversity of inputs available to work with labour (SD[M/L]), the lower the efficiency. In the current study, several other variables that capture the heterogeneity of the industry – variables that reflect the mechanism that might cause variations in productivity and thus lower efficiency levels – were also employed. The number of census-defined products classified to the industry (N5D), the variation in plant specialization (SD[HERF]), and the standard deviation in the plant-specialization ratio (SD[SPEC]) were all included. None of these was significantly correlated with efficiency at the 5 per cent level. Caves and Barton also include in their core explanatory variables a labour-conditions variable – the importance of full-time workers (FULL). As in the

Table 12-2. *Exogenous variables used in the analysis*

Variable	Definition
Competitive conditions	
CR4	Percentage of shipments accounted for by the four largest firms, 1970
XC	Excess concentration ratio defined as CONC minus the share that the four largest firms would have if they each operated one plant equal to MES (MES is the average plant size of those largest plants accounting for the top 50 per cent of shipments)
IMP	Imports divided by domestic disappearance, the latter defined as domestic production minus exports plus imports, 1970
EXP	Exports divided by domestic production, 1970
COMP	Exports less imports over exports plus imports, 1970
Product differentiation	
ADV	Inputs of advertising services divided by value of industry shipments, 1971
Occurrence of heterogeneity and change	
RD	Ratio of research-and-development personnel to all wage and salary earners, 1975
SD(M/L)	Standard deviation of the ratio of materials and energy expenses divided by the number of wage and salary workers, 1970
N5D	Number of five-digit ICC (Industrial Commodity Classification) commodities per four-digit SIC industry
SD(HERF)	Standard deviation of the plant level of product specialization, the latter defined using a Herfindahl index of the proportion of the plant's shipments classified to the nth four-digit ICC commodity, 1970
SD(SIZE)	Standard deviation of average plant-size based on salaried and production workers, 1970
SD(SPEC)	Standard deviation in the plant-specialization ratio
CVAR8	Coefficient of variation of the top eight firms, 1970
SUBOPT	Percentage of industry sales in Canadian plants that are smaller than the MES plant in the United States, the latter defined by ranking plants on the basis of size and choosing the one that divides the cumulative distribution of sales in two
KL	Capital–labour ratio for the industry, 1970
Geographic market heterogeneity	
REG	Dummy variable for an industry classified as being regional
Organizational influences	
Enterprise diversification	
COVE	Sales of plants in industry i belonging to enterprises in other industries divided by sales of all establishments in industry i, in 1970
Multi-plant operation	
MULT1	Sales of plants belonging to companies that are multi-plant operators divided by total sales in 1970
MULT2	Number of plants per enterprise, 1970

Table 12-2. *(cont.)*

Variable	Definition
Size of production units	
RPSIZE	Average plant-size of the largest plants that account for the top 50 per cent of shipments divided by industry shipments, 1970
RFSIZE	Average firm-size of the largest plants that account for the top 50 per cent of shipments divided by industry shipments, 1970
Labour relations	
UNION	Proportion of production workers who were union members, 1971
FULL	Importance of full-time workers as measured by the number of person hours worked by production workers divided by the number of production workers, 1970
Other	
NOBS	Number of plants on which the efficiency measure was based, 1970

Table 12-3. *Correlations between efficiency and industry characteristics*

Variable[a]	Correlation	Probability value[b]
CR4	−.10	.18
XC	−.20	.01
IMP	−.04	.60
EXP	−.03	.67
COMP	−.08	.27
ADV	−.19	.01
RD	−.07	.36
SD(M/L)	−.18	.02
N5D	−.12	.14
SD(HERF)	.04	.65
SD(SIZE)	.07	.36
CVAR8	−.08	.24
SUBOPT	−.08	.28
KL	−.26	.01
REG	−.02	.81
COVE	−.13	.09
MULT1	−.11	.14
MULT2	−.18	.03
RPSIZE	−.04	.59
RFSIZE	−.03	.69
UNION	−.12	.12
FULL	−.18	.02
NOBS	.08	.29

[a] For definitions of variables, see Table 12-2.
[b] Probability value of the null hypothesis that the correlation is zero.

United States, Canadian efficiency is positively related to the use of part-time workers.

In the U.S. study, the importance of competitive conditions proves difficult to discern. By itself, concentration is not significant, but when it is entered in a non-linear fashion, an effect is found. Efficiency first rises and then falls as concentration increases. In Canada, the concentration ratio is negatively correlated with efficiency. This is not inconsistent with the U.S. finding, because the level of concentration in most Canadian industries is higher than in U.S. industries. As is the case in the United States, export and import intensity in Canada are not closely related to industry efficiency. Nominal and effective tariff variables also are insignificant.

Similarities between the Canadian and U.S. results extend to the set of relationships outside the core variables. In both countries, geographic market heterogeneity has no robust effect, product differentiation is strongly associated with lower efficiency, and the labour-market variable (UNION) has a negative effect on efficiency that is only weakly significant.

An attempt was made to ascertain whether the strongly negative effect of concentration might be related to economies of plant scale rather than of multi-plant operation. To this end, the average plant size of the largest firms divided by market size was included (RPSIZE) as was excess concentration (XC). The former proxies the concentration effect due to plant-scale economies and the latter the concentration effect due to multi-plant ownership. The former is not significant, while the latter is negatively correlated with efficiency. Additional variables that captured the extent of multi-plant ownership in the industry (MULT1 and MULT2) also exhibit negative correlations with industry efficiency. Diversification across industries has a negative effect on efficiency, as does horizontal expansion within an industry.

While the results of the U.S. and Canadian studies are similar in many respects, there are two important differences. First, the number of observations is inversely related to efficiency in the U.S. study because of the "order" effect. The number of observations is not significantly correlated with efficiency in the Canadian study. Second, while the U.S. study finds that research-and-development intensity was significantly correlated with efficiency, this is not the case for Canada. One of the reasons for the difference may be the truncated nature of research and development in Canada. A substantial portion of the manufacturing sector in Canada is foreign controlled. If these firms perform their research and developement abroad and import the fruits of their discovery, domestic research-and-development ratios may not reflect the research intensity of the industry. In order to test for this phenomenon, two new variables were used. The first was technology payments made abroad divided by sales. The second was the sum of technology payments and domestic expenditure on research and development divided by sales. The technology-payments variable, like the employee-based variable, continues to be insignificantly correlated with efficiency. The variable that adds technology payments plus research-and-development expenditure is positively correlated with efficiency, but only marginally significant.

Industry efficiency, expressed in log-odds form, was regressed on the industry characteristics. The results of the regression are reported in equation 12-1.

$$EFF4 = 2.61 - 4.77 \text{ ADV} - 0.378 \text{ XC} - 0.001 \text{ N5D}$$
$$t = \quad (2.74) \quad\quad (2.98) \quad\quad (2.18)$$
$$\text{prob } t = \quad (.004) \quad\quad (.031) \quad\quad (.085)$$
$$- 0.768 \text{ FULL} - 0.0001 \text{ UNION} - 0.005 \text{ SD(M/L)}.$$
$$(1.75) \quad\quad (1.70) \quad\quad (1.80)$$
$$(.092) \quad\quad (.023) \quad\quad (.074)$$
$$R^2 = .16, \text{ d.f.} = 143, \text{ prob } f = .0001. \quad\quad (12\text{-}1)$$

When industry characteristics are considered simultaneously, the importance of the core set of variables found to be important in the U.S. study is confirmed. Product differentiation (ADV), labour-market conditions (FULL, UNION), variability of the factor–input ratio (SD[M/L]), concentration due to multi-plant activity (XC), and the diversity of products in an industry (N5D) all decrease efficiency.

Considering the various industry characteristics jointly in a regression may run afoul of multicollinearity. This problem is compounded here by the fact that some of the variables measure industry characteristics that are assumed to affect efficiency (competitive conditions), while others capture the mechanism by which inefficiency may develop (the degree of suboptimal capacity or the degree of diversity within an industry). The variables in this latter category also beg explanation and may themselves be related to basic industry characteristics like product differentiation, research and development, the state of industry competition, and organizational traits.

In order to ascertain the relative importance of the "determinants" of interindustry efficiency levels, a principal-component analysis was performed on the set of industry characteristics and the components were used in a regression. Principal-component analysis permits us to characterize the joint effects of the industry characteristics, since each of the components generated by the analysis is constructed as a weighted average of the original variables. Examining which of the original variables are heavily weighted in a component that significantly affects industry efficiency offers insight into how various industry characteristics tend to work together. The results are

$$\text{EFF4} = 0.70 - 0.098 \text{ PVAR2} + 0.061 \text{ PVAR3} - 0.056 \text{ VAR4}$$

$$t = \qquad (2.75) \qquad\qquad (1.94) \qquad\qquad (1.82)$$

$$\text{prob } t = \qquad (.01) \qquad\qquad (.05) \qquad\qquad (.07)$$

$$- 0.061 \text{ PVAR5} - 0.079 \text{ PVAR9} + 0.060 \text{ PVAR10}$$

$$(1.82) \qquad\qquad (2.57) \qquad\qquad (1.97)$$

$$(.07) \qquad\qquad (.01) \qquad\qquad (.05)$$

$$- 0.079 \text{ PVAR18}.$$

$$(2.52)$$

$$(.01)$$

$$R^2 = .166, \text{ d.f.} = 143.0. \qquad\qquad\qquad (12\text{--}2)$$

Table 12-4 reports the weights of the original variables.

Each of the significant components is heavily weighted on one of the variables that was previously found to be important; but there are other variables that come into play. The addition of these variables considerably enriches the interpretation of the process at work. The first component has a positive, though insignificant, effect on efficiency. It is the plant-scale portion of concentration – weighting both the four-firm concentration ratio (CR4) and relative plant size (RPSIZE) positively. The second component has a significant negative effect on efficiency. It represents multi-plant ownership in an industry – XC, MULT1, and MULT2 are all heavily weighted.[8] Relative plant size (RPSIZE) is negatively weighted and the regional variable is positively weighted in this component. Thus, inefficiency here is associated with multi-plant ownership, small plants, and regional production.

The third component has a positive effect on efficiency; it positively weights both comparative advantage (COMP) and export intensity (EXP), but negatively weights advertising intensity. This component represents resource-based industries that export a significant proportion of their production and do little advertising. The fourth component has a negative effect on efficiency: import intensity (IMP), advertising (ADV), and number of products (N5D) are included in this component with positive weights. In addition, suboptimal capacity (SUBOPT) has a positive weight. This component represents import-competing industries with a large number of products that are intensively advertised. The signs of the coefficients on these two components indicate that export industries are relatively efficient and that import-competing industries are less efficient.

The fifth component has a negative effect on efficiency: it combines a negative weight on export intensity and a positive weight on both the use of full-time employees and multi-plant ownership. Here, as elsewhere, it is a combination of factors that contributes to inefficiency.

The ninth and tenth components both represent regional industries, but they have opposite effects on efficiency. In both, the effect of advertising intensity and the use of full-time workers is to decrease productivity. The

Table 12-4. *Principal-component analysis of industry characteristics*

Variable					Eigenvector				
	PVAR1	PVAR2	PVAR3	PVAR4	PVAR5	PVAR6	PVAR7	PVAR8	PVAR9
CR4	0.47	-0.09	-0.09	-0.01	0.12	-0.02	0.06	0.05	-0.07
ADV	0.02	-0.02	-0.29	0.20	-0.10	-0.36	0.43	0.12	0.28
COMP	0.16	0.24	0.32	-0.11	-0.15	-0.09	-0.06	-0.49	0.04
RD	0.18	0.16	0.12	0.30	-0.03	-0.28	-0.15	0.09	0.30
MULT1	0.28	0.37	0.01	-0.10	0.16	-0.14	-0.05	-0.01	-0.14
MULT2	0.29	0.27	-0.14	-0.15	0.31	-0.13	0.04	-0.23	0.00
COVE	0.20	0.13	0.16	-0.03	-0.16	0.35	-0.17	0.39	-0.23
N5D	-0.10	0.01	0.15	0.16	0.00	-0.09	-0.14	0.09	0.12
REG	-0.08	0.23	-0.04	0.31	-0.07	-0.25	-0.04	0.15	0.37
EXP	0.19	0.01	0.39	0.16	-0.36	0.19	0.13	-0.37	0.09
IMP	0.02	-0.33	-0.07	0.38	0.05	0.21	-0.23	-0.23	0.08
CVAR8	0.44	-0.11	-0.02	-0.04	0.08	-0.12	0.06	0.02	-0.03
XC	0.02	0.48	-0.16	0.16	0.13	0.15	0.08	-0.06	-0.05
NOBS	-0.24	0.19	0.15	0.02	-0.22	-0.25	-0.26	-0.07	0.16
FULL	0.13	0.18	0.03	0.06	0.25	0.27	-0.41	0.21	0.44
SUBOPT	-0.16	0.05	-0.20	0.37	-0.03	0.27	0.39	0.03	-0.08
UNION	0.06	-0.10	-0.21	-0.23	0.07	0.42	0.15	-0.24	0.55
RPSIZE	0.30	-0.41	0.06	-0.12	-0.02	-0.12	-0.02	0.08	-0.01
SD(M/L)	0.19	0.15	0.24	0.04	-0.33	0.15	0.35	0.43	0.19
SDHERF	-0.16	-0.08	0.43	-0.02	0.40	-0.08	0.27	0.06	0.02
SDSPEC	-0.13	-0.05	0.42	-0.02	0.50	0.06	0.20	0.07	0.09

Table 12-4. (cont.)

| | | | | | Eigenvector | | | | |
Variable	PVAR10	PVAR11	PVAR12	PVAR13	PVAR14	PVAR15	PVAR16	PVAR17	PVAR18
CR4	0.13	0.04	-0.10	0.09	0.06	0.07	0.13	0.24	0.11
ADV	-0.40	0.12	0.19	0.39	-0.11	0.25	0.08	-0.02	-0.10
COMP	-0.33	0.15	0.08	0.04	0.25	-0.20	0.20	0.26	0.32
RD	-0.03	0.29	0.15	-0.65	0.23	0.14	-0.16	-0.02	-0.04
MULT1	0.15	-0.11	-0.03	0.04	0.10	0.03	0.09	0.03	-0.63
MULT2	0.04	0.03	-0.03	0.12	0.02	-0.21	-0.40	-0.59	0.26
COVE	-0.08	0.20	0.44	0.27	0.37	0.21	-0.05	-0.16	0.04
N5D	0.05	-0.55	0.23	0.16	0.18	-0.35	0.13	0.10	0.09
REG	0.56	0.29	0.29	0.14	-0.07	-0.29	0.12	0.08	0.02
EXP	0.12	0.10	0.03	0.07	-0.32	0.02	-0.06	-0.12	-0.39
IMP	0.29	0.23	0.11	0.24	-0.23	0.19	0.13	-0.06	0.25
CVAR8	0.22	-0.18	-0.12	0.04	-0.01	0.21	0.03	0.28	0.17
XC	0.10	-0.03	0.12	-0.21	-0.15	0.33	0.16	0.19	0.21
NOBS	0.16	-0.05	-0.43	0.29	0.29	0.46	-0.24	0.02	0.08
FULL	-0.36	0.19	-0.35	0.11	-0.18	-0.14	0.16	0.07	-0.07
SUBOPT	0.18	0.39	-0.32	0.03	0.38	-0.26	-0.08	0.20	-0.05
UNION	0.06	-0.32	0.12	-0.04	0.38	0.14	-0.03	-0.07	-0.13
RPSIZE	0.01	0.04	-0.16	0.21	0.15	-0.20	-0.03	0.02	-0.08
SD(M/L)	0.08	-0.20	-0.23	-0.12	-0.20	-0.05	-0.08	-0.14	0.28
SDHERF	0.11	0.08	-0.12	-0.01	0.17	0.17	0.54	-0.37	0.02
SDSPEC	-0.01	0.03	0.19	0.14	-0.13	0.06	-0.52	0.38	-0.02

ninth component, which has a negative effect on efficiency, represents regional industries with intensive advertising, suboptimal capacity, high unionization, and few part-time workers. The tenth component represents regional industries with little advertising and more part-time workers. The difference between the two components lies primarily in the existence of suboptimal capacity in the component that has a negative effect on efficiency.

The use of principal-component analysis to summarize industry characteristics confirms and extends the picture drawn by the simple correlation and regression analyses. Advertising is deleterious, not so much as an unconditional force giving rise to differential rents, but in conjunction with other factors that set the context for advertising: high import intensity, suboptimal capacity, and a large number of products. Export and import intensity both matter. Labour conditions also affect efficiency, but primarily in regional industries.

Turnover and industry efficiency

Most empirical studies of industry efficiency use single-period cross-sectional regressions (as was done in the first section of this chapter) and do not provide size-weighted measures. This methodology can miss the manner by which efficiency changes and the extent of the change. Changes in relative efficiency levels are important, as the evidence on the correlation between the estimates for 1970 and 1979 presented in Table 12-1 indicates.

Turnover and its relationship to productivity growth

Changes in efficiency occur as the productivity of individual establishments and their market shares change. When market shares are held constant, changes in the level of industry efficiency are a function of the extent to which productivity growth is spread evenly across establishments. The value of the efficiency measure does not change if productivity gains are spread equally across all establishments. Efficiency increases if the less productive firms make greater productivity gains over the period. Efficiency decreases if the most productive plants make the greatest productivity gains over the period.

When changes in productivity are not spread equally across establishments, changes in the efficiency measure depend on the initial positions of the productivity gainers and their share changes. If firms already at the frontier make the greatest productivity gains, then skewness in the distribution of productivity becomes greater. Since the efficiency measure used here involves both skewness and the relative shares of firms at the frontier, it will decrease unless the market share of productivity gainers also increases. The productivity gains and the market-share gains of these firms have opposite effects on the measure of industry efficiency. The larger the gain in market share, the greater the likelihood of improvements in the efficiency measure. The

Table 12-5. *Categories of plants for which changes in combined market shares are calculated, 1970–79*

Category	Definition
Plants gaining market share	
SH23	1979 market share of plants that were opened since 1970 by new firms (greenfield entrants)
SH13	1979 market share of plants newly constructed since 1970 by firms that continued in the industry between 1970 and 1979 (other births)
SHU	Market-share gain of continuing plants (gainers) between 1970 and 1979
Plants losing market share	
SH34	1970 market share of plants closed by 1979 that were owned by firms exiting the industry (closedown exits)
SH14	1970 market share of plants closed by 1979 that were owned by firms that continued in the industry throughout the period (other exits)
SHD	Market-share loss between 1970 and 1979 of continuing plants (losers)

relationship between market-share turnover and relative productivity performance is, therefore, of crucial importance. The categories that are used here to analyse the effects of turnover on efficiency are detailed in Table 12-5.[9]

Turnover between 1970 and 1979, as measured by market-share changes within four-digit industries, was substantial. In 1970, plants that were closed by 1979 accounted for 22.7 per cent of total shipments, on average. The largest proportion of plant closedowns (18.1 per cent of 1970 shipments) was accounted for by plants owned by firms that subsequently exited the industry. Some 4.6 per cent of 1970 shipments were in plants that were closed by 1979 by firms that would continue production in another facility in the same industry. The third category where market share was lost consists of declining continuing plants. The market share of these plants declined by some 14 per cent.

Gains in market share are spread across three categories. First, greenfield entrants accounted for some 16.1 per cent of market share in 1979. Second, new plants of continuing firms accounted for 5.2 per cent. The distribution of plant openings between new and continuing firms is similar to that of plant closedowns between exiting and continuing firms. Finally, gaining continuing plants acquired some 15.8 per cent of market share over the period.

Turnover and changes in efficiency

Market-share turnover also increased efficiency. The efficiency of each of the turnover categories is reported in Table 12-6.[10] Plants closed by exiting firms were less efficient than plants started by new firms. Plants

Table 12-6. *Efficiency measures[a] of turnover components, expressed as a proportion of potential efficiency, 1970–79*

Plant category in 1970	1970	1979	Plant category in 1979
Closedown exits	57.6	62.0	Greenfield births
	$(1.6)^b$	(1.5)	
Other exits	65.6	71.2	Other births
	(2.2)	(2.9)	
Plants gaining market			Plants gaining market
share, 1970–79	66.7	67.7	share, 1970–79
	(0.9)	(0.9)	
Plants losing market	69.0	56.7	Plants losing market
share, 1970–79	(0.9)	(1.2)	share, 1970–79
Mean	66.3	6.28	Mean

[a] These estimates employ the efficiency estimate used to derive EFF40 and EFF49.
[b] Standard error of the mean is in parentheses.

closed by continuing firms were less efficient than plants opened by continuing firms. In 1970 the continuing plants that were to gain market share differed very little in terms of efficiency from either those about to lose market share over the subsequent decade or the industry average. But this situation changed dramatically by 1979. Market-share losers had become much less efficient than market-share gainers. This pattern accords with the finding reported in Chapter 9 that changes in continuing plants' productivity and market share were positively correlated.

The contribution to the change in efficiency made by each of the new-plant categories and by the continuing plants that gained market share depends on the pattern of replacement. Each percentage point of market share captured by one of the "gaining" categories (SH23, SH13, SHU) in Table 12-5 comes at the expense of one of the "losing" categories (SH34, SH14, SHD). The contribution made to efficiency change by each of the gainers will depend upon how much of its increase in share comes from each category displaced and the difference between the efficiency of the two classes. This replacement pattern is described in Chapter 9.

Figure 12-3 shows the percentage that each of the gainers acquired from each of the losers. Greenfield entrants primarily replaced closedown exits, but about one-third of their gains came from declining plants. The gain in market share by continuing plants for the most part came from closedown exits. The largest part of the gain in market share by new plants of continuing firms came from declining plants, and the remainder came from plants that they themselves closed.

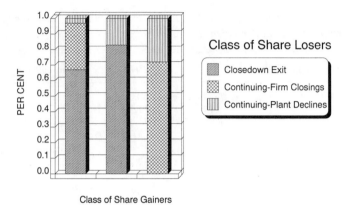

Class of Share Gainers

Figure 12-3. The proportion of share gains for greenfield entrants (left bar), other new plants (right bar), and continuing plants (middle bar) gaining market share coming from each class of share losers.

The turnover process clearly contributes to changes in efficiency. First, greenfield entrants were more efficient than both the categories they replaced (i.e., closedown exits and declining plants). In 1979 they were approximately 5 percentage points more efficient than closedown exits were in 1970; they were also about 5 percentage points more efficient in 1979 than were the remaining incumbent plants that had lost market share since 1970. Second, the plants opened by continuing firms replaced closed plants that were about 5 percentage points less efficient in 1970 and continuing plants that were about 15 percentage points less efficient in 1979. Third, the turnover associated with the replacement of declining continuing plants by continuing plants that gained market share would also have increased efficiency.

Despite the replacement of the less by the more efficient, the mean level of efficiency fell over the period. Continuing plants gaining share retained about the same level of efficiency, while those losing share declined substantially. Among other things, the failure of the gainers to make greater efficiency gains as a group and to take away even more market share from the losers than they did was one force contributing to the decline in average efficiency levels.

Nevertheless, the fundamental conclusion is that the turnover in market share associated with the competitive process contributed substantially to efficiency gains. Without this turnover, there would have been even greater declines in efficiency.

It is possible to estimate the joint impact of all the turnover categories on efficiency. The first requirement for this estimate is knowledge of the replacement pattern, previously described. The second prerequisite is an assumption

Table 12-7. *Contribution of turnover to efficiency (per cent)*[a]

Mean industry efficiency level, 1979	62.8
Mean industry level without turnover, 1979	58.7
Contribution of turnover category to difference	
Greenfield births	34.0
Other births	15.0
Continuing plants gaining market share	51.0

[a] See text for description of methodology.

about the level of efficiency as of 1979 that would have existed for plants in the two exit categories, SH34 and SH14 in Table 12-5, had they not been replaced. Here it will be assumed that the efficiency of each exit category would have been the same in 1979 as it was in 1970 relative to that of continuing plants that lost market share over the decade. This is a conservative assumption, because exiting plants fared even worse than declining plants over the decade.

Then the contribution that one of the entry or growth categories i made to efficiency by displacing category j ($DEFF_{ij}$) is calculated by

$$DEFF_{ij} = SHARE_i \times P_{ij} \times (EFF_i - EFF_j), \qquad (12\text{-}3)$$

where $SHARE_i$ is the increase in market share of the ith entry or growth category, P_{ij} is the proportion of the ith entry or growth category to come from the jth exit or decline category, and EFF_i, EFF_j is the efficiency of the ith entry or growth category or the jth exit or decline category in 1979.

The total effect of each entry or growth category is the sum of its effects across all exit and decline categories D to F in Table 12-5. The effect of turnover is then the sum of the effects of all categories in Table 12-5. The importance of each of these categories is expressed as a proportion of the total in Table 12-7. Without turnover, efficiency levels would have been 58.7 per cent rather than 62.8 per cent. Greenfield entry contributed 34 per cent of this improvement, other plant births some 15 per cent, and gains in market shares in continuing plants contributed 51 per cent.[11]

The determinants of turnover

Efficiency, then, is affected by, among other things, plant turnover, that is, the replacement of inefficient by efficient plants. The relationship between the amount of turnover and the level of efficiency is complex. The rate of technical progress and the capacity to adopt new processes will determine the rate at which those who are late in adopting new technology fall behind. By itself, this process increases the dispersion of productivity and decreases efficiency. However, if lagging firms lose sufficient market share, efficiency will not decline. The rate of turnover will, therefore, determine the extent to which efficiency is maintained in equilibrium.

In a world where efficiency did not vary, the two forces would be in balance. But equilibrium does not always prevail. Exogenous shocks may come in coordinated waves that cause efficiency levels across a wide variety of industries to change. In turn, turnover may intensify while efficiency is being restored to its previous levels. The intensity of turnover may, in this case, affect the speed of adjustment to exogenous shocks.

This tendency was at work in Canada during the 1970s. Caves and Barton (1990) postulate that growth in productivity produces a disequilibrating force, which temporarily results in lower levels of efficiency. The present study finds support for this proposition in Canada's experience. Between 1970 and 1979, the change in industry efficiency was negatively correlated with growth in real output per worker (−.25, significant at the 90 per cent level). This suggests that some changes in efficiency are brought about by the external shocks that lead to growth spurts. Just as revealing is the fact that the change in industry efficiency and the change brought about by market-share turnover reported in Table 12-7 are negatively and significantly correlated (−.24, significant at the 99 per cent level). Similarly, the market share of greenfield entrants is significantly negatively correlated with the change in efficiency. Thus, where efficiency was falling, there was more turnover and it contributed more to arresting the decline. Turnover appears to be part of an equilibrating process associated with rapid technological change.

Because the intensity of the turnover process affects the level of efficiency and its adjustment path, it follows that the determinants of turnover may be expected to affect both and that these determinants may differ somewhat from the determinants of industry efficiency at a point in time.

Modelling the turnover process

The turnover process has several components: three on the expansion side and three on the contraction side. Modelling each separately produces a large number of coefficients that have to be evaluated in order to estimate the net effect of the various determinants of efficiency. In order to simplify this system, an overall turnover equation – the sum of the market-share changes in the various entry and growth categories (GAIN) – is estimated. Since the turnover categories have different effects on changes in efficiency, weights were applied to each category. These weights reflected the contribution that a 1 per cent gain in that category had on changes in efficiency. They were calculated using the same assumptions employed for the estimates reported in Table 12-7.

The determinants of the turnover process are broken into three separate groups. The first consists of those variables that were presumed earlier in this chapter to affect industry-efficiency levels. They include some variables that engender change and others that tend to prevent change. Caves and Porter (1978) employ many of these variables to explain market-share change in incumbent firms.

The second set of variables are those traditionally used in entry and exit studies but not captured in the original set of variables used to explain efficiency.[12] These variables, with the exception of foreign ownership, can be classified as inducement variables that attract entry or reduce exit.[13] They are as follows:

> *G*: rate of growth in real shipments between 1970 and 1979
> VAR: variability of output around the trend growth line
> PR: average rate of profitability of the industry in 1970 and 1979
> PRFTGR: rate of growth in profitability in the period 1970–79
> FOR: proportion of shipments accounted for by foreign-controlled establishments in 1979

The third group of determinants consists of relative-productivity variables. It has been demonstrated that in the turnover process the less efficient are replaced by the more efficient, the less productive by the more productive. The differences between the productivity of various categories are taken here to represent the technological opportunities available to new participants. These variables are taken to proxy basic technological conditions that favour one or another form of turnover. For example, it is postulated that the market share captured by entrants is a function of the productivity advantage that entrants have over units that exit and over their prospective competitors: continuing plants that are growing and new plants of continuing firms.

Several measures are employed to represent the various factors at work. The first captures the extent to which the 1979 productivity of continuing plants that gained market share was higher than those losing market share:

> RLUD79: productivity of continuing plants in 1979 that gained market share between 1970 and 1979 divided by the productivity in 1979 of continuing plants that lost market share over the decade

Another set of variables compare the 1979 productivity of the two entrant categories with the continuing plant of gainers and losers:

> RLGU: productivity in 1979 of greenfield entrants relative to that of continuing plants that gained market share
> RLGD: productivity in 1979 of greenfield entrants relative to that of continuing plants that lost market share

RLNU: productivity in 1979 of new plants of continuing firms relative to that of continuing plants that gained market share

RLND: productivity in 1979 of new plants of continuing firms relative to that of continuing plants that lost market share

The third set of variables provides similar comparisons for 1970:

RLUD70: productivity in 1970 of continuing plants that gained market share between 1970 and 1979 divided by the productivity in 1970 of continuing plants that lost market share over the decade

RLCD: productivity in 1970 of closedown exits divided by the productivity in 1970 of continuing plants that subsequently lost market share over the decade

RLDD: productivity in 1970 of plants closed by firms that continued over the decade divided by the productivity in 1970 of continuing plants that subsequently lost market share over the decade

Finally, three variables represent the progress that resulted from the replacement of closedown exits by greenfield entrants, other exits by other births, and declining but continuing plants with gaining, continuing plants:[14]

RLUDDIF: RLUD79 – RLUD70, the growth in productivity of gainers relative to that of losers over the decade

RLGDIF: productivity of greenfield entrants in 1979 relative to that of continuing-plant market-share losers in 1979 minus the productivity of closedown exits in 1970 relative to that of market-share losers in 1970

RLODIF: productivity of other plant births in 1979 relative to that of continuing-plant market-share losers in 1979 minus the productivity of other plant exits in 1970 relative to that of market-share losers in 1970

The correlations among these measures are presented in Table 12-8. The degree of progress that is made in continuing plants (RLUDDIF) is the basic indicator of technical rivalry – of the potential for rivalrous behaviour without the creation of new plant. It is more highly correlated with RLGDIF than with RLODIF. Technological conditions that lead some continuing plants to outstrip others are also conditions under which new plants of entrants are substantially more productive than are closed plants of exiting firms.

The plant-replacement process among continuing firms (categories B and D in Table 12-5) is enhanced when new technology cannot be easily adapted to old plant. Productivity growth associated with the replacement process among continuing firms (RLODIF) is not as closely correlated with productivity differences that arise in continuing plants (RLUD79), as it is with gains associated with greenfield entry and closedown exit (RLGDIF). Thus, large

Table 12-8. *Correlation between measures of differential productivity growth*

	RLGU	RLGD	RLNU	RLND	RLUD79	RLCD	RLDD	RLUDDIF	RLGDIF	RLODIF
RLGU	1.0	.37 —[a]	.28 —[a]	.37 —[a]	-.14 (.07)	-.01 (.96)	-.05 (.59)	-.10 (.19)	.81 —[a]	.34 —[a]
RLGD		1.0	.12 (.20)	.35 —[a]	.85 —[a]	.05 (.55)	-.04 (.62)	.85 —[a]	.95 —[a]	.44 —[a]
RLNU			1.0	.82 —[a]	-.22 (.01)	.12 (.19)	.14 (.16)	-.18 (.05)	.05 (.55)	.70 —[a]
RLND				1.0	.33 —[a]	.09 (.30)	.10 (.28)	.29 —[a]	.27 —[a]	.85 —[a]
RLUD79					1.0	.02 (.77)	-.05 (.51)	.98 —[a]	.81 —[a]	.33 —[a]
RLCD						1.0	.18 (.05)	-.05 (.51)	-.27 —[a]	-.05 —[a]
RLDD							1.0	-.05 (.60)	-.09 (.30)	-.43 —[a]
RLUDDIF								1.0	.84 —[a]	.38 —[a]
RLGDIF									1.0	.84 —[a]

Note: The probability value of the null hypothesis that the correlation is zero is in parentheses.
[a] Represents a probability value of .001 or less.

Table 12-9. *Principal-component analysis of productivity variables*

	Eigenvector						
Variable	PPROD1	PPROD2	PPROD3	PPROD4	PPROD5	PPROD6	PPROD7
RLGU	0.39	0.40	0.51	−0.24	−0.18	0.44	0.39
RLNU	0.36	0.46	−0.51	0.18	−0.15	0.34	−0.48
RLCD	−0.04	0.48	0.31	0.25	0.74	−0.19	−0.16
RLDD	−0.26	0.30	0.07	0.70	−0.47	−0.19	0.29
RLGDIF	0.53	−0.17	0.42	0.09	−0.28	−0.49	−0.44
RLODIF	0.56	−0.00	−0.42	0.07	0.22	−0.37	0.57
RLUD79	0.24	−0.53	0.13	0.58	0.23	0.50	0.03

differences in productivity between greenfield entrants and closedown exits occur both when technological rivalry is manifesting itself in the continuing-plant population and when technological improvements are associated with the construction of new plants.

There are other indications that similar but not identical technical opportunities are at work across industries. There is a positive correlation between the productivity of greenfield entrants relative to that of losers (RLGD) and the disparity that develops in the continuing sector (RLUD79), and a negative relationship between the productivity of greenfield entrants relative to that of gainers (RLGU) and RLUD79. Thus, when productivity differentials are developing within the continuing sector, entrants do relatively well compared with those being displaced, but poorly, compared with the gainers. When new technology can be embodied very successfully in existing plants, entrants are not excluded from doing well, but they do not do quite as well as continuing plants that are gaining market share.

In order to distinguish the ways in which the various technological characteristics are combined within industries, the principal components of the relative productivity variables were derived (Table 12-9). PPROD1 positively weights most of the variables. PPROD2 represents situations where both RLGU and RLNU are high but RLUD79 is low. It denotes industries where new plants of both entrants and continuing firms do relatively well compared with the continuing plants that are gaining share, but where productivity differentials do not develop within the continuing sector. PPROD3 resembles PPROD2, except that greenfield entrants alone do well. RLGU and RLGDIF have positive weights, but RLNU and RLODIF have negative weights. This component represents situations in which technological advantage is related to new-plant construction by new firms, but is not as readily available to other plants, perhaps because patents matter more. PPROD4 represents situations conducive to the adoption of new technology by existing plants, reflected in the productivity differential that develops between continuing plants (RLUD79). PPROD5 designates situations in which the relative productivity of closedown exits (RLCD) is high, where the reason for exit must be found somewhere other than in initial-year productivity disadvantages. PPROD6 positively weights productivity differences between continuing plants (RLUD79) and the relative success of new plants (RLGU, RLNU). It differs from PPROD1 in that negative weights are attached to the growth in relative productivity of each of the corresponding plant exit and entry categories (RLGDIF, RLODIF), but a positive weight is given to the development of emerging productivity differences in the continuing-plant sector (RLUD79). PPROD6 represents industries in which dramatic change is occurring in relative productivity within the continuing-plant population and new plants of both kinds do relatively well, but exiting plants are not particularly inefficient at the beginning of the period. In such industries, turnover would be more closely related to rapid technological change over the period than to the elimination of plants that were particularly inefficient at the beginning of the period. This component represents technological rivalry experienced by both continuing firms and new firms. PPROD7, like PPROD3, positively weights greenfield entrants' success (RLGU), negatively weights the success of continuing firms' new plants (RLNU), and disregards productivity differentials that develop among continuing firms (RLUD79). The primary difference between PPROD7 and PPROD3 is that RLGDIF is negatively weighted in PPROD7, and positively weighted in PPROD3; RLODIF is positively weighted in PPROD7 but negatively weighted in PPROD3. PPROD7 represents situations in which greenfield entrants are doing well (RLGU), and continuing firms are making productivity gains with investment in new plant (RLODIF) but whose new plants are not doing very well relative to losing plants (RLNU).

Most studies of entry and exit or turnover among continuing firms have ignored the exogenous influence of changing technology and its influence on the turnover process. In order to characterize the process at work, the correlations were calculated among the total unweighted share gain (GAIN), the proportion of this total accounted for by each of the gaining and losing categories previously outlined in Table 12-5 (GAIN23,[15] GAIN13, GAINU, LOSS34, LOSS14, and LOSSD), and the relative-productivity components (Table 12-9). Overall, market-share change (GAIN) is most closely associated with PPROD2 and PPROD3. These components represent situations in which no substantial difference in productivity among continuing plants emerges and new plants do well relative to continuing plants. The proportion of market-share gains by greenfield entrants (GAIN23) is primarily related to PPROD6. The proportion taken by new plants of continuing firms (GAIN13) is positively related to PPROD1, but negatively related to PPROD2.

Table 12-10. *Principal-component analysis of inducement variables*

Variable	Eigenvector				
	PWEL1	PWEL2	PWEL3	PWEL4	PWEL5
G	0.70	−0.14	−0.15	−0.08	−0.68
VAR	0.04	0.62	0.53	0.52	−0.25
PRFTGR	0.18	−0.67	0.23	0.65	0.19
FOR	0.42	0.37	−0.60	0.35	0.44
PR	0.55	0.06	0.53	−0.41	0.49

The total turnover equation

Because the industry characteristics in the three sets of determinants are numerous, the principal components of each set were derived and used in a regression analysis. The principal components of the inducement variables (PWEL1 to PWEL5) are presented in Table 12-10. The results of the regression are reported in Table 12-11. To enable comparison with the determinants of efficiency, column 1 contains the signs of the components of the industry characteristics, mainly those found to be significant in equation 12-2. Column 2 contains the main regression results for the weighted turnover regressand (GAIN).

The inducement and the productivity components represent the disequilibrium forces that cause turnover. The following four variables in these two groups affect turnover. The inducement component PWEL3, with a positive coefficient, positively weights both average profitability over the decade and variability in demand. The inducement component PWEL5 has a negative but less significant coefficient; it negatively weights growth and positively weights profitability. The productivity components PPROD3 and PPROD6 positively affect turnover. Both of these components represent situations in which new plants are relatively productive compared with continuing firms. PPROD6 is the general technological-rivalry variable.

Five components from the industry-characteristics components affect turnover. Concentration associated with larger plant size (PVAR1) has a negative effect on turnover. Multi-plant ownership associated with low export levels and wide variability in plant-product diversification at the plant level (PVAR5) has a negative effect. Union activity associated with the lack of part-time workers, inward-bound diversification, and plant suboptimality (PVAR6) positively affect turnover.

The only component entering with the same sign into both the turnover equation (column 2) and the efficiency equation is PVAR5. However, this formulation of the turnover equation in column 2 does not allow for interaction

Table 12-11. *Determinants of plant turnover*[a]

| | Efficiency | | | | Turnover | | | |
| | (1) | | | (2) | (3) | | (4) | |
	Sign coefficient	Coefficient	t	Probability	Coefficient	Probability	Coefficient	Probability
PWEL3		.025	(2.0)	(.048)	.027	(.075)	.023	(.066)
PWEL5		-.018	(1.7)	(.097)	-.25	(.038)	-.021	(.071)
PVAR1	+	-.025	(2.1)	(.038)	-.31	(.011)	-.034	(.006)
PVAR2	–							
PVAR3	+							
PVAR4	–							
PVAR5	–	-.020	(1.8)	(.078)	-.021	(.053)	-.023	(.040)
PVAR6	+	.046	(4.0)	(.0001)	.048	(.0001)	.050	(.0001)
PVAR9	–							
PVAR10	+							
PVAR11								
PVAR16	–	-.021	(1.8)	(.063)	-.016	(.156)	-.020	(.078)
PVAR18	–	.024	(2.0)	(.051)	.019	(.110)	.019	(.109)
PPROD3		.021	(1.9)	(.055)	.017	(.098)		
PPROD6		.021	(2.0)	(.047)	.022	(.041)	.022	(.033)
PPROD7								
INTER					-.011	(.032)	-.012	(.018)
R^2			.41		.435		.42	
prob > F			.001		.0001		.0001	

[a] The interpretation of the principal components can be read from Tables 12-4, 12-9, and 12-10.

effects. It may be that the effect of the industry characteristic is to reduce the impact of the technological conditions represented by the productivity variables. This possibility was examined by entering interaction effects between the relative productivity components PPROD3 and PPROD6, and the components that had a negative effect on efficiency – PVAR2, PVAR4, PVAR5, PVAR9, and PVAR18. Individual terms entered on their own showed significance; but because of multicollinearity, this was not the case when several were entered simultaneously. In the end, PVAR2, PVAR4, and PVAR5 were summed and used interactively with the productivity component PPROD3 to form the variable INTER. The results with INTER added are reported in column 3. In this formulation, productivity component PPROD3 loses some of its significance, but the interaction term is significant and becomes even more so when productivity component PPROD3 is removed (column 4). The multi-plant-ownership component PVAR2, the import-advertising-suboptimal-capacity component PVAR4, and PVAR5 reduce the effect of productivity on turnover. These are the same characteristics found in industries with lower levels of efficiency.

Conclusion

Analysis of the turnover process can contribute in important ways to our understanding of competition. First, it provides a measure of its intensity. The extent to which market shares are changing provides a more direct measure of the intensity of the competitive process than do concentration measures. Second, an examination of the links between turnover and productivity change serves to emphasize the connection between productivity progress and the extent to which the new supplants the old.

This chapter adds another dimension to our understanding of turnover. It shows that turnover directly contributes to improvements in industry efficiency. Moreover, it is affected by many of the variables that influence the level of industry efficiency. Thus, this study provides a bridge between efficiency and turnover studies. Until now, the literature on efficiency has relied mainly on cross-sectional studies at a point in time. It was, therefore, difficult to ascertain whether the variables that were found to be related to efficiency were chance correlates. This analysis contributes to the debate by attempting to replicate the results of studies of similar economies. It demonstrates that efficiency in Canadian and U.S. manufacturing industries in the 1970s was related to many of the same industry characteristics.

Even more important, it establishes a link between turnover and efficiency. If the causes of efficiency are to be better understood, the forces that cause some firms to move ahead and others to fall behind must be examined. When technical change is the moving force, efficiency falls if the less efficient are not eliminated. This chapter documents how important this turnover process is in reducing inefficiencies. More importantly, it demonstrates that the forces that lead some industries to be less efficient at a point in time are contained in the forces that reduce the amount of turnover. That they can also restrain the turnover process that reduces the level of inefficiency lends credence to the cross-sectional results.

13

Firm turnover and profitability

There is no more important proposition in economic theory than that, under competition, the rate of return on investment tends toward equality in all industries.

George Stigler (1963: 54)

Introduction
Few other topics have received as much attention in applied studies in the field of industrial economics.[1] Despite the large number of studies in this area, few attempts have been made to measure the dynamics of the equilibration process and to relate them to specific industry characteristics.

Previous chapters have developed comprehensive measures of competitiveness and have examined the relationship between measures of competitiveness and measures of performance such as industry productivity or efficiency. This chapter explores the relationship between competitiveness and profitability.

The investigation focuses on three issues. The first is the degree to which profitability in various industries equates over time. The second is the extent to which differences in profitability are related to measures of firm turnover. The third is whether the speed with which industries regress to the mean is related to measures of industry turnover.

Profitability and competition
Previous studies
Studies of industry profitability have focused on the extent of cross-industry differences in profitability *levels* at a point in time and the degree to which these differences are perpetuated over time.

Stigler (1963) examines the time path of rates of profitability by correlating industry rates of return over time and reports that inter-industry rankings based on profitability changed slowly. The correlation between successive

328

years for 99 manufacturing industries in the United States was .69 in 1946–47 and had increased to .79 by 1956–57. Stigler also investigates the extent to which average profitability and the dispersion of profitability was lower in unconcentrated than in concentrated industries. Concentrated industries were found to have the same average rate of return as less concentrated industries but a larger dispersion in their rates of return. Industry rates in concentrated industries were more highly correlated over time than those in unconcentrated industries, indicating that there is greater stability in inter-industry differences in profitability in concentrated industries.

Other studies have used cross-sections to investigate the extent to which profitability is related to concentration. Usually relying on price–cost margins rather than rates of return, the majority of U.S. studies for the period up to 1970 find a positive relationship between price–cost margins and the concentration ratio (Schmalensee, 1989). While these studies suggest that the equilibration process is imperfect, they do not deal directly with the extent to which these imperfections are long-lived. Most only use data for single periods and do not directly measure the extent to which cross-industry patterns are stable over time.

The stability of the profitability–concentration relationship is challenged by Brozen (1971), who argues that if the competitive process works, the relationship originally discovered should disappear as the abnormal profits in concentrated industries are competed away over time. Using data for two separate years, Brozen suggests that this tendency could not be ruled out.

More recently, the dynamics of profitability over time has received more attention. Research has focused on the length of time over which profit differences at the firm level have been perpetuated. Using the profit histories of 551 U.S. firms over the period 1949–73, Mueller (1986) reports that profitability did not converge to a common value. Levy (1987) confirms differences at the industry level. In both studies, while industries are found to differ in their long-run profit levels, deviations from these levels are found to dissipate at a fairly rapid rate. More recently, this research has been extended to cover the performance of firms and industries across a wide range of countries (Mueller, 1990). Permanent differences in profitability are observed in most countries.

Profitability measures

Two standards have been used extensively to measure profitability – price–cost margins and rates of return. Price–cost margins capture the difference between total revenues and out-of-pocket costs. Rate-of-return variables measure the return earned by the capital invested in a firm.

Models of monopoly and oligopoly behaviour predict the relationship between the size of the price–cost mark-up and measures of concentration. If research is meant to test the validity of these models, the price–cost margin is the preferred measure. The rate of return provides a more direct estimate of the variable that is presumed to be equated by the competitive process – the return that is being *paid* to the capital that is performing the arbitrage. Since this chapter examines the extent to which profits move to a common norm, it focuses primarily on rates of return. But since the price–cost margin has been used so frequently, comparisons are made between the results obtained for rates of return and the price–cost margin.

The accounting rate of return, as commonly measured, may not accurately reflect the true profitability of an industry for several reasons. First, the rate in any one period will reflect the firm's history of investments. Since investment flows should be equating expected marginal returns in any one period and averages may lag behind the expected marginal rates of return, the average rates of return may move only slowly toward one another. Second, the accuracy of commonly used accounting rate-of-return statistics in measuring the internal rate of return being *earned* by investments in a firm has been questioned. Several studies (Stauffer, 1971; Fisher and McGowan, 1983) demonstrate that the rate of return, as it is usually estimated, does not perfectly measure the internal rate of return on funds being earned. Nevertheless, it probably ranks industries on the basis of profitability and tracks trends in profitability reasonably well (Stauffer, 1971; Salaman, 1985; Jacobsen, 1987). It should also capture changes in the rankings of industries on the basis of profitability, unless the accounting rules that affect the difference between accounting rates of return and the internal rate of return change substantially over time.

The shortcomings in accounting rates of return mean that even if competition is equating earnings at the margin, differences in measured rates of return across industries may not be completely extinguished in the long run or equilibration may not rapidly occur. Evidence that industry rates of return do not equate or that they do so very slowly should not be interpreted to mean that competitive forces are not working. But the tendency for industry profits to equate and the relative speed of equilibration offer useful information on the relative importance of competition across industries – especially if these differences can be shown to be related to the measures of competitiveness that have been developed in this study. It is these relationships that are investigated here.

This chapter mainly uses rates of return to investigate the equilibration process. Several are calculated from Statistics Canada's Corporation Financial Statistics.[2] The first is the after-tax total return to capital (PRCAP) – calculated as the return to equity plus interest, divided by the value of total equity plus debt. The second is the return to equity (PREQ) – residual profits after debt payments divided by the book value of equity. Finally, since the

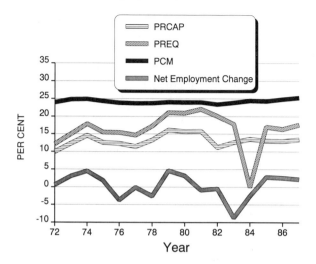

Figure 13-1. Mean profitability ratios (annual, 1972–87).

price–cost margin (PCM) has been used so frequently, it is employed here for comparative purposes. It is calculated as sales minus operating expenses divided by sales.

Data for the manufacturing sector are used to examine whether the competitive process serves to equate profitability across sectors. Accounting differences between manufacturing and resource firms are sufficiently large to produce permanent differences in profitability between firms in these sectors that have little to do with differences in the intensity of the competitive process.[3] It is likely that some accounting differences also exist within the manufacturing sector, but they are expected to be less severe.[4] Data are available on a consistent basis for 87 manufacturing industries for the period 1972–88.

The annual averages of the three ratios PRCAP, PREQ, and PCM for the period 1972–87 are graphed in Figure 13-1. Net employment change in the manufacturing sector is also presented to show the relationship between the measures of profitability and economic activity. The price–cost margin is relatively constant compared with both the return on equity and the return on capital. The two rates of return (PRCAP, PREQ) exhibit more volatility over the cycle. Price–cost margins do not closely reflect changes in the economy; rates of return do.

Since price–cost margins are relatively immune to economic conditions, they are poor measures of the extent to which inter-industry profitability differences change over time. Therefore, this chapter focuses primarily on rate-of-return measures.

There is still the question of which measure should be used for tracking the rate of return over time. Rates of return on capital are sometimes chosen because they are seen to be measuring total return, and are not therefore as likely to be affected by differences in debt–equity ratios. On the other hand, rates on capital are affected by long-term debt-financing decisions – commitments that cannot be changed quickly. They will not, therefore, quickly reflect marginal changes in the profitability of firms in the industry. The short-term effect of changes in industry conditions brought on by entry and exit, expansion and contraction by competitors, changes in international competitiveness, and technological advances are probably most quickly reflected in the equity rate of return.

Despite these theoretical arguments, as an empirical matter the choice of one measure may not matter if different rates of return yield basically the same result. Previous studies have suggested that this is likely to be the case. Rates of return are highly correlated – though rates of return and price–cost margins are not. This is also true of the Canadian manufacturing sector. The correlation between PRCAP and PREQ, when calculated over each year from 1972 to 1987, averaged .91. On the other hand, the correlation between PRCAP and PCM for the same period averaged .13 and that between PREQ and PCM averaged .07. The rates of return on equity and capital will both be used to examine the long-term differences in industry profitability.

Inter-temporal stability of industry profits

Three approaches are adopted to examine the inter-temporal stability of industry profits. First, the inter-temporal correlations of industry profitability are examined. Second, the history of industry profitability in broad industry groups is tracked. Finally, the equilibration process is summarized in two ways – first, by calculating the coefficients derived from representing the course of profits over time as an autoregressive process, and second, by graphing the rate at which an industry's profitability reverts to its mean.

Correlations

Correlation analysis provides a convenient summary of the extent to which inter-industry differences in profitability are perpetuated over time. Each profitability measure for all industries in a given year was correlated with the same measure for all industries in subsequent years for the period 1972–87. This gave a set of correlations for periods ranging from 1 to 15 years – 15 correlations for industry profitability taken one year apart, 14 for two years apart, . . . , and 1 for 15 years apart. In order to summarize whether the profit patterns across industries change as time passes, the correlations were averaged across all observations for periods of equal length. The results are presented in Figure 13-2, where the mean correlation coefficient is plotted

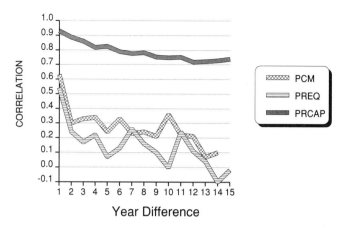

Figure 13-2. Cross-sectional industry correlation of profitability measures over time.

against the length of time between the industry profitability measures that were correlated.

The price–cost margin (PCM), which failed to reflect basic changes related to the business cycle, shows the most inter-temporal stability in industry rankings. The correlation for the price–cost margin is about .9 when it is calculated over an interval of one year and falls slowly to about .7 for intervals of 10 years. In contrast, the correlations for the two rate-of-return measures (PRCAP, PREQ) start between .5 and .6 and decline rapidly to between .2 and .3 after two years. These correlations are still significantly different from zero for the return on capital (PRCAP) up to a decade later – though they are not large. The correlations for the rate of return on equity (PREQ) fall to a level that is not significantly different from zero after five years.

Equity rates of return

An alternative way to depict cross-industry profitability differences over time is to track the average return of groups of industries ranked by profitability. In order to provide a summary of this process that is amenable to graphic representation, individual industries were ranked and divided into six groups on the basis of their rate of return on equity in 1972.[5] The average rate of return (PREQ) for these groups was calculated for each year from 1972 to 1987 (Figure 13-3). The averages and their standard errors are provided in Table 13-1. The means for the six groups in 1972, the year used for the initial ranking, show the most variability −6.4, 10.0, 11.5, 12.4, 13.8, and 18.3 per cent. By 1981, however, the group means were quite similar −21.6, 18.1, 20.3, 24.1, 26.1, and 22.5 per cent. With standard errors of the mean

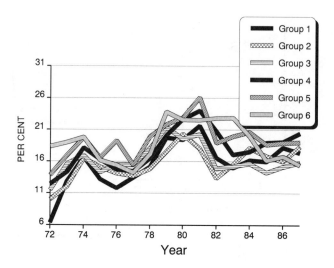

Figure 13-3. Average return on equity by industry group, based on 1972 profitability rankings (annual, 1972–87).

between 1.0 and 3.8, none of these profitability differences between groups in 1981 is significant.

The equilibration process depicted in Figure 13-3 examines the extent to which industries that differ substantially from one another, based on a 1972 ranking, do so in subsequent years. Other years can be used. The industries are ranked by 1979 profitability in Figure 13-4. Table 13-2 contains the means and the standard errors of the mean for the six groups based on 1979 equity rate-of-return rankings. Most of the differences in mean rates of return in 1979 emerge over the period 1975–79 and disappear over the period 1979–83.

The Canadian data, then, do not support the claim that the disparities in profits that exist at a point in time persist indefinitely. The ranking of industry profitability is not immutable. Correlations of profit rates decline rapidly as the length of time between periods is increased. A large part of the difference in industry profits when industries are ranked in one period disappears in subsequent periods.

Within this landscape of instability, certain patterns suggesting profit persistence do emerge. While industries change their relative profitability over time, the degree of change differs across the groups. The three least profitable groups show the greatest tendency to change relative positions with one another. The two most profitable groups also change relative positions with one another over time. But the two most profitable industries change position with the bottom four groups less frequently.

Table 13-1. *Mean return on equity in manufacturing industries organized by sextile group, ranked on 1972 profitability, 1972–82 (per cent)*[a]

	Group					
Year	1	2	3	4	5	6
1972	6.4	10.0	11.5	12.4	13.8	18.3
	(0.7)	(0.2)	(0.1)	(0.1)	(0.1)	(0.8)
1973	12.9	12.0	15.6	14.3	16.9	19.0
	(0.8)	(0.6)	(1.5)	(1.1)	(0.8)	(0.7)
1974	16.7	16.5	16.9	18.1	19.7	19.8
	(0.7)	(1.2)	(1.1)	(1.0)	(1.6)	(1.1)
1975	13.2	15.1	14.3	16.3	16.6	16.2
	(1.8)	(1.1)	(1.2)	(1.2)	(1.6)	(1.4)
1976	11.8	14.1	15.5	14.7	19.3	15.4
	(1.8)	(1.1)	(1.2)	(1.3)	(2.0)	(1.4)
1977	13.4	13.7	15.5	14.4	15.4	14.2
	(1.9)	(0.8)	(1.2)	(0.9)	(1.9)	(1.6)
1978	15.1	14.8	18.0	16.5	19.9	17.1
	(1.0)	(1.2)	(1.9)	(1.2)	(2.3)	(1.7)
1979	19.7	17.5	21.4	20.1	21.8	23.8
	(1.1)	(1.1)	(1.5)	(1.6)	(2.2)	(3.0)
1980	19.4	20.3	19.5	22.7	22.9	22.6
	(0.9)	(1.1)	(1.0)	(1.7)	(3.2)	(2.5)
1981	21.6	18.1	20.3	24.1	26.1	22.5
	(2.1)	(1.0)	(1.7)	(1.5)	(3.8)	(2.3)
1982	16.5	13.4	14.9	20.7	18.9	22.8
	(2.3)	(2.0)	(1.7)	(1.6)	(2.4)	(3.9)

[a] Standard error of the mean is in parentheses.

In order to depict the differences between the least and most profitable industries more clearly, all industries were grouped into only two classes based on 1972 return on equity, and their averages were tracked for the period 1972–81. The mean return on equity (PREQ) for each group, along with a 95 per cent confidence interval, are plotted in Figure 13-5. Industries that are in the most profitable group in 1972 maintain, on average, a level of profitability that is above the average of those industries in the less profitable group in 1972; however, the differences are not always significant. Figure 13-6 presents a similar picture using the rate of return on capital (PRCAP). Here too there are differences between the top and the bottom, but they are not always statistically significant.

This graphic representation demonstrates that there are elements of both change and stability in the profit histories of individual industries. Both

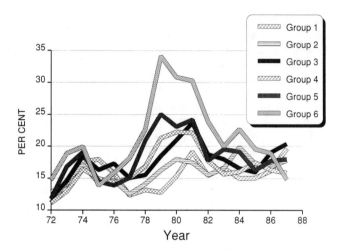

Figure 13-4. Average return on equity by industry group, based on 1979 profitability rankings (annual, 1972–87).

Table 13-2. *Mean return on equity in manufacturing industries organized by sextile group, ranked on 1979 profitability, 1975–83 (per cent)*[a]

	Group					
Year	1	2	3	4	5	6
1975	17.9	14.2	16.3	14.9	14.5	13.9
	(1.5)	(0.6)	(1.3)	(1.3)	(1.4)	(2.3)
1976	15.8	14.6	17.3	14.4	13.9	15.8
	(2.5)	(0.7)	(1.2)	(1.5)	(1.4)	(1.8)
1977	12.3	12.5	15.1	15.1	15.1	18.1
	(1.2)	(0.9)	(0.9)	(1.4)	(1.1)	(2.7)
1978	13.2	14.1	15.5	16.8	20.9	22.7
	(0.9)	(0.6)	(1.1)	(0.9)	(2.0)	(2.5)
1979	12.8	16.3	18.5	21.3	25.0	34.1
	(0.5)	(0.1)	(0.2)	(0.2)	(0.4)	(1.9)
1980	15.3	18.0	21.0	22.2	23.1	30.8
	(0.6)	(1.2)	(1.2)	(1.1)	(1.2)	(3.9)
1981	19.1	17.5	23.6	21.1	24.1	30.3
	(1.6)	(1.0)	(2.2)	(1.0)	(1.5)	(5.4)
1982	15.4	15.5	18.7	17.7	17.8	23.8
	(2.1)	(1.7)	(2.0)	(1.3)	(3.8)	(3.7)
1983	16.6	16.6	18.0	15.7	19.5	20.0
	(1.6)	(1.8)	(1.2)	(1.4)	(3.2)	(1.3)

[a] Standard error of the mean is in parentheses.

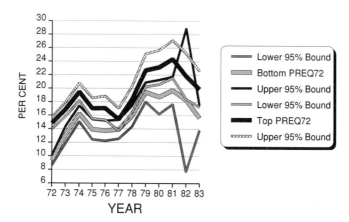

Figure 13-5. Average rate of return on equity for top and bottom profitability groups based on 1972 profitability ranking (1972–83).

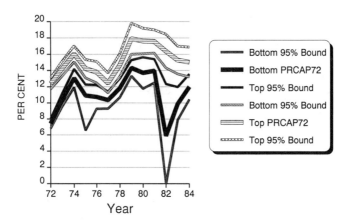

Figure 13-6. Average rate of return on capital for top and bottom profitability groups based on 1972 profitability ranking (1972–84).

tendencies need to be summarized if differences in an industry's competitiveness are to be related to them. This can be done by representing the adjustment path of profits over time as following an autoregressive process and by estimating parameters depicting several different characteristics of the profit history – both the long-run equilibrium and the speed of the adjustment process.[6] The change in profits between period $t(P_t)$ and period $t - 1$ (P_{t-1}) is taken to be a constant percentage of the difference between profits in period $t - 1$ and long-run equilibrium profits (P^*). That is,

Table 13-3. *Correlations between short-run and long-run rates of return on capital*[a]

	PRCAP72	PRCAP80	PRCAP85	PRCAP7286	LPRCAP	BETACAP
PRCAP72	1.0	.27	.36	.57	.50	−.17
PRCAP80		1.0	.43	.68	.68	−.38
PRCAP7286			1.0	.99	−.29
LPRCAP				1.0	−.29

[a] All correlations are significant at the 1 per cent level except for PRCAP72 and BETACAP, where the significance is only .11.

$$(P_t - P_{t-1}) = b \times (P^* - P_{t-1}). \tag{13-1}$$

Then the profit history of an industry follows the path

$$P_t = b \times P^* + (1 - b) \times P_{t-1}, \tag{13-2}$$

or

$$P_t = a + c \times P_{t-1}. \tag{13-3}$$

In this formulation, b represents the speed of adjustment. When b falls between 0 and 1, long-run profits can be represented as

$$P^* = a/c. \tag{13-4}$$

Equation 13-3 was estimated for the period 1972–86 using the rate of return on equity and on total capital. Estimates of an industry's equilibrium rate of return (P^*) were derived using both return on equity (LPREQ) and return on capital (LPRCAP). Similarly the speed of adjustment (b) is calculated for the return on equity (BETAEQ) and for the return on capital (BETACAP). Two questions arise. First, to what extent do measures of profitability taken at a point in time – which have been used previously in cross-sectional studies – reflect longer-run values? Second, do more profitable industries adjust more slowly?

Correlations between profitability for particular periods and the estimated parameters LPRCAP and BETACAP were used to address both questions (Table 13-3). The measures of profitability that were chosen were the average returns on capital for 1972 and 1973 (PRCAP72), 1979 and 1980 (PRCAP80), 1985 and 1986 (PRCAP85), and 1972–86 (PRCAP7286).

Opening-period profitability (PRCAP72) is related to profitability in subsequent years, but not strongly. Its correlations with profitability in the middle of the period (PRCAP80) and the end of the period (PRCAP85) are only

.27 and .36, respectively. While individual years do not correlate closely, profitability at the beginning of the period is more closely related with average profitability over longer periods. The correlation between beginning-year profitability (PRCAP72) and the average over the first period is .57. The correlation between opening-period profitability and the estimated long-run value of the return on capital (LPRCAP) is .5. Thus, the use of a particular year's profitability in place of long-run profitability in a cross-sectional regression can introduce a substantial error. Using average profitability for the entire period (PRCAP7286) in place of estimated long-run profitability LPRCAP would be less of a problem.[7]

The long-run profit value (LPRCAP) is negatively related to the speed of adjustment (BETACAP). Industries with higher profits adjust more slowly. This result differs somewhat from Khemani and Shapiro's (1990) finding that the speed of adjustment of firm profitability was higher for the two extremes of the distribution – the most and least profitable firms.

In order to investigate these relationships further, industries were divided into quartile groups on the basis of short-term profitability, and the mean estimates for LPRCAP and BETACAP calculated. In Khemani and Shapiro (1990), opening-year profitability was used to group the estimated parameters so as to examine the extent to which differences in opening-year profitability were perpetuated over time. In order to test whether the conclusion is sensitive to the year used for ranking, initial-, middle-, and end-period profitability (PRCAP72, PRCAP80, PRCAP85) were separately used to rank industries and to create quartile groups. The group means for the rate of return in the year used for ranking, the estimated long-run rate of return LPRCAP, and BETACAP are reported in Table 13-4; the first panel represents the grouping based on PRCAP72, the second represents that based on PRCAP80, and the third represents that based on PRCAP85.

Three conclusions stand out. First, short- and long-run profit rates are clearly related. The long-run profit value LPRCAP increases across the groupings and the differences are significant. The mean values of LPRCAP for each quartile group are remarkably similar for each of the three years chosen for groupings, even though the short-run means of PRCAP72, PRCAP80, and PRCAP85 differ across the panels. Second, the differences among groups in long-run profitability (LPRCAP) are less than the short-run differences in PRCAP72, PRCAP80, and PRCAP85. The range for LPRCAP is about 6 percentage points. The range for the short-run quartile group means is as high as 12 percentage points. Third, the speed of adjustment in the least profitable group is always more rapid than in the most profitable group. About 70 per cent of the difference between profits in a given year and the equilibrium rate of return LPRCAP is erased yearly in the least profitable group. It is only about 60 per cent in the most profitable group. This decline is fairly rapid and

Table 13-4. *Average short- and long-run return on capital, ranked by short-run profitability, selected years (per cent)*[a]

	Average profitability (PRCAP) for year of ranking	Average profitability (PRCAP), 1972–86	LPRCAP	BETACAP
Ranked on 1972–73				
Group 1	7.4 (0.8)	10.0 (0.8)	10.5 (0.9)	.73 (0.05)
Group 2	9.8 (0.4)	12.4 (0.4)	12.8 (0.5)	.64 (0.05)
Group 3	11.9 (0.4)	13.5 (0.4)	13.8 (0.5)	.66 (0.04)
Group 4	15.1 (0.7)	16.5 (0.7)	16.7 (0.8)	.61 (0.04)
Ranked on 1979–80				
Group 1	9.7 (1.0)	10.4 (0.5)	10.7 (0.5)	.73 (0.06)
Group 2	13.9 (0.1)	11.9 (0.5)	12.2 (0.5)	.73 (0.04)
Group 3	17.0 (0.3)	14.4 (0.5)	14.9 (0.6)	.61 (0.04)
Group 4	22.0 (0.5)	15.7 (1.0)	16.2 (1.0)	.58 (0.04)
Ranked on 1985–86				
Group 1	7.3 (0.4)	10.0 (0.6)	10.0 (0.6)	.72 (0.06)
Group 2	11.2 (0.2)	11.8 (0.7)	11.9 (0.7)	.63 (0.03)
Group 3	14.7 (0.2)	14.2 (0.3)	14.8 (0.3)	.69 (0.05)
Group 4	19.2 (0.7)	16.4 (0.7)	17.1 (0.7)	.61 (0.04)

Note: Standard error of the mean is in parentheses.
[a] Averages are taken across only those industries where $0 < |BETACAP| < 1$.

is not dissimilar to Khemani and Shapiro's estimates (1990) for a select sample of Canadian firms.

In conclusion, while much of the differences in short-run profit rates for Canadian manufacturing industries disappear quickly, in the long run some differences persist. Similarly, there are differences in the rates of adjustment.

Price–cost margins

Price–cost margins are poor statistics for investigating inter-industry-profitability dynamics, because they exhibit stability while the economic system does not.

Despite these shortcomings, price–cost margins can be used judiciously to investigate the nature of change. Since industry differences in price–cost margins mainly reflect differences in capital intensity, they should change slowly. Therefore, in this analysis, the mean price–cost margin of an industry is the focal point against which change is measured. An industry will be regarded here as being in disequilibrium when its price–cost margin differs substantially from its mean – earning higher than normal profits when the deviation from the mean is positive and lower than normal profits when the deviation is negative.

Volatility in an industry's profitability can be studied by examining the pattern of changes in the deviation of each industry's price–cost margin from its mean. Movements away from the mean represent disequilibration brought about by changes in demand or cost conditions; movements back to the mean represent reversals of the original forces that brought about disequilibrium and the adaptation associated with the entry of new firms and the exit of existing ones.

In order to examine equilibration and disequilibration, the industry values[8] of these deviations were ranked for *each* year from 1970 to 1986 and grouped into six categories. Group 1 consists of those industries whose price–cost margins were furthest below their mean in 1970 – the least profitable by their own historical standards. Group 6 contains those with the highest positive deviation above the mean – the most profitable by their own historical standards. The average deviations of the price–cost margins for each group were then calculated for all other years from 1970 to 1986 where the grouping for each of these years was based on the rankings of the original year.

Figure 13-7 presents the mean average deviation for the price–cost margin in each group for rankings based on 1970 values of the deviations. It demonstrates that deviations from mean values that existed in 1970 had mainly disappeared by 1976. Figure 13-8 contains the average deviation for each group based on the ranking of 1979 profitability values. Figure 13-8 shows that the deviations seen in 1979 emerged over a relatively short period – some four to six years – and disappeared in about the same time. Figures 13-7 and

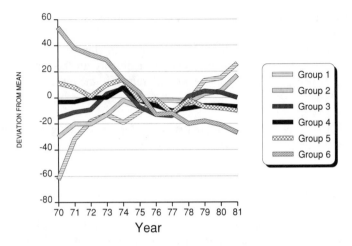

Figure 13-7. Mean deviation of price–cost margins of sextile groups based on 1970 profitability ranking (1970–81).

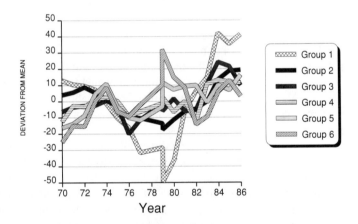

Figure 13-8. Mean deviation of price–cost margins of sextile groups based on 1979 ranking (1970–86).

13-8 show that the price–cost margins of individual industries are not stable. Moreover, there are certain similarities that suggest common patterns of movement away from and back toward equilibrium.

The representations of the disequilibrium process in Figures 13-7 and 13-8 describe that process for only two specific years – 1970 and 1979. In order to summarize the process that is continuously taking place each year as centripetal and centrifugal forces work against one another, industries were

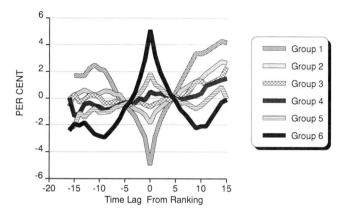

Figure 13-9. Trajectory of price–cost margins by sextile groups from time of ranking (1972–86). Price–cost margins are calculated as deviations from the mean.

ranked for all years between 1970 and 1986, and each industry was assigned to six groups for each year's ranking. The average deviation of each industry's price–cost margin from its mean was then calculated over the entire period for each group. This generated 16 case histories similar to those presented in Figures 13-7 and 13-8 that differ in terms of the year used to rank industries. These case histories track the emergence of differences across groups before the year of ranking and the extent to which the differences subsequently disappeared. These 16 cases were then averaged. These averages are summarized in Figure 13-9 for the lowest and highest two categories. The zero base year corresponds with the year when industries are ranked by profitability; a positive time lag corresponds with the number of years after the year of ranking; a negative value for the time lag corresponds with the number of years before the year of ranking.

The generality of the pattern depicted for 1970 and 1979 is confirmed. Over the period, the price–cost margin follows a cycle of about ten years. Five years before the year chosen for ranking, groups are virtually indistinguishable. The same is true five years later.

In the preceding section, the return on equity (PREQ) was used to examine the equilibration process. Two analytical techniques were used to estimate the speed of adjustment. Correlations of cross-industry profitability patterns over time demonstrate that after two years these patterns had substantially dissipated. When changes in profit rates were represented by an autoregressive process, the estimated coefficient of adjustment indicates that some 60 to 70 per cent of adjustment occurred in the first two years. It is therefore important to ask whether the graphic analysis used for price–cost margins yields results

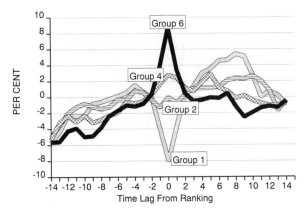

Figure 13-10. Trajectory of equity return by sextile group from time of ranking (1972–86). Equity return is calculated as deviations from the mean.

for the rate of return on equity that accord with the picture that emerged previously.

Figure 13-10 contains the trajectory of the highest and lowest two sextile groups using equity rates of return (PREQ). The trajectory is calculated as in Figure 13-9. The relative rankings in PREQ that are observable in any one period emerge over a three-year period and disappear equally quickly. This accords with the results of the regression analysis that about 65 per cent of the difference between existing and long-run profits is eroded each year. The equity rates of return yield a picture of a slightly faster equilibration process than do the price–cost margins, but the differences between them are not great. The choice of measure does not affect the conclusion that the profit-equilibration process inherent in each industry is relatively rapid.

Profitability and competition

The relationship between profitability and the intensity of competition is evaluated by examining the extent to which the various measures of intra-industry mobility are related to the two statistics characterizing the trajectory of industry profitability – the measures used to represent the long-run value of profitability and the speed with which profitability adjusts to disequilibrium situations. Previous studies of the determinants of inter-industry profitability differentials have generally relied on concentration as a measure of market structure – a measure that has been shown to be only imperfectly related to internal industry dynamics. One of the few exceptions is the work of Khemani and Shapiro (1990), which uses a measure of turnover – entry and exit – to examine the extent to which the speed of adjustment, but not the level of profits, is related to turnover. However, the entry and exit process is only one of many sources of expansion and contraction that might be expected to play an equilibrating role when profits deviate from their norm. Incumbents can open and close plants, as well as expand and contract existing plants. Acquisitions and divestitures shift control from one controlling group to another.

Since disequilibrium in profit levels caused by shifts in demand and cost factors can be eliminated in more than one way, this chapter employs several measures that capture diverse facets of the competitive process. Differences in equilibrium levels of profits and the speed of the adjustment process are related to the various turnover measures that have been developed in previous chapters.

There are two quite opposing views about the relationship that might be expected between profits and industry mobility. These will be referred to as the random-shock model and the life-cycle model.

The random-shock model would predict that profitability and turnover are negatively related. In this view, industry profits are held to follow a steady-state path, differing for each industry, that is continuously perturbed by random shocks. Such shocks cause profits in each industry to diverge from their long-run values. These influences are treated as transitory – as affecting only the short-run deviations of an industry's profitability around a longer-run trend. The shocks that cause an industry's profitability to diverge from its long-run mean are hypothesized to elicit turnover that returns industry profits to equilibrium. Higher than normal steady-state profits should be associated with less than normal entry and continuing-firm turnover in response to the random shocks that perturb profitability in the short run. Those industries that demonstrate less response to disequilibrium situations that develop over time are likely to be less competitive and therefore have higher profits. The reverse should hold for lower-profit industries. Therefore, turnover and profitability should be negatively related. Moreover, the speed of adjustment should be a function of the same turnover variables that are related to inter-industry profit differentials.

A life cycle model, on the other hand, would predict a positive relationship between profits and turnover in some industries. Mueller and Tilton (1969) identify four different stages in a life cycle of an industry characterized by a major innovation. In the first, the spread of innovation is limited. In the second, there is a rush of entry as technological knowledge spreads. In this stage, large and small firms coexist, the technology is not well understood, and there is large turnover. The third stage corresponds to the development of technological events such as increased specialization of research and development that favour large industrial corporations. The fourth stage sees standardization, the expiration of patents, and the reduction of technological barriers to entry. In the last stage, the intensity of entry depends upon the extent to which embedded knowledge or production economies are important.

Gort and Klepper (1982) in their study of the evolution of 48 new-product markets observe a close association between "rises and declines in the rate of innovation and the rate of entry into new markets". The first stage of the life cycle corresponds to initial commercial production and limited entry. The second stage is characterized by a large number of major innovations with significant consequences for the cost of production, a reliance on external sources of innovation, rapid entry, and a growth in the number of producers. In the third stage, the number of major innovations falls, minor advances become more prevalent, the accumulated experience of incumbents becomes more important, and entry and exit are roughly balanced. In the fourth stage, the number of new innovations falls dramatically, and entry by imitators becomes possible with the stabilization in technology. The number of firms falls as prices and profits come under pressure from entrants and the less efficient are forced to exit. In the mature fifth stage of the industry, entry and exit is once more balanced with a smaller number of participants than at the earlier stages.

In both of these cases, the early phase of an industry's life is characterized by high risk and high profitability. There is high entry and exit in the early phase as the production technology and marketing strategies change rapidly. In this period, which may last for a considerable period of time if scale economies do not develop, many small firms each compete on the basis of new products or technologies. Later in the life cycle, firms get larger as scale economies become more important, entry and exit decline, and risk falls as the technology and the product line mature. Profitability declines to reflect the lower risk of this period in the industry's life cycle. If this view is correct, turnover and profitability should be positively related.

In the case of the life cycle model, the relationship between the speed of adjustment and industry profits is unclear. High profits should be associated with high turnover. If that turnover leads to a large expansion in production from new firms or large contractions in production from exits in response to demand and supply shocks, then profitability and the speed of adjustment should be positively correlated. On the other hand, industries in the early phase of their life cycle may equilibrate very slowly. Turnover may be large because of slow equilibration. In this case, profitability and the speed of adjustment will be negatively correlated.

Rates of return and turnover

In order to investigate the relationship between rates of return and firm turnover, data from two quite different sources were brought together. The rates of return (PREQ, PRCAP) are derived from firm-level data that are calculated at the 1960 three-digit SIC level. The mobility measures are calculated at the 1970 four-digit SIC level. The official concordance was utilized to match the financial and the mobility data.

A procedure was carried out to allow for potential problems in the matching process. The financial data are collected at the firm level and the Census of Manufactures data are collected at the establishment level. In those industries where firm financial data assigned to a particular industry include a large amount of data from other industries, the profitability data and the mobility data may not be comparable.[9] In order to evaluate the resulting match, the price–cost margin derived from the financial statistics was correlated for each industry with the price–cost margin derived from the Census of Manufactures data for the period 1972–86. When the correlation was less than .2, the industry was dropped to create a second reduced sample of about 50 observations. Both the equilibrium rate (P^*) and the speed of adjustment coefficient (b) were correlated with the measures of mobility developed previously. This was done for the entire and the reduced samples.

Since the focus is on long-run values of profitability, measures of turnover are required that summarize the success of firms in displacing others over a fairly long period. Turnover measures that are calculated by comparing the status of firms in 1970 and 1979 are used. These capture the extent to which successful firms displace less successful firms.

Previous studies have wrestled with the question of whether net or gross measures of entry and exit should be the focus of attention.[10] The displacement of some firms by others is assumed to reduce profits where it leads to less oligopolistic coordination or where it adds substantially to industry capacity. Gross measures of turnover from entry and exit capture the total amount of change and might be expected to be related to situations conducive to breakdown in oligopoly coordination by the market leaders. But measures of gross turnover do not indicate whether turnover is adding much to industry capacity at the margin. If entry and exit affect only firms at the margin of the industry, then only if entry exceeds exit will larger incumbents lose market share and have to consider the threat of entry in setting their prices and quantities. In this case, the net contribution of entry and exit should be negatively related to profitability. When entry exceeds exit, downward pressure on profits might be expected. Kessides (1991) argues that the appropriate measures to capture this tendency are not gross entry and exit but net entry and exit. Rather than prejudge the issue, both were used here.

Gross turnover was measured with statistics that capture different aspects of the gross churning that takes place as some firms supplant others. The first group of statistics measure gross turnover due to entry and exit. TURNE is one-half the share of 1979 shipments accounted for by greenfield entrants plus the share of 1970 shipments accounted for by closedown exits. TURNEN captures the same phenomenon except that the share of entrants and exits is calculated in terms of the number of 1979 and 1970 firms rather than shipments, respectively. The second group of statistics capture various dimensions of gross change in the continuing-firm sector. In this category, TURNC is the sum of the market-share gain of continuing firms that increased market share and the absolute value of the decline in market share of those that lost market share. In addition, two measures were used that capture the extent to which continuing firms were opening and closing plants. TURNPS measures the share of total 1979 shipments accounted for by continuing firms' new plants plus the share of 1970 shipments in continuing firms' closed plants. TURNPN is the proportion in 1979 of the number of continuing firms that built new plant plus the proportion in 1970 of the number of continuing firms that closed plant. The third measure, TURNM, captures the amount of market share changing hands as a result of acquisitions and divestitures that are associated with firm entry and exit. TURNM is defined as the share of 1979 shipments in plants that were acquired by firms entering the industry plus the share of 1970 shipments in plants that were divested by firms leaving the industry.

The second set of turnover statistics capture several dimensions of the net effect of this turnover. Net change in entrants and exits is measured first by the difference between the share of shipments of greenfield entrants in 1979 and that of shipments of closedown exits in 1970 (ENTNETS), and second by the difference in the proportion of firms in each category (ENTNETN). Net change in the market share of continuing firms as a result of opening and closing plant (CONTNETS) is measured as the difference in the market share of new plants of continuing firms in 1979 minus the market share of closed plants of continuing firms in 1970. CONTNETN measures the same phenomenon using the difference in the proportion of continuing firms in the two categories.

The final set of statistics capture various aspects of instability. Two statistics are used to describe the regression-to-the-mean phenomenon. The first is the regression coefficient of 1979 market share on 1970 market share (REGSH).[11] The second is the correlation coefficient between 1979 market share and 1970 market share (CORSH). The third is the statistic suggested by Ijiri and Simon (1977) – the variance of the change in rank experienced by firms in an industry (RANK). The fourth is that suggested by Prais (1976) – the variance of growth rates for continuing firms in an industry (GROW).

Each of these measures was correlated with the estimates of long-run profitability. The average for the period 1972–81 and the estimated value of P^* for the rates of return on equity (LPREQ) and total capital (LPRCAP) were used to test for the robustness of the results. The correlations for average total return on capital (PRCAP7281) and estimated long-run return on capital

LPRCAP are reported in Table 13-5 for the entire sample and the reduced sample. Deleting the industries for which price–cost margins from the census did not correlate highly with the price–cost margins calculated from the financial statistics did not affect the results markedly.

There is support for the life cycle model in that gross turnover is larger in industries with higher profits. Turnover from entry and exit, using both the shares of shipments (TURNE) and the share of number of firms (TURNEN), is positively related to long-run profitability. Change among continuing firms (TURNC) also has a positive correlation but it is not significant. In order to sort out the relative importance of the two effects, the principal components of all the mobility measures were calculated. The first component weights both TURNE and TURNC highly and has a consistently positive correlation coefficient with the long-run profitability averages (PRCAP7281, PREQ7281) and the estimated long-run equilibrium rate of return, whether the latter is calculated using return on equity or return on capital.

Other measures of overall variability are also positively related to profitability. The variance in rank change (RANK) and the variability in growth rates (GROW) are positively related to long-run profitability. The statistics that capture the pattern of market-share change (REGSH, CORSH) also indicate that greater instability is correlated with higher profits. Industries where there is more regression to the mean or where the correlation of market shares is lower have higher profits.

The data reveal several other interesting relationships. Not all measures of gross turnover are positively associated with higher industry profitability. Two are associated with lower profitability. The statistics that capture plant opening and closing by continuing firms (TURNPS, TURNPN) are negatively related to profitability. The technical conditions that led to a productivity advantage for the new plants of continuing firms over their existing plants was one of the dimensions that affected overall turnover (see Chapter 13). These results add to that finding. The technical conditions that result in more new plant creation than expansion of incumbent plants by continuing firms are negatively associated with profitability.

The intensity of control changes (TURNM) also has a negative correlation with industry profitability that is often but not always significant. Industries with lower profits have experienced more control changes. This confirms the evidence that suggests that many of the control changes were related to a rationalization effect (Chapters 3, 10, and 11).

Evidence of the random-effects model can also be found in the correlations in Table 13-5. Net entry and profitability are negatively correlated and generally significant – whether net entry is measured by differences in the share of shipments of entrants minus exits (ENTNETS) or the percentage of firms that are entrants minus the percentage that are exits (ENTNETN). This

Table 13-5. *Correlations between long-run rate of return on capital and measures of turnover*

	Average PRCAP 1972–81		LPRCAP	
	Full sample	Reduced sample	Full sample	Reduced sample
Gross turnover				
Entry plus exit				
Shipment shares (TURNES)	.39*	.49*	.49*	.60*
Firm number shares (TURNEN)	.23**	.21	.27**	.25***
Continuing-firm change				
Share growth plus decline – shipments (TURNC)	.05	.06	.12	.16
Share of new plus closed plant – shipments (TURNPS)	–.18***	–.08	–.12	.02
Share of new plus closed plant – firm numbers (TURNPN)	–.28*	–.35**	–.24**	–.24***
Acquisitions plus divestitures Shipment shares (TURNM)	–.24**	–.11	–.39*	–.29**
Net turnover				
Entry minus exit				
Shipment shares (ENTNETS)	–.16	–.27***	–.28*	–.43*
Firm number shares (ENTNETN)	–.10	–.40*	–.15	–.56*
Continuing-firm plant birth minus closures				
Shipment shares (CONTNETS)	.02	–.06	–.02	–.04
Firm number shares (CONTNETN)	.08	–.02	–.01	–.02
Stability measures				
Regression-to-mean coefficient (REGSH)	–.08	.05	–.23**	–.15
Share-correlation coefficient (CORSH)	–.32*	–.31**	–.34*	–.34**
Variance of changes in firm rank (RANK)	.27**	.31**	.29*	.28**
Variance in firm-growth rates (GROW)	.15	.29**	.08	.16

Note: For definitions, see text.
* Significant at 1 per cent level.
** Significant at 5 per cent level.
*** Significant at 10 per cent level.

Table 13-6. *Average turnover measures by industry groups ranked on average return on equity, 1972–86*

| Variable | Profitability class | | | |
	1	2 (lowest)	3	4 (highest)
PREQ7286	13.1	15.8	18.2	22.9
TURNE	15.2	17.8	24.2	23.7
TURNEN	56.2	60.0	64.7	66.3
TURNC	15.8	15.0	17.2	17.4
TURNPN	12.6	9.6	9.1	9.5
CORSH	.89	.91	.86	.83
ENTNETS	1.5	−5.8	−5.8	−5.6
ENTNETN	1.7	−3.3	−5.6	−4.6
CONTNETN	2.6	−0.5	0.7	1.8

effect is generally robust to changes in the measure of profitability and to the sample used. On the other hand, the net change in the percentage of plants opened and closed by continuing firms (CONTNETS and CONTNETN) is not significantly correlated with industry profitability.

Correlations may be a useful method of summarizing data, but they do not reveal the magnitude of the differences in turnover across industries. Nor do they provide much detail about the pattern of differences in turnover in industries with different levels of profitability. To provide evidence on both these points, industries were ranked by the long-run average return on equity for the period 1972–86 (PREQ7286) and divided into quartile groups, and the means of the various turnover measures were calculated (Table 13-6). The two net entry statistics (ENTNETS and ENTNETN) show a discontinuity between the least profitable group (1) and the other three groups. The measures of turnover due to entry and exit (TURNE and TURNEN) increase uniformly as profitability increases. Turnover in the continuing sector (TURNC) does not increase uniformly. It is low in the two least profitable groups (1 and 2) and higher in the two most profitable groups (3 and 4). The difference between the gross market share changing hands within the continuing sector (TURNC) in the least profitable industry group and the most profitable industry group is only 2 percentage points, while it is some 8 percentage points for turnover due to entry and exit (TURNE).

These results may be attributable to some peculiarity in Canadian industrial policy that has protected atomistic industries and produced higher profitability in this sector. If this is the case, labour-intensive industries (like clothing,

Table 13-7. *Average entry and exit turnover for industry groups ranked by profit class (per cent share of shipments)*

| Industry group | Profitability class[a] | | | |
	1 (lowest)	2	3	4 (highest)
Natural-resources-based	13.5	16.2	22.2	15.6
Labour-intensive	21.0	25.2	27.9	32.8
Scale-related	10.6	8.9	17.1	27.4
Product-differentiated	9.8	20.7	27.8	21.4
Science-based	16.5	7.1	9.5	—

[a] Profitability class is based on the average return on equity, 1972–86.

Table 13-8. *Average entry and exit turnover for industry groups ranked by profit class (per cent share of firms)*

| Industry group | Profitability class[a] | | | |
	1 (lowest)	2	3	4 (highest)
Natural-resources-based	57.1	51.7	57.6	62.4
Labour-intensive	46.7	80.4	60.4	63.1
Scale-related	47.4	49.2	61.2	67.1
Product-differentiated	65.7	69.9	77.7	63.3
Science-based	54.4	37.3	55.2	—

[a] Profitability class is based on the average return on equity, 1972–86.

leather, and textiles), which have low barriers to entry and large gross turnover, would be more concentrated in the most profitable industries, and the aggregate results would merely reflect this fact. The positive relationship between profitability and turnover would then be the result of tariff policies as much as the operation of the competitive system.

In order to test this possibility, Canadian industries were divided into five groups using the taxonomy followed by the OECD – natural-resource-based, labour-intensive, scale-related, product-differentiated, and science-based.[12] When turnover measures were calculated for the different sectors across profit classes (based on PREQ7286), the patterns that were discovered at the aggregate level were found in many of the five sectors (Tables 13-7 to 13-11). In particular, gross entry and exit turnover increases with profitability for

Table 13-9. *Average correlation of 1970 and 1979 market shares for industry groups ranked by profit class*

Industry group	Profitability class[a]			
	1 (lowest)	2	3	4 (highest)
Natural-resources-based	.84	.94	.89	.88
Labour-intensive	.90	.87	.85	.80
Scale-related	.92	.92	.80	.72
Product-differentiated	.95	.88	.76	.84
Science-based	.93	.98	.77	—

[a] Profitability class is based on the average return on equity, 1972–86.

Table 13-10. *Average net entry rate for industry groups ranked by profit class (per cent share of firms)*

Industry group	Profitability class[a]			
	1 (lowest)	2	3	4 (highest)
Natural-resources-based	3.9	−6.3	−13.6	−2.1
Labour-intensive	14.9	−1.2	−4.5	−8.9
Scale-related	8.7	6.5	3.3	−5.3
Product-differentiated	8.5	8.2	−3.9	−4.5
Science-based	−4.7	−1.7	−15.3	—

[a] Profitability class is based on the average return on equity, 1972–86.

natural-resource-based, scale-related, product-differentiated, and labour-intensive industries. This relationship is present for entry and exit turnover calculated with share of shipments (Table 13-7) and for number of firms (Table 13-8). Similarly, the correlation coefficient between market shares in 1970 and 1979 falls as profits increase for all industry groups (Table 13-9). In conclusion, gross churning increases with profitability for many different industries.

The other relationships found in the aggregate data were also found at the sectoral level. Net entry was found to have a negative relationship with profitability when calculated at the aggregate level. The relationship between net entry and profitability exists for all the sectors (Table 13-10). Indeed, the

Table 13-11. *Average acquisition and divestiture turnover for industry groups ranked by profit class (per cent share of shipments)*

Industry group	Profitability class[a]			
	1 (lowest)	2	3	4 (highest)
Natural-resources-based	42.2	16.9	36.4	19.0
Labour-intensive	29.7	28.1	38.6	12.9
Scale-related	24.6	15.3	18.2	16.0
Product-differentiated	53.2	31.3	22.8	29.4
Science-based	25.8	21.1	2.8	—

[a] Profitability class is based on the average return on equity, 1972–86.

relationship is stronger at the sectoral level than at the aggregate level (Table 13-6). A strong negative association between profitability and the amount of market share turning over because of acquisitions and divestitures is also present in most sectors (Table 13-11).

Up to this point, only simple correlations between industry profitability and the intensity of competition have been used to investigate the determinants of inter-industry differences in profitability. Regression analysis provides a more comprehensive approach for sorting out the dominant effects of different variables.

Previous attempts to explain the determinants of industry profitability using regression analysis (e.g., Masson and Shaanan, 1987) postulate that an industry's profits (P_t) are a function of entry (E), barriers to entry (B), growth (G), and other factors (X), as in

$$P_t = p(E_t, B, G, X). \tag{13-5}$$

This equation is derived by postulating that inter-industry profitability differences are related to differences in the intensity of competition, measuring one aspect of competition with the turnover that comes from entry and exit (E), and substituting other factors (B, G, X) that determine the unmeasured aspects of turnover.[13] Thus, equations like 13-5 are specific versions of a more general hypothesis such as

$$P^* = F(C), \tag{13-6}$$

where C is the measure of the intensity of competition. Of course, the intensity of competition potentially encompasses many aspects of the process of competition – both measurable (T) and unmeasurable (OT). Thus,

$$C = G(T, OT).\tag{13-7}$$

If the traditional assumption that the turnover or mobility measures developed here and the ones that have not been measured are related to barriers (B) and other variables like growth (G), variability (VAR), research and development (RD), and advertising (ADV) is made, then the profit equation can be written

$$P = H(T, B, G, \text{VAR}, \text{RD}, \text{ADV}),\tag{13-8}$$

or

$$P = J(B, G, \text{VAR}, \text{RD}, \text{ADV}).\tag{13-9}$$

Equation 13-9 has been estimated because measures of the intensity of competition, either for entry and exit or for a broader group of measures, have been lacking. Since this is not a problem here, regressions using equation 13-8 were estimated with profit as the dependent variable. The regressors were the turnover measures developed here and other variables that capture market structure and technical factors that might create barriers to entry.

The first set of variables are used to measure market structure: the four-firm concentration measure (CR4), the Herfindahl index (HF), the marginal concentration ratio that captures the market share of firms ranked five through eight (MCR8), the size of this group relative to the top four (REL84), the variance of the logarithm of sizes (Prais' measure), VARS, the relative-firm-numbers ratio based on the Hannah and Kay measure of the equivalent numbers of firms (RELNUM), and the redundancy ratio based on the entropy index (RELRED). Principal components of the concentration measures (CR1–CR7) were estimated and used in the regression.[14]

The second set of variables, also described in Chapter 8, measure the importance of scale economies. They are the estimate of scale economies derived from a Cobb–Douglas production function (SCALE), the share of industry size accounted for by an MES plant (BMES), and the ratio of the value-added per worker in small plants relative to that of large plants (CDR). Once again, principal components of these variables (PSCL1–PSCL3) were used in the regression.[15]

The third set of variables, those that were found to be significant in previous profit studies,[16] are the rate of growth of real shipments between 1970 and 1979 (G), the variability of output around the trend growth line (VAR), research and development expenditures as a proportion of sales (RD), advertising expenditures as a proportion of sales (ADV), and the proportion of shipments accounted for by foreign-controlled establishments in 1979 (FOR).

Regressions of the relationship between profitability and turnover were estimated using both the return on capital and the return on equity. For each rate-of-return concept, average profitability over the period 1972–81 and

Table 13-12. *Regression of long-run return on capital (PRCAP) on turnover (average return, 1972–81)*

Variable	Parameter estimate	Probability[a] value
Full sample		
TURNC	−0.1128	.09
TURNM	−0.0003	.04
ENTNETS	−6.1900	.11
PSCL1	−0.0066	.11
IMP	0.0081	.01
FOR	−4.7398	.00
G	0.6737	.00
KL	−0.0002	.01
$R^2 = .486$		
Reduced sample		
TURNC	−0.1852	.06
TURNES	0.0965	.01
ENTNETN	−0.1001	.01
PCON7	0.1000	.04
IMP	0.0056	.02
FOR	−5.0971	.00
G	0.7641	.00
KL	—	—
$R^2 = .553$		

[a] The probability value of the t statistic ($|t| > 0$) for the null hypothesis that the coefficient is zero.

estimated long-run profitability (P^*) were each used as the dependent variable. The entire sample and the reduced sample were employed. Table 13-12 provides an example of the output of one of the estimates. The dependent variable is the average return on capital for the period 1972–81; the observations are drawn from the full and the reduced samples. In both cases, the turnover measures dominate the concentration and scale measures. Only one concentration and one scale measure enters each equation. In both cases, gross turnover for continuing firms (TURNC) and acquisition turnover (TURNM) are associated with lower profitability. Net positive entry (ENTNETS and ENTNETN) is associated with lower profitability. Growth is positively related to profitability, while industries with high foreign ownership have lower reported profits.

If all the estimated equations for the four different profitability measures (PRCAP7281, PREQ7281, LPRCAP, and LPREQ) and each of the two samples produced similar estimates, the reporting exercise would have to go no further. Unfortunately, this was not the case because a number of variables are collinear. Nevertheless, certain findings are robust to different choices of the profitability measure.

The first consistent finding is the negative coefficient associated with the net effect of entry minus exit. ENTNETS or ENTNETN invariably enters equation 13-8 with a negative sign. The second is that gross entry and exit, measured using firm shipment share (TURNE) or firm numbers share (TURNEN) often has a positive coefficient. Third, while the first component of concentration has a significantly positive correlation with profitability, if it is included in the regression analysis its effect is generally overwhelmed by the various turnover measures. In contrast, the third concentration component, when it is included, often has a significant negative coefficient. It captures the importance of the second tier of large firms (MCR8) – those ranked fifth through eighth. This is also the component that is related to the continuing-firm-mobility component (see Chapter 8). When this component in an industry is important, profits are lower. Perhaps equally significant, the mobility measures do not overwhelm the effect of this concentration measure, which suggests that MCR8 represents an aspect of competition that the mobility measures are not capturing. Fourth, the first scale component, which represents the scale coefficient from a Cobb–Douglas production function, generally has a significantly negative effect. Industries with economies of scale have lower profits. The extent to which this was the result of greater X-inefficiency was not investigated. Fifth, growth generally enters with a significant positive coefficient.

Equation 13-8 was estimated as if turnover was exogenous. Long-run profits were postulated to be a function of mobility; mobility was not postulated to depend on profits. If short-run profits were being used, this stance would be difficult to justify. But in the long run, it is the various facets of mobility such as entry and exit that determine long-run profits. Entry responds to movement of short-run profits away from the long-run equilibrium. If all industries experience the same number and magnitude of shocks, then long-run turnover such as entry and exit should be greatest where industries are most competitive, and thus negatively related to profitability. The fact that long-run profitability is a function of growth, however, suggests that the estimates of profitability that are used as dependent variables in the regression analysis are not entirely equilibrium values and that simultaneity may be a problem. The profitability equation was, therefore, estimated again, this time as part of a simultaneous system of equations (Table 13-13). The positive effect of gross entry and exit turnover (TURNEN), the negative effect of gross continuing-firm turnover (TURNC), and the negative effect of net entry (ENTNETN) continue to hold.

Table 13-13. *Determinants of long-run equilibrium return on equity (LPREQ) (reduced sample)*

Variable	Parameter estimate	t for H_0: parameter -0	Probability value[a]
TURNEN	0.3686	2.367	.024
TURNC	−0.8622	−2.567	.015
ENTNETS	−83.129	−1.93	.062
ENTNETN	−0.074	−0.13	.895
CONTNETN	0.103	0.42	.688
CONTNETS	0.179	0.28	.783
PMOB2	0.030	1.08	.287
NUMBER	−0.002	−0.25	.803
PCON3	0.076	2.60	.010
PCON4	0.042	1.19	.242
RD	942.966	4.25	.002
G	1.491	1.10	.278
VAR	−0.541	−0.85	.401
KL	−0.008	−1.67	.100
FOR	−12.434	−1.15	.256
$R^2 = .659$			

[a] The probability value of the t statistic ($|t| > 0$) for the null hypothesis that the coefficient is zero.

Rate of adjustment and turnover

The relationship between the rate of adjustment and industry turnover was also examined using correlation and regression analysis. Several robust findings emerged. First, the larger the rate of net entry, the faster the adjustment parameter. This confirms the predictions of the random-shock model. High rates of net entry facilitate the adjustment process. The second finding is that higher gross rates of entry and exit are associated with slower rates of adjustment. Thus, the life cycle model that emerges is one where industries with high rates of profitability are characterized by large gross turnover from entry and exit, and where this is not associated with positive net entry, the adjustment rates are relatively slow.

Other relationships that were more specific to the measure of profit used were found. Concentration leads to slower adjustment – but only for equity rates of return. The second-tier concentration component (MCR8) increases the speed of adjustment. Higher advertising increases the speed of adjustment for the equity rate of return but not for the rate of return on capital. Higher capital–labour ratios increase the speed of adjustment for the rate of return on capital, but not for the return on equity.

Conclusion

Mobility statistics provide a rich multi-dimensional description of the industrial system. Firm-size distributions remain relatively stable at the same time that firms are changing positions within industries. Instantaneous rates of change for entrants are not large; cumulative rates are substantial. A large amount of short-run job growth and decline in the continuing sector is transitory; nevertheless, longer-run rates of change indicate that structural shifts are taking place. Within industries, large amounts of market share are transferred from losers as a group to growing firms as a group; still, movements from one point on the extreme tails of the size distribution to another can take decades.

Like mobility statistics, industry profitability provides conflicting signals. There are aspects of instability and stability in the trajectories of industry profits. Correlations of industry profits over time decline dramatically as the period over which a comparison is being made is lengthened. Differences measured at any point in time contain a very substantial transitory element. Nevertheless, there is persistence in the differences in profitability across industries. Long-run profits in different industries do not equate. These differences could, of course, be due to measurement error. The fact that both the levels and the rates of adjustment are negatively related to net entry suggests that some of the difference is real.

The results also indicate that there is more than one relevant model of entry and exit. Most of the literature on entry has been built on the theme that profits are a function of entry barriers. In this case, profits should be negatively related to mobility. We find that profitability is lower in industries where there is more net entry. At the same time, empirical findings support the life cycle model. Industries with higher profits are those where there is both more entry and exit and general churning among continuing firms. However, high gross rates of entry and exit are associated with slower rates of adjustment. The churning that results from simultaneously high entry and exit is the result of industry conditions that lead to substantial changes arising from technological advances and demand shifts. These conditions allow for easy entry but also cause many to exit. Entry and exit together do not by themselves return these industries to equilibrium. The forces that move long-run profits away from equilibrium in these industries are more difficult to reverse even though there is a great deal of turnover within these industries.

14

Modelling entry

A structural determinant of market conduct and performance that is at least
as important as any other is the condition of entry to individual industries.
Joe Bain (1968: 251)

Introduction

Traditional models of the equilibrating process for markets stress the
role of entry. Positive economic profit results in entry. The process of entry
continues until each firm earns zero economic profit. Within this theoretical
framework, it is precisely excess economic profit that attracts new entry.

The field of industrial organization has modified the conventional micro-
economic view by stressing that adjustments to disequilibrium are not smooth
and that the path of adjustment in turn affects the level of equilibrium profits
in different industries. Certain factors such as advertising, research and development, and concentration have been hypothesized to act as entry barriers
and to perpetuate profit differences across industries.

Since the seminal works of Bain (1956) and Modigliani (1958), the economic profession has focused on the existence of entry barriers. Empirical
work on entry has generally used models that are based on the disequilibrium
view that entry occurs mainly in response to excess profits. The most widely
used models are the "limit-price" models of entry in which it is posited that
the profit level above which entry is attracted differs industry by industry and
is a function of entry barriers. Incumbents can set higher prices thereby
generating higher profits in industries with high barriers without attracting
entry. The level of price above which entry occurs is the limit price. Determinants of entry and their implications for market structure and performance
have traditionally been estimated by employing these types of models.[1]

Implicit in the limit-price model is the view that an entrant augments
existing output. Alternatively, the "stochastic-replacement" view of entry is
based on the assumption that entry is a dynamic process involving both

360

partial and complete replacement of existing firms by entrants (Baldwin and Gorecki, 1983; Shapiro and Khemani, 1987). The replacement view of entry presumes that entry can be expected even when price equals long-run average cost and industry profits are zero.

There are at least two reasons to expect entry even when industry profits are zero. First, to the extent that cost heterogeneity exists within an industry, low-cost firms can expect to enter and earn positive profit even if the industry reports zero economic profits as a whole. That is, some potential entrants who have cost advantages over some high-cost incumbents will enter and replace the high-cost incumbents. Second, a potential entrant can profitably enter if it expects to produce a superior product. In this case, entrants with high-quality products will replace incumbents with low-quality products, even though both entrants and incumbents have identical costs.

Most empirical attempts to estimate entry equations have been built on a limit-price type of model and have focused on the effect of entry barriers in raising the level of profits that can be earned by incumbents before entry is induced. Limit-price entry models purport to confirm the existence of entry barriers and, therefore, the existence of market imperfections.[2]

The evidence produced in previous chapters strongly suggests the aptness of the stochastic-replacement model. Entry rates are very similar to exit rates. Most entrants were found to displace exits.

When the stochastic-replacement phenomenon has been appended to the traditional limit-price model of entry, entry barriers have been found to be much less important (Baldwin and Gorecki, 1987b). This chapter examines the robustness of this finding. As is often the case in applied economics, interpretation of the significance of these differences is complicated by the fact that previous studies differ not only in terms of choice of model, but also in terms of how entry is measured – units of observation, units of measurement, type of entrants, and time period.

This chapter investigates the extent to which estimation techniques, model specification, and measurement alter the conclusion that entry is detrimentally affected by certain industry structural characteristics that have been described as providing barriers to entry.

The measurement of entry

Entry has been defined many different ways. Some have defined it as the birth of a producing unit, either a new plant or a new firm with a new plant – a greenfield entrant. Others have defined entry as the birth of a new legal entity. New legal entities may be associated with the birth of new plants, but they also include firms which enter an industry by acquiring existing firms. Both of these categories can be defined either in gross or in net terms. In the former case, entry is measured as the total number of plants (firms) entering an industry in a given period. In the latter case, it is the difference between the number of plants (firms) in two different periods.

This chapter uses a concept of entry implicit in the limit-price-entry literature – greenfield entrants. This is a relatively homogeneous category. The definition uses greenfield entrants rather than both greenfield and merger entrants, since the latter do not, initially at least, augment industry output. It focuses on gross measures rather than net entry measures, since the latter combine the effect of both entry and exit. It measures entry as new firms that build new plants and not new plants per se, since the latter include both greenfield entrants and plants that are built by incumbent firms. Failure to distinguish between new firms and existing-firm new-plant activity confuses entry with the expansion decisions of continuing firms. There are substantial dissimilarities in the determinants of greenfield and merger entrants, of greenfield entrants and the plant-creation process by continuing firms, and of gross and net entry measures (Baldwin and Gorecki, 1983, 1987b).

In order to test whether the existence of entry barriers depends on the unit of measurement used, the importance of greenfield entrants is measured in this chapter in terms of both their number and their size. The strength of the competitive forces associated with entry probably depends both on the number of entrants and the share of a market that is captured by the entrants. The two measures are related since the percentage of shipments in a market captured by entrants is equal to the count rate of entry times the average size of entrants relative to the population. High rates of entry that are calculated using count data may be negatively correlated with the relative average size of entrants, and therefore count-based rates and shipment-based rates need not be closely related. Thus, in testing for the importance of entry barriers, all three – the count of entrants, the shipments of entrants, and the average size of entrants – were used as dependent variables in the regression analysis.

A second test of the robustness of entry barriers is employed by using both short- and long-run data. Short-run estimates are derived by using two adjacent points of time; long-run estimates, by using two points removed from one another in time. Generally entrants are small at birth and many of the new-born do not survive infancy. Since the rate at which short-run performance translates into long-run market share may vary across industries, the determinants of both short- and long-run measures of entry were investigated separately.

Short- and long-run entry were estimated at the four-digit SIC level for the Canadian manufacturing sector using a longitudinal database that followed firms and plants between 1970 and 1979. Short-run rates of entry were estimated for each year between 1970 and 1979 and averaged. Long-run rates of entry were calculated as the number of firms in 1979 that had entered the industry since 1970. It is the total entry of all firms in each year since 1970 minus the deaths of entrants over this period.

The importance of entry is also evaluated in this chapter with a variable (RATIO) that measures the infant mortality rate. It is calculated as the long-run entry count divided by the sum of the short-run entry count. This is the proportion of all entrants over a decade that are still alive at the end of the period and is a direct measure of population continuance or an inverse measure of infant mortality.

Models of entry

The most common entry models follow the earlier work of Orr (1974), which posits that entry will occur whenever profits are above their entry-precluding levels. Following Orr, this model of entry is written as

$$E_{it} = f(P_{it} - P_{it}^*), \tag{14-1}$$

where E_{it} is the entry into industry i at time t, P_{it} is the entrant's perceived post-entry profit and P_{it}^* is the entry-precluding profit in industry i at time t.

The entry-precluding profit, P_{it}^*, depends on a vector of entry barriers, B, and a market risk variable, R. P^* (ignoring time and industry subscripts) can be specified as $P^* = h(B, R)$. As a consequence, the entry model in equation 14-1 may be written as

$$E = f(P, B, R). \tag{14-2}$$

E is expected to vary directly with perceived post-entry profit, P, and negatively with every component of B. It is, therefore, hypothesized that profit induces entry, whereas barriers to entry reduce entry.

In the estimations, expected profitability (P_{it}) is represented by two variables. The first (PR) captures the average profitability that entrants might expect to make in an industry over the period. It is represented by average industry profitability of continuing firms. Since the average does not incorporate information about the trend that might be expected to influence expectations about future profits, the growth in profits (GP) over the period is also included. Entry is expected to be greater in those markets where profits are growing.

Barrier variables (B) are represented by economies of scale (AVSZT), concentration (CR4), advertising intensity (ADV), and research and development intensity (RD). Market risk (R) is represented by volatility of market growth (VAR).

Equation 14-2 is an incomplete specification of entry since it does not consider stochastic aspects of entry. A substantial amount of entry simply replaces existing firms, and occurs even if economic profits are zero. Replacement entry is hypothesized to depend upon the size of the market. When firm count is used to measure entry, size of the market (S) is taken to be the number of firms in the industry (NF). When shipments of entrants is used as the dependent variable, size of the market is measured in terms of total industry shipments (TVS). The effect of the market-size variable can be interacted with the barrier variables to determine whether the magnitude of stochastic replacement is affected by the barrier variables.

The amount of entry should also depend on how easily entrants can enter and capture part of the market. A market with rapid growth is likely to be associated with new consumers, and therefore, there is a greater likelihood that new firms can gain market share. Positive growth in demand makes entry easier because the price level is less likely to fall after entry occurs. Existing firms may not respond adversely to the additional sales made by the entrants when their own sales are growing. In order to capture this part of the stochastic process, industry growth, G, is added to equation 14-2. Following Baldwin and Gorecki (1983, 1987b), an entry model that incorporates both stochastic-replacement and limit-price views of entry is specified as

$$E = f(S, G, P, B, R). \tag{14-3}$$

S, G, and P provide incentives to entry, whereas B and R provide disincentives.

Estimation procedures appropriate to count data

Prior empirical studies of entry have employed classical regression models of entry, and the principle of ordinary least squares has been the method of model estimation. However, entry data are non-negative integer-valued random-count data and deviate from classical regression assumptions. Since entry data are integer-valued and deviate from classical regression assumptions, the statistical specification of entry calls for a discrete-probability distribution.

In order to meet this requirement, an econometric model of entry is used that is based first on the assumption that each observation is drawn from a Poisson distribution and then from a negative-binomial distribution. This methodology is in the spirit of Hausman, Hall, and Griliches (1984) and Cameron and Trivedi (1986), who apply both the Poisson and negative-binomial regression to count data on firms' patenting activity and consumer demand for health care services, respectively. It is also in the spirit of Chappell, Kimenyi, and Mayer (1990), Mayer and Chappell (1992), and Papke (1991), who use Poisson regressions to study the entry behaviour of firms across industries in the United States.

For notational convenience, equation 14-3 is specified as

$$E_i = f(X_i), \qquad i = 1, 2, \ldots, n, \tag{14-4}$$

where $X_i = (S_i, G_i, P_i, B_i, R_i)$. E_i denotes the number counts of new entrants in industry i, and S_i, G_i, P_i, B_i, and R_i are the explanatory variables already discussed. Under the assumption that the data on entry are drawn from a Poisson distribution, the probability of observing a count of entry E_i in industry i is

$$\Pr(E_i) = \exp(-\lambda_i)\lambda_i^{E_i}/E_i!, \qquad E_i = 0, 1, 2, 3, \ldots, n. \qquad (14\text{-}5)$$

The mean and variance of E_i are equal to λ_i. To incorporate exogenous variables, X_i, which influence entry, including a constant, the parameter λ_i is specified to be

$$\lambda_i = E(E_i \mid X_i) = \exp(\beta X_i), \qquad (14\text{-}6)$$

where β is a parameter vector to be estimated. The Poisson parameter λ_i is a function of X_i and an unknown parameter vector, β.

There is one important restriction in the Poisson regression model. The Poisson has a conditional mean and variance of E_i given X_i that are equal. Many integer data sets do not satisfy this assumption. They are said to possess overdispersion when the variance is larger than the mean. If data show overdispersion, and the restriction of equality of mean and variance is imposed, estimates of the standard errors of estimated parameters will be unduly small.

Overdispersion can be incorporated into the count model. Following Gourieroux, Monfort, and Trognon (1984a, 1984b), a compound Poisson distribution is used that reduces to a family of the negative-binomial distribution (see Cameron and Trivedi, 1986).

The effect of entry barriers

The effect of entry barriers was investigated in four stages. The first uses the number of entrants as dependent variable and a traditional-entry equation that incorporates both the limit-price and stochastic-replacement views of entry. It compares the OLS estimates to those from the Poisson and the negative-binomial regression to show the improvements that are made by using the procedure that recognizes that entry is measured using integer-count data. The second section investigates the extent to which the effect of entry-barrier variables on the number of entrants is robust and whether different variants of the limit-price as opposed to the stochastic-replacement model are used. The third section examines the effect of using alternative measures of entry. Four different dependent variables are employed in this section – the number of entrants, the shipments of entrants, the average size of entrants, and the population-continuance rate of entrants. The fourth section asks whether changes occur when alternative specifications of the explanatory variables are employed. Alternative measures of both the barrier variables and profitability are used.

The effect of alternative estimation procedures

For comparison purposes, count data of entry were estimated with the number of greenfield entrants (E) as the dependent variable using a straightforward combination of the limit-price entry and the stochastic-replacement model. The implicit equation in linear form from the Poisson is

$$\exp(E) = a_1 \times S_i + a_2 \times G_i + a_3 \times P_i + a_4 \times B_i + a_5 \times R_i + \cdots .$$
$$(14\text{-}7)$$

The first estimate used OLS, the second was a count model using a Poisson regression, and the third was a count model that used a negative binomial. The latter two were estimated by maximum-likelihood procedures. Both long- and short-run data were used to examine whether the results depended on the time period chosen to measure entry.

The results are presented in Table 14-1. In both the long and the short run, the estimated standard errors of the Poisson and negative-binomial models are substantially lower than those of OLS estimates. These findings are consistent with those of Hausman, Hall, and Griliches (1984), and Cameron and Trivedi (1986). Although the Poisson point estimates and those in the negative-binomial model are similar in sign and magnitude, the estimated standard errors under the Poisson model are substantially smaller. This essentially reflects the consequence of imposing the restriction that the conditional mean and variance of the Poisson distribution are equal.

In order to choose between the Poisson and negative-binomial regressions, a test of the null hypothesis that the underlying model is Poisson, with mean = variance = $\exp(X)$, against the alternative that the model is a negative binomial, with mean = $\exp(X)$ and variance = $\exp(X)[1 + \exp(X)]$, is required. Both the Wald test and the likelihood-ratio test do this. The Wald statistic for testing the Poisson against the negative binomial is 8.65 and 8.54 for the long run and the short run, respectively. The corresponding likelihood-ratio-test statistics are, respectively, 848.20 and 15,428.78. Both the Wald and likelihood-ratio-test statistics are highly significant. Furthermore, the overdispersion parameter is significant. The data reject the equality of the mean and the variance, which is the key property of the Poisson model. The significance of the overdispersion parameter and both tests lead to the strong rejection of the Poisson model in favour of the negative binomial, which is therefore chosen for comparison to the OLS regression results.

The negative binomial and the OLS results for both the long and the short run show that entry is positively related to the existing number of firms (NF), the growth of shipments (GS), and risk, measured in terms of volatility of growth (VAR) (Table 14-1). In addition, the negative binomial has a significant and negative coefficient for two entry-barrier variables in both the short and the long run that were not significant in the OLS equation. These are plant-scale economies (MES) and concentration (CR4). Research and development

Table 14-1. *Comparison of estimation procedures for entry model, short and long run*

Measure	Long run			Short run		
	OLS	Poisson	Negative binomial	OLS	Poisson	Negative binomial
Constant	-4.995 (.500) [7.380]	3.587 (.000) [0.087]	2.848 (.000) [0.327]	-73.218 (.338) [76.190]	6.508 (.000) [0.022]	6.005 (.000) [0.359]
NF	0.294 (.000) [0.015]	0.003 (.000) [0.000]	0.005 (.000) [0.0004]	2.482 (.000) [0.066]	0.001 (.000) [0.000]	0.003 (.000) [0.0002]
PR	1.479 (.598) [2.795]	0.121 (.000) [0.025]	0.094 (.520) [0.146]	9.946 (.744) [30.390]	0.108 (.000) [0.008]	0.145 (.510) [0.221]
PRFTGR	0.166 (.911) [1.480]	-0.045 (.023) [0.020]	-0.062 (.372) [0.070]	-2.598 (.872) [16.030]	-0.054 (.000) [0.005]	-0.080 (.263) [0.072]
G	0.883 (.046) [0.439]	0.083 (.000) [0.006]	0.090 (.000) [0.022]	14.653 (.002) [4.675]	0.081 (.000) [0.002]	0.089 (.000) [0.019]
CR4	-0.074 (.427) [0.093]	-0.023 (.000) [0.001]	-0.018 (.000) [0.004]	-1.280 (.196) [0.986]	-0.027 (.000) [0.000]	-0.030 (.000) [0.004]
AVSZT	1.466 (.952) [24.060]	-2.971 (.000) [0.490]	-2.038 (.033) [0.955]	-77.137 (.768) [260.718]	-5.684 (.000) [0.174]	-2.158 (.014) [0.876]
RD	0.00004 (.999) [0.074]	0.006 (.000) [0.001]	0.005 (.362) [0.006]	1.191 (.141) [0.806]	0.011 (.000) [0.000]	0.013 (.005) [0.005]
ADV	-77.680 (.311) [76.360]	-9.904 (.000) [1.357]	-3.080 (.400) [3.649]	-515.700 (.533) [824.740]	-6.297 (.000) [0.335]	-0.408 (.902) [3.298]
VAR	0.084 (.018) [0.035]	0.003 (.000) [0.001]	0.004 (.012) [0.002]	1.247 (.001) [0.382]	0.003 (.000) [0.000]	0.003 (.046) [0.001]
Variance parameter α			0.372 (.000) [0.043]			0.487 (.000) [0.057]
Adj. R^2	.81			.93		
- log L		1016.099	591.998		8711.917	997.528

Note: The significance level of a two-tailed test for rejecting the null hypothesis that the coefficient is zero is in parentheses. Standard error of estimate is in brackets.

has a positive effect on entry in both the long and the short run but is only significant in the short run. Advertising is not significant either in the OLS or the negative binomial model.

Thus, choice of the negative binomial over the OLS overcomes earlier observations that entry barriers are positive but insignificant determinants of the entry process. The choice of the integer-count model substantially increases the significance of the effect of concentration and plant-scale-economies variables.

The limit-price and the stochastic-replacement models for count data

The effect of the estimation procedure was investigated in the previous section with an amalgam of the limit-price and the stochastic-replacement views of the entry process. The effect of changes in the specification of the entry model on the impact of entry barriers is examined in this section. Since the negative-binomial-regression technique was shown to be the preferred option, it is adopted in this section. Once more, entry is measured by the number of greenfield entrants in both the short and long run.

Three different models were estimated for the both the long- and the short-run entry count data. The first equation used just the variables that originate from a simple Orr-type model. These are profitability (PR), growth in profitability (PRFTGR), growth in sales (G), concentration (CR4), economies of scale (AVSZT), research and development (RD), advertising intensity (ADV), and demand variability (VAR). The second formulation added the industry size variable – number of firms (NF) to the first. The third formulation added an interaction term involving industry size and the entry-barrier variables – concentration (CR4), advertising intensity (ADV), research and development intensity (RD), and economies of plant scale (AVSZT).

The results are reported in Table 14-2. Columns 1–3 present the results for the long run; columns 4–6 present the results for the short run. The barrier variables that are significant in the simple limit-price model (columns 1 and 4) are also significant in the two models that incorporate the stochastic-replacement phenomenon (columns 2 and 3; 5 and 6). Concentration (CR4) and scale economies (AVSZT) negatively affect entry in all formulations.

Nevertheless, the size of the coefficient on the concentration variable decreases by about 50 per cent when the stochastic-replacement model (columns 2 and 4) is used. Moreover, in the third variant (columns 3 and 5), the fact that the scale-economies variable has a positive coefficient when interacted with a number of firms means that the effect of scale economies declines as the number of firms in the industry gets larger. Indeed, for all industries where the number of firms (NF) is greater than 30, scale economies will not have a negative impact on entry. Some two-thirds of the industries

Table 14-2. *Comparison of entry models: negative-binomial estimates*

Measure	(1)	(2)	(3)	(4)	(5)	(6)
Constant	4.561 (.000) [0.292]	2.848 (.000) [0.327]	2.498 (.000) [0.257]	7.944 (.000) [0.284]	6.005 (.000) [0.359]	5.409 (.000) [0.303]
PR	0.083 (.534) [0.133]	0.094 (.520) [0.146]	0.064 (.626) [0.131]	0.031 (.846) [0.160]	0.145 (.510) [0.221]	0.162 (.389) [0.188]
PRFTGR	-0.107 (.195) [0.083]	-0.062 (.372) [0.070]	-0.071 (.256) [0.062]	-0.103 (.220) [0.084]	-0.080 (.263) [0.072]	-0.073 (.257) [0.065]
G	0.131 (.000) [0.025]	0.090 (.000) [0.022]	0.056 (.001) [0.017]	0.108 (.000) [0.022]	0.089 (.000) [0.019]	0.052 (.002) [0.016]
CR4	-0.036 (.000) [0.004]	-0.018 (.000) [0.004]	-0.014 (.002) [0.005]	-0.049 (.000) [0.004]	-0.030 (.000) [0.004]	-0.025 (.000) [0.004]
AVSZT	-2.585 (.032) [1.210]	-2.038 (.033) [0.955]	-6.935 (.000) [1.414]	-2.160 (.039) [1.047]	-2.158 (.014) [0.876]	-5.642 (.000) [1.082]
RD	0.009 (.185) [0.006]	0.005 (.362) [0.006]	0.005 (.411) [0.006]	0.016 (.001) [0.005]	0.013 (.005) [0.005]	0.005 (.147) [0.004]
ADV	-6.206 (.116) [3.952]	-3.080 (.400) [3.649]	0.356 (.941) [4.839]	-4.552 (.231) [3.803]	-0.408 (.902) [3.298]	-0.696 (.882) [4.695]
VAR	0.002 (.370) [0.002]	0.004 (.012) [0.002]	0.004 (.002) [0.001]	-0.001 (.471) [0.002]	0.003 (.046) [0.001]	0.004 (.005) [0.001]
NF		0.005 (.000) [0.0004]	0.004 (.000) [0.001]		0.003 (.000) [0.0002]	0.004 (.002) [0.0005]
CR4 × NF			0.00003 (.487) [0.00005]			0.00002 (.368) [0.000002]
ADV × NF			-0.076 (.064) [0.041]			-0.015 (.636) [0.031]
RD × NF			-0.0007 (.313) [0.00007]			-0.000003 (.967) [0.00008]
AVSZT × NF			0.231 (.000) [0.042]			0.144 (.000) [0.024]
Variance parameter α	0.565 (.000) [0.065]	0.372 (.000) [0.043]	0.201 (.000) [0.026]	0.713 (.000) [0.086]	0.487 (.000) [0.057]	0.311 (.000) [0.039]
− log L	620.304	591.998	556.235	1033.470	997.528	958.751

Note: The significance level of a two-tailed test for rejecting the null hypothesis that the coefficient is zero is in parentheses. Standard error of estimate is in brackets.

fall into this category. Barriers matter – but not where firm numbers are relatively high.

In summary, the hypothesis that entry barriers exist is not rejected when the model specification is varied. Qualifications are, however, required about the extent to which they are important.

Alternative measures of the importance of entry

In each of the two preceding sections, entry is measured by the count of new firms. This section examines whether the determinants of entry remain the same when the unit of measurement that is used to define entry is changed. Four separate measures of entry are used to compare the robustness of our findings on the importance of entry barriers. Each of these is measured for both the long run and short run.

These measures are (1) the number counts of greenfield entrants (N23), (2) the amount of shipments by entrants (TVSE), (3) the average size of entrants (AVFZE), and (4) the ratio of the number of entrants in the long run to those in the short run (RATIO).

Each dependent variable is regressed on the same set of explanatory variables, with one exception. When entry is measured using the numbers count, the normalizing variable is the number of firms in the industry (NF); when entry is measured using shipments (TVSE), the normalizing variable is total value of industry shipments (TVS); for the average size of entrants (AVFZE), the normalizing variable is the average size of existing firms (AVFZ); for the population continuation rate, RATIO, it is the average size of entrants relative to the industry average size (RELSIZE).

Table 14-3 contains the results for the long run; Table 14-4, the results for the short run. The model was estimated using the negative binomial for the entry count measure and OLS for other variables.[3] A comparison of the entry count data and the industry shipments equations reveals that the latter has less explanatory power. A simple OLS of the counts data (not reported here) has a considerable higher adjusted R^2 than the OLS for shipments data – .81 as opposed to .41, respectively. This is because the explanatory variables do a poor job of describing the average size of entrants. The adjusted R^2 for the equation using the average size of entrant as the dependent variable was only .32. Despite this difference, most of the significant coefficients in the count and shipments equations tell the same story. Entry depends positively on size and growth of shipments, and negatively on concentration.

While these variables tell basically the same story for the count and shipments data, they do not always affect the average size of an entrant (AVFZE) in the same way. Growth positively affects average size of the entrant (AVFZE) and the success rate (RATIO), but in neither case is it very significant. Growth thereby affects the importance of entrants because it affects the number of

Table 14-3. *Comparison of entry measures: long run*

Measure	N23[a]	TVSE		ASE		RATIO	
Constant	2.923 (.000) [0.280]	19.207	(.000) [4.529]	8.837 (.132) [5.828]		0.051 [0.027]	(.060)
PR	0.125 (.411) [0.152]	−0.863	(.680) [2.090]	−2.514 (.351) [2.686]		−0.010 [0.012]	(.383)
PRFTGR	−0.033 (.602) [0.063]	−2.348	(.043) [1.152]	−2.854 (.057) [1.487]		−0.008 [0.007]	(.246)
G	0.082 (.000) [0.018]	1.024	(.002) [0.327]	0.621 (.138) [0.417]		0.003 [0.002]	(.153)
CR4	−0.018 (.000) [0.004]	−0.015	(.015) [0.062]	0.095 (.249) [0.082]		0.002 [0.000]	(.000)
AVSZT	1.806 (.038) [0.872]	27.703	(.127) [18.060]	45.760 (.051) [23.204]		0.086 [0.103]	(.406)
RD	0.004 (.377) [0.005]	0.094	(.095) [0.056]	0.168 (.020) [0.071]		−0.001 [0.000]	(.032)
ADV	−3.103 (.312) [3.069]	−78.861	(.166) [56.700]	−55.002 (.450) [72.518]		−0.308 [0.318]	(.335)
VAR	0.003 (.012) [0.001]	0.006	(.828) [0.027]	0.007 (.984) [0.034]		0.0003 [0.000]	(.096)
NF	0.005 (.000) [0.0004]						
TVS		0.000004 (.000) [0.000]					
AVPLZ				0.0001 (.001) [0.000]			
RELSIZE						−0.00002 (.195) [0.000]	
Adj. R^2		.41		.32		.25	
F		13.35		9.32		6.92	
Degrees of freedom		(9,148)		(9,148)		(9,148)	

Note: The significance level of a two-tailed test for rejecting the null hypothesis that the coefficient is zero is in parentheses. Standard error of estimate is in brackets.
[a] Excludes all zero value of the dependent variable.

entrants, not because it facilitates entrants of a larger average size. Growth also positively affects the success rate (RATIO), but the coefficient is not significant.

Concentration also has a different effect on entry counts than on average size. Higher concentration leads to fewer entrants, but it has a positive but insignificant effect on the average size of an entrant. There are, therefore, fewer entrants in concentrated industries, but the entrants tend to be bigger

Table 14-4. *Comparison of entry measures: short run*

Measure	N23	TVSE	AVFSE
Constant	6.005 (.000) [0.359]	44.698 (.000) [10.150]	3.818 (.132) [2.521]
PR	0.145 (.510) [0.221]	−0.266 (.954) [4.661]	−1.078 (.358) [1.169]
PRFTGR	−0.080 (.263) [0.072]	−3.687 (.135) [2.456]	−1.439 (.021) [0.618]
G	0.089 (.000) [0.019]	2.461 (.001) [0.719]	0.305 (.090) [0.179]
CR4	−0.030 (.000) [0.004]	−0.459 (.001) [0.014]	0.039 (.278) [0.036]
AVSZT	2.158 (.014) [0.876]	−69.727 (.084) [40.150]	22.089 (.030) [10.063]
RD	0.013 (.005) [0.005]	0.168 (.183) [0.126]	0.070 (.026) [0.031]
ADV	−0.408 (.902) [3.298]	−256.150 (.045) [126.976]	−47.916 (.132) [31.675]
VAR	0.003 (.046) [0.001]	0.036 (.537) [0.059]	0.004 (.797) [0.015]
NF	0.0003 (.000) [0.0002]		
TVS		0.003 (.000) [0.0003]	
ASF			0.151 (.000) [0.015]
Adj. R^2		.52	.45
F		20.98	15.70
Degrees of freedom		(9,156)	(9,156)

Note: The significance level of a two-tailed test for rejecting the null hypothesis that the coefficient is zero is in parentheses. Standard error of estimate is in brackets.

– probably because the cost disadvantages of small-scale entry are greater in these industries. Concentration is also associated with a significant positive effect on RATIO – the success rate of entrants.

Finally, it is noteworthy that industry variability has a significantly positive effect on numbers of entrants but not on average size. Variability perhaps leads to greater entry because highly cyclical industries require more entry for profit-equilibration purposes. Industries that experience more cyclical swings do not experience entry at larger average size, but they do have a higher success rate as measured by RATIO.

In conclusion, the entry-barrier variables that have been so often stressed in the literature are less important when we turn to measure the impact of entry in other than simple count terms. It may be that there are fewer entrants in concentrated industries, but the entrants in these industries tend to be larger, and therefore concentration does not have as great an effect on shipments captured by entrants as it does on their numbers. Moreover, entrants in concentrated industries have greater staying power. The number of entrants that survive is greater in concentrated industries.

Alternative measures of the profitability and entry-barrier variables

This section examines the effect of using alternative measures of the explanatory variables in the regression analysis. Both profitability and entry-barrier variables can be measured in more than one way.

In the first three sections, profitability has been measured as shipments minus materials and energy expenses minus wages and salaries divided by a measure of capital stock derived by the perpetual inventory method. The numerator comes from the Census of Manufactures and the denominator from a survey of investment. Alternatively, the profitability of an industry can be derived from income and balance-sheet data as profits divided by capital stock.

Concentration has been measured by the market share of the top four firms (CR4). The economies-of-scale variable that was used proxied the minimum-efficient-sized plant by the share of output accounted for by the plants in the top half of the size distribution, which Davies (1980b) has shown is just another measure of inequality. The structural characteristics that are associated with entry barriers can also be measured in a variety of other ways. Alternative measures for both concentration and scale economies were presented in Chapter 8.

In the case of the profit variable, no one measurement is inherently superior to another. On the one hand, using price–cost margins to measure profitability is imperfect because they contain a margin that includes payments for services and taxes. Other disadvantages of using price–cost margin data were discussed in Chapter 14. On the other hand, rates of return derived from balance-sheet data do not perfectly measure the concept of internal rate of return either.

The same indeterminacy exists for measures of entry barriers due to concentration. A number of measures of concentration have been derived. None is inherently superior to all others because there are different dimensions to market structure that are not captured by any one measure.

Since there are a large number of alternative measures, it is inappropriate to draw conclusions about the importance of entry barriers without some experimentation with alternative measures. However, there are too many alternatives for the analysis to proceed by including each potential candidate in a sequential fashion. The solution adopted here is to reduce each group of variables to its principal components and to employ these components in the regression analysis – as in the analysis in Chapter 8 that investigated the relationship between mobility and concentration.

The concentration variables are those used in Chapter 8 – the Herfindahl index (HF), the four-firm concentration ratio (CR4), the marginal-concentration ratio for firms ranked from number five to eight in an industry (MCR8), the size of the group of firms ranked from five to eight divided by the size of the top four firms (REL84), the variance of firm size (VARS), the relative redundancy ratio (RELRED), and the relative-numbers equivalent (RELNUM).[4]

The same set of plant-scale variables that were used in Chapter 8 are also employed. These include the economy of scale estimate derived from a production function (SCALE), the cost-disadvantage ratio (CDR – the ratio of the labour productivity of the smaller firms to that of the larger firms), and the Lyons estimate of minimum efficient scale (BMES – the size at which firms begin to build two plants rather than one).

The profitability variables include both those derived from balance-sheet data and from the Census of Manufactures price–cost data. Balance-sheet measures include both the return on equity and the total return on capital.[5] Several variants of each were employed. These include: the average rate of return on equity and on capital for the 1970s (PREQ7281 and PRCAP7281, respectively), the estimate of long-run equilibrium return on equity and on capital (LPREQ and LPRCAP, respectively) derived in the spirit of Mueller (1986) from an autoregressive process for the period 1972 to 1986, and the speed with which profit returns to equilibrium for both return on equity and on total capital (BETAEQ and BETACAP, respectively).

Three measures of profitability based on profit residuals from the census were used. The first is the average profitability of continuing plants that is used in the preceding section (PR). The second is a measure of the expected profitability of small plants (PRSMALL). This is defined as PR times the difference between the profitability of the largest firms in the industry and the smallest firms and captures what entering firms might expect if they base their expected profits not on average incumbent experience but on small-firm experience. The third census profit variable is the rate of growth in profitability (PR) between 1970 and 1979 (GP).

The principal components of the concentration variables were reported in Chapter 8. The first two components exhaust three-quarters of the total variance in the sample.

The principal components of the profit variables are presented in Table

14-5. The different profit measures are not highly collinear. The first component accounts for only some 29 per cent of the total variance of the sample; the second for 23 per cent, the third for 21 per cent. The first gives greatest weight to the equity and the total capital rates of return for the period 1972–81 (PREQ7281 and PRCAP7281). The second component primarily weights the census profit variables. It weights both the average (PR) and the expected small-firm performance (PRSMALL) equally. It varies inversely with both of these profit variables. Interestingly, the eighth component weights the same two variables but with opposite signs and varies directly with average profitability but inversely with small-firm profitability. The third component varies directly with average rates of return (PREQ7281 and PRCAP7281) and with the long-run estimated equilibrium rate of return on total capital (LPRCAP). The fourth profit component captures the speed of adjustment process with the largest weights on BETAEQ and BETACAP. It varies inversely with the rate of adjustment.

In order to use both sets of profit variables, data from the Census of Manufactures and the Corporation Financial Statistics were linked.[6] The numbers-count equation for long-run entry was then estimated with the concentration components (PCON1 to PCON7) replacing the concentration variable (CR4), the scale components (PSCL1 to PSCL3) replacing the scale variable (AVSZT), and the profit components (PPROF1 to PPROF9) replacing the profit variables (PR and PRFTGR). In keeping with the previous tests, both OLS and the negative binomial were employed.

The scale components by themselves had a negative effect on entry. When the scale components were included with the concentration components, they were always drowned out by the concentration components. This is not surprising. It was demonstrated in Chapter 8 that scale is an important determinant of concentration. When the various aspects of concentration are all entered with their components, there is little explanatory role that remains for scale. Therefore, the scale variables are omitted from the regression results reported here.

The results are presented in Table 14-6. Column 1 uses census profit variables PR and PRFTGR for comparison to the previous results. These estimates yield the same qualitative results as the more disaggregated data used in the previous sections. Profit is only significant at the 14 per cent level. The concentration and scale-barrier variables are highly significant in the negative-binomial formulation.

The second set of estimates reported in column 2 replaces the census profit variables – PR and PRFTGR – with average return on total capital (PRCAP7281). The significance of the profit variable remains about the same while the concentration and scale-barrier variables remain significant. Thus, the definition of profitability does not significantly affect the results.

Table 14-5. *Principal-component analysis performed on profitability variables*

Variable	Eigenvector								
	PPROF1	PPROF2	PPROF3	PPROF4	PPROF5	PPROF6	PPROF7	PPROF8	PPROF9
PREQ7281	0.3503	0.2270	0.4052	-0.3495	-0.1768	-0.5856	-0.0172	0.3574	-0.1929
PRCAP7281	0.4267	0.1884	0.4077	-0.1787	-0.0776	0.5197	-0.3046	-0.4459	-0.1287
LPRCAP	-0.1449	0.3639	0.5005	0.3537	-0.1234	0.0595	0.2489	0.0727	0.6204
LPREQ	0.4756	-0.1157	-0.1296	0.4962	0.1618	-0.0701	-0.5660	0.3005	0.2319
BETACAP	0.4046	-0.2378	-0.2533	-0.5151	-0.0249	0.1082	0.2501	0.0448	0.6100
BETAEQ	0.5169	-0.0544	-0.0952	0.4437	-0.0768	-0.1251	0.6070	-0.2727	-0.2391
PR	0.0168	-0.5147	-0.4246	0.0291	0.1912	0.4005	0.2368	0.5072	-0.2082
PRSMALL	-0.0875	-0.5113	0.3836	-0.0078	0.3272	-0.4364	-0.1039	-0.4927	0.1808
PRFTGR	0.0854	0.4258	-0.0391	-0.1071	0.8782	0.0169	0.1564	0.0380	-0.0314
Proportion of total sample variability accounted for	28.8	23.2	21.5	12.7	8.4	2.6	1.3	0.9	0.6

Table 14-6. *Comparison of entry models using different profitability measures: negative-binomial estimates*[a]

Measure	(1)		(2)		(3)	
Constant	5.857	(.000)	5.682	(.000)	5.233	(.000)
	[0.157]		[0.197]		[0.058]	
NF	0.0002	(.000)	0.0002	(.000)	0.0001	(.000)
	[0.00002]		[0.00002]		[0.0002]	
PR	0.157	(.140)				
	[0.107]					
PRFTGR	−0.002	(0.938)	−0.087	(0.005)		
	[0.030]		[0.031]			
G	4.868	(.000)	5.241	(.000)	5.178	(.000)
	[1.013]		[1.127]		[1.045]	
CR4	−1.612	(.000)	−1.201	(.000)		
	[0.236]		[0.239]			
AVSZT	1.447	(0.070)	1.049	(.197)		
	[0.799]		[0.814]			
RD	6325.220	(.127)	307.400	(.195)	249.600	(.313)
	[212.800]		[237.000]		[247.400]	
ADV	0.596	(.000)	0.753	(.000)	0.601	(.000)
	[0.607]		[0.074]		[0.057]	
VAR	−0.020	(.983)	−0.693	(.440)		
	[0.890]		[0.898]			
PRCAP7281			1.415	(.171)		
			[1.035]			
PCON1					0.167	(.000)
					[0.152]	
PCON2					−0.519	(.000)
					[0.037]	
PCON3					−0.156	(.004)
					[0.054]	
PPROF2					−0.026	(.288)
					[0.025]	
PPROF3					0.044	(.068)
					[0.024]	
PPROF4					0.085	(.000)
					[0.021]	
PPROF8					−0.176	(.034)
					[0.083]	
Variance parameter α	0.102	(.000)	0.112	(.000)	0.078	(.000)
	[0.004]		[0.004]		[0.003]	
$-\log L$	716.360		712.447		699.405	

[a] The significance level of a two-tailed test for rejecting the null hypothesis that the coefficients are zero is given in parentheses. Standard error of estimate is in brackets.

The results of adding various profit components that are related to the entry process are reported in column 3. The coefficients associated with the three concentration components (PCON1, PCON2, PCON3) indicate that concentration has significant negative effects on entry. The first component, which places large negative weights on the four-firm and the Herfindahl concentration measures, has a positive coefficient in the entry regression. Thus, industries where the four-firm concentration ratio and the Herfindahl measure are high have less entry. The other two concentration components have a negative effect on entry. The second component positively weights the share of the top four firms (CR4) and the share of the firms ranked five to eight (MCR8); the fifth component weights the Herfindahl measure and the relative-numbers ratio (RELNUM). Both the second and the fifth components emphasize the importance of the second largest tier of firms – but in different ways. A large presence by this group serves to further limit entry.

While the profit variables used previously do not possess much significance, there are four components – PPROF2, PPROF3, PPROF4, PPROF8 – that are related to entry. The two profit components that use the census margins – PPROF2 and PPROF8 – and inversely weight small-firm profitability have negative signs. The latter is significant; the former is not. Thus, higher small-firm profitability has a positive effect on entry. The profitability component that varies directly with average book value and estimated long-run profitability (PPROF3) has a positive effect on entry. The component that varies inversely with the speed of adjustment (PPROF4) has a positive coefficient. Where profits return to equilibrium more quickly, there is less entry.

In summary, profitability does matter. But it is a combination of different dimensions that would appear to most closely affect entry. In particular, it is a combination of overall profitability and whether smaller firms can expect to earn these profits that matters most in stimulating entry.

Conclusion

This chapter has investigated the robustness of the hypothesis that certain structural characteristics are barriers to entry. As often happens during robustness tests, we have learned not just whether a variable is important or whether a phenomenon exists, but instead the circumstances in which it matters.

When a more complex estimation procedure – regression for count data – was applied, the effect of entry barriers was more easily separated from that of other variables. Extension of the model substantiated the importance of entry barriers but found that they impeded entry only for industries in which there was a relatively small number of firms. This exercise confirmed that barriers have a non-linear effect.

Barriers were found to have a different effect on the number of entrants than on the average size of entrants and thus on the market share that entrants capture. Structural barriers reduce the number of entrants but do not have a negative effect on the average size of the entrant. If anything, they tend to increase the size at which entry occurs.

Finally, it is not so much industry profitability that has a positive effect on entry. It is the rate of small-firm profitability that attracts entrants. Greenfield entrants, we have seen, are generally small. Expectations of profitability are drawn from the experience of this small-firm population.

15

Conclusion

Industrial economics has a long empirical tradition. In order to contribute to it, this study provides new data on various facets of the internal dynamics of industries. It outlines the nature and the amount of dynamic change in an industry and describes how this change affects industry performance.

The evidence presented here tells us much about the competitive process. In doing so, it provides new insights and an improved understanding of phenomena that have long furnished the main fare for study in industrial economics.

New insights are provided into the way in which the various pieces of the various processes are put together. New data enable a more precise and comprehensive picture of the importance of entry and exit to be assembled. Both short- and long-run time periods are used to measure entry and exit. Facets of both greenfield and acquisition entry are described. The study also sets the process of entry and exit side by side with growth and decline in incumbent firms so that both their individual and their combined importance can be evaluated.

The study looks not just at the amount of turnover, but also at the effect of turnover on various measures of performance. It shows the relationship of turnover to productivity, efficiency, and profitability. By doing so, it confirms the importance of turnover and turnover measures. Together entry and exit along with growth and decline in the incumbent sector shift substantial amounts of market share from losers to gainers. Substantial productivity gains accompany this process. The study also shows that firm turnover is associated with improvements in efficiency and with the process that equilibrates profits across industries.

Finally, the research delineates the effects of control changes. Mergers are not associated with dramatic changes in the market share of the units that change hands. Indeed, changes in shares that accompany mergers are short-lived. But with a more comprehensive database and better data on the actual performance of plants that change hands, the study demonstrates that mergers also have real effects on labour productivity and profit margins.

380

This chapter briefly summarizes the findings in each of these areas and then places them in context by comparing the Canadian results with those of other countries.

Industry dynamics
Greenfield entry and closedown exit

The importance of entrants depends upon the probability of entry, on the size of entrants at birth, on the death rate of the new-born, and on the growth rate of survivors after birth.

When year-to-year data on entry and exit are examined, the process appears to be insignificant. Greenfield entrants, at birth, rarely account for more than 1 per cent of employment. Moreover, these entrants are initially small on average and, in their formative years, present little threat to large firms.

Entry turns potential into actual competition. Entrants are not instantly successful. The maturation process is often slow and painful. The infant mortality rate is high. Upward of 50 per cent of births die by their tenth birthday. Nevertheless, those infants who survive grow sufficiently to offset the deaths of their siblings. As a result, the share of each cohort increases slowly over time, and as more and more cohorts of entrants are born annually, the importance of new firms accumulates.

The data on entry and exit indicate that it is not a phenomenon confined to a group of firms that constantly churn at the margin of an industry. Greenfield firms that enter between 1970 and 1979 account for, on average, 16.1 per cent of 1979 industry shipments; in 1970, firms that close by 1979 account for 18.2 per cent of industry shipments.

Greenfield entry and closedown exit then have a significant cumulative impact when measured over a decade. Firms may start small and many may die during the maturation process, but the effect of successive cohorts cumulates to meaningful levels. Entry cannot be dismissed as being quantitatively unimportant, as some previous studies have done.

Acquisition entry and divestiture exit

Greenfield entry and closedown exit is the process that renews the firm population in the most direct sense. Resources are also transferred as a result of changes in control. When firms acquire control of plants in a new industry, entry occurs. It is not entry that, initially at least, creates new capacity. It is entry that leads to a change in the identity of a firm's controlling interests.

Important similarities between the two processes that generate entry and exit are outlined in this study. Like greenfield entry and closedown exit, acquisition entry and exit due to divestiture is relatively small when measured on an annual basis – averaging about 1 per cent per year when calculated in terms of the proportion of employment affected. Acquisition entrants follow a similar life cycle to greenfield entrants. Almost the same percentage of births in each category results in subsequent exits. Finally, the effect of successive cohorts of acquisition entrants also cumulates over time until it reaches economically significant levels after a decade. Establishments that were acquired by entrants to a four-digit industry between 1970 and 1979 account for 11.8 per cent of shipments in 1979, on average; establishments that were divested over the same period by exiting firms account for some 11.8 per cent of 1970 shipments, on average.

Although there are similarities between the two turnover processes, there are also important differences. The acquisition and divestiture process is more volatile than greenfield entry and exit. Whereas a cohort of greenfield entrants steadily gains market share over the decade considered here, a cohort of acquisition entrants gains market share only in the short run and then begins to decline. Greenfield entry and exit affect the small end of the firm-size distribution; acquisition entry and exit affect larger firms. Greenfield entry and exit is less in concentrated industries; acquisition entry and exit is greater in concentrated industries.

These differences suggest that the two processes are substitutes. The market for corporate control in concentrated industries leads to take-overs for large firms that are not living up to their potential. It is here that acquisition and divestiture are the primary form through which renewal occurs. In less concentrated industries, new ideas and production processes are more likely to be introduced via greenfield entrants. In small firms, decline is more likely to lead to exit than to take-over.

The lesson to be learned is that mergers provide an important source of turnover that brings new participants into an industry. Any evaluation of the importance of entry must consider the effect of entry via acquisition. Otherwise, an important component of the entry process will have been ignored. It is the joint effect of the two processes that has to be considered in evaluating the intensity of entry.

Over the decade of the 1970s, the cumulative effect of merger entry is just about the same as for greenfield entry. What is equally important, acquisition entry brings new participants into parts of the firm-size distribution and into industries where greenfield entry is less extensive. The quantitative importance of acquisition entry emphasizes the importance of the market for corporate control.

Change in the incumbent-firm population

In contrast to entry and exit, turnover in the continuing or incumbent sector appears large when measured on an annual basis. Annual employment rates of change in the incumbent-plant population average some 7 per cent between 1970 and 1982 – for both firms that grow and those that decline.

This is considerably more than either of the entry rates or exit rates. But much of the annual change in the incumbent population is ephemeral, the result of short-run transitory effects. The annualized long-run rates of change of those firms that grow between 1970 and 1979 average less than 2 per cent; for those that decline, 1 per cent.

Despite this difference between the volatility of incumbent firms in the short and long run, cumulative long-run change in the incumbent population is significant. Over 35 per cent of all firms existing in 1970 decline in absolute terms between 1970 and 1979. In 1970, these firms are on average some 50 per cent larger than those about to grow over the same period. The amount of growth and decline in each sector is large enough to change the relative size of the average firm in the two groups by 1981.

Substantial evidence shows that large firms generally decline and small firms grow. A comparison of the market share of a firm in 1979 to its share in 1970 reveals a regression-to-the-mean phenomenon. There is a continuous growth and decline process taking place that results in small firms displacing large firms.

Turnover is not confined to the smallest firms in an industry, nor are the largest firms immune to change. The three largest firms in an industry, on average, tended to lose almost one-quarter of their market share in the 1970s. It has long been argued that one of the characteristics of a market most relevant to an evaluation of the state of competition is the success of dominant firms in protecting their position (Gort, 1963). On average, the largest firms in an industry are already in decline because of the inexorable process that replaces the old with the new. Moreover, possessing a dominant position did not appear to protect firms. Across industries, the rate of decline in market share was not related to the size of the largest firm.

Differences between the dynamics of small and large firms were also examined. On average, small firms experienced more turnover than larger firms, but the differences are not large. Moreover, much of the difference results from a tendency of larger firms to experience less market-share gain, especially in industries where the largest firm possessed most of the market. The tendency to lose market share shows less differential across size-classes. Greater stability in the large-firm class is thus related more to this limiting effect due to their already large size than to their greater ability to control their environment.

This evidence points to the relevance of biological or evolutionary models that focus on growth and decline as opposed to models that presume the existence of a world of behemoths who have little to fear from competition.

Total turnover

Total change in this study is measured by the extent to which market share is transferred from exiting and declining plant to growing and entering plant. Greenfield entry and closedown exit lead to some 20 per cent of market share being transferred from losers to gainers over a decade. About the same market share – some 17 percentage points – is transferred as continuing firms change relative position. The total share being shifted is some 36 percentage points. If entry and exit due to acquisition entry and exit by divestiture are added, almost 44 per cent of market share is shifted to the successful from the unsuccessful.

While each of the turnover processes examined – greenfield entry and closedown exit, acquisition entry and divestiture exit, and continuing-plant turnover – is respectable by itself, it is the joint effect of the three that is striking. Taken together, the combined size of the three processes testifies to the intensity of competition.

Implications for market performance

The importance of turnover is evaluated in this study not just on the basis of its size, but also by its effect on industry performance.

Traditional approaches in industrial organization have relied upon profitability to measure performance and have estimated the extent to which market structure is related to profitability. These studies have two shortcomings. First, market structure is an imperfect proxy for the intensity of competition. Second, by relying on industry level rather than micro-data, existing studies have not been able to rule out the possibility that the relationship between profitability and concentration is the result of the superior efficiency of the largest firms.

These deficiencies are met here in two ways. First, micro-data are used to evaluate the performance of the plants that fall into different turnover categories. Second, several effects of turnover are investigated. The study first examines the effect of turnover on productivity and then investigates the extent to which turnover increases technical efficiency in an industry. The amount of technical efficiency depends on the dispersion of firm performance within an industry. It is a natural metric for the evaluation of turnover – a phenomenon deeply rooted in the notion of firm heterogeneity. Finally, the study examines the relationship between industry profitability and firm turnover.

Contribution to productivity

Most studies of productivity growth treat progress as manna from heaven. The role of competition is ignored. This study shows that intra-industry dynamics makes an important contribution to economic progress. Births are considerably more productive than deaths. Incumbent plants that gain market share become much more productive than those losing market share. Because of this, a large proportion of productivity growth in the 1970s is due to plant turnover. Greenfield entry contributes about 20 per cent of the total; continuing-firm plant births, about 7 per cent; and the replacement process within continuing plants, some 21 per cent. The world is not one where most firms make equal gains at the margin. Technical progress is not a disembodied phenomenon that can be studied as a simple matter of capital accumulation. Gains in productivity are associated with substantial shifts in market share.

This reinforces the admonition of those who have argued that a population of dynamic firms is the key to industrial success and that performance should be measured in terms of progress – not the static concept of inter-industry profitability differentials. The evidence developed in the Canadian studies demonstrates the linkage between turnover and progress. It also shows that adjustment does not occur in this world because a small number of workers are being made redundant at the margin in a large number of firms, as most firms adopt new techniques. Adjustment is required because a substantial number of jobs are being lost in firms that are either declining or exiting, while others are being gained in more successful firms. Adjustment problems arise because of the great heterogeneity in the response of different firms to exogenous events.

Relationship to technical efficiency

One of the few strands of empirical industrial economics to interest itself in firm heterogeneity is the X-efficiency literature. Economists like Leibenstein (1966) argue that the divergences in productivity or efficiency across firms are worthy of study. Recent work by Caves and Barton (1990) produces estimates of efficiency – the ratio of actual to potential output – and investigates which industry characteristics are related to efficiency.

This literature has not been able to show that these industry characteristics are also related to the process that generates inefficiency. This study, therefore, focuses on the extent to which turnover increases efficiency and whether the determinants of turnover are related to the same characteristics that are found to influence inter-industry differences in efficiency.

Each of greenfield entry and closedown exit, plant birth and death of continuing firms, and the displacement of declining plants with growing plants are shown to contribute significantly to improvements in industry efficiency. Of the gains that could be attributed to turnover, the proportion contributed by each of these sources is 34, 15, and 51 per cent, respectively. The intensity of competition, therefore, not only has a beneficial effect on average productivity; it also helps to bring more firms closer to the production frontier.

More importantly, turnover is shown to be related to the type of industry characteristics that are correlated with efficiency. Factors like advertising and import intensity, which have a negative effect on the level of industry efficiency, also have a negative effect on turnover.

Relationship to inter-industry patterns in profitability

The traditional literature uses profitability as a measure of performance and relates it to concentration. Traditionally, cross-industry differences in profitability provide the focus of these studies.

This approach relates the state of performance at a point in time to the state of competition as measured by the firm-size distribution at the same point in time. Because industry dynamics rather than statics is the focus of this study, the relationship between profitability and various dimensions of mobility is explored here. The extent to which profits regressed toward the mean between 1970 and 1979 is examined first. A strong regression to the mean is discovered. Despite this tendency, the study finds differences in profitability across industries that do not disappear over time. Therefore, the various components of the mobility measures are used to explain differences in these long-run profit levels. Long-run profitability is found to be lower where entry exceeds exit, thereby confirming the importance of net entry. On the other hand, profitability is higher in industries where the sum of greenfield entry and closedown exit is higher. Other measures of total turnover are also positively related to turnover. Once more, this emphasizes the need to utilize several measures of intra-industry change.

Concentration and firm turnover

Measures of firm turnover provide a rich description of the intensity of the competitive process. This is a sufficient reason for preferring these measures in addition to or in place of concentration statistics. Nevertheless, it is important to investigate the relationship between concentration and turnover since concentration measures are still all that are available to some researchers and continue to be used as guides for anti-trust work. Three findings suggest that concentration measures, when used alone, may produce misleading results.

First, while the concentration measure does not change much on average, there is considerable intra-industry change. Concentration measures thereby suggest stability; in reality, there is considerable underlying turmoil in an industry as firms shift relative position. Second, the concentration measure is not highly correlated with an important group of mobility measures. There are a number of different dimensions of intra-industry change. Inter alia, these dimensions include the extent to which firms change ranks, larger firms regress toward the mean, entry and exit is important, and whether much market share is redistributed among continuing firms. Turnover from entry and exit is most closely related to concentration; turnover in the continuing-firm sector is much less closely tied to concentration. Third, use of the concentration measure to choose a top quartile of industries most deserving of anti-trust attention does not yield the same list as would many of the mobility measures. These three findings suggest that concentration and mobility statistics provide separate information on aspects of competitiveness and need to be jointly employed in empirical analysis.

The study also asks how concentration statistics, along with mobility statistics, can be used to improve our knowledge of industry dynamics. To do so, we examine the relationship between concentration and mobility using an entirely different perspective. Rather than using concentration to predict mobility, we reverse the question and ask whether concentration could be better understood once mobility is known. Ijiri and Simon (1977) have argued that the distribution of firm size is determined by the type of stochastic process governing the growth and decline of firms. If so, concentration should be partially explained by mobility. This is the case for Canada. Along with measures of plant and firm scale, mobility is found to affect concentration. If the nature of intra-industry competition affects the size distribution, it is important to have measures of the former. It also suggests that the effect of behaviour, as manifested by firm turnover, on structure is significant. This confirms the desirability of treating structure as endogenous.

The merger process

The effect of mergers is a controversial topic. Many studies of the effect of mergers have been performed. Some use financial data. Others use stock-market data. As both Caves (1987) and Scherer (1988) note, the two sources differ in their evaluation of the success of U.S. mergers. This is also the case for Canada. Studies by the Royal Commission on Corporate Concentration (1978) find that mergers are not very successful. On the other hand, stock-market event studies done by Eckbo (1986) find the opposite result.

In order to resolve this conflict, the performance of the plants that underwent a change in control is examined. The industry share of these plants, their wage rates, their labour productivity, and their price–cost margins before and after the merger are compared. Both short-run and long-run effects are compared so as to distinguish between impacts that are immediate as opposed to those that are longer lasting.

The evidence for Canada suggests that, on average, mergers are not failures. While Mueller (1985) finds that mergers in the United States lose considerable market share, there is no evidence of this in Canada. When the natural regression-to-the-mean process is taken into account, market share is generally not lost in plants that undergo mergers. In the short run, plants that are taken over by entrants to the market experience an increase in market share. In the long run, there are few market-share effects. The evidence shows that this result differs by merger type. Related mergers, where the divesting party leaves the industry, are characterized by post-merger increases in market share.

Productivity effects also differ in the short and the long run. The productivity of plants acquired by entrants is slightly below the mean at the time of acquisition; it experiences a short-run increase in the period after merger. In the long run, there is some evidence of a sustained increase for related but not for unrelated mergers.

The clearest effect of mergers is on price–cost margins. In the case of both related and unrelated mergers, the plant's price–cost margin is not significantly different from the average price–cost margin of other plants in the same industry prior to the merger: it is afterward. Together, the results suggest that, although unrelated mergers have less of an effect on productivity, they increase profitability on average.

A considerable difference in the effects of mergers in different industries is discovered. Benefits are concentrated mainly in high-technology and product-differentiated industries. These are also the industries where foreign ownership is highest. However, the productivity-enhancing effect in these industries is the same for both domestic and foreign acquiring firms. It is the industry environment rather than the nationality of the acquirer that is the primary determinant of a merger's effect.

Together, the results on productivity and profitability indicate that mergers do not simply involve a meaningless churning of ownership. They contribute to real performance improvements, in terms of either plant productivity or profitability gains.

Greenfield entrants also bring new resources into an industry. Mergers bring in new actors. Both renew an industry, but in different ways. Greenfield entry has a particularly strong effect on productivity and efficiency. However, the impact of greenfield entry emerges only in the long run, and studies that focus on the short run will underestimate the impact of entry. The new-born require time to reach adolescence and begin to make a substantial contribution only when they become young adults.

Merger entry has greater short-run effects because it is used essentially to rescue a mature firm that has temporarily gone astray. The long-run effects are less because there is less room for improvement for an adult that has already proved its mettle. Improvement comes here from returning slightly subnormal performance to the mean. Nevertheless, it has a substantial overall effect because the affected businesses are large.

International comparisons

This section compares the dynamics of the market process in Canada to that of other countries. Some aspects of turnover will be similar in different countries because they stem from common forces that are so powerful they overcome inter-country differences; other aspects of turnover will differ because they are more dependent upon specific characteristics of national economies.

An international comparison is important; but a proper and exhaustive comparison requires as painstaking a measurement effort as has been undertaken here for Canada. Without that, a comparison of the results reported here for Canada with studies done for other countries is difficult. Definitions (i.e., for entry and exit), time periods, and the accuracy of databases differ across studies. Moreover, it is hard to find single sources for any one country that cover as many aspects of the turnover process as are examined here. Thus, comparisons of different aspects of market dynamics will involve different degrees of comparability. A detailed comparison must, therefore, remain the subject of another study.

Nevertheless, some of the topics covered here are dealt with elsewhere with data that are sufficiently comparable to the Canadian that comparisons are warranted. In what follows, we concentrate on drawing parallels to these studies. On the one hand, this involves attempting to generalize certain facts about the dynamics of markets. We also briefly discuss how these results fit into several themes found in industrial economics.

Entry

Entry and exit studies have begun to emerge in different countries (see Geroski and Schwalbach, 1991; Geroski, 1991). It is extremely difficult to evaluate the accuracy of most of the data used in these studies and, therefore, to compare the magnitude and relative importance of the entry process. Such a comparison requires the type of carefully constructed data provided in Chapter 6 of this study for the Canada–United States comparison. Despite these shortcomings, some robust common patterns emerge.

The general conclusion that flows from a perusal of international studies is that the number of entrants in any year is large relative to the existing stock; they are generally small and, therefore, capture only a small portion of output; they have high failure rates, but over time, they cumulate to gain a significant portion of many markets. Our finding that entry and exit are relatively unimportant in the short run, particularly when measured by employment or shipments affected, is consistent with European job-change studies (Johnson, 1986), with European entry studies (Geroski and Schwalbach, 1991; Boeri and Cramer, 1992), and with those for the United States (Davis and Haltiwanger, 1990, 1992). The high infant mortality rate is consistent with results for the United States (Churchill, 1955; Dunne, Roberts, and Samuelson, 1989) and for the United Kingdom reported in Geroski (1991). That exits are not confined to just recent entrants, but also occur among older, more established firms, is a result found in studies of business failures (Altman, 1983; Hudson, 1989). That an entry cohort initially gains market share, despite the high mortality rates of young entrants, implies that survivors grow faster than incumbents. This is consistent with Evans' (1987) and Dunne, Roberts, and Samuelson's (1989) finding that older firms tend to grow more slowly than younger firms. Finally, the substantial cumulative effect of entry measured over 5- or 10-year periods agrees with the results of Dunne, Roberts, and Samuelson (1988) for the United States.

Entry can be treated either as an error-correcting mechanism or as a dynamic evolutionary process. In the first case, entry serves to correct short-run disequilibria that may result in higher than normal profits. In the second case, entry is part of the process that involves the introduction of new products and processes to consumers. Most of the emphasis in the applied entry literature has been on the former. The evidence adduced here suggests that the entry serves both functions but that the error-correcting mechanism is the weaker of the two. Entry does respond to higher profitability, but the relationship was only isolated after a diligent search. Higher entry is related to reduced levels of profitability. More dynamic is the relationship of entry to growth. It is also part of the stochastic-replacement process that turns the existing population over. Entry serves to increase productivity. It boosts efficiency. It is part of the dynamic process that serves to renew industries and to facilitate technical progress and innovation. But it is only part of that process, and there are other important aspects to turnover.

Total turnover

In contrast to the interest in entry, comprehensive studies of total turnover from both entry and exit, growth and decline have received less attention from economists. Gort's (1963) earlier work was for a period shortly after the Second World War and is probably not directly comparable to our results for the seventies. Davies' (1991) study of the United Kingdom did not have plant-based data and had to work from public sources for data on total company sales. Firm data are notoriously difficult to assign to specific industries because firms span more than one industry.

Fortunately, there are many studies emanating from another literature – the job-change literature – that examine the importance of the employment growth and decline in firms and plants (Birch, 1987; Commission of European Communities, 1987; Leonard, 1987; Boeri and Cramer, 1992). These studies demonstrate that there are growing firms even in declining industries. Most employment change in the short run occurs because of employment changes in incumbent firms and not from entrants. Incumbent firms reverse their trajectory in the short run. Firms that grow fastest in one period have the greatest possibility of decline in the next. In the longer run, the importance of entry increases relative to the importance of change in the continuing-firm sector. These are some of the same patterns that have been demonstrated in this study.

The most important similarities, however, are to be found in the Canada–United States comparison, which was specially prepared for this study. The forces at work in Canada and the United States that lead to firm growth and decline produce similar results on a cross-sectional basis though job-change rates move in slightly different ways over time in response to differences in the business cycle.

This study also sheds light on the nature of the stochastic process at work in firm growth and decline. Growth in the incumbent population does not follow a strict Gibrat's process. Contrary to the results from Singh and Whittington (1975) for the United Kingdom, Canadian firms – at least large firms – exhibit a tendency to regress toward the mean. This is similar to the results reported by Hall (1987) for the United States.

Mergers

Mergers are examined in this study since they are one form of turnover, and a study of industry dynamics would be incomplete without their inclusion.

Mergers were found to have had a beneficial effect in Canada. Contrary to the case with entry, there are fewer studies in other countries that find the same positive results. Our results do, however, accord with Lichtenberg (1992) for the United States, who uses a similar set of administrative data derived from the U.S. Census of Manufactures. Our results do not concur with those of Ravenscraft and Scherer (1987) or with the international studies reported in Mueller (1980).

Therefore, there appears to be more cross-country differences for the merger results described herein than for the entry and turnover studies. It may be that the effect of mergers varies over time and across countries more than does the entry process. For instance, it might be argued that the diversifying mergers in the 1950–74 period covered in the Ravenscraft and Scherer work were generally inefficient while those in the later period covered by Lichtenberg had positive effects either because they were unravelling previous damage or because they were less oriented toward conglomerate activity. The Canadian mergers of the 1970s would then simply be interpreted as following the somewhat more beneficial pattern that develops in the United States by the 1970s. Indeed this explanation accords with Eckbo's (1986a) observations that his own results, which are based on stock-market data, are generally more favourable than comparable studies done for the United States.

Cross-country differences in merger effects may also result either from differences in the national economies or from the type of competition legislation in effect. During the 1970s, there was a considerable difference between the policy environment for mergers in Canada and the United States. On the one hand, Canadian competition legislation offered few restrictions compared to U.S. anti-trust policy. On the other hand, foreign investment legislation in Canada placed restrictions on foreign take-overs. Despite this difference, merger studies in Canada and the United States that use Census of Manufactures records show remarkable similarities. Moreover, in Canada, the greatest benefits associated with mergers are found in industries where foreign ownership is high and take-overs were most constrained by administrative restrictions. The tentative conclusion must be that the economic forces driving mergers are sufficiently strong to overcome these legislative differences.

It should be noted that the differences between the positive results found here as well as those in the Lichtenberg studies and the negative results found in many other case studies (e.g., Mueller, 1980) are related to at least three factors – the level at which the data are collected, the sample size, and the time horizon being used.

First, studies based on census data using establishment data have less difficulty in isolating the impact of a merger than do merger studies that compare two firms over time. Firms continuously remake themselves. Following a merger, some of the acquired plants are kept, some are sold yet again to others. Use of Census of Manufactures plant-based data allows a good part of these problems to be overcome in that the performance of those plants that are purchased and kept can be compared over time. Similarly, one can follow the plants that were originally owned by the acquirer over time. These plants can be grouped at the four-digit industry level, and thus the performance of different segments of acquired firms can be examined.

Second, even in the Canadian sample, many mergers have negative effects and the average effect is small. These differences are found to be statistically significant because of the large sample size that is being used.

Third, the effect attributed to mergers can be dependent on the period chosen for study. Mergers are only one event in the life of a firm. The effect of mergers is easiest to discern in the short run as existing plants whose productivity has declined experience a control change to redress deficiencies that have developed. This study has shown that, on average, there is a turnaround after a change in control. But other events – such as the natural regression to the mean – quickly superimpose themselves on the performance of merged firms.

There is one area in which the results here strongly parallel those found elsewhere. Previous studies for both Canada (Lecraw, 1977; Royal Commission on Corporate Concentration, 1978) and the United States (Ravenscraft and Scherer, 1987) have emphasized that related mergers are more likely to be successful than unrelated mergers. This study confirms this result. It also finds that diversification across industries – primarily unrelated diversification – reduces industry efficiency. On both counts, then, unrelated diversification is likely to have more negative than positive results.

This study has also made a first step in identifying areas in which mergers have the greatest beneficial impact. Mergers are more successful when they involve the transfer of intangible knowledge-based assets. It is precisely in those industries where there is greater synergy in asset use because of the intangible qualities of assets that are not readily transferred in arm's-length transactions and that require internalization where mergers have the greatest beneficial effects.

Efficiency

The preceding sections have outlined the considerable similarities between Canada and the United States with respect to the patterns of entry, exit, and turnover, as well as the effect of mergers. There are also similarities in terms of the factors associated with industry efficiency.

Technical efficiency in the United States has been found to be a function of competitive conditions such as concentration and the openness to trade, product differentiation characteristics, centrifugal forces leading to firm diversification across industries, and organizational issues that place pressure on management – the extent of diversification, multi-plant operations, unionization, and firm size (Caves and Barton, 1990). These results are confirmed here for Canada.

Efficiency changes are related to rapid shifts in the technological environment that produce new leaders and that gradually shift market share to these firms. As was the case with the United States (Caves and Barton, 1990), temporary spurts in productivity in Canada also lead to reductions in efficiency. Thus, leaders in productive efficiency may emerge quickly, but their acquisition of market share is sufficiently slow to produce overall efficiency losses at the industry level in the short run.

The study then confirms a process that has been found to be at work elsewhere; but it provides a new insight into the connection between turnover and efficiency. It shows that turnover increases the level of efficiency. Entrants are closer to the production frontier than the firms that they replace. The same industry characteristics are related to both efficiency and turnover. Thus, competitive conditions impede turnover, which in turn increases efficiency, thereby explaining the connection between competitive conditions and efficiency levels.

Profitability and firm turnover

The extent to which inter-industry differentials in profitability develop and persist have been the focus of several international studies (Connolly and Schwartz, 1985; Mueller, 1986, 1990; and Schohl, 1990). This research has found that profitability differences between firms do not disappear completely, though firm profits when disturbed from their long-run values return to these levels fairly quickly. Levy (1987) reports similar findings using U.S. industry-level data.

Some of these results are confirmed here for Canada. Much of the industry-profitability differences found in any one year tend to disappear within five years. However, there is still a difference in the long-run average profits across industries. Individual industries regress toward their own mean fairly quickly. These results are robust to the use of alternative measures of profitability.

New insights into the causes of the profitability differences are provided here by the analysis that relates profits to firm turnover. If turnover captures important aspects of competition and competition affects inter-industry profit differentials, these differentials should be associated with differences in turnover. This is the case. Lower profits are associated with greater net entry (gross entry minus exit), greater turnover in the incumbent population, and greater entry due to acquisition. These findings confirm that the measured profit differentials are probably not just the result of measurement problems and that turnover measures capture an important aspect of competitiveness.

Heterogeneity among firm populations

Our research provides several insights into the importance of heterogeneity. It emphasizes that markets are complex phenomena in which various forces – entry and exit, merger activity, incumbent growth and decline – are at work.

The effect of these separate forces is not felt equally in every industry. The intensity of the alternative forms of entry and exit are quite different in the large- and small-firm segments of an industry. Greenfield entry occurs more frequently in the small-firm segment of an industry. The primary source of new firms in the large-firm segment of an industry is merger entry.

This difference also extends across industries. Industries with higher levels of concentration have lower rates of greenfield entry but more entry due to control changes.

The pattern of replacement that occurs as firms vie for market share within an industry also suggests the existence of dichotomous groups that interact only at the margin. Greenfield entrants take market share away mainly from exiting firms. Growing incumbents mainly gain from incumbent firms in decline. An examination of differences between large- and small-firm turnover also confirms heterogeneity across size-classes that Newman (1978) stressed for the United States. The correlation of incumbent market-share change between large and small firms in an industry is not significant. This is suggestive of the type of mobility barriers studied by Caves and Porter (1977) for the United States.

There are also differences between domestic and foreign firms. The method of entry differs for these two groups. Much though not all of the difference is attributed to the industries in which they operate. Foreign firms tend to enter more commonly by means of plant acquisition than by construction of plant. In the case of plant acquisition, foreign acquisitions have a greater effect on productivity than do domestic acquisitions.

The internalization theory of multinational enterprise

The internalization theory of the multinational enterprise is given considerable support in this study. This theory posits that a reason for international investment is the existence of lumpy or intangible assets that can be used simultaneously in more than one market.

Previous studies of this hypothesis have tested whether the presence of multinationals occurs in industries with the specific proprietary rights that are posited to give foreign affiliates an advantage (see Dunning, 1992: 69–72, 160–64). Studies for Canada have found knowledge capital as expressed by research and development expenditures and professional employees in the total work-force, marketing expertise as represented by advertising-to-sales ratios, and coordination expertise from multi-plant activity to be related to the presence of multinationals in Canada (Caves, 1974; Caves et al., 1980).

The internalization theory of multinational enterprises was tested here jointly with a specific hypothesis about the market for corporate control. If mergers are an efficient way to deploy corporate resources and multinational presence serves primarily to extract gains from intangible assets that are not easily transferrable in arm's-length transactions, then we should expect mergers involving multinationals to experience especially large beneficial effects. This is the case. Foreign take-overs lead to increases in market share and relative productivity that are greater in sectors where intangible scientific and marketing expertise is highest. But productivity gains for foreign take-overs are not restricted just to these sectors. In other sectors, the gains are positive and greater than for domestic transfers. This supports the hypothesis that most control changes affecting multinational firms involve the transfer of specialized assets.

Technological change, innovation, and market structure

Cohen and Levin (1989) have noted the perceptible movement of research in industrial economics away from a concern with firm size and market structure toward consideration of the determinants of technical change in an industry. Phillips (1956, 1966, 1971) focuses on the relationship between the underlying science base and the intensity of product change and turnover of firms in an industry. Mansfield et al. (1977) emphasize the importance of entry in contributing to technological change. Acs and Audretsch (1990) emphasize the innovative capabilities of firms and how they differ between the small and large segment of each industry (see Baldwin and Scott, 1987).

While not directly focusing on technical change, this book contains much that is relevant to this issue. Schumpeter (1942) stressed the importance of "creative destruction" in the context of progress. Technical change and product innovation are behind the various aspects of turnover that are examined herein – of entry and exit, of growth and decline in incumbents, of take-overs that are used to exploit the emergence of new intangible assets that have resulted from knowledge creation.

Direct measures are provided here of the relationship between turnover and the technological environment. This study complements work done by Levin (1978) and Levin, Cohen, and Mowery (1985), who emphasize differences in technological opportunities across industries. In keeping with the possibility that there are similar but not identical technological opportunities across industries, the study's model of total turnover uses various measures of technological opportunities and finds that they have a significant effect.

This study also finds that entry is positively related to research and development. Research and development is greatest where new scientific developments are associated with investment in knowledge creation. Greenfield entry is positively related to research and development; the ratio of successful entrants to total entrants is negatively related to research and development. This suggests that certain technological environments foster not only turnover via entry but also increased exits. These industries then are in the phase where new ideas are being brought in by outsiders but where exits are also high (Gort and Klepper, 1982). Support for this hypothesis is found in our study of profit-equilibration process. Industries with higher research and development have higher profits. Industries with higher profits are also those with greater gross turnover as a result of higher entry *and* exit.

The Canada–United States comparisons provide the most compelling evidence that technology is the primary force driving cross-industry differences in turnover. Entry and exit rates at the industry level in the two countries are quite similar. So too is total job turnover, the effect of mergers, and the determinants of industry efficiency. The similarities between the two countries are remarkable in light of the differences between Canada and the United States in market concentration, plant size, openness to trade, and other industry characteristics. Explanations of these similarities are to be found in the common technological base – the production and marketing technologies – of industries in the two countries.

Feedback effects between structure and technological change

Technical change engendered, among other things, by developments in the science and the research and development base of an industry, leads to turnover and changes in market structure. Acs and Audretch's (1990) work stresses that the technology base affects innovation, which in turn determines market structure, and of course, that structure in turn affects the pattern of innovation.

This study confirms the connection between technological change and market structure. It not only provides evidence of a relationship between the technological environment and turnover, but it also establishes the link hypothesized by Simon between turnover and structure. Concentration is related both to the existence of scale economies and to the nature of the stochastic process at work.

Market imperfections

The applied literature that connects structure with performance may have become stale because of a reliance on single-period cross-sectional industry data and because of a dependence upon measures of concentration, but its insights need not be discarded for this reason alone.

This study emphasizes that new more efficient means of organization are brought about through turnover of various forms and that this turnover has beneficial effects on profit equilibration, productivity growth, and reductions in efficiency. But it is also true that change does not bring about an instantaneous transformation in the identity of the most dominant firms in an industry. In the midst of the seas of change, the larger boats appear to be more stable than others. Although the leading firm in an industry on average loses market share over a decade, less than 50 per cent of this group lose their premier ranking. Transition matrices show that movement across size-classes takes more than a decade on average for the larger firms. Moreover, inter- and intra-industry structural traits affect the speed and type of turnover bringing about the change. In industries with higher concentration, firms take longer to make the transition from one size-class to another, because market shares are skewed much more in these industries.

The chapter that models entry demonstrates that structural characteristics like concentration and scale economies are associated with fewer greenfield entrants. This is a common finding in other entry studies (Dunne and Roberts, 1991). However, we also note that concentration has a lesser impact on the share of new firms because concentration does not affect the average size of an entrant. We also find that although concentration and greenfield entry are negatively related, this is not the case for concentration and entry by acquisition. Indeed when both forms of entry are added together, the negative relationship between entry and concentration virtually disappears. Finally, although less net greenfield entry results in higher profits, the industries with less greenfield entry have higher acquisition entry rates, and acquisition entry rates are negatively related to profitability.

While concentration and entry are related, concentration and incumbent-firm turnover are not strongly associated. Shifts in market share in the incumbent population are not restricted by the relative size of the largest firms. This result is occasioned primarily by the fact that small-firm changes are unrelated to concentration. Large-firm changes are negatively related to concentration. Thus, the traditional measure of market structure that was devised to infer the intensity of competition among the largest firms is related to the internal dynamics of these firms, but not to the amount of turnover in smaller firms. This also provides additional evidence of heterogeneity between large and small firms.

Evidence on the relationship between the standard structural measures and performance measures is also produced by this study. Industry efficiency is negatively related to concentration and so is the total turnover that contributes to improving efficiency. Profitability differences are related not only to several turnover measures but also to concentration. While turnover measures were clearly shown to have a strong effect on each of these turnover measures, concentration captured an additional dimension that came through clearly in each area of performance. Concentration and turnover measures complement one another.

APPENDIX A: MEASURING FIRM TURNOVER –
METHODOLOGY

The study of firm turnover requires longitudinal databases that measure firm performance over time. These databases need to be comprehensive and reliable. Databases that are constructed only from the records of those companies that wish to be placed on files used for credit-rating purposes – like the Dun and Bradstreet records used by Birch (1979, 1981) and the U.S. Small Business Administration (1984) – are incomplete (see Johnson and Storey, 1985). Other databases, like the ones constructed by Storey (1985) and his colleagues in the United Kingdom, are built from different sources, none of which purports to be a complete census.

Problems can also arise with longitudinal databases if coverage is not current or if it changes over time because of a lag in adding new firms to a database or in purging it of firms that have exited. Sudden bursts of activity to catch existing firms that may have been overlooked or to purge the files of defunct producers can distort measured entry and exit.

Measuring entry and exit with the Canadian Census of Manufactures overcomes these problems in large part. First, these data are comprehensive in that they cover all firms in the manufacturing sector. Second, they are reliable. Third, they are timely, since the Canadian census is done annually. An effective method of finding new plants and firms exists – through the use of administrative tax files. Moreover, failure of a previously existing producer to file a census return is followed up by trained personnel to ascertain the status of the firm or plant.

Canadian Census of Manufactures data then provide the foundation for the databases used in this study; but, before turnover can be measured, the yearly census data have to be turned into longitudinal panel data. Constructing a longitudinal panel from data that were not originally collected with this objective in mind is complicated. This appendix describes the methodology that was employed to build such longitudinal panels for this study. It outlines the difficulties that arose and the choices that were made to resolve these difficulties.

Entry and exit involve the emergence of new producing units and the disappearance of old units. "New" and "old" can be defined in various ways. As a result, it is necessary to specify carefully the concepts being measured and the methods being used.

Several issues must be addressed. First, the type of study for which the entry and exit measures are going to be used needs to be specified. Measures that are useful for one type of study are not necessarily useful for another. Second, broad conceptual issues need to be resolved, such as what period is to be covered, what types of entry and exit are involved, and what level of industry detail should be provided. Third, problems that arise during the actual measurement process need to be solved. Each of these is discussed in turn.

Relating definitions to objectives

When administrative and survey data are used for purposes that were not originally envisaged, care must be taken. This is especially true when the appearance and disappearance of identification codes in these databases are used to define births and deaths. Identification codes can appear and disappear for a number of reasons, and it is possible that none satisfy the particular definition of entry and exit that the researcher has in mind.

There are many ways of defining a birth or death, since a firm is not defined by a single dimension but by a vector of characteristics. These include such variables as industry, ownership, country of control, size, company name, and the location and number of plants. The multi-dimensional nature of the firm would be unimportant if only one of these characteristics were required for defining births and deaths, or if all changed simultaneously. Neither is the case.

Different studies of the competitive process need different definitions of birth and death. If research is directed solely at the effect of new-firm creation on competition, then births should be defined as the creation of new entities. But new entities include both entry through greenfield plant construction (a category that depends upon the plant-status variable) and entry by acquisition of existing plants (a category that depends upon the ownership-status variable). The two forms of birth should be distinguished because they may have different effects on performance.

The wide range of interpretations that can be placed on the notion of entry and exit means that it is difficult to produce a single estimate that satisfies more than one purpose. Therefore, several databases were constructed for this study.

Conceptual issues

In creating the databases to measure turnover, decisions had to be taken on issues such as the appropriate level of industry aggregation, the production unit to be used, the time period selected for measurement, and the entry and exit categories to be employed.

The study employs a set of measures that look at the long and the short run, and measure entry to the manufacturing sector as a whole and to sub-sectors. One database uses annual data and defines entry and exit at an aggregate level – the manufacturing sector. The other database uses a longer period, defines entry at the four-digit industry level, and provides much more detail on the type of turnover.

The databases

The longer-run, four-digit-industry database

The first database measures longer-run entry and exit by comparing the status of production units in 1970 and 1979. It provides detail on both establishment and firm status and links the two. Therefore, it can be used to estimate plant and firm entry and exit. It also allows continuing-firm plant turnover to be measured so as to provide a standard of comparison for entering and exiting firms. It measures activity at a detailed four-digit SIC level.

A plant birth is defined as the appearance in 1979 of a plant in an industry that was not in that industry in 1970. A plant closure is equated with the 1979 disappearance from a four-digit industry of a plant identifier that had existed in 1970.

A firm entry is defined as the appearance of a firm code in 1979 in a four-digit industry that had not previously been attached to any other plant in the industry in 1970. A firm death occurs when the firm identifier attached to a plant in 1970 was no longer attached to any plant in the particular four-digit industry in 1979.

It should be noted that plants or firms that enter after 1970 and die before 1979 are not captured in the entry or exit measures derived from the long-term database.

Because of the link between the plant (establishment) and enterprise (firm) in the long-run database, it is possible to measure a number of different entry categories. These are summarized in the plant- and firm-status matrix presented in Table 2-1. The importance of the various categories can be measured using the number of establishments, firms, shipments, employment, or any other variable available from the Census of Manufactures.

The annual establishment and enterprise manufacturing databases

The second and third databases track the history of firms and establishments annually from 1970 to 1982. They are used primarily for short-term comparisons. Both define entry and exit at the manufacturing level as a whole. Establishment births are defined as plants that are new to manufacturing. New enterprises are defined in a similar fashion. Plants and firms that transfer from one four-digit manufacturing industry to another are not defined as entrants in these databases. Transfers into the manufacturing sector from other sectors – wholesaling, for instance – are included as entrants.

These databases use a less comprehensive entry and exit classification scheme than was used for the long-run analysis. For the establishment database, establishments are classified into three categories: those that are either newly created, closed, or continuing. In this database, no account is taken of the owning enterprise; therefore, whether the plant was acquired or divested is not considered. The enterprise database uses a more detailed classification scheme. On the entry side, new firms are divided into those that did so by greenfield plant construction as opposed to acquisition; on the exit side, firm deaths are divided into those associated with plant closing and those associated with plant divestiture.

Definitions of establishment and enterprise

In order to comprehend more fully the meaning of the entry and exit measures provided by the three databases, it is necessary to examine the definitions of establishments and enterprises used and to describe more fully the categories employed.

When measuring entry and exit, two basic units of production are identified. These are the establishment or plant, and the enterprise or firm. The terms "establishment" or "plant", and "enterprise" or "firm" are used interchangeably here. These terms need to be carefully defined if the Canadian data are to be compared, both with those from other countries and with other Canadian data sets.

An establishment is defined by Statistics Canada as "usually equivalent to a factory, plant, or mill".[1] This study focuses on establishments that are classified to the manufacturing sector.[2] The establishment is the basic statistical unit from which information is collected for the annual Census of Manufactures.[3]

An enterprise is defined as all establishments in the manufacturing and primary industries under common control. (See, for further details, Statistics Canada, 1979: 17–18; 1983: 23–25.) The concept of the enterprise does not necessarily coincide with the legal entity or what is sometimes referred to as the business or corporate entity.

> There is in fact an intermediate level of organization between the establishment and the enterprise, the legal entity. This is the ownership unit. Legal entities may be incorporated or unincorporated businesses, or individuals. One legal entity may own another legal entity; therefore, it is possible for an enterprise to control more than one legal entity, just as a legal entity may own more than one operating unit – an establishment. (Statistics Canada, 1983: 24)[4]

Since an enterprise is defined as the unit that groups all commonly owned establishments, subunits of an enterprise in a particular two-, three-, or four-digit industry can be created. Thus, firm entry can be measured at the individual-industry level or at the all-manufacturing-sector level.

For the purposes of this study, the finest level of detail (the four-digit level) is selected for the longer-run 1970–79 database. The annual entry and exit rates are measured at the all-manufacturing level.

Dating entry and exit

Each establishment in the Canadian Census of Manufactures is assigned a unique identification number, the record serial number or RSN.[5] This number remains with the establishment as long as it is included in the census (see McVey, 1981: 72). Each enterprise is also assigned a unique identifier – referred to here as the ENT code.[6] Unlike an establishment's RSN, the enterprise code can change when one enterprise purchases another.

A birth of a plant or enterprise is defined as the appearance of a new identifier code. An exit is defined as the disappearance of the code. If the code continues over the period being studied, the plant or firm is defined as continuing. In the short-run database, the status of establishments is compared in consecutive years from 1970 to 1982. In the longer-run database, their status in 1970 is compared with their status in 1979.

Exit and entry are defined first by the status – the continuation, the discontinuation, or the appearance – of the identification code of a plant and second, by the level of activity. Entrants are counted in the first year that the identifier appears and that the employment or value of manufacturing shipments is positive. Exits are defined as occurring in the first year prior to or equal to the disappearance of the identifier when employment in or the value of manufacturing shipments for the firm falls to zero.[7] Using the identification number only, and not taking into account whether production occurs, may cause the date of actual exit (based on production) to be estimated with a lag, since administrative systems and censuses are sometimes slow to purge themselves of defunct producers.

Validation of identifiers

Entry and exit are measured by examining changes in enterprise and establishment identifiers. This section examines the reasons why these identifiers appear and disappear.

The establishment code. Plant entry and exit are defined to occur with the appearance and the disappearance of an establishment code (the RSN). Whether this definition produces meaningful estimates of births and deaths depends upon the practice of the statistical agency in assigning establishment codes.

The closure of an establishment is usually grounds for the retirement of a code; but there may be situations where the old RSN code is dropped and a new one assigned. In these cases, deaths and births will be overestimated.

These situations occur because establishments, like firms, possess several characteristics. These characteristics can change during the lifetime of a plant and cause the administrative-coding system to assign a new plant number, thus giving the false appearance of a death. For instance, if a change in ownership triggers the reassignment of a code, then the death and birth in a database will not correspond to the opening and closing of a plant.

Statistics Canada's rule is to discard codes in the case of a continuing plant and to assign a new one only if the location, ownership, and name of the establishment *all* change simultaneously.[8] This rule precludes counting a change in the ownership or name of the plant as an establishment death.

The validity of the entry measures depends on the diligence with which Statistics Canada followed this rule. Two tests were employed to examine this. The first tested for false deaths. All the cases where a plant-identifier code that existed in 1981 had disappeared by 1985 were examined on the basis of their recorded name, ownership, and location to see if there were new plants for the year 1985 that were similar to the plants that had "died". This type of error would cause an upward bias in the plant birth and death rates. The second tested for the possible failure to record deaths. All plant-identifier codes that existed in 1981 and 1985 were examined to see whether any two were identical whose recorded name, ownership, and location all changed. These plants' 1981 identifier codes should have been changed and new ones assigned by 1985. This type of error would cause a downward bias in the plant death and birth rates. The errors in each case were less than 0.1 per cent and essentially offsetting.

Because of the criteria used to reassign RSN plant identifiers and the care taken by Statistics Canada in following this criteria, the emergence of new-establishment codes and the disappearance of old ones in the Canadian Census of Manufactures generally signifies "real" births and deaths. The ownership and name of a plant can change, but as long as the location does not, there will be no change in the identifier and no false indication of a plant birth and death.[9]

The enterprise code. Enterprise identifiers (ENT codes) can be used to track groups of establishments under common control. All plants in manufacturing, logging, and mining that are owned by the same enterprise are assigned the same ENT code. This code does not correspond with the legal entity, but relates to the concept of an enterprise that was discussed previously.

There are also legal entity (BRID) codes. New values of BRID codes are created and old ones discarded with a change in legal entity – such as an incorporation, an amalgamation, a reorganization of establishments, or a change in ownership. Since the identity of the legal entity changes much more frequently than does that of the enterprise that controls it, the exclusive use of a legal entity (BRID) code can generate "false" births and deaths. Births are considered to be false if they involve only minor changes that fall into neither the entry-by-building-new-plant category nor the entry-by-acquisition category.

In contrast with changes in legal entity (BRID) codes, changes in the ENT codes in the database are meant to reflect only major changes in enterprise organization. The appearance of an ENT code in an industry should signify the entry of an enterprise either by plant birth or by acquisition – where acquisition is broadly defined to include control changes that may not necessarily result in the merger of the facilities of the acquired firm with those of the acquirer. The disappearance of an ENT code should, likewise, signify an enterprise death. As was the case with establishments, the codes of continuing enterprises are not supposed to be retired and new ones assigned without good cause. However, the rules for reallocating the ENT codes of continuing enterprises are not as precisely specified as those for continuing establishments. The events that would have to be included in any definition are more complex. The rule as to name, location, and ownership for a plant identifier change would not suffice.

ENT codes are supposed to change only when a major event takes place in the life of the enterprise. The extent to which this occurs was carefully examined. All situations where the ENT code disappeared and was associated with the disappearance of an RSN were assumed to be valid events, because the validation check on the RSNs confirmed that births and deaths of establishments were correctly recorded. Thus, only continuing plants were checked for possible false changes in their ENT codes.

Continuing plants whose enterprise codes changed were classified into two groups. The first group consisted of those in which the change in the ENT code attached to the plant was associated with a major event that ruled out the possibility that a mere name change had led to the disappearance of the enterprise code. The remainder formed a second group, which was then examined for possible errors.

Three events were defined as sufficiently major to rule out minor organizational or name changes that might have prompted an ENT code to be improperly discarded. The first event was a change in the country of control assigned to a plant in 1970 compared with that of 1979.[10] If country of control changed, then it is reasonable to presume that a major shift in control of the firm has occurred. The second event was finding that either the acquiring firm or the divesting firm continued throughout the decade.[11] In the former case, this meant that the acquiring firm possessed a plant in some four-digit industry in 1970 other than the one in which the acquired plant was located in 1979. In the latter case, this meant that the firm, which exited an industry by divesting itself of plant, could be found in some other industry in 1979. Since in both cases one of the firms is an ongoing entity, changes in the ENT code are unlikely to have been the result of a minor organizational or name change. The third event was the presence of a horizontal merger. This occurred when the firm that entered by acquisition did so by acquiring plants from more than one enterprise. It is unlikely that this could have occurred without there having been a major organizational and control change.

When the major-event criteria were imposed simultaneously on both acquired and divested plants, there were only 8.6 per cent of all acquired/divested plants with about 9.5 per cent of shipments remaining that might *not* have been involved in a significant reorganization. The plants in the residual category were checked manually. Ultimately, 3.4 per cent of the original establishments with 1.6 per cent of employment turned out to have possibly experienced only a minor change in enterprise status like a name change. Reclassification of the group from acquisition and divestiture to continuing would not change the importance of these categories reported in the text.

Implementation problems

The broad conceptual issues of time horizon, industry detail, and the entry and exit categories to be adopted are relatively straightforward to resolve. More difficult are the problems associated with the peculiarities of individual databases that make precise measurement a problem.

In what follows, each of the databases is described in greater detail. Emphasis is given to the way in which measurement problems were resolved.

The long-run database

The long-run database was organized to provide the most detail on entry and exit, which are measured at the four-digit industry level. All the categories in Table 2-1 are used.

The sample. A sample of establishments from the Census of Manufactures was used to evaluate the importance of turnover. An establishment that is surveyed directly by Statistics Canada for the Annual Census of Manufactures may receive either a long form or a short form, which are distinguished as follows:

> The long-form is a fully detailed questionnaire sent to establishments with shipments above minimum sizes which vary by province and by industry and from year to year, designed to capture all but a small percentage of the shipments of the industry. In 1975 long-forms accounted for all but 4.1% of

the value of shipments of goods of own manufacture of the manufacturing industries. The short-form is a simplified, abbreviated questionnaire, bearing a closer resemblance to a typical income statement. It is sent to small manufacturers whose shipments fall below a minimum size. (Statistics Canada, 1979: 10)

Some very small plants do not receive either form. Data regarding them are taken from taxation administrative records in place of mailed questionnaires. In the late 1970s and early 1980s, small establishments accounted for 5 per cent or less of all manufacturing shipments: 2 per cent in 1970, 4.1 per cent in 1975, and 3.4 per cent in 1982 (Statistics Canada, 1979: 44). In 1970 they accounted for 40 per cent of all manufacturing-sector establishments, increasing to 50 and 53.9 per cent in 1975 and 1982, respectively.

The sample primarily used in this study excludes short-form firms[12] and focuses primarily on long-form firms. There are several reasons for focusing on the sample of establishments that filled out the long form. First, it is extremely costly to employ all records for the analysis. Second, it was initially felt that using the entire file might give rise to specious results. The creation and disappearance of short-form establishments may be sensitive to the diligence used in finding these small establishments. This, in turn, can vary year by year depending upon the budget constraints faced by the statistical agency and official concern about the paper burden imposed on smaller firms. Finally, using the long-form sample permits more characteristics of entrants to be measured consistently, because the long-form data contain more detailed information on plants' activities and because certain concepts, such as value-added, are defined differently for long- and short-form establishments (Statistics Canada, 1979: 42).

Since using the Canadian Census of Manufactures offers the advantage of extensive and accurate coverage, it is important to investigate the effect of choosing the long-form sample. The effects of using the long-form sample were evaluated by examining the coverage yielded by this sample and the differences between the rates of entry and exit yielded by the reduced sample and the entire census.

Table A-1 contains the proportions of all four-digit industries for which there were non-zero observations in each of the entry and exit categories. The coverage ratios are presented both for the entire set of establishments in each industry and for the long-form sample alone. It is evident that the choice of the long-form sample does not greatly affect coverage.

Table A-2 contains two estimates of the importance of the various entry categories using both number of establishments and the value of shipments. Table A-3 contains estimates of the importance of the exit categories using the two samples. In each case the first estimate uses the entire set of observations and the second uses the long-form sample. The importance of an entry or exit

Table A-1. *Proportion of industries with non-zero observations for the various entry and exit categories across 167 four-digit manufacturing industries, 1970–79 (per cent)*

	Firm status					
	Continuing		Entrant		Exit	
Plant status	Total sample	Long-form sample	Total sample	Long-form sample	Total sample	Long-form sample
Divested	32.9	32.3	—	—	91.0	91.0
Acquired	52.7	52.7	88.6	88.6	—	—
Born	74.8	73.6	99.4	94.0	—	—
Closed	74.9	74.8	—	—	97.6	96.4
Continuing	100.0	100.0	—	—	—	—

Note: See Table 2-1 for definitions of plant and firm status. All entry and exit categories are measured for the period 1970–79 and do not include plants that transfer from one industry to another.

category is measured relative to the totals for the set used – all observations in the first case, only long-form observations in the second. The estimates presented in Tables A-2 and A-3 are the average of the magnitude of each category taken across 167 four-digit industries.

It is evident that using the long-form sample affects the magnitude of entry and exit when numbers of establishments are used, but it has much less of an effect when shipments are used. Thus, the long-form sample may be employed to measure the shipment values affected by entry and exit without great distortion. This conclusion also applies to other measures of input or output.[13]

Units of measurement. The importance of entry can be measured either in terms of numbers of establishments and enterprises, or their outputs and inputs. Both sets of measures are used here. Entry and exit rates, when calculated using numbers, reveal whether entry and exit is easy; when they are calculated using a measure of output or input size, they reveal whether it is important. Both shipments and total employment (wage and salary earners) are used to measure size. Shipments is the most logical measure of the competitive process because it indicates what share of the market entrants are able to capture. Employment is also used to provide information on the contribution of entry and exit to job turnover.

Employment is derived from the total activity statistics in the census.[14] It

Table A-2. *Importance of categories for entry between 1970 and 1979 using alternative samples calculated as the mean across 167 four-digit industries (per cent)*[a]

Category[b]	Share of number of plants		Share of shipments	
	Total sample	Long-form sample	Total sample	Long-form sample
All entering firms[c]				
Plant birth (23)	36.9	18.8	14.4	11.5
Acquisition (22)	6.5	8.7	10.4	10.7
Plant transfer (26)				
No change in plant ownership	3.5	4.7	3.3	3.5
Change in plant ownership	0.6	0.9	1.0	1.1
All continuing firms				
Continuing establishments (15)	46.8	59.2	63.0	65.0
Acquired plant (12)	1.6	2.2	2.8	3.0
New plant (13)	3.6	4.6	4.2	4.4
Plant transfer (16)	0.5	0.7	0.9	0.9

[a] The mean is taken across all industries, including those that have a value of zero in a particular category.
[b] For definitions of categories, see Table 2-1 and the text.
[c] The importance of an entry category is measured as the number (shipments) of plants owned by firms in a particular category divided by all plants (all shipments) in an industry.

is reported as an annual equivalent. For example, if a plant employs 60 workers per month for six months, this is recorded as 30 person-years. This procedure might produce a downward bias in the estimates of entry and exit; in this example, 60, not 30 people are affected by the exit of the plant. This procedure, in turn, might bias downward calculated rates of entry and exit because, presumably, employment in continuing plants, which is the denominator of this calculation, will not be affected to the same degree by this factor. One approach would be to assume that entrants and exits are distributed uniformly across the year – that they have an average life of half a year. All raw employment figures for entry and exit would then be doubled. (See Statistics Canada, 1988, where this assumption is employed.)

This practice has not been followed here. The assumption is made that there is enough of a reporting lag in the census that employment totals for the first and last reporting year of an establishment are for essentially a full year's

Table A-3. *Importance of categories for exit between 1970 and 1979 using alternative samples calculated as the mean across 167 four-digit industries (per cent)*[a]

Category[b]	Share of number of plants		Share of shipments	
	Total sample	Long-form sample	Total sample	Long-form sample
All exiting firms[c]				
Plant death (34)	32.4	24.6	14.1	13.3
Divestiture (31)	8.5	10.0	12.5	12.7
Transfer (37)				
No change in ownership	3.8	4.3	3.4	3.5
Change in ownership	0.6	0.8	1.3	1.3
All continuing firms				
Continuing establishments (15)	50.6	55.3	62.9	63.4
Divested plant (11)	0.5	0.6	1.1	1.1
Closed plant (14)	3.3	3.8	3.7	3.8
Transfer (17)	0.4	0.5	0.8	0.8

[a] The mean is taken across all 167 industries, including those that have a value of zero in a particular category.
[b] For definition of categories, see Table 2-1 and the text.
[c] The importance of an exit category is measured as the number (shipments) of plants owned by firms in a particular category divided by all plants (all shipments) in an industry.

operation. This hypothesis was tested by examining employment in enterprises that exited, in both the year of exit and the preceding year. The differences were relatively minor and certainly not of an order of magnitude of 100 per cent, which is implied by the doubling rule.

Plant reassignment or transfer as entry. Establishment entry is defined as the appearance in the census records of a new plant that is assigned to a particular industry. A new plant may appear in a particular four-digit industry because it did not exist in the Census of Manufactures or because it existed previously in some other industry but was transferred to a new one.

An establishment is assigned to an industry on the basis of the commodities that it produces. If a plant's commodity output changes, the industry to which it is assigned by the census may change – though this is usually done with a lag in order to ascertain whether the change in output of the plant is permanent. Plants are transferred if they cease to concentrate on products assigned to one industry in favour of those assigned to another.

Transfers are important to studies of competition because they bring new participants into the industry. Since establishment entry and exit can be defined either inclusive or exclusive of plants that have been transferred from one industry to another, and some studies may want to know the size of this component, the magnitude of the plant-transfer category was investigated.

All continuing establishments that were assigned to an SIC code in 1979 that differed from that assigned in 1970 were defined as plant-transfer entrants to, in 1979, and plant-transfer exits from, in 1970, the relevant four-digit SIC industry. Plant transfers were divided into two categories – those attached to entering firms and those attached to continuing firms. In the former case, the plant transfer brought a new firm into an industry. In the latter case, the firm, whose plant was reassigned to a new SIC code, already possessed a plant there. A firm's status – new or continuing – depends on its possession of plant in a particular four-digit industry.

Tables A-2 and A-3 contain estimates of the magnitude of entry and exit through transfers. In Table A-2, the rate of new-firm entry through transfers was 4.6 per cent using shipments and the long-form sample. This rate is not greatly affected by the sample chosen. The rate at which new firms are brought into an industry by plant transfers can be broken into two subcategories. The first category (row 3) consists of plants that did not involve a change in plant ownership (3.5 per cent of total industry shipments). These might be included in the entry-by-new-firm new-plant category. Their shipments are equal to 30 per cent of the new-firm entry-by-plant-building category that does not include transfers (row 1). The second category (row 4) contains those that involved a change in plant ownership (1.1 per cent of total industry shipments using the long-form sample) and that might be included in the entry-by-acquisition category. This group is about 10 per cent of the entry-by-acquisition category that does not include plant switches (row 2).

The result for exits mirrors that for entries. Transfers that do not involve a change in ownership can increase the rate of firm exit by plant closure by 26 per cent.

Plant transfers by continuing firms are also important relative to new-plant creation by continuing firms. They account for 0.9 per cent of 1979 shipments (row 8) compared with de novo plant share for continuing firms of 4.4 per cent (row 7).

In conclusion, transfers cannot be ignored, because they have the potential to substantially affect the calculated long-term entry and exit rate.

Overlap in entry and exit categories. When entry and exit are defined in terms of number of plants, there are few problems of overlap. Plants fall exclusively into one or another category. There is potentially more overlap when the number of firms is used to measure entry. Firms may enter by building new plant, by acquiring new plant, or both. Continuing firms may build new plant, divest plant, and acquire plant. This creates the possibility that the percentages in various categories will not sum to 100.

In order to investigate the extent of this problem, the number of establishments and the number of firms in the various entry categories were estimated.[15] Across 141 four-digit manufacturing industries, an average of 24.6 firms per industry had entered by 1979. Of these, 4.9 entered by acquisition, and 21.7 entered by plant birth. Therefore, of the 24.6 entrants, an average of 2 entered over the period 1970–79 by both acquiring plant and building new plant. An average of 38.3 of the firms existing in 1970 exited over the decade, 7.2 by divestiture and 33.2 by plant death. Thus, of the 38.3 exits, an average of 2.1 exited over the period 1970–79 by both divestiture and death of plant (see Baldwin and Gorecki, 1983: 15, Table A-2).

In the continuing-firm category, which consists of firms that possessed plant in the industry in the initial and terminal years, there were an average of 50.3 firms. There were 49.8 firms owning plants that stayed in the industry over the decade, 1.6 firms that divested plant, and 3.7 that closed plant. The sum of the subcategories (55.1) is about 10 per cent greater than the number of continuing firms (50.3). Roughly the same overlap exists among entries when the number of continuing firms in 1979 is examined.

Measuring entry and exit in the short run

A number of problems had to be resolved when short-run entry into and exit from the manufacturing sector were measured. Two databases were created for this purpose. The first tracks establishments and the second tracks enterprises, annually, through the period 1970–82. The short-run databases measure entry and exit only at a high level of industry aggregation – the manufacturing sector as a whole.

The annual establishment database

The sample. Entry and exit data can be generated using all establishments, or only long-form or only short-form plants. It was decided to use only long-form establishments because, among other reasons, the constantly varying coverage of short-form plants (Statistics Canada, 1979: 12–13) would give rise to specious entry and exit – especially in the measurement of annual rates of entry and exit. In addition, the long-form data closely proxy the results of the total census for the longer run from 1970 to 1979 – at least when entry is measured by the amount of shipments or employment affected.

For the short-run database, using the long-form plants alone as a sample criterion is inadequate. Because the demarcation between short- and long-form plants changes over time, changes in entry and exit would emerge purely as a result of reclassification. This problem was resolved by taking as the longitudinal establishment sample all plants that completed a long form on at least one occasion. An establishment, then, is classified as entering in a particular year because it made its first appearance in that year and either was already a long-form establishment, or became one.

This technique reduces but does not eliminate the problems that shifting boundaries between short- and long-form establishments produce. It essentially smooths out the fluctuations by eliminating the most volatile component – establishments that are just at the boundary. Since the boundary changes are generally small, this is sufficient most of the time. There are two occasions when major changes in census coverage occurred. For these instances, corrections in the estimates of entry and exit were required.

Major revision in long-form plant coverage in 1975. During the early 1970s, Statistics Canada slowly raised the cut-off point between long- and short-form plants (Statistics Canada, 1979: 43–44). But in 1975, the cut-off point was increased dramatically in order to reduce the burden of responding for smaller manufacturers. As a result, the proportion of short-form establishments increased from 36.1 to 50.1 per cent between 1974 and 1975. There was no other increase in the proportion of establishments in the short-form category of a similar magnitude, though the proportion of short-form plants is drifting slowly upward over time. By 1983, it was 54.9 per cent of all establishments, compared with 50.1 per cent in 1975. Over the same period, the percentage of employees in short-form establishments increased slowly from 7.6 to 8.7 per cent.

The modified long-form sample adopted here mitigates the effects of the reclassification of the boundaries between long- and short-form establishments in 1975 on estimates of entry and exit. Those establishments that entered in 1975 using short forms but eventually used long forms – albeit in fewer numbers after 1975 because of the higher cut-off point used to define long-form plants – will still be caught. However, those establishments that would have made the transition from a short to a long form under the pre-1975 definition of a long-form plant, but do not do so under the new definition, will be missed.

That there is some reduction in measured entry because of the 1975 change is evidenced by the increase in the average size of entering establishments that occurred at this time. When the long-form sample is used, entering establishments averaged 20 employees per establishment between 1970–71 to 1972–73, but 28.1 employees per establishment between 1975–76 and 1980–81. The increase in average plant size occurred abruptly at the time of the reclassification of long-form and short-form establishments in 1975.

In order to calculate the effect of the 1975 redefinition on the estimated entry rates, the distribution of entrants in 1973–74 was truncated by removing the smallest entrants until the average size of those remaining was equal to the post-1975 size of the average entrant. On average, this required removing 32.1 per cent of entrants accounting for 4.5 per cent of employees of all entrants. This is the estimate of the percentage reduction in the pre-1975 entry figures required to make them comparable with those calculated for the remainder of the period.[16]

Relying on the long-form sample results in another measurement problem. The coverage of the establishment sample declines over time, reflecting the reliance on long-form firms in this study and their decreasing importance in terms of numbers of establishments. This should not greatly affect the rate of entry and exit when these are calculated as a proportion of the number of firms or establishments at a point in time. The bias will be even less when entry and exit are measured in terms of employment or shipments, because of the relatively small size of the short-form establishments. Nevertheless, annual rates of entry using the long-form sample are calculated only for the period up to 1982. After that year, not enough years are covered by the sample to capture fully the transition of a plant from short-form to long-form status. Therefore, it will increasingly underestimate entry rates.

Variation in census coverage. A problem also arose because there was a major change in the coverage of the Canadian Census of Manufactures. In 1972, Statistics Canada lost a source of administrative information used to identify possible new establishments (Potter, 1982: 21). A decline in coverage occurred that was not rectified until 1978 and, to a lesser extent, 1979.

If left uncorrected, this change would have overreported the amount of entry later in the 1970s and underreported both entry and exit in the mid-1970s. In order to correct it, the number of entrants and the employment associated with them that resulted from the increased coverage were identified and used to correct the entry and exit rates. For the 1978 and 1979 rates the overlap was simply subtracted.

The routine used for correcting previous years was more complicated. Because of the high death rate for new entrants, assigning the overlap for 1978 and 1979 to the earlier years would have understated earlier births. Instead, the following assumptions were made: first, that the total number of births missed was distributed across the years 1972 to 1977 in proportion to those actually reported;[17] and second, that the missed entrants died at the same rate after birth as those greenfield entrants actually reported. This allowed estimation of the missing entrants by year between 1972 and 1977. The employment was calculated by assuming that the number of employees in each missed birth was the same as the average in those actually captured.

The exit-rate data were also revised to allow for the fact that the under-coverage of entry in the mid-1970s would have produced a downward bias in calculated exit rates. Once again, the data for the exit rate of greenfield entrants was applied to the additional entrants. The corrections have little effect on the average rate of entry or exit over the decade. (More detail can be found in Baldwin and Gorecki, 1990b.)

The annual enterprise database

An enterprise is defined as all establishments in manufacturing and primary industries[18] under common control. If more of the enterprise's activity[19] is classified to a manufacturing industry than to any mining or logging industry, the enterprise is classified to the manufacturing sector. The sample for the short-run database consists of enterprises classified to the manufacturing sector.[20]

The previously given reasons for excluding short-form establishments also apply to enterprises that own short-form establishments. Such enterprises tend to be single-establishment enterprises, since establishments belonging to multi-industry, multi-establishment enterprises always complete long-form questionnaires (Statistics Canada, 1979: 43; McVey, 1981: 15). Establishments that belong to single-industry, multi-establishment enterprises are also likely to complete a long form (Statistics Canada, 1983: 15, Table 7). It was decided, therefore, to exclude enterprises that *always* owned only a single establishment (using the multi-/single-establishment code) that *always* completed a short-form questionnaire.

Treatment of temporary exits. In a small number of instances, a plant or all of the establishments owned by an enterprise fail to report for a given year, for whatever reason, but report in the years before and after that year. According to the rules already outlined, this should be classified as an exit and entry, rather than a continuing plant or enterprise. These situations were reclassified and the plant or firm was counted as continuing rather than as an exit or entrant.

The importance of plant transfers. At the aggregate level, an entry by plant transfer could occur if a firm began to manufacture products in a plant that had previously been used for wholesaling. It was felt that there would be relatively few reassignments of plants across sectors – at least compared with the number of reassignments within the manufacturing sector. Nevertheless, an effort was made to examine the importance of the phenomenon by examining the extent to which exiting firms purchased goods for resale – essentially a wholesaling activity. It was concluded that the majority of firm exits did not engage in much wholesaling activity before the exit, and the transfer category was relatively unimportant in the entry and exit rates calculated at the level of the manufacturing sector as a whole (Baldwin and Gorecki, 1990b).

Determination of entry and exit method. An enterprise may exit the manufacturing sector either by closing all of the plants it owns or by divesting them. Equally, an enterprise may enter the manufacturing sector de novo by building a new plant or by acquiring plants of existing enterprises. In the analyses of both long-run and short-run enterprise entry and exit, these methods of entry and exit were differentiated.[21]

In considering the method of entry in the short run, the following approach was used to determine if the firm entered by acquisition, as opposed to plant creation. If the entrant filed an annual Census of Manufactures questionnaire in a particular year *and* the establishment(s) it owned in that year existed in the previous year, the firm was classified as having entered by acquisition; if the plants did not exist in the previous year, the enterprise was classified as having entered by plant creation. The same approach was used to distinguish the method of exit: if the exiting firm last filed an annual Census of Manufactures questionnaire in a particular year and the plants it owned in that year were still alive in the next or subsequent year (but under a different owner), the firm was classified as exiting by divestiture; if the plants did not file an annual Census of Manufactures form in the next year, the firm was classified as exiting by closing plant.[22]

A classification problem may arise either if an enterprise enters by *both* acquiring plants and building new plants, or if an enterprise exits by *both* divestiture and by closing plants. This could be handled by counting the firm twice or by creating a new category – entry by both acquisition and plant opening. Alternatively, this firm could be assigned to one or other category on the basis of the relative importance of the plants created and the plants acquired.

The implications of using the first approach can be ascertained from the data that were employed to measure long-run entry and exit. While some firms entered both by building new plant and acquiring it, the overlap was relatively small. These data come from comparing firm status in 1970 and 1979. The possibility that a firm could enter by one route and then expand by the other should be greater for a 10-year period than for the 1-year period, which was adopted to measure short-run entry. There is less likelihood of overlap between the two methods of entry in a study that relies upon annual data.

It was decided that it would be appropriate to count an entrant as either entering by plant creation or by plant acquisition. Therefore, an enterprise entrant was assigned to one of the two entry categories on the basis of the employment in the plants created compared with that in the plants acquired.

APPENDIX B: DEFINITION OF CONCENTRATION AND MOBILITY MEASURES

Measures of concentration (based on shipments)

Measures that combine firm numbers with size inequality

CR(K)　　　Top-firm market share – the sum of the top i firms' market shares (S_i), based on domestic production:

$$\sum_{i=1}^{K} S_i$$

CRTR(K)　　The trade-corrected CR(K) measure: CR4, based on sales that include imports

ENT　　　　The entropy measure: $[-\Sigma\, S_i\, \ln(S_i)]$

ENTROPY　　The numbers equivalent of the entropy measure: the antilog of ENT

HAN(a)　　Hannah and Kay's (1977) numbers-equivalent measure:

$$\left[\sum S_i^a\right]^{1/(1-a)}$$

HCON　　　An index that captures the degree of concentration presented by the HF measure that varies from 0 to 1:

$$[N - (1/HF)]/[N - 1]$$

HF　　　　　Herfindahl measure – the sum of squared market shares of all firms classified to the industry:

$$\sum_{i=1}^{N} S_i^2 \quad \text{(varies from 0 to 1)}$$

HMOD　　　The firm equivalent derived from the Herfindahl index divided by the number of firms:

$$(1/HF)/N, \quad \text{where } N \text{ is the number of firms (varies from } 1/N \text{ to 1)}$$

HORV　　　Horvath's (1970) measure:

$$CR1 + \sum_{i=2}^{N}\left[S_i^2 \times (2 - S_i)\right]$$

MCR8　　　The share of the firms ranked from 5 to 8

REDUND   The entropy-based redundancy statistic:

                $(\ln N - ENT)$ (varies from 0 to $\ln N$)

RELNUM   The relative firm numbers, based on the entropy index: ENTROPY/N

RELNUM(I)   The firm-numbers-equivalent Hannah and Kay measure (HAN) using the parameter i divided by the number of firms in the industry

RELRED   Relative-redundancy ratio based on the entropy measure:

                REDUND/$\ln N$,   which varies from 0 to 1

RSBL   Rosenbluth's (1955) or Hall–Tideman's (1967) measure:

$$\frac{1}{2}\left[\sum_i S_i \times (i-1)\right]$$

Select aspects of the dispersion of the distribution

CRLDREQ   The slope of the share of the first 18 firms regressed against their respective ranks

CRSLOPE   The slope of the cumulative concentration ratio:

                [(CR8 + CR9 + CR10) − (CR2 + CR3 + CR4)]/6

CVAR8   The coefficient of variation of the top eight firms

PAR   The Pareto coefficient estimated using the approach suggested by Kwoka (1982) using the market shares of the leading two firms

REL21   The size of the second relative to that of the first firm

REL231   The share of the second and third relative to that of the first firm

REL84   The share of firms ranked 5 to 8 divided by those ranked 1 to 4

RELSK   The ratio of SKEWE to SKEWF

SKEWE   The ratio of the mean size of establishments in the top 50 per cent divided by the median-establishment size

SKEWF   The ratio of the mean size of firms in the top 50 per cent divided by the median-firm size

VARS   The variance of the logarithm of firm shares

Measures of mobility

Entry and exit (based on shipments): long run

SH22   The long-run rate of firm entry via the acquisition of plant; defined in terms of the importance of 1979 shipments of plants that entered the industry by acquisition between 1970 and 1979

SH23   The long-run rate of firm entry accomplished via the building of new plants; defined as the share of 1979 shipments in plants of firms that entered the industry between 1970 and 1979 by building new plant

SH31   The long-run rate of firm exit via the divestiture of plant; defined as the percentage of total 1970 shipments in plants belonging to firms that left the industry by 1979 because of divestiture

SH34   The long-run rate of firm exit resulting from plant closure, defined as the share of 1970 shipments in plants belonging to firms that left the industry between 1970 and 1979 because of plant closure

Existing firm activity (based on shipments): long run

SH11   The long-run rate of horizontal mergers; defined as the share of 1970 shipments in plants divested by 1979 by a firm that continued in the same industry

SH12   The long-run rate of horizontal mergers; defined as the share of 1979 shipments in plants acquired since 1970 by a firm in the same industry

SH13   The long-run rate of plant creation by continuing firms; defined as the share of 1979 shipments in plants opened by continuing firms since 1970

SH14   The long-run rate of plant closure by continuing firms; defined as the share of 1970 shipments in plants owned by continuing firms that have been closed by 1979

SHD   Market-share loss between 1970 and 1979 of continuing plants that lost market share (losers)

SHU   Market-share gain of continuing plants between 1970 and 1979 that gained market share (gainers)

Measures of share change (based on shipments)

BOTCHG   PASHIG calculated only for the smallest firms accounting for the bottom 50 per cent of shipments

BOTGR   The sum of the differences between the shares in 1979 and 1970 for the smallest firms accounting for the bottom 50 per cent of shipments

CONTNETS   The difference between continuing-firm plant openings and closings: SH13 minus SH14

ENTNETS   The difference between entry and exit: SH23 minus SH34

GAIN   The sum of SH23, SH13, and SHU

GAIN13   The ratio of SH13 to GAIN

GAIN23   The ratio of SH23 to GAIN

GAINU   The ratio of SHU to GAIN

PASHIG   The sum of the absolute values of the differences between firm market shares in 1979 and 1970 divided by 2

PASHIG1   The same as PASHIG except that each share change is weighted by the 1970 share

RANK   The standard deviation of the ratio of the share of the producer in 1979 to that in 1970

TOPCHG   PASHIG calculated only for the largest firms accounting for the top 50 per cent of shipments

TOPGR   the sum of the differences between the shares in 1979 and 1970 for the largest firms accounting for the top 50 per cent of shipments

TURNC   Turnover in continuing firms: PASHIG minus TURNE

TURNE   Total turnover due to greenfield entry and exit: the sum of SH23 and SH34 divided by 2

TURNM   Turnover due to acquisition entry and divestiture exit: the sum of SH22 and SH31 divided by 2

TURNPS   The turnover due to plant openings and closings in continuing firms: the sum of SH13 and SH14

Measures of share change (based on numbers of firms)

CONTNETN   The difference between continuing-firm plant openings and closings: SH13 minus SH14, where shares are measured using numbers and not shipments

ENTNETN   The difference between entry and exit: SH23 minus SH34, where shares are measured using numbers and not shipments

TURNEN   Total turnover due to greenfield entry and exit: the sum of SH23 and SH34 divided by 2, where shares are measured using numbers and not shipments

TURNPN   Total turnover due to greenfield entry and exit: the sum of SH23 and SH34 divided by 2, where shares are measured using numbers and not shipments

Measures of job turnover (based on employment)

ABNET   Absolute value of net change in employment

EXCESS   The rate of total job turnover in excess of that required to facilitate net change in jobs due to overall growth or decline, defined as the difference between SUM and the absolute value of NET

NEG   The rate of job decline as the sum of all employment losses in plants that declined between two periods (including exits) divided by total employment

NET   Net change in employment defined as the difference between POS and NEG

POS   The rate of job creation defined as the sum of all employment gains in plants that grew between two periods (including entrants) divided by total employment

SUM   Total job turnover defined as the sum of POS and NEG

Differential growth rates (based on shipments)

GROW   The variance in the growth rates of the producers in the industry in 1970 and 1979

Measures derived from regressions of 1979 share on 1970 share (shipments)

CORSH   The correlation between initial- and final-year share

REG   REGSH divided by the square root of CORSH – Gort's (1963) measure

REGSH	The coefficient from regressing final-year on initial-year share
REGSHINV	The inverse of the coefficient from regressing initial-year share on final-year share
STAB1	The absolute value of $(1 - \text{REGSH})$
STAB2	1 if REGSH is significantly less than 1; zero otherwise

Measures of transition from one size-class to another

Measures of length of stay

AVSTAY	The mean length of stay for all size-classes
STAY(i)	The average length of stay in size-class i (see Prais, 1955)

Transitional probabilities

ENMOB	The average proportion of producers in a size-class that have entered since the last period
ENTRYDIF	The difference between the top and bottom size-class entry rate
EXITDIF	The difference between the top and bottom size-class exit rate
EXMOB	The average proportion of producers in a size-class that have exited by the next period
MOB	The average proportion of producers in a size-class that have moved to another by the next period
P(ij)	The proportion of producers in size-class i of the first period that are in size-class j in the second
TOTMOB	The sum of PMOB and EXMOB, which is a measure of total movement by producers who both continue and exit

Note: If the suffix WTD is attached to PMOB, EXMOB, TOTMOB, or ENMOB, the proportion moving is weighted by the length of the move. The weights are the differences in the ranks of the mid-points of the size-classes.

Industry characteristics variable list

ADV	The advertising–sales ratio
AVFSZ	The average firm size, which is the total value of shipments of all entrants divided by the number of entrants classified to the industry
AVFSZE	The average firm size of entrants, which is total value of shipments divided by the number of firms classified to the industry
AVGSIZE	Employment-weighted average plant size
AVPLSZ	Average plant size
AVPLSZE	Average plant size of entrants
AVSZT	The average size (measured in total activity value of shipments of the smallest number of the largest plants accounting for 50 per cent of industry employment)
BETAEQ	The speed of adjustment of rate of return on equity to long-run levels
BETACAP	The speed of adjustment of rate of return on capital to long-run levels

BMES   The ratio of the minimum-efficient-sized plant (MES) divided by industry size, where MES is calculated as the Lyons (1980) branching estimate of MES

CA   Comparative advantage, defined as 1 plus (exports minus imports divided by the sum of exports and imports)

CDN   The proportion of industry shipment accounted for by foreign-owned enterprises. An enterprise is defined as foreign controlled if there is effective foreign control, although the percentage of stock owned by a foreign corporation may be less than 50 per cent

CDR   The cost-disadvantage ratio: the ratio of value-added per person-hour of the smallest plants accounting for 50 per cent of industry employment divided by the value-added per person-hour for the largest plants accounting for 50 per cent of industry employment

COMP   Exports less imports divided by exports plus imports

COVE   The sales of plants in industry i belonging to enterprises in other industries divided by sales of all establishments in industry i

CVAR8   The coefficient of variation of the size of the eight leading firms

EFF   A measure of efficency: the ratio of actual output to potential output, the latter defined as the efficient level of output per person multiplied by the level of employment in each establishment summed over all establishments in an industry

ERP   The effective tariff rate in the industry

EXP   The proportion of domestic production that is exported

FOR   The proportion of industry shipments accounted for by foreign-owned enterprises, an enterprise being defined as foreign controlled if there is effective foreign control, although the percentage of stock owned by a foreign corporation may be less than 50 per cent

FULL   The importance of full-time workers as measured by the number of person-hours worked by production workers divided by the number of production workers

G The rate of growth defined by the regression of the logarithm of the real value of shipments on time for the period 1970–79

GPROD   The growth in labour productivity

HERF4D   The Herfindahl index of plant diversity. It uses the proportion of the plant's shipments classified to the industry where the categories are the four-digit Industrial Commodity Classification (ICC) commodities produced by the industry

IHERF4D   The industry level of plant diversity: the weighted average (using plant shipments) of the individual plant measures of diversity

IMP   Imports divided by domestic market, which is production minus exports plus imports

KL   The capital–labour ratio, defined as the value of capital derived from the perpetual-inventory technique divided by total employment

LABOUR   Growth in labour productivity (value-added per worker)

LPREQ   The long-run return of equity

LPRCAP	The long-run return on total capital
MEST	The ratio of the minimum-efficient-sized plant (MES) divided by industry size, where MES is calculated as the average size of the largest plants that account for the top 50 per cent of shipments
MULT1	The sales of plants belonging to companies that are multi-plant operators divided by total sales
MULT2	The number of plants per enterprise
N4D	The number of four-digit ICC commodities per four-digit SIC industry
N5D	The number of five-digit ICC commodities per four-digit SIC industry
NF	The number of firms in the industry
NP	The number of plants in the industry
NOBS	The number of plants on which the efficiency measure was based
PCONT	The weighted gross rate of return of all firms that continued throughout the decade, where the weights used are firm value-added
PDIFF	The difference between the gross rate of return of the top half of the industry, ranked on the basis of size, and the gross rate of return of the bottom half
PCM	The price–cost margin, defined as the value of shipments minus wages and salaries minus intermediate materials and energy inputs all divided by shipments
PR	The profitability, defined as the shipments minus material minus wages and salaries (derived from census data) divided by capital stock (derived from the perpetual-inventory method applied to investment data)
PRCAP	The average rate of return on total capital derived from balance-sheet data
PREQ	The average rate of return on equity derived from balance-sheet data
PRSMALL	A measure of profitability for the year 1970 that combines overall profitability along with a measure of how well small firms do relative to large firms, defined as $(1 - \text{PCONT}) \times (\text{PDIFF})$, varies inversely with the difference between large- and small-firm profitability and directly with overall profitability
PRFTGR	A measure of the profit growth over the decade, defined as the ratio of the price–cost margin for the top half of the firm-size distribution in 1979 divided by that for 1970
RD	The ratio of research and development personnel to all wage and salary earners, 1975
RATIO	The ratio of long-term entry to the sum of short-term entry
REG	A dummy variable for an industry classified as being regional
RELSIZE	The average size of entrants relative to industry average size: AVPLSZE divided by AVPLSZ
RFSIZE	The average firm size of the largest plants that account for the top 50 per cent of shipments divided by industry shipments
RPSIZE	The average plant size of the largest plants (AVSZT)
SCALE	The estimate of scale economies derived using a Cobb–Douglas production function

SD(HERF)   The standard deviation of the plant level of product specialization, the latter defined using a Herfindahl index of the proportion of the plant's shipments classified to the nth four-digit ICC commodity

SD(M/L)   The standard deviation of the ratio of materials and energy expenses divided by the number of wage and salary workers

SD(SIZE)   The standard deviation of average plant size based on numbers of salaried and production workers

SD(SPEC)   The standard deviation of the plant specialization ratio

SPEC   The plant specialization ratio – the percentage of production in a plant of commodities belonging to the same industry to which the plant is assigned

SUBOPT   The percentage of industry sales in Canadian plants that are smaller than the MES plant in the United States, the latter defined by ranking plants on the basis of size and choosing the one that divides the cumulative distribution of sales in two

TVS   The total value of shipments in an industry

TVSE   The total value of shipments in entrants

UNION   The proportion of production workers who were union members, 1971

VAR   The variability of demand, defined as the standard deviations of the real value of shipments on time for the period 1970–79

XC   The excess-concentration ratio, defined as CONC minus the share that the four largest firms would have if they each operated one plant equal to MES. MES is defined as AVSZT

Principal components and canonical correlates used

CANCON   Canonical correlates of concentration variables

CANMOB   Canonical correlates of mobility variables

PCON(i)   The principal components of concentration variables

PPROF(i)   The principal components of profitability variables

PMOB(i)   The principal components of mobility variables

PSCL(i)   The principal components of scale variables

PVAR(i)   The principal components of a set of structural variables

PWEL(i)   The principal components of well-being variables

NOTES

Preface

1. For an evaluation of some of the databases that have been used, see Baldwin and Gorecki (1990b) and Johnson and Storey (1985).
2. See Baldwin and Gorecki (1990a) and Appendix A for a discussion of the database and the methodology used.

1. The dynamics of competition

1. See Ijiri and Simon (1977) for a compendium of these works.
2. For earlier studies, see Schneider (1966), Havrilesky and Barth (1969), Jacoby (1984), and Commission of Inquiry on the Pharmaceutical Industry (1985).
3. For instance, Baldwin and Gorecki (1987b, 1991) look at the extent of entry and exit; Hymer and Pashigian (1962) examine share change in the incumbent population; Joskow (1960) investigates the extent of rank change; Gort (1963), Singh and Whittington (1975), Hall (1987), and Prais (1976) examine the degree to which market shares regress toward the mean; and Prais (1955) looks at the extent to which there is mobility across size-classes.
4. See Appendix A.
5. Greenfield entry involves the entry of a firm by plant creation – as opposed to entry via merger. Closedown exit involves the exit of a firm by plant closedown – as opposed to exit via plant divestiture.
6. The primary focus is on acquisition entry and divestiture exit – that is, the entry of a firm via acquisition of a plant or the exit of a firm via divestiture of a plant.
7. A four-digit Canadian industry refers to the four-digit Standard Industrial Classification (SIC) level for Canada. See Statistics Canada, 1979.

2. Greenfield entry and closedown exit

1. For examples see the articles in the *International Journal of Industrial Organization* (1987: vol. 5, no. 1) and Geroski and Schwalbach (1991).

425

2. See the discussion of problems in Baldwin and Gorecki (1990b), particularly with respect to the use of Dun and Bradstreet data. For a study using national census data for the United States that avoids most of the problems in the literature and is comparable with the present study, see Dunne, Roberts, and Samuelson (1989).

3. See Johnson and Storey (1985) for a discussion of Dun and Bradstreet studies.

4. See Storey (1985) for a set of studies for the United Kingdom using specially constructed databases.

5. See OECD (1987) for a study that tries to reconcile the different definitions and coverage in France, West Germany, Japan, Sweden, Canada, and the United States.

6. Chapter 7 relates entry, inter alia, to productivity growth.

7. Plant-entry and -exit rates are also useful for job-creation and -destruction studies that focus on the relationship between change at the industry level and its effect on the labour force. This topic is covered extensively by Baldwin and Gorecki (1990b), using plant data.

8. The choice of the measure of size is somewhat arbitrary. If entrants are less productive than average, focusing on an input like labour rather than a shipments-based measure will increase the measured importance of entrants. In fact, entrants go from being less productive to being more productive than average over a 10-year period. Therefore, an employment-based measure overstates the importance of entry in its earlier years and understates its importance later on relative to a shipments-based measure.

9. Studies like those of Acs and Audretsch (1989a, 1989b) use the database generated by the U.S. Small Business Administration that combines both greenfield and acquisition entry.

10. Statistics Canada uses a number of different terms such as "business unit," "corporation," or "consolidated enterprise" to refer to a firm. For ease of reference, the term "firm" is used throughout as a generic term, and where necessary the particular meaning used is defined for the reader.

11. Several corrections were made to the raw data because of a change in the Census of Manufactures' coverage, among other things. For a discussion of the changes required, see Baldwin and Gorecki (1990a).

12. Not all years decline immediately. The exceptions are for entry in the late 1970s. This is partly because the entry data for 1978 included firms previously missed that were older and, therefore, did not die as quickly.

13. If employment were used rather than value-added, the results would show a decline in share after several years, which would give the impression that entry is less important than it is.

14. Panel C is derived from the uncorrected raw data on entry and exit (see note 10) and, therefore, does not correspond exactly with the results reported in Table 2-2.

15. Plant transfers that involve changes in ownership are excluded here. For the difference between the two types of plant transfer, see Appendix A.

16. If large firms are defined as having more than 100 employees, instead of being defined as in the top quintile of each industry, then over 33% of all exits over the decade occurred in large firms.

3. Entry, exit, and the merger process

1. Baldwin and Gorecki (1986b) define a merger as an acquisition by a consolidated enterprise of an unconsolidated enterprise (all commonly controlled establishments in an industry). This allows a merger between one consolidated enterprise and another to be divided into its horizontal and diversified components. A merger is classified as horizontal when the acquiring consolidated enterprise had an establishment in the same SIC class as the acquired unconsolidated enterprise.
2. Appendix A describes the database and the concepts used to measure mergers.
3. Lichtenberg and Siegel (1987) use a U.S. census of manufactures database to evaluate the effect of mergers.
4. Eckbo's (1986a) study relies on the Consumer and Corporate Affairs Canada merger register, which covers a very small portion of the total number of mergers that occurred over the period. Jog and Riding (1986) also use a small non-random sample for their study.
5. These data are taken from a database that was created by defining entry as a firm that was new to manufacturing as opposed to new to a subsector of manufacturing.
6. The measure uses only employment in those plants acquired or newly built, not total employment of the acquiring firm.
7. That is, an entrant is a firm that previously did not have any plant in manufacturing.
8. Entry and exit in Table 3-4 include the opening and closing of plants and the transfer of one plant to another industry when that transfer did not also involve an ownership or control change. When a change in control occurred, the transfer is classified as involving an acquisition entrant or a divestiture exit.
9. The effect of the merger process cannot be derived directly by taking the difference between the shares of acquired plants in 1970 and 1979 in the horizontal merger or the entry and exit categories. This is because some acquisitions of continuing firms come from other continuing firms and some come from exiting firms. The net effect of mergers on the continuing-firm sector is the difference between the share of plants acquired by continuing firms from exiting firms and the share that is divested by continuing firms and acquired by new firms.
10. These averages are calculated across all the four-digit manufacturing industries. Not all industries have the same amount of merger activity. Some 17% had mergers that transferred plant both from continuing firms to entrants and from exiting firms to continuing firms. In this group of industries, continuing firms expanded by 4.8 percentage points and mergers contributed some 3.5 percentage points of this.
11. Entrants are defined as new to the manufacturing sector as a whole. See Baldwin and Gorecki (1990a).
12. See Chapter 7 for a more extensive discussion of the replacement process.
13. This reduces the aggregation bias that would result from using fixed-boundary size-classes that are the same for all industries.
14. Even though Baldwin and Gorecki (1987b) find that slightly different variants worked better in the various regression equations, a common set was chosen here to facilitate comparison between equations. A more complex model is estimated in Chapter 14.

15. The results were robust to alternate specifications.
16. Only non-zero observations are used to explain variations in plant creation and merger intensity.
17. Entry share is measured in terms of employment.
18. See Appendix A for a discussion of the number of industries in which there is entry or acquisition activity.
19. See Scherer (1988: 76) for a discussion of the rate of divestiture of acquisitions.
20. These are as high as or higher than the rates of divestiture for the United States reported in Scherer (1988: 76) based on work by Ravenscraft and Scherer (1987) and Porter (1987).
21. Some successful take-overs will also result in exit. Take-overs whose sole purpose is to restructure a company and then resell it will also result in post-merger exit when the process of turn-around has been successfully completed – or at least started.
22. The correction factors were calculated in the following way. First, the annual exit rate through merger was calculated for 1970 firms. The correction factor was derived here as the ratio of the annual rate for this group divided by its mean. The reciprocal of this ratio was used to correct the divestiture rate of firms that had entered through acquisition. For entrants, the correction factor was calculated in a similar fashion, but using the annual exit rate for all establishments.

4. The rise and fall of incumbents

1. For a discussion of the difference between a consolidated firm defined at the level of the manufacturing sector and an unconsolidated firm defined at a four-digit industry level, see Appendix A.
2. A consolidated firm consists of establishments within manufacturing that are under common control.
3. Employment is used at this stage to measure changing relative position. Employment has intrinsic interest to those wanting to investigate the relationship between firm growth and decline and its potential impact on labour markets. It has the disadvantage that the employment decline category includes firms that are increasing their outputs and labor-productivity levels, although evidently they were not facing strong profit incentives to expand output at the margin. Later in the chapter, share of shipments is used to measure shifting relative position.
4. See Baldwin and Gorecki (1990b) for further discussion of the relative volatility of the different components.
5. See Baldwin and Gorecki (1990b) for a more extensive discussion of the characteristics of expansion and contraction measures using establishment rather than firm data.
6. See Chapter 2.
7. The OECD (1987) suggests that the minimum values of short-run change be used as a proxy for the amount of long-run or structural change. The results reported here suggest this is not always appropriate. The minimum value of the proportion of firms declining annually is close to the proportion that decline over longer periods. But the annualized longer-run decline rates are less than the lowest short-

run contraction rates. It is best, therefore, to concentrate directly on long-run comparisons and not to infer long-run behavioral characteristics from short-run data.

8. Another reason for focusing on individual industries is that a multi-industry firm may remain the same overall but its components at the individual industry level may change substantially. If this occurred often, aggregate data would underestimate change.

9. Hymer and Pashigian (1962) use this index to measure instability in an industry.

10. Market share is calculated using shipments.

11. Entry and exit due to acquisition are not counted as an entry or exit in this version. Share changes in the firm that was acquired are included in the share change associated with continuing firms.

12. In this formulation, the share change for divested firms is set equal to their share in 1970; that of acquired firms is set equal to their share in 1979.

13. Mergers are examined more extensively in Chapter 3.

14. No significant correlations were found between entry–exit and continuing-firm turnover within each group.

5. Patterns of large- and small-firm mobility

1. All turnover measures in this chapter are calculated for firms at the four-digit SIC industry level.

2. The maximum value the weighted index can take occurs when that firm that has closest to, but less than 50% of the market increases its share to 100% and all the rest decline to zero.

3. Entry and exit by acquisition were excluded from the calculations. In other words, all firms that existed in 1970 are treated as though they continued as separate entities until the end of the decade, even if they were acquired at some time during the decade. Since data are available for establishments in 1970 and 1979, it is possible to calculate the size in 1979 of the acquired establishments, even if the original firm had been subsumed into a larger unit.

4. It is the market share of the three largest firms plus one minus the market share of the fourth.

5. Once again, entry and exit by acquisition were excluded from the calculations.

6. The process was repeated twice, once for large and once for small firms. The last firm to be included in each sample was that just before cumulative output exceeded 50% of the total. Because it was rare to find a firm exactly at the 50% dividing line, the average share covered in each sample was slightly less than 50%. The turnover estimates were marked up by the ratio of 50 divided by the cumulative market share covered in each sample.

7. Each measure was inflated to reflect the fact that the procedure used to split the sample resulted in slightly less than 50% of market share being captured by each group.

8. These measures are described in note 6.

9. If only 1970 were used, all entrants would be assigned to the small size-class, since in 1970 entrants had zero market share.

10. Bartholomew (1973) contains a discussion of the assumptions needed to use transition matrices to estimate average length of stay.
11. See I. G. Adelman (1958) for the use of transition matrices to estimate structural change.
12. The exact value depends on the value of the variance in the growth rates.
13. The INST coefficient in the fourth row comes from the use of 1970 rank as an instrument (see Durbin, 1958).
14. Hall (1987) draws the same conclusion.
15. Including the industry effects did not change the conclusions.
16. For this exercise, acquisitions and divestitures were not considered as entry and exit.
17. These categories used the CR4 to define the industry groups. They are discussed at length in Chapter 6.

6. Plant turnover in Canada and the United States

1. See Caves (1989b: 1230–35) for a review of this literature.
2. The manufacturing sector in Canada is more concentrated than that in the United States. Baldwin, Gorecki, and McVey (1986) use matched data for 125 Canadian and U.S. industries to compare the average size of larger plants (those accounting for the top 50% of employment). Canadian plants were, on average, only about 70% the size of U.S. plants. They employ a similar matched panel of Canadian and U.S. industries and show that the usual four-firm concentration ratio averaged 56% in Canada but only 37% in the United States in the late 1970s. Neither of these concentration measures takes into account the effect of imports and exports on the size of the markets in the two countries. When corrections for imports are made, the difference in average concentration diminishes by some 7 percentage points to only about 12%, but there is still a gap.
3. Davis and Haltiwanger (1992) estimate that the average annual persistence rates for job creation and destruction are 68% and 81%, respectively.
4. See Baldwin and Gorecki (1990b) for a discussion of this problem.
5. A recent example of cross-country comparisons that needs to be treated cautiously can be found in a study by Cable and Schwalbach (1991), which compares international entry rates. Canadian entry data that were constructed especially for that study to include greenfield and merger entry are compared with U.S. data that cover basically only greenfield entry.
6. Previous chapters use a file that omitted firms filing short census forms. In this chapter, all establishments with five or more workers are included because the longitudinal (LRD) file for the United States covers only these plants.
7. Establishments that actually continue may be allowed to die in administrative files – that is, the old identifier dropped and a new one assigned – if there is a change in ownership or name. The Canadian longitudinal panel data were originally created with a strict rule for classifying a continuing establishment as a death: the name, location, and ownership all had to change. These rules were not originally applied to the U.S. data. When developing the LRD file in the United States, researchers have had to devise routines to detect false deaths. Until recently,

differences between the U.S. and Canadian data would lead to more deaths being recorded in the United States. By matching names and locations, researchers have edited the U.S. file to the point where the criteria used to classify plant deaths are very similar to those used in Canada.

8. Other measurement issues for Canada are covered in Appendix A and for the United States, in Dunne and Roberts (1986) and in Davis, Haltiwanger, and Schuh (1990).

9. Compare Dunne, Roberts, and Samuelson (1988, 1989) with Baldwin and Gorecki (1987b, 1990b).

10. Employment is defined here as the sum of production and non-production workers for both countries.

11. This point has been made previously by Birch (1981) for the United States and by Baldwin and Gorecki (1990b) for Canada.

12. Annual entry rates were not available for all years for the United States.

13. The average Herfindahl measure for Canada was used for this purpose. If the trade-corrected Herfindahl measure is used (see Baldwin, Gorecki, and McVey, 1986), the conclusion does not change.

14. See Davis and Haltiwanger (1991) for further discussion. Note that since the co-worker mean essentially involves squared plant employment in the numerator, it is functionally related to the Herfindahl index.

15. Average unionization, which turns out not to be a significant determinant of job turnover, is 38.3% in Canada and 24.8% in the United States and at the two-digit level has a correlation of .65.

16. Contrary to the earlier regressions, which used all two-digit industries, the long-run regressions had to omit several industries (tobacco, knitting mills, instruments, and miscellaneous) because a set of characteristics were not available.

17. See Ashenfelter and Card (1986), McCallum (1987), and Card and Riddel (1992).

7. Measures of market structure and the intensity of competition

1. See Boyle and Sorensen (1971) for an early attempt to evaluate mobility and concentration statistics.

2. For other work on concentration, see Department of Consumer and Corporate Affairs (1971), Marfels (1976), Royal Commission on Corporate Concentration (1978), and Khemani (1980, 1986).

3. Bain (1972: ch. 12) succinctly summarizes the importance to the SCP school of a stable market structure.

4. For a description of those few who investigated a feedback to structure, see Baldwin and Scott (1987: 99–105).

5. For descriptions of measurement and conceptual shortcomings, see Bain (1968: 124–33) and the papers by Miller, Conklin, and Goldstein in National Bureau of Economic Research (1955).

6. See Yamey (1985).

7. In Canada, the Royal Commission on Corporate Concentration (1978) and Khemani (1986) examine trends in concentration as part of attempts to assess changes in the competitive environment.

8. See, e.g., Adelman (1951), and Mueller and Hamm (1974).
9. For examples, see Sutton (1991).
10. Using the concentration ratio for 1975 confirms the picture of stability produced when the indices for just 1970 and 1979 are used.
11. See, e.g., Marfels (1971, 1972a), Aaronovitch and Sawyer (1975: 59–90), Curry and George (1983), and Waterson (1984: 166–74). Appendix B in the present study includes definitions of many of these indices.
12. See Waterson (1984) for this classification.
13. Occasionally, the CR4 index is supplemented here with the CR8 ratio.
14. A principal-component analysis that was conducted on various measures of the size distribution of firms suggested that the summary and discrete measures were about equally weighted in the first principal component. In other words, they were all capturing the same dimension of the firm-size distribution. The various measures used are defined in Appendix B.
15. Weighted concentration measures were also estimated, using industry value-added as weights. The same pattern of stability was found, but the change was somewhat greater. For example, the weighted CR4 index fell from .4952 in 1970 to .4638 in 1979.
16. See Bain (1968: 136–38), Green (1980: 45), and Department of Consumer and Corporate Affairs (1971: 21) for an application of the classification scheme to Canada.
17. The HF classification follows that employed by the U.S. Department of Justice (1982) in its merger guidelines. It uses a threefold classification: highly concentrated industries where competitive problems are likely to arise (.1800–1.00); industries where "competitive concerns associated with concentration become significant to the point at which they become quite serious" (.1000–.1799); and markets that are likely to perform quite well (0–.0999).
18. Many of these are defined in Appendix B and discussed in the references cited in note 5.
19. See, e.g., Hart (1971, 1975, 1979).
20. Simon and Bonini (1958) propose this measure.
21. This has been used by Caves et al. (1980: 229) in conjunction with CR4.
22. These numbers-equivalent measures are divided by NF to form the relative-number indices. The numbers-equivalent indices are defined as the number of equal-sized firms that would be required to derive the given value of an index. See Adelman (1969) for a discussion of the HF number equivalents.
23. The MCR8 measure is used by Miller (1971).
24. In measuring mobility, firm market shares in 1970 and 1979 are used. For the purpose of this exercise, firms that entered and exited through acquisitions and divestitures were not counted as entrants and exits. They were treated as continuing entities and their market-share change was included in the continuing-firm segment. For more detail on the procedure followed, see Chapter 5.
25. For definitions of TURNE and TURNC, see Chapter 4.
26. See Kalecki (1945), Steindl (1965), Prais (1976), Gort (1963), and McGuckin (1972).
27. In order to estimate the coefficient relating 1979 and 1970 market share, OLS was

used. See Chapter 5 for a discussion of the relationship between this estimate and others.

28. These are used because they correspond with the bounds used by Gort (1963). Alternative significance tests are described in Chapter 5.

29. McGuckin's work (1972) on the relation between entry and concentration finds a similar result.

30. Rank correlations yielded the same qualitative conclusions.

31. All firms were ranked on the basis of 1970 shipments to divide the sample into large and small firms. The technique is discussed in greater detail in Chapter 5.

32. Similar results are found if the HF classification described in note 11 is used instead.

33. STAB2 also had a significant relationship with concentration, with mean values of 0.96, 0.85, 0.66, and 0.44 across the concentration classes. This is partly the result of the regression coefficient being closer to one in concentrated industries and partly the result of there being fewer degrees of freedom in the concentrated industries and, therefore, less precision in the estimated coefficients.

34. See the discussion in Scherer (1980: 279–80), which attempts to determine the critical concentration ratio by finding that ratio at which there is a break in the concentration–profits relationship.

35. Using the HF classification scheme led to the identification of 34 problem industries. With one exception, these problem industries are identical to those found when CR4 is used.

8. The relationship between mobility and concentration

1. Principal-component rather than factor analysis is used for two reasons. First, factor analysis, with the indeterminacy associated with the choice of rotation, has a less than enviable reputation (Harris, 1975: 223). Second, it is less important to ask whether there are underlying factors that determine the various measures than it is to ascertain how many separate orthogonal components span each set of measures. This requires principal-component analysis.

2. Most of the commonly used concentration measures were highly correlated – at levels above .95.

3. Using the entire sample of mobility and concentration statistics did not change the qualitative conclusions.

4. This was derived using a weight of 1.1 in the formula for the Hannah and Kay firm-numbers equivalent. Using other weights (1.5, 2.0, 2.5, and 3.0) had little effect on the results reported here.

5. The subset of variables used here was chosen by determining which variables were most heavily weighted in the most important components when all variables were used and then by retaining the most important for the presentation here.

6. Ijiri and Simon (1977) suggest this as a measure of mobility.

7. Entry and exit due to mergers were not counted as part of market-share change for the calculation of TURNE and TURNC.

8. The principal-component analysis was performed on the normalized values of all variables.

9. Median values of the parameters are used.

10. In some analyses of the determinants of concentration, growth is included. It is omitted here because it is a determinant, not a dimension of mobility.

11. See, e.g., the discussion in Curry and George (1983).

12. SCALE uses OLS and a Cobb–Douglas production function because of the robustness of the results. For an extensive discussion of the methodology, see Baldwin and Gorecki (1986a).

13. When multi-plant operations were sufficiently infrequent to prevent the estimation of Lyons' MES, the average size of the four largest firms' plants was substituted. This only occurred in a small number of industries.

14. This is defined in Baldwin and Gorecki (1986a: 176).

15. Labour is measured by the number of wage and salary earners, and capital is measured by year-end gross capital stock in constant (1971) dollars.

16. These are defined in Baldwin and Gorecki (1986a: 173 and 182, respectively).

17. Caves et al. (1980: 50, Table 3.1).

18. In order, the combined components contain PMOB1, PMOB2 and PSCL1, PSCL2, PSCL3, PSCL4; none of the original components; PMOB3; none of the original components; PSCL5; none of the original components; and PMOB5. Only the second combined component groups two of the previously separate components together. This combined component is not significant in the regression.

19. Here the four-firm concentration ratio is used to investigate whether mobility as well as scale affects market structure. Alternatively, the principal components of structure could have been used as regressands. This produces the same qualitative conclusion. The first two components, which weight the main comprehensive measures, are related to entry and plant scale. The third component, which captures the importance of the secondary firms, is related significantly to the mobility variables that were found to be important in the canonical-correlation analysis, and also to certain of the scale variables. Therefore, the regression results reported for the four-firm concentration measure generalize to the various dimensions of market structure that were categorized in the first section of the chapter.

20. It is noteworthy that there is much less of a regression-to-the-mean phenomenon in Figure 8-5 than in Figure 8-2. In Figure 8-5, the industries with the greatest increase are, on average, less concentrated than those that experience a decrease in concentration; but the difference is much less than when industries are ranked from lowest to highest on the basis of their level of concentration in 1970. This means that increases are occurring more frequently but not exclusively in the least concentrated industries and decreases are occurring more frequently but not exclusively in the most concentrated industries.

21. Using concentration or changes in concentration may violate the homoscedastic assumptions required if OLS is to provide best-linear-unbiased estimators. To test for the robustness of the results, a logistic transformation of 1979 and 1970 concentration ratios was employed. The reverse regression yielded an estimate of adjustment that was greater than, not less than, one; the instrumental-variable technique using ranks on observed changes provided an estimate of the same coefficient of 1.25 with a standard error of 0.25.

9. Turnover and productivity growth

1. The data used here come from the yearly enterprise database and are discussed at length in Appendix A.
2. Real productivity is defined as value-added per worker divided by an output price index. The theoretical conditions for the use of an output price index are investigated by David (1961). This approach was chosen for the practical reason that the output price indices are more reliable than the implicit value-added indices that are available for this time period. In the end, the results were robust to other approaches. Experiments with real shipments per worker rather than with value-added per worker yielded the conclusion that turnover accounts for a significant proportion of total productivity growth during the decade of the 1970s.
3. Exiting firms are those that no longer own plant in the industry in question. They may continue to own plant in other industries. The data used here come from the long-run comparison of 1970 and 1979 plant status.
4. Transferred plants are those plants where the product mix changes sufficiently over the decade that they are reassigned from one industry to another by the census.
5. The proportions were calculated across all observations among the most and the least productive plants rather than calculating the mean of the proportion for each industry across all industries.
6. "High" was defined as a rate that increased a plant's relative share of continuing-plant sales.
7. See Leonard (1987) and Boeri and Cramer (1992), who show that while adjacent-year performance is correlated, correlations for longer periods of two, three, and four years are not significant.
8. Continuing plants that changed ownership were excluded so as to eliminate the effects of mergers. Their inclusion does not greatly change the ratios presented in Table 9-3.
9. Medians are used extensively as measures of central tendency, since the raw data on plant characteristics such as value-added per worker may have large outliers – due to incorrect data – that greatly influence means. For example, a plant with positive output but no employees listed would have infinite value-added.
10. These are the continuing plants that existed in the same industry in 1970 and 1979 and that did not experience a change in ownership over the decade. Adding those that changed ownership does not affect the reported ratios to any great extent.
11. Random fluctuations in demand may partially explain size-related productivity differentials – if a greater proportion of small than large firms have recently declined below optimum production levels and if such a decline leads to declines in productivity because fixed factors are not being optimally employed.
12. Both linear and log-linear forms were used. The conclusions were not affected by the type of functional form chosen.
13. The ratio of the median productivity in each group was calculated for each industry before the means were taken across all 167 industries.
14. These estimates are all means of the median estimates of the ratios taken at the level of the individual industry.

15. This is the formulation used by Hazledine (1985).
16. If continuing firms make large productivity gains over the period, the original-year shares – as in equation 9-16 – will be poor proxies if shares respond dramatically to changes in relative productivity. Nevertheless, it can be demonstrated that where the 1979 market share of continuing firms is underestimated by this assumption, the formula in equation 9-6 provides a lower bound for the effect of entry.
17. With this formulation, the difference in productivity between entrants and exits will be just the same as the difference in the growth in the continuing segment, but entry and exit will not be ascribed any importance.
18. New-plant creation includes both births and transfers.
19. The estimate covers those industries where positive real productivity growth occurred. Other samples had little impact on the estimates.
20. Hazledine employs indices of unit costs rather than changes in productivity.
21. The means are calculated across those industries where real productivity growth was positive.
22. Contrary to Table 9-3, continuing plants here include those that experience a change in ownership.
23. For simplification, plant openings and plant transfers are combined in SH23 and SH13.
24. Plant exits in each category include both plants that were closed and those that were transferred to another manufacturing industry.
25. Ordinary least squares was used. Seemingly unrelated least squares was also employed but made no difference.
26. The diagonal elements are SH23, U, and SH13 in lines 1, 2, and 3, respectively, of equation 9-15.
27. Second-order effects might also be postulated since SH23 and U were correlated. New-plant entrants compete with and displace some continuing firms that might otherwise have grown at the expense of the same groups that are being displaced by the entrants. But, presumably, the plants in the continuing sector whose market-share gain is smaller than it would otherwise have been were less productive than the entrants, so their contribution is less and not more than that of the entrants that displaced the groups actually losing market share. Therefore, these trade-offs were not pursued further.
28. The total predicted share loss using equation 9-14 is not equal to the actual total share loss. This is because the estimated share equations have statistical error terms. The approximation was quite good, on average. Nevertheless, there were some industries where the approximation of the displacement effect yielded by equation 9-15 was not very good. To handle this problem, the estimation procedure was modified slightly. The ratio of the predicted share of a displaced category relative to the actual share was calculated for each industry, and its inverse was used to correct each term a_{ij} in equation 9-19.
29. Each component of equation 9-21 was estimated for each four-digit manufacturing industry where real growth in productivity was positive.
30. The proportions of total estimated growth and not of actual growth were calculated so that the proportions would sum to one for the purpose of presentation.

Using actual growth as denominator did not affect the relative size of the various components.

31. The results are robust to the exclusion of outliers.

10. Merger success

1. See Caves (1987, 1989b) for a survey of this literature. See also Cowling et al. (1980) for a study of large mergers in Great Britain.

2. Lichtenberg and Siegel (1989a, 1989b) and McGuckin, Nguyen, and Andrews (1991) use this source to investigate the effects of mergers in the United States.

3. Ravenscraft and Scherer (1987) overcome some of these problems by using U.S. line-of-business data.

4. See Jarrel (1987) for a discussion of some of these innovations.

5. See Fisher and McGowan (1983) and Benston (1985). For an alternative position, see Mueller (1990: 8–14).

6. First, if relative plant and firm characteristics change rapidly, measuring the profitability or productivity in the initial period of plants that are subsequently merged may not reflect their status just before acquisition. Even more importantly, it may not reflect the situation that was responsible for the merger. Equally, their status in the final year may not reflect the effects of the merger. This problem is mitigated to the extent that trends are slow to emerge and – if there is enough persistence in profits and market share (as suggested by Mueller, 1986) – that longer time horizons provide the researcher with valuable information. Moreover, Chapter 9, which examines the 1979 status of plants that entered between 1970 and 1979 and the 1970 status of plants that exited between 1970 and 1979, finds significant differences between the productivity of entrants and exits and that of the rest of the population in each of these two years – even though the exits were to occur over the next decade and the entrants in 1979 could have been born any time during the preceding nine years. In this case, data for the year just prior to exit or just after entry were not required to show important differences between the plants that exited or entered and the rest of the population.

   The second problem with the methodology is that the firms being compared will not all be in the same position in any given year. Some will have been taken over at the end of the period; others will have been taken over at the beginning of the period. Nevertheless, with enough observations spread evenly throughout the decade, the average results may provide a discernible pattern.

   Third, measuring change using only two years could introduce a selection bias. Plants in 1970 that experience a change in control but exit prior to 1979 will be missed. On the other hand, plants in 1979 that entered after 1970 and that experienced a control change by 1970 will also not be considered. These last two factors, however, will probably offset each other (see Hall 1987).

7. See Rumelt (1974), Caves et al. (1980), and Lecraw (1984).

8. These averages do not include plants that were transferred from one industry to another and that changed control between 1970 and 1979.

9. The coefficient on category 12D is positive.

10. The productivity variable used throughout is value-added per worker. While there

are concepts that are more comprehensive, labour productivity was chosen for several reasons. First, it is interesting in itself. Second, it is subject to less measurement error than total-factor productivity concepts. Finally, movements in this variable are closely associated with relative growth and decline at the plant level, as Chapter 9 shows.

11. The relative productivity estimates for each industry were derived from the ratio-of-the-median estimate of productivity of the merged plants to the median estimate of productivity of continuing plants in the control group for each year. Medians were used to reduce the effect of outliers on the calculation of output per worker.

12. Value-added per worker was used.

13. The antilog was taken.

14. For example, for 1979 this is the sum of value-added in all plants acquired divided by the sum of all employment divided by the same ratio for all plants that continued over the decade without a change in ownership.

15. Thus, the weights for 1970 and 1979 are the relative shares measured in employment for that year.

16. The weighted relative productivity of acquired plants can increase over the decade because either the productivity of all plants goes up, the share of the most productive plants goes up more than those of the continuing sector, or some combination of the two.

17. See Brown and Medoff (1988) and Lichtenberg and Siegel (1989a, 1989b).

18. Wage rates are defined as wages paid divided by the number of production workers.

19. Salary rates are defined as salaries paid divided by the number of non-production workers.

20. This is similar to the findings of Pereboom, who uses data on wage contracts for the United States.

21. See Caves (1987) for a summary of the studies.

22. Profits are defined as value-added minus wages and salaries. All values are taken from the Census of Manufactures.

23. The parameter m is a function of p, the price and the exponent on labour in the production function.

11. Turnover in domestic and foreign enterprises

1. Gorecki (1976) finds that foreign-firm entry (defined as the change in the total number of firms) responds differently to concentration, growth, and profitability as compared with that of domestic-firm entry.

2. Lumpiness refers to a fixed cost or minimum capacity that may be large relative to a single market, for which declining marginal revenue deters full utilization. An intangible asset or skill is, of course, the limiting case of lumpy capacity – a public good belonging to the firm.

3. See Gilbert and Newbery (1988) and Caves and Mehra (1986).

4. See Dunning (1993: chs. 11 and 12) for a discussion of the role of the multinational in transferring technologies across national boundaries.

5. An international merger that extends multinational control of business assets can be horizontal (geographic extension), vertical, or diversifying with regard to the

product market(s) of the foreign acquirer. The evidence indicates that the horizontal and vertical mergers that were prevalent have given way somewhat to foreign investments that are diversifying in geographic terms and in terms of products (Hisey and Caves, 1985).

6. When a Canadian business unit is part of a multinational enterprise, the level of its reported productivity or profitability depends on transfer prices in its dealings with its corporate siblings. It is assumed that transfer-pricing practices may inject noise but do not systematically obscure the underlying economic relations.

7. The sample consists of establishments that were documented by the long and the short census forms and is therefore larger than the sample that was used in most other chapters, which consisted only of establishments completing the long form. The smaller sample was used previously because the estimation of turnover rates at the aggregate level was not very sensitive to the use of that sample (see Appendix A). However, the estimates for the particular industry groupings used in this chapter were sensitive to the sample chosen, and therefore the more comprehensive sample was used.

8. Productivity is defined as value-added per worker, the wage rate is defined as payments to production workers divided by number of production workers, and the salary rate is defined as payments to non-production workers divided by the number of non-production workers.

9. For example, relative output per worker was calculated as follows. The numerator is the sum of output divided by the sum of workers taken across all merged plants in one foreign-ownership industry group. The denominator is the sum of output divided by the sum of workers taken across all continuing plants that did not experience a control change in the same foreign-ownership industry group.

10. See Globerman (1979) for an earlier study of the difference between productivity of domestic and foreign firms.

11. The total number of plants per enterprise is not as good a measure of multi-plant activity because it varies among industries mainly with the number of single-plant firms. Not surprisingly, single-plant firms are more prevalent in industries with low foreign ownership.

12. The bounds for the specialization index are 1 when the output of the firm or plant is completely specialized and $1/N$ when it is spread equally across N industries or product lines.

13. Plants, of course, produce some products that are not classified to their primary four-digit industries, and these are included in panel D. To that extent, the lower bound shown in panel C is not constraining. Given the typically high plant-specialization ratios (the percentage of output produced by a plant that is classified to the SIC industry to which the plant is assigned), the constraint is still approximately relevant.

14. Plant size is also related to diversity and to the amount of foreign control in an industry (Caves, 1975). A regression procedure was used to control for plant size. The results show that the foreign–domestic differences were not solely due to differences in plant size.

15. Laiken (1973) finds no association between acquisition activity and financial performance among Canadian firms. Lecraw (1977) finds that large firms classified as unrelated diversifiers were heavily engaged in merger activity and tended

to report lower profits in the period 1960–75 than did less diversified firms (1977: Tables 13, 20). Using a sample of mergers obtained from the merger register of the Department of Consumer and Corporate Affairs by acquirers that were listed on the Toronto Stock Exchange, Jog and Riding (1988) and Tarasofsky (1991) find about equal numbers of post-merger failures and successes, where success is equated to profitability.

16. According to Reuber and Roseman (1969: 76–78), the most common explanations for mergers were the desire of the acquiree to sell and the acquirer to add capacity that is cheaper than de novo investment. Although acquirees were no less profitable than the firms acquiring them, losses were more common among the acquirees. Generalizing from case studies of large mergers, Lecraw (1977: 16–18) confirms the importance of sellers' initiatives; however, he ascribes importance to what was later called the "free cash flow" hypothesis that large enterprises undertake mergers when their cash inflow exceeds outlay on profitable reinvestments in their base activities plus normal dividends.

17. There are differences in the related spin-off–merger component. Transfers between continuing firms both of which are foreign – spin-offs to incumbents – show a differential pattern between domestic- and foreign-industry groups. The market shares of these foreign-to-foreign transfers increase in the low-foreign-ownership group and decrease in the high-foreign-ownership groups.

18. Related mergers and plant transfers between continuing firms are excluded from this estimate.

19. The greater productivity gain from related mergers might suggest monopoly rents. However, it should be noted that firms merging purely for monopoly profits generally must give up some market share to non-merging firms in order to increase their profit margins, unless they actually achieve a monopoly. This is not what happens here. Related mergers in industries dominated by domestic firms increase market shares (see Table 11-5).

20. The proportion of non-production workers in plants subject to control changes in the high-foreign-ownership group is lower than that in continuing plants before and after acquisition, and the proportion of non-production workers in new and closed plants in general declines with the extent of foreign ownership. These patterns suggest that in industries with high foreign ownership the high-ground positions of continuing units are held by foreign-controlled units that employ large proportions of non-production workers and are subject to low turnover. This is consistent with the evidence that foreign-to-foreign mergers vary with the extent of foreign control (see Table 11-5).

21. The weights are calculated vis-à-vis all plants in a foreign-ownership group, i.e., the summations of value-added and labour inputs are for all plants in a foreign-ownership industry group.

22. The weights are calculated vis-à-vis all plants in an industry, i.e., value-added and labour inputs are summed for all plants in an industry.

23. The term should not be given a normative connotation. All that is known is the level of average compensation in establishments that experienced a control change relative to that of continuing establishments that did not. No information is available here on whether compensation levels are above or below employees' opportunity costs in either group.

12. Industry efficiency and firm turnover in the Canadian manufacturing sector

1. See Caves and Barton (1990) for a summary of the literature.
2. See Farrell (1957) for an early attempt to classify the two types of inefficiencies.
3. See Timmer (1971), Forsund, Knox Lovell, and Schmidt (1980), and Schmidt (1985–86).
4. See Downie (1958) for one such attempt.
5. The similarities between the measures extended beyond the mean values reported here. Cross-industry correlations of the measures with one another were high. Correlations of the measures with industry characteristics were similar.
6. For further discussion of the database used and the definitions of the variables, see Baldwin and Gorecki (1986a) and Appendix B.
7. The correlations were estimated for both the entire sample and a reduced sample that eliminated those industries characterized by extreme values of the efficiency measure. Generally, the sign and the significance levels were very similar, suggesting that errors in observation may exist but are relatively unimportant.
8. The sign attached to PVAR18 strengthens the conclusion about the effect of MULT1.
9. For a description of the methodology used, see Appendix A.
10. These efficiency levels use the potential-output-per-person ratios derived from calculating the average value-added per worker in those plants that were most productive and that accounted for 40% of total value-added.
11. The contribution that each turnover category made to productivity growth can be usefully compared to these estimates. Almost half of productivity growth in the 1970s arose from turnover. Some 21% came from greenfield entry, some 7% from other new plants, and about 19% from gains in market share by continuing plants.
12. See Geroski and Masson (1987) for a general discussion of such models and Baldwin and Gorecki (1987b) for a specific application to the Canadian situation and more detailed definitions of the variables used here.
13. See Baldwin and Gorecki (1986a: App. A) for definitions of variables.
14. While these replacement assumptions distort reality slightly, they make the description of the ongoing replacement process much simpler (see Chapter 9).
15. Thus GAIN23 = SH23/GAIN.

13. Firm turnover and profitability

1. See Weiss (1974) and Schmalensee (1989) for a survey of the empirical studies.
2. See Statistics Canada (various years), Industrial Corporations, Financial Statistics, Cat. No. 61-003.
3. Khemani and Shapiro (1990) combine manufacturing and resource firms for their study of the extent to which firm profit differentials are perpetuated in Canada.
4. To reduce the problems that might have arisen from this source, top and bottom outliers in rates of return were deleted when averages were calculated.
5. In order to reduce the effect of error due to extreme accounting bias, the 10

industries with the highest and the lowest return on capital over the entire period were excluded. This does not change the qualitative results.

6. See Mueller (1987, 1990).
7. Return on equity also produces low correlations between profitability for individual years. Similarly, the correlations between the profitability for individual years (PREQ72) and the average (PREQ7286) are higher than those between individual years; however, compared with the results obtained using the return on capital, the return on equity for individual years is even less correlated with the estimated long-run return on equity (LPREQ), and the longer-period average (PREQ7286) is less correlated with the estimated long-run value (LPREQ).
8. For this exercise, four-digit Census of Manufactures data were used because they provide 167 industries with which to work, compared with 87 at the three-digit level in the financial statistics.
9. For a discussion of the accuracy of linking financial data to Census of Manufactures data, see Baldwin and Gorecki (1986a).
10. See the studies in Geroski and Schwalbach (1991).
11. The OLS estimate was used.
12. The method used to classify industries into these five classes was described in Chapter 11.
13. Even entry is often lacking in these analyses. Masson and Shaanan (1987) postulate entry to be a determinant of profitability and then omit entry from their list of regressors.
14. See Table 8-1 for a description of the components.
15. See Table 8-6 for the components of a slightly larger set of scale variables.
16. See Caves et al. (1980) and Masson and Shaanan (1987).

14. Modelling entry

1. See Geroski and Schwalbach (1991) for a survey of the results of applying this model to different countries.
2. See Cable and Schwalbach (1991) for a survey of the Orr-type results.
3. The negative binomial was also used for the shipments variable and a logistic transformation of the relative size and the population success rate was also employed; in all cases, the same qualitative results were obtained.
4. Chapters 7 and 8 define these variables.
5. See Chapter 13 for a definition of these variables.
6. See Chapter 13 for a discussion of the balance-sheet rate of return definitions.

Appendix A

1. As such, it excludes head offices and similar activities if they are located separately from the establishment or if they serve more than one establishment. For further details, see Statistics Canada (1979: 11–15).
2. An establishment may undertake a number of different activities. To be classified to the manufacturing sector, the preponderance of these activities (based on value-added) must be in manufacturing (Dominion Bureau of Statistics, 1970: 23–43).

3. There are a number of different reporting units under the Census of Manufactures, including head offices and other auxiliary facilities. Attention is paid here only to establishments. For further details, see Statistics Canada (1979: 10).

4. In order to determine whether one legal entity controls another, attention is paid to cases where, directly or indirectly, one company "has more than 50 per cent of the exercisable voting rights of the subsidiary corporation" (Statistics Canada, 1979: 17) and to cases of minority control "if factual information exists or acknowledgement by the entity in question is obtained" (Statistics Canada, 1983: 25).

5. In some instances, several establishments may file a combined record. In these cases, the original statistics are projected by Statistics Canada across the individual establishment, each of which has a separate RSN.

6. The longitudinal enterprise code was maintained for the purposes of estimating concentration and foreign ownership statistics.

7. The results indicate that there was little difference in the annual entry and exit rates calculated with and without these exclusion criteria.

8. Statistics Canada (1983) and "A Summary of the Establishment Description Tape File," Statistics Canada, unpublished internal working document (n.d.: 2, Appendix C-1).

9. This is often not true of databases used for U.S. studies that are generated from unemployment insurance or Dun and Bradstreet records. For a discussion of the problems with these databases, see Baldwin and Gorecki (1990b).

10. The country of control categories were Canada, United States, United Kingdom, other Europe, and other foreign.

11. A continuing firm is one that is in the same four-digit manufacturing industry in both the terminal and initial years of the comparison.

12. The data for small plants that are taken from taxation administrative records in place of a mailed short form and the short-form records are both referred to here, for convenience, as "short form."

13. Measures based on total employment are very similar to those based on shipments.

14. For a discussion of the total-activity concept used in the Census of Manufactures, see Statistics Canada (1979: 21–22). Measures of the employment size of enterprises cover all employment, including that in the headquarters – i.e., employment in ancillary units as well as that in operating establishments is included in the total.

15. This was done for a reduced 141-industry sample that excluded miscellaneous industries – a sample that was used for regression analysis of entry (Baldwin and Gorecki, 1983, 1987b). Only long-form establishments were used.

16. Although the cut-off point subsequently drifts upward, the increase in the percentage of short-form establishments by 1983 is relatively minor – only about 4 percentage points. In light of the relatively small correction required for entry rates at the 1975 revision, which increased short-form establishments by 14 percentage points, the corrections were taken no further.

17. Alternative assumptions about the distribution of omitted entrants were found to have little impact on the mean of the annual birth and death rates for the decade.

18. In the 1970 Standard Industrial Classification, these are Division 2, Major Group 1, Logging; Division 4, Mining (except Crude Petroleum and Natural Gas Industry and Major Group 5); and Division 5, Manufacturing. For full details, see Dominion Bureau of Statistics (1970: 17). In 1980, the value-added of enterprises classified to manufacturing was $66,472 million; to mining, $9,062 million; and to logging, $702 million (Statistics Canada, 1983: 15, Table VII).

19. Manufacturing value-added is used to classify the enterprise to a four-digit SIC on the basis of the largest unconsolidated enterprise owned by the consolidated enterprise. For details of these two enterprise concepts, see Statistics Canada (1983: 28–30).

20. Using this definition of enterprises, there were 30,160 manufacturing enterprises in 1980 (Statistics Canada, 1983: 15, Table VII); however, if a manufacturing enterprise is defined as all establishments classified to the manufacturing sector, then there would be 30,197 enterprises classified to the manufacturing sector (Statistics Canada, 1983: 21, Table XIII). Hence, in terms of numbers, it makes little difference how we define the universe of manufacturing firms.

21. This problem does not arise for establishment entry or exit. An establishment that exits the manufacturing sector – fails to file an annual Census of Manufactures questionnaire – is assumed to exist no longer. In the terminology used here, it has exited by closing. Similarly, establishment entry can only be the building of a new plant.

22. An alternative to matching whether an establishment filed an annual Census of Manufactures questionnaire in year t and $t + 1$ to determine whether the enterprise exited through closing plant is to refer directly to question 1.3.2 in the annual Census of Manufactures questionnaire, which asks, "Did this establishment go out of business during the reporting year?" to which the answer had to be yes or no (Statistics Canada, 1979: 79). Work by Statistics Canada's Business Micro-Data Integration and Analysis group suggests that matching the establishment annual Census of Manufactures questionnaire between year t and $t + 1$ is more reliable than accepting the answer to question 1.3.2.

REFERENCES

Aaronovitch, S. and M. C. Sawyer. (1975). *Big Business; Theoretical and Empirical Aspects of Concentration and Mergers in the U.K.* London: Macmillan.

Acs, Z. J. and D. B. Audretsch. (1989a). "Small-Firm Entry in U.S. Manufacturing". *Economica* 56: 255–65.

Acs, Z. J. and D. B. Audretsch. (1989b). "Births and Firm Size". *Southern Economic Journal* 56: 467–75.

Acs, Z. J. and D. B. Audretsch. (1990). *Innovation and Small Firms.* Cambridge, Mass.: MIT Press.

Adelman, I. G. (1958). "A Stochastic Analysis of the Size Distribution of Firms". *Journal of the American Statistical Association* 53: 893–904.

Adelman, M. A. (1951). "The Measurement of Industrial Concentration". *Review of Economics and Statistics* 33: 269–96.

Adelman, M. A. (1969). "Comment on the 'H' Concentration Measure as a Numbers Equivalent". *Review of Economics and Statistics* 51: 99–101.

Altman, E. I. (1971). *Corporate Bankruptcy in America.* Lexington, Mass.: Heath.

Altman, E. I. (1983). *Corporate Financial Distress.* New York: Wiley.

Ashenfelter, O. and D. Card. (1986). "Why Have Unemployment Rates in Canada and the United States Diverged?" *Economica* 53: supp.

Bain, J. S. (1956). *Barriers to New Competition.* Cambridge, Mass.: Harvard University Press.

Bain, J. S. (1968). *Industrial Organization.* 2d ed. New York: Wiley.

Bain, J. S. (1972). *Essays on Price Theory and Industrial Organization.* Boston: Little, Brown.

Baldwin, J. R. and P. K. Gorecki. (1983). *Entry and Exit to the Canadian Manufacturing Sector: 1970–79.* Discussion Paper No. 225. Ottawa: Economic Council of Canada.

Baldwin, J. R. and P. K. Gorecki. (1986a). *The Role of Scale in Canada–U.S. Productivity Differences in the Manufacturing Sector, 1970–1979.* Toronto: University of Toronto Press.

Baldwin, J. R. and P. K. Gorecki. (1986b). *Mergers and Merger Policy in the Canadian Manufacturing Sector: 1971–79.* Ottawa: Economic Council of Canada.

Baldwin, J. R. and P. K. Gorecki. (1987a). "The Impact of High Tariffs and Imperfect Market Structure on Plant Scale Inefficiency in Canadian Manufacturing Industries in the 1970s". *Recherches Economiques de Louvain* 53: 51–73.

445

Baldwin, J. R. and P. K. Gorecki. (1987b). "Plant Creation Versus Plant Acquisition: The Entry Process in Canadian Manufacturing". *International Journal of Industrial Organization* 5: 27–41.

Baldwin, J. R. and P. K. Gorecki. (1990a). "Measuring Firm Entry and Exit with Panel Data". In *Analysis of Data in Time*. Edited by A. C. Singh and P. Whitridge. Ottawa: Statistics Canada. 255–70.

Baldwin, J. R. and P. K. Gorecki. (1990b). *Structural Change and the Adjustment Process: Perspectives on Firm Growth and Worker Turnover*. Ottawa: Economic Council of Canada.

Baldwin, J. R. and P. K. Gorecki. (1991). "Firm Entry and Exit in the Canadian Manufacturing Sector". *Canadian Journal of Economics* 24: 300–23.

Baldwin, J. R. and P. K. Gorecki. (1993). "Dimensions of Labor-Market Change in Canada: Intersectoral Shifts, Job and Worker Turnover". *Journal of Income Distribution* 3: 148–80.

Baldwin, J. R., P. K. Gorecki, and J. McVey. (1986). "International Trade, Secondary Output and Concentration in Canadian Manufacturing Industries, 1979". *Applied Economics* 18: 529–43.

Baldwin, W. L. and J. T. Scott. (1987). *Market Structure and Technical Change*. London: Harwood.

Bartholomew, D. J. (1973). *Stochastic Models for Social Processes*. New York: Wiley.

Baumol, W. J. (1982). "Contestable Markets: An Uprising in the Theory of Industry Structure". *American Economic Review* 72: 1–15.

Benston, G. (1985). "The Validity of Profits-Structure with Particular Reference to the FTC's Line of Business Data". *American Economic Review* 75: 37–67.

Bevan, A. (1974). "The U.K. Potato Crisp Industry, 1960–72: A Study of New Entry Competition". *Journal of Industrial Economics* 22: 281–97.

Bhagwati, J. N. (1970). "Oligopoly Theory, Entry Prevention and Growth". *Oxford Economic Papers* (N.S.) 22: 297–310.

Birch, D. (1979). *The Job Generation Process*. Cambridge, Mass.: Massachusetts Institute of Technology Program on Neighborhood Change.

Birch, D. (1981). "Who Creates Jobs?" *Public Interest* 65: 3–14.

Birch, D. (1987). *Job Creation in America*. New York: Free Press.

Boeri, T. and U. Cramer. (1992). "Employment Growth, Incumbents and Entrants: Evidence from Germany". *Journal of International Industrial Organization* 10: 545–66.

Boyle, S. E. and D. Bailey. (1971). "The Optimal Measure of Concentration". *Journal of the American Statistical Association* 66: 702–6.

Boyle, S. E. and R. L. Sorensen. (1971). "Concentration and Mobility: Alternative Measures of Industry Structure". *Journal of Industrial Economics* 19: 118–32.

Branch, B. (1972–73). "Research and Development and Its Relation to Sales Growth". *Journal of Economics and Business* 25: 107–11.

Brown, C. and J. Medoff. (1988). "The Impact of Firm Acquisitions on Labor". In *Corporate Takeovers: Causes and Consequences*. Edited by A. Auerbach. Chicago: University of Chicago Press. 9–32.

Brozen, Y. (1971). "Bain's Concentration and Rates of Return Revisited". *Journal of Law and Economics* 13: 179–92.

Cable, J. and J. Schwalbach. (1991). "International Comparisons of Entry and Exit". In *Entry and Market Contestability: An International Comparison*. Edited by P. A. Geroski and J. Schwalbach. Oxford: Basil Blackwell. 257–81.

Cameron, A. C. and P. K. Trivedi. (1986). "Econometric Models Based on Count Data: Comparisons and Applications of Some Estimators and Tests". *Journal of Applied Econometrics* 1: 29–54.

Card, D. and W. C. Riddel. (1992). "A Comparative Analysis of Unemployment in Canada and the United States". In *Small Differences That Matter: Labour Markets and Income Maintenance in Canada and the United States*. Edited by D. Card and R. Freeman. Chicago: University of Chicago Press. 149–90.

Carroll, G. and D. Vogel, eds. (1984). *Strategy and Organization*. Boston: Pitman.

Carroll, G. and D. Vogel, eds. (1987). *Organizational Approaches to Strategy*. Cambridge, Mass.: Ballinger.

Caves, R. E. (1974). "Causes of Direct Investment: Foreign Firms' Share in Canadian and United Kingdom Manufacturing Industries". *Review of Economics and Statistics* 56: 279–93.

Caves, R. E. (1975). *Diversification, Foreign Investment, and Scale in North American Manufacturing Industries*. Ottawa: Economic Council of Canada.

Caves, R. E. (1982). *Multinational Enterprise and Economic Analysis*. Cambridge University Press.

Caves, R. E. (1987). "Effects of Mergers and Acquisitions on the Economy: An Industrial Organization Perspective". In *The Merger Boom*. Edited by Lynne Browne and Eric Rosengren. Boston: Federal Reserve Bank of Boston. 149–68.

Caves, R. E. (1989a). "Mergers, Takeovers, and Economic Efficiency: Foresight vs. Hindsight". *International Journal of Industrial Organization* 7: 151–74.

Caves, R. E. (1989b). "International Differences in Industrial Organization". In *Handbook of Industrial Organization*. Edited by R. Schmalensee and R. D. Willig. Amsterdam: North-Holland. 1225–50.

Caves, R. E. and D. R. Barton. (1990). *Technical Efficiency in the U.S. Manufacturing Industries*. Cambridge, Mass.: MIT Press.

Caves, R. E. and S. Mehra. (1986). "Entry of Foreign Multinationals in U.S. Manufacturing". In *Competition in Global Industries*. Edited by M. E. Porter. Boston: Harvard Business School Press. 449–81.

Caves, R. E. and M. E. Porter. (1977). "From Entry Barriers to Mobility Barriers". *Quarterly Journal of Economics* 91: 241–61.

Caves, R. E. and M. E. Porter. (1978). "Market Structure, Oligopoly, and Stability of Market Shares". *Journal of Industrial Economics* 26: 289–313.

Caves, R. E., M. E. Porter, A. M. Spence, with J. T. Scott. (1980). *Competition in the Open Economy: A Model Applied to Canada*. Cambridge, Mass.: Harvard University Press.

Chappell, W. F., M. S. Kimenyi, and W. J. Mayer. (1990). "A Poisson Probability Model of Entry and Market Structure with an Application to U.S. Industries During 1972–77". *Southern Economic Journal* 56: 918–27.

Churchill, B. (1955). "Age and Life-Expectancy of Business Firms". *Survey of Current Business* 35: 15–24.

Cohen, W. and R. C. Levin. (1989). "Empirical Studies of Innovation and Market

Structure". In *Handbook of Industrial Organization*. Edited by R. Schmalensee and R. D. Willig. Amsterdam: North-Holland. 1059–1107.

Commission of European Communities. (1987). *Job Creation in Small and Medium Sized Enterprises*. Vols. 1–3. Luxembourg: Office for Official Publications of the European Communities.

Commission of Inquiry on the Pharmaceutical Industry. (1985). *Report*. Ottawa: Minister of Supply and Services Canada.

Connolly, R. A. and S. Schwartz. (1985). "The Intertemporal Behaviour of Economic Profits". *International Journal of Industrial Organization* 3: 379–400.

Cowling, K., P. Stoneman, J. Cubbin, J. Cable, G. Hall, S. Domberger, and P. Dutton. (1980). *Mergers and Economic Performance*. Cambridge University Press.

Cowling, K. and M. Waterson. (1976). "Price–Cost Margins and Market Structure". *Economica* 43: 767–74.

Curry, B. and K. George. (1983). "Industrial Concentration: A Survey". *Journal of Industrial Economics* 31: 203–55.

Dansby, R. E. and R. D. Willig. (1979). "Industry Performance Gradients". *American Economic Review* 69: 249–60.

David, P. (1961). "The Deflation of Value-Added". *Review of Economics and Statistics* 44: 148–55.

Davies, S. W. (1980a). "Measuring Industrial Concentration: An Alternative Approach". *Review of Economics and Statistics* 62: 306–9.

Davies, S. W. (1980b). "Minimum Efficient Size and Seller Concentration: An Empirical Problem". *Journal of Industrial Economics* 28: 287–301.

Davies, S. (1991). *The Dynamics of Market Leadership in UK Manufacturing Industries, 1979–86*. London: London Business School, Centre for Business Strategy.

Davies, S. W. and B. R. Lyons. (1982). "Seller Concentration: The Technological Explanation and Demand Uncertainty". *Economic Journal* 92: 903–19.

Davis, S. and J. Haltiwanger. (1990). "Gross Job Creation and Destruction: Microeconomic Evidence and Macroeconomic Implications". *NBER Macroeconomics Annual* 5: 123–68.

Davis, S. and J. Haltiwanger. (1991). "The Distribution of Employees by Establishment Size: Patterns of Change and Comovement in the United States, 1962–85". Unpublished working paper.

Davis, S. and J. Haltiwanger. (1992). "Gross Job Creation, Gross Job Destruction, and Employment Reallocation". *Quarterly Journal of Economics* 107: 819–64.

Davis, S., J. Haltiwanger, and S. Schuh. (1990). "Published Versus Sample Statistics from the ASM: Implications for the LRD". *Proceedings of the American Statistical Association, Business and Economics Statistics Section*.

DeMelto, D. P., K. E. McMullen, and R. M. Wills. (1980). *Preliminary Report: Innovation and Technical Change in Five Canadian Industries*. Discussion Paper No. 176. Ottawa: Economic Council of Canada.

Department of Consumer and Corporate Affairs. (1971). *Concentration in the Manufacturing Industries of Canada*. Ottawa.

Deutsch, L. (1975). "Structure, Performance and the Net Rate of Entry in Manufacturing Industries". *Southern Economic Journal* 41: 450–56.

Dominion Bureau of Statistics. (1970). *Standard Industrial Classification, 1970*. Cat. No. 12-501. Ottawa: Minister of Supply and Services Canada.

Downie, J. (1958). *The Competitive Process*. London: Duckworth.

Dunne, T. and M. Roberts. (1986). "Measuring Firm Entry and Exit with Census of Manufactures Data". University Park: Department of Economics, Pennsylvania State University.

Dunne, T. and M. Roberts. (1991). "Variation in Producer Turnover Across U.S. Manufacturing Industries". In *Entry and Market Contestability: An International Comparison*. Edited by P. A. Geroski and J. Schwalbach. Oxford: Basil Blackwell. 187–203.

Dunne, T., M. Roberts, and L. Samuelson. (1988). "Patterns of Firm Entry and Exit in U.S. Manufacturing Industries". *Rand Journal of Economics* 19: 495–515.

Dunne, T., M. Roberts, and L. Samuelson. (1989). "Plant Turnover and Gross Employment Flows in the U.S. Manufacturing Sector". *Journal of Labor Economics* 7: 48–71.

Dunning, J. H. (1993). *Multinational Enterprises and the Global Economy*. New York: Addison-Wesley.

Durbin, J. (1958). "Errors in Variables". *Revue de l'Institut International de Statistique* 22: 23–32.

Eckbo, B. E. (1986). "Mergers and the Market for Corporate Control: The Canadian Evidence". *Canadian Journal of Economics* 19: 236–60.

Eckbo, B. E. (1988). "The Market for Corporate Control: Policy Issues and Capital Market Evidence". In *Mergers, Corporate Concentration and Power in Canada*. Edited by R. S. Khemani, D. M. Shapiro, and W. T. Stanbury. Halifax: Institute for Public Policy. 143–225.

Elliasson, G. (1985). *The Firm and Financial Markets in the Swedish Micro to Macro Model: Theory, Model, Verification*. Stockholm: Industrial Institute of Economic and Social Research.

Evans, D. S. (1987). "Tests of Alternative Theories of Firm Growth". *Journal of Political Economy* 95: 657–74.

Farrell, M. J. (1957). "The Measurement of Productive Efficiency". *Journal of the Royal Statistical Society* 120: 253–82.

Feldstein, M. (1974). "Errors in Variables: A Consistent Estimator with Smaller Mean Square Error in Finite Samples". *Journal of the American Statistical Association* 69: 990–96.

Fisher, F. M. and J. T. McGowan. (1983). "On the Misuse of Accounting Rates of Return to Infer Monopoly Profits". *American Economic Review* 73: 82–97.

Forsund, F. R., C. A. Knox Lovell, and P. Schmidt. (1980). "A Survey of Frontier Production Functions and Their Relationship to Efficiency Measurement". *Journal of Econometrics* 13: 5–25.

Friedman, M. (1955). "Comment". In *Business Concentration and Price Policy*. Edited by National Bureau of Economic Research. Princeton, N.J.: Princeton University Press. 213–18.

Gaskins, D. (1971). "Dynamic Limit Pricing: Optimal Pricing Under the Threat of Entry". *Journal of Economic Theory* 3: 306–22.

Geroski, P. A. (1989). "Entry, Innovation and Productivity Growth". *Review of Economics and Statistics* 71: 572–78.

Geroski, P. A. (1991). *Market Dynamics and Entry*. Oxford: Basil Blackwell.

Geroski, P. A. and R. T. Masson. (1987). "Dynamic Market Models in Industrial Organization". *International Journal of Industrial Organization* 5: 1–13.

Geroski, P. A., R. T. Masson, and J. Shaanan. (1987). "The Dynamics of Market Structure". *International Journal of Industrial Organization* 5: 93–100.

Geroski, P. A. and J. Schwalbach. (1991). *Entry and Market Contestability: An International Comparison*. Oxford: Basil Blackwell.

Gilbert, R. J. and D. M. Newberry. (1988) "Entry, Acquisition, and the Value of Shark Repellent". Working Paper No. 8888. Berkeley: Department of Economics, University of California.

Globerman, S. (1977). *Mergers and Acquisitions in Canada: A Background Report*. Royal Commission on Corporate Concentration. Study No. 34. Ottawa: Minister of Supply and Services Canada.

Globerman, S. (1979). "Foreign Direct Investment and 'Spillover' Efficiency Benefits in Canadian Manufacturing Industries". *Canadian Journal of Economics* 12: 42–56.

Goldshmid, H. J., H. M. Mann, and J. F. Weston, eds. (1974). *Industrial Concentration: The New Learning*. Boston: Little, Brown.

Gorecki, P. K. (1976). "The Determinants of Entry by Domestic and Foreign Enterprises in Canadian Manufacturing Industries: Some Comments and Empirical Results". *Review of Economics and Statistics* 58: 485–88.

Gort, M. (1963). "Analysis of Stability and Change in Market Shares". *Journal of Political Economy* 62: 51–61.

Gort, M. and S. Klepper. (1982). "Time Paths in the Diffusion of Product Innovations". *Economic Journal* 92: 630–53.

Gourieroux, C., A. Monfort, and A. Trognon. (1984). "Pseudo Maximum Likelihood Methods: Applications to Poisson Models". *Econometrica* 52: 701–20.

Grabowski, H. G. and D. C. Mueller. (1978). "Industrial Research and Development, Intangible Capital Stocks, and Firm Profit Rates". *Bell Journal of Economics* 9: 328–43.

Green, C. (1980). *Canadian Industrial Organization and Policy*. Toronto: McGraw-Hill Ryerson.

Grossack, I. M. (1965). "Toward an Integration of Static and Dynamic Measures of Industry Concentration". *Review of Economics and Statistics* 47: 301–8.

Grossack, I. M. (1972). "The Concept and Measurement of Permanent Industrial Concentration". *Journal of Political Economy* 80: 745–60.

Hall, B. H. (1987). "The Relationship Between Firm Size and Firm Growth in the U.S. Manufacturing Sector". *Journal of Industrial Economics* 35: 583–606.

Hall, M. and N. Tideman. (1967). "Measures of Concentration". *Journal of the American Statistical Association* 62: 162–68.

Hannah, L. and J. A. Kay. (1977). *Concentration in Modern Industry*. London: Macmillan.

Harris, R. J. 1975. *A Primer of Multivariate Statistics*. New York: Academic Press.

Hart, P. E. (1971). "Entropy and Other Measures of Concentration". *Journal of the Royal Statistical Society*. Series A. 134: 73–85.

Hart, P. E. (1975). "Moment Distributions in Economics: An Exposition". *Journal of the Royal Statistical Society.* Series A. 138: 423–34.

Hart, P. E. (1979). "On Bias and Concentration". *Journal of Industrial Economics* 27: 211–16.

Hart, P. E. and R. Clarke. (1980). *Concentration in British Industry, 1935–75.* Cambridge University Press.

Hart, P. E. and S. J. Prais. (1956). "The Analysis of Business Concentration: A Statistical Approach". *Journal of the Royal Statistical Society.* Series A. 119: 150–91.

Hausman, J., B. H. Hall, and Z. Griliches. (1984). "Econometric Models for Count Data with an Application to the Patents–R&D Relationship". *Econometrica* 52: 909–38.

Havrilesky, T. and R. Barth. 1969. "Tests of Market Share Stability in the Cigarette Industry, 1950–66". *Journal of Industrial Economics* 17: 145–50.

Hayek, F. (1948). *Individualism and the Economic Order.* Chicago: University of Chicago Press.

Hazledine, T. (1980). "Testing Two Models of Protection with Canada–United States Data". *Journal of Industrial Economics* 29: 145–54.

Hazledine, T. (1985). "The Anatomy of Productivity Growth Slowdown and Recovery in Canadian Manufacturing". *International Journal of Industrial Organization* 3: 307–26.

Hazledine, T. (1990). "Why Do the Free Trade Gain Numbers Differ So Much: The Role of Industrial Organization in General Equilibrium". *Canadian Journal of Economics* 23: 791–806.

Hisey, K. B. and R. E. Caves. (1985) "Diversification Strategy and Choice of Country: Diversifying Acquisitions Abroad by U.S. Multinationals, 1978–1980". *Journal of International Business Studies* 15: 51–64.

Horvath, J. (1970). "Suggestion for a Comprehensive Measure of Concentration". *Southern Economic Journal* 36: 446–52.

Hudson, J. (1989). "The Birth and Death of Firms". *Quarterly Review of Economics and Business* 29: 68–86.

Hymer, S. and P. Pashigian. (1962). "Turnover of Firms as a Measure of Market Behavior". *Review of Economics and Statistics* 44: 82–87.

Ibrahim, A. B. and J. R. Goodwin. (1986). "Toward Excellence in Small Business: An Empirical Study of Successful Small Business". In *La PME dans un Monde en Mutation.* Edited by P. Julien, J. Chicha, and A. Royal. Silery: Presse de l'Université de Québec. 223–30.

Ijiri, Y. and H. Simon. (1977). *Skew Distributions and the Sizes of Business Firms.* Amsterdam: North-Holland.

Jacobsen, R. (1987). "The Validity of ROI as a Measure of Business Performance". *American Economic Review* 77: 470–78.

Jacoby, N. M. (1984). "The Relative Stability of Market Shares: A Theory and Evidence from Several Industries". *Journal of Industrial Economics* 12: 83–107.

Jacquemin, A. (1987). *The New Industrial Organization: Market Forces and Strategic Behavior.* Cambridge, Mass.: MIT Press.

Jarrel, G. A. (1987). "Financial Innovations and Corporate Mergers". In *The Merger*

Boom. Edited by Lynne Browne and Eric Rosengren. Boston: Federal Reserve Bank of Boston. 52–73.

Jewkes, J., D. Sawers, and R. Stillerman. (1958). *The Sources of Invention*. London: Macmillan.

Jog, V. M. and A. L. Riding. (1988). "Post-Acquisition Performance of Partially Acquired Canadian Firms". In *Mergers, Corporate Concentration and Power in Canada*. Edited by R. S. Khemani, D. M. Shapiro, and W. T. Stanbury. Halifax: Institute for Public Policy. 233–52.

Johnson, P. (1986). *New Firms: An Economic Perspective*. London: Allen & Unwin.

Johnson, S. and D. Storey. (1985). *Job Generation – An International Survey: U.S. and Canadian Job Generation Studies Using Dun and Bradstreet Data: Some Methodological Issues*. Research Working Paper No. 1. Newcastle: University of Newcastle-upon-Tyne.

Joskow, J. (1960). "Structural Indicia: Rank-Shift Analyses as a Supplement to Concentration Ratios". *Review of Economics and Statistics* 42: 113–16.

Jovanovic, B. (1982). "Selection and Evolution of Industry". *Econometrica* 50: 649–70.

Kalecki, M. (1945). "On the Gilbrat Distribution". *Econometrica* 13: 161–70.

Kaplan, S. N. (1989). "The Effect of Management Buyouts on Operating Performance and Value". *Journal of Financial Economics* 24: 217–54.

Kessides, I. N. (1991). "Entry and Market Contestability: Evidence from the United States". In *Entry and Market Contestability: An International Comparison*. Edited by P. A. Geroski and J. Schwalbach. Oxford: Basil Blackwell. 23–48.

Khemani, R. S. (1980). *Concentration in the Manufacturing Industries of Canada: Analysis of Post-War Changes*. Ottawa: Minister of Supply and Services Canada.

Khemani, R. S. (1986). "The Extent and Evolution of Competition in the Canadian Economy". In *Canadian Industry in Transition*. Edited by D. McFetridge. Toronto: University of Toronto Press. 135–76.

Khemani, R. S. and D. Shapiro. (1990). "The Persistence of Profitability in Canada". In *The Dynamics of Company Profits: An International Comparison*. Edited by D. C. Mueller. Cambridge University Press. 77–104.

Kilpatrick, R. W. (1967). "The Choice Among Alternative Measures of Industrial Concentration". *Review of Economics and Statistics* 49: 258–60.

Kirzner, I. (1973). *Competition and Entrepreneurship*. Chicago: University of Chicago Press.

Knight, F. H. (1921). *Risk, Uncertainty and Profit*. New York: Harper.

Krause, W. and J. Lothian. (1988). "Measurement of and Recent Trends in Canada's Level of Corporate Concentration". Paper presented at the American Statistical Association Conference, New Orleans, August.

Kwoka, J. E., Jr. (1979). "The Effect of Market Share Distribution on Industry Performance". *Review of Economics and Statistics* 61: 101–9.

Kwoka, J. E., Jr. (1982). "Regularity and Diversity in Firm Size Distributions in U.S. Industries". *Journal of Business and Economics* 34: 391–95.

Laiken, S. N. (1973). "Financial Performance of Merging Firms in a Virtually Unconstrained Legal Environment". *Antitrust Bulletin* 18: 827–51.

Lecraw, D. J. (1977). *Conglomerate Mergers in Canada*. Royal Commission on

Corporate Concentration. Study No. 32. Ottawa: Minister of Supply and Services Canada.

Lecraw, D. J. (1984). "Diversification Strategy and Performance". *Journal of Industrial Economics* 33: 179–98.

Leibenstein, H. (1966). "Allocative Efficiency vs. 'X-Efficiency'". *American Economic Review* 56: 392–415.

Leonard, J. (1987). "In the Wrong Place at the Wrong Time: The Extent of Frictional Unemployment". In *Unemployment and Structure of Labor Markets*. Edited by K. Lang and J. Leonard. Oxford: Basil Blackwell. 141–63.

Levin, R. C. (1978). "Technical Change, Barriers to Entry, and Market Structure". *Economica* 45: 347–61.

Levin, R. C., W. M. Cohen, and D. C. Mowery. (1985). "R&D Appropriability, Opportunity, and Market Structure: New Evidence on Some Schumpeterian Hypotheses". *American Economic Review* 75: 20–24.

Levy, D. (1987). "The Speed of the Invisible Hand". *International Journal of Industrial Organization* 5: 79–82.

Lichtenberg, F. R. (1992). *Corporate Takeovers and Productivity*. Cambridge, Mass.: MIT Press.

Lichtenberg, F. R. and D. Siegel. (1987). "Productivity and Changes in Ownership of Manufacturing Plants". *Brookings Papers on Economic Activity* 3: 643–73.

Lichtenberg, F. R. and D. Siegel. (1989a). *The Effects of Leveraged Buyouts on Productivity and Related Aspects of Firm Behaviour*. Discussion Paper No. 89-5. Washington, D.C.: Center for Economic Studies, Bureau of the Census, U.S. Department of Commerce.

Lichtenberg, F. R. and D. Siegel. (1989b). "The Effect of Takeovers on the Employment and Wages of Central-Office and Other Personnel". *Journal of Law and Economics* 33: 383–408.

Lyons, B. R. (1980). "A New Measure of Minimum Efficient Plant Size in U.K. Manufacturing Industries". *Economica* 47: 19–34.

Mansfield, E. (1962). "Entry, Gilbrat's Law, Innovation and the Growth of Firms". *American Economic Review* 52: 1023–51.

Mansfield, E. (1983). "Technological Change and Market Structure: An Empirical Study". *American Economic Review* 73: 205–9.

Mansfield, E., J. Rapaport, A. Romeo, E. Villani, S. Wagner, and F. Husie. (1977). *The Production and Application of New Industrial Technologies*. New York: Norton.

Marfels, C. (1971). "A Guide to the Literature on the Measurement of Industrial Concentration in the Post-War Period". *Zeitschrift für Nationaloekonomie* 31: 483–506.

Marfels, C. (1972). "On Testing Concentration Measures". *Zeitschrift für Nationaloekonomie* 32: 461–86.

Marfels, C. (1976). *Concentration Levels and Trends in the Canadian Economy, 1965–1973*. Study No. 31 for the Royal Commission on Corporate Concentration. Ottawa: Minister of Supply and Services Canada.

Marshall, A. (1920). *Principles of Economics*. 8th ed. London: Macmillan.

Martin, S. (1979). "Advertising, Concentration and Profitability". *Bell Journal of Economics* 10: 639–47.

Martin, S. (1988). "Market Power and/or Efficiency?" *Review of Economics and Statistics* 70: 331–35.

Marx, K. *Capital*. 1966 edition. Moscow: Progress Publishers. Vol. 1.

Mason, E. S. (1939). "Price and Production Policies of Large-Scale Enterprise". *American Economic Review* 39 supp.: 61–74.

Masson, R. T. and J. Shaanan. (1987). "Optimal Oligopoly Pricing and the Threat of Entry: Canadian Evidence". *International Journal of Industrial Organization* 5: 323–29.

Mayer, W. J. and W. F. Chappell. (1992). "Determinants of Entry and Exit: An Application of the Compounded Bivariate Poisson Distribution to U.S. Industries, 1972–77". *Southern Economic Journal* 58: 770–78.

McCallum, J. (1987). "Unemployment in Canada and the United States". *Canadian Journal of Economics* 20: 802–22.

McGuckin, R. (1972). "Entry, Concentration Change and Stability of Market Shares". *Southern Economic Journal* 38: 363–70.

McGuckin, R. M., S. Nguyen, and S. Andrews. (1991). "The Relationships Among Acquiring and Acquired Firms' Product Lines". *Journal of Law and Economics* 34: 477–502.

McVey, J. (1981). *Mergers, Plant Openings and Closings of Large Transnational and Other Enterprises, 1970–1976*. Catalogue No. 67-507. Statistics Canada. Ottawa: Minister of Supply and Services Canada.

Miller, R. A. (1971). "Marginal Concentration Ratios as Market Structure Variables". *Review of Economics and Statistics* 53: 289–93.

Modigliani, F. (1958). "New Developments on the Oligopoly Front". *Journal of Political Economy* 66: 215–32.

Mueller, D. C., ed. (1980). *The Determinants and Effects of Mergers: An International Comparison*. Cambridge University Press.

Mueller, D. C. (1985). "Mergers and Market Share". *Review of Economics and Statistics* 47: 259–67.

Mueller, D. C. (1986). *Profits in the Long Run*. Cambridge University Press.

Mueller, D. C. (1987). *The Corporation: Growth, Diversification and Mergers*. London: Harwood.

Mueller, D. C. (1990). *The Dynamics of Company Profits: An International Comparison*. Cambridge University Press.

Mueller, D. C. and J. E. Tilton. (1969). "Research and Development Costs as a Barrier to Entry". *Canadian Journal of Economics* 2: 570–79.

Mueller, W. F. and L. G. Hamm. (1974). "Trends in Industrial Concentration". *Review of Economics and Statistics* 56: 511–20.

Mukhopadhyay, A. K. (1985). "Technological Progress and Change in Market Concentration in the U.S., 1963–77". *Southern Economic Journal* 52: 141–49.

National Bureau of Economic Research. (1955). *Business Concentration and Price Policy*. Princeton, N.J.: Princeton University Press.

Nelson, R. R. and S. G. Winter. (1978). "Forces Generating and Limiting Concentration under Schumpeterian Competition". *Bell Journal of Economics* 9: 524–48.

Nelson, R. R. and S. G. Winter. (1982). *An Evolutionary Theory of Economic Change*. Cambridge Mass.: Harvard University Press.

Neumann, M., I. Bobel, and A. Haid. (1982). "Innovations and Market Structure in West German Industries". *Managerial and Decision Economics* 3: 131–39.

Newbould, G. D. (1970). *Management and Merger Activity*. Liverpool: Guthstead.

Newman, H. (1978). "Strategic Groups and Structure–Performance Relationship". *Review of Economics and Statistics* 60: 417–27.

Organization for Economic Cooperation and Development. (1987). "The Process of Job Creation and Destruction". In *Employment Outlook*. Paris: OECD. 97–124.

Orr, D. (1974). "The Determinants of Entry: A Study of the Canadian Manufacturing Industries". *Review of Economics and Statistics* 56: 58–66.

Pakes, A. and R. Ericson. (1988). "Empirical Implications of Alternative Models of Firm Dynamics". A paper given at a conference entitled "Dynamic Aspects of Firm and Industry Behaviour". Cambridge, Mass.: National Bureau of Economic Research.

Papke, L. E. (1991). "Interstate Business Tax Differentials and New Firm Location: Evidence from Panel Data". *Journal of Public Economics* 45: 47–68.

Peltzman, S. (1977). "The Gains and Losses from Industrial Concentration". *Journal of Law and Economics* 20: 229–64.

Phillips, A. (1956). "Concentration, Scale, and Technological Change in Selected Manufacturing Industries, 1899–1939". *Journal of Industrial Economics* 5: 179–93.

Phillips, A. (1966). "Patents, Potential Competition and Technical Progress". *American Economic Review* 56: 301–10.

Phillips, A. (1971). *Technology and Market Structure*. Lexington, Mass.: Heath.

Porter, M. E. (1980). *Competitive Strategy: Techniques for Analyzing Industries and Competitors*. New York: Free Press.

Porter, M. E. (1985). *Competitive Advantage: Creating and Sustaining Superior Performance*. New York: Free Press.

Porter, M. E. (1987). "From Competitive Advantage to Corporate Strategy". *Harvard Business Review* May–June: 43–59.

Potter, H. D. (1982). "The Census of Manufactures and the Labour Force Survey: Some Experimental Approaches to Comparing Establishment and Household Survey Data". An occasional paper of the Analysis and Development Section of the Manufacturing and Primary Industries Division. Ottawa: Minister of Supply and Services Canada.

Prais, S. J. (1955). "Measuring Social Mobility". *Journal of the Royal Statistical Society*. Series A. 118: 56–66.

Prais, S. J. (1976). *The Evolution of Giant Firms in Britain*. Cambridge University Press.

Ravenscraft, D. and F. M. Scherer. (1987). *Mergers, Sell-offs and Economic Efficiency*. Washington, D.C.: Brookings Institution.

Reid, G. (1987). *Theories of Industrial Organization*. Oxford: Basil Blackwell.

Reuber, G. L. and F. Roseman. (1969). *The Take-over of Canadian Firms, 1945–61*. Ottawa: Queen's Printer.

Rohmer, P. (1986). "Increasing Returns and Long-run Growth". *Journal of Political Economy* 94: 1002–38.

Rosenbluth, G. (1955). "Measures of Concentration". In *Business Concentration and Price Policy*. Edited by National Bureau of Economic Research. Princeton, N.J.: Princeton University Press. 57–95.

Rosenbluth, G. (1957). *Concentration in Canadian Manufacturing Industries*. Princeton, N.J.: Princeton University Press.

Royal Commission on Corporate Concentration. (1978). *Report*. Ottawa: Minister of Supply and Services Canada.

Royal Commission on the Economic Union and Development Prospects. (1988). *Report*. Ottawa: Minister of Supply and Services Canada.

Rugman, A. M. (1980). *Multinationals in Canada: Theory, Performance, and Economic Impact*. Boston: Martinus Nijhoff.

Rumelt, R. P. (1974). *Strategy, Structure, and Economic Performance*. Boston: Division of Research, Graduate School of Business Administration, Harvard University.

Salaman, G. L. (1985). "Accounting Rates of Return". *American Economic Review* 75: 495–504.

Salter, W. E. (1966). *Productivity and Technical Change*. Cambridge University Press.

Saving, T. R., (1970). "Concentration Ratios and the Degree of Monopoly". *International Economic Review* 11: 139–46.

Scherer, F. M. (1980). *Industrial Market Structure and Economic Performance*. 2d ed. Chicago: Rand-McNally.

Scherer, F. M. (1983). "Concentration, R&D, and Productivity Change". *Southern Economic Journal* 50: 221–25.

Scherer, F. M. (1988). "Corporate Takeovers: The Efficiency Arguments". *Journal of Economic Perspectives* 2: 69–82.

Schmalensee, R. (1988). "Industrial Economics: An Overview". *Economic Journal* 98: 643–81.

Schmalensee, R. (1989). "Inter-Industry Studies of Structure and Performance". In *Handbook of Industrial Organization*. Edited by R. Schmalensee and R. D. Willig. Amsterdam: North-Holland. 951–1009.

Schmidt, P. (1985–86). "Frontier Production Functions". *Econometric Reviews* 4: 289–328.

Schneider, N. (1966). "Productivity Differentiation, Oligopoly, and the Stability of Market Shares". *Western Economic Journal* 5: 58–63.

Schohl, F. (1990). "Persistence of Profits in the Long Run: A Critical Extension of Some Recent Findings". *International Journal of Industrial Organization* 8: 385–404.

Schumpeter, J. A. (1939). *Business Cycles: A Theoretical, Historical and Statistical Analysis of the Capitalist Process*. New York: McGraw-Hill.

Schumpeter, J. A. (1942). *Capitalism, Socialism and Democracy*. New York: Harper.

Scitovsky, T. (1955). "Economic Theory and the Measurement of Concentration". In *Business Concentration and Price Policy*. Edited by National Bureau of Economic Research. Princeton, N.J.: Princeton University Press. 101–18.

Scott, J. T. (1982). "Multimarket Contact and Economic Performance". *Review of Economics and Statistics* 64: 368–75.

Scott, J. T. and G. Pascoe. (1987). "Purposive Diversification of R&D in Manufacturing". *Journal of Industrial Economics* 36: 193–205.

Shapiro, D. and R. S. Khemani. (1987). "The Determinants of Entry and Exit Reconsidered". *International Journal of Industrial Organization* 5: 15–26.

Shepherd, W. (1984). "Contestability versus Competition". *American Economic Review* 74: 572–87.

Simon, H. A. and C. P. Bonini. (1958). "The Size Distribution of Business Firms". *American Economic Review* 48: 607–17. Reprinted in Ijiri and Simon (1977).

Singh, A. and G. Whittington. (1975). "The Size and Growth of Firms". *Review of Economic Studies* 42: 15–26.

Spence, A. M. (1978). "Tacit Coordination and Imperfect Information". *Canadian Journal of Economics* 11: 490–505.

Statistics Canada. (1979). *Concepts and Definitions of the Census of Manufactures.* Cat. No. 31-528. Ottawa: Ministry of Industry, Trade and Commerce.

Statistics Canada. (1983). *Manufacturing Industries of Canada: National and Provincial Areas, 1983.* Cat. No. 31-203. Ottawa: Minister of Supply and Services Canada.

Statistics Canada. (1988). *Building a Longitudinal Database of Firms in the Canadian Economy: The Case of Employment Dynamics.* Ottawa: Minister of Supply and Services Canada.

Statistics Canada. (various years). *Corporation Financial Statistics.* Cat. No. 61-207. Ottawa: Minister of Supply and Services Canada.

Statistics Canada. (various years). *Industrial Corporations, Financial Statistics.* Cat. No. 61-003. Ottawa: Minister of Supply and Services Canada.

Stauffer, T. R. (1971). "The Measurement of Corporate Rates of Return: A Generalized Formulation". *Bell Journal of Economics and Management Science* 2: 434–69.

Steindl, J. (1965). *Random Processes and the Growth of Firms: A Study of the Pareto Law.* London: Griffin.

Stigler, G. J. (1963). *Capital and Rates of Return in Manufacturing Industries.* A study by the National Bureau of Economic Research. Princeton, N.J.: Princeton University Press.

Stigler, G. J. (1964). "A Theory of Oligopoly". *Journal of Political Economy* 62: 44–61.

Stigler, G. J. (1968). *The Organization of Industry.* Homewood, Ill.: Irwin.

Stigler, G. J. (1976). "The Xistence of X-inefficiency". *American Economic Review* 66: 213–16.

Storey, D. J., ed. (1985). *Small Firms in Regional Economic Development: Britain, Ireland, and the United States.* Cambridge University Press.

Sutton, J. (1991). *Sunk Costs and Market Structure: Price Competition, Advertising and the Evolution of Concentration.* Cambridge, Mass.: MIT Press.

Tarasofsky, A. with Ronald Corvari. (1991). *Corporate Mergers and Acquisitions: Evidence of Profitability.* Ottawa: Economic Council of Canada.

Tilton, J. E. (1971). *International Diffusion of Technology: The Case of Semiconductors.* Washington, D.C.: Brookings Institution.

Timmer, C. P. (1971). "Using a Probabilistic Frontier Production Function to Measure Technical Efficiency". *Journal of Political Economy* 79: 775–95.

United States Department of Justice. (1982). "Merger Guidelines". Reprinted in *Antitrust Bulletin* 27: 633–65.

United States Small Business Administration. 1984. "The Annual Report on Small Business and Competition". In Ronald Reagan. *The State of Small Business: A Report of the President.* Washington, D.C.: U.S. Government Printing Office.

Vanlommel, E., B. de Brabander, and D. Liebaers. (1977). "Industrial Concentration in Belgium: Empirical Comparison of Alternative Seller Concentration Measures". *Journal of Industrial Economics* 26: 1–20.

Waterson, M. (1984). *Economic Theory of the Industry.* Cambridge University Press.

Weiss, L. W. (1974). "The Concentration–Profits Relationship and Antitrust". In *Industrial Concentration: The New Learning.* Edited by H. J. Goldschmid, H. M. Mann, and J. F. Weston. Boston: Little, Brown. 184–233.

Yamey, B. (1985). "Deconcentration as Antitrust Policy: The Rise and Fall of the Concentration Ratio". *Rivista Internazionale de Scienze Economiche e Commerciali* 32: 119–39.

AUTHOR INDEX

459

SUBJECT INDEX

allocative efficiency, 299

barriers to entry
  contrasting effect: on entry vs.
    continuing-firm turnover, 78–9; on
    greenfield entry and merger entry, 60
  effect: on entry, 47–51, 365–78; on industry
    profitability, 354–8; on mobility, 84
  in models of entry, 363–5

Canada–U.S. comparisons; *see also* plant
    turnover
  determinants of industry efficiency,
    305–9, 393
  effect of mergers, 391–3
  industry characteristics, 119–20
  intra- vs. inter-industry job reallocation,
    147–9
  magnitude of entry and exit: short run,
    125–6, 390; longer run, 136–7, 138, 390
  magnitude of turnover: short run, 123–5,
    127–31, 390–1; longer run, 131–5,
    137–8, 390–1
  need for special data, 121–2
  profitability differences for industries, 393
  relation between turnover and industry,
    139–45
  structural vs. cyclical differences, 150–2
canonical-correlation analysis, concentration
    and mobility variables, 187–91
closedown exit
  average age of exiting cohorts, 19–21
  definition of, 10
  intensity of size-class differences, by
    industry, 27–8, 90–1
  magnitude: short run, 15–17; longer run,
    15–17
  measurement issues, 10–20
  measurement requirements, 9
  relative productivity of, 212, 215–16

competition
  Canada vs. United States, 119–20
  as complex process involving industry
    dynamics, 381–4
  contrasts provided by concentration
    and mobility measures, 54, 60,
    165–72
  displacement pattern resulting from,
    229–31
  effect on large vs. small firms, 82,
    89–92, 113–16,
  entry vs. incumbent turnover, 79–80
  firm life cycle, 117
  firm turnover, as a measure of, 177
  greenfield entry vs. merger entry, 54,
    60
  industry variation in turnover and
    mobility, 106, 113
  intra-group vs. inter-group, 238
  intra-industry change, relation to, 4
  manifestations: of greenfield entry, 8, 9,
    29; of incumbent turnover, 70–1, 80–1;
    of merger entry, 30
  market for corporate control, 239–40,
    265–6, 297
  measurement of, 3, 60–1
  rank changes, deficiencies as measures of,
    92–4
  regression to the mean, 65–8, 101–6
  relation to industry profitability, 328–9,
    344–6
  size-class differences in turnover, 27–8,
    89–90, 113–17, 427
  small- vs. large-firm change, 117–18,
    175
  as a state of affairs, 2
  static view provided by concentration
    measures, 174, 176–7
  stochastic processes, 2
  technological factors underlying, 150

463